lonely ⊕ planet

Mediterranean Europe

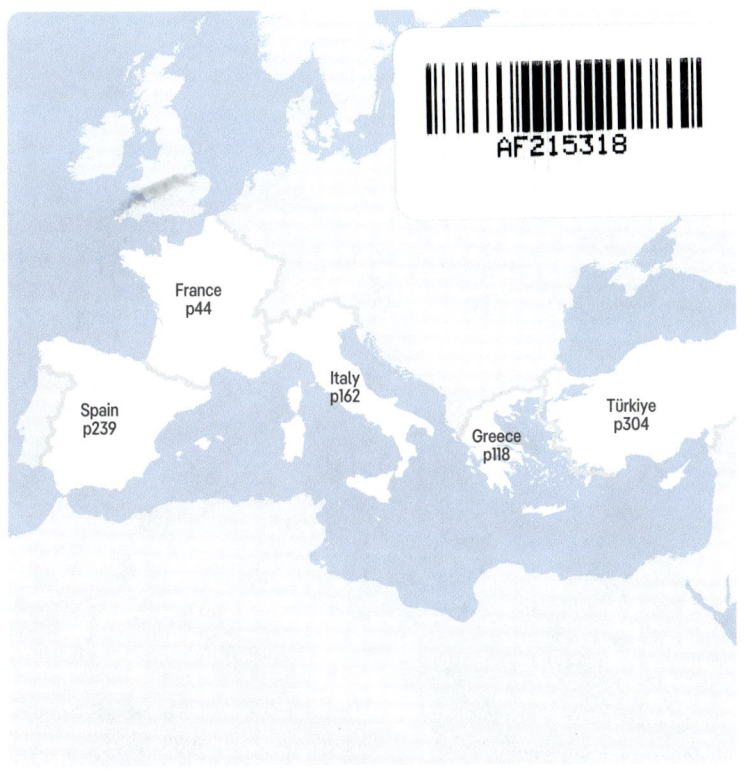

AF215318

France
p44

Spain
p239

Italy
p162

Greece
p118

Türkiye
p304

**Virginia Maxwell, Kate Armstrong, Cristian Bonetto,
Isabella Noble, Anna Richards**

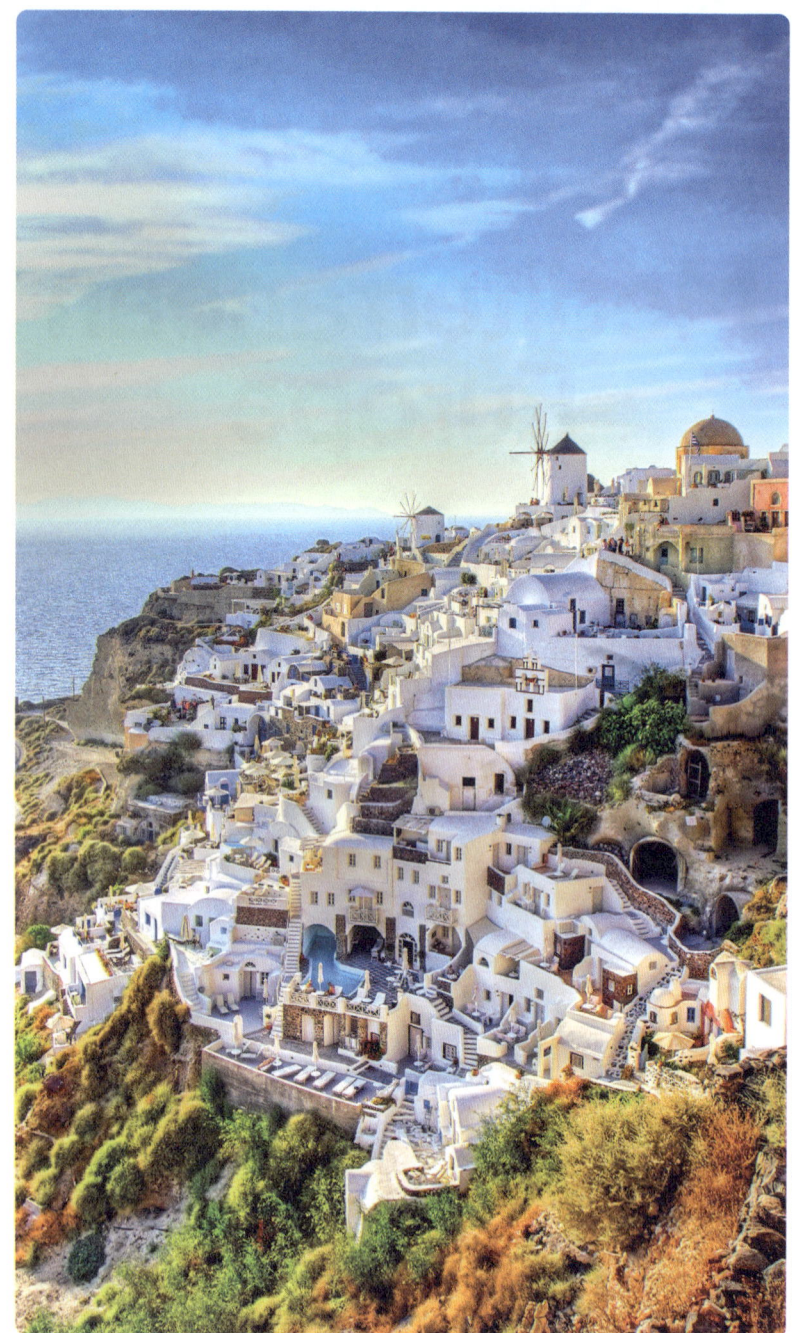

Oia, Santorini (p141), Greece

CONTENTS

Gargoyle, Notre Dame de
Paris (p55), France

Ponte di Rialto (p197), Venice, Italy

BTWIMAGES/SHUTTERSTOCK

Ferry on the Bosphorus (p315) and Süleymaniye Mosque (p314), İstanbul, Türkiye

MEDITERRANEAN EUROPE
THE JOURNEY BEGINS HERE

Ever since Homer described it as the 'wine-dark sea', writers have searched for superlatives when describing the Mediterranean. For me, it's the world's most exciting and evocative destination, one where history resonates and the triumvirate of family, faith and food underpins every culture. Over the years, Lonely Planet has sent me to 13 of the 22 countries around the Med for guidebook research (some on multiple occasions), so when the opportunity arose to work on this book, I jumped at the chance. I curated the Türkiye chapter in this edition, covering highlights as diverse as İstanbul's Old City, the Gallipoli battlefields, the ancient site of Ephesus and the sybaritic summer resort of Bodrum. And what this book makes crystal clear is the fact that Türkiye's extraordinary diversity of attractions isn't unique – all five countries covered are similarly diverse, offering compelling experiences for every type of traveller.

Virginia Maxwell

@maxwellvirginia

An Australia-based travel writer, Virginia is the author of Lonely Planet's Pocket İstanbul guidebook and has worked on multiple editions of the Türkiye guidebook, writing about Thrace & Marmara, the Aegean, the Mediterranean, Cappadocia and Central Anatolia as well as İstanbul.

My favourite experience is crossing from Europe to Asia on an **İstanbul ferry** (p315) and looking back at the minaret-studded Old City skyline as the ferry heads towards the Asian shore.

WHO GOES WHERE

Our writers and experts choose the places which, for them,
define Mediterranean Europe.

KIRK FISHER/SHUTTERSTOCK

Nafplio (pictured above; p136) is my Greek magnet. I love wandering through the alleyways and the fortresses to evoke aspects of the past. Even these days, as children play in the plazas, locals stroll along the waterfront, or when fishmongers bellow their prices at the bustling market, it feels as if the essence of life here continues as it has for centuries. While it gets busy, the crowds don't detract from Nafplio's soul: the bougainvillea-enshrouded Venetian houses, the maze of pedestrian lanes and the generosity of its locals.

Kate Armstrong

katearmstrongtravelwriter.com and @nomaditis.

Intrigued by the sight of her first kouros (ancient Greek statue) in her fine-arts studies, Kate first visited Greece aeons ago, and after returning regularly, she has finally put her roots down there. She writes for newspapers and magazines around the world, and has contributed to 65-plus Lonely Planet titles. She curated the Greece chapter.

ALESSANDRO TORTORA/SHUTTERSTOCK

It's hard to play favourites in Italy, but my heart belongs to **Naples** (pictured above; p212). Nowhere else thrills or moves me quite so deeply. It's a visceral, esoteric place – an Old-World New Orleans littered with contradiction, magic and a raw, relentless energy, both invigorating and fatalistic. As elegant and erudite as it is coarse and gritty, Napoli has almost 3000 years of tales to tell – in its ghostly catacombs, gilded royal palaces and painfully beautiful hilltop vistas. Dive in.

Cristian Bonetto

@cristian_alessandro_bonetto

Born in Australia, to Italian parents, Cristian has made a career from straddling two continents and cultures. A reformed playwright and TV soap writer, he has penned over 60 Lonely Planet titles – many covering his beloved Italy. When he's not in the Bel Paese, chances are you'll find him cycling through Copenhagen, chasing Old Hollywood in Los Angeles, or trading cat videos with his sisters in Melbourne. He curated the Italy chapter.

RALF LIEBHOLD/SHUTTERSTOCK

Few places feel as magical to me as the **Costa de la Luz** (p296) of Cádiz province, in southern Andalucía, where I spend time every year. It's something to do with the crisp natural light beaming across wild blonde beaches, catching a glimpse of Morocco just across the Strait of Gibraltar, and wandering for hours through the whitewashed streets of ancient, buzzing towns like Tarifa (pictured left) and Vejer. The food here is some of Spain's best, too.

Isabella Noble

@isabellamnoble

Andalucía-raised travel journalist Isabella Noble splits her time between Barcelona and Málaga and has written over 50 Lonely Planet guidebooks. She curated the Spain chapter.

PROCHASSON FREDERIC/SHUTTERSTOCK

My home, **Lyon** (pictured; p79), is wonderfully close to the Alps, making it a city for people who secretly hate cities. My perfect day in summer is spent hiking in the mountains; in winter I swap my hiking boots for skis. Come evening, you'll find me enjoying the buzz of the city, decimating my bank balance in a gourmet restaurant or wine bar.

Anna Richards

@annahrichards

Anna lives in Lyon with two French-speaking dogs that accompany her on many adventures, including guidebook research. She's won several awards for her work, but her proudest achievement is her bottomless capacity for fondue. She is the author of Paddling France for Bradt Guides. She curated the France chapter.

Paris
Sample the delights of the City of Lights (p50)

Lyon
Make a pilgrimage to France's gastronomic heartland (p79)

Florence
Admire Renaissance masterpieces in galleries and churches (p201)

San Sebastián
Eat, drink and party the nights away (p275)

Barcelona
Marvel at Gaudí's architectural flights of fancy (p259)

Rome
Walk in the footsteps of emperors and popes (p168)

Madrid
Feast on art, tapas and live flamenco (p244)

Pompeii
Evoke daily life in an ancient city (p217)

0   500 km
0   250 miles

Baltic Sea

TALLINN
ESTONIA

MOSCOW

RĪGA · LATVIA

RUSSIA

Caspian Sea

LITHUANIA

VILNIUS

RUSSIA

MINSK

BELARUS

POLAND

WARSAW

KYIV

UKRAINE

MOLDOVA

CHIȘINĂU

SLOVAKIA

BUDAPEST

Meteora
Meet monks
in their rocky
Byzantine-era
habitat (p132)

HUNGARY

İstanbul
Admire the world's most
magical skyline (p310)

Cappadocia
Float over fairy chimneys
in a balloon (p328)

Black Sea

Bafra

Trabzon

CROATIA

ROMANIA

İnebolu

Erzincan

B & H

BELGRADE

Zonguldak

Çorum

Sivas

Elazığ

SARAJEVO

SERBIA

BULGARIA

SOFIA

Edirne

İstanbul

ANKARA

TÜRKİYE

Kırşehir

Elbistan

Viranşehir

MONTENEGRO

Adriatic Sea

TIRANA

SKOPJE

Komotini

Serres

Dardanelles

Bursa

Polatlı

Cappadocia

Şanlıurfa

Bari

ALBANIA

Thessaloniki

Balıkesir

Adana

Lake al-Assad

Lecce

Ioannina

Larissa

Volos

Uşak

İzmir

Karaman

Suğla Gölü

Antakya
(Hatay)

Catanzaro

Meteora

GREECE

Çeşme

Epheus

Burdur

Taurus Mountains

Patras

ATHENS

Bodrum

Fethiye

Alanya

NICOSIA

Ionian Sea

Tripoli

Naxos

Rhodes Town

CYPRUS

Kalamata

Iraklio

Mediterranean Sea

Crete

Athens
Visit haunts
of ancient
playwrights and
philosophers
(p124)

Naxos
Laze on idyllic
white-sand
beaches (p142)

Ephesus
Walk down an ancient
processional way
(p322)

LIBYA

EGYPT

TASTE SENSATIONS

The cuisines of the Mediterranean countries are distinct, but share many qualities. Influenced by the landscape and climate, local cooks rely on olive oil and fresh herbs for flavour, and make great use of sun-kissed vegetables and fruit. The bounty of the sea is enjoyed at every opportunity, too – local seafood is fresh and delicious. Most importantly, food here is considered much more than fuel: it is the means by which people connect and celebrate.

Focus on Fish

When near the sea, it's sensible to feast on its bounty. Fresh seafood features on seasonally driven menus across the region.

Small Bites

Here in the Mediterranean, good things come in small packages. Graze on the starters and snacks known as mezes (pictured above), tapas, *pintxos* and antipasti.

Eat on the Street

Kebabs, souvlaki, crêpes, bocadillos, arancini – the tastiest and most affordable food in this part of the world is sourced at street stalls.

PLAN YOUR TRIP   OUR PICKS

BEST FOOD & DRINK EXPERIENCES

Spend an evening bar-hopping in ❶ **San Sebastián** (p276), snacking on plenty of *pintxos* (Basque tapas) along the way.

Nosh on perfectly grilled kebaps, modern Turkish tasting menus and decadently sweet baklava in ❷ **Beyoğlu** (p314), İstanbul's foodie hub.

Sample revered traditional dishes and wines from the Rhône Valley in the home of French gastronomy, ❸ **Lyon** (p79).

Make a gastronomic pilgrimage to ❹ **Bologna** (p192), home to the famous *ragù* and plenty of other taste temptations.

Appreciate a long and revered culinary tradition when eating simple but delicious Cretan food in the harbourside city of ❺ **Hania** (p153).

NOVAK LARISA/SHUTTERSTOCK

St Peter's Basilica (p177), Rome, Italy

ARCHITECTURAL MARVELS

The phrase 'spoiled for choice' certainly applies when considering what buildings to visit. Referring to UNESCO's World Heritage List is a good starting point, as it identifies many structures considered to be of major architectural significance. These range from little-known gems to iconic landmarks such as palaces, mosques and cathedrals.

Making a Pilgrimage

Consider building an itinerary around the work of a notable architect, perhaps Antoni Gaudí (Spain), Le Corbusier (France) or Andrea Palladio (Italy).

Visiting Etiquette

Dress modestly when visiting churches and mosques – save skimpy outfits for the beach. In mosques, women must wear headscarfs and everyone must remove shoes.

BEST ARCHITECTURAL EXPERIENCES

Marvel at the fantastical Barcelona buildings designed by Antoni Gaudí, including the utterly unique ❶ **La Sagrada Família** (p259).

Visit the Ottoman-era houses of worship that make the İstanbul skyline so magical, starting with the iconic ❷ **Blue Mosque** (p313).

Explore ❸ **Versailles** (p62), the vast estate and ornate château where the French kings and queens sequestered themselves.

Stand in Bernini's monumental piazza and admire Michelangelo's soaring dome at ❹ **St Peter's Basilica** (p177) in Rome.

Hike up steep steps to World Heritage–listed Byzantine monasteries teetering on towering rocky outcrops in Greece's breathtaking ❺ **Meteora** (p132) region.

CITY IMMERSION

What makes an experience great? Is it notable surrounds or delicious food? Or is it perhaps learning something or making new friends and acquaintances? All of these elements are in plentiful supply in the great cities of Mediterranean Europe, as are tempting shopping options, cultural events, outdoor activities and opportunities to party the night away.

Come Prepared

City neighbourhoods are best explored on foot, so be sure to bring comfortable walking shoes. If it's hot, a sunhat and water bottle are essential.

Green Retreats

When the crowds seem oppressive or the street noise overwhelms, take a break in a public park or garden like those of Rome's Villa Borghese (pictured; p179). These tranquil boltholes are usually easy to find.

Adjust Your Days

In summer, it's not unusual for locals to dine extremely late and indulge in afternoon siestas, meaning that restaurants, shops and offices adjust their hours accordingly.

BEST CITY LIFE EXPERIENCES

Stroll bustling boulevards and perennially packed plazas in the heart of ❶ **Madrid** (p244).

Follow the locals' lead to source bargains and indulgences in the historic and vibrant ❷ **bazaars** of İstanbul (p313).

Sail a toy boat, ride a carousel or play pétanque in Paris' flower-filled playground, the elegant ❸ **Jardin du Luxembourg** (p54).

Stroll through the colourful and chaotic morning produce market in Rome's ❹ **Campo de' Fiori** (p174).

Indulge in syrupy pastries and flaky *tiropita* (cheese pie) when wandering the streets of Greece's alluring second city, ❺ **Thessaloniki** (p133).

13

ANCIENT RUINS

The Mediterranean is the cradle of Classical civilisation and it has retained copious remnants of this glorious period, as well as traces of the even earlier Bronze Age. Ruined cities such as Ephesus, areas such as the Forum and Palatine in Rome or monuments such as the Parthenon tell us much about how the ancients lived, worked and worshipped.

BEST ANCIENT RUINS EXPERIENCES

Ponder the past in the huge, well-preserved **❶ Teatro Romano** (p258) in Mérida, once capital of the Roman province of Lusitana.

Walk in the footsteps of Cicero, Julius Caesar, the Emperor Augustus and his wife Livia in **❷ Rome** (p172) on the Palatino and at the Roman Forum.

Stroll along the temple-lined Curetes Way, the major thoroughfare of the still-majestic classical city of **❸ Ephesus** (p322).

Evoke daily life in a 1st-century CE Roman city when exploring the sprawling and well-preserved ruins of **❹ Pompeii** (p217).

Learn about Minoan civilisation when exploring the excavated courtyards, private apartments and baths at the **❺ Palace of Knossos** (pictured above left; p155) on Crete.

How Old Are These Places?

They're really old. The Palace of Knossos in Crete dates back to 1900 BCE and parts of the ruins at Troy to 3000 BCE.

Who Was Here First?

The Bronze Age civilisation of Crete (Minoan Phaistos Disc pictured above) flourished from about 3000 BCE, making it much older than Ancient Rome, which was founded around 753 BCE.

Fact or Fiction?

Some sites are mentioned in ancient myths or in texts like the *Iliad*, and though these accounts aren't grounded in fact, they make great pre-visit reading.

Museo del Prado (p250), Madrid, Spain

BEST MUSEUM EXPERIENCES

Admire works by Velázquez, Goya, Dalí and Picasso in the museums gracing Madrid's historic boulevard, the ❶ **Paseo del Prado** (p250).

Appreciate modern and contemporary Turkish art in the spectacular surrounds of the Renzo Piano-designed ❷ **İstanbul Modern** (p315).

Visit the Mona Lisa and other iconic artworks in the grand ❸ **Musée du Louvre** (p56), France's preeminent cultural institution.

Pay homage to the genius of Giotto, Botticelli, Michelangelo and other Renaissance masters at Florence's ❹ **Galleria degli Uffizi** (p203).

Prepare for your visit to the Western World's most important ancient site by browsing exhibits in the ❺ **Acropolis Museum** (p126).

MARVELLOUS MUSEUMS

Culture vultures are in for a treat when travelling this region. There are museums devoted to art and artists, to ancient sites and civilisations, to artefacts and cultures. Put simply, whatever your particular interest – shipwrecks or military battles, wine or space travel – there is likely to be a museum to match.

It's All in the Context

Museums can offer invaluable background information. Check out the Troy, Ephesus, Heraklion and Acropolis museums, for example, before visiting the associated ancient sites.

Make a Plan

Sometimes it's impossible to see everything in one visit. At major institutions such as the Louvre and Prado, prioritise the galleries according to your interests.

THE GREAT OUTDOORS

The beaches and turquoise waters of the Mediterranean and Aegean are magnets for sun lovers, who flock to city beaches and coastal resorts and towns in summer. For those who appreciate a more-tranquil beach experience, the occasional isolated cove or stretch of shoreline will oblige. Those who enjoy activities out of the water are also catered for, with ski sports, cycling, hiking and balloon rides among the many options available.

Beach Clubs

Many beaches are dominated by privately owned beach clubs where it's necessary to pay for a lounger and umbrella. These sometimes require advance booking.

The Perfect Balance

The preponderance of ancient settlements along the coast, such as Mycenae (pictured above), makes it possible to explore sites in the morning, then relax on a beach in the afternoon.

Dress Appropriately

If hiking, sturdy walking shoes and insect repellent are essential. And when hiking, cycling or on the beach or ski slopes, make sure you have sunblock and sunglasses.

BEST OUTDOOR EXPERIENCES

Cycle through saltpans to the idyllic beaches on Formentera's ❶ **Trucador Peninsula** (p288), then reward yourself with a swim in turquoise waters.

Float above valleys dotted with otherworldly fairy chimneys on an early-morning balloon ride in ❷ **Cappadocia** (p328).

Head to ❸ **Chamonix** (p73) in the breathtakingly beautiful French Alps to hike on Mont Blanc or brave the legendary off-piste ski route of La Vallée Blanche.

Wander the narrow Green-Blue walking trail linking the pretty-as-a-postcard fishing villages of Italy's famed ❹ **Cinque Terre** (p180).

Relax on the blindingly white sand of ❺ **Glyfada** (p142), one of the many alluring beaches on the Cycladic island of Naxos.

COUNTRIES

Find the places that tick all your boxes.

France

WINE, CHEESE AND WILDLY VARIED SCENERY

Few countries are as beloved as La Belle France. This is a place where the arts, fashion, food and wine are worshipped and where *joie de vivre* is a badge of honour. The population is multicultural and forward-looking; the landscapes are as varied as they are spectacular – it's an irresistible mix.

France
p44

Italy
p162

Spain
p239

Spain

A SOULFUL, SUNNY, FIESTA-LOVING LAND

It doesn't take much to fall in love with Spain. The locals are passionate about many things, including great food and wine, music, fiestas and outdoor activities. Here, you can walk pilgrimage routes, marvel at architecture, laze on sandy beaches and make new friends in neighbourhood bodegas – and that's just for starters.

Italy

EUROPE'S CULTURAL AND CULINARY PARADISE

Food, wine and culture reign supreme in Italy, contributing to the country's famed *dolce vita* (sweet life). The medieval city centres and photogenic rural landscapes here are nearly as impressive as the art-filled churches, museums and galleries – and that's really saying something. To paraphrase Julius Caesar: come, see and be conquered.

Türkiye

WHERE EUROPE AND ASIA MEET

Incorporating the lush fields of Thrace, a long and dramatic coastline and the sweeping steppes of Anatolia, Türkiye is a land of extraordinary beauty and contrast. Many empires have risen and fallen here, bequeathing magnificent monuments and contributing to the development of one of Europe's richest and most diverse cultures.

Türkiye
p304

Greece
p118

Greece

THE PLACE FOR EPIC ADVENTURES

This is the land of gods and heroes, a landscape celebrated in myth and traversed by travellers since ancient times. Ferry-hopping across the archipelagos and lazing on sun-spangled beaches is a highlight, but so too is dining in boisterous tavernas and visiting some of the world's most famous archaeological sites.

ITINERARIES

Along the Coast

Allow: 14 days   **Distance:** 3100km

Travellers have been traversing the shores of the Mediterranean for millennia, pausing in cities and on jewel-like islands along the way. This is one of Europe's great peregrinations, achieved on a mix of train, bus and ferry and easily extended from both its start and end points.

❶

BARCELONA ⏲ 3 DAYS

Start your coastal crawl in Catalonia's capital city, **Barcelona** (p259). Gaze in awe at Gaudí's extraordinary La Sagrada Família, stroll the length of the ancient boulevard of La Rambla (pictured) and plunge into the crowd at a city market. Before leaving, don't forget to pay your respects at the Museu Picasso and join locals for a midday tipple at a *vermuteria* (vermouth bar).

❷

MARSEILLE ⏲ 2 DAYS

Board a train and travel alongside the shore of the Mediterranean to **Marseille** (p96). Kick off your visit to this edgy French city by enjoying an aperitif on the cours Julien (to get into the local swing of things, choose a pastis; pictured), then wander the atmospheric side streets, dine on bouillabaisse and end the day listening to buskers playing on the frenetic main square.

❸

CINQUE TERRE ⏲ 2 DAYS

You'll need to take a mix of trains and buses to cross the Italian border and make your way to the historic port city of Genoa (Genova), from where you can take a short train trip to one of Italy's most stunning landscapes, the **Cinque Terre** (pictured; p180). The next day, walk the famous Green-Blue trail linking the five cliffside fishing villages.

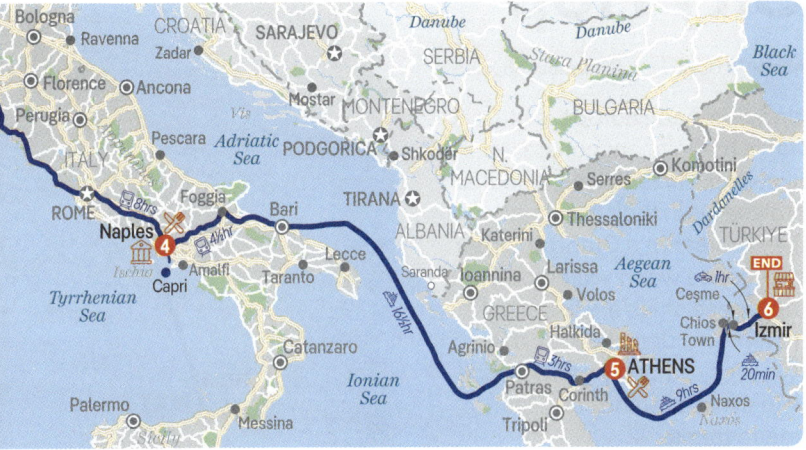

4 NAPLES ⏱ 3 DAYS

InterCity trains link La Spezia near the Cinque Terre with Rome, from where other services head to the gritty southern city of **Naples** (Napoli; p212). Spend a few days admiring the baroque architecture (pictured), visiting the stupendous archaeological museum, drinking Italy's best coffee and eating the world's best pizza.

🚢 *Detour: Take a short ferry ride to the island of **Capri** (p216), home to the famous Blue Grotto. ⏱ 6 hours.*

5 ATHENS ⏱ 2 DAYS

Trains link Naples with the port of Bari on the Adriatic Sea, from where ferries sail to the city of Patras in Greece's northern Peloponnese. Trains connect Patras with the ancient and always-alluring city of **Athens** (p124). Visit the Acropolis (pictured) and its museum, and dine in local tavernas. History is writ large here, as you'll discover when strolling the monument-laden streets.

6 İZMIR ⏱ 2 DAYS

Take a ferry across the Aegean to the island of Chios and then onto the Turkish resort town of Çeşme, from where you can make your way to the sophisticated city of İzmir. From here, you can promenade on the waterfront (pictured), eat great seafood and explore the labyrinthine Kemaraltı Çarşısı, one of Türkiye's most fascinating historic bazaars. To extend your holiday, head south to explore the idyllic **Turquoise Coast** (p325).

ITINERARIES

City Hop

Allow: 14 days **Distance:** 3839km

Mediterranean Europe is blessed with a magnificent constellation of capital cities. All major tourism drawcards in their own right, they represent a Grand Tour par excellence when visited on one trip. These cities are linked by multiple modes of travel; this two-week itinerary can be done with a mix of planes and fast-speed trains.

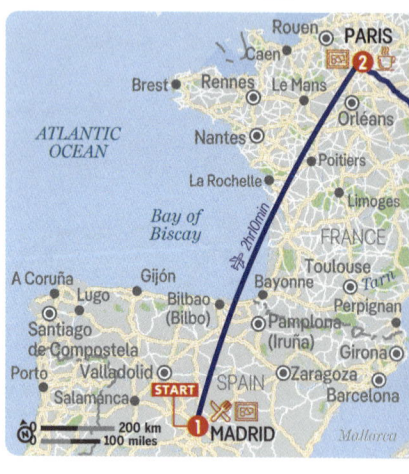

1

MADRID ⏱ 2 DAYS

Madrileños love a good party, and there's a constant celebratory vibe in their elegant and inclusive city. When here, visit the world-class art museums by all means, but save most of your energy for exploring the *barrios* (districts), wandering through grand plazas, checking out the bar and restaurant scenes, and visiting late-night flamenco venues (pictured).

2

PARIS ⏱ 3 DAYS

Ahh, Paris. First-time visitors to the **City of Light** (p50) will be instantly smitten with its charms; repeat visitors are sure to find new things to love. Wander the boulevards, marvel in art galleries and linger at pavement cafes – and that's just on day one. The arrondissements, the fashions, the cuisine and the *joie de vivre* can't be beaten – make the most of them.

3

MILAN ⏱ 2 DAYS

A TGV or Frecciarossa train can transport you from Paris to Milan in seven hours. Unlike many European cities, the attractions of **Milan** (p185) lie predominantly in its lifestyle rather than its monuments. That's not to discount top-tier attractions such as Leonardo's *Last Supper* (pictured), but what makes Italy's second city so compelling is its sense of style and sophistication.

FROM LEFT: OSCAR GONZALEZ FUENTES/SHUTTERSTOCK, MAZIARZ/SHUTTERSTOCK, MARK EDWARD HARRIS/GETTY IMAGES

4
ROME ⏱ 2 DAYS

All roads lead to **Rome** (p168). After arriving by train, tread in the footsteps of Julius Caesar and Mark Antony in the Ancient Forum, visit churches filled with Renaissance art, wander through fountain-filled piazzas and sample the *dolce vita* (good life) in the city's cafes and eateries (pictured).

5
ATHENS ⏱ 2 DAYS

Mix your trip up by taking to the air rather than the train tracks to reach **Athens** (p124). The main sights here are easily explored by foot – make the Acropolis, its museum and the National Archaeological Museum (pictured) your priorities, but don't forget to wander through the streets of the city centre, pausing for cups of strong Greek coffee along the way.

6
İSTANBUL ⏱ 3 DAYS

It's always a thrill to visit a new continent, but a long plane trip is usually involved. However, the flight from Athens to **İstanbul** (p310) takes only 90 minutes. Straddling Europe and Asia, this megalopolis has enough top-drawer attractions to keep visitors busy for weeks. Visit museums, monuments and bazaars (pictured) by day, and head to the entertainment hub of Beyoğlu at night.

High-speed train between Madrid and Barcelona

ITINERARIES

Exploring by Rail

Allow: 10 days   **Distance:** 2700km

It's comfortable, affordable, efficient and environmentally friendly – and for these reasons train travel in Europe is popular. French, Italian and Spanish trains and rail networks are great, and travelling between and around the three countries is easy as pie. So book your tickets, climb aboard and ride the rails

❶ VENICE ⏱ 2 DAYS

Traders and other visitors have been making their way to Venice (p193) for centuries. This ethereal floating city is one of the world's great travel destinations, one where vistas and monuments of extraordinary beauty are the norm rather than the exception. It's possible to get around by *vaporetto* (water bus), but the most serendipitous discoveries are made on foot.

❷ TURIN ⏱ 1 DAY

Fast and regional trains link Venice with **Turin** (p183), the capital of the Kingdom of Italy in the mid-19th century. There are ornate palaces, grand piazzas and parks aplenty, but the major draws here are its coffee (the city is the home of multinational brand, Lavazza) and its aperitivo culture – don't leave without enjoying a pre-dinner vermouth (pictured) or two.

❸ PARIS ⏱ 2 DAYS

Sleek Frecciarossa trains whisk passengers from Turin's sedate charms to glamorous **Paris** (p50) in a mere 6½ hours. Stay a couple of nights so that you can dine in style, indulge in some shopping, wander along the banks of the Seine and visit recently reopened Notre Dame (pictured). It's always difficult to leave – bribe yourself with the promise of a return visit.

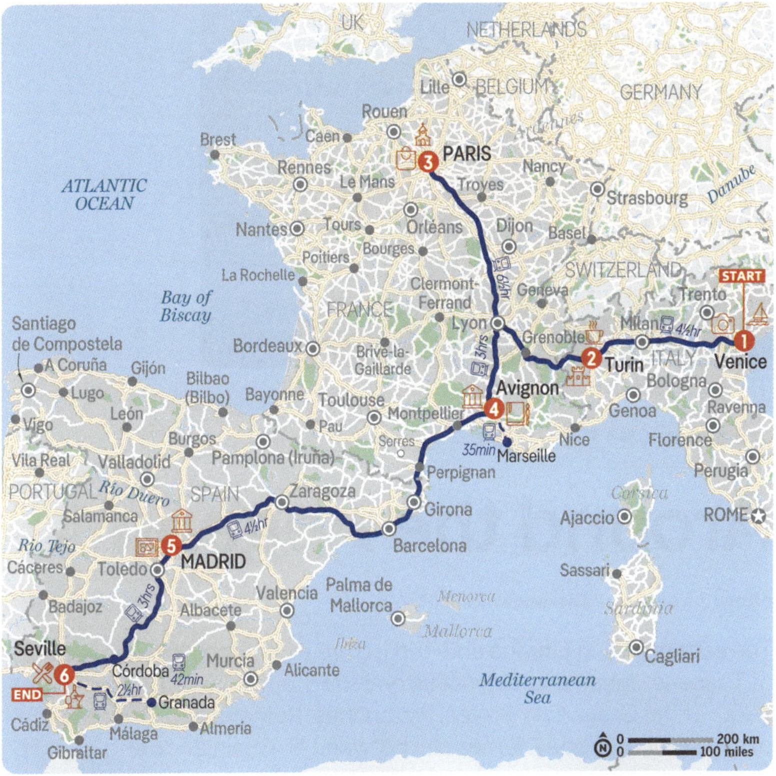

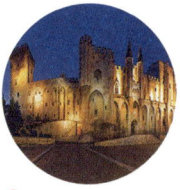

4 AVIGNON – 1 DAY

Regular Ouigo and TGV services head south to **Avignon** (p101) in Provence, once the centre of the Catholic world. Be sure to visit the medieval Palais des Papes (Pope's Palace; pictured), walk along the city ramparts and hum a few bars of the famous song at the city's ruined *pont* (bridge).

Detour: *The vibrant coastal city of* ***Marseille*** *(p96) is only a 35-minute train ride away. 4 hours.*

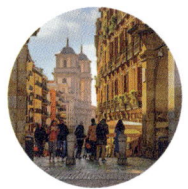

5 MADRID 2 DAYS

High-speed Renfe AVE trains carry passengers across the border and to **Madrid** (7¼ hours), stopping en route at both Barcelona and Zaragoza. Once in Madrid, it's customary to visit the Palazzo Reale and Museo del Prado, but once these are ticked off your list, there are plenty of further options to choose from; start in Plaza Mayor (pictured) and wander at will.

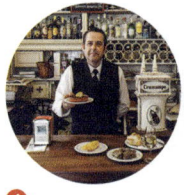

6 SEVILLE 2 DAYS

Continue onward to **Seville** (p289), the southern belle of Andalucia. The blend of cultural and artistic influences on show here is intoxicating, as is the range of tapas bars (pictured) and bodegas waiting for your custom.

Detour: *Two architectural marvels can be visited on easy trips from Seville: Córdoba's* ***Mezquita*** *(p294) and Granada's* ***Alhambra*** *(p297). ½ day Córdoba, 1 day Granada.*

FROM LEFT: KAVALENKAVA/SHUTTERSTOCK, CAVAN-IMAGES/SHUTTERSTOCK, MARGARET STEPEIN/LONELY PLANET

GEORGIOS TSICHLIS/SHUTTERSTOCK

Red (Kokkini) Beach (p142), Santorini

ITINERARIES

Around the Aegean

Allow: 2 weeks   **Distance:** 1300km

The waters linking Greece and Türkiye are where the mythical journeys of Theseus, Jason and Odysseus occurred; and where the naval fleets of the Greek City States, Byzantines, Romans and Ottomans once patrolled. Today, ferries sail between the mainlands and islands, making exploration easy, especially in the warmer months.

❶ ATHENS & AROUND ⏱ 3 DAYS

Spend a couple of days exploring central **Athens** (p124) and the surrounding countryside. The archaeological site of Ancient Delphi (pictured; p131) is a three-hour bus trip away, making it a good choice for a day trip.

🦭 *Detour: If you have additional time, consider a visit to the Byzantine monasteries perched on rocky outcrops in the **Meteora** (p132) region.* ⏱ *2 days.*

❷ CRETE ⏱ 2 DAYS

Fly or take a ferry to **Crete** (p152), the fifth-largest island in the Mediterranean and the largest in Greece. Laze on its famous beaches, savour the delectable local cuisine and explore the ruined Palace of Knossos (pictured), one of the world's most important archaeological sites.

❸ SANTORINI ⏱ 2 DAYS

From Crete, hop onto a ferry headed for the Cycladic Island of **Santorini** (p141), famous for its whitewashed villages surrounded by turquoise waters. If you're here between May and October, you'll have plenty of company (the island is a tourist magnet), but there are good reasons for its popularity, chief among them its incredible beauty.

FROM LEFT: KRECHET/GETTY IMAGES, ANDREI NEKRASSOV/SHUTTERSTOCK, OLGA GAVRILOVA/SHUTTERSTOCK

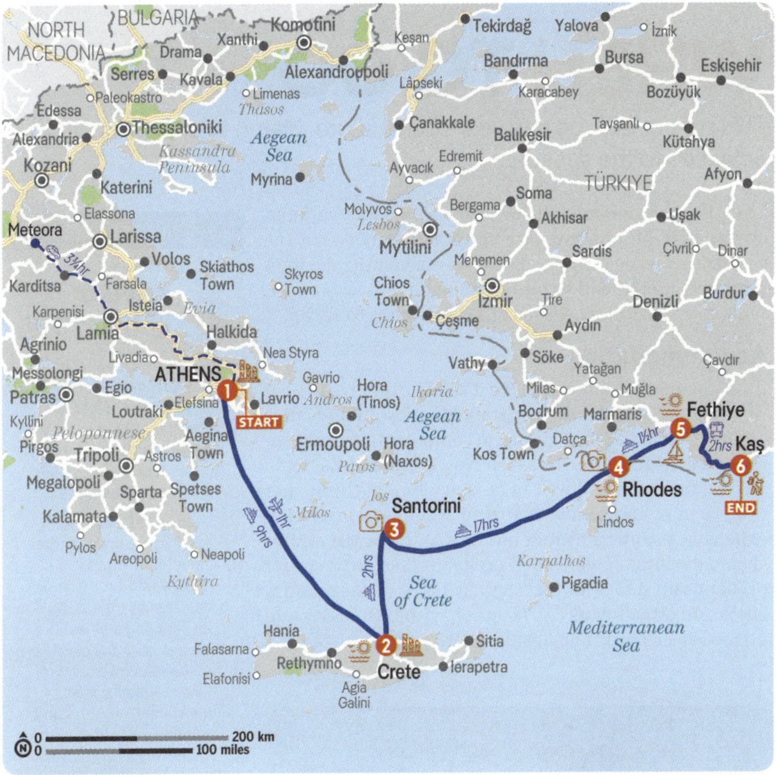

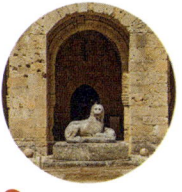

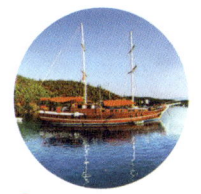

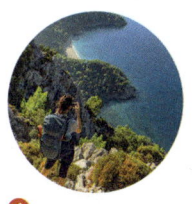

4

RHODES 3 DAYS

It's a 17-hour overnight ferry trip from Santorini to Rhodes. A change in Athens will be necessary if you opt to fly. Located in the Dodecanese group of islands in the southeastern Aegean, **Rhodes** (p144) has gorgeous beaches and a beautiful, World Heritage–listed Old Town that retains traces of its Classical, Medieval, Byzantine, Ottoman and Italian past.

5

FETHIYE 1 DAY

It's time to bid Greece farewell and sail onward to Türkiye. Ferries link Rhodes with two Turkish harbour towns: Marmaris and **Fethiye** (p325). From Fethiye, embark on one of the country's signature adventures, a multi-night *mavi yolculuk* (blue cruise) on a traditional *gület* (wooden yacht; pictured). Cruise stops usually include the famous Ölüdeniz beach and the island of Kekova.

6

KAŞ 3 DAYS

From Fethiye, take a local dolmuş (shared minibus) to the delightful former fishing village of **Kaş** (p325) on the Turquoise Coast. If you're keen to relax for a few days, this is a great choice – especially as some of Türkiye's best beaches and parts of the famous Lycian Way hiking trail (pictured) are nearby.

FROM LEFT: SAIKO3P/SHUTTERSTOCK, NEVIT DILMEN, CC BY-SA 3.0, VIA WIKIMEDIA COMMONS, MAZUR TRAVEL/SHUTTERSTOCK

WHEN TO GO

This part of Europe has year-round allure. Match your interests and activities to the seasons.

The Mediterranean coastline stretches a long way, and climatic conditions can vary considerably between the countries we cover in this book. As a general rule, temperatures inland will be high in summer and low in winter, making shoulder seasons the best times to travel.

Accommodation

Rates fluctuate wildly on the coast and in capital cities, but remain relatively stable year-round in most inland cities and regions. As a general rule, accommodation is cheapest and easy to source between November and Easter.

You'll need to book well in advance for anything near the beach or in the mountains in summer – prices are expensive in June and July, and can soar into the stratosphere during August when Europeans flock to the water or mountain slopes for their annual holidays. As a result, cities and large towns can be quiet, with businesses and attractions closed. The upside is lower hotel rates.

⊘ **I LIVE HERE**

SPRING COLOURS, SPAIN

Raquel Rivas is a photographer and business owner in Cómpeta (Málaga), where she also runs a sanctuary for rescued farm animals. @sarja_microsanctuary

Here in Andalucía, April and May are my favourite months. Each year, our yellow-and-brown land, dried out by the sun, puts on its spring clothes. The greens, reds and purples of the wildflowers return, along with the scent of the orange blossoms and endless birdsong, plus the many fiestas and ferias. Every year around this time, I say to myself, 'How lucky I am to be here'.

FROM LEFT: ROBERTO CALICINO/SHUTTERSTOCK, ANDREW PEACOCK/GETTY IMAGES

La Vallée Blanche, Chamonix (p73), France

SNOWFALL

There's consistent snowfall between January and March. Courchevel and Chamonix in France, and Cervinia and the Dolomites in Italy are popular destinations for powderhounds, but there are also opportunities to ski in Spain, Greece and Türkiye.

Weather through the Year (Capital Cities)

JANUARY	FEBRUARY	MARCH	 APRIL	MAY	JUNE
Avg. daytime max: **3–13°C**	Avg. daytime max: **4–14°C**	Avg. daytime max: **8–16°C**	Avg. daytime max: **12–20°C**	Avg. daytime max: **17–25°C**	Avg. daytime max: **22–30°C**
Days of rainfall: **5–16**	Days of rainfall: **5–14**	Days of rainfall: **5–12**	Days of rainfall: **6–10**	Days of rainfall: **5–9**	Days of rainfall: **3–8**

TOO HOT TO HANDLE

This part of Europe can be extremely hot in high summer, with temperatures hovering between the mid and high 30°Cs. If travelling at this time, make sure that you carry a water bottle and wear sunscreen, a sunhat and sunglasses.

Festivals & Events

Food markets, live music, human towers, fire-running and parades of fantastical Catalan creatures take over the streets during Barcelona's greatest annual celebration, the **Festes de la Mercè** (p266).
☀ **24 September**

Streets across Paris host free musical concerts and performances at the **Fête de la Musique** (Festival of Music; fetedelamusique-paris.fr).
☀ **21 June**

The ancient theatre at Epidaurus is one of a number of atmospheric venues where music, dance and theatre performances are staged during the **Athens Epidaurus Festival** (aefestival.gr).
☀ **June to August**

Madrid rolls out the red carpet in July to welcome LGBTIQ+ tourists from all over the world for Europe's largest Pride festival, **Madrid Orgullo** (p251; madridorgullo.com). Highlights include a parade. ☀ **First weekend after June 28**

Carnivals & Parades

In the lead-up to the 40-day Christian observance of Lent at the start of each year, joyous street carnivals are held in villages, towns and cities across Europe.

The narrow lanes of Venice throng with visitors wearing elaborate masks and costumes during the **Carnevale di Venezia** (carnevale.venezia.it), the most famous and elegant carnival in Europe.

Spain's most famously riotous carnival, the **Carnaval de Cádiz**, sees thousands of

costumed people singing and dancing in the streets over 11 fun-filled days.

Pasos (holy figures) are paraded through the streets, masquerades are held and 'flower battles' are fought during the **Carnaval de Nice** (nicecarnaval.com).

During **Semana Santa** (p291) in Seville, huge floats with revered statues are carried through the streets by religious penitents; the highlight is La Madrugá in the early hours of Good Friday.

⊕ I LIVE HERE

MOUNTAIN SPORT, ITALY

Denis Falconieri is a journalist and author for Lonely Planet Italia. Based in Aosta, he hikes, climbs and downhill skis.
@denisfalconieri

I love the mountains year-round. In February and March, the ski slopes in the Valle d'Aosta are stunning and there's no shortage of ski-trip opportunities. For climbing and tackling the *vie ferrate* (climbing routes), the Dolomites have magnificent rock faces, which are best in June and September.

Valle d'Aosta, Italy (p162)

WINDS

Two powerful winds can impact this region in winter and early spring: the southwesterly Lodos in Türkiye and Greece; and the northwesterly Mistral in southern France, the Balearic Islands and Sardinia. Both cause regular ferry cancellations. In summer, the Sirocco blowing north from Africa can also impact.

JULY	**AUGUST**	**SEPTEMBER**	**OCTOBER**	**NOVEMBER**	**DECEMBER**
Avg. daytime max: **24–33°C**	Avg. daytime max: **24–34°C**	Avg. daytime max: **21–29°C**	Avg. daytime max: **16–24°C**	Avg. daytime max: **9–18°C**	Avg. daytime max: **5–15°C**
Days of rainfall: **1–8**	Days of rainfall: **1–7**	Days of rainfall: **3–7**	Days of rainfall: **6–10**	Days of rainfall: **6–11**	Days of rainfall: **6–16**

FROM LEFT: AS PHOTO FAMILY/SHUTTERSTOCK, AMAZON_SPATULETAIL/SHUTTERSTOCK

Pompeii (p217), Italy

GET PREPARED FOR MEDITERRANEAN EUROPE

Useful things to load in your bag, your ears and your brain.

Clothes

Layers Bring an extra layer for spring or autumn evenings, and remember winter can be cold, especially inland.

Dining Out T-shirts and shorts are fine for most casual eateries, cafes and bars in summer, but pack a smart outfit for restaurants and clubs.

Rainwear A waterproof jacket is advisable, as most coastal destinations can have rain at any time.

Footwear Bring solid shoes for cobbles in historic city centres, and walking boots for coastal and mountain hikes.

Headgear A sun hat or cap is essential for Mediterranean summers.

Shawls Women will need a shawl to cover their heads when visiting religious buildings including mosques.

Manners

Polite greetings are important when meeting someone or entering a business (eg, shop or restaurant).

Queuing is accepted behaviour and attempts to 'queue jump' may cause trouble.

If you're invited out to dinner, your host will usually pick up the bill (and vice versa). Splitting bills is generally frowned upon.

When entering a Turkish home, remove your shoes.

Beachwear You'll need sandals or flip-flops for pebbly beaches. It's advisable that women wear caftans or sarongs when out of the water in Türkiye.

READ

Joie: A Parisian's Guide to Celebrating the Good Life (Ajiri Aki; 2023) How to acquire French *joie de vivre*.

La Bella Figura (Beppe Severgnini; 2007) A hilarious inside guide to how Italian minds work.

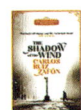

The Shadow of the Wind (Carlos Ruiz Zafón; 2001) Novel set in Barcelona in the mid-20th century.

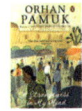

A Strangeness in My Mind (Orhan Pamuk; 2015) A wonderful evocation of İstanbul by the Nobel Laureate.

French Words:
Bonjour (bon-zhoor) – 'hello'
Au revoir (o-rer-vwa) – 'goodbye'
S'il vous plaît (seel voo play) – 'please'
Merci (mair-see) – 'thank you'
Oui (wee) – 'yes'
Non (non) – 'no'
Excusez-moi (ek-skew-zay-mwa) – 'excuse me'

Greek Words:
Geiá sou (yia-su) – 'hello'
Αντίο (a-*di*-o) – 'goodbye'
Parakaló (pa-ra-ka-*lo*) – 'please'
Efcharistó (ef-kha-ri-s*to*) – 'thank you'
Naí (ne) – 'yes'
Óchi (o-hi) – 'no'
Me synchoreíte (me sing-kho-ri-te) – 'excuse me'

Italian Words:
Buongiorno (bwon-*jor*-no) – 'hello'
Arrivederci (a-ree-ve-de-chee) – 'goodbye'
Per favore (per fa-*vo*-re) – 'please'

Grazie (*gra*-tsye) – 'thank you'
Si (see) – 'yes'
No (no) – 'no'
Mi scusi (mee *skoo*-zee) – 'excuse me'

Spanish Words:
Hola (*o*-la) – 'hello'
Adiós (a-dyos) – 'goodbye'
Por favor (por fa-*vor*) – 'please'
Gracias (*gra*-thyas) – 'thank you'
Si (see) – 'yes'
No (no) – 'no'
Perdón (per-*don*) – 'excuse me'

Turkish Words:
Merhaba (*mer*-ha-ba) – 'hello'
Hoşçakal (hosh-*cha*-kal) –'goodbye' when leaving
Güle Güle (gew-*le* gew-*le*) – 'goodbye' when staying
Lütfen (*lewt*-fen) – 'please'
Teşekkür (te-shek-*kewr*) – 'thank you'
Evet (e-*vet*) – 'yes'
Hayır (*ha*-yur) – 'no'
Bakar mısınız (bar-kar muh-suh-*nukz*) – 'excuse me'

 WATCH

All About My Mother (Pedro Almodóvar; 1999) This comedy-drama from the great Spanish director is rated among his best.

Eternity and a Day (Theo Angelopoulos; 1998) Palme d'Or winner at Cannes, this moving Greek film is set in Thessaloniki.

La Ch'tite Famille (Dany Boon; 2018) The second in Boon's iconic films about France's north–south divide.

La Dolce Vita (Federico Fellini; 1960; pictured) Marcello Mastroianni stars in Fellini's masterpiece, set largely in Rome.

Once Upon a Time in Anatolia (Nuri Bige Ceylan; 2011) Atmospheric film about a murder investigation in rural Türkiye.

LISTEN

Cositas Buenas (Paco de Lucía; 2004) Hugely popular album from a guitarist and composer recognised as a pioneer of new flamenco.

Elegy of the Uprooting (Eleni Karaindrou; 2006) Majestic live recording of Karaindrou's concert piece about the Greek-Turkish forced population exchanges.

Resonate (Papooz; 2024) A cult Paris-based duo elevate spirits with their upbeat mix of French folk, pop and rock.

Notto Siciliano (Lello Analfino & Shakalab; 2024) Features Sicilian hip hop-reggae band Shakalab with iconic rock singer Lello Analfino.

ARMANDO OLIVEIRA/SHUTTERSTOCK

Hiking the Camino de Santiago,
Santiago de Compostela (p277), Spain

TRIP PLANNER

PILGRIMAGE ROUTES

Pilgrims have been walking their way across Mediterranean Europe since the Middle Ages, and the number of people traversing the major pilgrimage routes has grown in recent decades. These days, most walkers follow these trails to appreciate nature, meet fellow travellers, enjoy physical exercise and enhance mindfulness rather than being motivated by religious zeal.

Pilgrimage Routes

CAMINO DE SANTIAGO

Called the Way of St James in English, the world's most famous pilgrimage route is actually a network of pilgrims' trails leading to the shrine of the apostle James in the cathedral of Santiago de Compostela in the Spanish region of Galicia.

Trails traverse parts of Spain, France and Portugal, with the most popular being the 800km **Camino Francés** (French Way; p256). Other trails include the 610km **Camino Portugués** (Portuguese Way); the 320km **Camino Primitivo** (Original Way); and the 508km **Camino del Norte** (Northern Way).

More information: saintjamesway.eu

VIA FRANCIGENA

Linking Canterbury Cathedral in the UK with St Peter's Basilica in Rome and then continuing to the southern Italian coast (the point from which ships to the Holy Land once departed), this 3000km trail crosses five countries, but its longest and most popular stretches are in France and Italy.

More informaton: viefrancigene.org

ST PAUL TRAIL

This 500km Turkish trail recreates the route taken by the Christian apostle Paul in 46 CE when he walked from Perge on the Mediterranean coast to the Roman garrison town of Antiochia-in-Pisidia east of

WHEN TO WALK

Avoid walking in July and August, when the trails can be unpleasantly crowded and the heat can be oppressive.

Camino de Santiago April to May and September to October

Via Francigena April to June and September

St Paul Trail Late April to June or late August to October

Camiño dos Faros April to June and September

Lycian Way April to May and September to October

Tour du Mont Blanc mid-June to mid-September

Lake Eğidir. It features spectacular mountain and lake scenery.

More information: *The St Paul Trail* (Kate Clow; 2013)

Other Long-Distance Walks

CAMIÑO DOS FAROS

Following the northwest Spanish coastline between Malpica de Bergantiños and Cabo Fisterra, the 200km **Camiño dos Faros** (Lighthouse Way; p279) has eight stages that can be walked individually or in pairs as day trips.

More information: caminodosfaros.com

LYCIAN WAY

Following the coastline of the Turkish Turquoise Coast (southwestern Mediterranean), the 540km **Likya Yolu** (Lycian Way) passes through pine and cedar forests beneath mountains rising almost 3000m. It features ruins of ancient Lycian settlements and remarkable coastal views that stretch as far as Rhodes.

More information: *The Lycian Way (Lik-ia Yolu) Topographic Map Atlas with Index 1:50000* (Sergio Mazitto; 2018)

TOUR DU MONT BLANC

A heavy-duty hike, this one-to-two-week 170km trail circles the massif and passes through mountainous terrain in France, Switzerland and Italy. The trail, which passes by glaciers, across high mountain passes and through alpine meadows, includes multiple ascents and descents.

For more information head to autour dumontblanc.com

WHAT YOU'LL NEED

Backpack
- The lighter, the better. A rainproof cover is a good idea.

Rain jacket
- Some hikers take an umbrella, too.

Layers
- Pack light but for all eventualities.

Water bottle or bladder
- Always carry adequate water.

Food
- Snacks for day hikes; meals for long hauls.

Walking stick
- Opt for a lightweight and foldable version.

Hiking boots
- These should be sturdy, broken-in and waterproof.

Plenty of socks
- Wool is best.

Long trousers
- These offer protection from sun, insects and vegetation.

Sun protection
- Sun hat, sun block & sunglasses.

First aid kit
- Don't forget insect repellent and a blister kit.

Camping equipment
- You may need tent, sleeping bag, sleeping mat and cooking equipment.

Tools
- Torch (flashlight), a trowel for toileting.

Phone and fully charged powerbank
- Vital in case of emergencies and for GPS readings.

NATALIA HANIN/SHUTTERSTOCK

Bœuf bourguignon

THE **FOOD** SCENE

Known for its gloriously fresh produce and diverse cuisines,
Mediterranean Europe is one of the world's great food destinations.

It's fair to say that the people of the Mediterranean are obsessed with food. The countries, cities and regions here possess delicious and distinctive cuisines that reflect their geographies – seafood is a staple around the coast, meat is more prevalent inland and the mountainous regions have long traditions of cheesemaking. There is one thing, though, that every Mediterranean cuisine has in common: a focus on fresh fruit and vegetables, harvests that come courtesy of the bountiful sun.

The food here has also been influenced by the traders and travellers who have traversed the Mediterranean over the centuries, bringing products and inspiration with them. The famed cuisines of Sicily and Andalucía, for instance, owe much to the aromatic spices, chilli and dried fruits

that characterise North African food. These days, the influx of people from far-away places means that it's now almost as common to eat couscous and curry as it is to feast on traditional dishes.

Put simply, the food you will eat here will be fresh, healthy, delicious and memorable. Enjoy!

Cheese

There are as many different types of cheese in this part of the world as there are artisanal cheesemakers. Cow, sheep, goat and buffalo milks are all used to delicious effect.

The French are perhaps the most cheese-obsessed of all Mediterranean people and their cheeses are among the best-known in the world – think Brie, Camembert, Chèvre, Comté and Roquefort among many others.

Best Mediterranean Dishes

BŒUF BOURGUIGNON

(France) Beef and red-wine stew – best eaten in Burgundy.

MOULES FRITES

(France) Mussels cooked in broth and served with skinny fries.

PULPO Á FEIRA

(Spain) Seasoned, boiled octopus that is a Galician speciality.

RISOTTO ALLA MILANESE

(Italy) Milanese rice dish prepared with bone marrow and saffron.

Challenging France in the contest for the best cheese crown is Italy, home to beloved products such as Parmigiano Reggiano, Grana Padano, Gorgonzola and mozzarella; parmigiano and Gorgonzola are made in the north of the country and the most highly regarded mozzarella (Mozzarella di Bufala Campana) is made in the south.

In Spain, Greece and Türkiye, tangy cheese made from sheep's and goat's milk is hugely popular – look for Greek Feta, Spanish *Queso Manchego* and Turkish *beyaz peynir* and Tulum.

Fish

When it comes to fish, the Mediterranean mantra is 'Keep it simple'. In Spain, Italy, Greece and Türkiye, fish and seafood is inevitably grilled or fried and the success of the dish hinges on the seafood's freshness rather than on technical wizardry. The French sometimes like to pimp their seafood up with pastry and cream sauces, but this is more prevalent inland than on the coast. The most famous seafood dishes are undoubtedly bouillabaisse, a fish stew from Marseilles in France, and paella, a rice and seafood dish from Valencia in Spain.

Bouillabaisse

Meat

This part of the world is paradise for lovers of cured meats. In Spain, *jamón* (ham) is treated reverently. Deep red and well marbled with buttery fat, it's an unctuous delight. There are many types of *jamón*, including *jamón serrano* (the most popular) and *jamón ibérico*, the elite Spanish ham.

Italians are, of course, famously obsessed with cured meats, which they usually eat as an antipasto. Popular products include

FROM LEFT: BIITU/GETTY IMAGES. KIKOSTOCK/SHUTTERSTOCK

Fiestas de la Vendimia

FOOD & WINE FESTIVALS

Mesir Macunu Festival (March) The Aegean town of Manisa marks the arrival of spring with concerts and distribution of its famous sweet paste.

Athens Street Food Festival *(athensstreetfoodfestival.gr;* May) Crowds flock to an old railway depot in Gazi over three weekends to snack on street foods.

Fiestas de la Vendimia (September) Jerez honours the Andalucian grape harvest with a foot-stomping festival.

Fête du Vin Nouveau et de la Brocante (p104; October) The main street of Chartrons in Bordeaux morphs into a party zone for two days to celebrate the new vintage.

Eurochocolate *(eurochocolate.com;* October) Perugia's medieval centre sets the stage for the city's homage to all things chocolate.

PIZZA MARGHERITA	DOLMADHES	MOUSAKAS	KÜNEFE
(Italy) Classic pizza topped with tomato, mozzarella and fresh basil.	(Greece) Either vine-leaf parcels, or hollowed-out vegetables, stuffed and baked.	(Greece) Luscious layers of aubergine, cheese sauce, minced meat and potato.	(Türkiye) Shredded-wheat dessert with pistachios, honey and sugar syrup.

Baklava

prosciutto (dry-cured ham made from the hind leg of a pig); salami (fermented and air-dried pork); *mortadella* (large pork salami incorporating a high percentage of fat); and *bresaola* (lean air-dried beef).

Meat features prominently on menus in most inland regions. In Spain, Italy and Greece it is closely associated with festivities – spit-roasted lamb and suckling pig are two favourite celebratory dishes. Grilled skewered meats are adored in Greece and Türkiye – the most beloved of these are the Greek souvlaki and its Turkish equivalent, the *şiş kebap. Köfte* and *keftedes* (meatballs) are equally popular.

Sweets

Sweets are eaten at different times of the day according to the country. Italians adore eating biscuits, tarts and sweet pastries at breakfast but often skip dessert at dinner, opting instead for fresh fruit. In Türkiye, sweets are often consumed as mid-afternoon treats. In France and Spain, any time of the day is the right time for something sweet – in Spain, for instance, it's not unusual for the locals to eat *churros con chocolate* (deep-fried doughnut strips for dipping in rich hot chocolate) for breakfast and enjoy a *crema catalana* as a dinner finale. In Greece, *loukoumadhes* (ball-shaped doughnuts dipped in honey and sprinkled with cinnamon or nuts) are a popular snack.

Avoid being drawn into any debate about the derivation of baklava – both Greece and Türkiye claim this treat of honey-drenched filo pastry packed with finely chopped nuts, and baklava-related arguments can get heated!

Vegetarian & Vegan Options

Salads and mezes will be your best friend if sticking to a vegan diet in this part of the world. Be aware that in Northern France, *frites* (fries) are traditionally double-fried in animal fat (suet or beef lard). Plant-based milks (oat, almond etc) are usually available in city cafes.

The Mediterranean love of fresh vegetables, pulses and cheese means that vegetarian options are easy to source. However, note that many cheeses are made with rennet, an enzyme derived from the stomach of a calf or young goat. Also be aware that stews and sauces that might appear vegetarian may include ham, especially in Spain. Chicken and meat stock is regularly used in sauces and soups – check before ordering.

SMALL DISHES

Small plates or bites enjoyed with drinks before lunch or dinner are a Mediterranean tradition. Called tapas and *pintxos* in Spain, mezes in Türkiye, *mezedhes* in Greece, *chicheti* and *stuzzichini* in Italy and *hors d'oeuvres* in France, these snacks are ordered from a bar menu or chosen from displays. Designed to be shared, they often end up being ordered in multiples in lieu of a full meal.

Like most food in this part of the world, these dishes differ from region to region. In Spain's Basque country, *pintxos* (bread with delicious toppings) are the snack of choice. In Venice, *chicheti* also tend to be bread with toppings (usually seafood). In Greece and Türkiye, dips are the undisputed kings of the meze and mezedhes tray – purees of fava (yellow split pea or broad bean), *taramasalata* (fish roe), tzatziki/*çacık* (yoghurt and cucumber) and *melitzanosalata*/baba ghanoush (roasted eggplant) are constants. Cured meats, fresh oysters and seafood are also popular.

Specialities

Dare to Try

SPAIN
Cabrales Pungent artisanal blue cheese.
Percebes Galician goose barnacles.

FRANCE
Canard à la presse Rouen's ghoulish 'n' glorious pressed duck.
Pied de cochon à la Ste-Ménéhould Boiled breaded pigs trotters.

ITALY
Lampredotto Cow's stomachs boiled, sliced, seasoned and served in a bread roll.
Pani cà meusa Sandwiches of beef spleen and lungs dipped in boiling lard.

GREECE
Kokoretsi Offal-stuffed lamb intestines wrapped around skewers and roasted.
Xoxlioi Cooked snails, sometimes prepared with courgettes.

TÜRKIYE
İşkembe çorbası Spicy beef tripe and garlic soup.
Kelle Paça çorbası Soup made with sheep's or goat's heads, hoofs and innards.

Snacks & Street Food

SPAIN
Bocadillos Filled bread rolls.

Arancini

Pa amb tomàquet Catalonia's beloved bread with tomato, salt and olive oil.

FRANCE
Crêpes & galettes Thin sweet and savoury pancakes with toppings.
Panisse Chickpea fritters, traditionally associated with Marseille.

ITALY
Arancini Sicilian fried balls of rice stuffed with *ragù* (meat sauce) and cheese.
Pizza al taglio Pizza by the slice.

GREECE
Koulouri Bread ring coated in sesame seeds.
Tyropita A filo pasty pie filled with a mixture of cheese and eggs.

TÜRKIYE
Balık ekmek Grilled fish served with salad between bread slices.
Döner Chicken or beef served with salad inside bread or a wrap.

MEALS OF A LIFETIME

Auberge Sauvage (p112) Fresh local produce dominates the menu at this Michelin-starred haven set in a 16th-century Mont St-Michel presbytery.

Arzak (p275) San Sebastián restaurant considered one of the world's best. Chefs create innovative dishes in its famous laboratory.

La Taverna di San Giuseppe (p209) Earthy and delicious traditional Tuscan flavours served in a 12th-century building.

Point A (p126) Classy hotel restaurant in Athens with stunning Acropolis and Acropolis Museum views.

Kybele Gastro (p322) Fine dining in a beautiful Selçuk setting, with distinctive and delicious mezes.

THE YEAR IN FOOD

SPRING

Markets are piled high with vegetables, including asparagus, broad beans, artichokes (pictured) and wild greens. Strawberry and green plum seasons kick off and cheesemaking kicks into gear. Easter means roast lamb.

SUMMER

The best time for fruit, with melons, nectarines, cherries, peaches, watermelons, apricots and figs everywhere. Fresh garlic and tomatoes enliven sauces and soups. Local catches include octopus (pictured) and lobster.

AUTUMN

Apples, grapes, chestnuts and pomegranates are harbingers of cooler weather. Menus celebrate mushrooms and game, and anchovy catches are abundant. White truffles (pictured) appear in September.

WINTER

Black truffles appear. Meat stews and hearty soups made with pulses (pictured) fend off the cold. Oranges are at their peak – try blood oranges and navels. Chestnuts are roasted and sold on the streets.

FROM LEFT: SARAH_DIAS/SHUTTERSTOCK, CHRISTOPHER MOSWITZER/SHUTTERSTOCK

Gorges du Tarn (p85), France

THE **OUTDOORS**

Those who like to keep active on their holidays will find plenty of opportunities in Mediterranean Europe, where the activities on offer cater for every interest.

Arranged in a jewel-like garland along the stunning coastline, the countries of Mediterranean Europe are justly famed for their beach cultures but offer many other outdoor-activity opportunities. As well as being home to some of the world's most famous hikes and pilgrimage routes (see p32), there are innumerable options for those wishing to embark on shorter walks or bicycle rides. Inland, rivers and lakes offer water sports aplenty, and majestic mountain ranges are the settings for adrenaline-pumping snow sports.

Hiking & Trekking

Spain is known as the home of the Camino de Santiago (p32), but there are plenty of other hiking options on offer. In the country's north, head to the Spanish Pyrenees, especially **Parque Nacional de Ordesa y Monte Perdido** (p272), which is home to the Valle de Ordesa, one of the most spectacular canyons in Europe. In the south, there are multiple day hikes and multi-day trails in the country's largest national park, the **Parque Nacional Sierra Nevada** (p298).

In France, hikers who follow the short but steep path from Chamonix up to **Lac Blanc** (p75) are rewarded with reflections of Mont Blanc captured in the water of the picture-perfect alpine lake. Unlike this famous trail, which is inevitably choked with people, the long-distance hiking trails around the **Gorges du Tarn** (p85) near Lyon are blissfully uncrowded.

Adrenaline Sports

DOWNHILL SKIING
Propel yourself down the 16km-long, near-vertical La Sarenne in **Alpe d'Huez** (p78) in the French Alps.

PARAGLIDING
Soar above the precariously perched Byzantine monasteries at **Meteora** (p132) in Greece.

VIA FERRATA
Don a harness and helmet to climb the scenic **Via Ferrata routes** (p189) around Lake Como in Italy.

FAMILY ADVENTURES

Cycle through the delightful Jardín del Túria (p283) in Valencia, stopping for a swim at Playa de la Patacona along the way.

Board a cable-car to reach the mountaintop Acropolis of the ancient city of **Pergamum** (p320) in Türkiye.

Embark on a two-day kayak trip along the rapids of the **Ardèche River** (p84), passing under an ancient rock arch on your journey.

Tour on two wheels through villages, vineyards and forests to visit grand châteaux in France's glorious **Loire Valley** (p86).

Float in a hot-air balloon high above the famous fairy-chimney rock formations in Türkiye's **Cappadocia** region (p326).

Climb the 251 steps to the top of the famous **Leaning Tower** (p210) in Pisa's Piazza dei Miracoli.

Walking the scenic Green-Blue trail linking the villages of the **Cinque Terre** (p180) in Italy is one of the country's iconic experiences. Equally unforgettable is the more challenging **Sentiero degli Dei** (p221) above Positano on the spectacular Amalfi Coast.

The famed landscape of **Meteora** (p132) in Greece offers plenty of hiking opportunities, including to cave hermitages and chapels set amid the landscape's extraordinary stone pillars. Other popular hikes include a 18km hike in the **Samaria Gorge** (p155) on Crete.

In Türkiye, hikers can spend days exploring the spectacular fairy-chimney-studded valleys near the village of **Göreme** (p326) in Cappadocia. Further east, the walk up to see the ancient statues on the mountaintop of **Nemrüt Dağı** (Mt Nemrut; p328) is memorable.

Water Sports

The most popular water sport here is, of course, swimming at the beach, and Spain, France, Italy, Greece and Türkiye are all blessed with beach-lined coastlines. The Foundation for Environmental Education has bestowed its Blue Flag certification on many of these beaches, signifying that their water and surrounds are clean and well managed. The beaches in Spain, Greece and Türkiye are particularly enticing – try the beaches on the **Costa de la Luz** (p296) and the **Balearic Islands** (p284) in Spain; on **Naxos** (p142) and **Kos** (p146) in Greece; and at **Patara** (p325) and **Çıralı** (p325) in Türkiye.

If you prefer to get your thrills on the water rather than in it, there are plenty of options. Kayakers can view Italy's **Cinque Terre** (p180) from the water, explore the stunning surrounds of the **Gorges du Tarn** (p85) in France, or paddle over the sunken ancient city of Simena near the island of **Kekova** (p325) in Türkiye.

Windsurfers and kitesurfers should head to Naxos in Greece or **Tarifa** (p296) in Spain; surfers will find the wild waves of the Atlantic more challenging than their Mediterranean counterparts – head to **Mundaka** (p275).

Sentiero degli Dei
(Path of the Gods; p221), Italy

MOON-BIKING
Tackle snowy trails in **Courchevel** (p74) in the French Alps astride a silent, electric snow bike.

ACRO-SPELEOLOGY
Take a guided experience mixing climbing and canyoning at the **Grottes de St-Christophe Caves** (p74) in France.

WILDLIFE SPOTTING
Spot Iberian lynx and Spanish imperial eagles on a 4WD safari in Spain's **Parque Nacional de Doñana** (p293).

MOUNTAIN BIKING
Zoom along oak-forest trails, across rock faces and through the verdant **Meteora Valley** (p133) in Greece.

Walking/Hiking

1. Parque Nacionalde Ordesa y Monte Perdido (p272)
2. Parque Nacional Sierra Nevada (p298)
3. Gorges du Tarn (p85)
4. Cinque Terre (p180)
5. Path of the Gods (p221)
6. Meteora (p132)
7. Nemrüt Dağı (p328)

Beaches

1. Costa de la Luz (p296)
2. Balearic Islands (p284)
3. Naxos (p142)
4. Kos (p147)
5. Presqu'île de Saint-Tropez Peninsula (p95)
6. Patara (p325)
7. Çıralı (p325)

Skiing/Snowboarding

1. Chamonix (p73)
2. Alpe d'Huez (p78)
3. Les Trois Vallées (p78)
4. Parc Nacional d'Aigüestortes i Estany de Sant Maurici (p272)

0 — 500 km
0 — 250 miles

ACTION AREAS

Where to find Mediterranean Europe's best outdoor activities.

Kayaking/Canoeing
1. Cinque Terre (p183)
2. Gorges du Tarn (p85)
3. Kekova (p325)
4. Ardèche River (p84)
5. Parc National des Calanques (p97)
6. Donostia-San Sebastián (p275)

Cycling
1. Jardín del Túria (p283)
2. Loire Valley (p89)
3. Meteora Valley (p133)
4. Ses Salines (p288)
5. Lake Annecy (p76)
6. La Vélodyssée (p106)
7. Corfu (p149)

THE GUIDE

Spain
p239

France
p44

Italy
p162

Greece
p118

Türkiye
p304

Chapters in this section are organised by countries, with each country split into hubs and their surrounding areas. Each hub includes unique experiences, local insights, insider tips and expert recommendations. It's also your gateway to the surrounding area, where you'll see what and how much you can do from there.

Gorges du Verdon (p99), France
BOIVIN NICOLAS/SHUTTERSTOCK

Curated by
Anna Richards

France

WINE, CHEESE AND WILDLY VARIED SCENERY

Endless coastline; mountains that provide thrills, be it summer or winter; and a gastronomy so good it invented Michelin stars.

Who doesn't dream of France? Ever since rich Europeans flocked to the Riviera in the 18th century and English alpinists conquered mountain peaks to unveil tourism in the Alps, it has been a highly desirable place to go.

A little bit of everything got sprinkled into the mix in France. Beaches along the Côte d'Azur that range from sugar-soft spun gold to rocky limestone inlets, mountain giants (including the highest peak in the Alps, Mont Blanc) that soften to hills peppered with lavender fields and olive groves in Provence, châteaux that span rivers and pierce the sky with a hundred turrets. Wherever you are in the country, you're never far from a wine region, and you can bet there'll be plenty of local, AOP cheeses too.

Throw in some of the most instantly recognisable monuments in the world – the Eiffel Tower, Notre-Dame and the Louvre to name a few – and it's no surprise that France consistently hits the headlines as 'the world's top tourist destination', notching up 100 million annual visitors in 2024. Making it even easier to get around responsibly, greening public transport and encouraging longer sojourns are top priorities for a country whose new 'dream big, live slow' road map has one overriding goal: becoming the global benchmark for sustainable tourism by 2030. Travel slowly, and if you can, avoid July and August.

EMPERORCOSAR/SHUTTERSTOCK

THE MAIN AREAS

For places to stay in France, see p112

MISTERVLAD/SHUTTERSTOCK

Left: Plateau de Valensole (p99), Gorges du Verdon; Above: Notre Dame (p55), Paris

LOIRE VALLEY	**PROVENCE**	**BORDEAUX**
Châteaux, vineyards and cyclepaths. **p86**	Sun, sea and rosé **p90**	Historic, wine-infused port city. **p102**

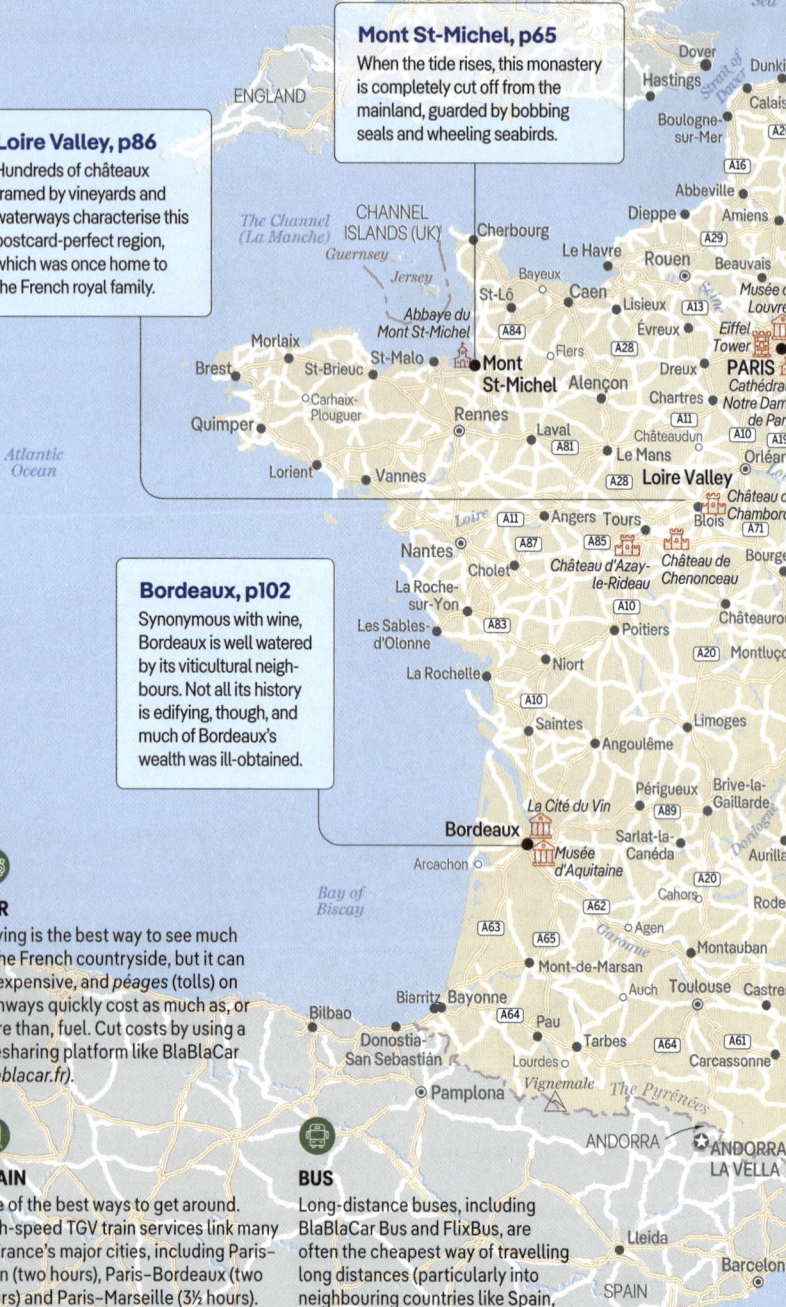

Mont St-Michel, p65
When the tide rises, this monastery is completely cut off from the mainland, guarded by bobbing seals and wheeling seabirds.

Loire Valley, p86
Hundreds of châteaux framed by vineyards and waterways characterise this postcard-perfect region, which was once home to the French royal family.

Bordeaux, p102
Synonymous with wine, Bordeaux is well watered by its viticultural neighbours. Not all its history is edifying, though, and much of Bordeaux's wealth was ill-obtained.

CAR
Driving is the best way to see much of the French countryside, but it can be expensive, and *péages* (tolls) on highways quickly cost as much as, or more than, fuel. Cut costs by using a ridesharing platform like BlaBlaCar (*blablacar.fr*).

TRAIN
One of the best ways to get around. High-speed TGV train services link many of France's major cities, including Paris–Lyon (two hours), Paris–Bordeaux (two hours) and Paris–Marseille (3½ hours). Slower, TER services also run between cities, as well as to more rural areas.

BUS
Long-distance buses, including BlaBlaCar Bus and FlixBus, are often the cheapest way of travelling long distances (particularly into neighbouring countries like Spain, Switzerland and Italy), although they tend to take longer than the train.

Find Your Way

Once the laughing stock of Western Europe for frequent strikes and delays, France's public transport is now one of the best out there. The strikes still happen, but they're generally scheduled in advance – check *cestlagreve.fr* for information.

Paris, p50

City of light and love, the place that inspired everyone from Hemingway to Fitzgerald, Paris' reputation precedes it.

French Alps, p72

Legendary for skiing, but increasingly a summer destination, as locals and tourists escape ever-common heatwaves to hike and mountain-bike through Europe's most dramatic scenery.

Lyon, p79

Hungry travellers arrive here guided by their stomachs, and find a city that's older than Paris, with architecture spanning Roman to Renaissance to avant-garde.

Provence, p90

A region that veers from wildly enthralling city life to tranquil village idyll – complete with fine wine, lavender fields and coastal castaway coves.

47

Plan Your Time

You could spend years in France and not see it all. If pushed for time, pick a region or two to savour.

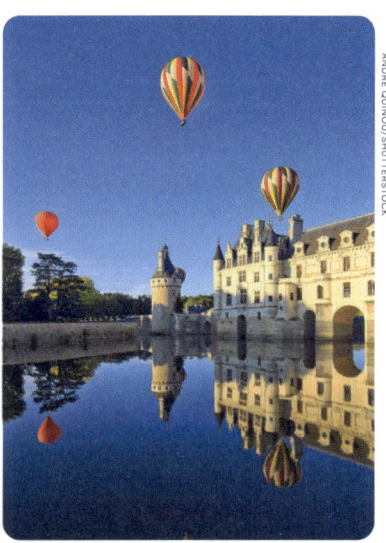

ANDRE QUINOU/SHUTTERSTOCK

Château de Chenonceau (p88), Chenonceaux

SEASONAL HIGHLIGHTS

France is strictly seasonal. Visit the Alps in May, for example, and you'll find very little open. Shoulder season often has the best of both worlds.

Paris in a Day

● Montmartre's slinking streets and steep staircases are enchanting, especially in the early morning when tourists are few. Head to the hilltop **Sacré-Cœur** (p59) basilica to soak up views over Paris. Wander down to Pigalle for lunch, to rub shoulders with fellow diners at the long tables at **Bouillon Pigalle** (p58).

● In the afternoon, potter through the Île de la Cité, site of **Notre Dame** (p55), painstakingly restored after the 2019 fire, and climb the 422 steps up the South Tower. Then put your feet up with a good book at **Shakespeare and Company** (p59).

● In the evening, ascend the **Eiffel Tower** (p50) to experience glittering *la ville lumière* (City of Light) by night, before changing perspective over dinner and drinks at floating restaurant **Francette** (p51), looking up at the tower.

FEBRUARY

It's the height of **ski season** in the Alps, but the school holidays mean sky-high prices and packed pistes in ski resorts. In Provence, Nice celebrates an epic **carnival** (p94) for a fortnight in late February and early March.

APRIL

The arrival of spring means **Lyon's rivers** come to life, with *péniche* (narrowboat) beer gardens spilling onto the banks. Water levels are high for **kayaking** the Ardèche River, although it's chilly for swimming.

MAY

In a month splattered with public holidays, many choose to *faire le pont* and take long weekends. **Cannes Film Festival** (p94) turns the city into a celebrity-spotting frenzy.

A Few Days Château-Hopping in the Loire

● Start at the **Château Royal de Blois** (p87), a compelling introduction to château architecture and the bloody history of the Loire, then stroll along the riverfront and up to Blois' medieval quarter. At dinner, sample a local dry white wine.

● Spend the next day exploring **Château de Chambord** (p87), its dazzling rooftop and the formal French gardens, and take a picnic lunch. Rent a bike/boat to enjoy in the sprawling grounds in the afternoon.

● On day three, explore the yew-tree maze and architecture at castle-turned-bridge, **Château de Chenonceau** (p88), much of which was designed by women. In the afternoon, drive to **Château de Villandry** (p89), famed for its unparalleled Renaissance gardens.

A Week in Provence

● Begin in **Marseille** (p96), France's second city. Marseille develops in dog years; however often you visit, there's always new hip restaurants and bars to discover, with grab-and-go street food on every corner. Take a day to escape the city to the **Îles du Frioul** (p96), only 20 minutes away.

● Once you've had your fill of edgy bars and street art, head to the splendid coastal **Calanques** (p97) on a build-your-own adventure: kayaking, hiking or even climbing. Next, head inland for an adventure fix at the **Gorges du Verdon** (p99), France's answer to the Grand Canyon. If you're touring in June or July, tack on a detour to the purple-hued **Plateau de Valensole's lavender fields** (p99). Finish up in Avignon to visit the **Palais des Papes** (p101).

JUNE	JULY	SEPTEMBER	DECEMBER
Lavender is everywhere in Provence; for a dreamy photoshoot, visit the **Plateau de Valensole** (p99) – responsibly. **Nuits de Fourvière** (p80) brings Lyon's Roman amphitheatre back to life with almost two months of concerts.	Thousands take to the streets to embrace the wild parties and living lesson in Basque culture during Bayonne's exuberant **Fêtes de Bayonne** (p107). The French summer holidays start in early July: expect crowds in the south.	The vendange, or **grape harvest**, begins in wine regions around the country. On the **Journées du Patrimoine** (usually the third weekend in September), many monuments usually closed to the public open their doors.	Strasbourg's **Christmas markets** light up the city. Expect fairy-light-covered craft stalls, mulled wine and treats. In the Loire, Christmas spirit takes hold at châteaux, including Azay-le-Rideau, Chenonceau and Villandry.

Paris

HERCULEAN CULTURE | HISTORY | JOIE DE VIVRE

GETTING AROUND

Most international airlines fly to Aéroport de Charles de Gaulle (28km northeast) or Aéroport d'Orly (19km south). Paris also has five major train stations with international service, and trains are the easiest public transport into the city. The metro is the fastest way to get around, and RER express trains save time crossing the city and serve the suburbs and airports. With no stairs, buses are good for parents with prams/strollers and people with limited mobility.

☑ TOP TIP

Craving green spaces? Join joggers, families and art lovers in the former royal hunting grounds, the **Bois de Boulogne** in western Paris, or **Bois de Vincennes** in the east.

A visit to the seductive French capital is a timeless experience. Be it sipping Champagne atop the Eiffel Tower, lunching cheek by jowl in a neighbourhood bistro, or people-watching on a buzzing cafe pavement terrace, the *art de vivre* (art of living) in the City of Light is utterly contagious.

Paris' cityscapes are instantly recognisable – Notre Dame cathedral, the iron Eiffel Tower, the Arc de Triomphe guarding the glamorous Champs-Élysées, lamplit bridges spanning the Seine, cafes spilling onto wicker-chair-lined streets. A short stay or first-time visit can entice you to linger in the historic centre – the Louvre, the islands, St-Germain and the Latin Quarter – with its myriad monuments and 'must-sees'.

Dining is a quintessential part of any Parisian experience, whether at intimate restaurants, Michelin-starred temples of gastronomy, *boulangeries* (bakeries) or lively street markets.

One of the world's great art repositories, Paris' priceless treasures are showcased in palatial museums, contemporary galleries and innovative multimedia spaces.

Exploring an Icon

Metal asparagus or iron lady?

Named after its designer, Gustave Eiffel, the **Eiffel Tower** *(toureiffel.paris, 2nd floor access using the stairs adult/youth/child from €14.50/7.30/3.70)* was built for the 1889 Exposition Universelle (World's Fair). It took 300 workers, 2.5 million rivets and two years of nonstop labour to assemble. Upon completion, the tower became the tallest human-made structure in the world (324m) – a record held until the 1930 completion of New York's Chrysler Building. A symbol of the modern age, it faced opposition from Paris' artistic and literary elite, and the 'metal asparagus', as some snidely called it, was originally

The Eiffel Tower and the Seine

SPARKLES & A PAINT JOB

Every hour on the hour, the entire tower sparkles for five minutes with 20,000 6-watt lights. They were first installed for Paris' millennium celebration in 2000 – it took 25 mountain climbers five months to install the current bulbs and 40km of electrical cords. For the best view of the light show, head across the Seine to the Jardins du Trocadéro. By day, admire the paintwork. Every seven years, a 50-person crew works at night to strip the old paint and then repaint the entire structure. The tower has sported six different colours throughout its lifetime. The most recent golden hue, unveiled for the 2024 Olympics, was the yellow-brown shade originally conceived by Gustave Eiffel.

slated to be torn down in 1909. It was spared only because it proved an ideal platform for the transmitting antennas needed for the newfangled science of radiotelegraphy. Now a local nickname for the tower is *La dame de fer* (Iron Lady). Of the tower's three floors, the 1st (57m) has the most space, with a broad wooden deck for lounging, but the least impressive views. The glass-enclosed Pavillon Ferrié houses an immersion film along with a small cafe, pizza bar and souvenir shop. This level also hosts the restaurant **Madame Brasserie**. Views from the 2nd floor (115m) are grand – impressively high but still close enough to see the details of the city below. Also up here are toilets, souvenir shops, a macaron bar and Michelin-starred restaurant **Le Jules Verne** (accessible by a dedicated lift in the south pillar). Views from the wind-buffeted top floor (276m) stretch up to 60km on a clear day. At this height the sweeping panoramas are more thrilling than detailed. You'll exit the lift onto a glass-enclosed level with directional panels orienting many of the world's cities. Then take one of the two small sets of metal stairs to the highest tier, which is open-air. Celebrate your ascent with a glass of bubbly from the Champagne bar at this topmost level – or

continued on p54

EATING NEAR THE EIFFEL TOWER: OUR PICKS

Les Deux Abeilles: Homemade delights await at this old-fashioned tearoom that's adored by regulars. *9am-7pm Tue-Sat* €

Bistrot des Fables: A zinc bar contributes to the old-world charm, along with traditional classics like herring potato salad, devilled eggs and beef stew. *hours vary* €€

Francette: Toast the tower from the deck of this floating restaurant moored right on the quay. For the best views, reserve an outside table. *noon-1am* €€

Arnaud Nicolas: The charcuterie maestro stocks a boutique and runs this restaurant with a lunch menu changing every two weeks. *noon-2.30pm & 7-10pm Tue-Sat* €€

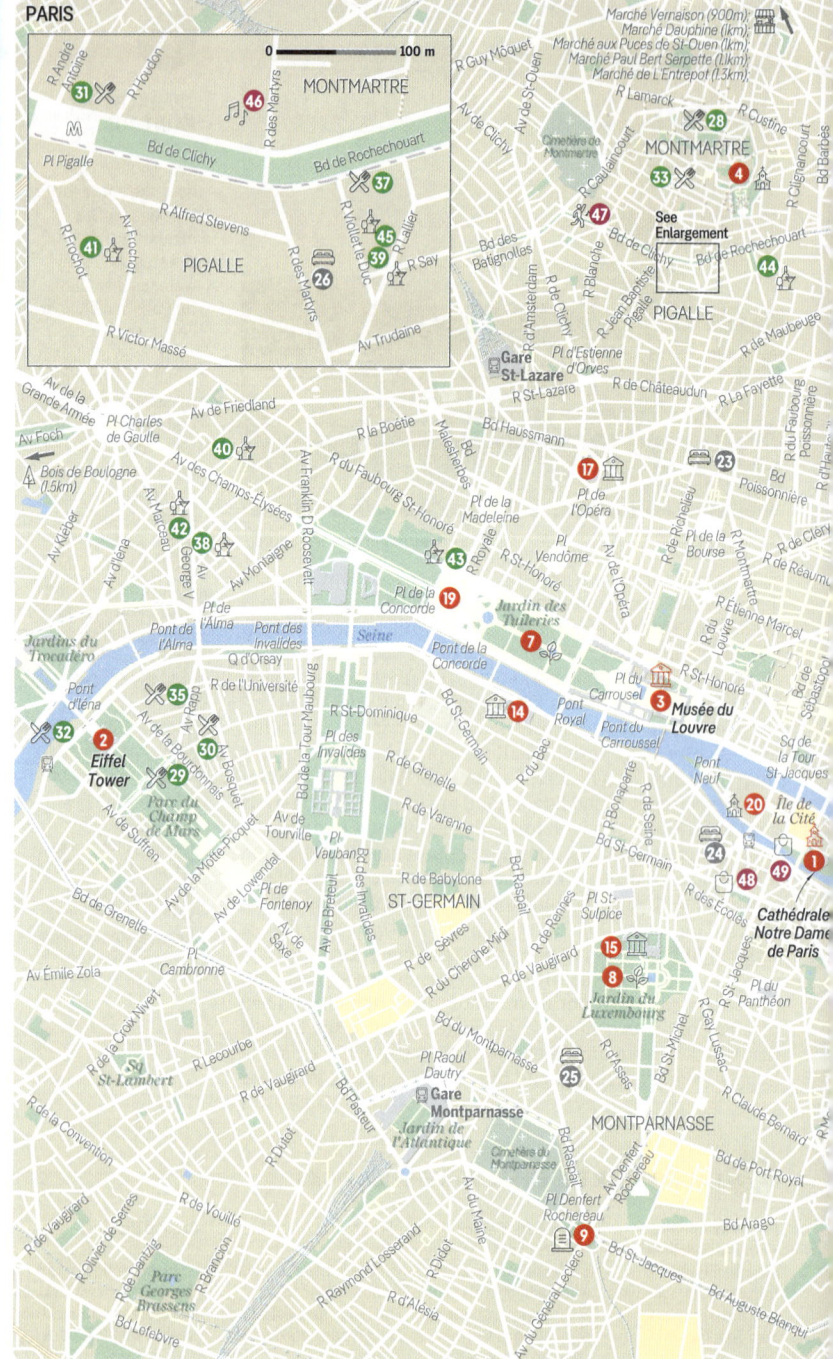

PARIS

0   100 m

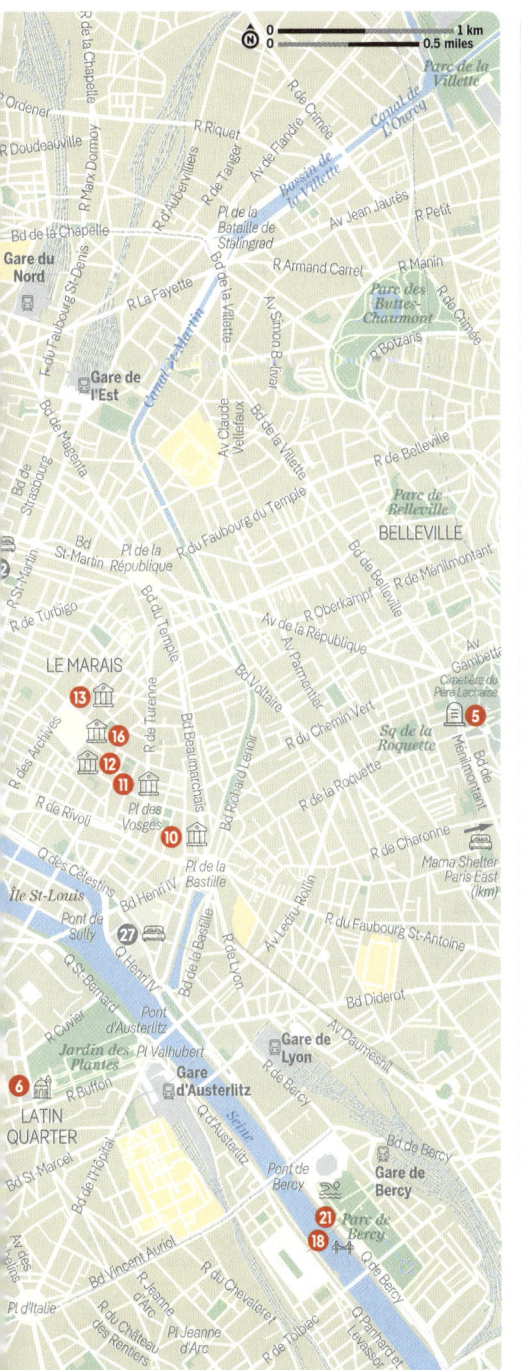

continued from p51

opt for mineral water, lemonade and macarons. Afterwards, peep into Gustave Eiffel's restored top-level office where wax models of Eiffel and his daughter Claire greet Thomas Edison. Somewhat unbelievably, there are also toilets up here.

Even on a good day the base of the Eiffel Tower can be a chaotic scrum of confused travellers; consider booking in advance. Generally attendance is lowest on Tuesdays, Wednesdays and Thursdays.

OFF WITH THEIR HEADS!

Created in 1772, **place de la Concorde** sits on what was once a dry moat and fields surrounding the **Jardin des Tuileries** and the former royal palace. It's famously where Louis XVI and Marie-Antoinette were guillotined in 1793 during the French Revolution, along with many others, gaining the square the name place de la Révolution. Renamed place de la Concorde in 1795, it was redesigned between 1836 and 1846 to add the two fountains, Fontaine des Mers and Fontaine des Fleuves, and the statues representing various French cities that sit around the edge of the square. But its most famous monument is the 3300-year-old Egyptian Luxor Obelisk, erected in 1836 after France received it as a gift from Egypt's ruler.

Impressionism & Architectural Innovation

See Monet's masterpieces

The second-most-visited museum in France after the **Louvre** (p56), the **Musée d'Orsay** *(musee-orsay.fr; adult/concession €16/13)* is housed in a former railway station and contains one of the most important collections of impressionist and post-impressionist works in the world (the 5th floor of the museum is largely dedicated to the movement). By tracing the galleries in a clockwise direction you'll get a fairly comprehensive overview from impressionism to postimpressionism to neo-impressionism. Here is where the movement's masterpieces, such as Monet's *Londres, le Parlement,* Van Gogh's *Starry Night over the Rhône*, and Edgar Degas' sculpture *La Petite Danseuse de Quatorze Ans* are exhibited alongside other fabled modern works, such as Cézanne's *Nature morte* series.

It's impossible to view the entire collection in one day – instead, pick one or two of the themes mentioned as entry points to discover the collection. Alternatively, take one of the museum's themed guided tours. Held daily in English, French and Italian, the 1½-hour tours are centred around fun themes such as masterpieces, animals and parties. Check the museum's website for departure times.

A Park Fit for a Queen

Royal gardens

A 22-hectare expanse along the southern edge of the Latin Quarter, the **Jardin du Luxembourg** *(free)* is a beloved Parisian playground for children and adults alike. Today the former residence of Marie de' Medici, Palais du Luxembourg, houses the French Senate, and the flower- and orchard-filled gardens are its official property. Highlights include the 17th-century Medici Fountain, the Orangerie greenhouse, **Musée du Luxembourg** *(museeduluxembourg.fr; charge varies according*

DRINKING NEAR THE CHAMPS-ÉLYSÉES: BEST HOTEL BARS

| **Le Bar at Four Seasons Hotel George V:** Cocktails crafted with the latest techniques at elegant and cosy gentlemen's-club-style bar. *5pm-1am* | **Bulgari Bar at Bulgari Hotel Paris:** Sleek black bar hidden at the back of Bulgari Hotel: a cool and sexy setting for after-dark cocktails. *10am-midnight* | **Les Ambassadeurs at Hôtel de Crillon:** One of Paris' most palatial hotels has an equally opulent bar (of course): the gilded gold Les Ambassadeurs. *5pm-1am* | **CopperBay at Hotel Lancaster:** Cool 10th arrondissement cocktail bar has opened up a third outpost inside the historic Hotel Lancaster. *5pm-1.30am* |

Palais du Luxembourg and Jardin du Luxembourg

to exhibition) and lovely statues scattered among treelined paths. In the spring and summer months, the pond springs to life, as toy sailing boats (available to rent) race across its waters. Tennis and pétanque courts, chess tables...there's a bevy of recreational activities, not to mention the delights for young children, including a playground and Paris' oldest merry-go-round, designed by Charles Garnier (the architect of the **Palais Garnier**), and topped with an ancient ring-tilting game that's a rite of passage for Parisian kids.

Gargantuan Gargoyles

The most famous cathedral in the world

Majestic and monumental, Paris' iconic French Gothic cathedral **Notre Dame** *(notredamedeparis.fr; treasury adult/ child €12/6)* reopened in December 2024 after the 2019 fire. Long considered the city's geographic and spiritual heart, it went through a massive restoration and, amazingly, because everything – including undamaged elements – was cleaned, the cathedral looks brand-new.

This is an actively working church, and also the capital's most visited free sight – more than 29,000 people come daily. The masterpiece we see today was begun in 1163 and largely completed by the early 14th century. It was badly damaged during the Revolution, prompting architect Eugène-Emmanuel Viollet-le-Duc to oversee extensive renovations between 1845 and 1864. That's when many of the magnificent forest of ornate flying buttresses that encircle the cathedral chancel and support its walls and roof were added. A constant queue marks the entrance to the Tours de Notre Dame *(tours-notre-dame-de-paris.fr)*, the cathedral's bell towers. Climb the 422 spiralling steps to the 69m top of the South Tower (the one on the right as you face the church). On your way up, you'll pass through a

REBUILDING NOTRE DAME

On the evening of 15 April 2019, a blaze broke out under the roof of Cathédrale Notre Dame de Paris. Firefighters were able to control the fire and ultimately save the church, but the damage was catastrophic. The restoration involved over 1000 artists and not only repaired fire-damaged elements, but cleaned and restored everything to the untarnished condition of the era of Viollet-le-Duc. It cost about €900 million (via donations).

continued on p58

SAIKO3P/SHUTTERSTOCK

TOP EXPERIENCE

Musée du Louvre

The Louvre is undeniably Paris' pièce de résistance, with 35,000 works of art on display, including iconic masterpieces, spread across four floors. Glancing at each piece for one minute would take 24 days without sleeping, not to mention the time needed to appreciate the museum's grand surroundings. Therefore, careful planning is essential to fully experience the world's largest art museum.

DON'T MISS

Mona Lisa

Winged Victory of Samothrace

Venus de Milo

The Sphinx's Crypt

Le Salon Carré

Cour Marly and Cour Puget

First Time at the Louvre?

Entering the museum for the first time can be intimidating. The key to approaching the vast collections of the Louvre is to consider them from two significant perspectives: Western Art spanning from the Middle Ages to the mid-19th century, and the art and crafts of five ancient civilisations that preceded and influenced it. Simultaneously, immerse yourself in the museum's captivating architecture shaped by multiple sovereigns. To navigate the museum, just remember that it is made of three wings: the parallel Richelieu (North), Denon (South) and Sully (East).

PRACTICALITIES
● louvre.fr/en ● adult/child €22/free ● 9am-6pm Thu & Sat-Mon, to 9pm Wed & Fri

The Louvre can be both awe-inspiring and overwhelming. Possibly the best way to visit it is to allow yourself to choose, explore and be pleasantly surprised. Don't worry about seeing every masterpiece – enjoy the journey itself!

Guided by Ancient Civilisations

The antiquities department showcases pieces dating from the Neolithic period to the decline of the Roman Empire. Exploring chronologically, the treasures of ancient civilisations will primarily lead you through the ground floor, with an additional area dedicated to Egyptian antiquities on level 1. Begin your journey in the Richelieu wing, exploring the Mesopotamian art (considered the earliest human civilisation). Continue to the Sully wing to descend into the Sphinx's Crypt and uncover Egyptian art. Proceed to the Denon wing to see Greek, Etruscan and Roman art.

Gardens of Sculptures

Sculpture enthusiasts should not miss the atmospheric Cour Marly and Cour Puget, on level 1 of the Richelieu wing. These indoor courtyards bathed in natural light house French masterpieces created under Louis XIV. The Cour Marly provides an atmospheric setting reminiscent of its original location in one of the king's residences. Interestingly, in an arrangement that may seem counterintuitive, ascending to the upper level will transport you back in time to medieval French sculpture. Moving through the Richelieu wing on the ground floor, you'll then encounter more sculptures from the 17th to 19th centuries.

A European Tour of Masterpieces

The top floors showcase European paintings and decorative arts from the Middle Ages to the mid-19th century. Many visitors explore these floors towards the end of their visit, following the sequential order of the rooms. If you're a painting enthusiast, you should prioritise these floors during your visit. They are must-visit areas for iconic artworks like the *Mona Lisa*, as well as monumental paintings such as the *Wedding at Cana* and the *Raft of the Medusa*. In addition, don't miss the impressive Great Gallery, the historic Salon Carré (the precursor to exhibition salons), and the opulent Galerie d'Apollon adorned with stunning murals and golden embellishments.

Around the Louvre, Around the World

As no ordinary museum, the Louvre takes you on a journey to different eras and continents. Don't miss the apartments of Napoléon III, almost untouched for nearly 150 years, at the end of the Richelieu wing on the first level. For a broader cultural experience, explore the small section dedicated to American, African, Asian and Oceanic arts, situated in a remote part of the Denon wing (access through level 1).

ANTIQUE MYSTERY

The oldest displayed piece is the statue of *Ain Ghazal* (Room 303, Sully Wing), unearthed in the 1980s in Jordan. Its subject is still a mystery: was it a man, a child, a god? In comparison, the *Winged Victory of Samothrace* and the *Venus de Milo*, both date back to the 3rd and 1st century BCE, which means more than 8000 years separates them from the enigmatic statue!

TOP TIPS

● Make sure to book your ticket online in advance, as you won't need to line up at the museum desk and there may be special offers available.

● The website is a valuable resource for finding inspiration and planning your visit, with thematic itinerary ideas.

● Arriving early will give you the opportunity to explore the galleries with fewer crowds.

● Wear comfortable shoes – you'll be walking through 403 halls and nearly 15km of corridors!

● If you're visiting with children, take a break at the Studio (Richelieu wing, level 1), which provides creative materials for them to enjoy.

FÊTE DE LA MUSIQUE

If you are in Paris on 21 June, the longest day of the year, get ready for the Fête de la Musique (Festival of Music). During this jovial annual celebration, which was launched in 1982 by the French government to encourage and support amateur music, the city's streets are filled all day and night with every kind of music genre imaginable. Concerts include big-hitter names, and are even held in unique venues, including the Louvre, but one of the best ways to experience the festival is to just stroll around by foot in neighbourhoods like Bastille, encountering concerts by chance. Check the full schedule at *fetede lamusique-paris.fr*, concerts generally run from 6pm to midnight.

PATRICK KERWIN/SHUTTERSTOCK

Sainte-Chapelle

continued from p55

room with displays on the cathedral's history before you reach the Galerie des Chimères (Gargoyles Gallery). These grotesque statues divert rainwater from the roof to prevent masonry damage, with the water exiting through their elongated, open mouths. Although they appear medieval, they were installed by Viollet-le-Duc in the 19th century. There's a 1000-visitor maximum per day, so book your timed-entry ticket in advance.

It is absolutely worth the fee to enter the *trésor* (treasury), which houses Notre Dame's dazzling sacred jewels and relics in the cathedral's southeastern transept. Check out the wonderful Les Camées des Papes (Papal cameos), sculpted with incredible finesse in shell and framed in silver. The 268 pieces depict every pope in miniature, from St Pierre to Benoît XVI.

Shimmering Stained Glass of Sainte-Chapelle

Glorious Gothic chapel bedazzlement

No sight in Paris is as dazzling as the radiant Holy Chapel called **Sainte-Chapelle** *(sainte-chapelle.fr; adult Jun-Sep €18, Oct-May €13, incl Conciergerie Jun-Sep/Oct-May €25/20, child free),* hidden away like a precious gem within the city's

EATING IN MONTMARTRE & PIGALLE: OUR PICKS

Aléa: Simple market-led cuisine. Local favourite. *noon-1.30pm & 7.30-9.30pm Wed & Thu, noon-1.30pm & 7.30-10pm Fri, noon-2pm & 7.30-10pm Sat, 12.30-2pm Sun €€*

La Part des Anges: Laid-back local spot with great traditional food like *magret de canard. 7pm-10.30pm Tue-Thu, 7pm-10.45pm Fri, noon-2.30pm & 7-11pm Sat €€*

Bouillon Pigalle: Terrific value, this *bouillon* is one of several not to miss for escargot and steak-frites. *noon-midnight Sun-Thu, from 11.30am Fri & Sat €*

Maggie: Vintage-style dining space (with vestiges of its days as a 1920s dancing hall) serves traditional French food. Rooftop bar with city views. *7-10pm Tue-Sat €€*

original, 13th-century Palais de Justice (Law Courts) and Palais de la Cité, the former royal residence. Paris' oldest, finest stained glass laces its sublime Gothic interior – best viewed on sunny days when light floods in, creating an entrancing rainbow of bold colours. Built in just six years and consecrated in 1248, it was conceived by French king Louis IX to house his collection of holy relics, including the famous Ste-Couronne (Holy Crown, Jesus' wreath of thorns), which he acquired in 1239 from the Emperor of Constantinople for a sum easily exceeding the amount it cost to build the chapel. There are discounts on entry on Wednesdays from April to September.

Beautiful Bookshops
English-language spots with Parisian soul

French literary giants and expatriate authors found creative refuge in both the city's cafes and bookshops, like the whimsical **Shakespeare and Company** (shakespeareandcompany.com), a hub for expats since 1919. There's also the cosy, Canadian-run **Abbey Bookshop** (abbeybookshop.org), where towering stacks of books and regular readings invite lingering. Along the Seine, the *bouquinistes* continue to sell vintage books, posters and magazines from green wooden stalls.

Where Cabaret Meets Cocktails
Glamour and after-dark revelry

Since the Belle Époque, Pigalle has been Paris' playground of after-dark pleasures. Its reputation truly took shape after WWII, when it became a hub for neon-lit sex shops, cabarets and smoky bars. While many of its infamous establishments are fading, Pigalle's spirit endures in legendary venues like the **Moulin Rouge** (moulinrouge.fr; adult €103), where since 1889, high-kicking dancers and extravagant sets bring the cancan to life in nightly shows at 9pm and 11pm. Cabaret **Madame Arthur** (madamearthur.fr) is a fun evening out of live music and gender-bending performances, keeping Pigalle's legacy of spectacle and seduction alive. Beyond the show lights, Pigalle's warren of small spaces has always been central to its illicit charm, once home to shadowy dens, opium-fuelled escapades and whispered rendezvous. Today, these tight quarters have found a new life as cocktail bars, where locals and visitors mingle over expertly crafted drinks. Spots like **Sister Midnight**, **Dirty Dick**, **Minore** and **Classique** shake up inventive cocktails, blending Pigalle's hedonistic past with a squeakier-clean present.

A Basilica With a View
Paris' sacred heart

Rising above Montmartre (the hill of martyrs), the **Basilique du Sacré-Cœur** (sacre-coeur-montmartre.com; adult/child/groups €8/5/6, tickets available on-site only, email for guided visits), dedicated to the Sacred Heart of Jesus, is a vantage point, a sanctuary, a Parisian rite of passage, and one of the

GHOSTS OF ARTISTS PAST

Pigalle has long been a stage for Paris' most electrifying performers and artists. In the late 19th century, Toulouse-Lautrec immortalised its cabarets, painting La Goulue and Jane Avril, the high-kicking stars of the Moulin Rouge. The district pulsed with bohemian energy, drawing poets and painters. By the 1920s, Josephine Baker mesmerised crowds at the Folies Bergère, while Édith Piaf sang in Pigalle's streets before becoming the soul of French chanson. Jazz musician and writer Boris Vian added his avant-garde flair to the area's clubs. After WWII, Pigalle's neon glow lit up a world of jazz, burlesque and underground culture. Today, its music halls, cabarets and cocktail bars keep the spirit of its legendary artists alive.

city's most visited landmarks. From its gleaming domes to one of the world's largest mosaics, its grandeur stuns. Designed in a striking Roman-Byzantine style, the basilica took five architects over four decades to complete (1875–1919). Visitors can climb the 300 steps to the dome for breathtaking panoramic views of Paris, while inside, chapels, stained-glass windows, and a crypt bathed in natural light create a contemplative atmosphere. The basilica's perpetual adoration prayer cycle, which began in 1885, continues uninterrupted, and on Sundays, the grand organ resonates through the sacred space during Mass and vespers. You can spend the night at the Basilica from 11pm to 7am if you pray for at least an hour, as part of the continuous prayer cycle, unbroken since 1885 (sign up on the Basilica website, dorms from €15).

Grab a Bargain

France's most famous flea market

Founded in 1885, the **Marché aux Puces de St-Ouen** *(puces deparissaintouen.com)* is the world's largest antiques market, located just beyond Paris' northern edge. It spans 12 distinct markets spread across 7 hectares, with antiques, vintage furniture, rare collectibles, fashion and curiosities. For serious collectors or intrigued wanderers, the mazelike alleys have endless inspiration and irresistible old-world charm.

The allure of Les Puces lies in the diversity and distinct rhythm and charm of each market. **Marché Vernaison**, the oldest, is a warren of open-air lanes lined with vintage postcards, embroidered linens and costume jewellery. **Marché Paul Bert Serpette**, the crown jewel, draws a discerning crowd of interior designers and collectors who come for 20th-century design icons, museum-worthy antiques and impeccably curated vignettes. Inside the vaulted glass pavilion of **Marché Dauphine**, the atmosphere is more freewheeling: vinyl records, retro cameras, tribal artefacts and the occasional taxidermied bird. **L'Entrepot** is one of the smallest markets but it's mighty and has a bunch of old zinc-top brasserie bars and spiral staircases from houses all over the country.

Haggling is part of the charm at Les Puces. Approach vendors with a smile, and you might knock 10% to 20% off the price. While some accept cards, cash is often preferred for smaller items or better deals.

Urban Swimming

Go for a dip in the Seine

In 1900, during the first edition of the Olympic Games in Paris, swimming races took place in the River Seine. Decades of industrialisation polluted the waters until a nadir was reached in the 1970s. After a mass clean-up operation, including the construction of water-treatment plants and rainwater-storage basins, swimming was possible once again for the 2024 Games. Since the summer of 2025, the public has also been able to bathe in the famous river,

MORE CITY DIPS
Urban 'wild' swimming is on the rise, and there are plenty of other European cities where you can take a plunge, including Barcelona, Amsterdam and Berlin.

Grande Mosquée de Paris

THE GUIDE

FRANCE PARIS

MARCHE DES FIERTÉS

Running in Paris since 1981, the **Marche des Fiertés** *(marchedes fiertes.org)* has its origins in the Gay Pride marches that began in New York. In Paris the annual parade is attended by over 500,000 people and includes support from more than 200 volunteers. Organisation of the event is led by the group Inter-LGBT, who brings together around 90 organisations. Their shared mission is to 'combat discrimination based on sexual orientation or gender identity, as part of the promotion of human rights and fundamental freedoms'. Open to all, whether you identify as an ally or part of the community, the event is a celebratory and political day filled with music, costumes, placards, floats, a final concert and dance-filled afterparties.

including at the **Bercy swimming area** by the **Simone de Beauvoir footbridge**. The area is supervised, marked with buoys and equipped with showers and lockers.

Calm at the Paris Mosque

A North African oasis for food and relaxation

One of the biggest mosques in France, and Paris' central mosque, the **Grande Mosquée de Paris** *(grandemosqueede paris.fr)* has a striking Moorish-style minaret, which peeks out from behind smooth white walls as you approach along the street. Visit the interior to see the intricate tile work and calligraphy. There is also a North African hammam (steam bathhouse) with timings for women and men, a pretty court-yard **restaurant** *(la-mosquee.com)* that serves delicious cous-cous, tagines and meat skewers, as well as a tearoom with sweet, fragrant mint tea and traditional cakes. There is also the possibility of smoking shisha in the front garden.

Pay Respects to Wilde & Morrison

The resting place of artists

When commissioned to design the new Parisian cemetery, **Père Lachaise**, in the early 19th century, architect Alexandre-Théodore Brongniart envisioned a space that would embody nobility without grandiosity, and simplicity without neglect, and invoke religious sentiments without fear. Inspired by En-glish gardens, the cemetery was meticulously planned, with winding paths and a significant portion dedicated to nature. Today, as you enter, the cacophony of the city fades away and the graves seamlessly blend into the undulating landscape, creating a feeling of beautiful strangeness, as if you were suspended between two worlds.

continued on p64

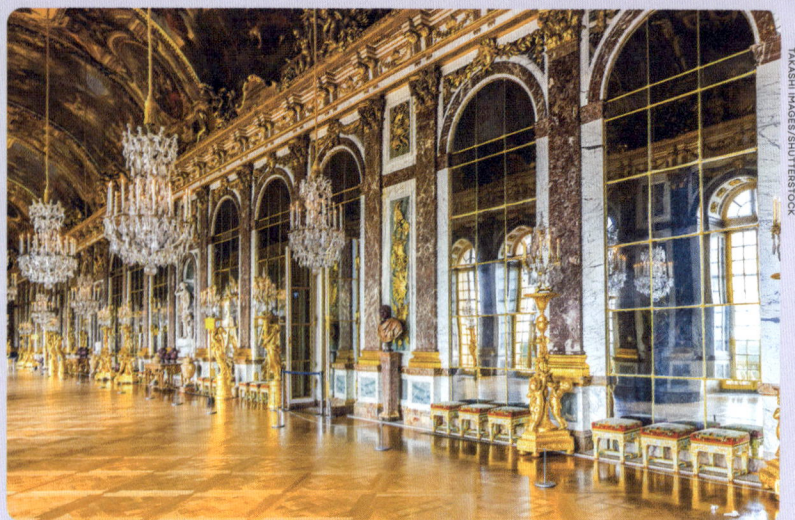

TAKASHI IMAGES/SHUTTERSTOCK

Hall of Mirrors

TOP EXPERIENCE

Versailles

Sprawling over 900 hectares, the monumental, 400-year-old Château de Versailles is France's most famous and grand palace. It's situated in the leafy, bourgeois suburb of Versailles, 22km southwest of central Paris. The estate is divided into three main sections: the 580m-long palace; the gardens, canals and pools to the west of the palace; and the Trianon Estate to the northwest.

DON'T MISS

The Palace

Hall of Mirrors

King's and Queen's State Apartments

Formal gardens and fountains

Lunch near the Grand Canal

History

The estate began in 1623 as a hunting lodge for Louis XIII. Subsequently, Louis XIV transformed it into a vast, baroque château. Some 30,000 workers and soldiers toiled on the property, the bills for which all but emptied the kingdom's coffers.

The Château de Versailles was the kingdom's political capital and the seat of the royal court from 1682 up until the fateful events of 1789 when revolutionaries massacred the palace guard. Louis XVI and Marie Antoinette were ultimately dragged back to Paris, where they were ingloriously

PRACTICALITIES
● en.chateauversailles.fr ● adult/child from €21/ free ● 9am-5.30pm Tue-Sun

guillotined. In the 19th century, Napoléon and Josephine lived on the estate, as did Charles de Gaulle in the 1940s.

The Palace

Work on the palace began in 1661 under the guidance of architect Louis Le Vau (Jules Hardouin-Mansart took over from Le Vau in the mid-1670s); painter and interior designer Charles Le Brun; and landscape artist André Le Nôtre, whose workers flattened hills, drained marshes and relocated forests as they laid out the seemingly endless gardens, ponds and fountains.

Le Brun and his hundreds of artisans decorated every moulding, cornice, ceiling and door of the interior with the most luxurious and ostentatious of appointments: frescoes, marble, gilt and woodcarvings, many with themes and symbols drawn from Greek and Roman mythology.

Few alterations have been made to the château since its construction, apart from most of the interior furnishings disappearing during the Revolution and many of the rooms being redecorated by Louis-Philippe (r 1830–48), who opened part of the château to the public in 1837. The château is in the final stages of a lavish €400 million restoration.

Hall of Mirrors

The palace's opulence peaks in its shimmering Galerie des Glaces (Hall of Mirrors). This 75m-long ballroom shines with 17 sparkling mirrored features comprising 357 individual mirrors on one side and an equal number of windows overlooking the gardens and the setting sun on the other.

King's & Queen's State Apartments

Luxurious, ostentatious appointments adorn every feature of the palace's Grands Appartements du Roi et de la Reine (the King's and Queen's State Apartments). Rooms are dedicated to Hercules, Venus, Diana, Mars and Mercury.

Other Notable Rooms

The **Galerie des Batailles** (Battle Gallery) is longer than the Hall of Mirrors and features 33 huge paintings that recall mostly forgotten French military victories. Savour the thematic decor in the **Salon de la Guerre** (War Room) and the **Salon de la Paix** (Peace Room), which bookend the Hall of Mirrors.

Gardens, Estate & Equestrian Academy

A walk through the sprawling and artful formal gardens, natural areas, huge Grand Canal and the Trianon palaces is a highlight. Or take in a horse show at the **National Equestrian Academy of Versailles**.

HISTORIC VERSAILLES

Don't miss the historic centre of Versailles town. Build a superb picnic at the market stalls of **Les Halles de Versailles** on the **place du Marché**. In the old St-Louis quarter, next to the **Cathédrale St-Louis**, the **Potager du Roi** (King's Kitchen Garden) dates from the time of gourmand Louis XIV.

TOP TIPS

● Prepurchase tickets on the château's website for a dedicated time slot.

● Consider getting tickets for a concert in the Royal Chapel or Royal Opera for a unique palace experience.

● Download the official Château de Versailles app – loaded with audio tours and info for the entire estate.

● The four-person rental electric carts are limited to a set route covering a fraction of the estate. Rental bikes and e-bikes allow the most freedom. Explore the Grand Canal with a rowboat. The shuttle train is very slow.

● Versailles is best reached by the RER C line, which ends at Versailles Château Rive Gauche (some trains continue elsewhere). Other stations with Versailles in their names are a much longer walk from the château and town centre.

BASTILLE'S ANCIENT FORTRESS

Nothing remains of Bastille's fortress, originally constructed in the 14th century to defend the eastern flank of Paris against the English during the Hundred Years' War. By 1417 the royal castle took on an unusual new aspect: it formally became a state prison, housing inmates for centuries until it was destroyed during the 1789 revolution. On 14 July 1789, the inhabitants of the Faubourg St-Antoine, sick of prolonged food shortages due to an ongoing siege of Paris, stormed Bastille prison. When the guards refused to surrender, rebels seized 250 barrels of gunpowder, freed prisoners and put the military governor's head on a pike. This was the first episode of the French Revolution.

MIKHAIL GNATKOVSKIY/SHUTTERSTOCK

Les Catacombes

continued from p61

Overlooked at the time of its inauguration, the cemetery faced challenges in gaining popularity due to its location far from the city. However, to enhance its appeal, the city of Paris relocated the graves of famous figures like Molière and La Fontaine. Over time, politicians, scientists, artists and writers followed, solidifying Père Lachaise's reputation as the eternal resting place of the renowned. Oscar Wilde's tomb has long been the object of passionate kisses believed to bring luck in love, and the ritual offerings left on Jim Morrison's grave perpetuate a cult (mainly based on alcohol). Download the cemetery map from a QR code at the entrance; this will help you locate specific graves and landmarks, and choose the right entrance. There are five different ones, but only three of them are near metro stations.

An Underground Ossuary
The ghosts of Paris past

In 1785, subterranean tunnels of an abandoned quarry were upcycled as storage rooms for the exhumed bones of corpses that could no longer fit in the city's overcrowded cemeteries. By 1810 the skull- and bone-lined catacombs – resting place of millions of anonymous Parisians – had been officially born.

The route through **Les Catacombes** *(catacombes.paris.fr; adult/child €31/12)* begins at its spacious entrance on av du Colonel Henri Rol-Tanguy. Walk down 131 spiral steps to reach the ossuary itself, with a mind-boggling number of bones and skulls of millions of Parisians neatly packed along the walls. Visits cover about 1.5km of tunnels in all, at a cool 14°C. People with claustrophobia may experience some anxiety in the confined environment. It's closed Mondays.

Mont St-Michel

BIODIVERSE BAY | TIDE-WALKING | WONDROUS ABBEY

For a millennium, Mont St-Michel has entranced visitors with majestic views that metamorphose with the tides. When the seas rise, a 1000-year-old Gothic abbey crowns the top of an island of craggy rock. Conceptualised from a dream in which an archangel bids a bishop to build a place of devotion in an impossible place, Mont St-Michel captures the imagination of anyone who crosses its sandy paths. The sometimes-island itself changes as quickly as the sea; only a handful of inhabitants live there in comparison to the millions of annual tourists who crowd the winding streets that ascend to the pointed top.

Once you've snapped your photo of the extraordinary sight and have heard the bells ring in the abbey, the next best step is to immerse yourself in the incredible biodiversity of the bay. With slow and careful observation and turning off the tourist paths, you can find yourself in a vivid, waking dream full of flora, fauna and culinary delights.

Nocturnal Visits & High Tide

A night visit to the bay

The traditional approach to the **Abbaye du Mont St-Michel** *(abbaye-mont-saint-michel.fr; adult/child €16/free)* is an established, elevated wood-plank path with guardrails, next to the road where shuttles ferry visitors back and forth all day. But in the spirit of Robert Frost: the road less travelled makes all the difference. If you're pressed for time, try to go as early as possible to avoid the crowds, and plan on eating and sleeping off the almost-island to avoid handing over a lot of cash for mediocre tourist traps.

Take the unconventional route and sink your toes in the sometimes-moving quicksand with local guide **Romain Pilon** *(labaiecderomain.fr; tours per person from €15)*, native of the bay and a guide for over two decades. Fishing enthusiasts can go shrimping with Romain during select windows throughout the year, usually mid-September through October and a short

GETTING AROUND

The nearest train stop is Pontorson (just short of five hours from Paris), where buses will take you 350m from the entrance of Mont St-Michel. But a car is your best bet to get around the bay and surrounding villages, though parking near Mont-St-Michel is pricey. Getting to the island of Mont St-Michel itself is fairly straightforward: walk or queue up for an all-day shuttle bus (free). To walk across the bay, it's best to hire a guide and check tide changes: *ot-montsaintmichel .com/marees.*

☑ **TOP TIP**

Avoid the summer months (July and August) for the best views and fewer crowds. If you find yourself here during high season, try to go at dusk or dawn to beat the rush.

BEST ANNUAL FÊTES/FESTIVALS IN NORMANDY

Dîner sur la Digue: Join thousands of guests at this dinner party alongside the boardwalk in Cabourg. Reserve, pack your picnic or grab a meal from vendors.

Cabourg Mon Amour Festival: Annual three-day, open-air music festival, with styles from electro to rap. *cabourgmon amour.fr*

Fête des Marins: Every Pentecost weekend (the seventh Sunday after Easter), get suited in sailor stripes in Honfleur for parades, concerts, photos and more.

Offcourts Festival: September festival celebrating French and Québécois short films. Free screenings, concerts and festivities.

American Film Festival: Each September, stars gather in Deauville to celebrate American cinema. *festival-deau ville.com*

MONT ST-MICHEL

⭐ **HIGHLIGHTS**
1 Abbaye du Mont St-Michel

⬤ **SLEEPING**
2 Auberge Sauvage

3 Camping La Baie du Mont St-Michel
4 Chambres d'Hôte Les Bruyères du Mont

🟢 **EATING**
see 2 Auberge Sauvage
5 La Brocante
6 Le Grillon
see 1 Le Logis Sainte Catherine

window in April. But year-round, the best way to see Mont St-Michel is with his 'Sortie Nocturnes'.

Night owls will meet at 7.30pm and then skulk around the bay as evening falls. Enter a hidden world over the next few hours, bathed in the light of the spectacular sunset and surrounded by the cries of geese and migratory birds – identified by your guide – and the moving waters and sound of the shifting shores. The visit ends at 11.30pm, cloaked in the mystical magic of night, where you'll emerge with uncovered secrets and views of the bay.

 EATING NEAR MONT-ST-MICHEL: OUR PICKS

Auberge Sauvage: Michelin-starred haven set in a 16th-century presbytery. Local produce and foraged delicacies dominate. *7.30pm-midnight Thu-Mon €€€*

La Brocante: Enjoy simple snacks, sandwiches, crêpes, coffees and wines in this retrofitted old auto shop. *10am-6pm Mon, Thu & Fri, 11am-6pm Sat & Sun €*

Le Grillon: Unpretentious and unfussy spot to taste lamb chops made from the sheep that graze the salty fields. *12.30-1.30pm Sat-Wed, 7-8.30pm Fri-Tue €€*

Le Logis Sainte Catherine: Rotating menu with innovative plates like *moussette* rillettes. Dazzling terrace, elegant decor. Book online. *hours vary €€€*

Abbaye du Mont St-Michel (p65)

Go Birding or Become a Bird

Bird-watching and paragliding

If you're travelling with a group, flock together and book the **Birding Bus** *(birding-msm.com; from €10)*, run by ornithologist and biologist-by-training Sébastian Provost, who showcases bird-watching as a fascinating artform that brings to life hidden worlds. At various points along the bay, you'll encounter birds, seals and even dolphins.

For those who like to fly solo, jump for a bird's-eye view of Mont St-Michel and its surroundings – literally. With experienced and competition-winning paraglider **Léo Hamard** *(parapenteenbaie.fr; flights from €80)*, you can float above the abbey and the bay like a bird. Watch your feet dangle and be dazzled by the singular feeling of lightness and freedom flying on the winds. Adrenaline junkies and first-timers alike can spring for the 'acrobatic' flight option (weather contingent) for a truly head-spinning flight. Reserve a date in advance online, but the jumping-off point is dictated by the winds.

MAD FOR MOUSSETTES IN MAY

Crab lovers, take note of *moussettes*, the nickname of a variety of young spider crab (under two years old) found all over fish markets in La Manche from April to June, and especially bountiful during the month of May. They're known for their sweet, subtle and abundant flesh; enjoy them without any condiments needed, although if you're partial to one, homemade mayonnaise is the most traditional (our advice: wear a bib and gloves to avoid the mess). You can buy them cooked or boil in water for 20 minutes. As a bonus, eating *moussettes* also helps out the local ecosystem, since the spider crabs have infiltrated the Normandy region and pose a threat to mussel producers.

Beyond Mont St-Michel

Explore the bucolic Norman countryside and wild Breton coast, toasting your adventures with crisp apple cider.

Places

GETTING AROUND

Various towns and cities like Le Havre, Étretat and St-Malo are easily accessible by direct trains from Paris. More isolated areas, including the D-Day beaches, require more planning, with sparse bus services. A car is most convenient to explore the less touristy areas (Breton highways are toll-free, Norman highways are not!). In both Normandy and Brittany, hiking and cycling are some of the best ways to take in coastal scenery.

To the east of Mont St-Michel, Normandy's breathtaking landscapes singlehandedly inspired the impressionist art movement; painter Claude Monet obsessively painted sunrise at Le Havre and his backyard water lilies in Giverny. From the world-famous and epically surreal Mont St-Michel abbey, all the way to the cliffs of Étretat, the Normandy coast is replete with famed destinations. History buffs can immerse themselves in D-Day reenactments, and even breakfast on tables made from reassembled German planes. Westwards, Brittany has some of nature's most wonderful sights with unspoiled rawness. Over 2000km of coastline, the ocean's mystical draw and mesmerising landscapes never fail to enchant visitors. That's got to be worth braving the rain.

Giverny
TIME FROM MONT ST-MICHEL: **3HR**

Skip the crowds at Monet's secret island

Monet's residence of over four decades, **Maison et Jardins de Claude Monet** (*claudemonetgiverny.fr; adult/child/under 7yr €12/6.50/free*) is a powerful testament to the lasting legacy of a visionary artist: his world-famous water lilies and his eccentric, brightly coloured home dotted with his collection of Japanese block prints are flocked to by thousands of tourists each year. The queue for the water lilies, which tears through the house at a frenetic pace, can be intimidating – but if you pause and gaze out of the window and focus on a flower, you'll surely be left with an impression of the painter's life. Reservations are strongly recommended (weekdays are slightly less crowded than the weekend) and beware of big holiday weekend crowds.

To contemplate his life with more breathing room, walk up to his humble grave and contrast it with the greatness of his legacy. Better yet, picnic at the lesser-known **Île aux Orties**, a patch of land Monet owned at the confluence of where the Epte River meets the Seine, that once turned into an island during heavy rain periods. To get there, walk past the windmill near the car parks the along the small rue des Batards

Maison et Jardins de Claude Monet, Giverny

until you reach the river for a more isolated experience of one of his rarer, inspired landscapes.

Étretat

TIME FROM MONT ST-MICHEL: **2½HR**

Coast along the renowned alabaster cliffs

France's famous and trafficked cliffs, Étretat's staggering arches have been sculpted over millennia by winds and the whims of the sea, and immortalised by Monet over 80 times. More recently, the cliffs have also unfortunately been the cause of deaths due to reckless photos – skip the selfies at the top and don't stray off established paths.

Falaise d'Aval and the adjacent Aiguille are the most iconic, featuring a needle shooting from the water alongside an arch; and the **Falaise d'Amont** has a bird's-eye view of Étretat. Hikes here are choose-your-own-adventure: opt for the steep steps to the neo-Gothic stone church, **Chapelle Notre-Dame-de-la-Garde**, for a peaceful (yet windy) picnic – the view from the church is better than a visit inside. Hardcore hikers, head to the intensive and rewarding five-hour Roc Vaudieu Loop. If you're short on time, take the Porte d'Amont Loop that starts at Chemin de Criquetot. To wade deeper into the waters, head to **Voiles et Galets** *(voilesetgalets.com; rentals from €15)* in Étretat for an unforgettable kayak or paddleboard ride

IN THE PATH OF RUSSIAN PAINTERS

Stretching just 1.1km, France's shortest river runs through **Veules-les-Roses**, a tiny village of idyllic windmills and thatched-roof cottages where Russian impressionist painters found endless inspiration during the 1850s. Along the river you can see the mill and watering hole, and beachside you can see the same sea as immortalised by painters Alexei Petrovitch Bogolyubov and Vassily Dmitrievich Polenov. Near the stone bridge near the source of the river, there's a watercress mill (also painted by Polenov), and today the watercress is still enjoyed by locals with an annual festival.

EATING IN GIVERNY: OUR PICKS

Au Coin du Pain'tre: Simple plates like quiches and baguette sandwiches. The highlight: relaxing over breakfast or lunch with a garden view. *9am-7pm* €

Cocorico: Pop-up food truck with fresh sandwiches, burgers and desserts at reasonable prices for a takeaway picnic, when the sun's out. *hours vary Apr-Oct* €

Les Nymphéas: Family-friendly garden restaurant: crêpes, fondue, raclette, burgers and salads. *9am-6pm Apr-Oct* €€

Oscar: Gourmet bistro in a stylish setting with refined plates by acclaimed chef David Gallienne. *10am-6pm Mon-Thu, to 9pm Fri & Sat* €€€

BEST WWII MUSEUMS/ MEMORIALS

Memorial Museum of Omaha Beach: Memorial of steel shooting out of the sand stops the breath, while well-curated museum pays tribute to fallen soldiers.

Utah Beach Landing Museum: Westernmost beach hosts one of biggest museums built on German fortifications. Glimpse an original B-26 bomber.

La Pointe du Hoc: View ravages of a battlefield and old bunkers at this powerfully sobering memorial point. Many stairs.

Overlord Museum: Collectors' paradise: restored trucks, vehicles, dioramas and veteran tributes.

Airborne Museum: Near historic church Ste-Mère-Église, this museum focuses on the airborne troops and hosts an original glider and a C-47 plane.

---

under some epic scenery; no reservations, as rentals depend on weather conditions. Don't miss a paddle out to the **Plage du Fourquet** to enjoy a secluded beach.

D-Day Landing Beaches

TIME FROM MONT ST-MICHEL: 1½HR

A night at a WWII museum

When US soldiers landed on Normandy's Omaha Beach on the morning of 6 June 1944, the ensuing crescendo to WWII left indelible scars on the French countryside. From west to east, the 80km stretch of sand comprises the American landing beaches of Utah and Omaha; Gold Beach, where the British landed; **Juno Beach** for the Canadians; and then another American landing destination, Sword Beach. Decades later, D-Day remains a monolithic legend that has left countless memorial and military sites, cemeteries, museums and remains of what was once the largest harbour in the world.

Bringing history to life are the wife-and-husband team behind guesthouse **D-Day Aviators Le Manoir** *(ddayavia torslemanoir.fr)*. Anne Florence and Paul Hontang are both pilots with passions. Paul is a history expert, constantly on the hunt to add to their impressive collection of war detritus: a plane cockpit adorns the living room, and guests breakfast on a table made from a German plane engine. Anne has a personal collection of over 500 dentelles, traditional lace bonnets and hats worn to signify the different life stages of a woman. Ask her for a peek in the garage next door. Situated in Arromanches-les-Bains, where the world's largest artificial harbour was assembled by the Allied Forces, the manor house is centrally placed for visiting all along the D-Day Landing Beaches and right next to the renovated **Musée du Debarquement** *(musee-arromanches.fr; adult/child €12.90/8.30)*, a stunningly detailed presentation of why and how the critical events of 6 June 1944 took place.

For a wilder ride, head to the family-friendly **La Batterie du Holdy Guesthouse** *(batterie-du-holdy.com)*, just south of Utah Beach. Be transported back to the events of 6 June 1944, with cinematic and immersive reenactments in the very buildings where WWII action took place. Booking a night here is well worth it – an impassioned Jeep tour is included without steep prices. The real goldmine is the anecdotes Jean generously shares with his guests, and the delight of breakfast served in a 1940s-era grocery store.

Go behind enemy lines

On the coast along the English Channel, known as La Manche, near Utah Beach, there are a few German artillery batteries to visit. The **Batterie de Crisbecq** *(batteriedecrisbecq. fr; adult/child €12.50/8.50)*, also known as the Battery of St Marcouf, is the largest and most spectacular. Built in 1941 by the German military engineering group Todt, the bunker today lets you walk in German soldiers' footsteps – the former trenches have been excavated and now serve as walking paths between the 22 blockhouses. View up-close battle scars, grenade traps and visible damage. The **Batterie d'Azeville** *(batterie-azeville.manche.fr; adult/child €8/4)* is smaller in scale, but stands intact today due to a one-in-a-million chance: on D-Day, an American destroyer successfully shot a shell through the opening of the blockhouses. The shell miraculously didn't explode but crossed through the blockhouse and ended up a dud behind the fields.

If you want to go underground in WWII sites, head to the under-the-radar **Radar Museum 1944** *(musee-radar.fr; adult/under 10yr €7.50/free),* a former German listening station that has preserved its original state. Run by friendly and impassioned volunteers, the guided visits at this lesser-known museum are well worth reserving in advance.

St-Malo

TIME FROM MONT ST-MICHEL: **50MIN** 🚗

Pirates and privateers

'Not French, not Breton, I am Malouin.' St-Malo's slogan sets the tone. Circled and protected by its commanding ramparts yet resolutely open to the sea, it takes great pride in its very distinctive identity. One of the most prosperous ports in France from the 15th century onwards, it became home to great seafarers such as Jacques Cartier, the first European to make his way to Canada in the 16th century. But St-Malo is most famous for the high number of privateers who enriched the city in the 17th and 18th centuries. Commissioned by the King of France to pillage enemy boats during war times, privateers owned hundreds of armed ships in the port of St-Malo towards the end of the 18th century. The city walls, which originally date back to the 12th century, were expanded and fortified to better defend these accumulated treasures, and quickly became emblematic of the city.

Standing imperiously on a rocky island facing the sea, St-Malo's **Fort National** *(fortnational.com; adult/child €5/3)* was built in 1689 and was originally intended to protect the city's port. Throughout the centuries, it has been the stage of legendary attacks and epic battles – and has also known darker days during WWII, when it was used as a prison by the Germans. The site is now open to visits every day in the summer, and during some school holidays and bank holidays. Opening hours depend on the time of the day: you'll need to wait for the tide to be low to walk across **Plage de l'Eventail** to reach the fort. You can book a 35-minute guided tour in English by email, with written translations also available in a number of other languages.

THE PRICE OF LIBERATION

The old town of St-Malo as we know it today came very close to not surviving at all. In August 1944, after four years of German occupation, St-Malo and its surroundings were relentlessly bombed by the Allies. When the city was liberated on 17 August 1944, 80% of the old town was destroyed. The ramparts, miraculously, were still standing. However, instead of razing the remains to the ground and rebuilding afresh, everything was reconstructed just as it was: a colossal, complex project that took years, including 18 months just to clear out the 500,000 cu metres of ruins. In 1972, when Cathédrale St-Vincent was inaugurated, St-Malo was officially completely restored.

 EATING IN ST-MALO: OUR PICKS

| **Doma:** A cosy room and a short, tasty menu based on seasonal produce that is reasonably priced. *noon-1.30pm Wed-Sat, 7.30-9.30pm Tue-Sat* €€ | **La Touline:** Classic crêperie with high-quality ingredients at the heart of the *intra muros. hours vary* € | **Les Flibustiers:** A warm spot with a terrace in the centre offering no-fuss *planches* (platters), salads, tartines, quiches and soups. *hours vary* € | **Bouliche:** Away from the crowds, near to Cité d'Alet, a local gem with creative plates. *noon-2pm Tue, 7-10pm Wed, noon-2pm & 7-10pm Thu-Sat* €€ |

French Alps

MOUNTAIN SCENERY | ADRENALINE | CHEESE

Places

Chamonix p73
Annecy p76
Alpe d'Huez p788

☑ TOP TIP

Travelling without kids? Take your skiing holiday in late January or late March: you'll miss all the school holidays (French and European) and rates are much lower. Low season in the Alps is from late April to early June and late September to late November, and many mountain towns all but shut up shop.

Heart-thumping adventure and pastoral tradition share the same starting gate in this high-octane playground, dedicated to safeguarding ancestral savoir-faire. The French Alps is where beauty of the most breathtaking nature and action collide. Glacier-carved national parks and shark-toothed mountain summits, ice-blue lakes and sky-high cols: the call of the wild is fierce in this eastern swathe of France, even more so for outdoor adventurers in town to bag the highest, longest feat – on skis, bike or simply your own two feet.

Rumbling across seven European countries, the Alps climax with western Europe's highest peak, Mont Blanc (4805m). The hypnotic snow-white crown of this storied mountain spirographs a kaleidoscope of magical shadows over the renowned ski and mountaineering town of Chamonix in Savoie (Savoy). Inhabited since prehistoric times, the French Alps have been fiercely contested since time immemorial. The desire to conquer that they arouse burns brighter

◈ GETTING AROUND

Embracing the *départements* (departments) of Savoie, Haute-Savoie and Isère, the French Alps cover a vast area – not easy to navigate swiftly, thanks to valleys and mountains blocking direct routes. Roads to many ski stations are steep and serpentine. Snow clearing is frequent, but winter tyres or chains stowed in your trunk are obligatory from November to March. Many cols (mountain passes) are snowbound and closed in winter; in early/late summer, check road conditions before setting out. Buses link Moûtiers train station with Les Trois

Vallées and Bourg-St-Maurice station with Val d'Isère/Tignes. Modane is the rail stop for the Vanoise, linked by bus to Bonneval-sur-Arc. For Chamonix, hop on the Mont Blanc Express train at TGV station St-Gervais-Le Fayet. The long-distance GR5 or Grande Traversée des Alpes walking trail crosses the entire French Alps en route from Lake Geneva to the Med (674km). Shorter trails tackle the entire region, and are the loveliest way of slow-hopping between remote hamlets, farms and mountain *refuges* (shelters).

FRANCOIS ROUX/SHUTTERSTOCK

Mer de Glace (p74), Chamonix

than ever regardless of the season, be it the Vallée Blanche ski descent or Europe's longest black run in winter, or epic hiking trails in summer (the Tour du Mont Blanc spans three countries). Lakeside towns like Annecy offer a choice between the slow pace of life – glacial dips and languid paddleboarding in the crystalline waters of Lake Annecy – or yet more adrenaline, and it's one of the most popular spots in the country for paragliding.

All that effort tends to work up an appetite, and culinary specialities in the French Alps are of the 'roll-me-down-the-mountain' type: belt-busting troughs of fondue, gooey tartiflette and heady raclette.

Chamonix

MAP p74

Off-piste ride of a lifetime

Free-rider king of the French Alps and springboard to some of Europe's most fêted mountain adventures, Chamonix has always been one ski spin ahead of the curve. Just walking down Chamonix's pedestrian main street, loomed over by Mont Blanc's snow-white dome, it's impossible not to feel a sassy new spring in your step: the palpable buzz and anticipation of the next outdoor thrill around the corner.

Tales of skiers cruising along and suddenly disappearing from sight are rife in La Vallée Blanche annals. Then again, skiing across a snow bridge and tumbling metres like a rag doll into a dark ice-blue crevasse as the ruptured bridge collapses happens with surprising frequency.

This is just one reason why Europe's most legendary off-piste ski route – an astounding 2800m descent through a landscape of eerie, unearthly beauty – must be tackled with a certified guide. Starting at a dizzying 3842m, at the top

MOUNTAIN TOOLKIT

Lift passes: Find details of all passes at *montblancnatural resort.com*.

Mountain guides: Compagnie des Guides de Chamonix *(chamonix-guides. com)*, inside the Maison de la Montagne, has guides for snowshoeing, ice-climbing, off-piste skiing, summer mountaineering, climbing and canyoning.

Trail access and conditions: The Office de Haute Montagne *(chamoniarde.com)*, also in Maison de la Montagne, has information on hiking, climbing and ski-touring trails – including trail conditions.

Chamonix mobile app: Tourist office app *(en.chamonix.com)*: weather forecasts, webcams, maps; purchase and top-up lift passes, too.

BEST ALTERNATIVE MOUNTAIN THRILLS IN THE FRENCH ALPS

Moon-biking: Ride snowy trails in Courchevel astride a silent, electric snow bike with front sled blade and rear caterpillar track.

Fat biking: Speed down on snow bicycles with ultra-fat tires in La Plagne.

Acro-speleology: Go with a guide to Grottes de St-Christophe caves for mixed climbing-canyoning in Massif des Chartreuse.

Electric mountain biking: Along the Via 3 Vallées, a 34km cycling itinerary links Courchevel, Méribel, Les Menuires and Val Thorens.

Mushing: Sled (up to 50km/h) with American Eskimo, Greenland or Alaskan dogs through sugar-dusted firs in several ski resorts

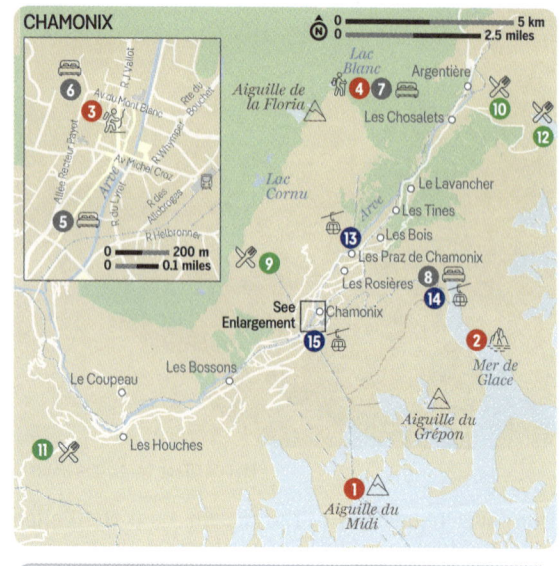

● SIGHTS	● SLEEPING	● EATING	● TRANSPORT
1 Aiguille du Midi	5 Hôtel Richemond	9 La Bergerie de Planpraz	13 Télécabine de la Flégère
2 Mer de Glace	6 La Folie Douce	10 La Crèmerie du Glacier	14 Télécabine de la Mer de Glace
● ACTIVITIES	7 Refuge du Lac Blanc	11 Les Vieilles Luges	15 Téléphérique de l'Aiguille du Midi
3 Compagnie des Guides de Chamonix	8 Refuge du Montenvers	12 Refuge de Lognan	
4 Lac Blanc			

cable-car station of the **Téléphérique de l'Aiguille du Midi** (*aiguilledumidi.montblancnaturalresort.com/en; adult/child return €78/66.30*), the challenging 20km ski route follows three serpentine glaciers down to the lower, moraine-scarred reaches of France's longest glacier, the **Mer de Glace** (Sea of Ice).

Here, at around 1700m, the glass-sided **Télécabine de la Mer de Glace** (*montenversmerdeglace.montblancnatural resort.com; adult/child return incl train, cable car & ice cave €39.50/33.60*) – a state-of-the-art cable car directly above an ice cave – whisks Vallée Blanche skiers back up to Gare du Montenvers at 1913m. From here Montenvers' cherry-red cogwheel train trundles down to Chamonix town in 20 minutes. This leg of the trip is also an exhilarating day trip for nonskiers year-round.

Late March to early April is the best time to tackle the Vallée Blanche, only suitable for confident skiers comfortable on black pistes and ungroomed terrain. Hook up with a guide from **Compagnie des Guides de Chamonix** (*chamonix-guides. com*) on a **small-group expedition** (*per person €155, plus lift passes €90*), with an overnight at 3613m at the **Refuge des Cosmiques** (*incl lift pass €425*) on the Col du Midi glacier or – most magically of all – on a **moonlight descent** (*2 people €430*).

Get up high on Chamonix's most popular hiking trail

Don trainers or sturdy walking shoes for the short but steep, rocky hike up to **Lac Blanc** (2352m). Despite horrific summertime crowds (avoid in July and August), marvelling at razor-sharp reflections of Europe's highest peak in the picture-postcard alpine lake is mind-blowing. Wild dipping in the crystalline water is prohibited.

Beat the crowds by hitting the trail at 8.30am when cable cars open; count three to four hours to cover the 8.5km return hike from the top of **Téléphérique de la Flégère** *(adult/child return €24/20.40)* at 1877m. Alternatively, overnight in Lac Blanc's lakeside mountain hut **Refuge du Lac Blanc** *(refuge-lac-blanc.fr; per person incl full board €85)* to gorge on sunrise views in splendid isolation. The WWII-era, 40-bed hut with basic cafe is open June to September.

Summiting the Aiguille du Midi

This rocky tooth of an alpine peak – **Aiguille du Midi** (3842m) in the Massif du Mont Blanc, easy to spot for miles around – ensnares France's highest cable-car station at 3777m, promising spine-tingling adventure for mountain enthusiasts and privileged access to a spectacular fairy-tale ice world for first-timers to high altitudes. Since it's weather dependent, check the website for variable hours *(aiguilledumidi.montblanc naturalresort.com; adult/child €88/68.90).*

The giddy anticipation of new heights to be conquered is electric as you glide from Chamonix's bottom Téléphérique de l'Aiguille du Midi cable-car station to its top station at 3842m. The change of cabin at mid-station Plan d'Aiguille du Midi (2317m) is a prime opportunity to grab a coffee or *vin chaud* (warm mulled wine) at mountain hut Bar Plan d'Aiguille and acquaint yourself with the numerous aiguilles sculpting Chamonix's distinctive skyline.

At the futuristic top station, dimly lit tunnels spaghetti from the cable car, past wintertime skiers donning crampons to tackle the Vallée Blanche off-piste descent, to a succession of outdoor panoramic terraces. Information panels identify what's what in the surrounding breathtaking sea of snowy peaks.

Follow signs to Le Tube – a 34m-long metal pipe wrapped around part of the rocky spur. Take your time to traverse the cylindrical walkway, perforated with five slit windows overlooking ant-sized rock climbers in summer dangling on Pointe Rébuffat. Information boards impress with mind-blowing facts such as the 300 cu metres of concrete, 80 tons of steel and 500-plus helicopter trips it took to construct this wild, gravity-defying gallery.

CHEESY SAVOYARD SPECIALITIES

Savoyard fondue: In Savoie equal parts of grated Comté, gruyere and Beaufort cheese are melted with white wine in a garlic-smeared pot.

Tartiflette: Reblochon sliced and layered between potatoes, diced bacon, cream and nuts in this classic oven-baked dish.

Raclette: Melted raclette – occasionally smoked/peppered – is scraped from a standing grill onto boiled potatoes.

Burgdorf: Slices of Abondance cheese are oven-baked with Savoie white wine, sweet Madeira wine, nutmeg and pepper until bubbling, crisp and golden.

Crozet gratin: Savoyard 'pasta' squares are oven baked with Beaufort or Reblochon to create a gooey, crisp-crust gratin.

 EATING IN CHAMONIX: BEST MOUNTAIN LUNCHES ——— MAP p74

| **Refuge de Lognan:** The blueberry tart is a rite of passage at this mountain shelter on Argentière's Intégrale run. Cash only. *noon-2pm Jun-Sep & Dec-Apr* € | **La Crèmerie du Glacier:** A 1920s forest cabin famed for gratins, fondues and *croûtes* (wine-soaked bread, oven-baked with toppings). *11:30am-3pm* €€ | **Les Vieilles Luges:** A roaring fire welcomes skis at the Old Sledges, an 18th-century farmhouse on the slopes in Les Houches. *12.30-3pm Tue-Sun Dec-Apr* €€ | **La Bergerie de Planpraz:** The cozy Sheepfold gazes at Mont Blanc from its sunny terrace perched at 2000m. Order fire-grilled meat. *noon-3pm Dec-Apr* €€€ |

Ride the lift up to Pas dans le Vide, a glass-walled and -floored cabin overhanging a 1000m drop which, at 3830m, sits just 12m short of the summit. This is the highest point of the Aiguille du Midi tourist site, and views down are predictably exhilarating or terrifying, depending on your head for heights.

Annecy

Timeless romance in a handsome old town

Colourful facades and flower-fringed canals characterise Annecy's Vielle Ville (old town), nicknamed 'Venice of the Alps'. Commanding views across ochre rooftops and flower-festooned canals to the lake and burly Massif des Bauges beyond, **Château d'Annecy** *(musees.annecy.fr; adult/under 12yr €7/free)* is the crowning glory. Residence to the Counts of Geneva in the 13th and 14th centuries, it was abandoned three centuries on.

From the château, drop steeply down along stone-paved Rampe du Château to prison-turned-history museum **Palais de l'Isle** *(adult/child €5/2.50)*. The best views of this eye-catching stone building, squatting on a triangular islet in the Canal du Thiou since 1325, are from Pont Perrière, the old town's distinctive canal bridge safeguarded by baroque **Église St-François de Salès**. The Venetian atmosphere here is undeniable.

Fly with the birds above Col de la Forclaz

It requires no skill – just guts or the dream to fly with birds – to paraglide over Lake Annecy. April to November, tandem flights take off from the **Site de Montmin** (1276m) up high near the **Col de la Forclaz** (1150m) at the lake's southern tip. They land 10 to 20 minutes later at official landing zones in Doussard (next to the D281) or in Perroix (2km south of Talloires).

Dozens of *parapente* (paragliding) schools offer tandem flights. Several operate from wooden huts at the Doussard landing field, from where minibuses shuttle clients up to the pass. In Annecy's old town, adventure-sports specialists **Takamaka** *(annecy.takamaka.fr; from €95)* has an office at 23 rue du Faubourg Ste-Claire where you can pick up info, check weather/flying conditions and reserve flights.

Paddling and surfing Lake Annecy

Don't let the garish rubber rings outside the *épicerie* (grocery) at the entrance to Doussard Plage on the lake's southern tip put you off. Once afloat a stand-up paddleboard (SUP), you'll find the serenity of less-tamed shores here is intoxicating.

BEST SWIMMING BEACHES

Imperial Beach: Picnic-friendly lawns, sandy beach volleyball court, pétanque, children's playground, concreted shallows to paddle in and seasonal beach bar – by Annecy's pre-WWI casino-turned-luxury hotel.

Marquisats Beach: Grass-fringed pebble beach, a 15-minute stroll from Annecy's Jardins de l'Europe on the western lakeshore.

St-Jorioz Beach: Lake Annecy's only natural sand beach is in St-Jorioz. Vintage diving tower (lifeguards July and August), changing cabins, showers and snack bar.

Angon Beach: Beach volleyball and pétanque, 2km south of Talloires.

Choseaux Beach–Clos Berthet: Untamed grass and pebbles in Sévrier, a 10-minute walk south from busy municipal beach.

 EATING IN ANNECY: OUR PICKS

Marché de la Vieille Ville: Open-air street market in the old town, stalls with Savoyard cheeses, charcuterie and food to go. *7am-1pm Tue, Fri & Sun* €

Les Baigneurs Café: Breakfast, brunch, specialist coffee and lunchtime tartines on a sun-soaked terrace. *8.30am-5.30pm Wed-Fri, from 9am Sat & Sun* €

Bon Pain Bon Vin: Local produce fuels this old-school buvette with 1960s interior, traditional cuisine and specials chalked on the board. *10am-1am* €€

Saba: Feast on creative French-Japanese fusion with local foodies at this sassy old-town bistro. *noon-1.30pm & 7-9pm Mon, Tue, Thu & Fri, 7-9pm Wed* €€€

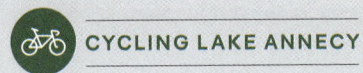

CYCLING LAKE ANNECY

Lap up big mountain views and bijou villages on this 42km lake-loop ride.

START	END	LENGTH
Annecy Town	Annecy Town	42km; 3–4 hours

Hire a bicycle/e-bike from **❶ Cyclable** (*annecy-bonlieu.cyclable.com*) and set off clockwise (300m elevation). Pick up the two-way cycling path in front of Veyrier-du-Lac, and cruise 6km alongside the D909, past Mont Veyrier (1291m) on your left. Climb up to place de l'Église in Menthon-St-Bernard, 3km south; its fairy-tale **❷ Château de Menthon-St-Bernard** is a 2km detour uphill. At **❸ Café de la Place**, refuel on coffee and a *tarte écureuil* (caramelised walnut tart) from the bakery.

Stay alert on the steep downhill swoop to Talloires. It was in this pretty lakefront village cradling 17th-century **❹ Abbaye de Talloires** that Cézanne painted in 1896. This is the lake's narrowest point where the built-up 'grand lac' (north) spills into the wilder 'petit lac' (south). Thirty minutes (8.7km) on a dedicated cycling path takes you to the lake's southern tip. Doussard is the springboard for walks in the **❺ Réserve Naturelle du Bout du Lac d'Annecy**. A greenway now takes you to Duingt: pedalling through a defunct railway tunnel heralds your arrival. Park and follow the footpath 10 minutes to hillside **❻ Grotte de Notre Dame du Lac** for breathtaking lake views. It's 13km back to Annecy.

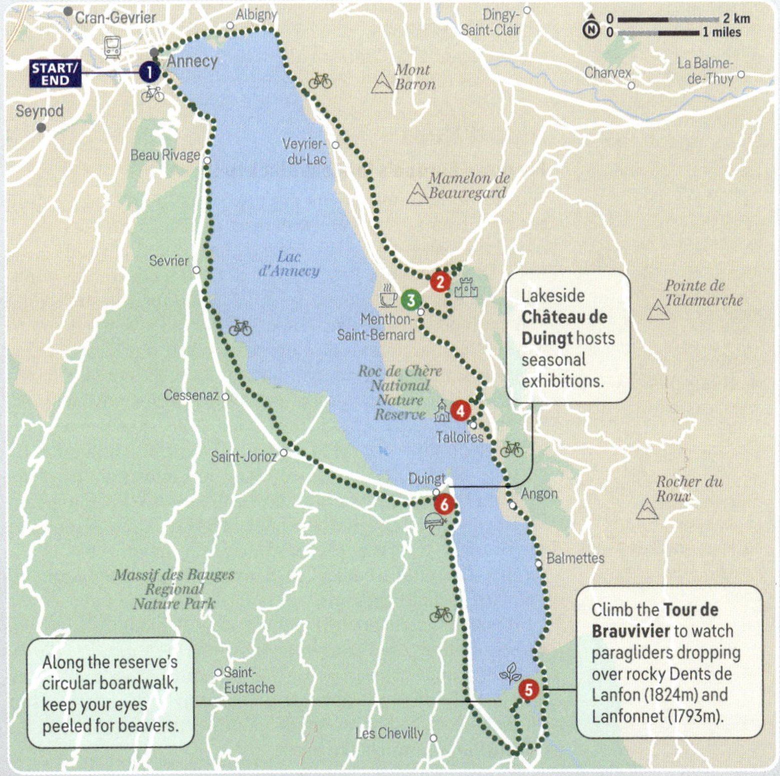

Lakeside **Château de Duingt** hosts seasonal exhibitions.

Along the reserve's circular boardwalk, keep your eyes peeled for beavers.

Climb the **Tour de Brauvivier** to watch paragliders dropping over rocky Dents de Lanfon (1824m) and Lanfonnet (1793m).

SKIING LES TROIS VALLÉES

The world's largest ski area connects three valleys with 600km of pistes and 200 lifts. Key resorts:

Méribel (1450m): Best for intermediate skiers: 150km of blue and red runs, two snow parks and a wild après-ski scene. Linked by gondola to budget Brides-les-Bains (600m). *(meribel.net)*

Courchevel (1850m): Tree-fringed playground for the super-rich; La Tania (1400m) lower down is less flash. *(courchevel.com)*

Val Thorens (2300m): Europe's highest ski resort, meaning the longest snow-sure season (usually late November to mid-May. *(valthorens. com)*

St-Martin de Belleville (1450m): Traditional village option: chic accommodation and dining ranging from gourmet mountain hut to Michelin-starred. *(st-martin-belleville. com)*

THOMAS DEKIERE/SHUTTERSTOCK

Paragliding over Lake Annecy (p76), Annecy

Help yourself to an inflatable board, paddle and life vest – via the Equip Sport app – from the ingenious SUP vending machine on the lawn section of Doussard Beach. April to October, head to beach cafe **Le Cadre** *(lecadre74.com)*, at the beach's opposite end by the pleasure port, where water-sports school **SkiWake74** *(skiwake74.com; rental per hr €17)* rents kayaks and SUPs. You can also water-ski, wakeboard or surf the waves of the latest speedboat here.

Alpe d'Huez

Fly down Europe's longest black run

Winter or summer, in the ski town of Alpe d'Huez, riding the two legs of the **Télépherique du Pic Blanc** *(skipass. alpedhuez.com)* up to Lac Blanc (2700m) and beyond to Pic Blanc (3330m) is dizzying. Prepare for bitter cold on the wind-whipped glacier – frequently -20°C in winter and -10°C on a sun-scorched spring day. A spectacular ski-swoosh down to Alpe d'Huez beckons – on Europe's longest black run, 16km-long **La Sarenne** with a 2km vertical drop. Except for a hand-ful of steep, ungroomed segments polka-dotted with moguls, the snowy descent is more like a wide, roller-coaster red with a maddeningly long green at the end. Skip the final 'flat' by cutting off at Pont du Gua to take the Chalvet chairlift up, then ski the red Campanules down. To admire Pic Blanc and its glacier in an alternative, magical light, ski La Sarenne at sunrise with a *pisteur* (ski patroller) or after sunset by head-torch with a guide; book at the tourist office *(alpedhuez.com)* on place Joseph Paganon.

Nonskiers zoom down Europe's longest black run on two wheels during April's Sarenne Snowbike *(skipass.alpedhuez .com/hiver/sarenne-snowbike)* and in July when thousands of intrepid bikers rip down ice, slush and rocks at speeds of up to 100km/h during Megavalanche, the world's longest downhill mountain-bike event.

Lyon

FINE WINE | UNPARALLELED DINING | VARIED HISTORY

First the Roman capital of the Gauls in the 1st century BCE, then European capital of the silk trade in the 16th century, Lyon's past has been multifaceted. As it industrialised and motorists began to pass through, it rose to prominence in the Michelin road guide, leading to the discovery of the city's unusual cuisine and *bouchon* restaurants.

Lyon today is wonderfully liveable, and still deservedly wears the crown as France's gastronomic capital. It has a sprinkling of everything: great food and wine, proximity to the mountains, immense parks, a buzzing nightlife (watered by fine wines from Beaujolais to the north and the Rhône Valley to the south), and architecture that yo-yos between Roman, Renaissance, Baroque and art deco. In recent years, the city council has invested in all things green, meaning that bike paths are often as wide as car lanes, and footpaths and parks run along much of the riverbanks.

> ☑ **TOP TIP**
>
> Some of the best art installations are under your feet. Incognito street artist Ememem is Lyon's answer to Banksy, only they're solving the city's pothole problem by filling them in with mosaics.

Before Lyon Came Lugdunum

Think about the Roman Empire

Until 43 BCE, Lyon was little more than a Gaulish village. Lucius Munatius Plancus, governor of Gaul, was sent to found a Roman colony by the Senate, and Lugdunum was born. Under Emperor Augustus (27 BCE to 14 CE) the city mushroomed, and many vestiges of its Roman origins are still standing today. The 1st-century-CE amphitheatre is home to summer

---

🧭 GETTING AROUND

Lyon's metro is comprehensive and reliable *(€2.10/journey)*. A **Lyon City Card** *(24hr/48hr/72hr/96hr €32/€44/€56/€68)* from **Only Lyon Tourist Office** includes entry into multiple museums, public transport, guided visits and certain boat trips. Download the

Vélo'v app (electric and regular bikes) for easy, pay-per-use rental in the city. To get to the city centre from the airport, take the **Rhône Express** *(rhoneexpress.fr; one way €15.20)*, or the C200 bus *(€2.10)* to **Vaulx-en-Velin La Soie** metro.

WHAT'S A BOUCHON?

In other parts of the country, a *bouchon* is either a wine cork or a traffic jam. In Lyon, they're meat-heavy traditional restaurants formerly run by *Mères Lyonnaises* (Lyonnaise mothers), who'd feed workers cheap, cheerful and filling plates of offal, washed down with red wine. Restaurants sticking to tradition dish up *andouillette* (sausages made from pig intestines), kidney and tripe, and many of the upmarket *bouchons* manage to make it quite palatable (though beware tourist traps in Vieux Lyon). The truly traditional even serve *mâchon*: bottomless brunch with a Lyonnais twist. Instead of eggs and avocado, the menu includes *rognons de veau* (calf kidneys) and *tête de veau* (calf's head) all washed down with large quantities of wine...at 9am.

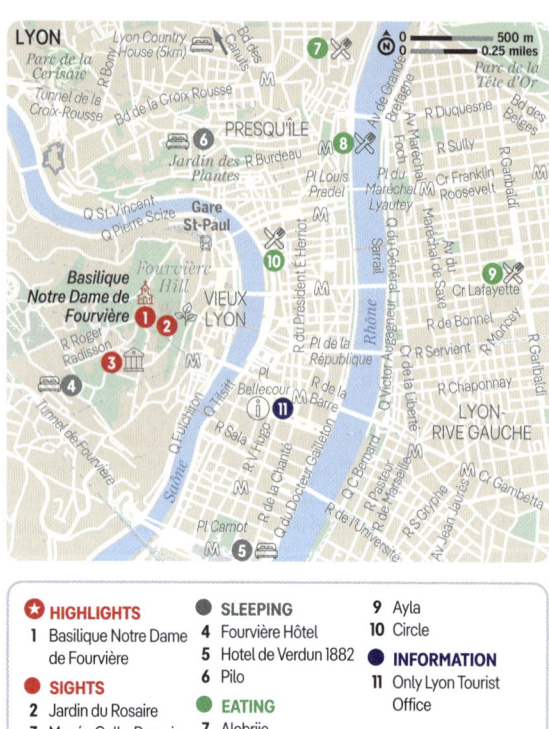

⭐ **HIGHLIGHTS**
1   Basilique Notre Dame de Fourvière

🔴 **SIGHTS**
2   Jardin du Rosaire
3   Musée Gallo-Romain de Fourvière

⚫ **SLEEPING**
4   Fourvière Hôtel
5   Hotel de Verdun 1882
6   Pilo

🟢 **EATING**
7   Alebrije
8   Astral

9   Ayla
10 Circle

🔵 **INFORMATION**
11 Only Lyon Tourist Office

concerts; **Nuits de Fourvière**, in June and July, is the largest. There's a great museum, the **Musée Gallo-Romain de Fourvière** (*lugdunum.grandlyon.com; adult/child €7/3*), that thoroughly explores Lyon's origins and has plenty of interactive displays for kids, including one section where they can dress up as gladiators.

Discover Secret Passageways

Traboules crisscross the city

Over 400 *traboules*, covered passageways originally used for transporting silk, wind their way through Lyon. Many are in private buildings, making them difficult to explore independently. Lyon's free **walking tour** (*freetourlyon.com*) – give what you like – in English and run by a Dutch expat, shows places many locals don't even know exist. Choose from a tour of Vieux Lyon (the Old Town), or Vieux Lyon and Croix-Rousse, and expect to return with a mine of fun facts. Who knew that the predecessor to computers was Lyon's silk-weaving Jacquard loom?

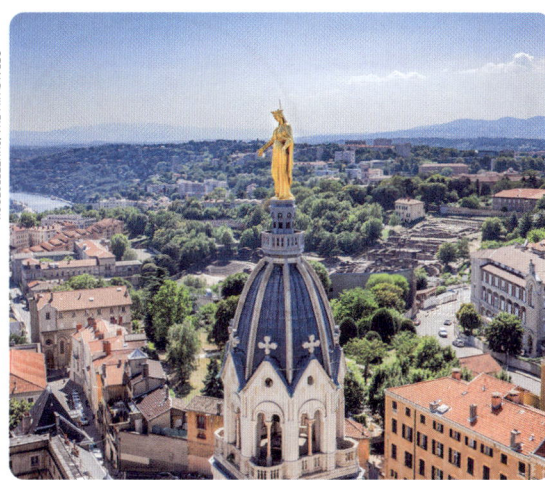

GERALD VILLENA/SHUTTERSTOCK

Virgin Mary statue, Basilica Notre-Dame de Fourvière

High on the Basilica Domes

A hill with history

It's difficult to imagine Lyon without **Basilica Notre-Dame de Fourvière** *(fourviere.org; free),* which dominates the skyline, but was only built at the end of the 19th century. The golden statue of the Virgin Mary predates the basilica: it was built by a local sculptor in 1852 and erected on the spires of the basilica to commemorate Lyon's liberation from the plague epidemic in 1643 (rumour has it that the disease never crossed the Rhône and stayed confined to the other side of Pont de la Guillotière).

Views from the top of Fourvière Hill are already impressive: they take in Lyon's twin rivers, the Saône and the Rhône, and (when you stand next to the basilica) the Alps. However, the highest point is from the basilica's domes. Inside the cathedral, stained-glass windows and ceilings adorned with golden stars and chandeliers of epic proportions create scenes straight out of a fairy tale. **Tours** *(booking.fourviere.org; adult/child €14/7)* run daily from April to September. To get here, take the funicular from Vieux Lyon, or walk up through **Jardin du Rosaire**.

WHY I LOVE LYON

Anna Richards,
Lonely Planet writer

Lyon bewitched me when I first visited as a backpacker over a decade ago. From our hilltop hostel we looked over the towers of Cathédrale St-Jean, cylindrical l'Opéra and silhouettes of the distant Alps. The scent of praline brioche wafted up from chimneys, and *péniches* sank lower into the Rhône under the weight of stomping feet dancing the night away in floating clubs. I've now lived here for years, but I'll never grow tired of discovering the latest fusion restaurant to open, or picnicking beside immense botanical greenhouses in urban parks. In winter I can go skiing all day and be back drinking Beaujolais on a boat bar at night – how many cities can you say that about?

✂ EATING IN LYON: PROPER GOOD GRUB

Circle: Six- or eight-course tasting menus where the quality of the simplest ingredients, like olive oil, shines through. *noon-1.15pm & 8-9.15pm Tue-Sat* **€€€**

Ayla: Franco-Lebanese sharing plates, as much of a feast for eyes as bellies. The tempura vine leaves stand out. *noon-2pm & 7.30-9.30pm Tue-Sat* **€€**

Astral: Classic French cuisine done well, managed by a young team. It also runs wine tastings in the cellar. *noon-2pm & 7-9.30pm Thu-Mon* **€€**

Alebrije: Franco-Mexican fusion from one of Lyon's top chefs, Carla Kirsch Lopez, who draws on inspiration from her two cultures. *7.30-9pm Tue-Sat* **€€€**

Beyond Lyon

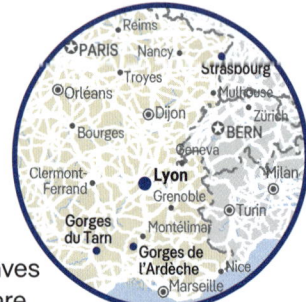

Towering limestone gorges, prehistoric caves and the seat of the European Parliament are easily reachable from Lyon.

Places

Limestone pillars higher than skyscrapers mask warrens of prehistoric caves, and forests teem with wildlife. The many twists and turns of the Ardèche River and Tarn River cut through their prospective limestone plateaus and snake through the middle to form the Gorges de l'Ardèche and the Gorges du Tarn. To the northeast, the impossibly photogenic city of Strasbourg is a flurry of twisting backstreets lined with crooked half-timbered houses, scenic canals, flower-filled courts and opulent shops. Inviting *winstubs* (traditional Alsatian taverns) cower beneath the soaring magnificence of the cathedral, a medieval marvel in pink sandstone. It may look like something out of a fairy tale, but Strasbourg has got its finger on the pulse, and this city is the seat of the European Parliament.

GETTING AROUND

Strasbourg is a major transport hub, and has high-speed (TGV) connections to Paris (from one hour 50 minutes). There's also an airport serving several European destinations.
  Strasbourg city centre is relatively small, so easy to walk.
  Both the Gorges de l'Ardèche and the Gorges du Tarn are difficult to reach using public transport: take a car to avoid wasting hours waiting for virtually nonexistent buses. The scenic roads with sweeping bends are popular with motorcyclists.

Strasbourg

TIME FROM LYON: **4HR**

Awe-inspiring architecture

Strasbourg walks a fine tightrope between France and Germany, and between a medieval past and a progressive future.
  Completed in all its Gothic grandeur in 1439, **Cathédrale Notre-Dame** *(cathedrale-strasbourg.fr; astronomical clock adult/child €4/2, platform €8/5)* is the unchallenged Strasbourg icon in the heart of the city. The lace-fine facade lifts the gaze little by little to flying buttresses, leering gargoyles and a 142m spire. The interior is exquisitely lit by 12th- to 14th-century stained-glass windows. We love the quirky Gothic-meets-Renaissance astronomical clock that strikes solar noon at 12.30pm with a parade of figures portraying the lives of the Apostles. A spiral staircase twists up to the 66m-high viewing platform. To appreciate the cathedral in peace, visit in the early evening, when the crowds have thinned.

Visit the European Quarter

About 2km northeast of central Strasbourg, the European Quarter is a city within the city, with its own architecture and unique energy. Overlooking the River Ill, the oval-shaped building of the **Parlement Européen** *(europarl.europa.eu)* is striking. You can take an audioguide tour or sit in on debates ranging from lively to yawn-a-minute.

Cathédrale Notre-Dame's astronomical clock, Strasbourg

A futuristic glass crescent, the Council of Europe's **Palais de l'Europe** *(coe.int)* across the River Ill can be visited on free one-hour weekday tours (ask to join a group); see the website for reservations. You can also take a virtual tour at *70.coe.int/virtual-tour-en.html.*

It's just a hop across the Canal de la Marne to the swirly silver **Palais des Droits de l'Homme** *(European Court of Human Rights; echr.coe.int),* the most eye-catching of all the EU institutions. It ensures that 46 European states abide by the European Convention on Human Rights.

Gorges de l'Ardèche

TIME FROM LYON: **3HR** 🚗

Prehistoric cave paintings

Grotte Chauvet 2 *(grottechauvet2ardeche.com; adult/child 10-17/under 10yr €18/9/free)* may be a replica of the original cave, which is closed to the public to avoid damaging the cave paintings, but it's a good one. The original, discovered in 1994, is a UNESCO World Heritage Site, and features cave paintings thought to be over 30,000 years old, composed of handprints and sketches of cave bears, cave lions and mammoths. From the paintings it's possible to deduce incredible amounts of information, including the rough age and the gender of the artists. The replica includes exceptionally informative guided

DINING AT A WINSTUB

For a memorable culinary experience in Strasbourg, dine at a *winstub:* a traditional Alsatian restaurant renowned for its warm, homely atmosphere. Most dishes are based on pork and veal; specialities include *baeckeoffe* (meat stew), *wädele* or *jambonneau braisé* (braised pork knuckles), *fleischschnäcke* (minced meat rolls) and *choucroute garnie* (sauerkraut garnished with meat or fish). Vegetarians can usually order *bibelaskäs* (soft white cheese mixed with fresh cream) and *pommes sautées* (sautéed potatoes). Also look for restaurants serving *tarte flambée* (a thin-crust pizza dough topped with crème fraiche, onions and lardons). Alsatian specialities are best accompanied with Alsatian white wines.

✗ EATING IN STRASBOURG: OUR WINSTUB PICKS

Chez Yvonne: Near the cathedral, Chez Yvonne is an institution. Traditional decor and excellent Alsatian dishes. *11.45am-2pm & 6.30-10pm Tue-Sat* €

Le Tire-Bouchon: Arguably the best *choucroute* of Strasbourg is served at this snug, amiable *winstub. 11.30am-9.30pm* €

Au Pont Corbeau: The essence of Alsace quaintness: dark timber, checked tablecloths and hearty grub. *noon-2pm & 7-9.30pm Mon-Fri, noon-2pm Sun* €

Le Clou: The menu is packed with classics – *wädele, bibelaskäs* – all of which marry nicely with a glass of local pinot noir. *11.45am-2.30pm & 6-10pm* €

KAYAKING THE ARDÈCHE RIVER

A roller-coaster adventure by water through France's prehistoric playground. Shorter 7km and 13km routes are also possible.

START	END	LENGTH
Vallon Pont d'Arc	Sauze	32km; 7 hours/2 days

Kayaking the Ardèche River reaches motorway levels of busy in high season; a website is in place to predict how busy the river will be. Canoë Malin can be consulted via the tourist office website (*gorges-ardeche-pontdarc.fr*).

Start at ❶ **Vallon Pont d'Arc**: it's a sprawling mass of rental shops without a clearly defined centre. There's plenty of choice and, so long as your kayak is seaworthy, rentals are much of a muchness, supplying laminated maps and a watertight tub for your belongings, and organising your return transfer at the end of whichever distance you choose to tackle. Aigue Vive (*aigue-vive.com*) is helpful and efficient.

It doesn't take long to reach the showstopper, the ❷ **Pont d'Arc** (4km), but what those who've taken the land route don't see are the caves inside the rock arch itself. By kayak, you can dip in and out of the caves and crane your neck to take in the 54m-high rock from the water.

Keep moving with the current, over rapids (Grade II/Grade III) and between limestone cliffs, to reach two wild campsites: ❸ **Bivouac de Gaud** and ❹ **Bivouac de Gournier**. If splitting the trip over two days, you'll need to camp at one of these. For the final few kilometres to ❺ **Sauze**, the limestone cliffs shrink, and you can often see vultures wheeling overhead.

Pont d'Arc is a 60m rock arch created by thousands of years of water erosion.

Sauze is the end of the (watery) road, with several riverside restaurants and bars.

Bivouacs Gaud and Gournier are open April to September. Obtain a camping permit *(€16.50)* from the tourist office in Vallon Pont d'Arc.

Gorges du Tarn

visits and immersive sound-and-light shows. The visit lasts approximately one hour; factor in extra time for the sound-and-light show. Audioguides in English available.

Gorges du Tarn

TIME FROM LYON: 3½HR

Road trips and watery adventures

One of France's most spectacular natural wonders, the Gorges du Tarn, is found in the zone where the Cévennes becomes the Causses: a biodiverse region of shifting mountain-scapes. If you have a car, prepare for one of the country's truly spectacular, and slightly unnerving, drives. The gorge runs for around 50km, but a good entry point is the pretty village of Ste-Énimie. From here, the D907 balcony road scrapes its way past vertiginous cliffs, which occasionally hang right over the road.

Midway along is the stunning La Malène village, the best point to go boating. **Les Bateliers des Gorges du Tarn** (*gorgesdutarn.com; €26*), the revered local boaters, steer you down the river in a green wooden boat. Kayaking and canoeing are popular alternatives, and the river is safer for beginners here than Ste-Énimie. **Canoë 2000** (*canoe-kayak-gorgesdu tarn.com*) and **Canoe au Moulin de la Malène** (*canoeblanc. com*) rent all the necessary equipment and drive you back to the village at the end. In **Ste-Énimie**, try **Canoë Méjean** (*canoe-mejean.com*). Back on the road, at **Le Rozier** you can turn east into **Gorges de la Jonte**, which has another stunning gorge drive on wider, less crowded roads.

BEST LONG-DISTANCE HIKES NEAR THE GORGES DU TARN

For more information, see *gr-infos.com*.

GR67: Considered the ultimate guide to the Cévennes on foot, the 130km GR67 is a loop hike that begins and ends in Anduze, summiting Mt Aigoual.

GR68: The GR68, aka the Mont Lozère loop, never actually climbs the mountain, rather using it as the axle around which the 115km hike revolves.

GR736: From Albi to Villefort, this 317km route encompasses the entire Causses et Cévennes.

GR4: Passes through the Causses et Cévennes on its way from the Atlantic to the Mediterranean.

GR70: The Stevenson Trail, famously trekked by Robert Louis Stevenson and his donkey Modestine, running from Le Puy-en-Velay to Alès.

 EATING IN GORGES DU TARN: BEST RESTAURANTS

L'Alicanta: Seasonal ingredients (often linked to beef, pork or lamb) with good-value set menus in Le Rozier. *7-8.30pm* €€

Le Petit Paris: Try regional dishes, such as *aligot* (cheesy mashed potato served with sausage) in Ste-Énimie. *hours vary Fri-Tue* €€

Capluc Kfé: Charcuterie and cheeseboards, river trout and *aligot* with pork sausages in onion gravy are hearty at this Le Rozier favourite. *hours vary* €€

Auberge du Moulin: Terrace dining in Ste-Énimie, overlooking the gorge, with French cuisine staples such as roast leg of lamb with vegetables. *Thu-Tue Apr-Oct* €€

Loire Valley

Le Mans · St-Calais · Orléans · Vendôme · Beaugency · La Flèche · Château de Loir · **Blois** · **Chambord** · Romorantin-Lantheney · **Villandry** · Tours · Amboise · Vierzon · **Chenonceaux** · **Azay-le-Rideau** · Loches · Châtellerault · Châteauroux

RIVERSIDE CASTLES | VINEYARDS | SERENE CYCLING

Places

Blois p87
Chambord p87
Chenonceaux p88
Villandry p89
Azay-le-Rideau p89

 TOP TIP

Thirsty? Head to one of the Loire's many *guinguettes*. A kind of pop-up riverbank restaurant with a beer-garden vibe, *guinguettes* originated in Paris during the Belle Époque. Open from spring to early autumn, they bring together wooden furniture, deckchairs, hanging fairy lights, local wine, tasty food and, often, live music.

If you're looking for French splendour, style and gastronomy, the Loire Valley will exceed your expectations, no matter how great. Poised on the crucial frontier between northern and southern France – and just a short train or *autoroute* (tolled motorway) ride from Paris – the region was once of immense strategic importance. Kings, queens, dukes and nobles came here to build feudal castles and, later on, sumptuous Renaissance pleasure palaces – that's why this fertile river valley is sprinkled with hundreds of France's most opulent aristocratic estates, many sporting crenellated towers, soaring cupolas and twinkling banquet halls.

The Loire, much of it a UNESCO World Heritage Site, is also known for its outstanding wines – reds, whites, rosés and sparkling – and vineyards stretch along both banks of the Loire from the Blésois, westward through Touraine and Anjou, to the Atlantic. A network of walking trails, bike paths and tertiary roads makes it easy to visit both glittering châteaux and vine-encircled *domaines* (wine-growing estates) in a single afternoon.

Fans of French urban life will find medium-sized cities that are renowned for their *douceur de vivre* (the gentle pleasures of life), with verve and energy added by tens of thousands of students. Tours, Angers and Nantes are graced with handsome avenues, historic

---

GETTING AROUND

Having your own wheels is the easiest and quickest way to visit châteaux and vineyards, but if you stay in the city centre in Tours, Angers and Nantes, a car can be a liability, as parking is in short supply and is time-limited and/or pricey. Tours-Centre, the Loire Valley's main rail hub, has direct services to over a dozen Loire destinations.

Direct TGV trains link Paris Montparnasse with St-Pierre-des-Corps (3km from Tours), Angers-St-Laud and Nantes. Zipping along backroads on a *vélo* is a fantastic way to tour the Loire.

quarters traversed by narrow medieval streets and excellent (and moderately priced) dining, as well as an abundance of lovely gardens and romantic riverside promenades.

Blois

Royal château with a bloody history

Seven French kings lived in the **Château Royal de Blois** *(chateaudeblois.fr; adult/child €14.50/7.50)*. Its four grand wings were built during four distinct periods in French architecture: Gothic (13th century), Flamboyant Gothic (1498–1501), early Renaissance (1515–20) and classical (1630s). You can easily spend a half-day immersing yourself in the château's dramatic and bloody history and its extraordinary architecture. An informative audioguide costs €3; a HistoPad, offering augmented-reality views, is free at the *consigne* (checked-luggage facility). The most sumptuous part of the Gothic wing is the richly painted Estates General Room, from the 13th century. The King's Chamber was the setting for one of the bloodiest episodes in the château's history, the assassination of Duke Henri I de Guise in 1588.

Every night from early April to late September, a 45-minute **Son et Lumière** *(adult/child €12/7.50),* held in the interior courtyard, brings the château's history and architecture to life with dramatic lighting and narration.

Chambord

The Loire's most magnificent château

One of the crowning achievements of French Renaissance architecture, the **Château de Chambord** *(chambord.org; adult/child €19/free)* – with 426 rooms, 282 fireplaces and 77 staircases – is the largest, grandest and most visited château in the Loire Valley. Rising through the centre of the structure, the world-famous double-helix staircase ascends to the great lantern tower and the rooftop, where you can gaze out across the vast grounds and marvel at a mind-blowing skyline of cupolas, domes, turrets, chimneys and lightning rods. To add virtual-reality furnishings to some of the rooms, pick up – at the entrance to the château itself – a HistoPad tablet computer *(€6.50, 1½ hours)*. In July and August, hour-long guided **tours** *(adult/child €7/4)* in English begin daily at 11.15am; reserve online or at the ticket counter.

FRANCE LOIRE VALLEY

WINE TOURING IN THE LOIRE

It's easy to put together a web of wonderful wine-tasting itineraries in the Loire, drawing on 350 wine cellars producing reds, rosés, whites, dessert wines and crémants (sparkling wines). A tourist office or *maison des vins* (wine visitor centre) can supply you with local options and – assuming it's reissued – *À la Découverte des Vins de Loire* (Discovering Loire Wines): a free map with an excellent, colour-coded presentation of the winegrowing areas that stretch from Blois to the Atlantic. It is produced by the region's winegrowers' association, Vins de Loire *(vinsdeloire. fr);* its website has plenty of information in English and downloadable brochures under 'Tourist circuits'.

EATING IN BLOIS: OUR FRENCH PICKS

Poivre et Sel: Traditional French cuisine served on rustic tables, with old-style wood beams overhead. *noon-1.45pm & 7-9.30pm Mon-Sat* €€	**L'Arboré Sens:** A city-centre brasserie with a pretty terrace, a good selection of salads, reasonable prices and, on some evenings, live music. *11am-midnight Mon-Sat* €	**Côté Loire-Auberge Ligérienne:** On the riverfront, French cuisine in a rustic dining room and, when it's warm, on a lovely terrace. *noon-1.30pm & 7.30-9pm Tue-Sat* €€	**Au Rendez-Vous des Pêcheurs:** Elegant bistro specialising in fish (salmon, cod, zander), served on gorgeous ceramic plates. *12.15-1.15pm & 7.15-8.30pm Tue-Sat* €€€

VINEYARD-HOPPING & FLOATING ABOVE THE VINEYARDS

Private companies offer well-organised minibus tours that take in various combinations of châteaux, sometimes coupled with vineyard visits, as well as specialised tours featuring cycling or wine-tasting. Tourist offices and their websites have details. Floating peacefully in a *montgolfière* (hot-air-balloon) is a gorgeously romantic way to see the Loire countryside. Operated by about a dozen companies, flights are generally possible from April to October, weather permitting, with departures early in the morning or in the evening. Tourist offices (eg Tours and Amboise) and their websites can provide contact information and help with reservations.

Château de Chenonceau, Chenonceau

The château is surrounded by Louis XIV-style formal gardens (château tickets required) and extensive grounds (open 24 hours). At the Embarcadère (boat dock), rent bicycles, quadricycles, electric golf carts and electric boats from early April to October. Outdoor spectacles held in the warm season include a 45-minute **equestrian show** *(adult/child €18/14.30, adult incl château €32)* in which horses and colourfully clad riders take you through five centuries of Chambord's history. Shows are held from early April to September and begin at 11.45am and/or 4pm from Tuesday to Sunday.

Chenonceaux
Elegant arches and delightful gardens

Spanning the languid Cher River atop a graceful arched bridge, the **Château de Chenonceau** *(chenonceau.com; adult/child €18/15)* is one of France's most elegant castles. It's hard not to be moved and exhilarated by the glorious setting, the formal gardens, the magic of the architecture and the château's fascinating history. Chenonceau is largely the work of several remarkable women – hence its nickname, the Château des Dames. The distinctive arches and the eastern formal garden were added by Diane de Poitiers, mistress of Henri II. Catherine de Médici completed the château's construction and added the yew-tree maze and the western rose garden. The most singular contribution of Louise of Lorraine's was her black-walled mourning room on the top floor, to which she retreated when her husband, Henri III, was assassinated in 1589.

The château's pièce de résistance is the 60m-long, checkerboard-floored Grande Galerie over the Cher River, scene of many an elegant party hosted by Catherine de Médici and Madame Dupin. Used as a military hospital during WWI, it served from 1940 to 1942 as an escape route for *résistants*, Jews and other refugees fleeing from the German-occupied zone (north of the Cher) to the Vichy-controlled zone (south of the river). There's an excellent 1¼-hour audioguide *(€5)* in 12 languages. Chenonceau's elegant restaurant, L'Orangerie, serves brunch-style French meals from noon to 3pm and becomes a *salon de thé* (tearoom) from 3pm to 4.30pm You can taste Touraine wines in the château's historic wine cellar, the Cave des Dômes (closed November to January). Chenonceaux (the name of the village has an X at the end) is an easy train ride from Tours.

Villandry

Exquisite gardens à la Française

The gardens of the **Château de Villandry** *(chateauvillandry. com; adult/child €14/8, gardens only €8.50/5.50, winter €2)* are among France's most beautiful, with more than 6 hectares of cascading flowers, ornamental vines, manicured lime trees, razor-sharp box-hedges and tinkling fountains. Try to visit when the gardens – all of them organic – are blooming (ie between April and October). Tickets are valid all day (get your hand stamped if you leave). An audioguide costs €4. For many, the highlight is the 16th-century-style *Potager Décoratif* (Decorative Kitchen Garden), where cabbages, leeks and carrots create nine geometrical, colour-coordinated squares.

Azay-le-Rideau

Renaissance castle par excellence

Romantic, moat-ringed **Château d'Azay-le-Rideau** *(azay-le-rideau.fr; adult/child €16/free)*, built almost exactly 500 years ago on a natural island in the middle of the Indre River, is wonderfully adorned with elegant turrets, exquisitely proportioned windows, delicate stonework and steep slate roofs. The famous, Italian-style loggia staircase overlooking the central courtyard is decorated with the salamanders and ermines of François I and Queen Claude. Audioguides *(€3; 1½ hours)* are available in five languages. From mid-July to late August, you can take a *flânerie nocturne (nighttime stroll; adult/child €8/4)* around the illuminated gardens, accompanied by ancient music, from nightfall until 11.15pm.

CYCLING THE LOIRE

The Loire Valley is fabulous cycling country – pedal through villages, vineyards and forests on your way from one château to the next. **La Loire à Vélo** *(Loire by Bike; loirebybike.co.uk)* maintains 900km of signposted routes from Nevers to the Atlantic; pick up a free guide from a tourist office or access information (details on route options and bike hire) from the website. Individual *départements*, including Indre-et-Loire (Touraine), Loir-et-Cher (Blésois) and Maine-et-Loire (Anjou), have their own cycling networks and brochures. Les Châteaux à Vélo *(chateauxavelo.co.uk)* maintains over 500km of marked bike routes in the Blésois. The Geovelo smartphone app recommends routes that follow bike paths and avoid heavy traffic.

THE GUIDE

PROVENCE FRANCE

Provence

SEDUCTIVE BEACHES | LAVENDER FIELDS | COLOURFUL CITIES

 TOP TIP

Don't dismiss Provence in winter. The crowds have left and prices are much lower, but the temperature remains balmy. Some of the best parties happen in winter, including Nice's carnival, which lasts for two weeks each February.

When you find yourself awash in Provence's famous light, it becomes clear why so many artists have been magnetically drawn here for centuries, seeking to unlock something bigger than themselves. This land epitomises springtime, having inspired great post-impressionist painters Cézanne and Van Gogh to create their seminal works. As the mistral wind howls down the Rhône Valley towards the sea, slamming the wooden shutters of homes throughout the night and clearing the skies for what feels like endless sunshine, it creates a climate that is not only inviting for travellers but also ideal for farming. Sampling the fresh produce nurtured here is an essential part of the journey, especially in the busy markets and endless stretches of vineyards. For a month or two every year, from June to early July, the region glows purple as Provençal lavender comes into bloom.

The region's palpitating heart is Marseille, France's second-largest city, with its vibrant cultural energy, street art, eclectic nightlife and world-class dining scene. It's constantly evolving, and increasingly attracts partygoers looking to discover 'France's Berlin'. To the east, the Côte d'Azur, France's glittering

GETTING AROUND

Away from the coast, driving in this region can be a joy. To spontaneously stop in tiny villages or wind your way to far-flung vineyards is a luxury. Provence is one of the best cycling areas in France, thanks to its endless backroad options. In the cities, ditch the car as fast as you can. Marseille has two metro lines and an extensive bus network, while Nice is best explored by bus or tram. Both cities also have pay-per-use bike-rental schemes.

The comprehensive ZOU! bus service runs lines all around the region. Great for connecting villages and sights, but, with infrequent services, it's not so great if you want to dine at a restaurant outside of town or have booked accommodation in the countryside. However, it is a good way of avoiding extortionate parking charges and summer traffic jams along the coast.

blue coast, maintains its glorious longtime allure with its intoxicating mix of sun, sea, culture, food and wine. The sun shines down 300 days a year on Nice's Renaissance old town, movie capital Cannes and the glitzy beach clubs of St-Tropez.

Whether you're stretched out by the sea, driving quiet countryside roads or lost in nature, Provence is a sensuous Mediterranean experience waiting to be discovered.

Nice

MAP p92

Soak up the history

Nice's UNESCO heritage can be seen in around 800 buildings across the city, and their art deco detailing and Belle Époque flourishes can be admired from the street. The excellent Explore Nice Côte d'Azur app *(explorenicecotedazur.com/ en/discover-the-unesco-heritage-routes)* organises some of the most noteworthy sites into a series of self-guided neighbourhood walks, complete with a pop-up historical outline of each building listed. You can also deep dive into this protected heritage at the **Musée Massena** *(massena-nice.org; adult/child €10/free)* on the **Promenade des Anglais**. Much of the permanent collection is dedicated to the history of Nice.

Cycling the Prom

The combo of Nice's public e-bike fleet and the dedicated, flat bike lane that extends the entire 6km length of the Promenade des Anglais (and then some) is one of the city's best pairings. The Prom is scattered with bike pickup and drop-off points.

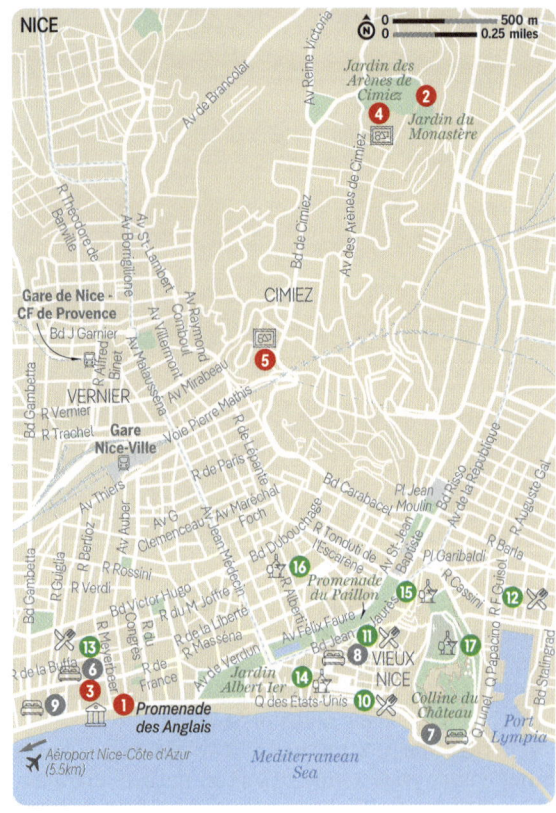

★ HIGHLIGHTS
1 Promenade des Anglais

● SIGHTS
2 Monastère Notre Dame de Cimiez
3 Musée Masséna
4 Musée Matisse
5 Musée National Marc Chagall

● SLEEPING
6 Hostel Meyerbeer Beach
7 Hôtel La Pérouse
8 Hôtel Rossetti
9 Le Negresco

● EATING
10 Babel Babel
11 Lavomatique
12 Le Bistrot de Jan
13 Le Canon

● DRINKING & NIGHTLIFE
14 Cave Bianchi
15 Cave de la Tour
16 La Part des Anges
17 Rouge

Propelled by the battery and the fresh sea air, you'll reach **Aéroport Nice-Côte d'Azur** in less than 20 minutes (if starting out at the eastern end opposite the arcades of **Vieux Nice**).

Two masters and their museums

It is a truth universally acknowledged that the light on the Côte d'Azur has an allure unlike anywhere else in the world. Countless artists have been drawn to the region in search of it: two in particular have left their mark (or, perhaps it's the other way around?): Marc Chagall and Henri Matisse. Dedicated museums to both artists occupy sprawling grounds in

 EATING IN NICE: OUR PICKS ──────── MAP p92

| **Lavomatique:** Trendy bistro with natural wines in Vieux Nice. Shared plates cooked in an open kitchen. *noon-1.45pm & 7-10pm Tue-Fri, 7-10pm Mon* €€ | **Babel Babel:** Med cuisine, served across from the Med. Don't miss the panisse with homemade za'atar. *10am-midnight Mon, Thu & Sun, to 2am Fri & Sat* €€ | **Le Bistrot de Jan:** More casual sibling to the Michelin-starred Jan next door. The decor is straight from a design magazine. *noon-3pm & 7pm-12.30am Tue-Sat, 11am-3pm Sun* €€ | **Le Canon:** Neighbourhood fave with a hyperlocal focus: each farmer is named on the menu. *noon-2pm Mon, Tue, Thu & Fri, 7.30-11.30pm Mon-Fri* €€ |

VV SHOTS/SHUTTERSTOCK

Musée Massena (p91), Nice

Cimiez, the leafy residential neighbourhood in the north of Nice, and can be visited on the same day. Start at the **Musée National Marc Chagall** *(musees-nationaux-alpesmaritimes .fr/chagall; adult/child €10/free)*, where the most extensive public collection of the Belarusian artist's work hangs. The 12 monumental canvases depicting scenes from the Old Testament are spellbinding in colour and detail, and will linger in your memory long after you've left. A further 20 minutes' walk (or Ligne d'Azur bus 5) and you'll arrive at the **Musée Matisse** *(musee-matisse-nice.org; adult/child €10/free)*. The setting, in a coral-red Genoese villa dating from the 17th century, is magic, with olive groves and ancient ruins. Matisse is buried in the **Monastère Notre Dame de Cimiez** at the eastern end of the parkland. Both museums are closed Tuesdays.

The coolest street in town

The strip and the surrounding streets of **rue Bonaparte** are Nice's hip LGBTIQ+ district, having earned the nickname le petit Marais, a nod to Paris' famous bohemian gay quarter. A part of the road is painted rainbow, à la San Francisco's Castro District, and the stretch between place Garibaldi and place du Pin is now fully pedestrianised. This is where you should head if you are looking for a guaranteed evening buzz,

WHAT IS NIÇOISE CUISINE?

Nice's street-food culture, including chickpea-based *socca* and panisse, *pan bagnat (salade niçoise* in a bread roll) and *pissaladière* (onion-topped dough), is based on the colourful vegetables and legumes that thrive in the poor, water-deprived soils of the Mediterranean coastline. It feels closer to Italy in nature and flavour than the heavier, sauce-based cuisine of northern France. The city brims with cheap and cheerful street-food stops, as well as more classic local bistros. If you see the Cuisine Nissarde sticker displayed at a restaurant's entrance, you know their dishes respect local culinary traditions. Beyond the traditional places, a new wave of chefs is putting a fine-dining twist on local dishes, elevating them to a semi-gastronomic standing.

THE GUIDE

FRANCE PROVENCE

DRINKING IN NICE: BEST WINE BARS

MAP p92

Rouge: Sleek spot just back from Port Lympia serving up stylish, modern tapas plates, washed down with organic wines. *noon-10.30pm*

Cave de la Tour: Enjoy 1940s jazz, an interior that has hardly changed, and Nice wine by the glass. *8am-2.30pm & 6-8.30pm Tue-Sat, 8am-12.30pm Sun*

La Part des Anges: A treasure of natural and organic wines in the city centre; voted best wine bar in France in 2020. *10am-8.30pm Mon-Sat*

Cave Bianchi: History seeps out of every nook of this atmospheric Vieux Nice wine shop and bar across from the Opera. *9.30am-7.30pm, to 10.30pm Fri & Sat*

Jardin Exotique d'Èze, Èze

BEST EVENTS IN NICE

Carnaval de Nice: For two weeks in late February and early March, floats and flower battles take over the streets. One of Europe's brightest carnivals, running since the Middle Ages.

Lou Queernaval: France's first queer carnival runs adjacent to the Carnaval de Nice; expect glitter, dazzling floats and drag queens.

Nice Jazz Festival: Jampacked four-night calendar of performances in Jardin Albert Ier, and fringe concerts popping up all around town.

Pink Parade (Pride): Crowds swarm Nice's main streets for July's Pink Parade (Pride); the afterparty lasts all night.

Noël à Nice: Sip bubbles with fresh oysters and ride on a giant Ferris wheel; festive Nice lights up during December.

as new bars or restaurants are always opening – just remember that you're still in the provinces, and even the most lively bars shutter by 1am, particularly out of season.

Èze

Exotic flowers and panoramic sea views

Although you'll increasingly need to swerve around selfie-stick-wielding visitors as you meander through it, the **Jardin Exotique d'Èze** *(jardinexotique-eze.fr; adult/child €5/free)* is still one of the region's most delightful experiences. Around the ruined 12th-century château above the terracotta rooftops of the village, a peaceful cactus garden grows: it's more than worth the entry fee for the sweeping sea views that extend beyond Cannes alone.

Cannes

Festival fever

For two weeks every May, Cannes rolls out the red carpet for a galaxy of stars during the annual **Festival de Cannes** (the Cannes Film Festival). The harbourfront **Palais des Festivals et des Congrès** is the epicentre. For the remainder of the year, the gloss barely fades. Follow the trail of over 400

EATING & DRINKING IN CANNES: OUR PICKS

Poissonnerie Forville: Fish counter outside Marché Forville serving fresh treats such as oysters and sea urchins (in season). *7am-2.30pm Tue-Sun* €€

Le Pompon: A menu of creative small plates that changes daily with the season. Colourful ingredients and beautiful presentation. *12.15-1.30pm & 7.15-9.30pm Tue-Sat* €€

Bar Fouquet's: Hôtel Barrière Le Majestic's bar serves artful cocktails, where homemade bitters, jellies, even edible perfumes, are standard. *10am-midnight*

Maison Grenache: Atmospheric wine bar next to the Marché Forville with ultra-knowledgeable owners. *9am-5pm, to 10.30pm Fri & Sat*

stars who have cast their handprints in stainless steel along the **Chemin des Étoiles** (path of stars) outside the Palais. Dates for **tours** *(adult/child €6/3)* inside the Palais are only scheduled six weeks in advance by the tourist office (conveniently housed in the building), depending on the upcoming event calendar, and are only in French. When visits do run, you're given a 1½-hour behind-the-scenes insight into one of cinema's most legendary venues.

St-Tropez
Life's a beach

Sexy St-Tropez might be the most desired destination on the Côte d'Azur and a byword for lithe, tanned bodies dancing on tables at trendy beach bars along buttercream Plage de Pampelonne, but it hasn't always been the jet-set magnet it is today. The sleepy fishing village was thrust into the global spotlight in the 1950s, when a young Brigitte Bardot filmed *And God Created Woman* here. If bling isn't your thing, that doesn't mean you should bypass St-Tropez. Meander cobbled lanes in the old fishing quarter of La Ponche, watch games of pétanque beneath plane trees on place des Lices, fill your picnic basket at its produce market (don't forget a bottle of local rosé), or hike along the coast from beach to beach on the Presqu'île de Saint-Tropez peninsula. Just be aware: in summer, every inch of space is jampacked.

The seaside scene revolves around sandy clubs and restaurants, all with their own style. Most are open May to September, and advance bookings are highly recommended. Beaches also have public areas where you can lay down your towel. The 5km-long, celebrity-studded **Plage de Pampelonne** is the most famous of the beaches and has the largest selection of exclusive clubs and restaurants. It's the place to see and be seen – you'll want to reserve a lounger and lunch. Atmosphere? Indulgence, glitz and relaxation. **Le Club 55** *(leclub55.fr)* is the longest-running Pampelonne club, originally the crew canteen during *And God Created Woman* and still catering to incognito celebs. **Nikki Beach** *(nikkibeach.com/sttropez)* is favoured by dance-on-the-bar glitterati, and those who just want to be seen. For a more chill vibe, try **Le 1051** *(le1051.com)*.

Looking for a quieter beach experience without sacrificing luxury? Book ahead for **La Cabane Méditerranée** *(laca banemediterranee.com; loungers from €30)*, on the edge of **Plage d'Héraclée**. About 10km further south from St-Tropez, the beach is wilder than Pampelonne, and the club is tucked into the edge of a rock.

Hit the open seas

Get out on the water to take in the gorgeous coast. It can be as easy as taking a ride on **Les Bateaux Verts**, with boat excursions throughout the region. Or opt for a water-skimming catamaran on Golfe de St-Tropez at sunset with **Sport De-couverte** *(sport-decouverte.com; €40)*, where you can sip an *apéro* suspended in the nets of the catamaran, sandwiched between the blues of the sea and the sparkling sky.

BEST ARTS EXPERIENCES & EVENTS IN CANNES

Festival d'Art Pyrotechnique: Global competition to win best fireworks show crown. Six nights in summer.

Les Plages Électroniques: Epic three-day dance festival on the beach: eight stages and over 50,000 festivalgoers. In August.

Musée Bonnard: Neoimpressionist painter Pierre Bonnard (1867–1947) was known as the Painter of Happiness, and Le Cannet, at Cannes' northern fringes, was his happy place.

La Malmaison: Showcase of contemporary art in a historic, renovated building.

Le Suquet des Artistes: Small but avant-garde exhibition space in the former city morgue that brings local artists to the fore.

CLEANLINESS IS CLOSE TO GODLINESS

Following the cholera outbreaks of the early 1830s, which claimed thousands of lives, a plan was devised to improve public health by channelling water from the Durance River in the Alps. By 1869, Marseille's **Palais Longchamp** was opened to the public as a 'hymn to water', celebrating this remarkable engineering achievement.

Marseille's famous soap (Savon de Marseille) also played a significant role in reducing infant mortality and the spread of contagious diseases during the 19th century. Originally made with olive oil and free of colouring and perfume, it now comes in various shapes and smells. The **Savonnerie Marseillaise de la Licorne** has free daily tours of its factory.

STEFANO BOLOGNINI/SHUTTERSTOCK

Chateau d'If, Marseille

Marseille
MAP p96

Mix with the locals in lively squares

Marseille has an edge. France's second-largest city puts its arms around you as a drunken friend would – passionately and deliriously. It is a city that revels in its status as France's underdog. Sooner or later, you'll end up on the **cours Julien** (known locally as 'le cours Ju') for a drink, and for good reason. As a pedestrian area slathered with street art and bohemian yearnings, this is the home of some great bars and restaurants, which remain open day and night. Wander the narrow side streets, packed with bookshops, galleries and tattoo parlours, until you reach the noisy and elongated main square, a destination for a solid night out, and a microcosm of the city itself. You are likely to hear boomboxes blasting, guitars strumming and African drums pounding as soon as the sun comes out.

Place Jean-Jaurès, also known as La Plaine, is another vast square surrounded by bars and restaurants. For years it has been the battleground for left-wing militants and artists. Buzzing day and night in the spring and summer months, it remains a beating heart for locals escaping the tourist traps, whether in the bars or in the public seating areas beneath the trees. La Plaine is only a 10-minute walk east from cours Julien.

Escape to the Château d'If

For a quick and easy trip out to sea, hop on the Frioul-If ferry to Marseille's closest islands: the Île d'If (for historians) and the **Îles du Frioul** (for nature lovers). Commanding access to Marseille's Vieux Port, the **Chateau d'If** *(chateau-if.fr; adult/child €7/free)* was immortalised by Alexandre Dumas in his classic 1844 novel, *The Count of Monte Cristo*. At the 16th-century island prison with three towers, one giving a great view across the bay, you can wander unaccompanied or visit with an audio or guided tour; the contrast between the cells for the wealthy and the dungeon pit strikes a tone. This is the ferry's first stop; it's 20 minutes from the Vieux Port.

MARSEILLE

Mediterranean Sea

See Enlargement

Marseille

Île Ratonneau

Île Pomègues

La Pointe-Rouge

Parc National des Calanques

Mont Puget

Les Goudes

Callelongue

Île de Jarre

Île Calseraigne

Île de Riou

Allées Léon Gambetta, Bd de la Libération, Cours F. Roosevelt, THIERS, La Canebière, Pl Jean Jaurès, R des Trois Mages, Cours Lieutaud, R Ste Pierre

0 —— 200 m
0 —— 0.1 miles

0 —— 2 km
0 —— 1 miles

⭐ **HIGHLIGHTS**
1 Parc National des Calanques

🔴 **SIGHTS**
2 Calanque de Morgiou
3 Calanque de Sormiou
4 Château d'If
5 Cours Julien
6 Îles du Frioul

7 Palais Longchamp
8 Place Jean-Jaurès

⚫ **SLEEPING**
9 Hotel Peron
10 La Relève
11 Le Ryad

🟢 **DRINKING & NIGHTLIFE**
12 Bar des Maraîchers

13 Grand Bar du Chapitre
see 10 La Relève
14 PMU le blabla

🔴 **SHOPPING**
15 Bière de la Plaine
16 Cristal Limiñana
17 Savonnerie Marseillaise de la Licorne

It's another 15 minutes to the next stop, the Port du Frioul, your entry point to two of the Îles du Frioul, Pomègues and Ratonneau, which are connected by a dam. Attacking the unspoiled jagged rock of Pomègues is liberating. Following the seawall after you dock will lead to the Fort de Cavaux, leaving you lost at sea on an uninhabited island, revisiting ghosts in the bunkers of WWII. The island of Ratonneau has a few small shops and restaurants and is popular for its beaches and tiny village. There's a chapel that resembles a Greek temple and the ruins of the Hôpital Caroline, which once housed quarantined travellers, but the highlight is the St-Estève beach, where you can swim safely, protected from the wind.

The ticket pier for **lebateau ferries** (*lebateau-frioul-if.fr; 1/2 islands return €11.10/16.70*) is at the Vieux Port. When facing the port, get in line at its large booth on the left. The Château d'If is closed on Mondays.

Outdoor adventures in the Parc National des Calanques

It feels like a miracle to find a refuge like the **Parc National des Calanques** only a short distance from Marseille. In parts

THE GUIDE

FRANCE PROVENCE

DISCOVER THE HISTORY OF PASTIS

The apéritif pastis is easy to spot: a milky-looking concoction served in a tall glass that adorns outdoor tables across Provence. In 1932 in Marseille, Paul Ricard developed his aniseed-and-liquorice-based liqueur (*pastis* means 'mix' in Occitan) after absinthe was banned in France for fear it caused hallucinations and madness. Since then, it has become a drink that is synonymous with the city. Ricard may now be part of a multinational conglomerate based in Lille, but there are still independent producers in Marseille where you can arrange a visit, including **Cristal Limiñana** (*cristal-liminana.com*) and the independent brewery **Bière de la Plaine** (*Distillerie de la Plaine; @distillerie_de_la_plaine*).

WHAT IS A CALANQUE?

Calanques are coastal geological features typical of the Mediterranean region. These picturesque coves, formed in limestone and located between Marseille and Cassis, are characterised by steep cliffs rising above vibrant turquoise waters. When the sun shines, the small beaches within these narrow bays, comprising either pebbles or fine sand, attract crowds. Escaping to them has become a way of life for city dwellers, leading to various regulations protecting the natural sites. Access by car can be challenging, and most routes are closed between June and October as the arid conditions during this period place the parks at a high chance of wildfires. The strong mistral winds that can sweep through the area further intensify the risks.

MARAKOB5/SHUTTERSTOCK

of this diminutive 85-sq-km patch of scrubby promontories, it's easy to believe you're miles from civilisation. Then a twist in a pine-clad gully reveals the entirety of France's second metropolis spread out within apparent touching distance; the *calanques* (inlets) appear almost as its uninhabited suburbs. But with their light-shifting geometry, rich plant and animal life and idyllic hidden coves, Les Calanques are so much more than that. They are beloved of the Marseillais, who come for the sun and to hike over pine-strewn promontories, mess about in boats and generally refresh their souls.

Of the many *calanques* along the coastline, the most easily accessible are **Calanque de Sormiou** and **Calanque de Morgiou**. Remote inlets such as **Calanque d'En-Vau** and **Calanque de Port-Miou** take dedication and time to reach, either on foot or by kayak. Note that overland access is often limited from June to September, due to fire danger; always check first on the app: *calanques-parcnational.fr/fr/application-mobile -officielle-mes-calanques*. The app is also excellent for up-to-date info on the park and activities. There is also a reservation system in place for two of the most popular *calanques* in summer: **Calanque de Sugiton** and **Calanque des Pierres Tombées**. See *calanques-parcnational.fr*.

DRINKING IN MARSEILLE: BEST PASTIS BARS

MAP p96

Bar des Maraîchers: Listen to '80s radio hits with owner, Serge, who features in his own hilarious fresco of the *Last Supper. 3pm-2am*

Grand Bar du Chapitre: A young crowd in a leafy square at the top of the main thoroughfare, La Canebière. *10am-12.30am*

PMU le blabla: Super cheap and one of the best suntraps protected from the wind in the city. *6.30am-9pm*

La Relève: In the Endoume neighbourhood. Pastis can still be fancy and here it's served with great food and music. *8am-10pm Mon-Sat, 9am-5pm Sun*

Calanque d'En-Vau

LOOK UP

The Gorges du Verdon is home to one of France's most impressive bird populations, including griffon, cinereous and Egyptian vultures. These massive birds ride the thermals above the cliffs, often visible from Route des Crêtes or trail lookouts. Bring binoculars and look for their broad wingspans and slow, soaring flight – especially active on warm afternoons with rising air currents. The two-hour **Treguier Botanical Trail** (start/finish Moustiers-Ste-Marie) is a relatively easy circular walk; great for spotting birdlife. Spring is the best time for twitchers, although the wallcreeper bird tends to only make an appearance in winter.

There's no shortage of outdoor activities here: hiking, kayaking, stand-up paddleboarding, swimming, diving and rock climbing are all incredible. You'll find guides and gear rental in both Marseille and Cassis. From October to June, hiking trails lead through the maquis (scrub). Marseille's tourist office leads guided walks and has an excellent hiking map of the various *calanques,* as does Cassis' tourist office. For access by public transport take bus 19 from Marseille's Castellane bus station down the coast to its terminus at La Madrague, then switch to bus 20 to Callelongue. Note that the road to Callelongue is only open to cars on weekdays from mid-April to May and closed entirely from June to September.

Gorges du Verdon
Sustainable lavender visits

Dive into the new face of ecologically responsible lavender production by visiting an organic lavender farm on the **Plateau de Valensole**. To start with, look for the lavender fields that have let golden grass grow up between the rows of purple – these farms are doing their part to preserve the soil for the next generation. Many farms are open year-round to guests, but run special tours during the harvest season. And no visit would be complete without trying some lavender-based products straight from the source, such as essential oils, soaps and perfumes produced on-site using sustainable methods.

The lavender fields of Valensole are usually the highlight of a photography tour of Provence. Visit in late June or early July, but no later. During this time, the fields are alive with colour and fragrance, providing a stunning backdrop for your photos. To get the perfect shot, you'll have to get up early – sunrise has the longest 'soft-light' period, which reduces shadows and harsh glare. Don't go tramping in the fields,

LAVENDER FARMS ON THE PLATEAU DE VALENSOLE

La Ferme du Riou: This organic farm runs distillery visits during the harvest season and farm visits year-round.

Lavande Bio Berenger: Organic producer with a cabin in the fields during harvest season. Otherwise, stop into the shop in Valensole.

Lavandes Angelvin: Runs distillery visits during high season and guided visits on Tuesdays at 3pm.

Terraroma: Very photogenic lavender and almond farm, with a few sunflower fields to complete the mosaic.

Les Lavandes d'Isabelle et Sébastien: Technically off the plateau and closer to Manosque, this little family lavender farm is less crowded and has a small boutique to find your favourite products.

ZORAN PAJIC/SHUTTERSTOCK

Tablet in use, Palais des Papes, Avignon

but tread carefully between rows – these are precious crops for local farmers. What to wear? Consider colours that will complement the lavender fields. Soft pastels, earthy tones and neutral colours work well in this setting. Avoid wearing bright colours that may clash with the lavender or draw too much attention away from the landscape's natural beauty.

Hike the Sentier Blanc-Martel

This 16km one-way trek from **Chalet de la Maline** to **Point Sublime** is one of France's most legendary hikes. Named after the first geologists to explore the canyon, the trail hugs the cliffs and drops down to the riverbed, with ladders, tunnels and dizzying views along the way. It's demanding but not extreme – suitable for fit beginners with proper footwear. Book the Navette Blanc-Martel *(navette.parcduverdon.fr)* in advance for transport to the trailhead and pickup at the end. Hikers should carry plenty of water, snacks and a torch for the tunnel. Get an early start to avoid the heat and crowds.

Cycle the Route des Crêtes

This 24km balcony road loops out from La Palud-sur-Verdon, rising over 650m in elevation and offering heart-stopping views straight into the canyon. Originally designed for motorised day-trippers, parts of the Route des Crêtes are now restricted or closed to vehicles on select days, giving cyclists a stretch of silence and space. The ride is challenging but manageable with an e-bike – rentals are available in La Palud. Spring and autumn are the best times to ride, with cool weather and lighter traffic. Stop at *belvédères* (lookouts) along the way, where vultures and climbers share the same dizzying vertical playground. A helmet, water and good brakes are essential.

Raft the Verdon River

From April to June, when the river is flowing strong, rafting the Verdon is a wild, splashy ride through limestone corridors and rolling rapids. Most trips depart from Castellane, on the gorge's eastern end. Rapids range from easygoing to intense (Class I to IV), making this a good fit for both beginners and adrenaline junkies. Book ahead with a certified company such as **Yeti Rafting** (*verdon-rafting.net; per person from €40*) – gear and guides are included. Minimum age varies by route (usually seven to 16), and all participants must be able to swim. It's a half-day adventure that takes you deep into the canyon, with moments of calm water to catch your breath between the thrills.

Avignon

The home of seven popes

The vast rooms and shady arcades of 14th-century **Palais des Papes** (*palais-des-papes.com; adult/child €12/€6.50*) give a glimpse into medieval life, when Avignon was the centre of the Catholic world. A visit is supported by tablets (available in multiple languages) that digitally restore lost frescoes and furniture. It's a surprising example of tech that genuinely deepens the experience, bringing rooms to life with audio-visual storytelling and changing art installations. The **Great Chapel** represents the largest covered space in the palace. Construction began in 1348 but was slowed by the Black Death pandemic. In the 14th century, the windows were of stained glass with a carpeted floor and walls covered with drapery dominated by green tones.

Buy tickets online to save time at the entrance, especially during the busy summer season and July theatre festival, and don't miss the Jardins du Palais, designed in the English style and accessible from the former apartments of the Pope – his place for wandering reflection.

THE GREAT SCHISM

Avignon first gained its ramparts – and reputation for arts and culture – during the 14th century, when Pope Clement V fled political turmoil in Rome. From 1309 to 1377, seven French-born popes invested huge sums in the papal palace and offered asylum to Jews and political dissidents. Pope Gregory XI left Avignon in 1376, but his death two years later led to the Great Schism (1378–1417), during which rival popes (up to three at once) resided at Rome and Avignon, denouncing and excommunicating one another. Even after the matter was settled and an impartial pope, Martin V, established himself in Rome, Avignon remained under papal rule. Avignon and Comtat Venaissin (now the Vaucluse *département*) were ruled by papal legates until 1791.

EATING IN AVIGNON: BEST RESTAURANTS

Numéro 75: Chic restaurant in a *hôtel particulier* with a private courtyard, excellent Med menu and stellar wine list. *noon-2.30pm & 7-10pm Mon-Fri* €€€

Graines de Piment: Good-value, tasty bistro on place de la Principale that gives disadvantaged youth a chance to gain work experience. *12.15-1.30pm Mon-Fri* €

Fou de Fafa: Four-course dinners at this Avignon staple, drawing on Mediterranean and Provençal cuisines. Reserve. *7-11pm Thu-Mon* €€

L'Épicerie: Classic French bistro with rustic decor in the heart of old Avignon. Plenty of hearty meat-based dishes; vegan options too. *noon-2.15pm & 7-10pm Thu-Mon* €€

Bordeaux

WINE | GASTRONOMY | ART AND ARCHITECTURE

Bordeaux's mood board hasn't changed since French novelist Victor Hugo (1802–85) visited in 1839, waxing lyrical in letters to his wife back in Paris about the city's elegant squares and quaysides, fountains and monumental theatre that reminded him of Versailles. He wrote 'and you will love Bordeaux, even if you only drink water'.

Bordeaux's heady cocktail of old and new – not to mention its legendary wine cellars, bistros, *bars à vin* and restaurants bursting with prestigious vintages – is as intoxicating as ever. From this Gallo-Roman city's golden past as medieval wine trader and key port in Europe during the Age of Enlightenment, to famous vineyards, a spirited student population and a buoyant undercurrent of creativity, France's sixth-largest city brims with surprising and enthralling stories at every turn. Paired with an exceptional dining scene and captivating river life, there is no tastier marriage.

The Epic Story of Bordeaux Wine

Learn and taste in city museums

Bordeaux's intoxicating wine story begins in the ancient trading district of riverside Chartrons. The city's life-blood wine trade originates here. Discover the role of *négociants* (merchant traders) in the 18th and 19th centuries at the **Musée du Vin et du Négoce** *(museeduvinbordeaux.com; adult/child*

 GETTING AROUND

Tram line A is the cheapest, quickest way to get into town: 45 minutes from **Aéroport de Bordeaux** *(bordeaux.aeroport.fr)* in Merignac, 10km west. The same tickets *(single/10-ticket card €1.90/15)* are valid on Bat3 riverboats, likewise run by public-transport company

TBM *(infotbm.com)*. TBM's public bike-sharing scheme **Le Vélo** has stations with classic and electric wheels all over town. Free-floating electric scooters by **Pony** *(getapony.com)* and **Dott** *(ridedott.com)* fill the gaps.

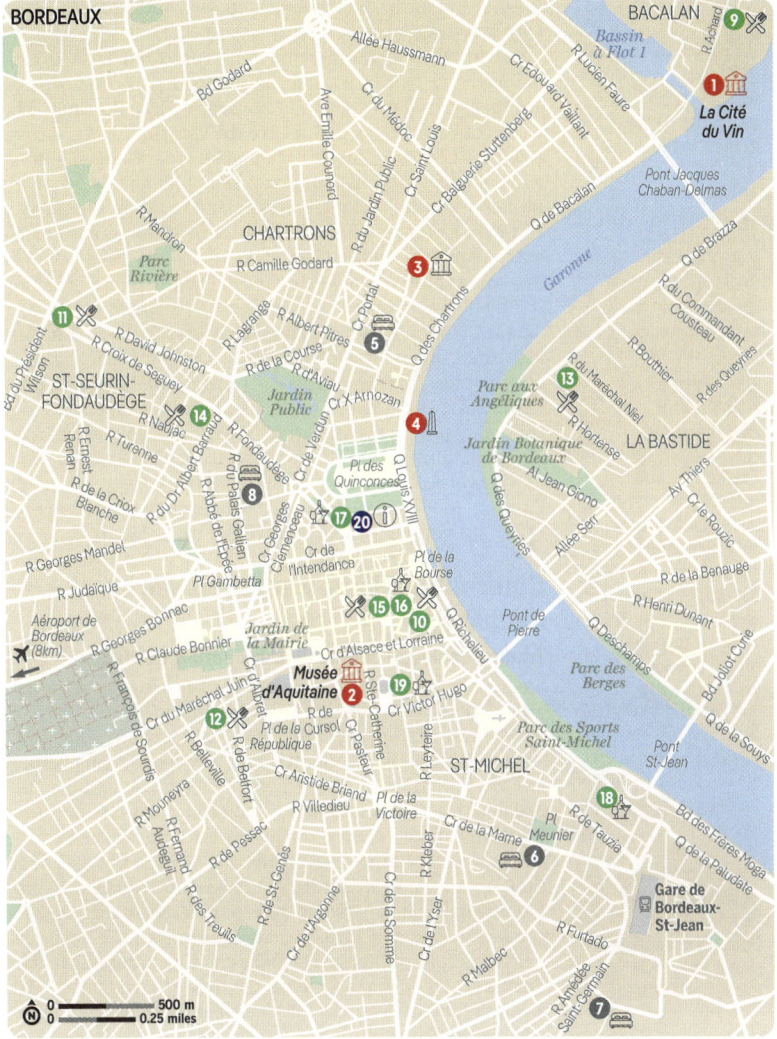

BORDEAUX

⭐ HIGHLIGHTS
1 La Cité du Vin
2 Musée d'Aquitaine

🔴 SIGHTS
3 Musée du Vin et du Négoce
4 Statue of Marthe Testas

⚫ SLEEPING
5 Chez Dupont
6 Hôtel La Zoologie
7 Jost
8 La Maison du Lierre

🟢 EATING
9 Bar de la Marine
10 Chiocchio

11 Le Pavilion des Boulevards
12 L'Univerre
13 Magasin Général
14 Ressources
15 Soif

🟢 DRINKING & NIGHTLIFE
16 Aux Quatre Coins du Vins
17 Bar à Vin
18 Le Point Rouge
19 Wine More Time

🔵 INFORMATION
20 Bordeaux Tourist Office

**WHERE TO
TASTE WINE IN
BORDEAUX**

Jane Anson,
Bordeaux wine
critic and author of
*Inside Bordeaux: The
Châteaux, The Wines
and the Terroir,* shares
her recommenda-
tions. *@jane.anson*

Start with the
**Mémoires et
Partages** *(memoires
etpartages.com)*
walking tour about
colonial trade. It has
lots of wine links
and you'll learn an
important part of
Bordeaux history not
often talked about.

Visit restaurants
with the best wine
lists: **L'Univerre**
and **Le Point Rouge**
are very good, and
Ressources is one of
my favourites.

Some great wine
bars not to miss
include **Wine More
Time**, **Aux Quatre
Coins du Vins** and
Le Bar à Vin at the
Conseil Interprofes-
sionnel du Vin de
Bordeaux (CIVB).

€12/free), in an Irish merchant's house from 1720. Visits end
with a tasting.

Nearby, viticultural merriment morphs Chartrons' quaint
main street, rue Notre Dame, into a street-party zone during
October's two-day Fête du Vin Nouveau et de la Brocante. The
wine trail continues at **La Cité du Vin** *(laciteduvin.com;
adult/child €22/9)*, Bordeaux's emblematic 'Guggenheim of
wine' in a curvaceous building resembling a wine decanter.
Immersive exhibits (lots of sniffing and smelling – it's great!)
end with a glass of *vin* or grape juice in 8th-floor bar Le Bel-
védère. April to October, taste while you tour on a one-hour **Via
Sensoria tour** *(adult/child €22/9)* led by an English-speaking
sommelier, with four wine-and-season pairings.

Back in the old-town quarter of St-Pierre, indulge in a wine
apéritif at the hallowed **Bar à Vin** *(baravin.bordeaux.com;
glass of wine from €2.50)* inside the **Maison du Vin de Bordeaux**. Artworks from the 1950s, including tapestries and
stained glass, further illustrate Bordeaux's epic wine story.
End with dinner at **Soif** *(soif-bordeaux.com; 7-11pm Fri-Mon,
12.30-2pm Sat & Sun)*, a five-minute walk away on rue du
Cancera, to dine in the company of organic, natural wines by
brilliant boutique winemakers you've never heard of.

Confronting History at the Musée d'Aquitaine

Trading enslaved people in 18th-century Bordeaux

Spanning Gallo-Roman times to the present day, the evocative **Musée d'Aquitaine** *(musee-aquitaine-bordeaux.fr;
adult/child €4.50/free)*, closed Monday, is a captivating waltz
through urban history. But it's not all swashbuckling heroics
and viticultural swag. Bordeaux's backstory gets grim on the
2nd floor where chronological exhibits move into 18th-century
Bordeaux and its pivotal role in transatlantic trade and the
trade of enslaved people. During the 480 'triangle' expeditions organised from Bordeaux between 1672 and 1837, some
130,000 to 150,000 Africans were 'purchased' in exchange for
goods and later sold on as enslaved persons in the Americas.

En route, pay your respects to the emotive statue of **Marthe
Testas** (1765–1870) gazing out at the river on quai Louis XVIII,
a young East African girl purchased at the age of 16 by Bor-
delais traders.

 EATING IN BORDEAUX: FAVOURITE TERRACES

Magasin Général:
France's largest organic
restaurant, with vintage
sofas. *8am-7.30pm
Mon-Fri, from 9am Sun, to
11.30pm Fri, 9am-11.30pm
Sat €*

Bar de la Marine: Nothing
beats the €20 three-
course lunch served in a
summer flower garden
in Bacalan. Cool 1950s
memorabilia too. *9am-
5pm Mon-Fri €*

Chiocchio: Tasty Franco-
Tuscan fare on an urban
terrace, foxy street art and
prime people-watching
on cafe-beaded place
du Palais. *noon-3pm &
7-11.30pm Mon-Sat€€*

**Le Pavilion des
Boulevards:** Seasonal
gastronomy on terracotta-
paved patio perfumed with
magnolia. *noon-2pm Wed,
noon-2pm & 8-10pm Tue &
Thu-Sat €€€*

Beyond Bordeaux

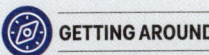

An unmatched sensory feast, trips beyond Bordeaux deliver pink-hued cities, go-slow sea adventure and France's finest wine.

Bordeaux is a gateway to vine-ribboned countryside and Atlantic Coast sand dunes. North, where the Dordogne and Garonne Rivers meet, spills the Gironde Estuary and the prestigious vineyards of the Médoc. South of the city, the Côte d'Argent (Silver Coast) takes centre stage with endless shimmering-gold beaches backed by dark-green pine forests. Surfers catch waves and enjoy incredible sunsets in celebrity Biarritz, while Basque culture reigns supreme in Bayonne. To the southeast, the pink city of Toulouse feels lived in and laid-back, thanks to its large student population, yet still has lofty dreams of aiming for the stars: it's a hub for the manufacture of airplanes and rockets.

Places

St-Émilion p105
Arcachon p106
Bayonne p106
Biarritz p107
Toulouse p108

St-Émilion
TIME FROM BORDEAUX: 1HR 🚗

Visit an eco-winery and lunch between vines
The first vines were planted on the picturesque Troplong Mondot estate carpeting the highest point of St-Émilion in the 1700s, and by 1745 the winemaker was rich enough to have a handsome château built from the local creamy limestone on his land. Today, guided tours of **Château Troplong-Mondot** (troplong-mondot.com; 90min guided tour with tasting €50) walk you around one of the region's most innovative, green-thinking wineries. Vineyards are ploughed exclusively by a dozen hefty working horses; a pig and several hens recycle organic waste; and the estate's swanky barrel cellar with 12m-high cathedral ceiling is underground to avoid spoiling the centuries-old bucolic landscape.

Tours end with tastings of two vintages and there's a swish boutique where you can buy the premier *grand cru* wines. Alternatively, reserve a table at the château's Michelin-starred

---

🧭 GETTING AROUND

A car isn't vital along the southwest coast, but needed in rural areas and those with poor public transport (northern part of the Médoc and the Basque hinterland). High-speed TGVs service Bordeaux, Biarritz and Bayonne (four hours direct from Paris Montparnasse).

Toulouse also has TGVs to Paris Montparnasse (just under five hours), and regular trains to Spain. Walking or cycling the city centre is easiest. Toulouse also has a well-served international airport.

LA VÉLODYSSÉE

As its evocative name suggests, **La Vélodyssée** *(cycling-lavelodyssee. com)* is a coastal odyssey by *vélo* (bike) along France's Atlantic Coast, linking Roscoff in Brittany with Hendaye on the French–Spanish border, 1270km away in Pays Basque.

The scenic Gironde stretch is 81km (four hours) from the tip of the Médoc south to Lacanau, just north of the Bassin d'Arcachon. Flat and reasonably unchallenging, the well-marked cycling itinerary kicks off with ethereal sea and Cordouan lighthouse views from Pointe de Grave (it's 108 steps up the cape's own, 28m-tall Phare de Grave lighthouse) before plunging through pine forests and past sand dunes, beaches, lake and lagoon on its route 7.5km south to Soulac-sur-Mer and beyond.

restaurant, Les Belles Perdrix *(weekday lunch/dinner menus from €50/85)*, overlooking vines, to indulge in outstanding modern French cuisine and perfect pairings. It's 20 minutes (2km) on foot from St-Émilion village to Troplong-Mondot.

Arcachon

TIME FROM BORDEAUX: 1HR

Climb Europe's largest sand dune

Breathtakingly cold in winter and as hot as burning coals in the height of summer it might be, but barefoot is the most thrilling way to romp around the golden sands of Europe's largest dune. Local lore claims the shifting **Dune du Pilat**, 10km south from Arcachon, has swallowed trees, a road junction, even a hotel. What is certain is the spectacular panorama from the top. Looking west, see sandy shoals at the mouth of the Bassin d'Arcachon, Cap Ferret and bird-rich Banc d'Arguin. Facing east, dead black trees killed by forest fires polka-dot rich green forest.

April to November, a staircase – around 150 steps – is built on the dune's eastern slope to help tourists stagger breathlessly to the top. Otherwise, use the locals' 'secret' shortcut to arrive midway up the dune: uphill past fashionista lunch hangout **La Co(o)rniche** on av Louis Gaume, then right onto the unmarked footpath between the bike stand and No 31 on av des Dunes. To understand the fragility and diversity of Pilat's vulnerable sand scape, join a guided nature walk, sunrise or sunset hike, telescope workshop or storytelling sessions organised by the **Espace Accueil** *(ladunedupilat.com)* at the dune entrance. Snack bars and eco-boutiques here only sell local artisan fare.

Bayonne

TIME FROM BORDEAUX: 2HR

Learn about traditional Basque culture in Bayonne

Funerary rites, fishing, folklore, pastoral life and *pelota*: Petit Bayonne's riverfront **Musée Basque et de l'Histoire de Bayonne** *(musee-basque.com; adult/under 26yr €8/free; closed Mon & Thu)* has brought Basque history, culture and crafts vividly to life since 1924. Its 20 rooms fill a 17th-century warehouse, built on the wharf by a merchant to store his goods once offloaded from the ship. Get orientated with a scale model of Bayonne port in 1805, showing Grand Bayonne, which the Romans founded on a hill between the town's two rivers, and Petit Bayonne on the Nive's opposite riverbank, which flourished as a trading and shipbuilding hub from the 12th century. Spot the Gothic twin spires – one now clean-cream, the other

 EATING & DRINKING IN ARCACHON: OUR PICKS

La Pâtisserie de Ma Fille: Gourmet breakfasts, brunch, crêpes and cakes on market square place des Marquises. *8am-7pm Mon-Thu, to 10pm Fri-Sun* €€

Café de la Plage – Chez Pierre: A Mira craft beer brewed next door in La Teste-de-Buch or lavish shellfish platter: this timeless seafront duo delivers. *8am-2am* €€

Coquille: All-day ceviche, burgers, bowls, salads and meat/fish mains in a cosy, sea-inspired bistro near the market. *9am-midnight Tue-Sat, to 4pm Sun* €€

Club Plage Pereire: Enjoy oysters, seafood, cocktails and a great gin made from Cognac vine blossoms at this pop-up on Plage Pereire. *10am-midnight Apr-Sep* €€

Dune du Pilat, Arcachon

dirty dark-grey – of 13th-century **Cathédrale Ste-Marie** *(free)* and its peaceful cloister on place Louis Pasteur, and the 17th-century ramparts encircling the city.

Don't miss the rooms dedicated to *pelote Basque (pelota)* – the catchall name for more than a dozen traditional Basque ballgames, including *main nue* (played barehanded) and *jaï alaï* (the most high-octane variant). Art, short films and players' kit shine light on the rules, the *fronton (pelota* court), how to use the scoop-like basket called a *chistera*, etc. Post-museum, pass by **Trinquet St-André**, a 17th-century covered *jeu de paume* court on rue du Jeu de Paume, later adapted for *pelota*. Enjoy a drink in its bar-brasserie from 1943 and catch a game in action.

Biarritz

TIME FROM BORDEAUX: **2HR**

Lunch cheap on oysters and white wine

Fashionable surf villages and fishing ports bead the seashore south of Biarritz. Ruins of medieval ovens once used to melt whale blubber rub shoulders with trendy beach bars, bodegas and eco-boutiques. *Pintxos, poissons* and paella at Biarritz' renowned bistro-bodega **Bar Jean** *(barjean-biarritz.fr)* has been a Biarrot rite of passage since 1930. The round-the-clock festive vibe on the street terrace alone is memorable (unusually, food is served nonstop from 10.30am to 1am).

FÊTES DE BAYONNE

Thousands of revellers fill Bayonne for five days during July's Fêtes de Bayonne *(fetes. bayonne.fr)*. White with a red sash and neck-scarf is the non-negotiable dress code. The street revelry starts on the last Wednesday in July or first in August with the traditional throwing of the city keys from the balcony of Bayonne's town hall. Fireworks and a *bal* (dance) follow. Brass bands, DJs and choirs perform all over town and there's folk dancing, *pelota*, omelette championships, espadrille throwing, tugs-of-war and stone lifting in *festivals de force basque* (strength competitions). Thursday's Journée des Enfants has kids' activities. Less savoury are the Basque *courses des vaches* ('running of the bulls' but with horned cows) and *corridas* (bullfights).

 EATING IN BAYONNE: GOOD-VALUE DINING

Bistrot Pépite: Modern bistro fare: duck hearts with port, curried mussels, veggie beignets. *7.30-9.30pm Tue-Fri, noon-1.30pm & 7.30-9.30pm Sat* €

Cantine du Musée: Excellent-value bistro serves seasonal Basque fare with lashings of 'bonne humeur'. *12.15-1.30pm Tue, 12.15-1.30pm & 7.30-9.30pm Wed-Sat* €€

Cidrerie Ttipia: A juicy *txuleta* (beef steak) for two, fries, salad and a cider is the thing at this rustic, noisy cider hall. *noon-2pm & 7-11pm Tue-Sat, noon-2pm Sun* €€

Basa: Good-value lunches in a brasserie with peaceful garden patio. Try smoked octopus with beetroot and caramelised dill. *noon-10pm Mon-Sat, to 2pm Sun* €€

ANIBAL TREJO/SHUTTERSTOCK

BEST BIARROT BEACHES FOR SURFING & SUNBATHING

Grande Plage: Biarritz' main golden-sand beach, much-loved since the days of Napoléon II and Eugénie.

Plage de la Côte des Basques: Long golden sand beach with trendy bars. A surfers' and sunset lovers' favourite.

Plage d'Ilbarritz: Another strip of powder-soft sand, enlivened with the summer terrace of beach bar Blue Cargo, a dance floor after dark.

Plage de l'Océan: Fringed by protected sand dunes and a golf green, this is the wildest of Anglet's back-to-back swathe of sand beaches. Sunset drinks at beach bar Ozeanoa are a must.

Plage des Sables d'Or: Cafes, surf shops and several sandy beach-volley courts in Anglet.

Capitole, Toulouse

To keep things cheap, dive into **Les Halles** *(halles-biarritz. fr; 6/12 oysters with glass of wine €8/14)* opposite. Swimming with the day's catch from 7.30am to 2pm daily, the fish hall buzzes with vendors flogging crab claws, whelks, seasonal sea urchins and an ocean of fish. Oyster farmers shuck various sized *huîtres* for seafood lovers to devour standing up or slurp around shared tables on a no-frills mezzanine upstairs.

Toulouse
TIME FROM BORDEAUX: 2½HR

It's a Capitole idea to visit Toulouse

Toulouse's city hall, the **Capitole** *(free)*, demonstrates many facets of the city's cultural character. With its rose terracotta and white brick neoclassical facade, complete with eight pink and cream marble Corinthian columns, it is one of Toulouse's signature buildings. The exterior's architectural display is balanced by the interior's impressive frescoes and paintings, which decorate the chambers and halls. Enter from the **Place du Capitole**, the city's social focal point; its perimeter arcades are packed with patrons of its Belle Époque bistros and brasseries. Inside, follow the entry signs through security. Once through, climb the elegant main staircase, overlooked by Renaissance-style murals. At the top, local artist Henri Martin's huge postimpressionist canvases fill Salle Henri-Martin, while painted scenes from Toulouse's history

 EATING IN BIARRITZ: HIP PICKS IN BIBI BEAURIVAGE

Bleach: Lunch with sassy locals over homemade food in a retro, 1950s-styled cafe in Biarritz' coolest no-tourists 'hood. *9am-3pm Mon-Fri* €

Club Sandwich: Chicken burgers, truffle clubs, falafel salad by day. Vinyl nights, DJ sets, club nights come dark. *noon-3pm & 7pm-midnight Tue-Sat, noon-3pm Sun* €

Restaurant Hernani: Spend an evening in Spanish Basque country at this lively bodega. The sangria flows. *7.30-11pm Tue-Sat* €€

Chéri Bibi: Off-grid modern neighbourhood bistro: expertly curated local produce with natural wines on a wooden people-watching deck. *7pm-midnight Thu-Sun* €€

decorate the **Salle des Illustres** (Hall of the Illustrious). The southern end of the building hosts the **Théâtre du Capitole** (*opera.toulouse.fr*), where the city's ballet and opera companies perform regularly. Try to catch one of the occasional €5 lunchtime recitals (book in advance).

Towpath adventures

The Canal de Garonne runs east from the Atlantic; the Canal du Midi runs west from the Mediterranean. They meet in Toulouse, forming one continuous, navigable coast-to-coast waterway. Exploring the towpaths, which are shaded by regimented parades of plane trees, can be as simple as a leisurely stroll or a daylong cycling trip. For the latter, rentals are available from the city's 400 bike stations using the véloToulouse (*velotoulouse.tisseo.fr*) bike-sharing app.

A more substantial waterway, the Garonne River cleaves its way through the heart of the city. Get onto the water with **Les Bateaux Toulousains** (*bateaux-toulousains.com; from €8*), with 30-minute cruises from July to October. The same boats are used for canal cruises from March to June.

Conquering the skies

Toulouse has long been seen as the world capital of aeronautics. And aviation, space and technology enthusiasts have not one, but four major landmarks in store. Of them, the most impressive is **Aeroscopia** (*aeroscopia.fr; adult/child €15/12*), which brings together scores of planes, among them some of the world's largest. You can walk through a Concorde (its 1970s style seats and complex control panels preserved in place behind perspex) and an Airbus A380 on the tarmac outside, where parts of the fuselage and flooring are stripped back to expose the complicated wiring. Nearby, **Ailes Anciennes Toulouse** (*Old Wings Toulouse; aatlse.org; €7*), open only a few days a week, holds a fine collection of 47 heritage planes, including a French Dassault Mirage, British De Havilland Vampire T11, and a US Lockheed T-33 Shooting Star. **Let's Visit Airbus** (*manatour.fr; adult/child €16/13*) runs tours of the Airbus Factory.

Nothing martials humanity's scientific advances like the exploration of space. Toulouse's contribution to our airborne feats beyond the stratosphere are celebrated at the vast **Cité de l'Espace** (*cite-espace.com; adult/child €29/22.50*) space museum. Highlights include boarding a Mir space station, riding the Apollo mission simulator and seeing real pieces of moonrock.

CITY OF VIOLETS

It is dubbed the Rose City but Toulouse is also a city of violets. Specifically, the flowers that are cultivated locally in winter and used to make *liqueur de violette* (a popular ace up the sleeve with local mixologists); *violettes de Toulouse* candies; and Paris-Toulouse pastries, consisting of hazelnut praline and violet-infused Chantilly cream. If used well, violet flowers create a subtle fragrant note, rather than the soapy flavour you might expect. To buy violet products, check out **La Maison de la Violette**, a shop in a canal barge. In a nod to this violet heritage, the local football team, Ligue 1's Toulouse FC, play in purple and even released a third kit in the 2024–25 season emblazoned with violet flowers.

EATING IN TOULOUSE: OUR PICKS

Chez Tran: Playful neon lighting and paper lanterns. Try its signature bo buns. On rue Pargaminières, known as the 'street-food half-mile'. *hours vary* €

Au Bon Graillou: Try the excellent-value seasonal three-course menu for lunch, using ingredients from Marché Victor Hugo downstairs. *noon-3pm Tue-Sun* €€

L'Oncle Pom: Sagely takes a potato-forward approach: first, select your preparation (gratin, French fries etc) before choosing a meat or fish to accompany. *hours vary* €€

Restaurant Emile: Michelin Guide–level *cassoulet* served in clay bowls. Book ahead for terrace seating. *noon-1.30pm & 7.30-9.30pm* €€€

HELP ME PICK:

Where to Taste Wine

The French thirst for wine dates to Roman times when oenophiles identified fertile pockets of Gaul to plant *vignobles* (vineyards) to spawn France's most celebrated wine regions: Burgundy, Bordeaux, Champagne, Alsace, the Loire and Rhône valleys, Provence and Languedoc. Quality wines in France are Appellation d'Origine Contrôlée (AOC) or Appellation d'Origine Protégée (AOP): the wine has met stringent regulations governing where, how and under what conditions it was grown and bottled. Some regions have a single AOC (like Alsace); others dozens. Bordeaux has 65!

Where to go if you love...

Full-Bodied Reds

Monks in Burgundy began making wine in the 8th century, believing divine spirits in the soil spoke to them through wine. Burgundy vineyards remain small and are divided into *climats* – a viticultural patrimony UNESCO-listed since 2015. Winegrowers in **Côte d'Or**, **Chablis**, **Châtillon** and **Mâcon** produce small quantities of excellent reds from pinot noir grapes. The best Bourgogne vintages demand 10 to 20 years to age. Despite Burgundy's global fame (and the sky-high prices its wines now fetch), many winemakers remain modest – owner-operators who prune their own vines and consider themselves caretakers rather than creators.

Bubbles

Champagne's beloved bubbles were once thought to be a fault in the region's still wine. It wasn't until Dom Pierre Pérignon, a Benedictine monk at Hautvillers Abbey, started to master the art of winemaking that the sparkling wine began to be appreciated. 'Come quickly, I am tasting the stars!' is what he reportedly exclaimed upon tasting Champagne in 1693. For centuries, Champagne was the celebratory drink for French coronations, giving it the reputation as 'the wine of Kings and the King of wines'. Today, the famous Champagne houses welcome visitors to underground caverns, perfectly manicured vineyards and exquisite tasting rooms.

BARNALINI/SHUTTERSTOCK

Crisp Whites

The Loire Valley produces France's greatest variety of wines, some in troglodyte caves. Light delicate whites from **Pouilly-Fumé**, **Vouvray**, **Sancerre**, **Bourgueil** and **Chinon** are excellent. Muscadet, cabernet franc and chenin blanc grapes contrast with chardonnay grapes that go into Burgundy's great whites. There are also plenty of reds, particularly in Chinon, most made from cabernet franc grapes, aged in caves carved out of *tuffeau*, the soft local limestone, which offers the ideal temperature and humidity.

Pale Rosé

Chilled, fresh pink rosé wines are synonymous with the hot south, and 80% of the wine produced in Provence is rosé. **Côtes de Provence**, with 20 hectares of vineyards between Nice and Aix-en-Provence, is France's sixth-largest appellation. Look for rosés from **Bandol**, **Coteaux d'Aix-en-Provence**, **Palette** and **Coteaux Varois**.

Map labels: Caen, Rouen, Reims, PARIS, Metz, Champagne, Strasbourg, St-Malo, Nancy, Alençon, Chartres, Colmar, Rennes, Laval, Le Mans, Sens, Troyes, Mulhouse, Vallée de la Loire, Orléans, Auxerre, Chablis, Angers, Bourgueil, Blois, Côte d'Or, Besançon, Nantes, Tours, Sancerre, La Tour du Pouilly Fumé, Dijon, SWITZERLAND, Chinon, Bourges, Bourgogne, Châtillon, Châtellerault, Châteauroux, Poitiers, Mâcon, Niort, Villefranche-sur-Saône (Marathon du Beaujolais), Annecy, La Rochelle, Limoges, Clermont-Ferrand, Lyon, Chambéry, Saintes, Angoulême, ITALY, Périgueux, Brive-la-Gaillarde, Grenoble, Bordeaux, Valence, Médoc (Marathon de), Montélimar, Provence, Montauban, Nîmes, Avignon, Nice, Toulouse, Montpellier, Arles, Palette, Cannes, Bayonne, La Celle (Coteaux Varois), Pau, Béziers, Aix-en-Provence, Marseille, Carcassonne, Narbonne, Bandol, Toulon, SPAIN, GERMANY, 100 km, 50 miles

HOW TO

Burgundy Wineries are almost impossible to visit; buy from *négociants* (wine merchants) in specialist wine shops instead.

Champagne Most Champagne houses are in Reims, Épernay or in between the two. Tastings often require reservation and include a tour, and are much more expensive than in other wine regions, starting from €27 per person.

Loire Valley Hundreds of vineyards welcome visitors, although advance reservations are preferred. Visit *vinsdeloire.fr/caves -touristiques* for information and an interactive map.

Provence Many vignerons (growers) open their doors to visitors; taste two or three vintages before buying. In Provence fill your own container with cheap *vin de table* (table wine) at the local wine cooperatives.

Oeno-tourism

E-bike tours are common in areas like Beaujolais, Jura and the Loire; or in the Dordogne and Ardèche, wake up to sunrise yoga sessions among the vines. In the Alps, try heady combinations like snowshoe walks to taste wine in forest tipis, or take blind tasting up a level by combining speleology and wine tasting in the Ardèche's caves. Wine-infused runs are increasingly popular, too. The Marathon du Médoc is now almost 40 years old, and obtaining a place is reminiscent of getting tickets for Glastonbury or Coachella. Bigger and more popular year-on-year, the riotous Marathon du Beaujolais is a popular alternative, but even that sells out well in advance. Look out for smaller wine runs, and prepare to don full fancy dress.

When buying wine from a shop, visit a caviste rather than a supermarket. Often the price difference is nominal, and they'll have a greater selection of wines from small producers.

Places We Love to Stay

€ Budget €€ Midrange €€€ Top end

Paris
MAP p52

Hôtel Chopin € A rare budget hotel in Paris, and in the unique location of one of the city's historical *passages couverts*. This historic hotel originally opened in 1846 and features classic, period-inspired rooms overlooking the Paris rooftops.

People Marais € This modern hostel is built for community, with well-equipped dorms, communal kitchens, and a light-filled sociable cafe and restaurant.

123 Sebastopol €€ A cinema-themed hotel, where each floor is dedicated to a film director or film-music composer, with an entertaining atmosphere. It is family-friendly and conveniently located between Sentier and Le Marais.

Hôtel des Académies et des Arts €€ An effortlessly cool design hotel housed in the building where Modigliani once had his studio (book room 52 if you want to sleep in it). The hotel also has its own art atelier downstairs.

Hotel Dame des Arts €€ This hip hotel is one of St-Germain-des-Prés coolest addresses, with design-led rooms and a rooftop terrace with fantastic views that pulls in locals as well as guests.

Hôtel HoY €€ One of the most restful places to stay; there's a yoga studio and in-room mats. The highlight is the ground-floor flower shop and the excellent MESA, serving up creative plant-based dishes steeped in Latin American flavours.

Mama Shelter Paris East €€ This cool Philippe Starck–designed, 170-room hotel draws a younger, creative crowd to its off-grid location, thanks to its bold industrial decor, rooftop bar and playful touches such as cartoon-mask lampshades.

Mont St-Michel
MAP p66

Chambres d'Hôte Les Bruyères du Mont € Find an enchanted garden and gracious host Nadine in this guesthouse near Mont St-Michel.

Camping La Baie du Mont St-Michel €€ A well-maintained, no-frills campsite with friendly hosts and plenty of hot water for showers.

Auberge Sauvage €€€ Farmhouse chic aesthetic with a garden and tennis courtyards – and a Michelin-starred restaurant.

Annecy

Hôtel du Château €€ Family-run hotel in Annecy with panoramic breakfast terrace and free parking, on a hill across from the château's imposing gatehouse.

Chamonix
MAP p74

Le Chamoniard Volant € Veteran favourite of climbers and ski bums on a budget, with bunk dorms and communal kitchen in a self-catering chalet.

Hôtel Richemond € Third-generation family hotel, with old-school rooms in a grand old building from 1914; exceptional value.

La Folie Douce €€ The famous après-ski brand's only hotel parties hard inside a monumental Belle Époque palace.

Refuge du Montenvers €€ Mourn France's longest but fast-melting glacier at this elegant grand dame, an 1880 vintage with chic retro-styled rooms, restaurant and summer terrace above Mer de Glace.

Lyon
MAP p80

Pilo € Almost too stylish to be a hostel, with oodles of plants, Friday-night DJ sets alfresco, boules pitches and frequent visiting tattoo artists.

Hotel de Verdun 1882 €€ Beautiful rooms in a historic building formerly belonging to the founders of Lyonnais institution Brasserie Georges.

Lyon Country House €€ A breath of fresh air just 15 minutes from the city centre, with lodges, treehouses and suites.

Fourvière Hôtel €€€ Chic, upmarket hotel in a former convent. The old altar and confessional booths spill over with house plants.

Loire Valley

Hôtel de Biencourt € Just 150m from the entrance to Azay-le-Rideau, 17 charming rooms in a one-time school from the 17th and 18th centuries.

Côté Loire-Auberge Ligérienne € Facing the river in Blois, this establishment – an inn since 1675 – has eight spotless rooms, some with 350-year-old beams and/or great Loire views.

Le Bois des Chambres €€ A very classy 39-room hotel, 300m from Chaumont-sur-Loire, that occupies a 19th-century barn and ecofriendly, modern pavilions surrounded by gardens.

Hôtel Le Grand Monarque €€
An 18th-century coaching inn transformed into a charming hotel just five minutes on foot from the château. Rooms are spacious, with a mix of 21st-century mod cons and antique touches.

Relais de Chambord €€€
Chambord's former kennels are now a luxury hotel with an unbeatable château-adjacent location, country-chic rooms, a sensational bar, a spa and a *bistronomique* restaurant.

Nice MAP p92

Hostel Meyerbeer Beach €
Friendly hostel with a cracking city-centre location, just three minutes from the beach. Dorms are mixed.

Hôtel Rossetti €€ Charming three-star boutique hotel with seven rooms in the shadow of Cathédrale Ste-Réparate in Vieux Nice. The hidden terrace is lovely.

Hôtel La Pérouse €€€ Clinging to the Colline du Château with a hidden pool and sea views, this delightful four-star hotel is one of Nice's finest.

Le Negresco €€€ The grande dame of Nice's hotels, set across from the beach. Each room is unique and styled to a theme. The art collection is priceless.

Marseille MAP p97

Hotel Peron €€ Wes Anderson–style hotel with views of the corniche and beyond. Art deco from every angle and a friendly reception.

Le Ryad €€ North African–inspired hotel that has a sanctuary of a garden to drink fresh mint tea in after a long day.

La Relève €€ There are only four rooms, so book in advance for this 1950s-inspired guesthouse that is attached to a very cool bar in the 7e.

St-Tropez

Hôtel Ermitage €€ Self-consciously retro, with sweeping views over town.

Hôtel Lou Cagnard €€€ Lovely jasmine-scented garden patios and welcoming feel. Open year-round.

Bordeaux MAP p103

Jost € A new-gen lifestyle hostel with a Spritz-fuelled bar around a rooftop pool (guests only). Tip-top Italian tapas too.

Chez Dupont €€ B&B-style rooms decorated with vintage furniture and curiosities, on Chartrons' old-world main street.

La Maison du Lierre €€ As serene as its name, the House of Ivy has quaint boutique rooms and serves breakfast in a vine-draped garden.

Hôtel La Zoologie €€€ Four-star luxury in Bordeaux's historic Institute of Zoology, a glorious 1903 mashup of brick, stone and glass.

Hotel Peron, Marseille

Practicalities

MONEY & CURRENCY
The currency in France is the euro (€). Payment by card is widespread and can be contactless up to €50; smaller shops can impose a minimum payment (€10 or €15). In rural France, many B&Bs, *fermes auberges,* produce markets and taxi drivers don't accept cards. You cannot hire a car without a credit card.

BILLION PHOTOS/SHUTTERSTOCK

SMOKING
Smoking in France is illegal in indoor public spaces, summer forests and – since July 2025 – in public parks and gardens, beaches, bus shelters, sports facilities and outdoor spaces around schools.

HEALTHCARE
Pharmacies – an illuminated green cross indicates they're open – sell a wide range of medicines without *ordonnance* (prescription). Details of the closest *pharmacie de garde* open at night and on Sundays are displayed in pharmacy windows. Call 118 or Europe-wide 112 for an ambulance.

LGBTIQ+ TRAVELLERS
The rainbow flag flies high in France. 'Laissez-faire' perfectly sums up France's liberal attitude towards homosexuality and people's private lives in general, in part because of a long tradition of public tolerance towards unconventional lifestyles.

OPENING HOURS
In many French towns and villages, shops close on Monday.
Banks 9am–noon and 2pm–5pm Monday to Friday or Tuesday to Saturday
Bars 7pm–1am
Cafes 7am–11pm
Clubs 10pm–3am, 4am or 5am Thursday to Saturday
Restaurants Noon–2.30pm and 7pm–9pm or later six days a week
Shops 10am–noon and 2pm–7pm Monday to Saturday

ACCESSIBLE TRAVEL
France presents constant challenges for *visiteurs à mobilité réduite* (visitors with reduced mobility) and *visiteurs handicapés* (visitors with disabilities), but inroads are being made into helping them get around more easily. Paris metro is not good for accessibility, but Paris buses are 100% accessible.

PUBLIC HOLIDAYS
New Year's Day 1 January
Easter Sunday & Monday Late March/April
May Day 1 May
WWII Victory Day 8 May
Ascension Thursday May; 40th day after Easter
Pentecost & Whit Monday Mid-May to mid-June; seventh Sunday after Easter
Bastille Day (Fête Nationale) 14 July
Assumption Day 15 August
All Saints' Day 1 November
Remembrance Day 11 November
Christmas Day 25 December

Language

Standard French is taught and spoken throughout France. This said, regional accents and dialects are an important part of identity in certain regions, but you'll have no trouble being understood anywhere if you stick to standard French.

Basics

Hello. Bonjour. *bon-zhoor*
Goodbye. Au revoir. *o-rer-vwa*
Yes. Oui. *wee*
No. Non. *non*
Please. S'il vous plaît. *seel voo play*
Thank you. Merci. *mair-see*
Excuse me. Excusez-moi. *ek-skew-zay-mwa*
Sorry. Pardon. *par-don*
What's your name? Comment vous appelez-vous? *ko-mon voo-za-play voo*
My name is ... Je m'appelle ... *zher ma-pel ...*
Do you speak English? Parlez-vous anglais? *par-lay-voo ong-glay*
I don't understand. Je ne comprends pas. *zher ner kom-pron pa*

Directions

Where's ...? Où est ...? *oo ay ...*
What's the address? Quelle est l'adresse? *kel ay la-dres*
Could you write the address, please? Est-ce que vous pourriez écrire l'adresse, s'il vous plaît? *es-ker voo poo-ryay ay-kreer la-dres seel voo play*
Can you show me (on the map)? Pouvez-vous m'indiquer (sur la carte)? *poo-vay-voo mun-dee-kay (sewr la kart)*

Signs

Entrée Entrance
Fermé Closed
Ouvert Open
Sortie Exit
Toilettes/WC Toilets

Time

What time is it? Quelle heure est-il? *kel er ay til*
It's (8) o'clock. Il est (huit) heures. *il ay (weet) er*
Half past (10). Il est (dix) heures et demie. *il ay (deez) er ay day-mee*
Morning Matin. *ma-tun*
Afternoon Après-midi. *a-pray-mee-dee*
Evening Soir. *swar*
Yesterday Hier. *yair*
Today Aujourd'hui. *o-zhoor-dwee*
Tomorrow Demain. *der-mun*

Emergencies

Help! Au secours! *o skoor*
Leave me alone! Fichez-moi la paix! *fee-shay-mwa la pay*
I'm ill. Je suis malade. *zher swee ma-lad*
Call ... Appelez... *a-play*
  a doctor un médecin. *un mayd-sun*
  the police la police. *la po-lees*

Eating & Drinking

What would you recommend? Qu'est-ce que vous conseillez? *kes-ker voo kon-say-yay*
Cheers! Santé! *son-tay*
That was delicious. C'était délicieux! *say-tay day-lee-syer*

NUMBERS

1
un *un*
2
deux *der*
3
trois *trwa*
4
quatre *ka-trer*
5
cinq *sungk*
6
six *sees*
7
sept *set*
8
huit *weet*
9
neuf *nerf*
10
dix *dees*

TRAVELVIEW/SHUTTERSTOCK

Charles de Gaulle airport

Arriving

For many, touchdown in Paris, at Charles de Gaulle or Orly airports, is their first taste of France, although there are international airports across the country. Trains link much of continental Europe and the UK with France, with many ferry connections joining the UK to northern France, too. Cruises dock on much of the French coast, particularly along the Mediterranean.

By Air
Charles de Gaulle, Paris, is the largest international airport in France, and most flights linking non-European countries arrive here. There are international airports in Lyon-St-Exupéry, Marseille-Provence, Nice-Côte d'Azur, Bordeaux-Mérignac and Toulouse-Blagnac, among others.

By Train
Eurostar *(eurostar.com)* is currently the only trans-Channel service to the UK; book tickets to/from London St Pancras in advance for best rates. Renfe *(renfe. com)* runs France–Spain connections, and Trenitalia *(trenitalia.com)* serves the France–Italy route.

MONEY
Currency Euro (€)

CREDIT & DEBIT CARDS
Some metro systems (including Lyon) accept contactless card payments. In other cities, like Paris, you'll need to buy a rechargeable Navigo card.

ATMS
ATMs – *points d'argent* or *distributeurs automatiques de billets* – are the cheapest and most convenient way to get euros, usually offering the best exchange rates. Cashpoints connected to Visa/MasterCard/Cirrus/Maestro networks are situated in all cities and towns, on central squares, outside banks on main streets and inside large supermarkets.

Getting Around

There's excellent public transport but you'll also want your own wheels to explore deeper. EU nationals don't need a visa to visit France, but by the end of 2026, it is anticipated that arrivals from the UK, US, Canada and New Zealand, among others, will have to fill in a pre-arrival, online form to meet the EU's new electronic vetting system *(etiasvisa.com)*.

Train & Bus

France's SNCF rail network has frequent services (both high-speed TGVs and regional TER trains). Principal rail lines radiate out from Paris, making services between towns on different spokes slow or nonexistent. Bus services are reduced weekends and school holidays.

GREGORY_DUBUIS/GETTY IMAGES

Bicycle & E-Bike

Dedicated cycling paths are widespread; many skirt canal towpaths or retired railway lines *(voies verts* or greenways). Long-distance itineraries like La Vélodyssée (p106) favour roads with light traffic and are ideal for bike-packing. Bike rental – road and mountain bikes, regular and electric-assisted – is omnipresent.

Hiring a Car

Driving is a delight in backstage France, but a car is a liability in traffic-plagued city centres. Find rental agencies at airports and by train stations; many offer electric cars. Some cities have a public car-sharing scheme, ideal for an out-of-town day flit. Consider car-sharing platforms *ouicar.fr* and *fr.getaround.com*.

Using Motorways

Autoroutes (motorways) command *péages* (tolls). Take a ticket on entering, pay when exiting. Cash payers: drive into a tollbooth displaying a green arrow – booths showing a white card symbol only accept cards. Check traffic conditions, motorway services etc on *bison-fute.gouv.fr*.

Ridesharing

Covoiturage (ridesharing) in France is a national institution. BlaBlaCar *(blablacar.fr)* is the most popular app, connecting passengers with drivers. In towns and cities, hitchhikers can stand in front of an *'Arrêt sur le pouce'* sign to be picked up by a vetted driver in the Rézo Pouce network *(rezopouce.fr)*.

DRIVING ESSENTIALS

Any car entering an intersection (including a T-junction) from a road on your right has the right of way unless street signs indicate otherwise.

There's generally a tollbridge, but some motorways have phased this out; pay within 72 hours online at *sanef.com*.

Approx. €1.72/L

Curated by
Kate Armstrong

Greece

THE PLACE FOR EPIC ADVENTURES

Greece's legendary status is defined by its astonishing ancient civilisations, stunning azure seas, fresh culinary delights and mind-blowing museums.

Greece is a legendary destination in every sense. Literally speaking, it's where many myths of gods and giants originated, and it's not hard to see why. With wide skies, an island-speckled ocean and a varied and stunning terrain, it's made for adventure, relaxation and imagination.

You can evoke the essence of Ancient Greek civilisation at the Acropolis in Athens, consult the oracle at Delphi and reach lofty heights in the monasteries of Meteora in central Greece. Then wander under clear blue skies and white domes of the Cyclades, or even live out your inner knight in Rhodes' medieval Old Town. Eat your way through the local dishes in Crete and wander through fortresses and the ancient Palace of Knossos.

As for Greek cuisine? *Nostimo!* (Delicious!) Greek food is renowned across the globe for its wholesome, hearty dishes and philosophy of simple but superior-quality local ingredients, from mountain meats and coastal seafood to wild herbs and vegetables. And Greeks love eating out, sharing impossibly big meals with family and friends in a drawn-out, convivial way. Whether you're eating octopus at a seaside table or sampling a contemporary lamb recipe under the floodlit Acropolis, dining out in Greece is never just about what you eat but the whole sensory experience.

Finally, whether you're after beaches, ancient sites, mountain walks or city life, Greece has you covered.

IMARZI/SHUTTERSTOCK

THE MAIN AREAS

ATHENS
Greece's riveting, ancient capital.
p124

**CENTRAL &
NORTHERN GREECE**
Full of history, with Greece's coolest city.
p130

PELOPONNESE
Filled with amazing archaeological sites.
p136

CYCLADES
Blue, white, gorgeous and ever popular.
p140

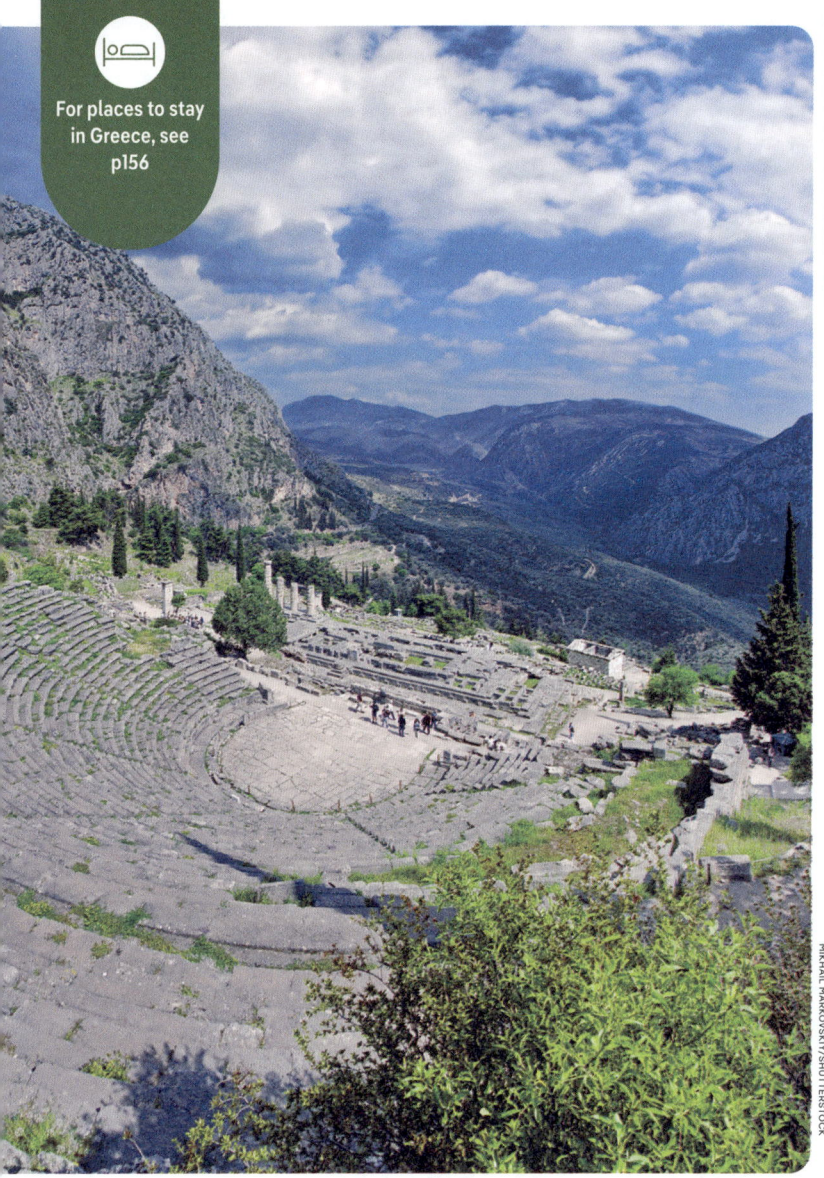

For places to stay in Greece, see p156

MIKHAIL MARKOVSKIY/SHUTTERSTOCK

Left: Grilled octopus; Above: Ancient Delphi (p131)

DODECANESE
A stunning array of history and beauty.
p143

CORFU
A pearl of the Ionian Islands.
p148

CRETE
Cretan cuisine, Minoan civilisation and fun.
p152

0 ——— 100 km
0 ——— 50 miles

Central & Northern Greece, p130

The focus is Meteora, famous for its Byzantine monasteries; Delphi, the centre of the ancient world; and Thessaloniki, Greece's creative city-by-the-sea.

Corfu, p148

Stroll atmospheric alleys between two fortresses, and explore world-class museums and gilded churches, all set against Venetian, French and British architecture.

Peloponnese, p136

Home to Nafplio, Greece's first capital, amazing archaeological sites of Mycenae and Epidavros, and Ancient Olympia, the spiritual home of the modern Olympics.

BULGARIA

NORTH MACEDONIA

Prilep
Ohrid
Lake Prespa
Lake Ohrid
Bitola
Florina
Korça
Kastoria

Gevgelija
Doirani
Paleokastro
Kilkis
Kajmakčalan
Edessa
Naoussa
Giannitsa
Veria
Alexandria

Sidirokastro
Serres
Kerkini Reservoir
Dram
Kaval
Strymonas

Thessaloniki
Katerini
A24

Vlorë
ALBANIA
Mt Grammos
Mt Smolikas
Konitsa
Grevena
Metsovo
Ioannina
Igoumenitsa
Parga

Lecce
Otranto
ITALY
Saranda

Ptolemaida
A2
Kozani

Mt Olympus
Thermaic Gulf

Ionian Sea

Corfu
Palaio Frourio
Corfu Town
Achilleion Palace
Mon Repos
A2

Moni Megalou Meteorou
Kalambaka
Elassona
Trikala
Larissa

Paxi
Preveza
Arta
A5
Lefkada Town
Lefkada
Fiskardo
Ithaki
Argostoli
Kefallonia
Sami

Karditsa
Farsala
Volos
Skiathos
Skiathos Town
Alonnis
Skopelos

Karpenisi
A3
Lamia
A1
Isteia
Kymi

Agrinio
Messolongi
Nafpaktos
Ancient Delphi
Itea
Livadia
Mt Parnassos
A1
Halkida
Loutraki
Thiva
Agios Konstantinos

Gulf of Corinth
Patras
A8
Egio
Xyiokastro
A5
Kyllini
Amaliada
Pirgos
Olympia Archaeological Museum
PELOPONNESE
A7
Corinth
A8
Tripoli
Nafplio
Megalopoli
Kyparissia
Astros
Theatre of Epidavros

Agios Nikolaos
Zakynthos
Zakynthos Town

ATHENS
Acropolis
Piraeus
Acropolis Museum
Aegina Town
Aegina
Poros Town
Hydra Town
Hydra
Spetses Town
Spetses

Evia
National Archaeological Museum
Karyst
Rafina
Lavr

Kalamata
Sparta
Mt Profitis Ilias
Pylos
Kardamyli
Areopoli
Gythio
Neapoli

Mediterranean Sea

Kythira

Antikythira
Venetia Harbou

Kissamos
Hania
Paleohora
Hora Sfakio
Gavdos

Find Your Way

Given its complex geography, Greece has an extensive network of domestic flights. Ferries link all the islands. Buses run on the larger islands, and a car or motorbike is the best way to explore most islands.

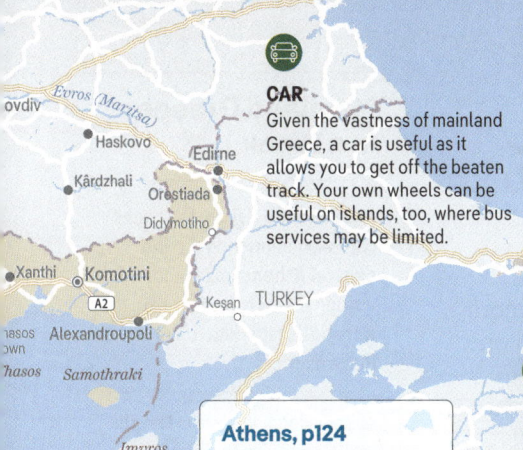

CAR
Given the vastness of mainland Greece, a car is useful as it allows you to get off the beaten track. Your own wheels can be useful on islands, too, where bus services may be limited.

BOAT
Greece's extensive ferry network includes fast modern ferries and overnight boats with cabins. Departures are subject to delay during poor weather. Schedules change annually, and services are greatly reduced between mid-October and Easter. In high season, book ahead. For schedules and tickets, *ferryhopper.com* is reliable.

Athens, p124
Ogle world-renowned treasures in one of the cradles of civilisation, from the Acropolis to the historic backstreets.

BUS
The bus network on larger islands and in Athens is comprehensive and fares are cheap; buy tickets at the office (sometimes on board). Corfu (and some other Ionian islands) can be reached from Athens by bus – the fare includes ferry ticket price. Village services can be more limited.

Cyclades, p140
Be mesmerised by white-and-blue architecture, dramatic cliffs and epic sunsets. The largest island, Naxos, has ancient ruins, mountain hamlets and white-sand beaches.

Dodecanese, p143
The historic centre of the Dodecanese, Rhodes Town is a medieval time capsule, while Kos Town is a charmer, with fabulous ancient ruins and more.

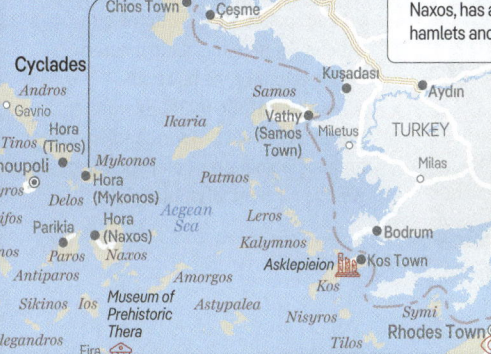

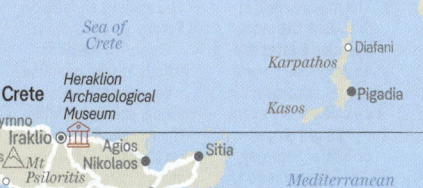

Crete, p152
Explore Minoan culture at the Palace of Knossos, enjoy the best of fresh and local Cretan cuisine, and hike through gorges to open sea.

121

Plan Your Time

You can choose to spend more time in Athens and visit just one (or two) islands, or go crazy and do a ferry-heavy (or flight-focused) whirlwind trip to get a taste beyond the mainland.

Erechtheion, Acropolis (p125)

YASEMIN OZDEMIR/SHUTTERSTOCK

Mainland Greece in a Week

● Spend two days in the Greek capital, meandering around **central Athens** (p124) and visiting the **Acropolis** (p125), the **Acropolis Museum** (p126) and the Plaka district.

● Then catch the bus to **Delphi** (p130) and enjoy the sacred ruins. Alternatively, head to **Meteora** (p132) to visit the monasteries before hiking through the surreal landscape (connections are difficult and time-consuming between Delphi and Meteora).

● Afterwards, catch another bus to **Thessaloniki** (p133) and indulge in the city's restaurants, museums and artistic spaces, before returning to Athens. Another mainland itinerary option is to take the bus from Athens to **Nafplio** (p134). Explore the historic town and surrounding archaeological sites before heading west to **Ancient Olympia** (p139).

SEASONAL HIGHLIGHTS

Greece is a year-round destination. Many islands are 'closed' during winter. What you're looking for should dictate when you go.

FEBRUARY

With fewer tourists, it's a great time for sightseeing – you won't have to push through crowds at the major sights like the Acropolis or Roman Agora in Athens.

APRIL/MAY

The main festival in the Greek Orthodox calendar, **Easter** has an emphasis on the Resurrection, meaning it's a celebratory event. The highlight is midnight on Easter Saturday, when fireworks and a procession hit the streets.

JUNE/AUGUST

The ancient Theatre of Epidavros and Athens' Odeon of Herodes Atticus are the headline venues of Greece's annual cultural shindig. The **Athens Epidaurus Festival** (p139) features music, dance, theatre and much more.

Two Weeks to Explore

● Follow the **Athens** (p124) itinerary, then on day three catch the bus to **Delphi** (p130) for a night to experience the sacred ruins, and return to Athens.

● Next, fly to **Corfu** (p148) and spend several days exploring the Old Town and the **Achilleion Palace** (p151) before enjoying a beach day. Take a one-hour ferry to **Paxi** (p151) where you can relax for a day or two amid the olive groves, seaside villages and beach coves.

● Return to Corfu and take the ferry to Igoumenitsa, where you can catch a bus to Kalambaka (via Ioannina) for **Meteora** (p132). Fill two days with visits to the rock monasteries and outdoor pursuits before heading back to Athens.

Ten Days to Travel Around

● Start on Crete by flying in to **Hania** (p153). Spend a day strolling the Venetian fortifications or people-watching from a cafe by its charming harbour. Enjoy a day trekking the **Samaria Gorge** (p155) and another day at the Minoan ruins of **Knossos** (p155) and the state-of-the-art **Heraklion Archaeological Museum** (p154) in Iraklio.

● From Iraklio, either fly to **Rhodes** (p144) or get the twice-weekly, 11-hour ferry (less time from Sitia). On historic Rhodes, explore its atmospheric medieval **Old Town** (p145).

● To end your journey, take a three- to five-hour ferry ride to the island of **Kos** (p146). Here, experience its own ancient Old Town, before venturing out to beaches and archaeological sites.

SEPTEMBER

In early September, sample widely at the **wine festival** (p138) that celebrates the Nemea region's *agiorgitiko* red grape with tastings, concerts and more.

OCTOBER

A simple 'no' (ohi in Greek) was the famous response when Mussolini demanded passage for his troops on 28 October 1940. Now, **Ohi Day** is a national holiday with remembrance services and parades.

NOVEMBER

Around 150 films are crammed into 11 days of screenings, alongside concerts, exhibitions, talks and theatrical performances at the **Thessaloniki Film Festival** (p135).

DECEMBER/ JANUARY

This season brings joyful, light-festooned harbours, honey cookies and good cheer. New Year's Day brings the **Feast of Agios Vasilios** (St Basil), a church ceremony. This is time for the *vasilopita* (cake with a lucky coin).

Athens

ANCIENT LANDMARKS | ARCHITECTURE | CONTEMPORARY CULTURE

 TOP TIP

You could skip all the sights in Athens and still feel you have the city's pulse just by strolling along the pedestrian Dionysiou Areopagitou street around sundown. Lights glow on the Acropolis above, and the road is filled with tourists, snack vendors, musicians and local couples out for a promenade.

Cradle of European civilisation and democracy, Athens is a master of reinvention, serving a thrilling mashup of architectural gravitas, bodacious street life and inspiring creativity. With both grace and grunge, Athens creates a heady mix of ancient history and contemporary cool. The cultural and social life of the city plays out amid and within ancient landmarks, and the magnificent Acropolis remains the hub around which Athens' neighbourhoods revolve. This citadel crowns a rocky outcrop with ancient temples (including the jewel, the Parthenon) and serves as a daily reminder of Greece's heritage and the city's many transformations.

With a past rooted in mythology, drama, philosophy, Byzantine churches and, more recently, the 2004 Olympic Games, the city continues to pulse with art, community spirit and political debates. It's a must for most visitors to Greece. Athens can be chaotic, but take the pressure off by people-watching at a cafe or retreating to a wooded hilltop.

GETTING AROUND

The transit system uses the **Ath.ena Ticket**, a reloadable card available from metro ticket offices and machines. Load it with credit, rides (*€1.20 each, discount for 5 or 10*) or travel pass (*24 hours/5 days €4.10/8.20*). These exclude airport transfer. Three-day tourist tickets (*€20*) include airport transfer. Swipe at metro turnstiles or, on buses/trams, validate in the machine. One swipe gives you 90 minutes, including transfers.

The Piraeus port is massive – 12 quays from which ferries and cruises depart to most Greek island groups and the Peloponnese. The metro line 1 (green) and suburban rail line 3 (blue) from Athens terminate at gate E7. A free shuttle bus runs regularly along the northern quays inside the port from gate E7 to E1.

Direct bus X96 to Eleftherios Venizelos International Airport stops outside the metro and along the road outside the port. The T7 tram departs from outside E8. Bus 040 goes to Athens, as does express X80 (May to October).

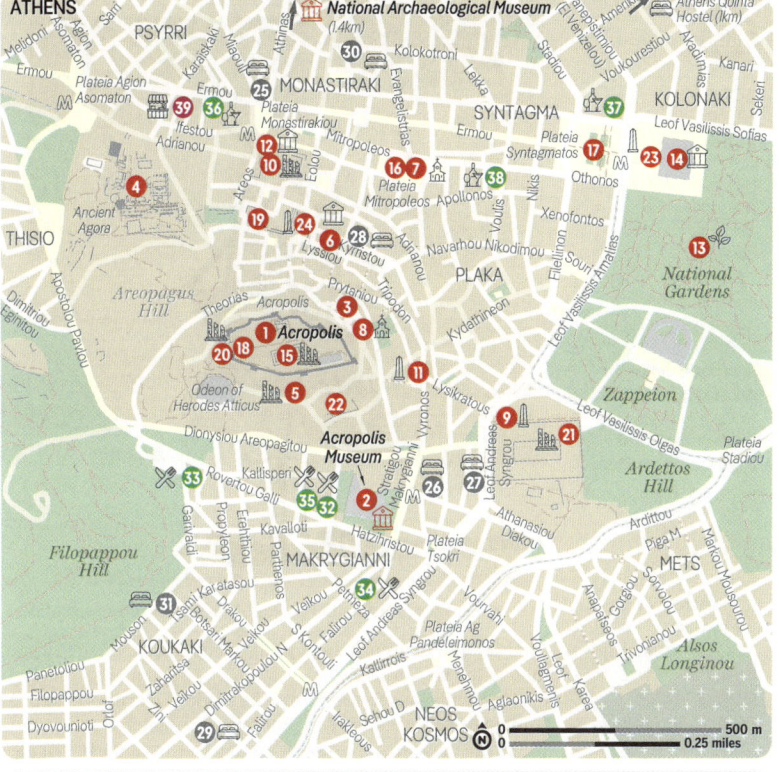

ATHENS

Athens' Crown Jewel

Epic monuments and vistas at the Acropolis

The **Acropolis** (*odysseus.culture.gr; adult/child €30/free*)
is the most important ancient site in the Western world, and
a glimpse of this magnificent monument cannot fail to exalt
your spirit. Crowned by the Parthenon, it's visible from almost everywhere in Athens. Its marble gleams white in the

ACROPOLIS MUSEUM PLANNING TIPS

Buy tickets for the Acropolis Museum online to skip the queue.

Bring a smartphone and headphones to download and listen to the audio guide, or register online for occasional guided tours (included in the ticket price). You'll need the registration code to attend.

Leave time for the fine museum shops and the film describing the history of the Acropolis (on the top floor).

The last admission is 30 minutes before closing, and the galleries are cleared 15 minutes before closing, starting at the top floor.

The ground-floor shop and cafe are accessible without a ticket.

Every Friday and Saturday the 2nd-floor restaurant is open until midnight.

THANASIS F/SHUTTERSTOCK

Evzones (presidential guards), Tomb of the Unknown Soldier

midday and takes on a honey hue as the sun sinks, then glows above the city by night.

On the hill's southern slopes, the modern **Acropolis Museum** holds its treasures. The Dionysiou Areopagitou promenade links the museum and site – it's a tourist throughway, but also a favourite spot for locals to stroll at sundown. Entering from the southeastern entrance (near the museum), you come to the ancient **Theatre of Dionysos** before ascending the stairs towards the **Asclepieion** temple ruins. Continue on the trail and, as you climb the final steps, look up to see the **Temple of Athena Nike**. Then, like so many pilgrims before you, pass through the **Propylaia**, the monumental entrance to the Acropolis. The **Parthenon**, one of the largest Doric temples ever completed in Greece, looms before you.

Ancient Masterpieces

Admire the treasures of the Acropolis Museum

The state-of-the-art **Acropolis Museum** (*theacropolismuseum.gr; adult/child €20/free*) displays the surviving treasures

EATING AROUND THE ACROPOLIS: STYLISH SPOTS

Mani Mani: i Dig into herb-filled cuisine from the Mani peninsula region in the Peloponnese, like seafood orzo with wild fennel. *2-11pm* €€

GH Attikos: Greek classics in a casual, airy setting with Acropolis views and an open terrace. *noon-4pm & 6-9pm Mon-Sat* €€

Ellevoro: Family-run, decorated with candles and mini-chandeliers and serving trad Greek dishes. *7pm-midnight Wed-Mon, from noon Sun* €€

Point A: Rooftop restaurant of the Herodion Hotel, with stunning Acropolis and Acropolis Museum views. *7pm-midnight* €€€

from the temple hill, with emphasis on the Acropolis as it was in the 5th century BCE, the apotheosis of Greece's artistic achievement. Layers of history are revealed and interpreted: glass floors expose subterranean ruins, and the Acropolis itself is visible through the floor-to-ceiling windows, so the masterpieces are always in context.

As you enter the museum, look down through the glass floor to view the ruins of an ancient Athenian neighbourhood that were uncovered during the museum's construction and had to be preserved and integrated into a new building plan.

The Finest Collection of Greek Antiquities

A pilgrimage to the National Archaeological Museum

Housed in an enormous 19th-century neoclassical building, the 11,000 treasures of the **National Archaeological Museum** *(namuseum.gr; adult/child €12/free)* date from prehistoric to Classical periods – a comprehensive overview of historic Greek art. It's impossible to appreciate all the exquisite sculptures, pottery, jewellery and frescoes in one go, and whatever you see will be a treat. You'll need time here to do it justice or make a beeline for the big-ticket items: the Mask of Agamemnon, Vaphio gold cups, the colossal Sounion Kouros and the Antikythera Mechanism.

Watch the Changing of the Guard

A photo op at the Tomb of the Unknown Soldier

Located on Athens' principal plaza, Plateia Syntagmatos, an essential photo op is of the traditionally costumed *evzones* (presidential guards) flanking the **Tomb of the Unknown Soldier**, a cenotaph dedicated to Greek soldiers killed in war, which stands just below the neoclassical **Parliament** building. Every hour, on the hour, the guard changes. On Sunday at 10.30am, a whole platoon, accompanied by a band, sets off from the Presidential Guard complex on Irodou Attikou, and marches down Vasilissis Sofias to the tomb for the 11am ceremony. The *evzones'* uniform of the fustanella (skirt) and pompom shoes reflects the attire worn by the klephts, the mountain fighters of the War of Independence.

GUIDED TOURS

On Foot: Athens Walking Tours *(athenswalkingtours. gr)* and **Alternative Athens** *(alternative athens.com)* have expert guides. **This is Athens** *(thisisathens. org)* has a free program to team up visitors with locals for themed walks.

By Bike: E-bike tours by **We Bike Athens** *(webikeathens.gr)* in Thisio, **Solebike** *(solebike.eu)* near the Acropolis and **Roll in Athens** *(facebook. com/rollinathens)* near Syntagma take the strain out of pedalling uphill. **Coco-Mat.Bike Tours** *(coco-mat. bike)* in Gazi gains cool points for unique ash-wood-frame bikes (regular and e-bikes). Or rent your own bike at **Funky Ride** *(funkyride.gr)*.

On the Bus: Hop-on, hop-off with **City Sightseeing Athens** *(city-sightseeing.com)* or **Athens Happy Train** *(athenshappy train.com)*.

DRINKING IN MONASTIRAKI & SYNTAGMA: ROOFTOP BARS

A for Athens: The rooftop cafe-bar at this Monastiraki hotel is grand, with sweeping 360-degree views. *4pm-midnight*

Couleur Locale: In a Monastiraki arcade, this all-day bar-restaurant has Acropolis views. *10am-2am Sun-Thu, to 3am Fri & Sat*

Metropolis Roof Garden: Head to the top of luxe Electra Metropolis Athens Hotel for creative cocktails and inventive cuisine. *1-6pm & 7-11pm*

GB Roof Garden: Glam it up on the top of the Grande Bretagne Hotel on Plateia Syntagmatos, with radiant Acropolis views. *1pm-2am*

Central Athens Meander

Boisterous, monument-packed central Athens is best explored on foot. The historic centre and the main archaeological sites, major landmarks, museums and attractions, are quite close to one another. The main civic hub of Athens, Plateia Syntagmatos, merges into the historic Plaka and Monastiraki neighbourhoods, which mesh one into the next and make for a super stroll (3km, three hours) for soaking up the city-centre history and life.

❶ Plateia Syntagmatos

Plateia Syntagmatos, considered the centre of Athens, has been a favourite place for protests since the rally that led to the granting of a constitution on 3 September 1843. Time your visit with the hourly changing of the guard at the **Tomb of the Unknown Soldier** (p127) in front of Parliament.

❷ Temple of Olympian Zeus

Stroll through the lush **National Gardens**, exiting south to the striking **Temple of Olympian Zeus** or what remains of the largest temple ever built. Teetering on the edge of the traffic alongside the temple, **Hadrian's Arch** is the ornate gateway marking the boundary of Hadrian's Athens.

❸ Lysikrates Monument

Cross Leoforos Vasilissis Amalias and walk up Lysikratous into Plaka. Built in 334 BCE, the **Lysikrates Monument** is the only remaining example of monuments that once lined this street to the **Theatre of Dionysos** (p126), site of dramatic contests.

PIC MEDIA AUS/SHUTTERSTOCK

Temple of Olympian Zeus

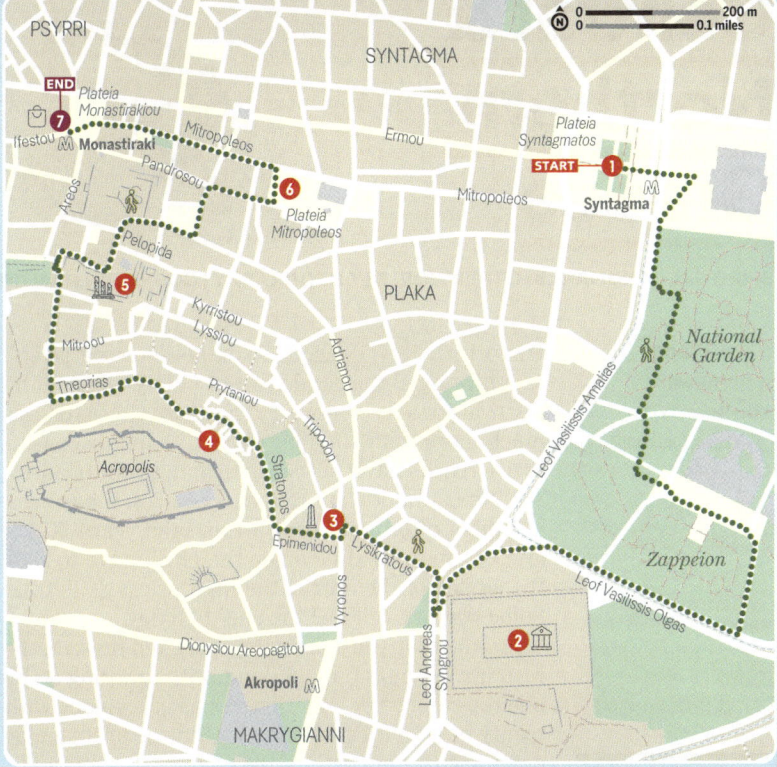

The monument commemorates one chorus' victory.

4 Anafiotika

Ascend the Epimenidou steps, turn right into Stratonos, and **Church of St George of the Rock** marks the entry to **Anafiotika**, a picturesque maze of whitewashed houses. Explore a bit, then emerge at Theorias road, above the old Athens University (1837–41). Descend on pedestrianised Diaskouron for views of the **Ancient Agora**.

5 Roman Agora

Descend as far as the ruins of the **Roman Agora** where you can see its **Tower of the Winds**, a classical time-and-weather station. Across the road, duck into **Bath House of the Winds**, a historical Turkish

hammam. Northeast of the Roman Agora, the ruins of **Hadrian's Library** sit next to 1759 **Mosque of Tzistarakis**.

6 Plateia Mitropoleos

Jaunt north to **Plateia Mitropoleos**, where you'll find Athens Cathedral and its smaller, more historically significant neighbour, 12th-century **Church of Agios Eleftherios**, which was built from pieces of ancient temples and earlier Christian monuments.

7 Monastiraki Flea Market

Cruise up Mitropoleos and you'll reach colourful, chaotic Plateia Monastirakiou. To the left, down Ifestou, is **Monastiraki Flea Market**, a gateway to shopping throughout the district.

Central & Northern Greece

SPIRITUAL LANDMARKS | OTHERWORLDLY GEOGRAPHY | COSMOPOLITAN CITY

Places

Historical sites, dense forests, fast-flowing rivers, sapphire-hued seas and vibrant villages framed by warm hospitality: central and northern Greece deliver much more than you may expect. Delphi is considered Greece's navel of the Earth and, as one of antiquity's most important religious centres, it has been a symbol of unity of over a thousand years. Kings and commoners alike made the pilgrimage to seek the advice of the oracle, the high priestess Pythia. Some visitors still feel the energy today.

Also the centre of spirituality, past and present, the Meteora region is breathtaking, with towering rocky outcrops topped by teetering monasteries, along with plenty of activities to enjoy within the spectacular environs. In the north of the country, the stimulating and stylish city of Thessaloniki always surprises and is considered Greece's most cosmopolitan city (shhh, don't tell the Athenians). Expect excellent cuisine, bars and shopping here, too.

☑ TOP TIP

The shoulder seasons (April, May, September and October) are the best months of the year to visit Delphi and Meteora. You won't get blasted by the sun yet everything is open and the crowds are manageable. In spring, the surrounds are abloom with wildflowers.

Delphi

Legend has it that Zeus released two eagles from opposing ends of the Earth to locate its centre. They crossed paths above Delphi. In the 8th century BCE, the cult of Apollo was established here. Leaders and commoners alike from the Mediterranean and Asia Minor made the pilgrimage to the oracle of sacred Delphi to consult a mysterious high priestess, Pythia,

 GETTING AROUND

Central Greece is the country's largest region. Meteora (Kalambaka) is easily reached by train from Athens; for Delphi, catch a direct KTEL bus from Athens' Liosion bus terminal. Connections between Delphi and Meteora are surprisingly tricky. There are limited bus services, though these are long and you must change at Trikala, 22km east of Kalambaka. For exploring central Greece, having a car is best as it allows you to reach historical sites, remote mountain villages and far-flung beaches.

CENTRAL & NORTHERN GREECE

APOLLO'S VOICE: THE ORACLE

Perched in the Temple of Apollo, the Delphic oracle ranked high among the sacred sites of Ancient Greece. Devotees flocked here asking for Apollo's guidance in making decisions. Wars were fought, colonies created, marriages sealed, leaders chosen and journeys begun on the strength of the oracle's advice.

Apollo's instrument of communication, the Pythia (priestess), was usually an older woman who sat on a tripod in the temple. Although there's no evidence for the theory that she inhaled vapours of ethylene from cracks in the rocks below the sanctuary, evidence shows she made her prophesies in a trancelike state.

The Pythia's pronouncements were notorious for their ambiguity, which left the interpretation up to the recipients.

who prophesied on everything from matters of the heart to a city-state's decision to go to war. The joy of staying right in the town of Delphi is that you can easily walk to all the ancient sites and museums.

One of Greece's top sights

As you ascend the archaeological site of **Ancient Delphi** (*ody sseus.culture.gr; incl museum adult/child €20/free*), look out across the olive-grove-carpeted valley and Gulf of Corinth below, close your eyes and tap into Delphi's divine energy. Get here early to avoid the crowds, take snacks and water. And time!

Like the original pilgrims, start your visit at the **Sanctuary of Athena Pronaia**, a 20-minute walk east past the region's highlights while taking in the sweeping views down to the Gulf of Corinth. The fenced site is always open. You'll pass the **Castalian Spring**, a sacred source for Delphi.

You can scamper about the hilly site in a sweat-soaked, manic hour, but why? It's better to take it slow, ponder the many individual features and tease out the surviving nuances. Gaze out over the views and find quiet, shady spots to contemplate the deep meaning it has held over the millennia. Just thinking of the countless feet that have trod the **Sacred Way** and who they've belonged to, will give all but the dullest minds pause.

Taking a tour with a local guide is a wonderful way to evoke the sense of place. Try English-speaking **Penny Kolomvotsou** (*kpagona@hotmail.com*).

Treasures and masterpieces

Save the unmissable **Delphi Archaeological Museum** (*ody sseus.culture.gr; incl site adult/child €20/free*) for the afternoon, when the outdoor sites swelter in the midday sun. Entry is by time slot, so reserve ahead. You'll gain a clearer

METEORA'S HISTORY

The name Meteora is derived from the Greek adjective *meteoros*, meaning 'suspended in the air' (the word 'meteor' comes from the same root).

Hermit monks began inhabiting the scattered natural caverns of Meteora during the 11th century. By the 14th century, the power of the Byzantine Empire was waning, and with Turkish incursions into Greece on the rise, monks fled the bloodshed for a safe haven here.

Ruins of abandoned communites in sites that now seem utterly inaccessible dot the area. Removable ladders were used at first. Later, windlasses hauled the monks up in nets. When curious visitors asked how frequently the ropes were replaced, the monks' straight-faced reply was 'when the Lord lets them break'.

JOAQUIN OSSORIO CASTILLO/SHUTTERSTOCK

Sphinx of the Naxians, Delphi Archaeological Museum

understanding of the context of where the treasures were found. You can have a deeply rewarding visit in under two hours and you'll come away with a clearer picture of how lavish Ancient Delphi must have been and the wealth it attracted. Get more info on selected exhibits in 3D via the Digital Delphi phone app or the comprehensive *Delphi Monuments and Museum* by Photios M Petsas.

The collection starts with some impressive bronze works: a bronze figurine believed to depict Apollo, the forerunner of stone-carved *kouros* statues; the **Sphinx of the Naxians** (560 BCE), with the face of a woman, the body of a lion and the wings of a bird; and the crown jewel, the life-size **Bronze Charioteer** (478–474 BCE).

Meteora

Meteora's otherworldly stone pillars rise up vertically from the vast Thessaly plain. This geological marvel came about some 11 million years ago: earthquakes, wind and rain gradually sculpted a mass of rocks, sand and sediment. It's hard to comprehend how monasteries were built atop these precipitous cliffs and into rockfaces.

Has a fabulous beer menu of regional brews!

 EATING IN DELPHI: OUR PICKS

Taverna Gargadoyas: Welcoming, no-frills traditional taverna at the west end of town, serving great grilled meats. *1-11pm* €

Dion Tavern: Classic Greek dishes, like rice-stuffed tomatoes and souvlaki, are well executed. Tables inside and out; stark decor. *noon-11pm* €

Taverna Vakhos: Well-crafted Greek fare, including vegan dishes; seasonal artichokes and mountain herbs from the garden. *noon-10.30pm* €

To Patriko Mas: Elevated views to go with the elevated Mediterranean fare. Game casseroles are a speciality. *noon-3pm & 6-10pm* €€

Free-climbing, cave-dwelling ascetics were the first to make Meteora home in the 11th century. Deemed a holy place, Meteora was where the first Orthodox monastic communities formed in the 12th century. At its peak, 24 monasteries were hosted here; today, six remain active and open to visitors in this UNESCO-listed destination.

Moseying about monasteries

There's enough variation between the opening hours of Meteora's monasteries that crafting an itinerary is a bit like a jigsaw puzzle. As always, try to hit top sights such as Moni Megalou Meteorou as early as possible.

All six of Meteora's monasteries – **Moni Megalou Meteorou, Moni Varlaam, Moni Agiou Stefanou, Moni Agias Varvaras Rousanou, Moni Agias Triadas** and **Moni Agiou Nikolaou Anapafsa** – are impressive in their own way. With precision planning, you might see four in one day, but this would be a stunt. To enter the monasteries, visitors are required to cover their shoulders and legs; shawls are available to buy or borrow at most monasteries. Be prepared to scale between 140 and 300 steps at all but the accessible Moni Agiou Stefanou.

Each monastery charges the same admission *(adult/child €5/free)*. Good sources of information include **Visit Meteora** *(visitmeteora.travel)* and the **Kalambaka Tourist Office** *(infotouristmeteora.gr)*.

Thessaloniki

Map p134

It's easy to fall in love with Thessaloniki. Greece's second-largest (and arguably coolest) city is built along the water, and the view over the Aegean Sea to snowcapped Mt Olympus is superb. Old and new coexist in architectural anarchy: here, the ruins of Byzantine churches give way to 1960s apartment blocks, and Ottoman-era *hammams* and historic buildings have been repurposed into art spaces, cafes, bars and shops.

Boardwalk empire and people-watching

Walking along the waterfront promenade is a way of life in Thessaloniki. It even has its own word in Greek: *volta*. Start walking the Nea Paralia from the port, where a crop of new cafes and restaurants have opened up in this once seedy area. Head towards the 15th-century **White Tower** *(lpth.gr; adult/child €6/free)*, Thessaloniki's most iconic image, and continue to the strikingly contemporary **Thessaloniki Concert Hall**. The total distance is 3.5km.

EATING & DRINKING IN KASTRAKI & KALAMBAKA: OUR PICKS

| **Taverna Gardenia:** Kastraki taverna with a huge front patio and snug old-fashioned interior. Open-air grill/spit-roast mains. *12.30-11pm* € | **Qastiro:** Stylish wine bar in Kastraki serving Med-accented meals from a short menu. Enjoy quality coffee on the stone terrace. *10am-midnight* €€ | **Fortounis Tsipouradiko:** Long-standing Kalambaka *ouzerie* (place serving ouzo and food) that gets a lively, late crowd. *11am-midnight* € | **Ambrosia Taverna:** Modern Greek place in Kalambaka that does creative fresh fare served with aplomb. Fine wine list. *noon-11pm* €€ |

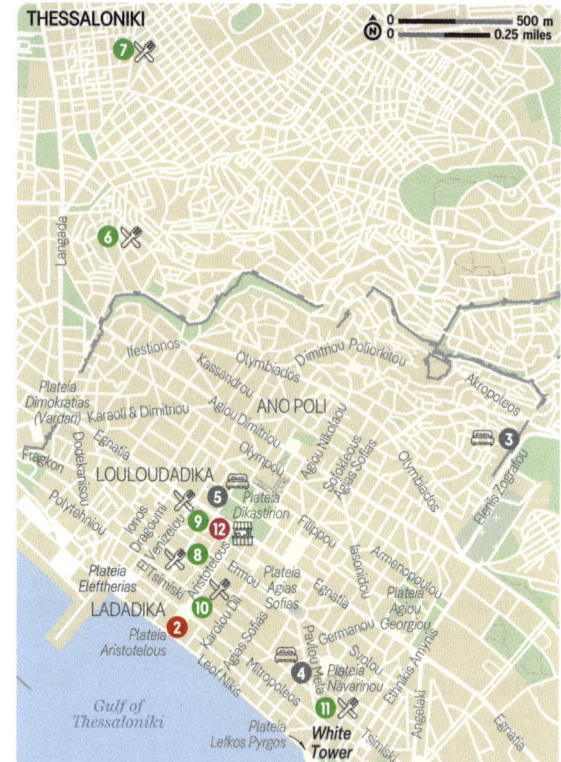

THESSALONIKI

HIGHLIGHTS
1 White Tower

SIGHTS
2 Plateia Aristotelous

SLEEPING
3 Little Big House
4 Trilogy House
5 Zeus is Loose

EATING
6 Bougatsa Bantis
7 Milano Bakery
8 Modiano Market
9 Stou Mitsou
10 Terkenlis
11 Trigona Elenidis

SHOPPING
12 Kapani Markete

Afterwards, relax in **Plateia Aristotelous**, Thessaloniki's heartbeat. It's a cross between a Parisian boulevard, Bologna's covered arcades and Venice's Piazza San Marco, with an unmistakably Greek flair. Elsewhere, the port of Thessaloniki is the city's hotbed for contemporary art. Just up from the port is the **Ladadika** neighbourhood, where former brick warehouses have been converted into tavernas, cafes and bars.

Thessaloniki's markets

Rich in both history and culinary delights, Thessaloniki is a city that can be best appreciated through its markets.

 EATING IN THESSALONIKI: BEST PASTRY SHOPS ———— MAP p134

Milano: Hands down the city's best *tiropita* (cheese pie) can be found at this bakery in the Neapoli neighbourhood. *8am-7pm* €

Trigona Elenidis: A flaky triangle stuffed with custard and dripping in sweet syrup, the *trigona* found here is a hallmark Thessaloniki dessert. *9am-11pm* €

Bougatsa Bantis: Salty cheese or sweet custard is layered in filo, cut in squares and served warm. It's the ideal breakfast. *6.30am-2.30pm* €

Terkenlis: *Tsoureki* is a slightly sweet, yeasted loaf with a mastic flavour; try it covered in chocolate and stuffed with chestnut puree. *7am-11pm* €

White Tower (p133), Thessaloniki

The **Modiano Market** (*agoramodiano.com*) was originally built in 1930 by renowned local Jewish architect Eli Modiano, and quickly became the centre of daily life for Thessalonikians. Today, the revamped, cavernous, glass-and-brick structure is home to dozens of stalls, divided into 'neighborhoods' by food type. From fruits and veg to syrupy pastries to third-wave coffee, you can find almost anything here. The space is now also used for events and concerts.

Food lovers should make a beeline for the **Kapani Market** (*kapani.gr*). Located in the city centre, this is the place to stock up on Greek products like mountain tea, mastic from Chios and pine-tree honey. In addition to non-perishables, you can stroll through the fresh fish and meat sections. Grab lunch at **Stou Mitsou**, a *tsipouradiko* selling delicious grilled and fried dishes between the market stalls.

LIGHTS, CAMERA, ACTION

Each year, Thessaloniki hosts its **international film festival**, the most important silver-screen event in the country. First launched in 1960 as a national film festival, it has adapted to the times: in its earliest years, it focused on New Greek Cinema, and then, following the end of Greece's military dictatorship, the festival promoted much more political cinema. These days, the focus is still on arthouse cinema, with an emphasis on voices from the Balkans. For 11 days each November, the city is awash in screenings, premieres, lively talks and discussions. It's an event cinephiles shouldn't miss. See *filmfestival.gr* for more info.

Peloponnese

ARCHAEOLOGICAL WONDERS | ANCIENT OLYMPIA | MYTHICAL MOMENTS

Places

Nafplio p136
Ancient Mycenae p138
Epidavros p139
Ancient Olympia p139

 TOP TIP

Nafplio is a good base from which to explore the sites of Mycenae and Epidavros; for Ancient Olympia, it's best to spend a night or two in Olympia.

With secluded beach coves, bucolic cypress forests, lofty peaks and concealed villages, mainland Peloponnese has the charm of a seasonal island all year round. The region is legendary – fables are central to its culture and landscape. It's where many a Greek god and human hero performed their deeds in historical sites, classical temples, Mycenaean palaces, Byzantine cities and Venetian fortresses. You can commune with the ghost of Agamemnon at Mycenae, a once-great civilisation, or test your sprinting skills at Ancient Olympia, spiritual home of the Olympics. Or recite the lines of Oedipus at the Theatre of Epidavros and be captivated by Mystras where the Byzantine civilisation ended in the 14th century. If 'ancient' isn't your thing, explore the natural surroundings instead. The region's cuisine is among the best in Greece thanks to its fresh seafood, mountain meats and wild greens. The Peloponnese has the best of everything.

Nafplio

Explore the Old Town Nafplio

Nafplio is one of Greece's prettiest towns and admirers revel in its knockout waterside location. The town is a sum of its

---

🧭 GETTING AROUND

The Peloponnese is one of Greece's largests region with distinct sub-areas and varied topography. Various KTEL bus networks link main towns and remote villages throughout the region. Buses run from Athens to both Nafplio and Ancient Olympia. For the former, you can take a direct bus or, if you're in or near the Peloponnese, you can change at the interchange known as KTEL Isthmus, located near the Corinth Canal and gateway to the region. Similarly, to get to Ancient Olympia from Nafplio, you'll need to head first to KTEL Isthmus and change buses at Pyrgos, from where you can get a small train or bus to Olympia. Apart from this train, the main train network no longer operates in the region, except for the *proastiako*, a handy suburban network that runs between Athens Airport and Kiato, on the outskirts of Corinth (town). For remote regions, having your own wheels allows you more access.

THE ANCIENT ACRONAFPLIA

Panagiotis Zotos is a history lover and co-owner of **Pension Marianna** (hotelmarianna.gr).

What is Acronafplia? An 'acro-polis' was the upper fortified part of town where, when attacked, the locals went for protection. Acronafplia is Nafplio's oldest castle; it dates to Mycenaean times (1750 BCE). Over time, different conquerors changed its fortifications. Finally, when it was no longer considered secure, it moved to Palamidi (16th century).

Why visit? It's a beautiful and quiet place, especially at sunrise. When you walk inside, you feel like you're in the pages of history; you can see the different architectural styles and construction stages over the different periods.

Another interesting fact? The name Nafplio means 'ship'. When you're up here, you understand why: it feels like you're sailing through the ocean waters.

parts: enchanting narrow streets, elegant Venetian houses and neoclassical mansions.

All alleys seem to lead to the bustling **Plateia Syntagma**, the heart of the Old Town. Here, the cafes afford views of the **Trianon**, a former mosque, the handsome former **National Bank building** (1932) and the **Archaeological Museum** (odysseus.culture.gr; adult/child €10/free), a former Venetian warehouse. The outstanding collection includes bronze armour from near Mycenae.

The **Peloponnesian Folklore Foundation Museum** (bpf. gr; adult/child €5/free) displays Greek cultural items. Further on is **Plateia Kapodistrias**, named after Ioannis Kapodistrias, the first governor of the modern Greek state, who was murdered outside the church of Aghios Spiridonas. A block south of here is the **Land Gate**, identifiable by the lion carving. In the first Venetian occupation it was the only entrance to the city by land.

Power to the fortresses

Nafplio's imposing landmark, the citadel known as **Palamidi** (odysseus.culture.gr; adult/child €20/free), stands on a 216m-high outcrop of rock. An hour or so within its walls will give you time to wander the grounds and enjoy bird's-eye views over the sea and landscape. Built by the Venetians between 1711 and 1714, the fortress is regarded as a masterpiece of military architecture. To get there, you can go by road via taxi or tackle the 911 steps that begin southeast of the bus station. Climb early or towards sunset.

Back on the waterfront, boats run the five-minute journey (half-hourly) between the waterfront and the **Bourtzi** (incl boat ride €12), an islet fortress about 500m off the port. A

THE WINE ROUTES OF NEMEA

The rolling hills 37km northwest of Nafplio are part of the Nemea region, one of Greece's premier wine-producing areas that's particularly famous for its *agioritiko* grape and full-bodied reds. Look out also for wine made from *roditis*, a local variety of white grape. Nemea has been known for its fine wines since Mycenaean times, when nearby Phlius supplied the wine for the royal court at Mycenae.

There are dozens of wineries in the region. Many of these are open to the public; for tastings, most – but not all – require bookings. Visits usually include a winery tour and a tasting, sometimes with accompanying nibbles. To hop between vineyards, you'll need your own transport.

A **wine festival** in early September marks the beginning of the vintage.

Lion Gate, Ancient Mycenae

half-hour or so allows time to 'recreate' the events of the fortress 'of the rock'. Constructed between 1471 and 1472 by the Venetians, it helped defend the city for 350 years under different conquerors. Explanatory signs are in English.

Ancient Mycenae

Where myth and history are linked

The region's must-see historical attraction is **Ancient Mycenae** *(odysseus.culture.gr; adult/child €20/free),* 24km northwest of Nafplio, in the barren foothills of Mt Agios Ilia and Mt Zara. Ancient Mycenae was the home of the legendary King Agamemnon, ruler of the Greeks during the Trojan War. It was, for four centuries in the second millennium, the most powerful kingdom in Greece. One of Greece's most impressive ancient sites, it provides context to understanding Mycenaean influence over Ancient Greece.

KTEL buses from Athens and Nafplio drop you at Fichti village; it's an uphill slog for 3.5km to the site. It's easiest to have your own wheels.

EATING IN NAFPLIO: OUR PICKS

Pidalio: A 10-minute walk west of the Od Town, Pidalio prepares some of the best mezedhes around. Just ask locals. *1.45-11.15pm Wed-Mon* €€	**I Gonia Tou Kavalari:** Some of the best contemporary Greek mezedhes around, from *spetsofaï* (sausage) to *apaki* (fried pork). *noon-late* €€	**To Omorfo Tavernaki:** Modern twist to traditional cuisine: creative salads and excellent meats, plus tasty starters. Always busy. *11.30am-late Fri-Wed* €€	**Antica Gelateria di Roma:** Nafplio's original gelateria, run by Italians – as genuine as they come. Handmade on premises, any flavour is good. *9am-1am* €

MATYAS REHAK/SHUTTERSTOCK

Epidavros

The stage of ancient dramas

Built of limestone, yet one of the best-preserved Ancient Greek structures in existence, the late-4th-century-BCE **Theatre of Epidavros** (*argolisculture.gr; incl Sanctuary of Asclepius adult/child €20/free*) will have you singing. Part of the Sanctuary of Asclepius (an ancient health sanctuary), and considered to have played an important role in the cultural life of ancient times, it's renowned for its symmetry and amazing acoustics; a coin dropped in the theatre's centre can be heard from the highest seat. The theatre is now used for performances during the annual **Athens Epidaurus Festival** (*aefestival.gr*).

In high season, buses head here from Nafplio. If visiting by car, follow the signs to Ancient Theatre (not to P Epidavros or A Epidavros).

Ancient Olympia

In the footsteps of glory

It's worth the energy to reach Olympia, if only for one impressive site. This is **Ancient Olympia** (*odysseus.culture.gr; adult/child €20/free*), birthplace of the modern Olympic Games, where states come together for the sake of friendly competition just as they did here some 2800 years ago. This atmospheric site is also fun: sprint the 192.27m in the stadium and the ghosts of cheering crowds are guaranteed to make your skin prickle. At the ruins of the gymnasium, conjure up an aroma of sweat and oil (athletes smeared their bodies with this).

There's no right way to approach the site; the QR code at the entrance helps recreate the buildings in 3D, thereby revealing the sanctuary's former glory, and there are good information panels in Greek, English and German. But you'll need at least half a day for the site and Archaeological Museum. Archaeological or sports buffs might like one to two days to visit all museums. A guide will bring the site alive.

One ticket includes access for one day to the **Archaeological Site of Olympia**, **Olympia Archaeological Museum**, the **Museum of the History of the Olympic Games in Antiquity**, and the **Museum of the History of the Excavations in Olympia**. These are located within walking distance of the site, on the way to Olympia village.

 DRINKING IN NAFPLIO: OUR PICKS

Allotino: The place to be seen for daytime coffee and evening cocktails. Also serves salads and club sandwiches. *8am–3am*	**Mavros Gatos:** Nafplio's popular hangout, especially the young and trendy, with music and good drinks. *8am–3am*	**A!Ladokampos Gold:** Olive oil and wine tastings (think organic wine) in this store-cum-bar run by a Greek-American. *10am–12.30am Wed-Mon*	**3Sixty:** A posh wine bar in a hotel of the same name, it has a more international feel, a snob factor and high-end cocktails. *9am–midnight*

Cyclades

INCREDIBLE VISTAS | BEACHES | BLUE-AND-WHITE DOMES

Places

Santorini (Thira) p141
Naxos p142

✅ TOP TIP

If flying, give yourself extra time when leaving from Santorini Airport as the small terminal can be mayhem. Fira can become crammed with people, especially when the cruise ships are in port.

What do you think of when you think of the perfect Greek island? Why, one of the Cyclades, of course. This circular archipelago is Greece from central casting: rugged, sun-drenched outcrops of rock anchored in turquoise waters and strewn with gleaming white hamlets and blue-domed churches. Add to that a fabulous set of culinary flavours, fantastic hiking, plentiful beaches and a good dose of sophistication, and you really get the best of Greece's ample charms.

Of all of the Cyclades, one island seems to be the principal actor. Santorini (Thira) exudes in-your-face charm, including sheer cliffs and a snowdrift of white Cycladic houses. But beauty brings admirers and the island is slammed by them in peak season (so much so that the strain on the infrastructure is a huge concern). The more relaxed alternative, Naxos, has an entrancing variety of attractions including grand beaches, mountains and a lovely historic town.

🧭 GETTING AROUND

Conventional and fast ferries connect both Santorini and Naxos with Athens' Piraeus and Rafina ports. Ferries also link the two islands (two to three hours). In Santorini, Athinios port sits at the cliff base; buses and taxis meet ferries and cart passengers up to Fira. Consult **KTEL Santorini Buses** *(ktel-santorini.gr)* for schedules and prices. May to September buses are overcrowded. Having a car is the best way to explore the island, but traffic in high season is a menace. Fira's taxi stand is on Dekigala, near the bus station.

Naxos' small airport has several daily flights to/from Athens. Buses leave from the end of the ferry quay in Hora; timetables are posted outside the bus information office. While there are frequent buses to the villages, they can take a long time to get there and back. Buy tickets from the office or the machine outside (not from the bus driver). For larger exploration, get your own wheels; taxis are useful only for short hops.

Ancient Thera:
Perched on a
mountaintop, the
town was first settled
by the Dorians in the
9th century BCE and
remains a maze of
Hellenistic, Roman
and Byzantine ruins.

Ancient Akrotiri: In
1967, excavations in
Santorini's southwest
uncovered this
ancient Minoan
city buried beneath
volcanic ash from the
eruption of 1613 BCE.

**Museum of
Prehistoric Thera:**
Fira's standout has
extraordinary finds
excavated from
Akrotiri, a wealth of
Minoan frescoes,
ceramics and a
17th-century-BCE
gold ibex figurine.

Gyzi Megaron:
Displays fascinating
photographs of the
1956 earthquake,
centuries-old maps
of the Cyclades
and medieval
manuscripts.

**Archaeological
Museum:** Impressive
artefacts and marble
statues excavated
from Akrotiri and
Ancient Thera.

Santorini (Thira)

Booming caldera town and more

Santorini's main town, **Fira**, is a busy place, its caldera edge
layered with swish cave hotels, infinity pools and restaurants.
It's backed by narrow streets packed with shops, and more
bars and restaurants. Sitting 220m below Fira – three minutes
by cable car, or 587 steps on foot – the **Old Port** (Fira Skala)
is mainly used by cruise-ship passengers visiting for a day.
Santorini Cable Car (*scc.gr; adult/child €10/5*) is swamped
with those same passengers, especially in the morning and
afternoon. Views over the multicoloured cliffs are breathtaking, and come sunset, crowds gather at the caldera edge.

Fira merges into two more villages: **Firostefani** (about a
15-minute walk north) and posher **Imerovigli** (about a half-
hour walk from Fira). All are loaded with stores – browse for
original art, ceramics, woodwork, local foodstuffs, high-end
fashion and junk. Fira is also the island's nightlife hot spot.
Nine kilometres further on, with white dwellings hewn into
the volcanic rock, **Oia** is a gleaming gem and a famous place
to watch a sunset. It, too, gets packed – your only hope is to

EATING IN SANTORINI: OUR PICKS

Aroma Avlis: Part of the
Artemis Karamolegos
winery, this terrific
restaurant does brilliant
things with local
ingredients. *1-11pm* €€

Fistikies: Head to this
restaurant in an elegant
courtyard in Kamari for
seafood, pasta and Greek
fare. *2-11pm* €€

Pelican Kipos: Gorgeous
garden and good food in
central Fira, plus a good
selection of wines. *8am-
11.30pm* €€

To Krinaki: Superb, all-
fresh, all-local ingredients
are paired with local beer
and Santorini-grape wine;
just east of Oia. *noon-11pm*
€€€

BEST BEACHES ON NAXOS

Agios Prokopios: Sandy and shallow beach set in a sheltered bay south of Cape Mougkri.

Agia Anna: Merging with Agios Prokopios, this is a stretch of crowded white sand, with development along its length.

Glyfada and Plaka: Sandy beaches and turquoise waters, with accommodation and restaurants, perfect for a chilled-out stay.

Mikri Vigla: Golden granite boulders divide the beach into two; it's big on the kitesurfing scene, with reliable wind conditions.

Pyrgaki: Windsurfing and kitesurfing spot reachable via an unpaved road past the Aliko promontory.

Hawaii Beach: Shines with calm, limpid blue waters just north of the promontory.

venture out in the very early morning. Walking here takes three hours (9.1km); bring water, sunscreen and a hat.

For swimming, the famous **Red (Kokkini) Beach**, near Ancient Akrotiri in the south, has particularly impressive red cliffs, loungers and restaurants. You can walk from a parking lot over the eastern point to reach it. Or, catamaran cruises from all over the island plus caïques from pretty **Akrotiri Beach** go there and on to the sheltered cove of **White (Aspri) Beach** before visiting **Black (Mesa Pigadia) Beach**, with a beachside taverna.

Naxos

The largest of the Cyclades – and a centre of Classical Greece and Byzantium, with Venetian and Frankish influences – Naxos impresses. Its main town of Hora backs a lively waterfront with a web of steep cobbled alleys climbing to its dramatic hilltop *kastro,* a testament to three centuries of Venetian rule. Within easy reach are excellent beaches, fascinating mountain villages, inspiring ancient sites and bizarre-looking marble quarries.

Labyrinthine old town and ancient icons

Hora (Naxos Town) is enchanting, especially with the remnants of the fortified Venetian **kastro** looming above the waterfront. This was the seat of power for Marco Sanudo, the 13th-century Venetian who founded the town and made Naxos the heart of the Duchy of the Aegean. The tangle of steep footpaths is divided into two historic Venetian neighbourhoods: Bourgos, where the Greeks lived, and the hilltop Kastro, where the Roman Catholics lived.

Hora is easily managed on foot, though it's almost impossible not to get lost in the old town, but it's just as easy to find your way again. And that's half the fun. Within the *kastro,* the remnants of Sanudo's castle, the **Tower of Sanoudos**, is surrounded by gorgeous Venetian mansions.

Reach the two marble columns with a crowning lintel of the **Temple of Apollo** via a causeway to Palatia islet.

 EATING IN HORA: OUR PICKS

Avaton 1739: Atop Hora's *kastro*, don't miss the exalted panorama – a favourite for sunset cocktails and creative cuisine. *8.30am-2am* €€

O Apostolis: Occupying a tiny plaza right at the heart of labyrinthine Bourgos, with good traditional dishes in a pretty courtyard. *7pm-midnight* €€

Doukato: Magical setting in a former monastery, with top Naxian specialities like *kalogeras* (beef, eggplant and cheese). *6pm-midnight* €€

Kamaraki: Excellent taverna frequented by locals, with traditional dishes such as *horta* and fried fish, and tables in a pretty alley. *noon-11.30pm* €

Dodecanese

STUNNING COVES | VARIED LANDSCAPES | ANCIENT CULTURES

Timeless charm and natural beauty, historic ruins and tranquil beaches – welcome to the Dodecanese, which has all that epitomises old Greece. Meaning '12 islands' (these are the main ones, though there are more), the archipelago curves through the southeastern Aegean parallel to the ever-visible shoreline of Türkiye. The footprints of everyone from Greeks and Romans to crusading medieval knights and Byzantine and Ottoman potentates to 20th-century Italian bureaucrats are found here.

Admittedly, Rhodes and Kos are magnets for package tourism and cruise-ship crowds, but you can find your own corners on each of these islands. They offer two very different experiences, so you can commune with the ghosts of the knights over one or two nights in Rhodes, and the ghost of Hippocrates in the Asklepieion, an ancient healing centre in Kos, the next. Both islands also have beautiful beaches that are perfect for swimming.

Places

Rhodes Town p144
Kos Town p146

☑ TOP TIP

If you're only visiting Rhodes for a short time, perhaps as part of an island-hopping itinerary, there's plenty to see in Rhodes' Old Town without venturing further afield. Beware that in high season, the Old Town gets terribly crowded with tourists.

 GETTING AROUND

Direct ferries connect Rhodes with Kos (between two and four hours, depending on the service).

Rhodes has an excellent bus network. Buses leave from the urban bus stop on Mandraki Harbour; buy tickets on board. If you're based in Rhodes Old Town, you can't drive into that district, so it makes sense to rent a car only for the actual day(s) you'll use it. Rhodes Town's main taxi rank is on the northern edge of the Old Town, just east of

Plateia Rimini; a board displays set fares for specific destinations.

In Kos, cycling is very popular, with plenty of bicycles for hire, and it's a great way to get around. Cycle lanes thread all through Kos Town, with the busiest route running along the waterfront to connect the town with Lambi to the north and Psalidi to the south. Taxis congregate on the south side of the port. The line of boats moored in Kos Town offer excursions around Kos and to nearby islands.

RHODES' HISTORY

The Minoans and Mycenaeans established early outposts on Rhodes, around the 16th century BCE, followed by the Dorians. Over the next centuries, Rhodes switched allegiances like a pendulum between Athens, Persia, Sparta and Alexander the Great; the island was assimilated into the Roman Empire in 70 CE, then the Byzantine province of the Dodecanese. When the Crusaders seized Constantinople, it was granted independence. Later, the Genoese gained control followed by the Knights of St John, who ruled Rhodes for 213 years from 1309. They were ousted after two sieges by the Ottomans, who were kicked out by the Italians nearly four centuries later. In 1947, after 35 years of Italian occupation, Rhodes, along with the Dodecanese Islands, became part of Greece.

Rhodes Town

Rhodes Town sits at the island's northern peak and is made up of the Old and New Towns, each its own entity. Sealed like a medieval time capsule behind a double ring of high walls and a deep moat, the Old Town is a magical labyrinth. The New Town is a modern Mediterranean resort, with busy beaches, nightlife and waterfront bars.

Trace the history of the knights

An easy walk down the somewhat forbidding **Street of the Knights** is the quintessential Rhodes Town experience, not least because its architecture speaks of the various historical

 EATING IN RHODES TOWN: BEST RESTAURANTS

Paradosiako Kafeneio I Symi: Rhodes' cutest terrace and some of the best seafood and fish you're likely to taste. *1-11pm Mon-Sat €€*

Romios Restaurant: Traditional, elegantly presented Rhodian dishes in a tree-canopied Old Town courtyard. *noon-midnight €€*

Kelari Pantieras: Taste the meze and listen to live bouzouki music in this gorgeous neighbourhood taverna. *5pm-midnight Mon-Sat €*

4 Rodies: Eat perfectly prepared Rhodian dishes in the leafy garden of this locally loved, family-run restaurant. *1.30-11pm Wed-Mon €€*

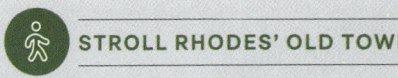

STROLL RHODES' OLD TOWN

A walk around the historical capsule of Rhodes' Old Town will take you through millennia of history.

START	END	LENGTH
D'Amboise Gate	Jewish Museum of Rhodes	2.5km; 2–3 hours

Start from the 16th-century **❶ D'Amboise Gate**, one of the most impressive of the nine approaches to the Old Town; it's protected by two massive concentric towers. Go down Orfeos and turn into the Street of the Knights. The austere mansions (known as inns) that line the arrow-straight streets of the **❷ Knights' Quarter** were home to the medieval occupying army of the Knights of St John.

From the outside, the 14th-century castle-like **❸ Palace of the Grand Master** looks much as it did when erected by the Knights Hospitaller, though it has fascist-style interiors. Walk to Apellou street and the **❹ Archaeological Museum**, located inside the magnificent 15th-century Knights' Hospital.

Carry on south down Apellou, and you'll reach Sokratous street and **❺ Hora**, the so-called Turkish Quarter that occupies the central bulk of the Old Town. Look out for the **❻ Mosque of Suleyman**, built in 1522 to commemorate the Ottoman defeat of the knights, and renovated in 1808 (not open to visitors). The peaceful **❼ Muslim Library**, founded in 1793, sits in an inviting little garden courtyard opposite the mosque.

Head back down Sokratous to the Old Town's southeast corner and the **❽ Jewish Quarter**, once home to a population of 5500 Jewish people. End the walk at the **❾ Jewish Museum of Rhodes**, entered via the 1577 Kahal Shalom Synagogue.

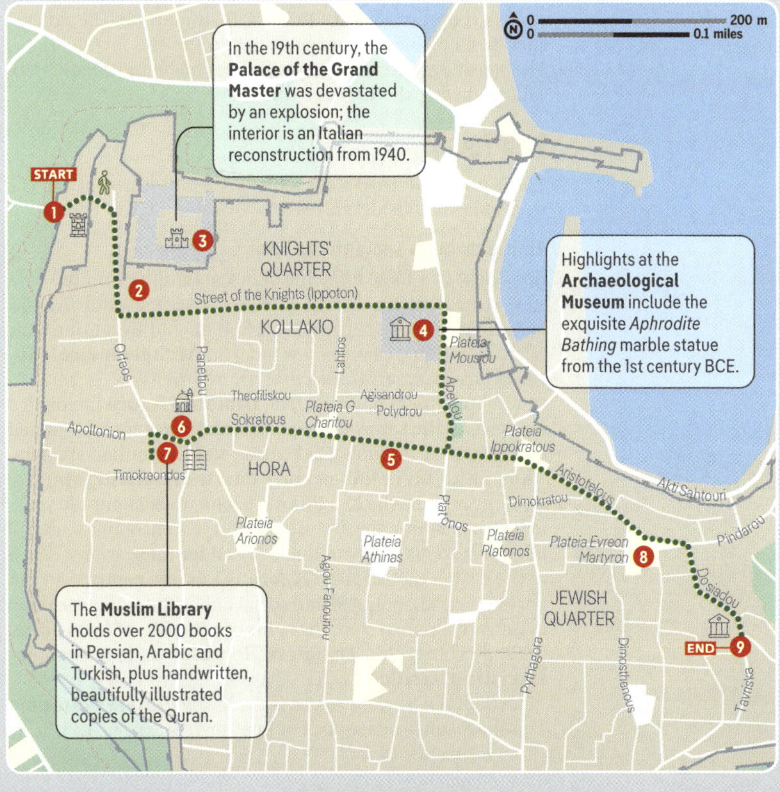

In the 19th century, the **Palace of the Grand Master** was devastated by an explosion; the interior is an Italian reconstruction from 1940.

Highlights at the **Archaeological Museum** include the exquisite *Aphrodite Bathing* marble statue from the 1st century BCE.

The **Muslim Library** holds over 2000 books in Persian, Arabic and Turkish, plus handwritten, beautifully illustrated copies of the Quran.

START
❶

❸

KNIGHTS' QUARTER

Street of the Knights (Ippoton)
❷

KOLLAKIO

Lahitos

❹ Plateia Mousiou

Orfeos

Panetiou

Theofiliskou

Plateia G Charitou

Agisandrou Polydrou

Sokratous

❻

Apollonion

❼

Timokreontos

HORA

Apellou

Plateia Ippokratous

❺

Aristotelous

Akti Sahtouri

Platonos

Dimokratou

Pindarou

Plateia Arionos

Plateia Athinas

Agiou Fanouriou

Plateia Platonos

Plateia Evreon Martyron

❽

Desarou

Pythagora

Dimosthenous

JEWISH QUARTER

END ❾

Tavriska

0 200 m
0 0.1 miles

rulers of this Mediterranean island. It should take you no more than 20 minutes.

From the 14th century, this was home to the Knights Hospitaller who ruled Rhodes. The knights were divided into seven groups, according to their birthplace and language, each responsible for a specific section of the fortifications. The street's modern appearance owes much to Italian restorations during the 1930s.

Kos Town

Kos is an island ringed by some of the finest beaches in the Dodecanese, considerable wilderness and a lively capital.

Amble through ancient Kos Town

Kos Town is a handsome harbour community, fronted by a superb medieval castle and somehow squeezed amid an array of ancient ruins from the Greek, Roman and Byzantine eras.

The main square houses a wonderful **Archaeological Museum** *(archaeologicalmuseums.gr; adult/child €10/free)* in a superb Italian-era building. The **Dimotiki Agora** (municipal market), in the same square, is a great place for well-priced local produce, mythological curios and Kalymnian sponges.

Kos' magnificent 15th-century **Castle of the Knights** *(kos. gr; free),* built by the Knights of St John, took about 130 years to build, meaning the architectural styles encompass several historic periods. Parts of it are closed for renovations. South of the castle, the **Ancient Agora** is Kos' old centre – an important market, political and social hub. Landmarks include a massive, columned stoa, the ruins of a **Shrine of Aphrodite**, the 2nd-century-BCE **Temple of Hercules**, and a 5th-century **Christian basilica**.

North of the Ancient Agora is the lovely **Plateia Platanou**. The charm and sedate pace of Kos Town is experienced at its

TRABANTOS/SHUTTERSTOCK

Asklepieion, Kos

best in this lovely cobblestone square. Sitting in a cafe here, you can pay your respects to **Hippocrates' plane tree**. Hippocrates himself is said to have taught his pupils in its shade – though this is legend, since plane trees don't usually live for more than 200 years.

Discover the ancient site of healing

The island's most important ancient site, **Asklepieion** (*kos. gr; adult/child €15/free*) stands on a pine-covered hill 3km southwest of Kos Town, commanding lovely views towards Türkiye. A religious sanctuary devoted to Asclepius, the god of healing, it was also a healing centre and a school of medicine. It was founded in the 3rd century BCE, according to legend by Hippocrates himself, the Kos-born 'father' of modern medicine. He was already dead by then, though, and the training here simply followed his teachings. Bus 3 runs hourly from Kos Town to the site. It's also a pleasant, if uphill, bike ride.

BEST BEACHES ON KOS

Magic Beach: Great spot for a nature-based experience with few(er) resources, in the island's southwest.

Exotic Beach: If you like to get into your birthday suit, this spot near Magic Beach is the nudist option.

Lagada Beach: Lovely and simple, also referred to as Banana Beach.

Agios Stefanos Beach: Sadly, this beach has been ruined by a massive resort behind it. Nevertheless, the small beachfront promontory has the photogenic islet of Kastri, topped with a tiny church, within swimming distance offshore.

Agios Theologos Beach: On the west coast, backed by meadow bluffs carpeted in olive groves, it feels far removed from the resort bustle.

EATING ON KOS: OUR PICKS

Haihoutes: In a ghost village, this tastefully restored cafe serves history, traditional food and good coffee. *3pm-midnight* €

O Makis: In Mastihari, this is a genuine Greek experience with friendly Makis, serving seafood and grills at incredible prices. *10am-midnight* €

Oria Taverna: Walk up for 15 minutes to this idyllic taverna, near old Pyli Castle, for the best views on Kos and traditional food. *9am-9pm* €

Restaurant Agios Theologos: Set above Agios Theologos Beach, this much-loved seafood taverna enjoys the best sunsets in Kos. *10am-9pm* €€

Corfu

COSMOPOLITAN VIBE | MIGHTY FORTRESSES | REGAL REFUGE

 TOP TIP

Parking and car congestion can be a nightmare in Corfu Town. It's best to find a space where you can leave your car; the centre is largely pedestrianised and you won't need it while you're in town.

Still recognisable as the idyllic refuge where the ship-wrecked Odysseus was soothed and sent on his way home, Corfu – one of the seven main Ionian Islands – continues to attract travellers with its lush scenery, bountiful produce and pristine beaches. While certain parts of the island have succumbed to overdevelopment, it's possible to escape the crowds.

Imbued with Venetian elegance, historic Corfu Town (Kerkyra) stands halfway down the island's east coast. Located between two strongholds (each topped by a fortress built to withstand Ottoman sieges), the UNESCO-listed Old Town unfolds as a tight-packed car-free warren of cobbled lanes. Some are lined with fine restaurants, lively bars and intriguing shops; others exude a timeless charm, with flowery side alleys and weathered facades. The Old Town's majestic architecture includes the splendid Liston arcade, high-class museums, and many churches.

By day, streets buzz with cruise-ship passengers and day-trippers; come evening, the atmosphere thrives around teeming bars.

GETTING AROUND

Corfu's Old Town is compact and mostly pedestrianised, so getting around is best done on foot.

Corfu City Bus *(astikoktelkerkyras.gr)* serves points around Corfu Town and the nearby communities in central Corfu; most lines depart from the main local bus station near San Rocco Sq (aka Plateia Theotoki). Line 15 goes to the airport and the port, New Limani. Buy tickets at vending machines or kiosks; tickets bought from bus drivers are more expensive.

Buses to destinations in northern and southern Corfu leave from the **Green Buses** *(ktelkerkyras.gr)* terminal in the New Town, a 15-minute walk south of the centre. Green Buses has frequent services to major beaches and island communities, the port and airport. Services are reduced on weekends and outside peak season.

To thoroughly explore the island, you'll need your own transport. Car and motorbike rentals are widely available at the airport, in Corfu Town and at the resorts. Prebook in summer.

CORFU

BEST ORGANISED TOURS

Corfu Walking & Food Tours: Guided tours of Corfu's Old Town, plus island coach tours, including a Durrell-themed one. *(corfuwalkingtours. com)*

Corfu Perspectives Guided Tours: Insightful tours focus on Corfu's lesser-known sides, personalities and locations. *(corfu guidedtours.com)*

Aperghi Travel: Island hikes, from guided one-day treks up Mt Pantokrator to two-week self-guided Corfu Trail expeditions. *(aperghitravel.gr)*

S-Bikes & Cycle: Acharavi-based company leads guided mountain-bike tours around northern Corfu and e-bike tours of Corfu Town. *(cyclecorfu.com)*

Ionian Cruises: Day cruises to Paxi and Antipaxi, to Parga and Syvota islands and across to Albania. *(ionian-cruises.com)*

HIGHLIGHTS
1 Palaio Frourio

SIGHTS
2 Archaeological Museum
3 Byzantine Museum of Antivouniotissa
4 Casa Parlante
5 Church of Agios Spyridon
6 Corfu Museum of Asian Art

7 Liston
8 Neo Frourio
see 6 Palace of St Michael & St George
9 Spianada

SLEEPING
10 Bella Venezia
11 Locandiera

EATING
12 Chrisomalis

13 Marina's Taverna
14 Papagiorgis
15 Tsipouradiko
16 Venetian Well

DRINKING & NIGHTLIFE
17 Imabari Seaside Lounge

INFORMATION
18 Aperghi Travel

A Stroll Through History

Explore Corfu's Old Town

A Corfu Town landmark, the elegant **Liston** is an arcaded building dating back to Corfu's Napoleonic occupation (1807–14). These days, it houses see-and-be-seen cafes. Across the grassy expanse known as the **Spianada**, the imposing **Palaio Frourio** *(odysseus.culture.gr; adult/child €10/free)* fortress was built in the 14th century by the Venetians to

149

Neo Frourio

defend against Ottoman attacks. Previously, it enclosed the entire Byzantine city within massive stone walls; spend half an hour clambering up to the viewpoints.

After a sightseeing respite at **Imabari Seaside Lounge** on Faliraki Beach, follow the waterfront to reach a pale-yellow 15th-century church that houses the **Byzantine Museum of Antivouniotissa** *(odysseus.culture.gr; adult/child €5/3)*. Then wander through a web of lanes and alleyways, where bougainvillea plants blaze in pink and red across pastel-painted walls.

The **Church of Agios Spyridon** shelters the remains of Corfu's patron saint. Cross the pretty Plateia Agios Spyridon for an ice cream at **Papagiorgis** *(papagiorgis.gr)*, an old-school patisserie from 1924, before popping into **Casa Parlante** *(casaparlante.gr; adult/child €10/6)* to gain the sense of the lifestyle of a 19th-century merchant family.

On the other side of town looms the **Neo Frourio** *(odysseus.culture.gr; adult/child €5/free)*, or New Fort, another Venetian masterpiece of military engineering built in the 16th century. The bastion can be accessed via the stairway at the western end of Solomou. It's open from April to October.

Eastern Masterpieces

Greece's only collection of Asian art

Looming over the northern end of the Spianada is the neo-classical **Palace of St Michael and St George**. Built by the British as a residence for the high commissioner, it also served as the seat of the Ionian Parliament and summer palace of the Greek royal family. Today, it's home to the prestigious **Corfu Museum of Asian Art** *(matk.gr; adult/child €10/free)*, which features 15,000 artefacts, mostly from Japan and China, donated by private collectors.

Archaeological Treasure Chest
Catch a glimpse of Corfu's distant past

South of the city centre, the **Archaeological Museum of Corfu** *(adult/child €10/free)* should be on the to-do list of anyone interested in Ancient Greek history and art. Its fine collection of pieces unearthed around the island provides an insightful survey of Corfu's rich archaeological heritage, from prehistoric to Roman times.

Forest, Royals & Ruins
Discover Corfu's regal connections at Mon Repos

The rambling wooded estate of **Mon Repos** sits partly on top of Palaeopolis, an ancient settlement dating back to the 8th century BCE. The park's centrepiece is a neoclassical mansion, showcased as the **Museum of Palaeopolis** *(odysseus. culture.gr; adult/child €10/free)*. It was built in 1830 as the summer retreat of Corfu's British governors and used as a residence by Greek royals from 1864 until 1967. Perhaps its biggest claim to fame is as the place where Prince Philip of Greece, later Duke of Edinburgh and husband of Queen Elizabeth II, was born in 1921.

Mon Repos is about 2km south of the Old Town and served by bus 2a from the Spianada or San Rocco Sq. Pack a picnic and water, as there are no cafes or shops on the grounds or nearby.

Royal fans, garden lovers and mythology buffs should make the 10km trip south to **Achilleion Palace** *(achillion-corfu. gr; adult/child €7/5)*, the splendid summer retreat of Empress Elisabeth of Austria, aka Sissi. It was completed in 1892, and Sissi only got to enjoy a few years here before her tragic assassination in 1898. To get here, hop on Blue Bus 10 at San Rocco Sq.

PAXI & ANTIPAXI

A mere 10km off the south of Corfu island, and measuring 13km from tip to toe, Paxi packs a lot of punch in its pint-sized frame. Its sublime beaches are bound to bring a smile to your face. Facilities are concentrated in three peaceful harbour villages on its eastern shores – Lakka, Loggos and the ferry port of Gaios. The vibe is laid-back but sophisticated. From Gaios, it's a short hop to sister island Antipaxi, a wonderful day-trip destination for its beach coves.

Paxi does not have an airport. Passenger-only ferries operated by Joy Cruises, Lefkada Palace and Kerkyra Lines serve Paxi from Corfu Town, while Kamelia Lines leaves from Lefkimmi in southern Corfu (free bus shuttle from Corfu Town). Kerkyra Lines and Kerkyra Seaways link Paxi with Igoumenitsa.

 EATING IN CORFU TOWN: OUR PICKS

Tsipouradiko: Pick from plenty of mezedhes at this rustic old mansion with tables under a tree and occasional live music. *6.30pm-midnight* €€

Chrisomalis: Going strong since 1904, this little taverna was a Durrell family fave. Warm service and good people-watching. *12.30pm-midnight* €€

Marina's Taverna: Tables strewn around a cobbled square, and home-cooked dishes made from tried-and-true family recipes. *noon-midnight* €€

Venetian Well: Local recipes elevated with contemporary techniques and cosmopolitan flair. It's tucked on a romantic square. *7-11.30pm* €€€

Crete

STUNNING COASTS | VIBRANT CULTURE | HISTORIC WONDERS

Places

☑ **TOP TIP**

Hania is known for having some of the best food on the island, from prized meats to seasonal vegetables. Be sure to try cheeses, preserves and olive oil.

Crete is a treasure chest of splendid beaches, ancient marvels and striking landscapes, weaving in entrancing cities and throwback villages where residents share uniquely Cretan traditions. There's something undeniably artistic in the way Crete's landscape unfolds, from the sun-drenched beaches in the north to the rugged canyons spilling out at the cliff- and cove-lined southern coast. In between, valleys cradle moody villages, and round-shouldered hills are the overture to often snow-dabbed mountains.

Crete's natural wonders are equalled only by the richness of its history. The Palace of Knossos is but one of many vestiges of the mysterious ancient Minoan civilisation (as seen in the unmissable Archaeological Museum in Iraklio). Then there are Venetian fortresses, Turkish mosques and Byzantine churches – Hania and Rethymno showcase these spectacularly. The island's beauty is rivalled by its food, with rural tavernas often producing their own ingredients and catching their own seafood.

🧭 **GETTING AROUND**

KTEL buses serve the island and link Iraklio, Hania and Rethymno. Local buses head from Iraklio to the Palace of Knossos.

If you're driving to Hania, park on the periphery (there are car parks to the south) and walk to the Old Town. From the airport, insist to your driver that they stick to the posted fixed price before setting off.

The historic quarter of Rethymno is mostly car-free and best enjoyed on foot. Parking is always a problem; try the huge car park east of the Municipal Park or the paid parking on Kriari. The bus station is at the western edge of the commercial centre.

Most places of interest in Iraklio are within the city centre, which is largely pedestrianised. Leave the car in your hotel garage, a 24/7 car park or use the free parking at the Cultural Centre on Giannikou. The airport is 4km east of the centre; access is a breeze. The ferry port is even closer.

CRETE

Sea of Crete

Kolymbari · Stavros
Kissamos · Hania
Panormo · Bali
Georgioupolis · Rethymno
Samaria Gorge · Perama
Sougia · Mt Pahnes
Paleohora · Agia · Plakias · Spili
Roumeli · Hora · Agia Galini
Sfakion · Zaros
Tymbaki
Mires · Pyrgos

Dia

Iraklio · Palace of Knossos
Anogia · Malia · Agios
Arhanes · Kastelli · Neapoli · Nikolaos · Sitia · Palekastro
Agia Varvara · Mt Dikti · Istron · Mohlos
Arkalokhorion · Myrtos · Makrygialos · Zakros
Arvi · Ierapetra · Xerokampos

Gavdos

Gaidouronisi (Hrysi)

Koufonisi

Libyan Sea

0 — 50 km
0 — 25 miles

Hania

Hania (also spelt Chania) is Crete's most evocative city. Wandering its tangle of alleys and lanes is one of the island's pleasures. It was historically the seat of Venetian, Turkish and then Cretan rule, and remnants of Venetian and Turkish architecture abound, with ancient synagogues, plus old townhouses now transformed into atmospheric restaurants and boutique hotels.

Explore the Venetian Harbour

There are few places where Hania's historic charm and grandeur are more palpable than in the **Venetian Harbour**. Lined by pastel-coloured buildings that punctuate a maze of narrow lanes lined with shops and tavernas, its oldest parts date to the 15th century. The eastern side is dominated by the domed **Mosque of Kioutsouk Hasan**, now an exhibition hall. On the west side, short and steep streets lead up to the remains of the Venetian fortifications. (It's worth ascending the steps for the somewhat hidden high Venetian-era terrace, to enjoy views across the city and harbour.)

Heading east around the harbour, the restored **Grand Arsenal** houses the **KAM Centre of Mediterranean Architecture**. Continuing on, the somewhat dilapidated, 15th-century **Neoria**, or **Venetian shipyards**, are a historic treasure hiding in plain sight.

Following the waterfront out onto the 14th-century **breakwater**, you can clamber over the huge blocks of stone as you take in captivating views back to the Old Town. Imagine the port filled with Venetian sailing ships laden with valuable cargo. Parts of the magnificent 21m-high **lighthouse** date to 1595. It was rebuilt by the Egyptians in the 1820s in the shape of a minaret.

HANIA TOURS & INFO

Boats of every shape and size tour Hania's harbour and coast, especially at sunset. Touts offer a choice of glass-bottom, vintage or sailing boats and more. Some tours are all-day affairs and visit the remote beaches on the Rodopou Peninsula and **Balos Beach** on the Gramvousa Peninsula, which are difficult to reach via land.

Tours on land cover much of Western Crete. Check durations carefully – for instance, the trip for the hike in the **Samaria Gorge** lasts from dawn until after dusk.

Hania's **municipal tourist office** (explorechania.gr) has limited hours but is an excellent resource for special events and getting around the region without a rental car. Check its official website and phone app.

Heraklion Archaeological Museum, Iraklio

MILAN GONDA/SHUTTERSTOCK

Treasures in the Archaeological Museum of Chania

For greater historical insight, don't miss the **Archaeological Museum of Chania** (amch.gr; adult/child €15/free) where artefacts from across the island are displayed in two light-filled galleries, with plenty of signage offering details and context. For time out, relax in the breezy cafe with views from the deck to the Aegean. The museum is 1.5km east of the Old Town. Come in the afternoon, and after the visit walk back along the shoreline for pre-sunset views plus glimpses of hidden beaches below a tiny park and the remains of waterfront tanneries that were a major Hania industry 100 years ago.

Iraklio

Minoan culture at the Heraklion Archaeological Museum

Snake goddesses, bull leapers and the Prince of the Lilies are among the intriguing characters you'll encounter in the unmissable **Heraklion Archaeological Museum** (heraklion museum.gr; adult/child €12/free). This is the world's premier museum of the Minoan culture, widely considered the first civilisation in Europe. Reaching a peak of development beginning in 2000 BCE, their art, architecture and culture are celebrated in the 27 rooms of this visitor-friendly museum.

A two-hour spin around here will greatly enhance your understanding of Cretan history, help put any archaeological site on Crete in context, and shine a spotlight on aspects of daily life and the development of Cretan societies. It's best to visit after 3pm in summer when it's less busy. The simple

EATING IN HANIA: BEST TAVERNAS

Pinaleon Fine Kitchen: A menu of the greatest hits of Greek classics is served in this spiffy yet unpretentious corner taverna. 1-10pm €€

Kouzina Epe: Stylish cafe on a relaxed square serving an appealing mix of modern Greek fare and daily specials. noon-7.30pm €€

Christostomos: Behind the harbour, popular for its classic Cretan cuisine cooked over wood or in a pot with homegrown ingredients. 1-11pm €€

Kalderimi: A traditional, busy taverna in Topanas. Cretan standards cooked with creative flair, plus dishes from around the Med. 8.30am-11pm €€

cafe is good for refreshments and has shady outdoor seating overlooking architectural digs.

Palace of Knossos
The grand capital of Minoan Crete

Crete's must-see attraction is the **Palace of Knossos** *(knossos-palace.gr; adult/child €26/free)*, just 5km south of Iraklio. Combining a visit here with Iraklio's excellent Archaeological Museum is highly recommended and will give unparalleled insight into Crete's Minoan civilisation. The setting is awe-inspiring and the ruins and recreations impressive, incorporating an immense palace, courtyards, private apartments, baths, lively frescoes and more. To beat the crowds and avoid the heat, get to Knossos either at 8am or after 3pm. Skip ticket-booth queues by buying timed-admission tickets online. Plan on spending at least two hours to do the place justice.

Samaria Gorge
Crete's world-class hiking

Samaria Gorge *(samaria-gorge.gr; adult/child €10/free)* is one of Europe's top geological wonders. The best way to experience the gorge is by hiking its 18km length from the starting point in the hillside village of **Xyloskalo** near Omalos. You begin at an elevation of 1230m and end at sea level. The national park ends at the 13km mark just north of the almost abandoned village of **Palea Agia Roumeli**, from where it's a further 3km to the sea. All along the route stay alert for *kri-kri,* a mountain goat that's native to Crete, and enjoy the wildflowers blooming in profusion.

Day trips to the gorge are heavily marketed to tourists across Crete and it gets crowded in summer. Start as early as you can manage to get ahead of the crowds. The park's north entrance is open from 7am to 1pm May to October. After closing, visitors are not permitted to walk on the entire trail, as everyone needs to be out of the park by 4pm. Sturdy shoes are a must. Day trips to Samaria Gorge start at the park entrance and include a pick-up from either Sougia or Hora Sfakion, after a ferry ride from Agia Roumeli. The Samaria Gorge website has excellent details on the hike and how to get there.

BEST WINERIES BEYOND IRAKLIO

Boutari Winery: One of Greece's largest wine producers has a vast, airy tasting room in Skalani.

Stilianou Winery: Rustic and down-to-earth, it specialises in organic wines made with local varietals only; in Kounavi.

Titakis Wines: Huge facility and garden in Kounavi, with sample plots of 11 Cretan varietals.

Digenakis Winery: In Peza, with an artful tasting room and unusual vintages.

Agelakis Winery: In a bare-bones facility around a Peza courtyard. Vines cover just 4.5 hectares.

Domain Paterianakis: This organic specialist has views as big as its tasting room off the main road in Alagni.

 EATING IN IRAKLIO: OUR PICKS

Peskesi: Culinary magic forged from family-farm ingredients and served amid unpretentious sophistication in a Venetian mansion. *1pm-1am* €€

Thigaterra: This rustic-elegant slow-food champion at Ammoudara Beach gives traditional Greek dishes the next-gen workout. *4pm-midnight* €€

Vourvouladiko: Turkish-infused Cretan cuisine in an enchanted Lakkos garden with historic photographs. A genteel retreat. *7pm-1am* €€

Apiri: Stylish but relaxed corner bistro with a tightly curated menu of modern Greek cuisine, cocktails and craft beer. *noon-midnight* €€

Places We Love to Stay

€ Budget €€ Midrange €€€ Top end

Athens
MAP p125

Athens Backpackers € Aussie-run backpackers near the Acropolis, with spotless dorms, a courtyard, well-stocked kitchen and busy social scene. Also has Athens Studios.

Athens Quinta Hostel € Friendly hostel in an old Exarhia mansion, furnished with velvet sofas and patterned tile floors.

Marble House Pension € In a quiet cul-de-sac in Koukaki, this pension offers well-maintained rooms and one apartment; some have small balconies. Air-con is extra.

Athens Gate €€ Stunning views over the Temple of Olympian Zeus from the spacious front rooms, and a central (if busy) location.

Athens Muses Suites €€ Renovated townhouse up on the slopes of Plaka with small, well-kept rooms.

Mosaikon €€ One in a cluster of high-end, reasonably priced suite hotels in the heart of Monastiraki.

Neoma €€€ Light and airy, with sensational Acropolis views from the rooftop bar and pool, on the edge of Filopappou Hill.

Delphi

Fedriades Hotel € Attractive, value-for-money three-star hotel with comfortable, family-friendly rooms and terrific mountain views. Breakfast features homemade food. Free bikes.

Hotel Tholos € Minimalist (not to say humdrum), central and great value. Has sea-view balconies and caring owners.

Meteora

Meteora Central Hostel € Well-managed spot in Kalambaka and one of Greece's best hostels. Dorm rooms are spotless, with good lockers; also private doubles.

Doupiani House €€ Breakfast in a carefully tended garden with uninterrupted Meteora views at this warmly welcoming family-run Kastraki hotel.

Thessaloniki
MAP p134

Zeus is Loose € Hostel (or rather, poshtel) with a muted colour scheme, big windows, sleek furniture and a rooftop bar.

Little Big House € Choose from private doubles or small dorms in this cute and eclectic hostel in charming Ano Poli.

Olganos VL €€ Lovely, family-run boutique hotel in the old Jewish quarter of Veria, close to all the archaelogical sites.

Trilogy House €€ Design buffs will feel at home in this restored 1920s building, where modern fixtures mix with neoclassical lines.

Nafplio

Pension Marianna €€ Vibrant place with convivial owners, Greek *filoxenia* (hospitality) and wide-vista setting – you can't get better for value. Organic breakfasts.

Aetoma €€€ Intimate yet comfortable, the five rooms in a classic mansion have dark, heavy and stylish furnishings. Generous traditional breakfast.

Grand Sarai €€€ This renovated pink mansion is sleek and modern on the inside, with stylish rooms. Most have marvellous views; some have balconies.

Olympia

Hotel Pelops €€ Our pick for Olympia's most welcoming lodgings, with comfortable rooms and a delightful, sunny lounge. Greek-Australian Suzanne is a fount of knowledge.

Pension-Tavern Bacchus €€ Located only a few kilometres from the ancient site in the village of Ancient Pissa, this pleasant spot has wonderful valley views, a swimming pool and a decent tavern.

Santorini (Thira)

Spiros & Hiroko Hotel €€ Behind a huge bloom of geraniums on Perissa's main street, Japanese-Greek couple Hiroko and Spiros run an immaculate 10-room hotel. No kids.

Aroma Suites €€ Overlooking the caldera at the quieter southern end of Fira, this boutique hotel has charming service and six cave-house rooms and suites.

Chelidonia Traditional Villas €€€ Traditional Oia cliffside dwellings that have been in the owner's family for generations. It has beds in cosy alcoves, and private patios with caldera views.

Villa Blanca €€€ A superb option away from the crowds amid Megalohori's vineyards, this luxury villa is built in traditional Cycladic style with a hot tub and ocean view.

Naxos

Hotel Grotta €€ Located on high ground overlooking the *kastro* and Hora, this excellent family-run hotel has immaculate rooms, great sea views, and a cool indoor hot tub.

Hotel Glaros €€ A well-run and immaculate 13-room boutique hotel with an indoor hot tub. The beach is only a few steps away. Adults only.

Rhodes Town

S Nikolis Hotel €€ Set across several restored buildings and a flowery courtyard, the stylish, split-level rooms feature four-poster beds, marble floors and stone walls. Breakfast is superb.

Marco Polo Mansion €€ This 15th-century pasha's house lovingly recreates an Ottoman ambience. Some rooms are in the mansion itself; the rest open onto the stunning garden.

Spirit of the Knights €€€ With their thick rugs, dark woods, stained-glass windows and sense of tranquillity, the six opulent suites in this gorgeous boutique hotel ooze medieval atmosphere.

Kos Town

Hotel Afendoulis € There may be plusher hotels in Kos, but none with such spirit. Clean rooms with small balconies, a homely lounge area and delicious breakfasts.

Kos Aktis Art Hotel €€€ Bedrooms are minimalist affairs of glass, light and wood. The view of the Aegean and, by night, Bodrum glittering like a giant chandelier is romantic.

Corfu

MAP p149

Locandiera €€ This stylish guesthouse in a historic building in Corfu Town is a standout for its superb breakfasts and rooms with a subtly artsy vibe.

Manessis Apartments €€ Lovely two-bedroom apartments with balconies facing Kassiopi's harbour, framed by flower-filled gardens and managed by a caring owner who ensures everything goes smoothly.

Rolling Stone €€ Indie travellers' favourite on Kontogialos (Pelekas) Beach, with a shared outdoor kitchen and hosts who organise

barbecue evenings and boat rides to hidden caves.

Bella Venezia €€€ This city hotel in a neoclassical villa on a peaceful street features compact but well-equipped rooms and a flowery breakfast terrace.

Hania

Kumba Hostel € Restored, hip hostel east of the centre. Bright cafe–bar, spacious and modern dorms, and rooms that are quiet and comfortable.

Ionas Boutique Hotel €€ Historic building with nine contemporary rooms and a rooftop terrace, located in the labyrinth old Splantzia quarter.

Malmo Historic Hotel €€ Beautifully restored hotel arching over the pedestrianised street in Splantzia. Rooftop deck; nightlife is right outside the door.

Iraklio

Intra Muros Boutique Hostel € Family-run and central, with a fully equipped communal kitchen and a veranda for socialising.

Olive Green Hotel €€ Contemporary hotel with minimalist white and olive-green decor. It gets eco-cred from solar panels and sustainable building materials.

Lato Boutique Hotel €€ Iraklio goes Hollywood – with all the sass but sans the attitude – at this mod boutique hotel overlooking the old harbour.

Hotel Grotta, Naxos

Practicalities

FAMILY TRAVEL

Greeks love children, and yours will be fussed over wherever you go. While there may not be specific tourist infrastructure for families, the country is crammed with fascinating history, thrilling ferry rides and sandy beaches. Children receive discounted admission at nearly all museums and sights.

SVEN HANSCHE/SHUTTERSTOCK

SMOKING

Be aware: while smoking is prohibited in all enclosed public spaces, including restaurants and bars, enforcement can be lax. And outdoors (including restaurant/ bar terraces) is another matter – it's permitted (and enjoyed) by many.

HEALTH & SAFE TRAVEL

Probably the biggest danger travelling in Greece is heatstroke; much of Greece experiences seaside breezes, so it's easy to become overexposed to the sun without realising it. Be careful, too, at isolated swimming spots that may have powerful currents. Mosquito repellent can be hard to find; bring some with you. Cannabis is illegal and brings heavy fines and/or imprisonment.

VISAS

Visitors from the UK, Canada, New Zealand, the US and Australia are among nationalities that can stay for up to 90 days in any six-month period without a visa.

OPENING HOURS

Opening hours vary throughout the year, the following are high-season hours.
Banks 8.30am–2.30pm Monday to Thursday, 8am–2pm Friday
Restaurants 11am–11pm
Cafes 9am–midnight
Bars 8pm–late
Shops 8am–3pm Monday, Wednesday and Saturday; 9am–2pm and 5.30pm–9pm Tuesday, Thursday and Friday

LGBTIQ+ TRAVELLERS

Same-sex marriage was legalised in Greece in 2024; attitudes to the LGBTIQ+ community have grown more liberal across Greece. However, the Orthodox Church plays a prominent role in shaping society's views, so attitudes outside major cities and gay-friendly islands are more conservative.

PUBLIC HOLIDAYS

New Year's Day 1 January
Epiphany 6 January
Lent First Sunday in February
Greek Independence Day 25 March
Good Friday April/May
Orthodox Easter Sunday April/May
May Day (Protomagia) 1 May

Whit Monday (Agiou Pnevmatos) 50 days after Easter Sunday
Feast of the Dormition 15 August
Ohi Day 28 October
Christmas Day 25 December
St Stephen's Day 26 December

Language

With just a little Modern Greek under your belt, you'll have a richer understanding of this language's impact on contemporary Western culture; and even if you learn only the very basics, your travel experience will be the better for it.

Basics

Hello. Γειά σας. ya·sas (polite/plural)
Γειά σου. ya·su (informal/singular)
Good morning. Καλημέρα. ka·li·*me*·ra
Good evening. Καλησπέρα. ka·li·*spe*·ra
Goodbye. Αντίο. an·*di*·o
Yes./No. Ναι./Όχι. ne/o·hi
Please. Παρακαλώ. pa·ra·ka·*lo*
Thank you. Ευχαριστώ. ef·ha·ri·*sto*
Sorry. Συγγνώμη. sig·*no*·mi
My name is ... Με λένε …
me *le*·ne …
Do you speak English?
Μιλάτε αγγλικά mi·*la*·te an·gli·*ka*
I (don't) understand.
(Δεν) καταλαβαίνω.
(dhen) ka·ta·la·*ve*·no

Directions

Where is ...? Πού είναι …;
pu *i*·ne …
What's the address?
Ποια είναι η διεύθυνση
pia *i*·ne i dhi·*ef*·thin·si
Can you show me (on the map)?
Μπορείς να μου δείξεις
(στον χάρτη)
bo·*ris* na mu *dhik*·sis (ston *har*·ti)

Signs

ΕΙΣΟΔΟΣ Entry
ΕΞΟΔΟΣ Exit
ΠΛΗΡΟΦΟΡΙΕΣ Information
ΑΝΟΙΧΤΟ Open
ΚΛΕΙΣΤΟ Closed
ΓΥΝΑΙΚΩΝ Toilets (Women)
ΑΝΔΡΩΝ Toilets (Men)

Time

What time is it? Τι ώρα είναι;
ti o·ra *i*·ne
It's (2 o'clock).
Είναι (δύο η ώρα). *i*·ne (*dhi*·o i o·ra)
It's half past (10).
Είναι (δέκα) και μισή. (*dhe*·ka) ke mi·*si*
today σήμερα *si*·me·ra
tomorrow αύριο *av*·ri·o
yesterday χθες hthes
morning πρωί pro·*i*
(this) afternoon
(αυτό το) απόγευμα
(af·*to* to) a·*po*·yev·ma
evening βράδυ *vra*·dhi

Emergencies

Help! Βοήθεια! vo·*i*·thya
Go away! Φύγε! *fi*·ye
I'm lost. Έχω χαθεί. e·kho kha·*thi*
There's been an accident.
Έγινε ατύχημα. e·yi·ne a·*ti*·hi·ma
I'm ill.
Είμαι άρρωστος. *i*·me *a*·ro·stos (m)
Είμαι άρρωστη. *i*·me *a*·ro·st (f)
I'm allergic to (antibiotics).
Είμαι αλλεργικός/αλλεργική
(στα αντιβιωτικά).
i·me a·ler·yi·*kos*/a·ler·yi·*ki* (m/f)
(sta an·di·vi·o·ti·*ka*)

Eating & Drinking

What would you recommend?
Τι θα συνιστούσες;
ti tha si·ni·*stu*·ses
That was delicious.
Ήταν νοστιμότατο!
i·tan no·sti·*mo*·ta·to
Cheers! Εις υγείαν! is i·*yi*·an

NUMBERS
1
ένα e·na
2
δύο dhi·o
3
τρία tri·a
4
τέσσερα
te·se·ra
5
πέντε pen·de
6
έξι e·xi
7
επτά ep·ta
8
οκτώ ok·to
9
εννέα e·ne·a
10
δέκα dhe·ka

MARKUS MAINKA/SHUTTERSTOCK

Eleftherios Venizelos International Airport

Arriving

While it's possible to drive south via the Balkans, many visitors arrive by air into Eleftherios Venizelos International Airport (Athens) or one of the four other international airports. Visitors from the UK, Canada, New Zealand, the US and Australia are among nationalities that can stay for up to 90 days in any six-month period without a visa.

By Air
Greece is easy to reach by air, particularly in summer. There are five main international airports: Athens and Thessaloniki, as well as two on Crete and one on Rhodes. Kos and Corfu receive year-round flights and these increase in high season.

By Boat
Ferries reach Greece from ports in Italy (Ancona, Bari, Brindisi). Services to Patras are useful for the Peloponnese (specifically Ancient Olympia), while those that head to Igoumenitsa are handy for ongoing journeys to Kalambaka (Meteora) or Delphi. See *ferryhopper.com*.

MONEY
Currency: Euro (€)

CREDIT & DEBIT CARDS
Big resorts and hotels accept payments by credit and debit card, but family-owned properties often don't. MasterCard and Visa are the most widely accepted.

CASH
Cash is accepted everywhere and helps businesses avoid extra fees from banks (and in some cases, the tax office). ATMs are found at banks in cities and towns.

TIPPING
Hotels Tip porters €1 per bag and housekeepers €1 per night.

Restaurants Even if a service charge is included, a small tip is customary for good service. Round up the bill or tip around 10%.

Taxis Not expected but rounding up to nearest euro is a welcome gesture.

Getting Around

Given its complex geography, Greece has an extensive network of domestic flights and ferries. Intercity buses (KTEL network) are frequent, cheap and air-conditioned; services to remote villages are limited though not impossible. A car remains the best way to explore off-the-beaten track locations, but roads can be narrow and winding, especially in mountainous terrain and mountain villages.

LYDIAREI/SHUTTERSTOCK

Boat
Greece's network of ferries includes fast modern ferries and overnight boats with cabins. For safety, departures are subject to delay during poor weather. Schedules change annually, and services are greatly reduced between mid-October and Easter. In high season, book ahead.

Bus
The bus network is comprehensive and fares are cheap. It's mostly run by public companies under the **KTEL** (ktelbus.com) umbrella. Towns on the mainland have frequent connections to Athens. The island of Corfu can also be reached from Athens by bus (ferry ticket may be included).

Taxi
Taxis are widely available in Greece. They are reasonably priced by European standards, making them a viable alternative to hiring a car if you aren't exploring much. Beware of meter scams. In Athens, useful apps to avoid rip-offs include Beat and Uber.

Car Hire
Hire cars are available on all but the smallest islands; local firms often have the best rates. Some islands are becoming jammed with hire vehicles, and parking can be challenging in summer. You'll need a good dose of road smarts.

Driving Conditions
Main highways in Greece are in good condition. However, some island roads aren't paved. Road surfaces are also prone to weathering and subsidence, and roads passing through mountainous areas can be littered with rocks (or, in winter, ice and snow).

DRIVING ESSENTIALS

Drive on the right

50   **120**

Speed limit is 50km/h in urban areas, 90km/h on secondary roads and 120km/h on highways

0.05

Blood alcohol limit is 0.05%

Curated by
Cristian Bonetto

Italy

EUROPE'S CULTURAL AND CULINARY PARADISE

World-famous art, architecture, food and passion, wrapped up in some of Europe's most magnificent natural landscapes.

A favourite destination since the days of the 18th-century Grand Tour, Italy may appear to hold few surprises. Its iconic monuments and masterpieces are known the world over, while cities like Rome, Florence and Venice need no introduction.

Yet Italy is far more than the sum of its sights. Its fiercely proud regions maintain centuries-old customs and culinary traditions, making the country feel more like a collection of mini nations – each with its distinct identity, specialities, architecture and festivals. After all, Milan and Turin are closer to Paris and Munich than they are to Palermo, while the latter's souk-like markets and Arabesque flourishes serve as a constant reminder that Tunis is much closer than Rome.

The extraordinary contrasts extend beyond the lively streets and piazzas, spilling into the very landscapes that frame them. Italy offers an amazing suite of natural backdrops: icy northern Alps and glacial lakes, gentle Tuscan hills, vertiginous Campanian coastlines and spitting Sicilian volcanoes. Few countries can claim such breadth and beauty in such a compact area.

Then, Italy has always had a knack for superlatives – from ancient glories and Renaissance masterpieces to fashion, design, food and wine. No other country matches its number of UNESCO World Heritage Sites, and few others seduce with such effortless style and heart-on-sleeve charm. *Benvenuti* to Europe's most intoxicating, theatrical stage.

RAUL JICHICI/SHUTTERSTOCK

THE MAIN AREAS

For places to stay in Italy, see p232

SERGEY NOVIKOV/SHUTTERSTOCK

Left: Tuscany (p201); Above: Cattedrale di Santa Maria del Fiore (p205), Florence

TRAIN & BUS

Fast, efficient and well connected, Italy's train network is best for travelling between major cities and along the coast. It works in conjunction with an efficient regionalised bus network, which can be useful for reaching smaller towns.

CAR

Cars aren't needed for getting around Italian cities and major towns, where historic centres are walkable and public transport is generally reliable. Beyond urban areas, a car offers flexibility to explore rural, off-the-beaten-track locations at your own pace.

FERRY

Ferry and hydrofoil services connect the Italian mainland to various islands, including regular overnight services between Naples and Sicily. Regular high-speed hydrofoils run year-round between Naples, Capri and other islands in the Bay of Naples, with seasonal services connecting Amalfi Coast towns.

Northern Italy, p180

Operatic encores in Milan, glittering mosaics in Venice, stunning hikes along the plunging Cinque Terre: Italy's well-heeled north isn't short of blockbuster moments.

Florence & Tuscany, p201

Birthplace of the Renaissance, Florence is Italy's preeminent city of art. Hop between masterpieces, then detour to a Tuscan town or an infamously crooked tower.

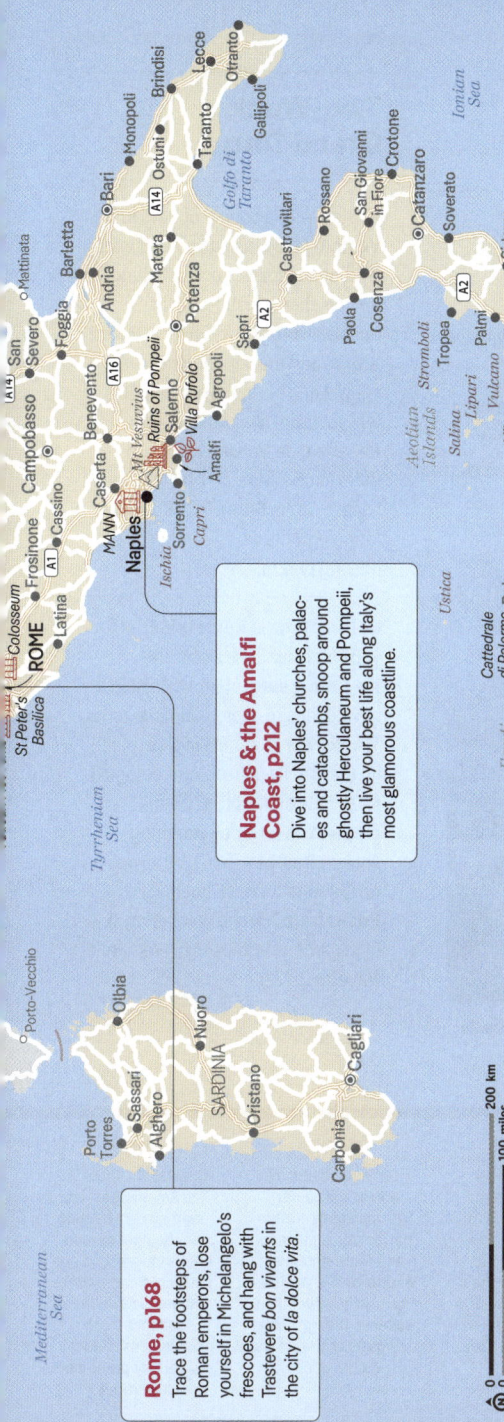

Sicily, p223

A heady, cross-cultural mash-up: wander Palermo's Arab-Norman landmarks, go baroque in Catania, soak up Taormina's *White Lotus* vibes and lose yourself in Syracuse's luminous, labyrinthine streets.

Naples & the Amalfi Coast, p212

Dive into Naples' churches, palaces and catacombs, snoop around ghostly Herculaneum and Pompeii, then live your best life along Italy's most glamorous coastline.

Rome, p168

Trace the footsteps of Roman emperors, lose yourself in Michelangelo's frescoes, and hang with Trastevere *bon vivants* in the city of *la dolce vita*.

Find Your Way

We've zoomed in on some of Italy's top offerings, from ancient ruins in Rome, Naples and Sicily to art-slung palaces in Florence, Venice and Milan. Speckled in between – spectacular natural highs and some lesser-known treasures.

100 miles
200 km

Plan Your Time

It's tempting to cram as many must-sees as you can into a single trip. High-speed trains make hopping between highlights easy, but also consider focusing on a smaller corner of the country. You won't be disappointed.

ARCADY/SHUTTERSTOCK

Villa Rufolo (p222), Ravello

Two-Week Grand Tour

● Start with a couple of days in **Venice** (p193), losing yourself in its Byzantine mosaics and art-slung palace, then whistle-stop in bookish **Bologna** (p191) for crooked towers and proper *bolognese*. A couple of days in **Florence** (p201) lets you skim the cream of its Renaissance treasures, among them Michelangelo's brawny *David*, while a day in **Siena** (p208) means lounging in its world-famous, Palio-hosting piazza.

● Three days in **Rome** (p168) lets you catch headline sights like the **Colosseum** (p169), while also having time to explore atmospheric **Trastevere** (p178). In **Naples** (p212), hit the **MANN** (Museo Archeologico Nazionale di Napoli; p215) in preparation for a day exploring ancient **Pompeii** (p217). Wrap up on the Amalfi Coast, boating in **Positano** (p221) and wandering sky-high gardens in impossibly romantic **Ravello** (p222).

SEASONAL HIGHLIGHTS

Spring and autumn are ideal for sightseeing. Summer heat packs the coasts, while winter snows fuel alpine skiing.

JANUARY

January is ideal for rugging up and strapping on skis in the Alps: the snow is generally solid, and the slopes are a little calmer after the Christmas and New Year's holiday rush.

APRIL

Springtime blooms across the country, with mild temperatures perfect for sightseeing and hikes among the wildflowers. Crowds are generally lighter than summer, though Easter brings busy streets and higher prices.

MAY

Coastal hot spots like the Amalfi Coast and Taormina are buzzing as shoulder season brings longer days and pleasant temperatures without the sweltering summer crush. Epicureans hit local markets for prime-time asparagus.

Six Northern Days

● Strut straight into Italy's fashion-and-finance capital, **Milan** (p185), for a couple of days. Scale its spindly **Duomo** (p187), take in Leonardo da Vinci's **The Last Supper** (p188) and dive into the Navigli's canal-side **aperitivo scene** (p188). Book ahead to catch a show at the world-famous opera house **La Scala** (p185).

● Head west for a few days in Italy's former capital, **Turin** (p183) – elegant, faintly French and home to royal palaces, grand cafes and the **Museo Egizio** (p185), Europe's greatest repository of Egyptian antiquities. Then, trade the city's stately arcades for the dramatic coast of the **Cinque Terre** (p180). Spend another two days or so hiking between its pastel villages, take a dip in turquoise coves and linger over Liguria's famous seafood, pesto and focaccia.

Sicily in Short

● Time-poor? Sicily's Ionian Coast delivers easy-to-reach thrills, from ancient Graeco-Roman ruins and jaw-dropping coastal towns to baroque splendour and vibrant street life. Start with two days in **Syracuse** (p229), indulging in Ortigia's island charm and roaming the vast **Parco Archeologico della Neapolis** (p231).

● Then continue up the coast to **Catania** (p226), Sicily's second-largest city, where UNESCO-listed piazzas, stuccoed churches and a raucous fish market make light work of a couple of days. The dining is sensational and its youthful, student energy invigorating. Then slow down with a day or so in polished **Taormina** (p228). Stroll old-world alleys, savour clifftop views of moody Mt Etna, and catch a moonlit show at the resort town's spectacular, millennia-old **Teatro Greco** (p229).

JUNE
School is out and the summer holidays begin, with tourist numbers increasing significantly across the country. Warm days and evenings herald outdoor festivals, from opera and theatre to Pride parades.

JULY
Hot days, packed beaches, and wild blueberries in full bloom. Outdoor festivals continue and Siena's Piazza del Campo hosts the thrilling horse race **Palio** (p210) on 2 July (a second edition is held on 16 August).

OCTOBER
While central and southern Italy still enjoy mild days, northern regions may see the season's first snow. Leaves are ablaze and autumn produce shines, from pumpkin-filled tortellini to roasted chestnuts.

NOVEMBER
Truffle season hits its peak in northern Italy, especially for the prized white Alba truffle. Gourmands flock to truffle festivals and waiters shave it fresh over steaks, pastas and warming risottos.

Rome

ROMAN ARCHITECTURE | BAROQUE LANDMARKS | LA DOLCE VITA

 TOP TIP

Trastevere's riverfront is the place to be in summer as the Lungo il Tevere street carnival revs into action. Stalls, pop-up bars, restaurants and even dance floors set up on the waterfront between Ponte Sisto and Ponte Sublicio between June and September.

Ever since its golden age as the ancient *caput mundi* (world capital), Rome has been seducing visitors. Its thrilling cityscape, piled high with martial ruins and monuments, is achingly beautiful, and its museums and churches harbour some of Europe's finest masterpieces.

Managing the twin demands of tourism and modern civic life has increasingly become a reality of governing Rome, a city whose population of 2.7 million is dwarfed by the annual influx of Italian and foreign visitors. The result of all this is a city that can sometimes appear to be living on the edge of perpetual chaos. And while Rome is undeniably busy, and is often scruffy and noisy, it's not the giant free-for-all it's occasionally portrayed as. Look closer and you'll see most drivers are wearing their seatbelts, and that few people are smoking in banned public places. In Rome, first impressions can be gloriously misleading.

Ancient Rome

Just to the south of the city centre, Ancient Rome is a thrilling mix of ancient treasures, iconic monuments and mesmerising views. This is where you'll find Rome's most celebrated ruins and showstopping landmarks: the Colosseum, Palatino (where

continued on p172

🧭 GETTING AROUND

Rome is best explored on foot: the main sights are clustered in and around the *centro storico* (historic centre), the centre is relatively flat, and traffic is restricted in many areas. Driving is stressful, parking scarce and scooters better left to locals. Public transport fills the gaps: the metro (lines A and B) links Termini to the Colosseum and the Vatican. There are no metro stations in the *centro storico,* but you can walk from Barberini, Spagna and Flaminio stations. Spagna is also useful for Villa Borghese. Buses cover much of the *centro storico* and trams run to Trastevere. Tickets are easy to buy at stations and kiosks.

Colosseum

The Colosseum is the most thrilling of Rome's ancient monuments, an electrifying, spine-tingling sight commissioned by Vespasian in 72 CE and inaugurated by Titus in 80 CE. This is where gladiators met in mortal combat and prisoners fought off wild beasts in front of baying, bloodthirsty crowds. Two thousand years on and it remains the city's most popular attraction.

VIACHESLAV LOPATIN/SHUTTERSTOCK

Making the Most of Your Visit

Even without a ticket, the outer walls – originally covered in travertine and with statues in the niches – impress. The upper level, punctuated by square window openings and slender Corinthian pilasters, had supports for 240 masts, which held a giant awning over the arena.

Once you make it inside, steep steps lead to the first and second tiers. From here you can look over the partially rebuilt arena floor and down into the underground areas. On the 2nd floor you'll also find the small **Museo del Colosseo** illustrating the Colosseum's history. You'll need a Full Experience ticket (€24) to gain access to the upper floors, where women spectators would have sat. The Full Experience ticket also allows you to walk on the arena floor and explore the subterranean sections, which once served as the stadium's backstage.

Demand for all tickets is high, so book well in advance, even a month ahead for peak periods; check the website for details. You can buy same-day tickets (subject to availability) at ticket offices on Piazza del Colosseo (credit/debit cards only) and Largo della Salara Vecchia.

TOP TIPS

● Tickets include the holder's name, so bring photo ID to enter.

● Reckon on about an hour inside the Colosseum. Try to visit first thing or late afternoon, when it's cooler, less crowded and there's better lighting.

● Free interactive audio guides are available on the official MyColosseum app.

PRACTICALITIES
● colosseo.it ● adult/reduced €18/2 ● 8.30am–1hr before sunset, last entry 1hr before closing

ROME

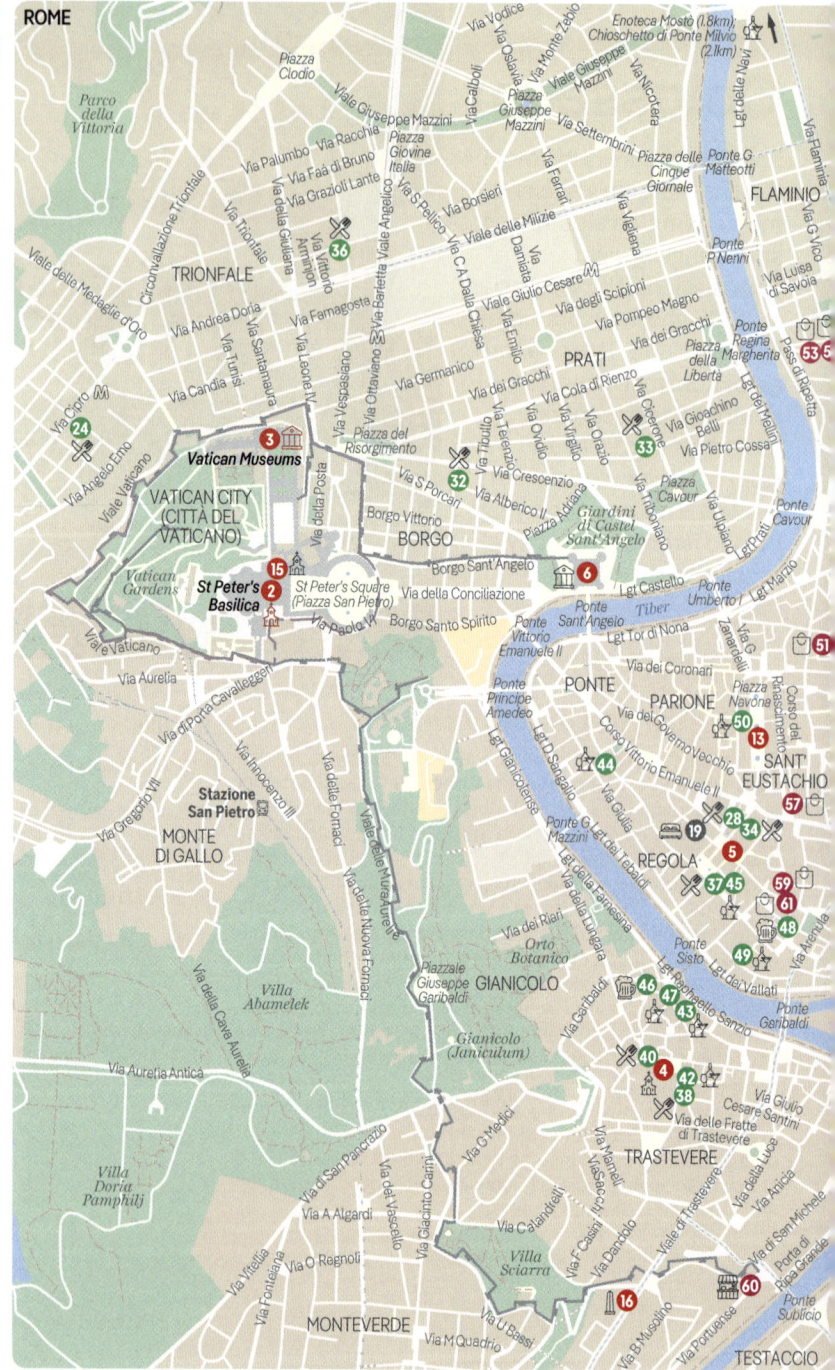

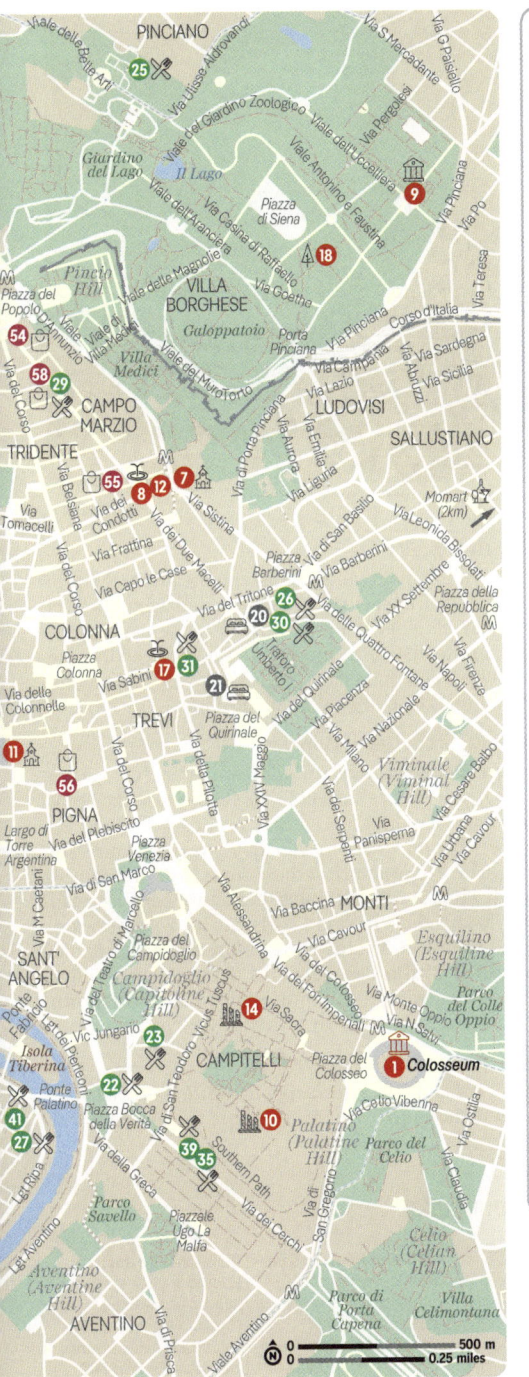

ANCIENT HIGHLIGHTS

Darius Arya, a Rome-based archaeologist, highlights some must-sees. @dariusaryadigs; ancientromelive.org

The Forum and Palatino are the real heart of Rome's history. You'll want to get the Super pass to have access to the 'secret' sites and monuments like Santa Maria Antiqua and the Curia Iulia. Due to new openings, everyone should walk up Domitian's ramp (which once connected to the palace on top) and through the substructures of the Domus Tiberiana.

For the Colosseum, try to take the elevator ride to the top or the hypogeum (underground chambers). They are both wonderful experiences that bring you closer to the Colosseum's history.

RESUL MUSLU/SHUTTERSTOCK

Pantheon

continued from p168

it all began with Romulus and Remus) and the Roman Forum. Unsurprisingly, it's a touristy part of town and while it's busy during the day, it's quiet at night with little in the way of after-hours action. Realistically, most of the people you'll come across will be fellow sightseers but look closely enough and you can still find the odd glimpse of local life.

Explore the heart of Caput Mundi

The **Roman Forum** (*colosseo.it; adult/reduced incl Colosseum & Palatino from €18*) was ancient Rome's showpiece, a vibrant centre of temples, basilicas and bustling public spaces. Today its ruins impress, but you'll need imagination – or a good guide – to picture them in their prime. Near the Forum's eastern entrance, the **Arco di Tito** (81 CE) celebrates the victories of Vespasian and Titus. To its right, **Via Sacra** leads into the Forum's heart, passing the **Tempio di Vesta**, where virgins tended the flame. The **Tempio di Giulio Cesare** marks the spot where Julius Caesar was cremated, while the 6th-century **Chiesa di Santa Maria Antiqua** harbours early Christian frescoes.

Roam where emperors slumbered

Palatino (*Palatine Hill; colosseo.it; adult/reduced incl Colosseum & Roman Forum from €18*) is Rome's mythical

 EATING IN ANCIENT ROME: OUR PICKS

Alimentari Pannella Carmela: A workaday food store ideal for sandwiches. *8.30am-2.30pm Mon-Sat, 5-8pm Mon-Fri* €

Osteria Circo: This Circo Massimo *osteria* specialises in traditional Italian fare and hearty Roman pastas. *12.30-3.30pm & 7.30-11.30pm* €€

47 Circus Roof Garden: Rooftop restaurant offering Mediterranean cuisine and sunset *aperitivi* (from 4pm). *noon-3.30pm & 7-10.30pm* €€€

Ristorante Ad Hoc: Housed in a 16th-century *palazzo* on the Circo Massimo. Modern Italian cuisine and national wines. *7-10.30pm Fri-Wed* €€€

birthplace, where Romulus supposedly founded the city in 753 BCE. Archaeology reveals Iron Age huts from the 9th century BCE. Later, emperors lived in palatial luxury, most notably in Domitian's 1st-century palace, divided into the public **Domus Flavia**, private **Domus Augustana**, and sunken **stadio**. Highlights include Augustus' frescoed **Casa di Augusto**, the **Orti Farnesiani** gardens with stunning Forum views, and the towering **Domus Tiberiana**, the Palatino's first palace. The **Museo Palatino** chronicles the hill's development, though you'll need a Forum Pass Super *(€18)* or Full Experience *(€24)* ticket to access the museum, as well as the Aula Isiaca and Loggia Mattei, Casa di Augusto and Domus Tiberiana. Allow about three hours to explore the Palatino and adjoining Forum.

Centro Storico

A tangled knot of cobbled alleyways, Renaissance palaces and baroque piazzas, Rome's *centro storico* (historic centre) is the city many visitors come to find. The Pantheon and Piazza Navona are the star turns, but walk around and without even trying you'll come across a whole host of monuments, museums and churches, many containing masterpieces. But it's not all high culture. There's plenty of fun to be had just strolling the area's theatrical streets, taking in its romantic nooks and enjoying the many boutiques, cafes, *trattorias* and bars. Just make sure to bring some comfortable shoes for the uneven cobbles.

Admire an engineering marvel

Built by Hadrian around 125 CE on the site of Marcus Agrippa's earlier temple, the 2000-year-old **Pantheon** *(pantheon roma.com)* is the best-preserved of Rome's ancient monuments. Step through its immense bronze doors and you're met with the largest unreinforced concrete dome ever built – a feat so breathtaking it inspired Michelangelo before he designed the dome of St Peter's Basilica. The temple-turned-church, whose tombs include that of Raphael, is best visited early to avoid the biggest crowds, and it's wise to book **tickets** *(portale.mu seiitaliani.it; adult/reduced €5/2)* online in advance to skip long queues. Return at night to see it illuminated.

Pose on a perfect piazza

A cinematic sweep of fountains and baroque *palazzi* (mansions), **Piazza Navona** has long been a hub of city life. For close on 300

WATER FOUNTAINS

Sightseeing can be thirsty work in Rome. Fortunately, you can get free drinking water throughout the city, courtesy of 2500 or so fountains known as *nasoni* (or 'big noses'). First introduced in the 1870s, these cast-iron fountains supply a constant flow of safe, refreshingly cool, *acqua potabile* (drinking water), which you can use to fill up your bottles or drink directly. To do so, block the main spout and cup the water as it spurts through the hole in the top of the nozzle. You'll find *nasoni* in Piazza della Rotonda and Piazza Navona, among other places. To locate the nearest one to you, check out the free app Acea Waidy Wow.

A hip trattoria with piazza seating.

EATING & DRINKING IN THE CENTRO STORICO: OUR PICKS

Osteria La Quercia: On a charming square near Piazza Farnese eat Lazio regional classics. *noon-3.30pm & 7-11.30pm* €€

Ditirambo: Central location, informal vibe and seasonal, organic cuisine. Roman pastas to thoughtful vegetarian offerings. *12.30-3pm & 6.30-11pm* €€

Rimessa Roscioli: Gourmets adore this place, with its wine-pairing dinners, tastings, tours and classes. Book ahead. *5-11pm Mon-Sun* €€

Luciano Cucina Italiana: Near Campo de' Fiori, this spot serves renowned carbonara and inventive mains. *12.15-3pm & 7.15-11pm* €€€

BEST SHOPS FOR SOUVENIR HUNTING

Aldo Fefè: Pick out a beautifully hand-painted notebook or picture album created by master craftsman Aldo Fefè.

Salumeria Roscioli: Rome's most celebrated deli, with a range of cured hams, cheeses, wines, olive oils and balsamic vinegars.

Confetteria Moriondo & Gariglio: A historic confectioner's specialising in delicious handmade chocolates, many prepared according to original 19th-century recipes.

Emporio Centrale: Choose from a 500-strong range of vintage Italian household goods and products made by artisans and long-standing Italian companies.

Ibiz – Artigianato in Cuoio: For wallets, bags, belts and sandals hand-crafted at this family-run leather workshop.

years it hosted Rome's main market, and still today it attracts a daily circus of street artists, hawkers and tourists. It stands on the 1st-century **Stadio di Domiziano**, whose underground remains can be visited from Via di Tor Sanguigna. The piazza's centrepiece is Bernini's 1651 **Fontana dei Quattro Fiumi**, featuring four river gods. Dominating the square's western flank, the domed **Chiesa di Sant'Agnese** in Agone was designed by the revered baroque architect Francesco Borromini. To catch the piazza at its most alluring, come first thing in the morning before the crowds or after dark when the fountains are illuminated.

Browse on the Campo

Hanging out on a busy piazza is a quintessential Roman experience. And nowhere does piazza life quite like **Campo de' Fiori**. Colourful, noisy and always busy, the square hosts a well-known market during the day and teems with life at night as visitors and young locals pack its restaurants and brash bars.

Amid the piazza's hurly-burly, you'll see a statue of a hooded monk. This is the philosopher Giordano Bruno, who was burned here for heresy in 1600.

Tridente & Trevi

Tridente, named after the three streets that form a trident as they lance off Piazza del Popolo, is a glamorous district, full of old money, fashionable bars and swish hotels. It's also Rome's premier shopping district, home to luxury designer boutiques and flagship stores. But once the shops close, the area quietens, leaving few after-hours distractions.

To the south, the Trevi Fountain stands out in a knot of dark, narrow streets, which teem throughout the day as crowds stop off to toss their coins into the *Dolce Vita* fountain.

Climb some famous steps

Few spots in Rome are as iconic (or romantic) as **Piazza di Spagna**, especially in April or May, when its famous Steps are adorned with azaleas. Once dubbed *'il salotto di Roma'* (Rome's parlour), the square takes its name from the 17th-century Spanish embassy still standing here. At its heart is Pietro and Gian Lorenzo Bernini's **Fontana della Barcaccia**, which depicts a seemingly sinking boat. Rising above, the 1725 Scalinata della Trinità dei Monti – better known as the **Spanish Steps** – links the piazza to the 16th-century **Chiesa della Trinità dei Monti** and its striking frescoes. Make sure not to sit on the Steps as hefty fines apply.

 DRINKING IN THE CENTRO STORICO: OUR PICKS

L'Angolo Divino: Near Campo de' Fiori, this snug wine bar serves interesting Italian wines and tasty dishes. *11am-3pm Tue-Sat & 5pm-1am Mon-Fri*

Open Baladin: Modern pub near Campo de' Fiori with 40 craft beers on tap and up to 100 bottled brews. *noon-1am, to 2am Fri & Sat*

Il Goccetto: An old-school *vino e olio* (wine and oil) shop with a bottle-lined interior and a fabulous wine list. *noon-midnight Tue-Sat, from 5pm Mon*

Terrazza Borromini: Bask in sunset views over Piazza Navona from this rooftop bar atop a 17th-century *palazzo.* Reservations recommended. *noon-midnight*

ZOIA KOSTINA/SHUTTERSTOCK

Spanish Steps, Piazza di Spagna

Relive a Fellini scene

The **Trevi Fountain** is Rome's most famous, and most flamboyant, baroque masterpiece. Designed by Nicola Salvi in 1732, it fills an entire piazza, with Oceanus riding a shell chariot, tritons and seahorses symbolising the sea's moods. Fed by the Aqua Virgo aqueduct, it will be forever tied to Fellini's *La Dolce Vita,* in which a glamorous Anita Ekberg wades through its waters (don't try it – bathing is banned). Spot the odd stone urn on the right, rumoured to have been placed there by Salvo to block the view of a rude, meddling barber during construction. And don't skip the ritual: back turned, eyes closed, coin tossed with your right hand over your left shoulder.

Vatican City & Borgo

The Vatican City sits across the river to the northwest of the historic centre. Officially it's an independent sovereign state – the world's smallest, with an area of 44 hectares – but in practice it's more like a city neighbourhood. It's also one of Rome's most visited areas, home to priceless treasures and revered masterpieces, many housed in St Peter's Basilica, the Vatican Museums and Sistine Chapel.

A short walk from St Peter's Square, Castel Sant'Angelo looms over the quaint Borgo district. Originally, this was a much larger medieval quarter, but much of it was destroyed in 1936 to make way for Via della Conciliazione.

TRIDENTE'S BEST SHOPS

Bomba: Designer Cristina Bomba's atelier creates gorgeous pieces that hit the wallet hard but are oh so worth it.

Artisanal Cornucopia: Jewellery, handbags and homeware are for sale at this stylish independent boutique on Via dell'Oca.

Borsalino: On Piazza del Popolo, Borsalino showcases headwear for both men and women, selling classic and newer models.

Fabriano: Fabriano stocks stylish stationery, including delightful leather-bound journals and notebooks, at its store in Via del Babuino.

c.u.c.i.n.a.: If you've always dreamed of owning a *caffettiera* and other Italian kitchen essentials, then this is the place for you.

 EATING AROUND TRIDENTE & TREVI: OUR PICKS

Colline Emiliane: Regional delicacies of Emilia-Romagna, according to what's in season. *12.45-2.45pm & 7.30-10.45pm Tue-Sat* €€

Hostaria Romana: A textbook Italian *trattoria* serving up delicious Roman classics. *12.30-3pm & 7.15-11pm, closed Sun & Mon lunch* €€

Il Chianti: Enjoy Tuscan classics, from soups to steaks, or select pizzas at this ivy-clad location. *noon-1am* €€

Da Edy: A chic restaurant, with high-ceilinged interiors and painting-covered walls. *noon-3pm & 6.30-11pm Mon-Sat* €€

Vatican Museums

The Vatican Museums claim more masterpieces than some countries, and with 7km of exhibition halls, they are rightly considered one of the world's greatest art museums. While exploring the entire complex would take several days, even a single visit is sure to leave you star-struck as you take in its never-ending collection of world-famous artworks, culminating in Michelangelo's frescoes in the Sistine Chapel.

ANTON_IVANOV/SHUTTERSTOCK

Galleria delle Carte Geografiche

Must-See Treasures

Start your explorations by heading to the **Pinacoteca**, often overlooked but full of treasures, among them a trio of works by Raphael, Leonardo da Vinci's *San Gerolamo* and Caravaggio's moving *Deposizione*.

The ground-floor **Museo Pio-Clementino** houses classical sculptures, and many top pieces are found in the Cortile Ottagono, including the *Laocoön* and *Apollo Belvedere*. Elsewhere, the Sala delle Muse houses the famous *Torso Belvedere*, while the Sala Rotonda displays the towering bronze *Hercules*.

The Simonetti staircase leads up to the popular **Galleria delle Carte Geografiche**, a 120m-long corridor adorned with Renaissance topographic maps. The so-called **Stanze di Raffaello**, once part of Pope Julius II's private apartments, astounds, with its frescoes by Raphael and his pupils, including *La Scuola di Atene* and scenes of Constantine.

They're a fitting prelude to the grand finale – the inimitable **Sistine Chapel**. Start by gazing at Michelangelo's ceiling from the east wall, then take in the *Last Judgement* on the western wall and the side frescoes of Moses and Christ. Just remember photography is strictly forbidden in the Sistine Chapel. Time wise, allow at least three hours to cover the Vatican Museum's highlights.

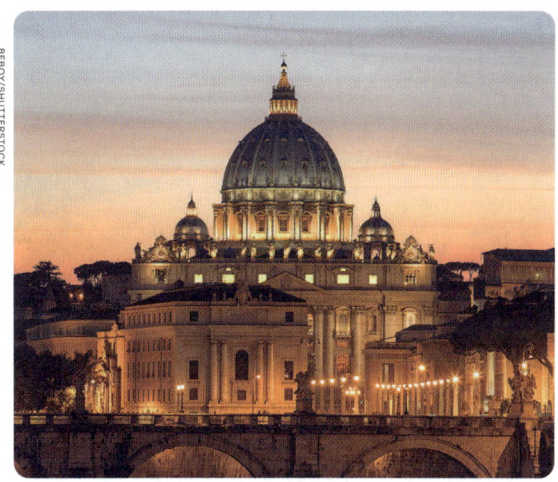

BEBOY/SHUTTERSTOCK

Vatican City (p175)

Make a pilgrimage to St Peter's

St Peter's Basilica *(basilicasanpietro.va)* is the pinnacle of Rome's artistic and architectural brilliance. Built over St Peter's supposed burial site, Constantine's 4th-century church gave way to the current basilica, consecrated in 1626. Inside lies Michelangelo's hauntingly beautiful *Pietà,* a red floor disc marking Charlemagne's coronation spot, and Bernini's towering baldachin, soaring beneath Michelangelo's 133m-tall dome. Don't miss the bronze statue of St Peter, its foot worn smooth by centuries of pilgrims' caresses. Dress modestly (cover shoulders and knees), and plan to visit at lunch or late afternoon to avoid the longest lines. To the right of the main portico is entry to the dome, which offers magnificent views of the city.

Scale a mighty fortress

With its distinctive round keep, **Castel Sant'Angelo** *(castel santangelo.beniculturali.it; adult/reduced €16/2)* is an immediately recognisable landmark. Built as a mausoleum for Emperor Hadrian, it was converted into a papal fortress in the 6th century. Nowadays it houses a fascinating collection of paintings, sculpture, military memorabilia and medieval firearms. Many of these weapons were used by soldiers fighting to protect the castle, which is linked to the Vatican by a 13th-century passageway, the Passetto di Borgo.

VATICAN CURIOSITIES

The Vatican is quite the curious place, besides being a repository for some of the world's greatest artworks. It might be a tiny pocket of Rome, but officially it's an independent state, the world's smallest, complete with its own flag, army (the Swiss Guards), postage stamps, licence plates and, of course, head of state (the pope). And another thing – while Italian is widely spoken throughout the Vatican, Latin is technically the official state language. That means that if you want to withdraw some money at a Vatican ATM, you will find Latin among the possible language options.

EATING IN VATICAN CITY, BORGO & AROUND: OUR PICKS

Bonci Pizzarium: Some of Rome's best sliced pizza, served with tonnes of creative toppings. *11am-11pm Tue-Sat, 11am-3pm & 5-11pm Sun* €

Il Sorpasso: A popular spot in Prati, serving everything from salads to pizza to *trapizzini* (pizza pockets). *9am-1am Mon-Fri, 9.30am-1am Sat* €€

Osteria dell'Angelo: Authentic neighbourhood *trattoria* offering fixed-price menus. *12.30-2.30pm & 7.30-11pm Mon-Fri, 7.30-11pm Sat* €€

L'Arcangelo: Treading the line between informal and chic, this restaurant enjoys a stellar local reputation. *7.15-10.45pm Mon-Sat* €€€

COBBLESTONES & PIETRE D'INCIAMPO

It pays to look down as you're walking your way through Trastevere, and not just because its oh-so-picturesque cobblestones can be notoriously treacherous and slippery, especially when wet. But among the regular cobblestones, you will sometimes find gilded *pietre d'inciampo* (stumbling stones). Every single one of these bronze squares is engraved with the name of a Jewish Roman citizen and marks the spot where he or she was rounded up by Nazi troops during WWII and deported to one of the Reich's concentration camps. More than 1000 Jewish residents were forcibly removed from their homes, and many of the stones appear in a group with several others – marking where entire families were taken.

Pincio Hill, Villa Borghese

Museum highlights include the papal apartments on level five and the terrace, immortalised by Puccini in his opera *Tosca*, from where you can enjoy a truly spectacular view over Rome.

Trastevere

On the left bank of the Tiber – hence the name *trans Tevere*, 'across the Tiber' – Trastevere is one of Rome's most attractive areas, an endlessly photogenic pocket of cobbled lanes, medieval piazzas and ochre, ivy-clad *palazzi*. It's beautiful any time of day but really comes into its own at night when street sellers set up camp on its picturesque alleyways and crowds swarm to its many restaurants, bars and cafes.

This beauty and carnival-like atmosphere has made it popular with visiting students and foreign home buyers. But while gentrification has undeniably changed the area, it hasn't eradicated its unique character.

Ponder medieval mosaics

The **Basilica di Santa Maria in Trastevere** is one of Rome's oldest churches dedicated to the Virgin Mary. Tradition places its founding in the 3rd century, though the current building

Located right in the heart of Trastevere.

 EATING IN TRASTEVERE: OUR PICKS

Tonnarello: Always packed but rightfully so, since it serves up all the delicious staples of Roman cuisine. *11am-11pm* €€

Da Enzo: Tiny *trattoria* with a menu made from locally sourced Lazio ingredients. *12.15-3pm & 7-11pm Mon-Sat* €€

Osteria Nannarella: A great place to sit down and enjoy everything from carbonara to fried artichokes. *11.30am-11.30pm* €€

Trattoria da Teo: A textbook *trattoria* that's perfect for digging into platefuls of Roman standards. *12.30-3pm & 7.30-11.30pm Mon-Sat* €€

– featuring 24 Roman columns from the Baths of Caracalla and stunning medieval mosaics – is a 12th-century rebuild. The portico was added at the beginning of the 18th century, with various pieces of Roman marble forming another informal mosaic to echo those found inside. Legend holds the basilica stands atop a miraculous oil fountain, marked inside near the altar, though scholars suggest it may have been a polluted water source. To catch the mosaics in the best light, visit early morning or late afternoon.

Treasure-hunt at a flea market

Every city needs its own giant flea market, and the **Mercato di Porta Portese** fills that role for Rome. With more than 500 stalls selling everything from secondhand clothes and everyday home stuff to antiques, paintings, books and picture frames, the sprawling open-air market takes over the area around Porta Portese every Sunday morning. While undoubtedly chaotic, it's the perfect way to truly immerse yourself in the local atmosphere of Trastevere.

Villa Borghese

For a leisurely stroll, a family bike ride or an outdoor yoga class, **Villa Borghese** is the place. The gateway to Rome's affluent northern suburbs, it's the city's central park – an 80-hectare oasis of shadowy glades, gardens and grassy banks. Among its attractions is a small boating lake, the Giardino del Lago; a panoramic viewing terrace on the Pincio Hill; and several excellent museums, including the superlative Museo e Galleria Borghese.

Schmooze with the masters

Set in a lavishly decorated villa, the **Museo e Galleria Borghese** *(galleriaborghese.beniculturali.it; adult/reduced €17/4)* boasts some of the city's greatest Renaissance and baroque masterpieces. Among them are Bernini's *Apollo e Dafne* and *Ratto di Proserpina,* not to mention Canova's daring depiction of Napoleon's sister, Paolina Bonaparte Borghese, as *Venere vincitrice.* Caravaggio dominates Sala VIII with six intense canvases, including his much-loved *Giovane col Canestro di Frutta.* Upstairs, Titian's early masterpiece *Amor Sacro e Amor Profano* is one of the museum's most prized works. Tickets must be booked in advance, with timed-entry ensuring you can savour the highlights sans the hordes. Bring photo ID.

GOFFREDO MAMELI

The Palazzo Corsini was the theatre of one of the most violent battles of the Siege of Rome of 1849 – and among the many soldiers who were fatally wounded was a poet and patriot named Goffredo Mameli, barely in his early 20s. His compositions included the 1847 'Canto degli Italiani', literally 'Song of the Italians'. His fellow patriot Michele Novaro arranged it into music, and that song is now known as the 'Inno di Mameli', or 'Hymn of Mameli' – Italy's national anthem, recognised as provisional in 1946 and made official in 2017. While Mameli's original text includes six verses and a refrain, the anthem is performed by repeating the first verse twice and adding the refrain at the end of the second repetition.

DRINKING IN TRASTEVERE: OUR PICKS

Ma Che Siete Venuti a Fà: A paradise for beer lovers, with a wide selection of beers on tap and by the bottle. *11am-2am*

Meccanismo: Cool, hip and good at any time of day, from morning coffee to afternoon tea or late-evening cocktails. *8am-2am*

Freni e Frizioni: Cool, lively and with a young crowd. Ideal for an afternoon *aperitivo* or post-dinner cocktail. *6.30pm-2am*

Bar San Calisto: Packed with locals at every hour of the day and night. Come here for a taste of authentic Trastevere. *6am-2am*

Northern Italy

ICONIC CHURCHES | OPULENT PALACES | STUNNING HIKES

Places

TOP TIP

If you plan on buying Murano glass, beware of foreign-made imposters. As a rule of thumb, if it's not expensive, it's probably not made locally (expect to pay upwards of €35 for a single handblown tumbler). Certified artisans are listed on *muranoglass.com* and display 'Vetro Artistico Murano' labels.

Italy's well-heeled north is the country at its most powerful and creatively charged. Home to names like Missoni, Maserati and Kartell, it's here that Italian style, creativity and flair reach their enviable zenith, shaping trends across the world. Its biggest city, Milan, is the country at its sharpest and chicest – a place where past and future collide with spectacular effect. Celebs and mere mortals sigh collectively over villa-flanked Lago di Como, while others fall madly for Liguria's wilder, equally stunning Cinque Terre. Do you feast in mouthwatering Bologna, museum hop in orderly Turin, or catch a summer opera in Verona's ancient Roman arena? Then, of course, there's the fairest of them all: Venice. The world's most improbable masterpiece, no city quite blurs the line between reality and fantasy like this one. Tread lightly and respectfully, and it promises to reward you with its own extraordinary treasures.

Cinque Terre

Clinging like timeworn citadels to Liguria's precipitous coast, Cinque Terre – namely Riomaggiore, Manarola, Corniglia, Vernazza and Monterosso al Mare – are five diminutive fishing villages linked by a network of ancient cliff-side footpaths that are

---

🧭 GETTING AROUND

Spanning several regions – including Lombardy, Piedmont, Liguria and the Veneto – northern Italy is well served by trains, buses and tolled *autostrade* (freeways). Frequent high-speed services link Turin and Milan with Verona, Venice, Bologna and cities further south, while *regionale* (regional) trains and buses connect smaller towns.

Milan and Venice are major international gateways, with airports offering domestic and global connections. Outside urban areas, driving can be rewarding, but Liguria's cliffside roads are not for the faint-hearted, especially in summer.

Within cities, public transport – including buses, metro lines, trams, and in Venice, *vaporetti* (passenger ferries) – makes getting around easy. For short distances, walking remains the most convenient option.

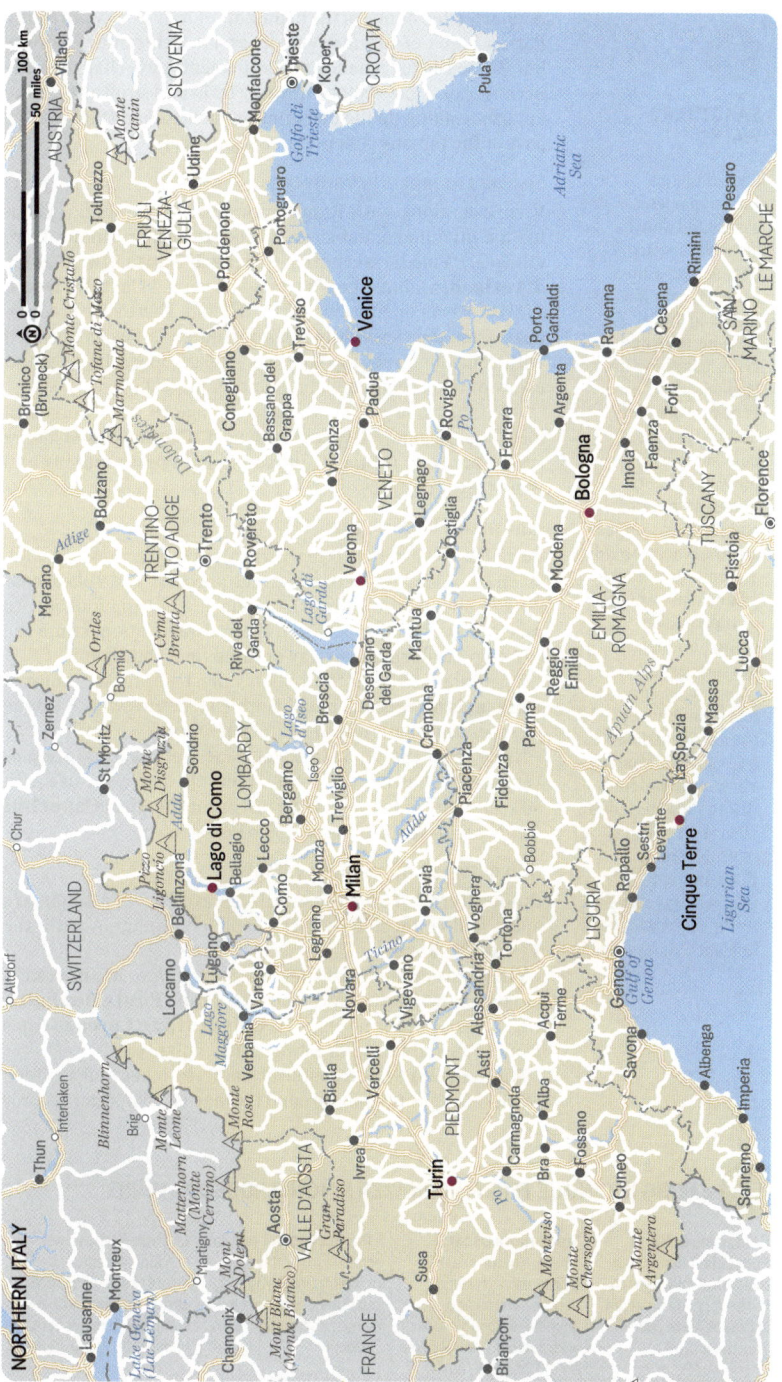

NORTHERN ITALY

100 km

50 miles

SANCTUARY WALKS

Each of Cinque Terre's villages is associated with a medieval sanctuary bequeathed with a holy Marian icon. Reaching these religious retreats, high in the hills above the Mediterranean, used to be part of a hefty Catholic penance but, these days, the walks through terraced vineyards and soporific villages are a heavenly reward in themselves. All the pilgrimages involve a little climbing on well-trodden but surprisingly uncrowded trails and each church has its own features and nuances, from Vernazza's **Madonna di Reggio** on the edge of an ancient wood, to the **Madonna di Montenero** perched high above Riomaggiore with brilliant coastal views.

regularly cited as one of the highlights of Italy. It's a valid claim. Bar an influx of summer visitors and a 19th-century railway line, these ruggedly handsome settlements have changed little in centuries. Most visitors arrive by train and stroll around the villages soaking up the maritime ambience. Some tackle all or part of the famous Green-Blue walking trail.

Fish and focaccia in Vernazza

Vernazza, along with Riomaggiore, is imbued with a genuine fishing village ambience. Unlike the other Cinque Terre villages, its medieval church, **Chiesa di Santa Margherita d'Antiochia**, abuts the water, and its ruined **Castello Doria** (tickets €2) is open to visitors (although there's little to see apart from the views). Main thoroughfare Via Visconti is lined with delicious street-food options – gelato, focaccia slices and cones of fried seafood – and one-of-a-kind shops.

Vernazza is, arguably, the best village to get involved in local cooking and tasting experiences. **Cinque Sensi** (5sensivernazza.com; from €50) offers excellent pesto-making and wine-tasting classes.

Find peace in Corniglia

Corniglia is the only village with no direct sea access, although steep steps lead down to a picturesque cove. The village consists of one narrow street that ends at a clifftop lookout. To reach the village proper from the railway station, climb the 377-step Lardarina stairway or jump on a shuttle bus.

Corniglia harbours the region's most impressive church, **Chiesa San Pietro**, a small Gothic structure with baroque frescoes and sombre 18th-century paintings.

Aside from the popular Green-Blue trail heading west to Vernazza, you can hike east to Manarola on free-to-use path 583. En route, don't miss wine tasting at **Cantina Cappelini** (cantinacapellini.it) just outside Volastra.

Hop between the eastern villages

Cinque Terre's two closest villages are barely a kilometre apart and connected by a strollable cliff-hugging path, the **Via dell'Amore**.

Vineyards cram narrow terraces high above **Manorola**, a village known for its cafes and panoramic **Punta Bonfiglio**. On Piazzale Papa Innocenzo IV, **Chiesa di San Lorenzo** dates from 1338 and houses a 15th-century polyptych.

Riomaggiore has a couple of small churches and a ruined castle. Most people hang around the marina, where multistorey

EATING IN CINQUE TERRE: VERNAZZA & MONTEROSSO AL MARE

Il Massimo della Focaccia: Monterosso beachfront bakery with the best crispy focaccia in Cinque Terre. *9am-7pm Thu-Tue* €

Trattoria da Oscar: Tiny family-run joint in Monterosso's historic centre; outstanding anchovies, *vongole* (clams) and gnocchi. *noon-2.30pm & 7-9.30pm Sat-Thu* €€

Il Porticciolo: All-natural gelato in fruity flavours, including Greek yoghurt and honey, right next to Vernazza's harbour. *10am-7.30pm* €

La Torre: Handsome outdoor restaurant beside an old watchtower high above Vernazza with a steep climb to get here. *noon-4pm & 6.30-10pm* €€

Chiesa di Santa Margherita d'Antiochia, Vernazza

pastel houses glow romantically at sunset. This is the best place in Cinque Terre to rent a kayak or organise a diving or snorkelling excursion. A short walk to the east brings you to pebbly, wave-battered **Spiaggia di Fossola**.

Kayak the coast

Laced with caves and beaches, some of them only accessible by boat, Cinque Terre lends itself to the pulse-raising pursuit of sea-kayaking. When the weather is cooperating, it's possible to paddle into the harbours of all five towns in one day. Riomaggiore is the best launch point and has a reliable rental point, **Cinque Terre Adventure** *(cinqueterreadventure.com; kayak rental 1/2hr €10/20)*, in the marina. For extra safety and insider knowledge, join a guided trip.

Turin

Turin has abundant history moving through its streets and sailing down its river, the mighty Po. What was once a small settlement of the Taurini people in the 3rd century BCE became a Roman colony first and a Renaissance duchy after. But most of Turin's current look comes from the 19th and 20th centuries: grand royal palaces in the city centre, which speak to its former status as a capital of the Kingdom of Italy and seat of the country's royal family, and industrial suburbs

PARCO NAZIONALE DELLE CINQUE TERRE INFO

The whole Cinque Terre area is part of the **Parco Nazionale delle Cinque Terre** *(parconazionale 5terre.it)*. Park authorities maintain the various hiking trails that surround the five villages and preserve the surrounding seas, which are included in a protected marine area. The park's useful website is worth visiting when you are planning your trip, and there are also information points at each Cinque Terre train station and in La Spezia. Check out the two options for the Cinque Terre Card ahead of your visit. Opt for the Trekking Card if you just want to hike on the SVA between the villages, and the Treno MS Card if you want to also include unlimited train travel.

 EATING IN CINQUE TERRE: CORNIGLIA

Ristorante Cecio: Large portions of risotto, pasta and fish served by charismatic staff who treat you like family. *noon-3pm & 6.30-10pm* €€

Alberto Gelateria: Often touted as offering the best ice cream in the five villages, using local herbs to augment its fruity flavours. *9am-10pm* €

Pan e Vin: Friendly staff serve hearty breakfasts, focaccia sandwiches, wine and the best Nutella cake on the Riviera. *7am-8pm Fri-Wed* €

Enoteca Il Pirun: Spread across two floors of an old village house, this trad *trattoria* offers earthy Cinque Terre classics. *noon-3pm & 7-10pm* €€

THE HOLY SHROUD

Don't expect to see the Holy Shroud when you visit the **Cattedrale di San Giovanni Battista** – it's usually kept locked inside a very specific case to prevent any damage, and pilgrims can only stop in front of the chapel that houses it. The Shroud is, however, exhibited to the public at irregular intervals – with years potentially separating them, considering the last ones were in 2013, 2015, 2020 and 2021, with some of the viewings only being via TV. These are always announced beforehand on its official website (*sindone.org*). If you happen to visit around the time of an *ostensione* (showing) and want to take advantage, prepare for some considerable queues.

Palazzo Reale, Turin

dating back to when Turin was one of the engines behind Italy's modernisation process.

Tap into the city of kings

The **Palazzo Reale** *(museireali.beniculturali.it; full/reduced €15/2)* was once the official residence of the House of Savoy. Close by is **Palazzo Madama**, also used by members of the royal family as a residence. Both palaces are museums in their own right, but also host exhibitions. Passing through the Palazzo Reale's courtyards will lead you to the relaxing **Giardini Reali**.

Just off the side of the Palazzo Reale, the **Cattedrale di San Giovanni Battista** contains the **Chapel of the Holy Shroud**, which houses the famous Shroud of Turin, believed to be the cloth used to wrap the body of Jesus Christ after his crucifixion.

Piazza-hop *alla torinese*

The quickest way to gain a sense of Turin's atmosphere is to get lost in the perfectly parallel, grid-like streets of its city centre. Linger in its piazzas, like **Piazza Statuto** – not too far from the Porta Susa railway station – or the sprawling

EATING IN TURIN: OUR PICKS

Barbagusto: Tiny, cosy and featuring a menu bursting with all the delicacies the Piedmontese culinary tradition has to offer. *12.30-3.30pm & 7.30-10pm Wed-Sat, 7.30-10pm Sun €*

Osteria Antiche Sere: Your textbook Turin restaurant in both looks and food, on a quiet street away from the most beaten tourist tracks. *7.30-10.30pm Mon-Sat €€*

Pasticceria Ghigo: This incredibly *torinese* cafe is perfect for sitting under the Via Po porticoes. Try their *nuvola*, a little *pandoro* (sweet bread) that's renowned throughout the city. *7.30am-8pm €€*

Vintage 1997: Enjoy a Michelin-starred meal at this elegant place. Tasting menus include local dishes and quirkier creations. *12.30-2.30pm & 8-11pm Mon-Thu, 12.30-2.30pm & 7.30-11pm Fri, 7.30-11pm Sat €€€*

Piazza Vittorio Veneto, or the tiny **Piazza Carlo Emanuele II**, which locals know as 'Piazza Carlina'.

Getting from one to the other is simple, thanks to Turin's porticoes. When put together, the city's monumental porticoes are almost 20km long, lining the major avenues of its centre and allowing people to be outside even when the weather isn't the nicest.

Enjoy a museum day

Rainy days are the perfect occasion to explore one of Turin's many museums. History buffs can head to the **Museo Nazionale del Risorgimento Italiano** *(museorisorgimento torino.it; full/reduced €10/8),* housed inside the magnificent **Palazzo Carignano**, or the nearby **Museo Egizio** *(museo egizio.it; full/reduced €18/3),* which hosts the second-largest collection of Egyptian antiquities after the one in Cairo. If you prefer cinema, then head to the **Museo Nazionale del Cinema** *(museocinema.it; full/reduced €16/14),* located inside the skyline-defining **Mole Antonelliana**.

For something a little different, car lovers should try the **Museo Nazionale dell'Automobile** *(museoauto.com; full/ reduced €15/12)* a few kilometres outside the city centre.

Milan

MAP p186

Milan is an industrial powerhouse, a fashion capital and global trendsetter in architecture and design. The birthplace of Prada and Alfa Romeo, Italy's wealthiest city continues to nurture innovation, but for many residents its finest attributes have nothing at all to do with financial clout or iconic labels. This is a place of countless, only-in-Milan experiences. It's sinking into a red velvet chair and waiting for the curtain to rise at La Scala. Or enjoying a balmy summer evening at a canal-side cafe while watching the world stroll past, wandering through a provocative art installation or happening upon a glowing Duomo at sunset.

Watch the curtain rise at La Scala

One of the most famous opera stages in the world, **La Scala** *(teatroallascala.org)* is where Maria Callas made her debut, Verdi triumphed and Toscanini established his legacy as a virtuoso conductor. Sitting in the crimson and gilt boxes of Teatro alla Scala among the Milanese dressed to impress is one of those moments you won't forget. The opera season kicks off on 7 December, the day of Sant'Ambrose – Milan's patron saint – and it typically runs until mid-July. If you're not a fan

LOCAL DRINKS

If you want to truly take a sip of Turin, then you can't leave the city without having tried two of its most typical drinks. First up is the *bicerin* (quite literally 'small glass' in the local dialect), a shot of espresso carefully layered with chocolate and milk. Try it at **Caffè al Bicerin**, where it was supposedly invented at the beginning of the 18th century. Then there's vermouth, an aromatised and fortified wine whose modern version was first produced right here in Turin around the same time the *bicerin* was invented. It's usually drunk as an *aperitivo,* even though you'll find that a good number of the city's cafes serve it around the clock.

EATING NEAR MILAN'S DUOMO: OUR PICKS

MAP p186

Trattoria Milanese: Generous goblets of wine, hearty servings of traditional Milanese (try pan-fried risotto). *noon-2.30pm & 7-10.30pm Mon-Fri* €€

Peck: Restaurant and deli; Milanese specialities like *osso buco* (veal and vegetables in broth) and *mondeghili* (meatballs) with chicory. *9am-7.30pm Tue-Sat, from 3pm Mon* €€

Rinascente Food Hall: On the 7th floor of Rinascente department store; excellent options include Il Bar, with Duomo views. *10am-midnight* €€

Il Marchese: A beautiful courtyard and photogenic bar, with decadent dining on Roman specialities like pasta carbonara. *12.30pm-2am* €€€

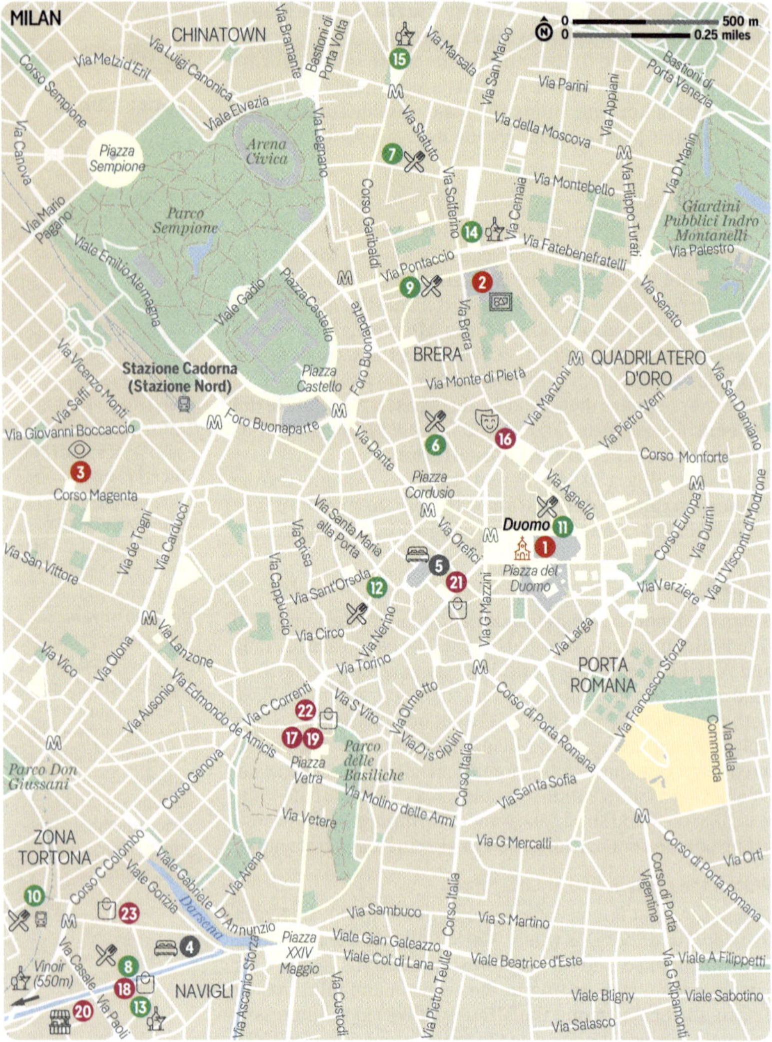
MILAN
0 500 m
0 0.25 miles
CHINATOWN
Via Melzi d'Eril
Via Luigi Canonica
Corso Sempione
Viale Elvezia
Via Bramante
Bastioni di Porta Volta
Via Marsala
Via San Marco
Via Parini
Bastioni di Porta Venezia
Via Canova
Piazza Sempione
Arena Civica
Via Legnano
Via Statuto
Via della Moscova
Via Appiani
Via Mario Pagano
Parco Sempione
Corso Garibaldi
Via Solferino
Via Cernaia
Via Montebello
Via Filippo Turati
Via D Manin
Giardini Pubblici Indro Montanelli
Via Palestro
Viale Emilio Alemagna
Via Fatebenefratelli
Via Pontaccio
Viale Gadio
Piazza Castello
Foro Buonaparte
Via Brera
Via Senato
Via Vincenzo Monti
Stazione Cadorna (Stazione Nord)
Piazza Castello
BRERA
QUADRILATERO D'ORO
Via Monte di Pietà
Via Manzoni
Via San Damiano
Via Saffi
Via Giovanni Boccaccio
Via Dante
Via Pietro Verri
Corso Monforte
Corso Magenta
Piazza Cordusio
Via Agnello
Via de Togni
Via Carducci
Via Santa Maria alla Porta
Via Orefici
Duomo
Corso Europa
Via Durini
Via U Visconti di Modrone
Via San Vittore
Via Brisa
Piazza del Duomo
Via Cappuccio
Via Sant'Orsola
Via Verziere
Via G Mazzini
Via Circo
Via Nerino
Via Lanzone
Via Larga
Via Vico
Via Olona
Via Torino
PORTA ROMANA
Via Ausonio
Via Edmondo de Amicis
Via C Correnti
Via Olmetto
Via S Vito
Via Disciplini
Corso di Porta Romana
Via Francesco Sforza
Via della Commenda
Parco Don Giussani
Piazza Vetra
Parco delle Basiliche
Corso Genova
Corso Italia
Via Santa Sofia
Via Molino delle Armi
Via Vetere
ZONA TORTONA
Via G Mercalli
Corso C Colombo
Viale Gorizia
Viale Gabriele D'Annunzio
Via Arena
Darsena
Corso di Porta Romana
Via Orti
Corso di Porta Vigentina
Via Sambuco
Via S Martino
Corso Italia
Piazza XXIV Maggio
Viale Gian Galeazzo
Viale Col di Lana
Viale Beatrice d'Este
Via Casale
Vinoir (550m)
Via Ascanio Sforza
Via Pietro Teulié
Viale A Filippetti
NAVIGLI
Via Custodi
Via G Ripamonti
Viale Bligny
Viale Sabotino
Via Paoli
Via Salasco

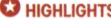

HIGHLIGHTS
1 Duomo

SIGHTS
2 Pinacoteca di Brera
3 The Last Supper

SLEEPING
4 Maison Borella
5 Spadari al Duomo

EATING
6 Il Marchese
7 Le Tre Regioni
8 Luca & Andrea
9 Osteria da Fortunata
10 Osteria del Binari
11 Rinascente Food Hall
12 Trattoria Milanese

DRINKING & NIGHTLIFE
13 Mag Cafè
14 N'Ombra de Vin
15 Radetzky Cafe

ENTERTAINMENT
16 Teatro alla Scala

SHOPPING
17 Cavalli e Nastri Uomo
18 Dischivolanti
19 Frip
20 Mercatone dell'Antiquariato
21 Peck
22 Scout
23 Tenoha

Duomo, Milan

LA SCALA TICKETS

Tickets with a full view of the stage typically cost from €65 to €320. Buy tickets online or from the box office up to four months before the performance. The box office also sells discounted same-day tickets, available online two hours before the performance or from the box office one hour before opening.

Keep in mind that the cheapest seats (which can start at €10) may be partial or no view. Located in the highest galleries, you'll either be forced to stand or crane your neck just to put a face to those angelic voices. But you'll still get to revel in the butterflies-inducing energy of a performance at La Scala – at an unbeatable price.

of operatic glory, you can also see theatre, ballet and classical-music concerts here year-round (except during August).

Swoon over the Duomo

Milan's pink-marble **Duomo** *(duomomilano.it)* was begun by Giangaleazzo Visconti in 1387. Canals were dug to transport the vast quantities of marble, and new technologies invented to cater for the never-before-attempted scale. During his stint as king of Italy, Napoleon offered to fund its completion in 1805. Neo-Gothic details were piled on – the petrified pinnacles, cusps, buttresses, arches and more than 3000 statues are almost all 19th-century additions.

Inside, stare up, and up, to the enormous stained-glass windows, with 144 panes illuminating stories from the Bible. Climbing to the roof terraces, you'll be within touching distance of the elaborate 135 spires and their forest of flying buttresses. The good-value €22 combination ticket covers the cathedral, roof terraces and more.

Trawl the Pinacoteca

Upstairs from Brera Academy, the **Pinacoteca di Brera** *(pinac otecabrera.org)* houses Milan's impressive collection of old masters, much of it 'lifted' by Napoleon during his Italian campaigns.

EATING & DRINKING IN BRERA: OUR PICKS

MAP p186

Le Tre Regioni: Tiny family-run deli – compile a delicious sandwich from quality cold cuts and Lombard cheeses. *7.30am-8pm Mon-Sat* €

Radetzky Cafe: Fabulous banquette and window seating on a stylish, pedestrianised strip make it popular for an *aperitivo*. *8am-2am* €€

N'Ombra de Vin: Atmospheric former Augustine refectory with top wines, meat boards and tapas-style dishes. *10am-midnight Mon-Wed, to 1am Thu-Sat, 6pm-midnight Sun* €€

Osteria da Fortunata: Go early to beat the long lines at this perennially popular spot, famed for its homemade pasta. *noon-12.30am* €€

BOUTIQUES & INDIE SHOPS

Running directly south of the Duomo, the Via Torino chain shops gradually morph into the city's hippest streetwear strip, Corso di Porta Ticinese.

Frip: The small boutique is a showcase for avant-garde fashion, from cutting-edge to more subtle designs.

Cavalli e Nastri Uomo: A beautifully curated collection of vintage menswear. The women's store is across the street.

Dischivolanti: This canal-side shop is a must for vinyl lovers, with a great selection of classic and hard-to-find LPs.

Tenoha: Direct from Tokyo, this Japanese concept store features beautiful objects for home and wardrobe, plus a stylish restaurant and bar.

Scout: Affordable, attractive and well-made basics by the well-known Italian retailer.

Rembrandt, Goya and van Dyck are included, but you're here to see the Italians: Titian, Tintoretto, Veronese and the Bellini brothers. Much of the work has tremendous emotional clout, notably Mantegna's brutal *Lamentation over the Dead Christ*. Allow several hours to cover 38 rooms at a reasonable pace. Among the highlights is Room IX, a showcase of Venetian Renaissance masters. Don't miss Caravaggio's *Cena in Emmaus* (Supper at Emmaus) in Room XXVIII, or the Rubens, Van Dyck and Jan Fyt paintings in Rooms XXXI and XXXIII.

Attend the Last Supper

Milan's most famous painting, Leonardo da Vinci's **The Last Supper** *(cenacolovinciano.org/en),* is hidden away on a wall of the refectory adjoining the Basilica di Santa Maria delle Grazie. Depicting the moment when Jesus drops the bomb of his impending betrayal, the mixed reactions of his disciples rendered through their gestures and expressions – what da Vinci described as 'motions of the soul' – are utterly enthralling. The illusion of a 3D space created by various tricks of perspective only adds to the image's realism. Online reservations are released quarterly (mid-March for June, July or August visits); tickets go quickly. If sold out, book a **Viator city tour** *(from €80),* which guarantees a visit.

Hang out by the canals

Milan was once laced with waterways that da Vinci himself had a hand in developing. Sadly, in the 1930s the fascist regime closed them for supposed hygiene reasons and to accommodate the increasing number of cars. Now you can have a drink on the photogenic **Naviglio Grande** and **Naviglio Pavese**, and imagine what might have been. Naviglio Grande is *the* place for *aperitivo* and on Saturday nights it feels like the whole city is here. On the last Sunday of the month, it hosts the **Mercatone dell'Antiquariato** *(navigliogrande.mi.it),* a sprawling antiques market.

Lago di Como

Set in the shadow of the snow-covered Rhaetian Alps and hemmed in on both sides by steep, verdant hillsides, Lago di Como (aka Lake Lario) is spectacular. Shaped like an upside-down Y, the lake is littered with villages, including exquisite Bellagio. Where the southern and western shores converge is the lake's main town, Como, an elegant, prosperous city that was once a powerful rival of Milan. Among the area's siren

EATING & DRINKING IN NAVIGLI: OUR PICKS

MAP p186

Luca & Andrea: Tiny place overlooking the canal. Chalkboard menu of classic fare with standouts like *osso buco* and summer pastas. *8am-2am* €€

Osteria del Binari: Bedrock of quality Milanese fare with a Liberty Style design interior and garden terrace. *7am-3pm & 7.30pm-1am* €€

MAG Cafe: Canal-side cocktails crafted with curious herbs and syrups, served in vintage glassware by knowledgeable barkeeps. *9am-2am*

Vinoir: Small, spare bar at Navigli Grande's quieter end, harbouring unusual natural wines and delicious small plates. *noon-3pm & 5pm-midnight*

Bellagio and Lago di Como

calls are extraordinarily sumptuous villas, often graced with gardens bursting with plant and animal life. The mountainous terrain provides numerous opportunities for bird's-eye views of the lake. Prepare to swoon.

Ride the cable car to Brunate

The 1894 **Funicolare Como–Brunate** (*funicolarecomo.it; one way €3.60*) takes seven minutes to trundle up to the quiet hilltop village of **Brunate** (720m), revealing a memorable perspective of mountains and lakes. Once at the Brunate funicular stop, continue to nearby baroque **Chiesa di San Andrea**. With its faded pink exterior and giant bell peeking out of the tower, it's hard to miss. If you want to keep going, allow another 30 minutes or so for the steep walk (1.3km) up to **San Maurizio**. There you can scale 143 steps to the base of **Faro di Volta**, a lighthouse built in 1927 to mark the centenary of the physicist Alessandro Volta's death.

Fall in love with Bellagio

Flanked by blue waters and lined with villas, cypress groves, oleanders and lime trees, **Bellagio** lives up to its moniker as the 'pearl' of Lago di Como. From the port, wander up the stony stairs of Salita Serbelloni, stopping to peruse the wine and silk shops. At Via Garibaldi, if you turn left and walk for

THE VIA FERRATA

Alberto Trombetta, founder of Lake Como Adventures. *@lakecomoadventures*

The *via ferrata* is basically a system of steel cables and ladders secured to a rockface that allows you to safely travel up a steep mountain. Nowadays, there are 15 or so *via ferrata* around Lake Como that provide the next big challenge when it comes to hiking. You'll find all different levels – easy, medium and hard – and *via ferrata* are free and open to all. The only gear you need are the harness and clip system, a helmet and decent hiking shoes. Those who aren't ready to go alone can hire a guide, who can help you find the perfect *via ferrata* for your fitness level.

 EATING & DRINKING IN BELLAGIO: OUR PICKS

Enoteca Cava Turacciolo: Bellagio's most charming wine bar is in a candlelit, stonewalled space down a lane near the waterfront. *noon-11pm Thu-Tue* €

Trattoria San Giacomo: Cosy spot in the heart of town, with reasonably priced homemade pasta and lake fish. *noon-2.30pm & 7-9.30pm Wed-Mon* €€

La Grotta: Satisfying pizzas, pastas and seafood in an understated dining room with vaulted ceilings. *noon-2.30pm & 7-9.30pm Tue-Sun* €€

Dispensa 63: Small, creative, seasonally inspired menu with hits like risotto with scallops and roe. *noon-2pm Thu-Sat & 7-9pm Tue-Sat* €€€

10 minutes you'll hit **Punta Spartivento**, the northernmost tip of the town where there's a swath of green and pretty views. You'll pass the town's brick Romanesque church en route, worth ducking into for its stark simplicity. But the real stars of Bellagio are its **villa gardens**.

Hike Menaggio's ancient pathways

A narrow cobblestone lane that was once part of a Roman road along the western side of Lago di Como has been preserved in sections. The **Antica Strada Regina** traverses wooded greenery, passes through age-old villages and offers fine views over the shoreline – at times from 150m heights. One of the best sections to walk is the 7km stretch (about a three-hour walk) between Menaggio and Rezzonico. If you don't want to walk back, return on the C10 bus (22 minutes).

Verona

Best known for its Shakespeare associations, Verona attracts a multinational gaggle of tourists to its pretty piazzas and knot of lanes, most in search of Romeo and Juliet. But beyond the heart-shaped kitsch and Renaissance romance, it's a bustling city whose centre is dominated by a mammoth, remarkably well-preserved 1st-century amphitheatre, the venue for an annual summer opera festival. Add to that countless churches, a couple of architecturally fascinating bridges, regional wine and food from the Veneto hinterland and some impressive art, and Verona shapes up as one of northern Italy's most attractive cities.

Beyond Romeo and Juliet

Avoid the crowds leaving lovelorn graffiti at **Casa di Giulietta** *(adult/reduced €22/13)* – which some might say is...ahem... much ado about nothing.

Verona's actual teen lovers climb up to the hilltop terraces of **Castel San Pietro** for spectacular views. Art lovers shouldn't miss the **Galleria d'Arte Moderna Achille Forti** *(gam.comune.verona.it; adult/reduced €6/4)*, nor the extraordinary **Palazzo Maffei** *(palazzomaffeiverona.com; adult/reduced €15/13)*, overlooking wonderful **Piazza delle Erbe**.

Veronetta, on the right bank of the Adige, is the authentic part of the city. It's home to the beautiful Renaissance garden **Giardino Giusti** *(giardinogiusti.com; adult/reduced €13/9)* and the striking **Teatro Romano e Museo Archeologico**

EATING IN VERONA: OUR PICKS

Café Carducci: Storied 1920s-style bistro in classic surrounds (mirror-lined interior, linen-topped tables with candles). Exquisite for charcuterie and local cheeses. *8am-3pm & 6-10pm Tue-Sat* €

Hostaria la Vecchia Fontanina: The tables at this historic eatery fill mostly with Italians – a good sign. Excellent food at easy-to-digest prices. *noon-2.30pm & 7-10.30pm Mon-Sat* €

Osteria da Ugo: Back-alley *osteria* with a wonderful courtyard; Veronese specialities are executed with creative flair and smart service. *noon-2.30pm & 7.30-10.30pm Mon & Wed-Sat, noon-2.30pm Sun* €€

Casa Perbellini: World-class, three-star Michelin dining, such as warm spaghetti, lemon, anchovy, chicken and spring-onion emulsion (tasting menus from €220). *12.30-2pm & 7.30-9pm Tue-Fri, 12.30-2pm Sat* €€€

(museoarcheologico.comune.verona.it; adult/reduced €9/6), both worthwhile pit stops.

An arena of arias

The eighth-biggest amphitheatre in the Roman Empire and predating the Colosseum in Rome, the 1st-century **Arena di Verona** *(arena.it; adult/reduced €12/9)* is an engineering marvel. Book tickets online to avoid long queues, then pass through its ancient corridors to re-emerge into the massive, sunlit stone arena (head to the top!).

The arena is at its best during the **Arena di Verona Opera Festival** *(arena.it; tickets €30-365)*, which runs from June to September and draws international stars. There's no need to spring for top-end tickets – the numbered stone steps are fine. Rent a cushion and prepare for an unforgettable evening.

Bologna

Bologna is a city of two intriguing halves. One side is a high-tech city located in the super-rich Po valley, where opera-goers waltz out of regal theatres and into some of Italy's finest restaurants. The other is a bolshie, politically edgy city that hosts the world's oldest university and is famous for its graffiti-embellished piazzas filled with tipsy students.

No wonder Bologna has earned so many historical monikers: *La Grassa* (The Fat One) for its rich food legacy, *La Dotta* (The Learned One) for its university, and *La Rossa* (The Red One), a nod to its medieval terracotta and long-standing penchant for left-wing politics.

A medieval marvel

The foundations of Bologna's forward-thinking ethos were laid in the Middle Ages. Home to the world's oldest continually operating university, founded in 1088, the city welcomed everyone from Dante to Petrarch.

On this day-long sojourn, all roads lead to 13th-century **Piazza Maggiore**, dominated by **Basilica di San Petronio** *(basilicadisanpetronio.org)*. On the western flank is **Palazzo Comunale (Palazzo d'Accursio)**, home to the Bologna city council since 1336 and the **Collezioni Comunali d'Arte** *(museibologna.it; adult/reduced €6/4)*, a collection of 13th- to 19th-century paintings, sculptures and furniture. Head up the attached 13th-century **Torre dell'Orologio** *(Clock Tower; bolognawelcome.com)* for panoramic views, including of the

A DAY OFF IN BOLOGNA

Daniele Bendanti, chef at **Oltre**, one of the city's top modern *trattorias*, shares some insights from his days off in the city. *@d.bendanti*

You can't miss a great breakfast at **Gino Fabbri Pasticcere** *(ginofabbri.com)* in La Caramella, a bit outside Bologna but worth it. Take a nice walk at **Giardini Margherita**, the city park that raised me. Eat something from Alessandro, my meat supplier at **Macelleria Con Cucina Agnoletto Bignami** *(facebook.com/Macelleria.Agnoletto.Bignami)*, and stop for a glass of wine or two at the **Osteria del Sole**. Towards evening, cuddle up with a nice plate of *tagliatelle* at **All'Osteria Bottega** *(osteriabottega.com)*, where I worked as a chef for five years and to which I'm very attached.

 EATING IN BOLOGNA: OUR PICKS

I Panini di Mirò: Friendly Mirò holds court at this glorified food stall with over 50 versions of great-value gourmet *panino* (roast pork, caramelised onions, pecorino). *noon-11pm* €

Delizie Bolognesi: Forging incredible, seasonally driven gelato, often with surprising local ingredients. Try Nettuno (Cervia salt, Bourbon vanilla, Sorrento lemon, orange-scented pistachio brittle). *11am-midnight Tue-Sun* €

Al Sangiovese: A convivial husband-and-wife team as generous with their portions as they are with their hospitality runs this somewhat off-the-beaten-path *trattoria*. *12.15-2.30pm & 7-10.30pm Mon-Sat* €€

Oltre: Trendy Oltre bucks tradition with creative nightly specials, without foregoing outstanding modern takes on classics. *12.30-2.30pm & 7.30-11pm Mon, Sat & Sun, 7.30-11pm Thu & Fri* €€€

SAN MARCO'S BEST SHOPPING

Piedàterre: Stylish, colourful *furlane* (Venetian slippers), hand-stitched by Italian artisans.

Merchant of Venice: Locally inspired perfumes, toiletries and home fragrances sold in a neo-Gothic pharmacy.

Giuliana Longo: A milliner and living institution, crafting everything from fascinators to classic Panamas.

Rubelli: Silk foulards and lavish handbags from a world-renowned textile house.

Chiarastella Cattana: Elegant, understated tablecloths, napkins, tea towels, cushions, robes and more from Venetian textile designer Chiarastella Cattana.

Libreria Linea d'Acqua: A high-end treasure trove of antiquarian books, first editions, maps, sculptures and engravings driven by a genuine love of Venice.

COLLECTION MAYKOVA/SHUTTERSTOCK

Torre degli Asinelli and Torre Garisenda, Bologna

leaning 97.2m-high **Torre degli Asinelli** and its neighbour, **Torre Garisenda**. Finally, there's **Basilica di Santo Stefano** *(santostefanobologna.it),* a labyrinth of interlocking ecclesiastical structures dating to the 11th century.

Taste-test the city

A misnomer, spaghetti *bolognese* is about as Bolognese as Yorkshire pudding, and Bologna's fiercely traditional *trattorias* don't serve it. Instead, the city prides itself on a vastly superior meat-based sauce called *ragù*, which sees slow-cooked minced beef and pork added to a *soffritto* (sautéed onions, celery and carrots), enlivened with a liberal dash of red wine and simmered for hours.

Ragù is one of a long list of renowned specialities birthed in the kitchens of what is arguably Italy's culinary capital, Emilia-Romagna. Lasagne, tortellini, *mortadella* and *passatelli* (pasta made with breadcrumbs, eggs and Parmesan) all hail from here.

It's generally difficult to eat badly in Bologna (though you'll need reservations at the best places, at least a week in advance). At **Trattoria Bertozzi** *(trattoriabertozzibologna.it; meals €30-45),* locals in the know indulge in authentic local

DRINKING IN BOLOGNA: OUR PICKS

Enoteca Storica Faccioli: This storied – if somewhat touristy – *enoteca* features Italy's best natural, organic and biodynamic juice. *4-10pm Mon-Wed, from noon Thu-Sat*

Ruggine: Locally driven craft mixology down a serene alleyway near Piazza Maggiore: house-made shrubs, Venetian aperitifs, Romagnan brandies. *6pm-1am*

Le Serre dei Giardini Margherita: Bologna's unique alfresco bar; a part co-working/event space and vegetarian restaurant immersed in greenery. *8am-midnight Mon-Fri, from 9am Sat & Sun*

Il Punto: Bologna's best and most Italian-focused craft-beer bar, with eight taps and 150 choices by the bottle. *6pm-12.30am Tue & Sun, to 1am Wed-Thu, to 2.30am Fri & Sat*

specialities. And at richly traditional **Al Cambio** *(ristoranteal cambio.it; meals €42-55)* the incredible lasagne is the pinnacle by which all others are judged. Make these your can't-miss meals in Bologna (reservations mandatory).

Walk it all off around the city's old food market, a squared grid of narrow lanes just off the southeast corner of Piazza Maggiore known as the **Quadrilatero**. For a deeper dive into local kitchens, get cooking with **Cesarine** *(cesarine. com; per person €65-214).*

Venice

MAP p194

The French novelist Marcel Proust famously declared: 'When I went to Venice, I discovered that my dream had become – incredibly but quite simply – my address'. In this city of masks, storybook palaces and ghostly winter fogs, the line between reality and fantasy can be very thin indeed.

For over 1000 years, Venice was the capital of the Republic of Venice, a sovereign state which, at its peak, ruled lands as far away as the Peloponnese, Crete and Cyprus. Trading with Asia Minor, Persia and the Mongol Empire, La Serenissima was also one of the world's most cosmopolitan commercial hubs, its *calli* (streets) graced with the silks, spices and languages of distant lands. This melting pot would leave an indelible mark on the city's architecture, cuisine and culture. To this day, these worldly influences are palpable, whether it be in the Islamic flourishes of its Palazzo Ducale or the sweet-and-sour flavour of the city's signature *sarde in saor* (deep-fried sardines).

Eye-up Venice's keepsakes

Taking up most of the Procuratie Nuove and Procuratie Nuovissime (Ala Napoleonica) wings of Piazza San Marco, **Museo Correr** *(correr.visitmuve.it; adult/reduced €14/11)* offers a crash course in Venetian history, with an inventory that includes Doge Francesco Morosini's buff coat and sword.

Part of the 1st floor houses the **Museo Archeologico Nazionale** and its Graeco-Roman relics. If you're pressed for time, skim it and focus instead on Museo Correr's old globes and maps, its extraordinary cache of weapons and trophies from Venetian battles, and the magnificent reading room of the 16th-century **Biblioteca Nazionale Marciana**. Upstairs, the **Pinacoteca** explodes with four centuries of masterpieces, including works by Paolo Veronese.

continued on p197

THE CAPPELLA MARCIANA CHOIR

Marco Bellussi, director and composer. *@bellussiteatro*

Attend Sunday morning mass at the **Basilica di San Marco** (p196) to hear the magnificent Cappella Marciana choir, which has performed at the church for more than 700 years. Occasionally the choir performs works in the Venetian polychoral style, a Renaissance-era technique that sees it split into two 'competing' formations *(cori battenti)*. The architecture is perfectly suited to this stereophonic sound, turning the basilica itself into an instrument. In my opinion, Cappella Marciana performs the most interesting music on normal, non-festive Sundays. This might mean works by Andrea Gabrieli, Giovanni Pierluigi da Palestrina, Baldassare Galuppi or Antonio Lotti. You might even hear contemporary works composed by the choir's current director, Marco Germani.

✂ EATING IN SAN MARCO: OUR PICKS

MAP p194

Rosticceria Gislon: Historic, canteen-style joint famous for deep-fried street food, including croquettes and deep-fried mozzarella. *9am-9.30pm* €

Ai Mercanti: Top chefs and sommeliers dine here for the modern, produce-driven dishes and artisanal wines. *1-2pm & 7-10pm Tue-Sat* €€

Rossopomodoro: Neapolitan chain serving decent pizzas, pasta dishes and grazing platters in upbeat, modern digs. *11.30am-11.30pm* €€

Chat Qui Rit: Refined, creative cooking celebrating top-tier Italian produce and subtle Asian accents. *noon-3pm & 6-10pm Tue-Sat* €€€

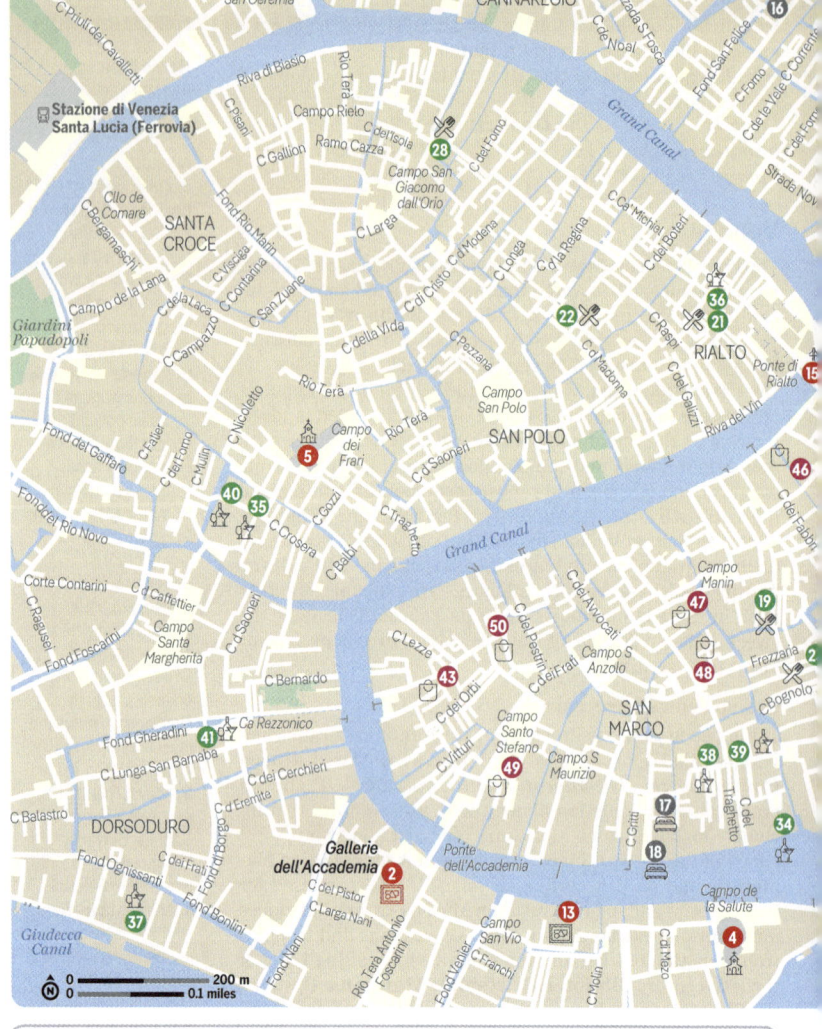

VENICE

★ HIGHLIGHTS
1 Basilica di San Marco
2 Gallerie dell'Accademia

● SIGHTS
3 Basilica dei Santi Maria e Donato
4 Basilica di Santa Maria della Salute
5 Basilica di Santa Maria Gloriosa dei Frari
6 Burano
7 Chiesa di San Martino Vescovo
8 Murano
9 Museo Correr
10 Museo del Merletto
11 Museo del Vetro
12 Palazzo Ducale
13 Peggy Guggenheim Collection
14 Piazza Baldassare Galuppi
15 Ponte di Rialto

● SLEEPING
16 3749 Ponte Chiodo
17 Giò & Giò
18 Gritti Palace

● EATING
19 Ai Mercanti
20 Alla Maddalena
21 All'Arco
22 Antiche Carampane
23 Chat Qui Rit
24 Crema Gelato
25 Osteria Acquastanca
26 Osteria Ai Bisatei
27 Osteria al Duomo
28 Osteria La Zucca
29 Panificio Pasticceria Marangon

30 Rossopomodoro
31 Rosticceria Gislon
32 Trattoria al Gatto Nero
33 Venissa Osteria

● **DRINKING
& NIGHTLIFE**
34 Arts Bar
see 18 Bar Longhi
35 Café Noir
36 Cantina Do Mori

37 Experimental Cocktail
Club
38 Il Caravellino
39 Library Bar at Nolinski
Venezia
40 Malvasia all'Adriatico
Mar
41 Osteria ai Pugni

● **SHOPPING**
42 Cesare Toffolo

43 Chiarastella Cattana
44 De Biasi
45 Fornace Mian
46 Giuliana Longo
47 Libreria Linea d'Acqua
48 Merchant of Venice
49 Piedàterre
50 Rubelli
51 Venini
52 Wave Murano Glass

● **INFORMATION**
53 Ateneo San Basso Left
Luggage Office

Basilica di San Marco

In a city packed with architectural wonders, nothing trumps the Basilica di San Marco for sheer spectacle. In 828 CE, wily Venetian merchants allegedly smuggled St Mark's corpse out of Egypt in a barrel of pork fat to avoid inspection by Muslim authorities. Venice built a basilica around its stolen saint in keeping with the city's own sense of supreme self-importance.

PAOLO GALLO/SHUTTERSTOCK

TOP TIPS

● Dress modestly, covering knees and shoulders.

● Arrive early to avoid queues or purchase 'Skip the Line' tickets online; leave large bags at **Ateneo San Basso Left Luggage**.

● The **Campanile** *(adult/under 7yr €10/free)* offers 360-degree lagoon views, but book 'Skip the Line' tickets in high season.

PRACTICALITIES

● basilicasanmarco.it
● admission from €3
● 9.30am-5.15pm, museum & loggia only 9am-2pm Sun

Unmissable Highlights

Church authorities in Rome disapproved of Venice's self-glorification, but the city defiantly created a private chapel for its Doge that outshone the official cathedral. After the original St Mark's burned, the basilica was rebuilt twice, with the current incarnation completed in 1094.

Its facade ripples like a wave, with five portals capped by mosaics and arches, and four bronze horses prancing above the central doorway. Enter beneath the ornate triple arch of porphyry columns and reliefs from the 13th to 14th centuries. The oldest mosaic (1270) sits above the far-left portal, showing St Mark's stolen body arriving here.

Inside, 8500 sq metres of mosaics – many with 24-carat gold leaf – glitter with divine light. The narthex holds the oldest mosaics of apostles with the Madonna, standing sentry by the main door for more than 950 years.

Treasures abound: the **Pala d'Oro** *(€5),* studded with 2000 gems; the **Tesoro** *(€3)* with Crusader booty, a Byzantine chalice and Archangel Michael icon; and the **Museo** *(€7),* with close-ups of the mosaics and piazza views from the Loggia dei Cavalli. The most unforgettable experience? An **After Hours tour** *(walksofitaly.com; from €139),* which includes the crypt.

continued from p193

The Doge's palace

For over seven centuries, Venice's spectacular **Palazzo Ducale** (*palazzoducale.visitmuve.it; adult/reduced incl Museo Correr from €25/13*) was the city's seat of government, enduring storms, fires, conspiracies – and even Casanova, who famously escaped the attic prison. The site likely became the Doge's residence in the 10th century, but the current palace began taking shape around 1340. The 1443 **Porta della Carta**, facing the Piazzetta, welcomed dignitaries into the **colonnaded courtyard**. Today, entry is from the waterfront side of the building, which leads into its colonnaded courtyard. From it, the **Scala d'Oro** leads to Palladio's **Sala delle Quattro Porte**, while the **Sala Consiglio dei Dieci** is where Venice's star chamber plotted under a Veronese ceiling. The vast **Grand Council Chamber**, with Tintoretto's gigantic *Paradise,* once hosted elections and ducal audiences, while the **Armoury** displays weapons and fragments of frescoes. Cross the **Bridge of Sighs** to the eerie **Prigioni Nove**, complete with graffitied cells.

The worthy, 60-minute **Secret Itineraries Tour** *(adult/reduced €32/20)* uncovers the **Pozzi** wells, top-secret **Chancellery**, and the **Piombi** attic prison where Casanova was imprisoned in 1756. Book both standard entry tickets and Secret Itinerary Tours online in advance to avoid queues.

Ponder Titian's masterpiece

Built for the Franciscans in the 14th and 15th centuries, the **Basilica di Santa Maria Gloriosa dei Frari** (*basilicadei frari.it; adult/reduced €5/2*) has none of the flying buttresses, pinnacles and gargoyles typical of international Gothic – but its vaulted ceilings and broad, triple-nave, Latin-cross floor plan give this minor basilica a grandeur befitting the masterpieces it contains.

Its undisputed star is Titian's restored 1518 altarpiece *Assunta* (Assumption), one of Italy's greatest Renaissance artworks and also the world's largest wood-panel painting.

The church harbours works by other Venetian greats as well, among them Bellini and Donatello, not to mention a rare Monks' Choir area dating from 1468. Among the numerous monumental tombs is that of Antonio Canova, designed by the sculptor himself and home to his heart.

Cross the Rialto at dawn

The best time to experience Venice's world-famous **Ponte di Rialto** is early in the morning (before 8.15am). Uncluttered

---

VENICE FROM THE WATER

Steven Moore, TV presenter, *Antiques Roadshow* judge. @mrstevenmoore

Some visitors think gondola rides are tacky, but they're actually a fabulous experience. Many gondoliers know Venice intimately, so instead of asking them to sing you 'O Sole Mio', ask them to point out any interesting details about the buildings. Golden hour, when the sun is beginning to set, is especially magical. Evening rides are also wonderful: look up and you might catch a glimpse of a chandelier or a ceiling fresco.

If you've got an hour to kill, take the *vaporetto* up or down the Grand Canal. From tip to toe it's around 40 minutes. I prefer the number 2 *vaporetto* over the 1: it's generally quieter and has less stops.

🍸 **DRINKING IN SAN MARCO: OUR PICKS** ———————— MAP p194

Bar Longhi: Superlative martinis and bellinis in sumptuous surrounds on the Grand Canal. Expensive but magical. *11am-1am*	**Il Caravellino:** Historic restaurant bar with handsome wood panelling, leather armchairs and classic drinks. *8.30am-11pm*	**Library Bar at Nolinski Venezia:** Posh hideaway, with floor-to-ceiling bookshelves, Simon Buret ceiling art and creative libations. *5pm-12.30am*	**Arts Bar:** Cocktail den inside the St Regis Hotel serving clever libations inspired by Venetian artworks and architecture. *6.30pm-12.30am Tue-Sat*

GUGGENHEIM

Karole PB Vail, Director Peggy Guggenheim Collection, granddaughter of Peggy Guggenheim.

When visiting the Peggy Guggenheim Collection, get up close to the paintings to appreciate their superb execution. Note the thickness of the paint in Jackson Pollock's *Alchemy* and the meticulousness of Leonora Carrington's *Oink (They Shall Behold Thine Eyes)*. Joan Miró's wonderful Dutch *Interior II* is a bit of a riff on Jan Steen's 17th-century painting *The Dancing Lesson*, but Miró made it all his own in a very entertaining, surreal way. I also love the work of Yves Tanguy, who painted surreal, dreamlike landscapes. The collection is very rich in sculpture; look for Jean Arp's *Head and Shell*, the first sculpture Peggy Guggenheim bought.

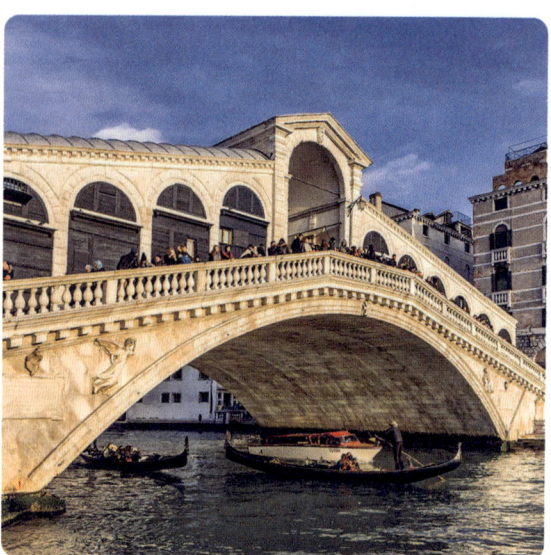

KIEVVICTOR/SHUTTERSTOCK

Ponte di Rialto (p197), Venice

by tourists and awnings, you'll be able to fully appreciate its elegant Renaissance lines and the superb view from its balustraded decks. Below you, the city prepares for another busy day: sharply dressed commuters spill out of *vaporetti* (small passenger ferries) and delivery workers unload restaurant supplies from bobbing boats. Costing 250,000 gold ducats and completed in 1592, the Istrian-stone bridge is the work of Antonio da Ponte, whose nephew Antonio Contino would go on to design San Marco's Bridge of Sighs.

Admire Venetian greats

Tracing the development of Venetian art from the 14th to 19th centuries, the unmissable **Gallerie dell'Accademia** (*gallerie accademia.it; adult/reduced €15/2*) contains more murderous intrigue, forbidden romance and shameless politicking than the most outrageous Venetian parties. Room 5 harbours Giovanni Bellini's sublime *Madonna and Child between Saints Catherine and Mary Magdalene* while Room 8 claims two Giorgione masterpieces: *Old Woman* and *The Tempest*. Even more commanding is Paolo Veronese's monumental *Feast in the House of Levi* in Room 10, condemned by Inquisition leaders for depicting dogs, drunkards, dwarves, Muslims and

---

 EATING IN SAN POLO & SANTA CROCE: OUR PICKS ──────── MAP p194

All'Arco: Epicureans relish All'Arco's market-fresh seafood *cicchetti* (Venetian tapas) and in-the-know wines by the glass. *10am-2.30pm €*

Cantina Do Mori: Venice's oldest *bacaro* (bar), with interesting pan-Italian wines and tasty *cicchetti* and cheeses. *8am-7.30pm Mon-Sat €*

Osteria La Zucca: Daily changing menu of delicious vegetarian and meat dishes; book ahead. *noon-2.30pm & 7-10.30pm Mon-Sat €€*

Antiche Carampane: Book ahead for market-driven Venetian classics. Near Ponte de le Tette. *12.30-2.30pm & 7.30-10pm Tue-Sat €€€*

Reformation-minded Germans cavorting with apostles. Another highlight is Gentile Bellini's recently restored *Miracle of the Reliquary of the Cross at San Lorenzo Bridge* in Room 20. Allow at least 1½ hours for a visit, and avoid high-season queues by arriving at opening time or after 4pm.

Picasso, Pollock and Peggy

Set aside a couple of hours for the **Peggy Guggenheim Collection** *(guggenheim-venice.it; adult/reduced €16/9)*, one of Italy's finest modern-art museums. Occupying an unfinished 18th-century Grand Canal *palazzo*, it was once home to American arts doyenne Peggy Guggenheim.

Works on display rotate, but look out for early works by Picasso and Mondrian – among them Picasso's *A Poet* (1911) and Mondrian's *Ocean 5* (1915) – as well as Magritte's enigmatic *Empire of Light* (1953–54). Another highlight: *Alchemy* (1947), one of Jackson Pollock's first revolutionary 'poured' paintings. A spirited advocate for contemporary Italian art, Guggenheim also influenced the reappraisal of artists such as Umberto Boccioni, Giacomo Balla and Giorgio de Chirico.

The gallery's **Nasher Sculpture Garden** includes works by Henry Moore, Alberto Giacometti and Isamu Noguchi.

Ponder a mystical basilica

Sitting on over a million tree trunks at the mouth of the Grand Canal, Baldassare Longhena's **Basilica di Santa Maria della Salute** *(basilicasalutevenezia.it; church free, sacristy adult/reduced €6/4)* is the Senate's *grazie* to the Madonna for saving the city from the plague of 1630–31. Inside, the lines of the building converge beneath the dome to form a vortex on the inlaid marble floors: esoteric types believe that the central black dot radiates healing energy. The **sacristy** houses Titian's self-portrait in the guise of St Matthew and Tintoretto's made-to-measure *Wedding Feast of Cana*. For a divine view, climb the basilica's iconic **dome** *(adult/reduced €8/6)*.

Observe master glassblowers

The interlinked islands of **Murano** have been synonymous with glassmaking since the 13th century, and despite being extremely touristy, some of its furnaces offer fascinating glassblowing demonstrations. Among these is certified traditional furnace **Wave Murano Glass** *(wavemuranoglass.com)*, where you can watch the blowers from the entry to the factory for free, join an in-depth tour (€29 for 45 minutes) or take a two-hour beginners' course (€245).

MURANO'S BEST IN GLASS

Venini: Even if you don't have the cash to buy a Venini, pop by to see Murano glass at its finest.

De Biasi: These certified Murano artisans design their own jewellery, picture frames, bottle stoppers and even chopsticks.

Cesare Toffolo: Mind-boggling miniatures are the trademark here, along with featherlight drinking glasses and glossy black candlesticks.

Fornace Mian: Shuffle past the typical Murano kitsch and you'll find one of the best ranges of classic stemware on the islands.

Wave Murano Glass: This team of young artisans offers a modern take on ancient traditions.

DRINKING IN DORSODURO: OUR PICKS

MAP p194

Malvasia all'Adriatico Mar: Waterside spot offering natural, small-scale wines from the Adriatic region. *5-10pm Mon & Tue, from 11am Wed-Sun*

Osteria ai Pugni: Hefty selection of wines by the glass plus *aperitivo*-friendly nibbles by Ponte dei Pugni. *10am-10.30pm Mon-Sat*

Experimental Cocktail Club: Seriously curated cocktail menus at the Zattare's old Adriatic Naval Company. *6.30pm-1am Sun, Mon & Thu, to 2am Fri & Sat*

Café Noir: Gritty, friendly, boho-spirited bar with a long list of cocktails and a faithful student following. *7am-2am*

VINE REVIVAL

If you were ever invited to dinner with the Doge, chances are you would have been served dorona, a local varietal that was golden hued and highly prized.

Venice's devastating 1966 flood was thought to have wiped out the remaining dorona vines, meaning the wine of the Doges was lost for ever. That is, until 2002 when winemaker Gianluca Bisol stumbled across golden grapes growing on Torcello. He subsequently tracked down another 88 vines and used them to revive an ancient vineyard enclosed by medieval walls on Mazzorbo.

Venissa now sells bottles of the liquid gold in handblown Murano glass bottles embossed with gold leaf. Tours and tastings are available.

You'll need about an hour to explore the excellent **Museo del Vetro** *(museovetro.visitmuve.it; adult/reduced €10/7.50)*, which recounts the backstory of glassmaking.

A short walk away is the remarkable, 12th-century **Basilica dei Santi Maria e Donato** *(adult/reduced €3.50/1.50)*, lavished with intricate mosaics.

See where Venice began

Torcello is one of the lagoon's most tranquil islands. But 1500 years ago, it was a different story. The first lagoon island to have been settled, it was once the site of a major city, with nine churches, two abbeys and its own bishop. The Byzantine-Romanesque **Basilica di Santa Maria Assunta** *(adult/child €6/5)* served as his cathedral. The oldest parts of the building date from 639, making it by far the oldest church on the lagoon.

Inside, grab an audio guide to decode the basilica's astonishing 12th-century mosaics, and make time for the **Museo di Torcello** *(adult/reduced €3/1.50)* across the square, which outlines the island's history.

Combine your Torcello trip with Burano, and avoid Mondays when the museum is closed.

Slow the pace

Famed for its lace and technicolour buildings, **Burano** has become a popular destination for social-media hacks seeking a bright backdrop for posing purposes. After you've snapped a trillion photos of the multihued houses of the outer canals, inevitably you'll find yourself on bustling **Piazza Baldassare Galuppi**.

Here, call inside the 16th-century **Chiesa di San Martino Vescovo** *(parrocchiadiburano.weebly.com; admission free)* to see Giambattista Tiepolo's 1725 *La Crocifissione* and the *Madonna di Kazan,* a 19th-century Russian icon considered a masterpiece of enamelwork.

Across the square, give yourself an hour to explore the **Museo del Merletto** *(museomerletto.visitmuve.it; adult/reduced €5/3.50)*, which tells the story of Burano's revered lace industry.

From Burano, a bridge reaches tiny **Mazzorbo**, perfect for a mind-clearing walk or a feast at vine-flanked **Venissa Osteria** *(venissa.it)*.

EATING ON MURANO: OUR PICKS

MAP p194

Panificio Pasticceria Marangon: Grab a morning pastry from this local bakery. *6.30am-1pm Mon-Sat, plus 5-7pm Mon, Tue & Thu-Sat* €	**Osteria Ai Bisatei:** Glassblowers come here for plates of fried fish, seafood risotto and *spaghetti vongole. 11.30am-2.30pm Thu-Tue* €	**Osteria al Duomo:** Dishes up bowls of pasta and excellent pizza within a walled garden. *noon-2.30pm & 6.30-9pm Fri-Wed* €€	**Osteria Acquastanca:** The best restaurant on Murano serves mainly seafood dishes. *noon-3pm Mon-Sat, plus 7-9.30pm Mon & Fri* €€€

Florence
& Tuscany

ICONIC LANDMARKS | RENAISSANCE ART | MEDIEVAL TOWNSCAPES

Stretching along the Tyrrhenian Sea below Liguria and Emilia-Romagna, Tuscany beckons with its wealth of historic sites scattered on the changing landscapes that slope down from the Apennines to the coast. Fortified palaces and ancient *case-torri,* the tower houses erected by wealthy pre-Renaissance families, define skylines, as do the stone-built bell towers of Gothic and Romanesque churches continuously visited by long-distance pilgrims for nearly a millennium.

The region's capital and undisputed headliner is Florence (Firenze), cradle of the Renaissance and home to an embarrassing wealth of cultural riches (even by Italy's inimitable standards). While it's easy enough to stay put in Florence, Tuscany's cypress-lined countryside rewards the curious. Of all the region's hilltop towns, few match Siena, where winding medieval streets lead to an extraordinary cathedral and storybook square. Closer to the coast, scholarly Pisa beckons with more than just its vertically challenged tower.

Places

Florence p201
Siena p208
Pisa p210

☑ TOP TIP

Summers can be scorching hot in Florence. If you're climbing the Duomo, Giotto's Campanile or the Torre di Arnolfo, keep in mind that hundreds of narrow steps await. People have fainted in the past – avoid the middle of the day when booking your tickets.

Florence

MAP p204

Few cities are so compact in size or so packed with extraordinary art and architectural masterpieces at every turn. The

 GETTING AROUND

Frequent high-speed trains connect Florence to other major Italian cities, including Rome, Bologna and Milan. High-speed and *regionale* (regional) trains connect Florence to Pisa, while a reasonably extensive regional bus network includes *corse rapide* (express services) between Florence and Siena. Other bus routes in Tuscany can involve long trips.

Florence itself is small and best navigated on foot; most major sights are within easy walking distance. Nonresident traffic is banned from the historic centre, and parking is an absolute headache and best avoided. Trams run between Florence Airport and the city's main train station, Firenze Santa Maria Novella.

urban fabric of this small city, on the banks of the Arno river in northeastern Tuscany, has hardly changed since the Renaissance and its narrow cobbled streets are a cinematic feast of elegant 15th- and 16th-century *palazzi,* medieval candlelit chapels, fresco-decorated churches, marble basilicas and world-class art museums brimming with paintings and sculptures by Botticcelli, Michelangelo et al. Unsurprisingly, the entire city centre is a UNESCO World Heritage Site.

Florence's centre of power

For over 700 years, **Palazzo Vecchio** has housed Florence's government, and it's still home to the mayor's office today. Built in 1299 above a Roman theatre, the fortress-like palace was designed by Arnolfo di Cambio and later expanded by the Medici.

Buy a **ticket** *(bigliettimusei.comune.fi.it; adult/reduced €12.50/10)* to see the vast Salone dei Cinquecento, begun in 1494 under preacher Savonarola and later transformed by Vasari with grand scenes of Florentine victories and a ceiling celebrating Cosimo I de' Medici.

Snoop around the private quarters, including Duchess Eleonora di Toledo's chapel by Bronzino and the Sala delle Udienze, awash with frescoes by Furio Camillo. Also, don't miss

T PHOTOGRAPHY/SHUTTERSTOCK

Salone dei Cinquecento, Palazzo Vecchio, Florence

Donatello's *Judith and Holofernes* and Ghirlandaio's *Apoteosi di San Zanobi*. The **Secret Passages tour** *(musefirenze.it/en/attivita/percorsi-segreti; €5)* reveals Francesco I's hidden Studiolo of rare and curious treasures.

Cross the Ponte Vecchio

Built in 1345, Florence's **Ponte Vecchio** is one the city's best-known symbols, both because of its unusual architecture and its convoluted past. Originally, the bridge was mainly populated by *beccai* (butchers), but in 1593 Grand Duke Ferdinando I, who could not stand the smell of meat and the insalubrious state of the market, evicted all businesses involved in 'vile arts', allowing only goldsmiths and jewellers to trade on the bridge. The 48 jewellery stores perched on the bridge survived the 1944 bombing of the city – all other bridges in central Florence were destroyed – and the major flood that hit the city in 1966.

Feast on masterpieces

The **Galleria degli Uffizi** *(uffizi.it; adult/reduced €25/2)* is one of the world's greatest museums, home to masterpieces from Giotto to Caravaggio. Commissioned in 1560 by Cosimo I

continued on p206

THE 1993 BOMBING OF THE UFFIZI

In 2021 the 4.4m-tall **Albero della Pace** (Peace Tree) – a bronze olive tree created by sculptor Andrea Roggi – was placed in Via dei Georgofili, behind the Uffizi, to commemorate one of the darkest days in Italy's recent history. In the early hours of 27 May 1993, a car bomb exploded, killing five people and injuring 48. Besides the loss of human life, the detonation devastated the Torre dei Pulci housing the Accademia dei Georgofili and the Uffizi. The bomb had been placed in a parked car and detonated by remote control by the Mafia, which had escalated its tactics in response to the tightening of prison laws for those involved in organised crime.

Beloved eatery near Dante's museum.

 EATING IN DUOMO & SIGNORIA: OUR PICKS

MAP p204

Osteria Nuvoli: People spill onto the sidewalk with vino in hand, or enjoy authentic Tuscan fare at a table in the cellar. *8am-9.30pm Mon-Sat* €

I Buongustai: The sisters running this historic *trattoria* on Via dei Cerchi serve homemade Tuscan pastas. *noon-3.30pm Mon-Sat* €

Da' Vinattieri: Traditional Florentine street food, with 18 different fillings for your *schiacciata* (flat bread) – or try the Florentine tripe. *11.30am-7.30pm Mon-Sat* €

Maledetti Toscani: The 'cursed Tuscans' are far from blasphemous when it comes to food – enjoy one of their rustic sandwiches on the go. *8.30am-7pm Mon-Sat, 10am-5pm Sun* €

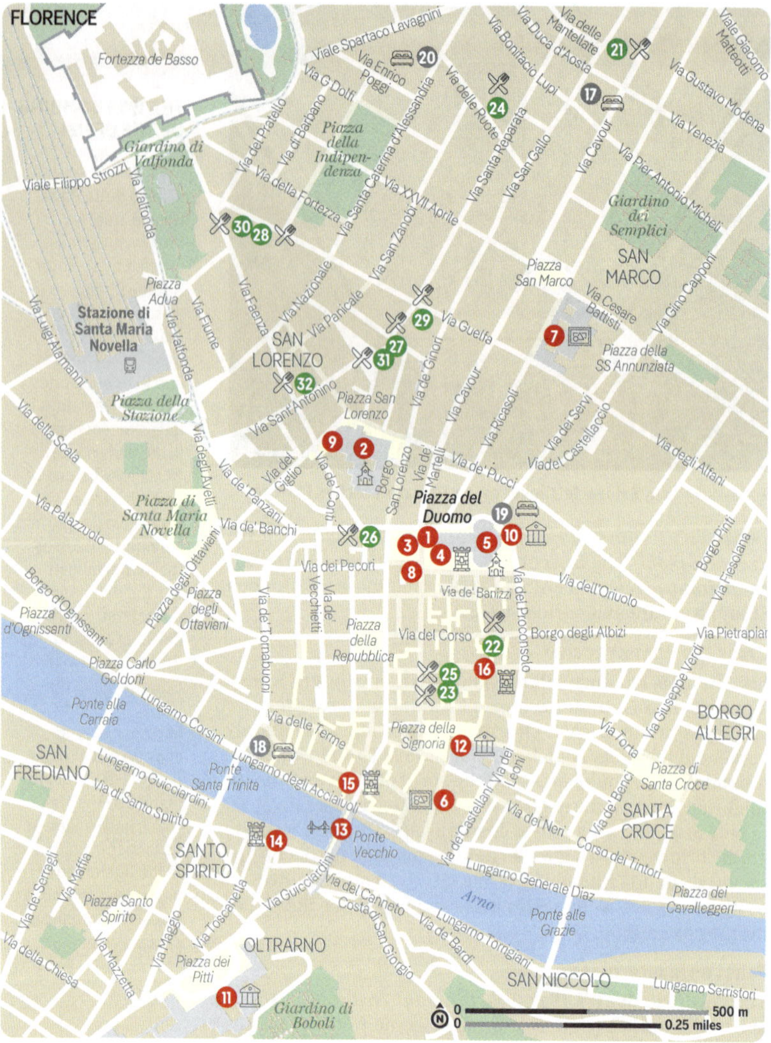

FLORENCE

Fortezza de Basso

Giardino di
Valfonda

Viale Filippo Strozzi

Piazza
della
Indipen-
denza

Piazza
Adua

Stazione di
Santa Maria
Novella

Piazza della
Stazione

SAN
LORENZO

Piazza San
Lorenzo

Piazza di
Santa Maria
Novella

Piazza
degli
Ottavieni

Piazza Carlo
Goldoni

Ponte alla
Carraia

SAN
FREDIANO

Piazza Santo
Spirito

SANTO
SPIRITO

OLTRARNO

Piazza dei
Pitti

Giardino di
Boboli

Giardino
dei
Semplici

SAN
MARCO

Piazza
San Marco

Piazza della
SS Annunziata

Piazza del
Duomo

Piazza
della
Repubblica

Piazza della
Signoria

Ponte
Santa Trinita

Ponte
Vecchio

Arno

Ponte alle
Grazie

SAN NICCOLÒ

BORGO
ALLEGRI

Piazza di
Santa Croce

SANTA
CROCE

Piazza dei
Cavalleggeri

0   500 m
0   0.25 miles

Piazza del Duomo

Nearly six centuries have passed since Filippo Brunelleschi completed the cupola topping the Cattedrale di Santa Maria del Fiore, providing Florence with an architectural landmark that would be revered for centuries. But the octagonal dome is only the most visible of the many treasures on Piazza del Duomo, where Gothic and Renaissance masters left an indelible mark on the city's identity.

Cattedrale di Santa Maria del Fiore

Designed by Arnolfo di Cambio and consecrated in 1436, the **Cattedrale di Santa Maria del Fiore** is crowned by Brunelleschi's revolutionary dome, inspired by Rome's Pantheon. Highlights include Ghiberti's stained-glass windows, a vast marble floor by Pollaiolo, and Vasari and Zuccari's *Last Judgement* fresco, best admired while climbing the 463 steps to the cupola's rooftop. The current neo-Gothic facade was added in the 19th century.

Giotto's Campanile

The 85m-tall bell tower of Santa Maria del Fiore was initiated by Giotto in 1334 and completed by Andrea Pisano and Francesco Talenti after Pisano died in 1337. The **Campanile di Giotto** encloses a narrow 414-step staircase leading to the panoramic platform Talenti added in 1359.

Battistero di San Giovanni

A prime example of Florentine Romanesque architecture, the piazza's octagonal **baptistery** was consecrated in 1059. Andrea Pisano and Lorenzo Ghiberti created its monumental bronze doors. Inside, stunning 13th-century mosaics are being restored and are viewable on scaffolding **tours** (*duomo.firenze.it; €65*).

Museo dell'Opera del Duomo

Many original sculptures from Piazza del Duomo now reside in the **Museo dell'Opera del Duomo**. Highlights include baptistery doors by Pisano and Ghiberti, and a reproduction of Arnolfo di Cambio's 1296 facade.

TOP TIPS

● The cathedral's ground floor is free, but a ticket is required for the cupola.

● Three passes are available: Ghiberti, Giotto and the all-inclusive Brunelleschi. Purchase online in advance.

● Before leaving Piazza del Duomo through Via dei Calzaiouli take a moment to admire the 1358 Gothic **Loggia del Bigallo**.

PRACTICALITIES
● duomo.firenze.it
● adult/reduced from €15/5 ● hours vary

BELOW THE DUOMO

What is commonly referred to as the 'crypt' was in fact a welcome centre for pilgrims travelling along the ancient Via Francigena, the 3000km medieval route between Canterbury and Rome. Pilgrims would descend into the rooms below the cathedral to admire the vivid 13th-century cycle of biblical frescoes decorating the walls – well-earned spiritual wonder and respite to weary, faith-filled travellers. Hidden for centuries beneath layers of history, the rooms were only rediscovered in 1999, revealing a breathtaking visual narrative of faith and artistry. The frescoes' vibrant colours remain remarkably intact, their preservation owed to the absence of sunlight and humidity. Today they stand as an essential piece of the city's rich medieval heritage.

continued from p203

and designed by Vasari, the U-shaped palace once housed government offices before becoming a gallery under Francesco I. Admire its symmetrical facade from Piazza della Signoria before ascending to the 2nd floor via the Scalone Granducale. Highlights include Botticelli's *Nascita di Venere* (1485), the octagonal Tribuna degli Uffizi, and Michelangelo's *Tondo Doni* (1504–06), his only existing panel painting.

Don't miss the restored **Terrazzo delle Carte Geografiche**, covered in handpainted 16th-century maps. Later, encounter Leonardo, Raphael, and Roman sculptures in the **Sala della Niobe**. On the 1st floor, the Collezione degli Autoritratti showcases 250 self-portraits, while the final stretch includes Caravaggio's chilling *Giuditta che Decapita Oloferne* (1620). Book tickets in advance online.

Where the powerful prayed

Built over a 4th-century church, the **Basilica di San Lorenzo** (*sanlorenzofirenze.it; adult €9*) became the Medici family church in the 15th century. In 1425, Cosimo the Elder commissioned Brunelleschi's elegant redesign; his tomb now lies in the crypt-turned-museum, Museo del Tesoro di San Lorenzo. Nearly a century later, Pope Leone X, son of Lorenzo the Magnificent, asked Michelangelo to revamp the facade – but the Carrara-marble plan was never realised, leaving the exterior bare. Inside, *pietra serena* columns frame masterpieces like Filippo Lippi's *Annunciazione Martelli* (1440), Rosso Fiorentino's *Sposalizio della Vergine* (1523) and Donatello's sculpted pulpits (1460). Brunelleschi's *Sagrestia Vecchia* (Old Sacristy), left of the altar, is a highlight, decorated with Donatello's sculptural details. Before exiting, look up to the **Tribuna delle Reliquie** above the main portal, designed by Michelangelo.

Mingle with the Medicis

Matching their opulent palaces, the Medicis' final resting place is a grandiose masterpiece. Enter the **Museo delle Cappelle Medicee** (*bargellomusei.it/musei/cappelle-medicee; adult €9*) from the rear end of the Basilica di San Lorenzo in Piazza di Madonna degli Aldobrandini to find yourself under the 59m-high cupola of the Cappella dei Principi, where the Cosimo I, Francesco I and Cosimo III tombs are surrounded by the city's Florentine mosaic, or *commesso*. Continue to the **Sagrestia Nuova**, the marble hall designed by Michelangelo, where Lorenzo the Magnificent and his brother Giuliano are

Cooking up Tuscan classics for over a century.

 EATING IN SAN LORENZO & SAN MARCO: OUR PICKS

Trattoria Guelfa: Select a first and second course from the hand-written menu that changes daily. *noon-2.45pm & 7-10.45pm* €

Trattoria Mario: Bustling *trattoria* serving authentic Tuscan cuisine. No reservations. *noon-3pm Mon-Sat, 7.30-10pm Thu & Fri* €

Il Vegetariano: Vegetarian dishes, freshly made savoury cakes and a variety of teas. *12.30-2.30pm Mon-Fri, 7.30-10.30pm Mon-Sun* €

Antica Trattoria da Tito: The walls are covered in scrawled messages from past customers testifying to its popularity. Book ahead. *12.30-3pm & 7-11pm Mon-Sat* €€

Michelangelo's *David*, Galleria dell'Accademia

FLORENCE'S TOWER HOUSES

The stone-built *case-torri* (tower houses) that dot Florence's heart are a fascinating architectural remnant of the Middle Ages. These residential structures rise above the city's red rooftops, taking you back to an era when powerful families erected hermetic homes to protect themselves from enemy attacks and show off their wealth. The towers generally had a rectangular or square base and could have up to six or seven storeys. About 50 *case-torri* still stand. The best-preserved ones are the **Torre della Castagna**, the **Torre degli Amidei** and the **Torre de' Barbadori**. You can even sleep in one – the hotel **Antica Torre di Via Tornabuoni 1**, offering spectacular 360-degree views over the city from its crenellated rooftop.

buried. This smaller room, built between 1520 and 1534, is adorned with monumental sculptures whose details are elevated by two carefully constructed sources of natural light, which Michelangelo viewed as an essential element of his design.

Make a date with David

Michelangelo's iconic *David* is one of hundreds of artworks at the **Galleria dell'Accademia** (*galleriaaccademiafirenze. it; adult/reduced €16/2),* from 13th-century gilded panels to Bartolini's neoclassical busts. Originally a Medici drawing academy (1563), it became a public museum in 1784. At the heart of the Sala del Colosso stands Giambologna's dynamic plaster *Ratto delle Sabine* (1581), surrounded with works by Lippi, Perugino and Botticelli. Before reaching *David,* pause at Michelangelo's four intentionally unfinished *Prigioni* (1519–34), marble figures straining to escape their stone prisons. Waiting at the end of the gallery is *David* (1504) himself, a 5m marble icon of freedom and beauty sculpted by Michelangelo at just 29. Book tickets on the website (there's a €4 reservation fee). Entry is free on the first Sunday of the month, but expect queues.

MAP p204

Trattoria Palle D'Oro: Ideal lunch break, with simple Tuscan dishes. *noon-3pm & 7-10.30pm* €

Ristorante Cafaggi: Local favourite offering changing seasonal classics in an old-school atmosphere. *12.30-3pm & 7-10pm Mon-Sat* €

Osteria Pepó: Book ahead to secure a spot at this popular place serving generous portions of pastas and meats. *noon-2.30pm & 7-10.30pm* €€

Osteria Vecchio Cancello: This quirkily decorated *osteria* is known for its calm atmosphere and its steaks. *noon-2pm & 7-10pm Wed-Mon* €€

THE MEDICIS' BALLS

As you stroll through San Lorenzo, you'll inevitably spot the Medicis' emblem hanging on many of the neighbourhood's buildings. The shield adorned with six or seven spheres continues to loom over Palazzo Medici Riccardi, the Biblioteca Medicea Laurenziana and the ceiling of the Basilica di San Lorenzo. No one knows exactly what the balls of the Medicis' emblem mean. One hypothesis suggests that they represent the marks left by the Mugello Giant on the shield of Averardo, an ancestor of the Florentine rulers. A more worldly take on the story says that the spheres are simply coins, linking the family with their banking activities.

Trawl treasures at the Pitti

Dominating its namesake piazza, stately **Palazzo Pitti** (*uffizi .it/en/pitti-palace; adult €16*) became the Medici residence in 1549 and was later expanded by court architect Bartolomeo Ammannati. Start in the Galleria Palatina to explore the Sala di Ulisse, with works by Raphael and Vasari, then continue to the Sala dell'Iliade, where paintings by Andrea del Sarto surround Bartolini's *La Carità* under a Homeric ceiling. In the Sala di Apollo, meet Cosimo I's court jester Morgante, painted nude by Bronzino. Upstairs, the Galleria d'Arte Moderna showcases neoclassical sculptures by Canova, as well as Romantic and Macchiaioli works. Don't miss the Museo della Moda e del Costume, tracing Italian fashion from Eleonora di Toledo to Prada. Back on the ground floor, the dazzling Sala di Giovanni da San Giovanni, frescoed in 1635, celebrates a Medici wedding with trompe l'oeil splendour.

Siena

MAP p209

Unlike other major medieval powers, Siena could not rely on access to rivers or seas for transport and trade. Still, the city, nestled on three hills, flourished during the 13th century, developing a political system that would guarantee a period of peace prolonged enough to allow the development of one of Italy's most influential universities and one of Europe's richest art collections. Traces of this legacy are still visible today, starting from the architecture of the enchanting Piazza del Campo, the city's main square, to the Duomo, one of Tuscany's most impressive cathedrals.

Explore a theatrical square

Siena's shell-shaped **Piazza del Campo** has been the city's civic and political heart since the 12th century. Its transformation began with the 13th-century construction of the Gothic Palazzo Pubblico. Strict urban planning laws ensured architectural harmony, with double- or triple-arched windows and no balconies. The square, divided into nine segments, hosts December's **Mercato del Campo** (*mercatonelcampo.it*) and, most famously, the Palio horse race (p210). A 19th-century copy of Jacopo della Quercia's **Fonte Gaia** (1419) stands at its northern edge. Originally topped with a Venus statue, the fountain was altered after the Black Death, when religious authorities blamed pagan imagery for the plague. The statue's remains were reportedly buried in Florentine lands to wish the enemy an equal misfortune.

Art for the powerful

Flanked by the 88m **Torre del Mangia**, Siena's iconic **Palazzo Pubblico** was built between 1288 and 1342 as the seat of the Government of the Nine. Today, it houses the extraordinary **Museo Civico** (*museocivico.comune.siena.it*), showcasing centuries of Sienese art. Highlights include Martino Bartolomeo's *Sixteen Virtues* fresco and Spinello Aretino's *Storie di Alessandro III* in the Sala di Balìa, and Simone

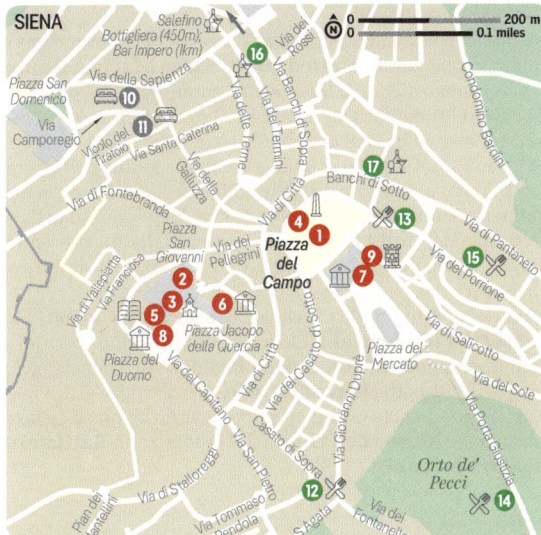

SIENA

Salefino (450m);
Bottiglieria (450m);
Bar Impero (1km)

Piazza San Domenico

Via Camporegio

200 m
0.1 miles

MAP p209

MICHELANGELO'S DRAWING ROOM

In 1975 a series of wall drawings was discovered behind a layer of plaster in a storage room below the New Sacristy of the **Cappelle Medicee** (p206). The sketches were attributed to Michelangelo, who's believed to have hidden in this room in 1530, fearing retaliation from Pope Clement VII, a member of the Medici family, due to work done for the republican government during the brief period when the Medici were ousted from Florence. Fifty years after the discovery, Michelangelo's drawing room has opened to the public for the first time. A test run of guided tours was held in 2024 – tickets were sold out immediately and new dates have yet to be announced. Keep an eye on *bargellomusei. beniculturali.it* for updates.

⭐ **HIGHLIGHTS**
1 Piazza del Campo

🔴 **SIGHTS**
2 Battistero di San Giovanni
3 Cattedrale di Santa Maria Assunta
4 Fonte Gaia
see 6 Museo Civico
5 Museo dell'Opera Metropolitana

6 Palazzo Pubblico
7 Porta del Cielo
8 Torre del Mangia

🔴 **ACTIVITIES**
9 Libreria Piccolomini

⚫ **SLEEPING**
10 Albergo Bernini
11 Hotel Alma Domus

🟢 **EATING**
12 La Taverna di San Giuseppe

13 Osteria Le Logge
14 Ristorante All'Orto de' Pecci
15 Ristorante Gallo Nero

🟢 **DRINKING & NIGHTLIFE**
16 Gastronomia Morbidi
17 Trefilari Wine Bar

Martini's *Maestà* (1312) in the Sala del Mappamondo. The star attraction is Ambrogio Lorenzetti's *Buon Governo* fresco cycle (1337–39) in the Sala della Pace, a powerful allegory of good government in city and rural life. And if the message wasn't clear enough, opposite the fresco you can see the *Effetti del Cattivo Governo,* the effects of a bad government.

 EATING IN SIENA: OUR PICKS MAP p209

Ristorante Gallo Nero: Named after the black rooster icon of Chianti, Gallo Nero is worth visiting for its truffle *pappardelle* alone. *noon-2.30pm Thu-Sat, 7-9.30pm Mon-Sat* €€

Ristorante All'Orto de' Pecci: Behind the Torre del Mangia, this garden-restaurant is run by a co-op serving seasonal dishes made from ingredients grown on-site. *12.30-2.30pm & 7.30-10.30pm Tue-Sun* €€

La Taverna di San Giuseppe: Prepare for a Tuscan-flavours overload in this historic spot inside a 12th-century building with an Etruscan foundation. *noon-2.30pm & 7-9.30pm Mon-Sat* €€€

Osteria Le Logge: This Sienese institution breathes tradition from every pore, starting from the in-house underground cellar. *noon-2.30pm & 7-10.15pm Mon-Sat* €€€

SIENA'S PALIO: A HEARTFELT HORSE RACE

Piazza del Campo has been the heart of Siena since the Middle Ages. Today it remains the focal point during the **Palio**, a traditional horse race held on 2 July and 16 August, where Siena's *contrade* (districts) compete to win the *drappellone,* a painting displayed in the winning district's museum. Leading up to the race, centuries-old rituals are observed, including neighbourhood decorations, horse assignments, open-air dinners and horse blessings in local churches. Originating from 1633 Assumption celebrations, the Palio involves a historical parade, jockeys in traditional costumes and three laps around the sand-covered piazza. The event is deeply rooted in local culture – this is not a tourist attraction but a heartfelt celebration for all communities involved.

Marvel at the Duomo

No matter how many other Tuscan churches you've seen, Siena's Romanesque-Gothic **Cattedrale di Santa Maria Assunta** *(operaduomo.siena.it; adult/child from €14/3)* astonishes. The polychrome facade, begun by Giovanni Pisano in 1287 and completed by Giovanni di Cecco in 1376, features copies of Pisano's statues (the originals are in the Museo dell'Opera del Duomo) and a rose window added in 1288. Inside is the cathedral's famed mosaic floor, produced by over 40 artists from the 14th to 19th centuries and partially uncovered in July and from mid-August to mid-October (arrive early during these periods).

Year-round highlights include Nicola Pisano's pulpit, the **Libreria Piccolomini** frescoed by Pinturicchio, Bernini's sculptures, and the Altare Piccolomini with Michelangelo niches. Tours of the **Porta del Cielo** offer a unique attic view. Buy Duomo tickets online to skip queues; combined tickets include the **Museo dell'Opera del Duomo** and **Battistero di San Giovanni**.

Pisa

Once a maritime power to rival Genoa and Venice, modern Pisa is best known for an architectural project gone terribly wrong. But the world-famous Leaning Tower is just one of many noteworthy sights in this compelling city. Education has fuelled the local economy since the 1400s, and students from across Italy compete for places in its elite university. This endows the centre of town with a vibrant cafe and bar scene, balancing an enviable portfolio of well-maintained Romanesque buildings, Gothic churches and Renaissance piazzas with a lively street life dominated by locals rather than tourists.

Piazza dei Miracoli's sights

Piazza dei Miracoli is far more than the **Leaning Tower**, though its 251 steps and iconic tilt remain a must-see. Completed in 1370 but only stabilised in the late 20th century, the *torre pendente* is a medieval marvel. The adjacent **Duomo di Pisa**, built from 1063 with a dome added in 1380, incorporates materials looted during Pisa's Sicilian campaign, while the **Museo dell'Opera del Duomo** houses sculptures by Nicola and Giovanni Pisano and Bonanno Pisano's bronze Porta di San Ranieri. The piazza's **Battistero di San Giovanni** is the world's largest baptistery and home to Nicola Pisano's Carrara marble pulpit. Make time also for **Camposanto cemetery** to

DRINKING IN SIENA: OUR PICKS

MAP p209

Salefino Bottiglieria: An extension of the homonymous restaurant, this natural-wine-focused *enoteca* is an ideal spot for discovering new labels. *6pm-1am Mon-Sat*

Bar Impero: Excellent cocktails are served under the tall, vaulted ceilings of this historic bar near Porta Camollia. *7am-midnight*

Trefilari Wine Bar: Get the evening going with a couple of glasses of wine sourced from small regional producers. *4pm-2am Tue-Thu, 2pm-2am Fri-Sun*

Gastronomia Morbidi: The artisanal products displayed at this deli-bar will make your mouth water. *9am-7.30pm Mon, 8am-8pm Tue-Thu, to 9pm Fri, to 7.30pm Sat, to 3pm Sun*

ZEVANA/SHUTTERSTOCK

Duomo di Pisa and the Leaning Tower, Pisa

view Buffalmacco's impressive fresco *Il Trionfo della Morte,* and for the **Museo delle Sinopie**, to eye-up rare preparatory sketches for Renaissance frescoes.

Five centuries of Tuscan art

Despite housing one of Italy's most valuable collections of medieval art, the **Museo Nazionale di San Matteo** *(adult/ reduced €5/2)* doesn't receive much attention from visitors. The precious collection of paintings and sculptures produced between the 12th and 16th centuries includes works by Masaccio, Beato Angelico, Benozzo Gozzoli, Nicola and Giovanni Pisano, Donatello and Michelozzo. It's contained in a former Benedictine convent founded in the 11th century overlooking the Arno.

SOLVING THE TILT

After its completion in 1370, Pisa's bell tower continued to slowly tilt southward for over six centuries, defying gravity and baffling architects through the ages. Only in the 1990s did engineers finally find a solution to stabilise its fragile foundation, through a pioneering technique known as 'controlled sub-excavation', which involved the careful removal of small quantities of soil from beneath the north side of the structure. Over the past three decades the tower has straightened by as much as 4cm, and is now tilted by 'only' 3.97° – and, remarkably, it's now considered as stable as it has ever been, secure for generations of future visitors to take a dubious photo of themselves pretending to prop it up.

 **EATING IN PISA: OUR PICKS**

Numeroundici: No reservations, no frills. Order at the counter, sit at a wooden table and enjoy one of the daily specials. *noon-10pm Mon-Fri, from 7pm Sat* €

Trattoria Sant'Omobono: Walk past the market stalls into this *trattoria* that seems sustained by a Corinthian column in the middle of the room. *12.30-2.30pm & 7.30-10pm* €€

Osteria di Culegna: With exquisite ravioli and a wide selection of meaty mains, this family-run *osteria* offers up authentic Tuscan flavours. *12.30-2.30pm & 7.30-10pm* €€

Trattoria da Stelio: Stelio has spent most of his life serving loyal returning customers after half a century of cooking simple, traditional classics. *noon-3pm Mon-Fri* €€

Naples & the Amalfi Coast

STREET LIFE | ARCHAEOLOGY | SPECTACULAR COASTLINES

Places

Naples p212
Herculaneum p216
Capri p216
Pompeii p217
Amalfi Coast p220

 TOP TIP

The popularity of Naples' Quartieri Spagnoli has seen holiday accommodation proliferate in recent years, making housing increasingly scarce or too expensive for residents. Consider staying in an adjacent neighbourhood and then heading in for meals or experiences. It really helps.

If you picture Italy, much of it is likely infused with the lore of Campania. Perhaps it's the holy chaos of Naples, Vespas buzzing down ancient alleys while women hang laundry above, chatting animatedly with neighbours. Or the glittering island of Capri, playground of the rich, powerful and artistic for millennia. Then, you might be conjuring the plunging seascapes of the Amalfi Coast: vertical towns crossed by lemon-coated zigzag alleys that seem to rise straight out of the Mediterranean. Yes, any one of these things might well be on your mood board. The good news? It's all real, all waiting for you. Of course, the reason it will feel familiar is because much of it has been discovered already, so prepare yourself for high-season crowds. But there's plenty left to explore and still more than a few corners that will seem like a delicious secret. No matter where you go, there will be magic.

Naples

MAP p214

Italians sometimes joke that there's Italy and then there's Napoli – so singular is its character, so potent its historical legacy. And yet so few visitors are prepared for its uniqueness and capacity to surprise.

Its story begins with the Greek colony of Neapolis, founded in 474 BCE. Norman, Spanish and Bourbon rulers made

🧭 GETTING AROUND

Frequent high-speed trains connect Naples to Rome and other major Italian cities. Circumvesuviana trains connect Naples to Herculaneum, Pompeii and Sorrento.

Frequent ferries connect Naples to its bay islands, including Capri, where buses traverse the island. Ferries sail between Capri and Sorrento, while the extensive SITA bus network covers the Amalfi Coast. In Naples itself, the dense city centre is best explored by foot, though use a little more caution in crowded places and at night. Mass transport – buses, funiculars, the metro – is essential for making it up to hilltop areas like Capodimonte and Vomero. Driving in Naples is unnecessary and highly discouraged, as is driving along the Amalfi Coast in high season.

NAPLES & THE AMALFI COAST

Avellino

Monte Vergine

Avella

Nola

Marigliano

Pomigliano d'Arco

Acerra

San Gennaro Vesuviano

Palma Campania

Sarno

Nocera

Cava

Mt Finestra

Vietri sul Mare

Cetara

Golfo di Salerno

Salerno

Tramonti

Maiori

Minori

Ravello

Atrani

Amalfi

Conca dei Marini

Amalfi Coast

Pimonte

Agerola

Bomerano

Riserva Statale Valle delle Ferriere

Mt Sant'Angelo a Tre Pizzi

Nocelle

Praiano

Pompeii

Terzigno

Somma Vesuviana

San Giorgio a Cremano

Mt Vesuvius (Vesuzio)

Torre Annunziata

Castellammare di Stabia

Vico Equense

Positano

Colli di Fontanelle

Moiano

Piano di Sorrento

Sorrento

Sant'Agata sui Due Golfi

Massa Lubrense

Termini

Mt San Costanzo

Marina del Cantone

Marina Grande

Capri Town

Capri

Anacapri

Mt Solaro

Herculaneum

Portici

Torre del Greco

Naples

Golfo di Napoli

Giugliano in Campania

Marano di Napoli

Qualiano

Aversa

Caivano

Casavatore

Bagnoli

Pozzuoli

Campi Flegrei

Baia

Bacoli

Lago d'Averno

Lago d'Fusaro

Torregaveta

Lido di Licola

Villaggio Coppola

Golfo di Gaeta

Procida

Procida

Casamicciola

Lacco Ameno

Ischia

Ischia

Forio

Mt Epomeo

Sant'Angelo

Tyrrhenian Sea

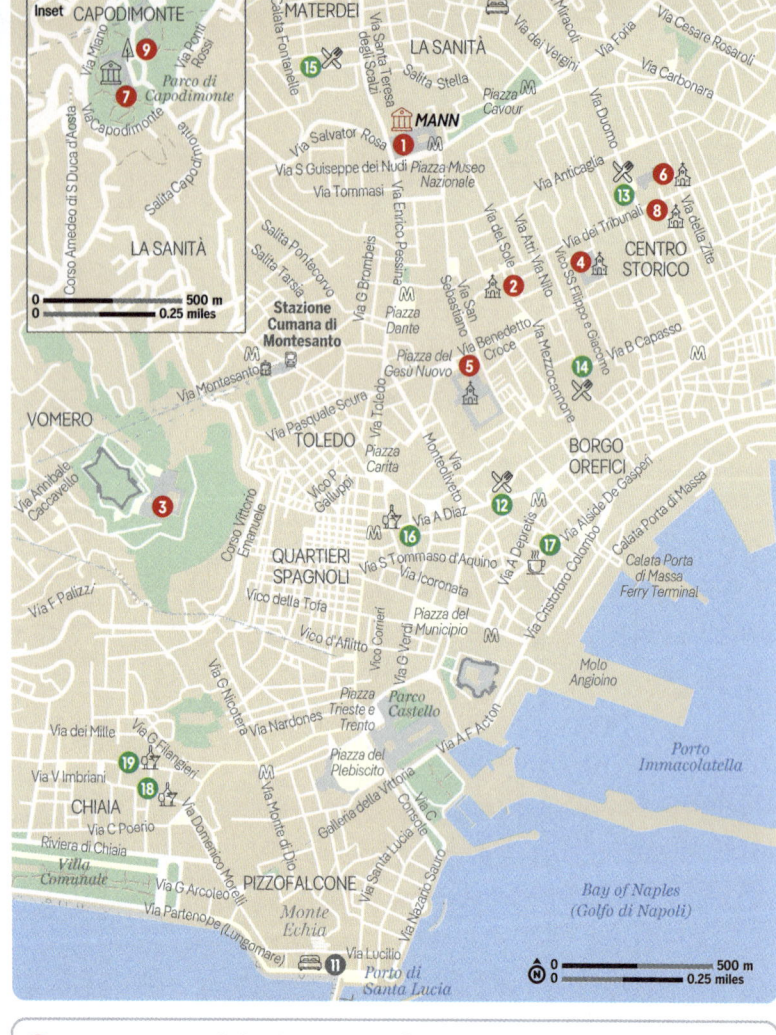

NAPLES

Inset: CAPODIMONTE

0	500 m
0	0.25 miles

★ **HIGHLIGHTS**	5 Complesso Monumentale di Santa Chiara	● **SLEEPING**	15 Pizzeria Starita
1 MANN	6 Duomo di Napoli	10 Atelier Inès	● **DRINKING & NIGHTLIFE**
● **SIGHTS**	7 Museo di Capodimonte	11 Grand Hotel Vesuvio	16 Astronomia Bar Segreto
2 Cappella Sansevero	8 Pio Monte della Misericordia	● **EATING**	17 Bar Mexico
3 Certosa e Museo di San Martino	9 Real Bosco di Capodimonte	12 Aria Restaurant	18 Chandelier
4 Chiesa e Chiostro di San Gregorio Armeno		13 Januarius	19 Enoteca Belledonne
		14 La Locanda Gesù Vecchio	

Naples wealthy, leaving behind architectural splendours like the imposing Castel Sant'Elmo and the Palazzo Reale. Today, it's a deliciously layered, always surprising beast – gritty yet aristocratic, unrelenting yet deeply humane, a maze of glittering ballrooms and bellowing street life.

Indeed, Naples is exactly what you expect while being not what you expect at all.

Witness a miracle

San Gennaro's blood – reputedly saved by a devotee after his rather gruesome death in 305 – has become famous for its miraculous liquefaction on the first Saturday in May, 19 September and 16 December. On these days, thousands flock to the **Duomo di Napoli** *(free) t*o witness this miraculous event. Whether it's truly the blood of San Gennaro (or whether it's blood at all) is impossible to say: the Catholic Church prohibits anyone from opening the two hermetically sealed ampoules. Besides, it hardly matters. Those who gather do so out of reverence for their city as much as for their saint.

On any day, the Duomo is worth a visit for its artistic treasures, among them a breathtakingly frescoed **Chapel of San Gennaro**.

Wander the Museo Archeologico Nazionale di Napoli

The largest museum in central Naples, **MANN** *(mann-napoli.it; adult/reduced €20/2; closed Tue)* is also one of Italy's most important archaeological repositories. Its vast collection of Greek and Roman antiquities includes the monumental Farnese Bull, priceless Roman bronzes, and exquisite mosaics recovered from the ruins of Herculaneum and Pompeii. MANN also houses the second-largest collection of Egyptian artefacts in the country, spanning seven rooms and six centuries. Then there's the museum's blush-inducing Secret Room, home to over 250 pieces of erotica (gathered mainly from excavations at Pompeii and Herculaneum) that once titillated the Bourbon monarchy.

Escape to a hilltop palace and wood

The Royal Palace of Capodimonte began life in 1738 when Charles III originally planned to build himself a hunting lodge on the hill above Naples but pivoted to a palace that could accommodate both his expanding court and the priceless art he'd inherited from his mother, Elisabetta Farnese.

That palace is now the **Museo di Capodimonte** *(capodimonte.cultura.gov.it; adult/under 18 €15/free),* whose magnificent

BEST SACRED ART IN THE CENTRE

Cappella Sansevero: Houses the iconic *Cristo Velato* statue, whose realistic marble folds and delicate contours have attracted admirers for centuries. *(museosansevero.it; adult/reduced €12/8)*

Pio Monte della Misericordia: Contains Caravaggio's *Sette Opere della Misericordia. (piomontedellamisericordia.it; €10)*

Chiesa e Chiostro di San Gregorio Armeno: The frescoes of San Gregorio Armeno here are among the best examples of Luca Giordano's intricate work in central Naples. *(free)*

Complesso Monumentale di Santa Chiara: An explosion of colourful majolica tilework set over 72 octagonal columns that connect to similarly decorated benches framing a lush private garden. *(Chiostro di Santa Chiara; monastero disantachiara.it; adult/reduced €7/5)*

✂ EATING IN NAPLES: OUR PICKS

MAP p214

Pizzeria Starita: A constant contender for best in the city, and even if it's franchised, it's still stellar. *noon-3.30pm & 7pm-midnight Tue-Sun* €€

La Locanda Gesù Vecchio: Traditional recipes, local ingredients and a broad selection of wines. *2-3.30pm & 7-11pm Tue-Sun* €€

Aria Restaurant: This intimate Michelin-star restaurant elevates Neapolitan street food. *7.30-11pm Mon-Sat* €€€

Januarius: The cuisine is classical Neapolitan with down-to-earth products, but the fresco ceilings are out of this world. *1-3pm & 7.30-11pm Wed-Mon* €€€

collection includes a Caravaggio in situ, where it was meant to be, as well as contemporary works from artists like Mimmo Paladino and Umberto Manzo.

Done, get some fresh air at the **Real Bosco di Capodimonte**, the palace's 124-hectare former royal forest.

Explore a panoramic charterhouse

The paradoxical density and splendour of central Naples is hard to grasp when you're amid it, so spend a few hours surveying it from the hilltop **Certosa e Museo di San Martino** *(adult/reduced €6/2)*. Originally a Carthusian monastery built between 1325 and 1368, it's now home to priceless frescoes and paintings by Neapolitan baroque masters such as Jusepe de Ribera and Cosimo Fanzago. The cloisters here are among the most beautiful in Italy, adorned and altered over the centuries by some of the country's finest artists, most importantly architect Giovanni Antonio Dosio in the 16th century and baroque sculptor Cosimo Fanzago a century later.

Herculaneum

Head back to 79 CE

The same eruption that destroyed Pompeii in 79 CE buried **Herculaneum** *(coopculture.it/en/poi/archaeological-park-of -Herculaneum)* under a volcanic mudslide. This site is more manageable than Pompeii and has an incredible array of artefacts. Among the highlights is the **Casa dei Cervi**, a two-storey villa that belonged to a noble family with a twisted sense of humour: cross the courtyard to see marble deer attacked by dogs and a drunkenly inappropriate Hercules. The **Casa Sannitica**, built in the 2nd century BCE by the Samnites, is a portal into Herculaneum's pre-Roman past, with wooden lattice fences, an impluvium and a fresco of the rape of Europa, while the vaulted rooms of **L'Antica Spiaggia**, likely port warehouses, became a refuge during the eruption. Equally intriguing is the **Terme Suburbane**, featuring intricate mosaics, and the **Casa del Tramezzo di Legno**, which preserves a folding wooden screen and bedframe.

Capri

Encounter the magical Blue Grotto

The world-famous **Grotta Azzurra** (Blue Grotto) is a spectacular natural phenomenon, although – fair warning – the tourist crush and breakneck pace of the experience may taint

---

HELP KEEP COMMUNITIES ALIVE

Naples' Quartieri Spagnoli has been synonymous with social decline for many years. However, thanks to the grassroots work of cultural associations, artists and residents, the neighbourhood has become a unique heritage site, a place that welcomes visitors with pride. Yet many people are forced to live on meagre incomes, and life remains difficult. It often means that they adapt in creative ways, and this might look charming to the outside eye. But these are real people living real lives – something to keep in mind when visiting. If you want to take a picture of someone or their home, ask first. If they say no, don't take it personally. The difference between gawking and engaging begins with our approach to delicate situations.

DRINKING IN NAPLES: OUR PICKS

MAP p214

Bar Mexico: This 1960s relic in Piazza Garibaldi serves a thick, sugary rocket fuel that will remind you why you're here. *5.30am-8pm Mon-Sat*

Astronomia Bar Segreto: A speakeasy that'll take a moment to find but is worth the search for its inspired drinks and service. *8pm-2am Thu-Tue*

Enoteca Belledonne: Stellar wine bar with a great selection of finger foods and a cosy setting. *hours vary*

Chandelier: You'd best reserve a table. Your reward is incredible drinks and abundant snacks. *8am-3pm*

Pompeii

The once-thriving city of Pompeii was buried under a layer of lapilli (burning fragments of pumice stone) by the eruption of Vesuvius in 79 CE. The result is a remarkably well-preserved slice of ancient life, where visitors can walk down Roman streets and snoop around millennia-old houses, temples, shops, cafes, amphitheatres and a brothel.

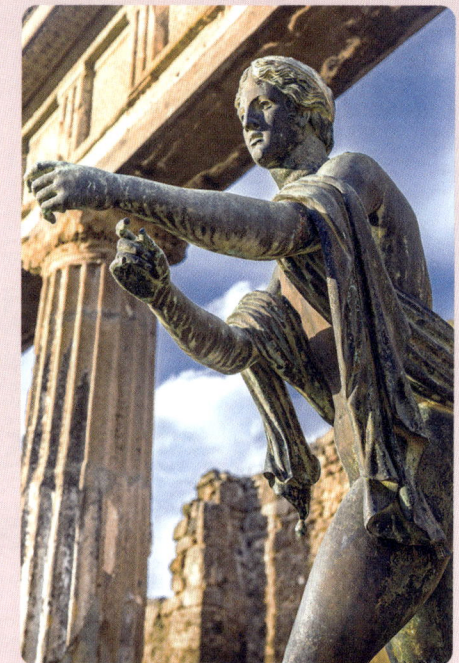

Top Sights

The Romans were nothing if not entertainers, and the 20,000-seat **Anfiteatro** (Amphitheatre) at the park's eastern end is proof of their love for the stage.

Pompeii's main piazza, the **Foro**, was the seat of religious, commercial and political life. It's best to end your day here because even when it's not summer the sun can be punishing.

The restored 90-room **Villa dei Misteri** dates to the 2nd century BCE. The Dionysiac frieze spans the walls of the large dining room and is one of the biggest and most arresting paintings from the ancient world.

The site of **Insula dei Casti Amanti** was first uncovered in 1912 and has since been discovered to include a room decorated with mythological figures, charcoal drawings made by children in a service courtyard, and an entrance hall where the skeletons of two eruption victims were found. You can watch the process of bringing Pompeii to life, as well as an innovative effort to bring photovoltaic panels onto the site, which was designed as part of the Pompeii for All initiative and has access for travellers with disabilities.

TOP TIPS

● Always enter the park via the less-crowded Amphitheatre entrance. Crowds are thickest in the morning; take the afternoon to explore.

● You should only buy your tickets directly through the Pompeii website.

● The excellent audio guides are multilingual.

PRACTICALITIES

● pompeiisites.org
● adult/reduced from €18/2 ● 9am-7pm Apr-Oct, to 5pm Nov-Mar

HERCULANEUM'S FRESCOES & MOSAICS

Pompeii may have more frescoes and mosaics, but Herculaneum is no slouch in the art department. Check them out in these fascinating dwellings and temples.

Casa dello Scheletro: Spectacular *lararium* (shrine) inlaid with impossibly tiny mosaic tiles.

Casa di Nettuno e Anfitfrite: Intricate and vivid mosaic depicting Neptune and Aphrodite.

Colegio degli Augustali: Frescoes of Hercules fighting the good fight.

Casa dell'Atrio a Mosaico: This sea-view villa's floor is entirely covered in floral and geometric mosaics.

Casa del Gran Portale: Beautiful brick lintel entrance, and fascinating wall decorations of birds and bizarre designs.

RUI VALE SOUSA/SHUTTERSTOCK

your buzz. The grotto opens at 9am, but try to get here as early as possible to (slightly) shorten your wait. A ticket to the grotto costs €18 for a five-minute tour; duck as the gondolier ushers the boat inside, lest you crack your head open on the rock. Inside, the waters glow electric blue and the gondoliers serenade you with Neapolitan classics.

Ride a heavenly chairlift

From **Anacapri**'s Piazza Vittoria, the chairlift **Seggiovia del Monte Solaro** (*montesolarocapri.it; one way/return €11/14*) whisks riders up to **Monte Solaro**, Capri's highest peak. The 13-minute 589m ride up provides unforgettable views of terraced vineyards, white houses and lemon groves, with the Gulf of Naples and the Amalfi Coast winking in the distance.

Vertigo? You can also get to the top on foot by following Via Axel Munthe to Via Salita per il Solaro. Go right, then look for the iron crucifix marking La Crocetta pass. A left turn will take you to the hermitage of **Santa Maria a Cetrella**; turning right will get you to the summit. The hike takes about an hour each way.

 EATING & DRINKING NEAR POMPEII: OUR PICKS

Melius: Gourmet deli-restaurant offering dishes made with local ingredients such as Graniano pasta or anchovies from Cetara. *9am-2pm Tue-Sun, 5.30-10pm Tue-Sat* €€

Zi'Caterina: Spacious old-school restaurant that looks touristy but serves delicious traditional southern Italian food. *noon-midnight* €€

La Bettola del Gusto: Highly innovative Italian food such as seared-octopus couscous, made with proudly artisanal ingredients. *12.30-3pm & 7.30-11pm Tue-Thu & Sun, to midnight Fri & Sat* €€

Na' Pasta: Excellent pastas and a magical parmigiana makes the tight seating entirely worth it, especially after a few glasses of local wine. *12.15-7pm Tue-Sat, to 8pm Sun* €€

Seggiovia del Monte Solaro, Capri

SEA MONSTERS & MERMAIDS

Capri's most iconic natural sight is undoubtedly the **Faraglioni** rock formation. The Faraglioni is formed by three stacked crags just off the island's coast: the 109m-high Saetta; Stella with its 60m-long central cavity; and Scopolo, home of the blue lizard, native only to Capri. Here swimmers revel and lovers kiss for luck as they sail through Stella's cavity. They must not know the legends.

The Faraglioni, like many of Campania's natural phenomena, are linked to Greek myth. Homer believed they were boulders hurled at Ulysses by the cyclops Polyphemus. Virgil thought they were the legendary home of murderous mermaids, waiting to lure sailors to death. Squint a little. Don't they look like a sea monster?

Live it up in Capri Town

Capri Town's beauty is iconic. It's no wonder. Its white-washed labyrinthine streets – with their tiled courtyards and hand-painted ceramic street signs, shaded by purple blooms – are the ultimate Italian island dreamscape.

Your first port of call is **Piazza Umberto I**, called La Piazzetta by locals. It's perfect for people-watching, though your nosiness will cost you – an espresso can set you back €8. Wander side streets like **Via Le Botteghe**, peppered with luxe boutiques and restaurants. In Via Vittorio Emanuele, a queue leads to **Gelateria Buonocore**, famous for its freshly pressed waffle cones. Continue on to **Via Camerelle**, Capri's bougainvillea-strung haute couture street.

Escape to the gardens

For a break from Capri Town's bustling centre, escape to the tranquil **Giardini di Augusto** and nearby **Certosa di San Giacomo**. Built in 1371, the *certosa* (Carthusian monastery) houses 17th-century frescoes in its church and revolving modern-art exhibits. Meanwhile, the Giardini di Augusto

EATING ON CAPRI: OUR PICKS

Salumeria da Aldo: A well-stocked Marina Grande minimart with a delicatessen where you can get a freshly made *panino* (sandwich). *7am-9pm* €

Pescheria Le Botteghe: Fish market with a raw bar and restaurant serving fishburgers and seafood pastas. *8am-3pm & 7-11pm, to 1pm Mon* €€€

Gennaro Amitrano: Michelin-star seafood restaurant at Marina Piccola, with elegant farm-to-table fare. *12.30-2.30pm & 7.30-10.30pm* €€€

La Capannina: A family-run traditional restaurant (established 1931) for dinner or drinks. Book ahead. *12.15-3pm & 7.15-11.30pm* €€€

THE BEST BEACHES ON CAPRI

Bagni di Tiberio: Take a *gozzetto* (dinghy) to this chic pebble beach (entry €20), once Emperor Tiberius' bathing grounds – next to the ruins of one of his villas.

Marina Grande Beach: Free beach popular with day-trippers for its proximity to the port; large, boisterous stretch of pebbles and *lidos* (stretches of sand) with lots of families.

Marina Piccola: Petite (free) pebble beach with views of the Faraglioni and water that's always warm and still. Enjoy lunch and snacks at the various *lidos*.

Isole Faraglioni: This cliff 'beach' and diving point is stunning, but its beach clubs Da Luigi and La Fontelina are reservation only. Shuttle-boat service.

Spiaggia del Faro (Anacapri): Luscious cliff beach with views of the historic lighthouse; enjoy light lunches and *aperitivi* at the beach's *lidos*. Spectacular sunsets.

Bagni Regina Giovanna, Amalfi Coast

rewards with soaring views of Marina Piccola and the Faraglioni. Time your visit for the spring bloom for a particularly beautiful experience. Just outside the gardens, you'll find the entrance to **Via Krupp**, a 1.5km paved hairpin path leading down to **Marina Piccola** and a refreshing dip in the sea (the bus will take you back up).

Amalfi Coast

If you're looking for a secret corner of paradise, you're 1000 years too late to the Amalfi Coast. But who cares? It remains transformatively beautiful. Stretching 50km along the southern side of the Sorrentine Peninsula, the UNESCO-protected Costiera Amalfitana is a postcard-perfect vision of shimmering blue water fringed by vertiginous cliffs on which cling whitewashed and pastel-hued villages and terraced lemon groves. You won't be able to see it all, and you'll ruin your time trying. But choose wisely and you'll find yourself grinning like a fool at your luck.

Go beyond the souvenirs

Sorrento's historic centre offers much more than kitschy souvenirs. At the edge of town lies haunting **Il Vallone dei**

DRINKING ON CAPRI: OUR PICKS

Giardino Mediterraneo: Chic outdoor cocktail lounge in a historic lemon grove. Enjoy tranquil views and lemon cocktails. *10am–midnight, to 8pm Sun & Mon*

Bianca by La Palma Hotel: Super luxe cocktail lounge in the new La Palma hotel, with bespoke cocktails, a restaurant and a rooftop view. 'Island chic' dress code. *7pm–1am*

Taverna Anema e Core: Bar with live music, DJ sets and a full menu of cocktails on Via Sella Orta. No dress code. A Capri institution. *11pm–4.30am*

Hangout Capri: Capri Town gastropub serving steaks plus classic and inventive cocktails in a cool, relaxed atmosphere. *11.30am–4pm & 6.30pm–2am*

Mulini and its ruins of ancient wheat mills. A short walk away, **Piazza Tasso** is the city's convivial living room. From here, follow Via Luigi de Maio to the **Chiesa and Chiostro di San Francesco**, where pagan, Roman and medieval architecture make an evocative backdrop for art exhibitions. Make a stop at the nearby **Sedile Dominova**, a fresco-covered 14th-century nook that once served as a place for nobles to congregate, and check out the tiny **Chiesa dei Santi Felice e Baccolo**, home to *intarsio* (inlaid wood) master Giuseppe Rocco.

Swim like a queen

When Queen Giovanna II of Anjou-Durazzo wanted to escape the 14th-century bustle, she came to the dazzling natural pools beside a vast Roman villa outside Sorrento. Known today as **Bagni Regina Giovanna**, they can get crowded in summer but they're free, almost surreal in beauty, and worth the hike. Spend half a day and picnic at the ruins of the Pollio Felice villa above the pools. To reach them, take Via Capo from Sorrento to Traversa Punta Capo. Stop at the *alimentari* (deli) for a sandwich and water, then continue down the Traversa until it becomes a footpath that leads to a steep staircase.

Take to the sea

The best way to enjoy **Positano** may be from the sea, but ferries and group tours can be crowded and private tours can be exorbitant. Family-run **Bluestar Positano** *(bluestar positano.it)* offers a range of tours for every budget and timeframe. Early-bird and sunset tours offer a 1½-hour ride around the coast. The best part? Many of the boats are traditional wooden *gozze*.

The boat ride to **Adolfo** *(daadolfo.com)* might be short, but this throwback beach club and restaurant is one of the greatest reminders of how life used to be in Positano. You can only make reservations by telephone, and their distinctive boat is the only ride available from Positano town. Make sure you reserve sunloungers as well as lunch.

Hike the Path of the Gods

In the 1980s hikers christened an ancient, panoramic shepherd's trail the **Sentiero degli Dei** (Path of the Gods). Stretching 6km each way, it is indeed heavenly – running from Agerola (Bomerano) to Nocelle above Positano, and taking three to five hours to tackle. It's moderately challenging, with several route options; the most popular is Bomerano to Nocelle (mostly downhill), reachable by bus from Amalfi.

SONGS OF SORRENTO

It's not just the Sirens who composed intoxicating odes to Sorrento. Throughout the years some of Italy's most famous songs have been written in or about the city. 'Torna a Surriento', composed in 1894 by the De Curtis brothers, is one of the most famous examples of the *canzone napoletana* and has been recorded by singers all over the world. There are few songs so well known (and heartbreaking) to Italians as Lucio Dalla's 'Caruso', a tribute to the great opera singer and his lover. Indeed, the Bologna-born Dalla is considered by many to be an honorary citizen of the town, in honour of the song.

 EATING & DRINKING IN AMALFI: OUR PICKS

Pasticceria Pansa:	**Trattoria dei Cartari:**	**Donna Stella:** Pizzeria	**Ristorante La Caravella:**
More than just morning coffee and *cornetti* (croissants), with plenty of non-alcoholic options. *7.30am-11pm* €	Head towards the paper museum for a locals-approved meal with the freshest catch in town. *noon-3.30pm & 7-10.30pm Tue-Sun* €€	in an atmospheric lemon grove that serves delicious pizza plus salads. *11am-4pm & 5.30-10pm Wed-Mon* €€	Michelin-starred restaurant with tasting menus featuring local specialities. *noon-2pm & 7-10pm Wed-Mon* €€€

BEST AMALFI SHOPPING

Dalla Carta alla Cartolina: Magical paper shop with art exhibits, near the famous Museo della Carta. Drop postcards in a mailbox and see its beautiful story come to life.

JP Boutique: Signature Amalfi designs, gauzy fabrics and unique accessories from an Amalfi-born artist and illustrator with a flair for the dramatic.

L'Altra Costiera: The best place in Amalfi for locally sourced ceramics from up-and-coming and established artists, many from Vietri sul Mare.

La Scuderia del Duca: Tucked behind the Terminal restaurant at the port, this place is full of great antiques and funky paper crafts that make excellent gifts.

Continue to Positano or return by public transport. The trail is well signposted, but consider getting a guide to explain the surrounding area and make sure you're OK. Also, wear good shoes, carry water, a windbreaker and prepare for crowds. With care, it's an unforgettable experience.

Dig deeper in Amalfi

Amalfi has always been a central point on the coast, and it remains so today. Pass through the vaulted arches to Piazza Duomo, dotted with historic coffee bars and dominated by the Arabic-Norman **Cattedrale di Sant'Andrea**.

The town centre was constructed in the 10th and 11th centuries, when Amalfi was a powerful maritime republic and the natural landscape lent itself to a fortification in the hills. Neighbourhoods followed suit and almost disappear into the stone, so sticking to the main drags means you'll likely miss them. So wander just a bit and you'll find yourself in a very local world of covered walkways and ancient alleys.

Find romance in Ravello

High above the coast, **Villa Rufolo**, just off Ravello's Piazza Duomo, was founded in the 13th century. In its 700 years, it's been the residence of King Robert of Anjou and several popes. Its history is evident in the 14th-century entrance tower, Gothic gateway, Moorish courtyard and 19th-century cascading gardens and lavish sitting rooms with sweeping Gulf views. It's not hard to see how it inspired Wagner in the second act of his opera *Parsifal*.

A 10-minute walk away is **Villa Cimbrone** and its gasp-inducing Terrace of Infinity, 280m above sea level. Both villas are swank hotels. If you're looking for somewhere to splash out, you could do worse. Otherwise, sip at Villa Cimbrone's **Grotto di Eva** garden bar.

DRINKING IN POSITANO: OUR PICKS

Franco's Bar: It would be criminal not to try to get here, even though the prices might magically swallow your wallet. *5pm-midnight*

Il San Pietro di Positano: You can't get much higher up and you won't get much more dramatic; worth the hike and the prices. *Apr-Oct*

Fly: Come on, when's the last time you had it large? Start here and continue below at Music on the Rocks. *6pm-2am*

Bar Internazionale: The closest you'll get to no frills in town, with locals stopping in for their own *aperitivo. 7am-11pm Thu-Tue*

Sicily

GRAECO-ROMAN RUINS | GOLDEN MOSAICS | STREET MARKETS

Everything about the Mediterranean's largest island is extreme, from the beauty of its rugged landscape to its hybrid cuisine and flamboyant architecture. Sicily is intense, ancient and contradictory, and every corner reveals the same incongruous mash-up of old and new, chaos and calm.

Now an autonomous region in Italy, the island was hotly contested for centuries – the ancient Greeks, Carthaginians and Romans all fell into its devilishly handsome lair. Later rule by Byzantines, Saracens, Normans, Germans, Angevins and Spanish blessed Sicily with artistic and architectural riches that remain star attractions.

The rich Sicilian kitchen, crafted from multiple cuisines, only intensifies the sensory feast. Island produce – sun-spun capers and cherry tomatoes, olives, creamy almonds and pistachios, pomegranates, wild saffron, farm-churned ricotta, shellfish, tuna and swordfish – has been the magic ingredient ever since Bacchus planted vines near Taormina and the Greek god of blacksmiths fired up his forge inside Mt Etna. Come curious. Come hungry.

Places

Palermo p224
Catania p226
Taormina p228
Syracuse p229

☑ **TOP TIP**

Late spring and early autumn are ideal times to visit Sicily; temperatures are warm but not extreme, prices are lower and crowds much more manageable than they are in July and August.

 GETTING AROUND

Regular car-passenger ferries cross the Strait of Messina from the Italian mainland to Sicily. Once on the island a flurry of high-speed hydrofoils and slower *traghetti* (ferries) sail to Sicily's offshore Aeolian and Egadi islands. Boats run year-round, with reduced schedules in winter.

Driving in traffic-busy Palermo and Catania is a headache, but motoring along the coast and inland is pleasurable and scenic. The A18 and

A20 *autostrade* (motorways) are toll roads. Away from towns, electric-vehicle charging stations are scarce. Trains and buses link Ionian coastal cities; buses offer faster links than trains between Palermo and Catania. Private operator **Ferrovia Circumetnea** (*circumetnea.it*) runs trains around Mt Etna villages. Island-wide, Sunday services are limited.

SICILY

Ustica

Aeolian
Islands

Stromboli

Filicudi   Salina   Panarea

Alicudi

Lipari Town   Lipari
                Vulcano

Castellammare
del Golfo

San Vito
Lo Capo   Terrasini

Palermo   Capo   Milazzo
                 d'Orlando Patti   Messina
Trapani   Partinico   Bagheria Cefalù Santo   Barcellona
                                         Stefano di Sant'Agata   Reggio di
           Alcamo   Termini   Camastra   di Militello   Calabria
Firvignana Salemi   Imerese
                      Pizzo Carbonara   Castelbuono   Taormina
Marsala   Corleone   Troina Bronte Randazzo   Naxos
           Petralia   Giarre
Castelvetrano Soprana Nicosia   Agira Adrano Mt Etna Aci Acireale
Mazara del   Menfi   Mussomeli   Paternò
Vallo   Enna
           Ribera   Aci
       Sciacca   Caltanissetta   Catania
Raffadali Canicatti Barrafranca Piazza Armerina
           Favara   Mazzarino   Scordia   Lentini
Agrigento   Ravanusa Caltagirone   Augusta
                 Licata   Niscemi Vizzini
                         Gela Comiso   Palazzolo   Syracuse
Mediterranean   Vittoria   Ragusa Acreide
Sea   Scoglitti   Noto   Avola
                           Marina di Modica Ispica Rosolini
                           Ragusa Scicli Pozzallo Pachino

0 ——— 50 km
0 ——— 25 miles

Palermo

Nearly 3000 years old, Palermo was conquered by the Arabs in 831 CE and, when the Normans invaded in 1072, Roger I (1031–1101) made the old Greek port the seat of his enlightened 'kingdom of the sun', encouraging resident Arabs, Byzantines, Greeks and Italians to remain.

Contemporary Palermo is stitched from rebellion, bravery, squalor and solidarity. It's a place where roving street vendors sell *pani ca meusa* (Sicilian bread roll stuffed with sautéed beef spleen) from hand-pushed carts, and locals chat in Italian, Albanian and Arabic. Be inquisitive. Peek into every citrus-filled cloister, cherub-spun chapel or trash-strewn back alley. You'll be astonished by what you find.

Royal tombs and a rooftop walk

The 13th-century **Cattedrale di Palermo** *(cattedrale.pal ermo.it; adult/child €12/6)* is a larger-than-life example of Sicily's unique Arab-Norman architectural style. Its interior safeguards royal Norman tombs containing two of Sicily's greatest rulers – Roger II and Frederick II of Hohenstaufen.

Save the best for last: the cinematic spiral up 110 steep stone steps to the cathedral's expansive roof terraces (open until

Cappella Palatina, Palermo

DARE-TO-TRY STIGGHIOLA

At quick glance it looks like an ordinary sausage. It's not. Introduced to the city by the Greeks 2000 years ago, Palermo's beloved *stigghiola* sees veal, lamb or goat intestines wrapped around a spring onion or leek, seasoned with parsley and flamed to a crisp on a charcoal- or wood-fired grill. It's deemed both a delicacy and an icon of Palermo's sizzling street-food scene.

Several market stalls and *trattorie* or fast-food joints with street kitchens at Palermo's oldest street market – **Mercato di Ballarò** – grill *stigghiola* on home barbecues in the street. The snack is always served chopped in chunks, salted and doled out on a plastic plate with a wedge of lime.

midnight once-weekly in summer), with an unmatched city panorama. Visit at the end of the day to savour the setting sun recasting the city in spectacular pink.

Save cents with a **combined ticket** *(adult/child €15/8)* covering the cathedral (the tombs, crypt, apse, treasury and rooftop) and 15th- to 18th-century art in the neighbouring **Museo Diocesana di Palermo**.

Explore an Arab-Norman wonder

Norman Sicily's cultural complexity is beautifully evoked at Palermo's star attraction: **Cappella Palatina**, awash in gold mosaics from 1130. It's squirrelled away like a jewel inside **Palazzo dei Normanni** *(federicosecondo.org; adult/child €19/11),* built by conquering Arabs in the 9th century.

Wind up the stone staircase in the 17th-century Maqueda courtyard to the 2nd floor, where treasures include the Hall of Viceroys, lit up in Murano glass; the Hall of Mosaics, decorated with secular mosaics; and the soaring square tower of the Hall of Winds.

Visit Friday to Monday when the Royal Apartments are also open, and cover up – short skirts, shorts and bare shoulders are forbidden in the chapel.

 EATING & DRINKING IN PALERMO: OUR PICKS

Da Mimì di Guglielmo Damiano: Locals claim this Il Capo icon fries up the city's finest arancini (stuffed rice balls). *7.15am-10pm Mon-Sat, from 10am Sun* €

Moltivolti: You'll be hard-pushed to find a cooler co-working space, cafe, kitchen cooking up world cuisine (vegan included) and late-night bar. *9am-midnight* €

Ciccio in Pentola: Creative fish and seafood dishes paired with excellent service make this elegant *ristorante* a local foodie favourite. *noon-3.30pm & 7-11pm* €€

Gagini: Experience gourmet heaven at the contemporary kitchen of Italian-Brazilian chef Mauricio Zillo – Palermo's only Michelin-starred address. *12.30-2.30pm Wed-Sun, 7.30-10pm Tue-Sun* €€€

BEST SHOPPING: SLOW DESIGN ON VIA VITTORIO EMANUELE

Angela Tripi: Teeny terracotta *presepi* (crib figurines) in a 15th-century *palazzo* courtyard at Via Vittorio Emanuele 452.

Naná Aristova Jewels: Sicilian volcanoes inspire the contemporary jewellery by a Siberia-born Palermo-adopted jeweller at No 314.

Barbisio: Palermo's spiffiest hat shop at No 286 is a 1949 vintage. Buy a Sicilian *còppola* (flat cap).

Sicilia Inspired: Modern art, including drawings in Etna lava pigments, at No 292.

Rogato: 'Bags with history' are crafted from recycled materials at this boutique at No 130.

La Cittàcotte di Vincenzo Vizzari: Purchase a terracotta miniature of a Palermo church, palace or orange tree; No 120.

Fontana dell'Amenano, Catania

Sunset drinks at the Fountain of Shame

So scandalised were Sicilian churchgoers by the flagrant nudity of cheek-baring nymphs and frolicking river gods on Piazza Pretoria's monumental **Fontana Pretoria** that they dubbed it Fontana della Vergogna (Fountain of Shame). Designed by Florentine sculptor Francesco Camilliani between 1554 and 1555 for the Tuscan villa of Don Pedro di Toledo, it was bought by Palermo in 1573 in a bid to outshine Messina's newly crafted Fontana di Orione.

The play of light on the nudes posing in the fountain's tiered basins is theatrical any time of day – and never the same twice. Come sunset, enjoy it from above over alfresco drinks at rooftop bar **Le Terrazze del Sole** *(6pm-midnight Mar-Oct).*

Catania

The days when travellers avoided Sicily's second-largest city are long gone. Despite first-glance chaos and scruffiness, Catania has magnetic pull, brimming with youthful energy and earthy spirit. A smart base for Ionian coast trips or Mt Etna climbs, it delivers both convenience and intrigue.

UNESCO-listed, Catania rose from two disasters: Etna's 1669 lava flow and the 1693 earthquake that killed 12,000. baroque

DRINKING IN PALERMO: OUR PICKS

Altrove Bar: Italian craft beer, cocktails and killer margaritas lure a local crowd to this hip bar on Via Discesa dei Giudici. *5.30pm-1.30am Mon, to 2am Tue-Thu, 10am-1am Fri-Sun*

Tatum Art: Jazz lovers enjoy the intimacy of this small venue; reserve tables online. In summer concerts shift to seaside Mondello. *7pm-1am Tue-Sat, to midnight Sun*

Malox Cult: Don't miss the house Negroni (mixing Bulldog gin with Cinzano 1757 and Bèrto Bitter) at this cult bar with terrace on Piazzetta della Canna. *5.30pm-2am*

Botanico: Late-night music and cocktails down an alley festooned with greenery and street art. *6.30pm-2am Tue-Sun*

palazzi and churches, designed by Giovanni Vaccarini, sprouted from volcanic rock. Roman ruins sit beneath ornate facades, street art enlivens bohemian alleys, and *pasta alla Norma* (pasta with eggplant and ricotta) is served in ancient lava tubes – urban discovery here is intoxicating and richly layered.

Trawl a mouthwatering market

Tables groan under the weight of all manner of sea life at Catania's open-air fish market, **La Pescheria** *(closed Sun)*. Visit early morning – it opens at 7am and is being hosed down by 1pm. Access to the market, through a passageway by the side of gushing **Fontana dell'Amenano** (1867) on Piazza del Duomo, only adds to the theatre.

Grab a pew at **Scirocco Sicilian Fish Lab** *(sciroccolab.com)*, with a terrace overlooking the market on Piazza Alonzo di Benedetto, and enjoy the show over a paper cone of battered fish or deep-fried Etna pasta in cuttlefish-ink sauce. For fish without bones, order *cartoccio di mare senza spine.*

Delve into Catania's spiritual and social heart

Begin with *paste di mandorla* (almond sweets) at **Prestipino**, its contrasting white limestone and black volcanic-sand plaster typical of Catania's baroque architecture. Energised, explore the showpiece **Cattedrale di Sant'Agata**, final resting place of Catanian composer Vincenzo Bellini (1801–35).

The 360-degree panorama from the rooftop terraces of **Museo Diocesano** *(museodiocesanocatania.com; terrace €3, adult/child museum €7/4, with Roman baths €10/6)* is a perfect introduction to Catania. The museum's star attraction is a jewel-drenched, silver reliquary bust of Catania's patron saint Agata. Nearby is Piazza del Duomo's **Fontana dell'Elefante** (1736), a smiling black-lava elephant from Roman times, surmounted by an Egyptian obelisk.

Give in to Sicilian baroque

If you only have time for just one church, make it **Chiesa di San Benedetto** *(monasterosanbenedettocatania.it; adult/ child €6/4; open Tue, Fri & Sat)*. Sweeping up the monumental staircase of angels into the 18th-century church, nothing prepares you for its sumptuous interior of white stucco, coloured marble, the rare jasper altar with gold inlays and graphic ceiling frescoes painted between 1726 and 1729 by Messina artist Giovanni Tuccari. His depiction of St Agatha

BEST ROOFTOP CLIMBS

Chiesa Badia di Sant'Agata: Enjoy a 360-degree city panorama from the church's terrace.

Monastero dei Benedettini di San Nicolò l'Arena: Climb 141 steps up to the church roof in the monastery complex on Piazza Dante.

Chiesa di San Giuliano: There are heavenly views from this 18th-century jewel climax with 34 dizzying steps across a cupola to its crowning iron crucifix. A must.

Museo Diocesano: Admire black-stone Via Etnea marching north to Mt Etna from rooftops above Piazza del Duomo.

Ostello degli Elefanti: Only Catania could have its city hostel in a 17th-century *palazzo* with rooftop bar, open to all.

EATING IN CATANIA: OUR PICKS

Nuova Trattoria del Forestiero: Wholesome, no-frills fare including a superlative *pasta alla Norma* typical to Catania. *1-3.30pm & 6.30-10.30pm Tue-Sun* €

Mè Cumpari Turiddu: Small producers and Slow Food sensibilities underpin the sophisticated, classically inspired dishes at this vintage-styled place. *noon-2.30pm Sat & Sun, 7-10.30pm daily* €€

Canni e Pisci: Fashionable, contemporary meat and fish restaurant, with pavement terrace next to Palazzo Biscari. *1-3pm Sun, 8-11.30pm Tue-Sun* €€

Coria: Ultimate modern Sicilian epicurean treat: five- to eight-course tasting menus between moody art works by Etna painter Nunzio Fisichella. *12.30-2.30pm & 7.30-10pm Tue-Sat* €€€

BEST STREET-FOOD BITES

Coppa di frittura di paranza: Traditional paper *coppa* or cone (*cartoccio* on some menus) of battered, deep-fried fish and seafood, usually squid, shrimps, anchovies, mullet and cuttlefish – served with lemon or lime to squeeze on top.

Sardine a beccafico: Stuffed and fried sardines.

Panelle di ceci: Deep-fried chickpea fritters, sometimes spiced with fennel seeds. Best devoured as an *aperitivo* with an Ionian coast craft beer: Birra Messina is a favourite.

Polpo arristo o bollito: Fried or boiled octopus.

Caponata con spada: Cold, sweet-and-sour Sicilian stew of aubergine, onion, pepper and celery with swordfish; *con polpo* mixes in octopus.

being tortured, in a lunette above the altar, is a masterpiece. Visit at noon when the ferocious ringing of church bells adds unparalleled drama to the frescoes.

Taormina

Yes, it's unashamedly touristy and expensive, but Taormina merits a day or two at least. After all, it's one of Sicily's most popular summer destinations for good reason, with an ancient amphitheatre, superb people-watching and hypnotic vistas in spades – all from the town's spectacular perch on the side of a seaside mountain.

Founded in the 4th century BCE, Taormina prospered under the Greek ruler Gelon II and later under the Romans, but fell into quiet obscurity until its 18th-century comeback as a Grand Tour playground for wealthy aristos.

A fashionable hike and *passeggiata*

Outside sweltering July and August, hilltop Taormina is best explored on foot. Walk up from seaside **Mazzarò** (or ride the cable car), from where 700-plus steps (2.2km, 45 to 60 minutes) zigzag from Via Nazionale (SS114), opposite the staircase to Isola Bella. Plunge through 19th-century city gate **Porta Messina** and follow **Corso Umberto I**, past the crenellated,

DRINKING IN CATANIA: OUR PICKS

Vermut: Vermouth, vino, *salumi* (charcuterie) and 20-plus versions of the ubiquitous spritz keep this budget-friendly hot spot pumping. *11am-2am*	**Bohème Mixology Bar:** Intimate cocktail den decked out in mismatched furniture, gilded mirrors and the odd gramophone. Creative syrups made from scratch. *6pm-2am*	**Black Sheep Beer Store:** Craft beer and cocktail bar with stupendous burgers oozing creativity and artisan produce. *7pm-1am Tue-Sun*	**Razmataz:** Sip wine with bohemians under a huge tree on a village-esque square off Via Etnea. *noon-1am Mon-Sat*

Teatro Greco, Taormina

BEST BEACHES AROUND TAORMINA

Isola Bella: Small, chic, pebble beach in Mazzarò, linked to the Isola Bella nature reserve by a shingle isthmus.

Spiaggia di Mazzarò: Shingle beach in Mazzarò. Rent boats here, and bag a table for an unforgettable seafood lunch at peerless *trattoria* Il Barcaiolo.

Baie delle Sirene: Cut down hidden steps by Mazzarò's Atlantis Bay hotel to access tiny Mermaid's Bay, dotted with rocky islets. Snorkelling heaven.

Spiaggia di Spisone: Shingle-sand beach with a free public section and private beach clubs, a 10-minute walk from Mazzarò.

Spiaggia di Mazzeo: The sandiest option, 3km north of Lido Mazzarò.

Arab-influenced **Palazzo Corvaja** (now the tourist office) and baroque **Chiesa di Santa Caterina d'Alessandria**.

Grab a filled-on-the-spot *cannolo* (pastry shell with a sweet filling of ricotta or custard) at **Pasticceria Gelateria D'Amore** to enjoy on Piazza IX Aprile, then continue west through 12th-century clock tower **Torre dell'Orologio** into Piazza del Duomo. End in soothing **Villa Comunale**, the public gardens that are open until midnight in summer.

Showtime at an ancient theatre

Suspended between sea and sky, Taormina's **Teatro Greco** (*parconaxostaormina.com; adult/child €14/7),* built in the 3rd century BCE, is the world's most dramatically situated Greek theatre. Bag a ticket for an evening summer concert and enjoy the thrilling double act: opera, dance or theatre on stage and – if you're lucky – an erupting Etna beyond. Outside of performances, visit early morning to dodge the worst of the high-season crowds.

Syracuse

More than any other city, Syracuse (Siracusa) encapsulates Sicily's timeless beauty. Ancient Greek ruins rise out of lush

EATING IN TAORMINA: OUR PICKS

Bam Bar: Traditional *granita* served in a ceramic-tiled interior, with terrace seating. Go for a seasonal fruity flavour – lemon, fig, melon or peach. *7.30am-10.30pm* €

Gustibus: Six-table bistro adjoining a gourmet grocery, with a menu venerating Sicilian cheese, salami and fresh produce. End with a glass of Limonetna (lemon liqueur). *noon-10.30pm* €€

Tischi Toschi: Chocolatey *caponata* (sweet-and-sour aubergine stew), wild-fennel 'meatballs' and rosemary-infused liqueur. *1-2pm Fri-Sun, 7-10pm daily, shorter hours winter* €€

Osteria RossoDiVino: The day's catch, seasonal produce and wine by independent producers in a romantic, candlelit courtyard. *noon-2.30pm & 7-10.30pm Wed-Mon* €€€

GOLDEN AGE

After its founding by Corinthian colonists in 734 BCE, Syracuse flourished, becoming a rich commercial town and regional powerhouse. Victory over the Carthaginians at the Battle of Himera (480 BCE) paved the way for a golden age: art and culture thrived, and the city's tyrannical kings commissioned impressive public buildings.

The finest intellectuals of the age flocked to Syracuse, cultivating the sophisticated urban culture that was to see the birth of comic Greek theatre. Syracuse's independence abruptly came to an end in 211 BCE when invading Romans breached the city's defences, devised by Archimedes, and took control. Under Roman rule Syracuse remained Sicily's capital but the city's glory days were over. Decline set in.

citrus orchards, cafe tables fill baroque piazzas, and honey-hued medieval side streets tango to the sea. In its heyday this was the largest city in the ancient world, bigger than Athens and Corinth.

Its 'once upon a time' begins in 734 BCE, when Corinthian colonists landed on the beautiful island of Ortygia (Ortigia), setting up the mainland city four years later. Almost three millennia on, the ruins of that city constitute one of Sicily's greatest archaeological sites, with cathedral-like caves and an amphitheatre hosting magical evening performances.

Walk the island's perimeter

Count less than an hour (longer with stops) to walk the perimeter of **Ortygia**; its sea-facing terraced houses and labyrinthine alleyways are what a Syracuse visit is all about.

Drink in views of the mainland from **Forte San Giovannello**, part of the island's 16th-century fortification system. Walk to **Forte Vigliena** – watch waves crash against the crenellated fort walls and take a dip with the locals. On the island's southern tip, visit 13th-century **Castello Maniace** *(adult/reduced €6/3)*, a stone fortress built for Emperor Frederick II and host to July's electronic-music festival **Ortigia Music**.

Continue along the western shore to **Fonte Aretusa**, a spring turned pretty pond. End on the pedestrian jetty – magic at sunset.

Kick back on a showpiece square

Soak up the city's warm cream and ochre palette on vast **Piazza del Duomo**, with a sweep of golden-stone *palazzi* that could be spun from sunlight. Along the side of the **Duomo** *(adult/child €2/1)*, spot thick Doric columns incorporated into the cathedral's structure.

Next door, 17th-century **Palazzo Arcivescovile** safeguards a library with rare 13th-century manuscripts and **Chiesa di Santa Lucia alla Badia**, a nuns' parlour with a beautiful blue majolica floor. Allow time for people-watching over a spritz at **Gran Caffè del Duomo** or a cone filled with pistachio, lemon or chocolate ricotta cream from hole-in-the-wall **I Cannoli del Re**.

Go Greek at the ruins

It's wild to think you can sit in the theatre where playwright Aeschylus watched his tragedies unfold. Hewn in the rocky hillside in the 5th century BCE and rebuilt two centuries

EATING IN SYRACUSE: OUR PICKS

Divino Mare: Graze on Roman-style artichokes, oysters, cured meats and cheese at this wine bar by the market. *noon-3pm & 6-11.30pm Tue-Sat* €

A Putia delle Cose Buone: Creative home-style dishes brimming with local seafood, veggies etc; generous portions and a lovely atmosphere. *noon-11pm Wed-Mon* €€

Cortile Santo Spirito: Fine dining in a 17th-century *palazzo* on Ortygia's southern tip, with plant-based, seafood and meat tasting menus. *12.30-3.30pm & 7.30-10pm Tue-Sun* €€€

Don Camillo: Sterling service and innovative Sicilian cuisine in a refined setting; a Slow Food gourmand must. *1-2.30pm & 8-10.30pm Mon-Sat* €€€

Castello Maniace, Syracuse

later, Syracuse's **Teatro Greco** remains one of Sicily's most prestigious theatres, and watching a summertime play here is unforgettable.

Pre-performance, ramble around ancient Greek Syracuse in **Parco Archeologico della Neapolis** *(parchiarcheologici .regione.sicilia.it/siracusa-eloro-villa-tellaro-akrai; adult/ child €17/free, incl Museo Archeologico €18)*. Scan the QR code at the ticket booth for a map marked with three walking itineraries, 45 to 90 minutes long.

End at the **Museo Archeologico Paolo Orsi** *(adult/child €10/free, incl Parco Archeologico €18),* a one-stop shop covering Syracuse's ancient backstory.

BEST SWIM SPOTS

Solarium Forte Vigliena: Metal stairs lead to rocks below, next to Forte Vigliena. Limited space, deep water.

Spiaggia Diane nel Forte: In summer a wooden platform by the rocks to Forte Vigliena creates this seasonal urban beach.

Spiaggia di Cala Rossa: Small crescent of sandy beach near Ortygia's southeastern tip – always packed.

Solarium Zefiro: Below Fonte Aretusa, a private 'beach' with sunloungers and parasols (reserve online), music and drinks on a wooden platform. Come dusk, it morphs into a sunset lounge bar. *zefirosolarium.it*

Solarium Zen: Private *lido* and late-night lounge bar, with loungers on terraces and decks between rocks, in new-town Syracuse. *instagram. com/zensiracusa*

 DRINKING IN SYRACUSE: OUR PICKS

La Barca: Sip Negronis aboard a boat at Ortygia's marina, with occasional film screenings on deck, live music and excursions out to sea. *4pm-midnight Tue-Thu, 5pm-1am Fri & Sat*

Mi Ka Tù: Views of sundown's fireball sun slipping into the sea stun at this stylish wine-bar terrace on bar-lined Via Castello Maniace. *noon-midnight*

Cortile Verga: Enjoy drinks and chilled music in an 18th-century courtyard at one of Ortygia's top cocktail bars. *5.30pm-12.30am*

Ortigia Mare Escursioni: Admire the sunset from sea with an *aperitivo in barca* ('evening drinks afloat'); book excursions at the seasonal stand on Ponte Umbertino. *hours vary*

Places We Love to Stay

€ Budget €€ Midrange €€€ Top End

Rome
MAP p170

Night and Day € On narrow, historical Via Rasella, a short walk from Trevi Fountain, is this simple, laid-back hostel-style guesthouse.

Navona Essence €€ On a quiet backstreet near Campo de' Fiori in the *centro storico,* this snug boutique hotel is well placed for pretty much everywhere.

Palazzo Scanderbeg €€€ Located in a 15th-century *palazzo* around the corner from the Trevi Fountain, with comfortable and elegant rooms.

Cinque Terre

Hotel Gianni Franzi €€ Smallish rooms loaded with an atmospheric mix of antique furniture and simple traditional architecture in Vernazza. Spectacular breakfasts served on a shared terrace.

Hotel Porto Roca €€€ On a vantage point high above Monterosso with the SVA trail running right past, this 43-room hotel is the pinnacle of luxury in Cinque Terre.

Turin

Combo Torino € A modern and bright hostel with a Japanese-inspired feel and beautiful communal spaces.

Palazzo Chiablese €€ Nestled in a little alleyway just off the Palazzo Reale, this B&B features beautifully decorated rooms halfway between the contemporary and the antique.

Milan
MAP p186

Maison Borella €€ Overlooking the Naviglio Grande, this charming canal-side hotel with an inner courtyard has appealing rooms with parquet floors and exposed-beam ceilings.

Spadari al Duomo €€€ Milan's original design hotel, with its stylish rooms like miniature galleries showcasing the work of emerging artists.

Lago di Como

Hotel Borgo Antico €€ Hits all the right notes, with attractive rooms, helpful staff, ample breakfasts and a quiet location a 10-minute walk from the centre of Como (town).

Miralago €€ A delightful B&B in Pescallo (a 10-minute walk from Bellagio's centre), Miralago has bright, attractive rooms and a small garden.

Verona

Corte delle Pigne €€ Set around a quiet internal courtyard, this tiny three-room B&B is two short blocks from Piazza dei Signori.

Due Torri Hotel €€€ This former Della Scala palace exudes luxury, with velvet-clad sofas, tapestry-clad walls and burnished antiques.

Bologna

Dopa Hostel € Stylish hostel featuring recycled design touches, classy tiled bathrooms and a great communal kitchen.

Bologna nel Cuore €€ Intimate and immaculate lineup of rooms and apartments run by friendly art historian Maria; divine breakfasts.

Venice
MAP p194

3749 Ponte Chiodo € A charming little B&B in Cannaregio with period furnishings, canal views and a private front garden. It's a short walk from superb neighbourhood wine bars.

Giò & Giò €€ A classic hideaway in San Marco, with floor-to-ceiling silk draperies, subtle rococo flourishes and heirloom furniture pieces. Angle for a room overlooking the gondola stop.

Gritti Palace €€€ High-end perfection, set in a 1525 Doge's palace on the Grand Canal and lavished with rare marble, Rubelli silk damask, precious artworks and antiques.

Florence
MAP p204

Plus Hostel € This mega-hostel on Via Santa Caterina d'Alessandria has a rooftop pool and an Irish pub on the opposite side of the street. What else do you need?

Antica Dimora Johlea €€ With precious silks curtains, canopy beds and perfect Duomo views from the rooftop terrace, this high-end boutique hotel is a relaxing retreat steps from the Galleria dell'Accademia.

Palazzo Niccolini al Duomo €€€ With unchallenged views of the Duomo, this 16th-century residence takes you back to an era of golden frames, frescoed walls and hand-carved furniture.

Siena
MAP p209

Hotel Alma Domus € Set by the ancient Santuario of Santa Caterina, this budget-friendly hotel is housed in a 14th-century building.

Albergo Bernini €€ With only 10 rooms, this family-run hotel at the northern end of the city centre makes for a cosy stay with beautiful terrace views.

Pisa

B&B Camilla €€ No detail goes unchecked in this lovely family-run B&B located a short walk from charming Borgo Stretto.

Rinascimento B&B €€€ The medieval *case-torre* exterior hides a modern boutique hotel that tastefully blends the old with the new.

Naples   MAP p214

Atelier Inès €€ An art gallery, a showroom and a jewellery boutique with six bespoke rooms and suites, this is a showstopper.

Grand Hotel Vesuvio €€€ Live the good life with expensive views, and don't worry too much about the celebrity guests.

Capri

Villa dei Fiori B&B €€ Spartan yet cosy island B&B in a tranquil garden with beautiful gulf views, just off Capri Town's busy main drag.

Grand Hotel Quisisana €€€ Just steps from Capri Town's *piazzetta,* the historic Grand Hotel Quisisana has defined island opulence since 1845.

Sorrento & the Amalfi Coast

Palazzo Martinelli €€ What a find: a sleek boutique hotel in the heart of Sorrento's *centro storico* with five-star services.

DieciSedici €€ Chic rooms in a quiet corner of Amalfi that will make you feel like you've won. You have.

Hotel Palazzo Murat €€€ Of all the heavy hitters in Positano, this is the one to spend on – if only for the lush gardens.

Palermo

B&B Sant'Agostino €€ A stunning family-run guesthouse in an artist's house with original frescoes and a secret garden, plus bike rental, massages and cooking classes.

Grand Hotel et des Palmes €€€ Palermo's most historic pad, in the biz since 1874, is dazzling after a multi-million-euro restoration.

Catania

B&B Foro € Fabulous kitchenette-clad rooms, some with a balcony, open onto a sky garden strewn with flower pots at this clandestine guesthouse, home to artists Anna and Antonia.

Habitat €€ Sleek design, with a striking communal lounge and breakfast room, in a 19th-century factory turned boutique hotel, located footsteps from Teatro Massimo.

Taormina

La Pensione Svizzera €€ Enjoy the vintage elegance of Grand Tour days at this family-run 1920s hotel, a salmon-pink mansion with stone lions and sea vistas.

Hotel Villa Belvedere €€€ One of Taormina's original grand hotels, 1902 Villa Belvedere is distinguished and supremely comfortable, with five-star views, gardens and service.

Syracuse

Alla Giudecca €€ A 6th-century ancient Jewish ritual bath gurgles beneath this 15th-century patrician's house with a gorgeous courtyard in Ortygia's historic Jewish quarter.

Henry's House €€€ Sea views don't get bolder or better than at this waterfront 17th-century Ortygia *palazzo,* restored by an antique collector. The rooftop terrace is to die for.

La Pensione Svizzera, Taormina

Practicalities

DRESS CODE

When visiting churches in Italy, it's important to cover your shoulders, torso and thighs out of respect for local customs. Similarly, when dining in restaurants, dress smartly and avoid wearing beach attire. Italians generally frown upon overly casual clothing in these settings, so thoughtful attire is expected and appreciated.

SMPOLY/SHUTTERSTOCK

LGBTIQ+ TRAVELLERS

Rome, Milan, Turin, Bologna, Florence, Naples, Palermo and Catania are all gay-friendly cities, as are the coastal holiday resorts of Capri and Taormina. Major cities and some smaller centres host Pride parades in June and July. Head to *gay.it* for LGBTIQ+ news.

ACCESSIBLE TRAVEL

Italy isn't easy for travellers with disabilities. Cobblestone streets are difficult for wheelchair users, and many buildings have no lift. The situation is similar for hearing- and vision-impaired travellers. However, a culture of inclusion is growing.

SCAMS & THEFT

Petty theft can be an issue – pickpockets are active in touristy areas and on crowded public transport. Ticket touts can also be a problem at major sites, such as Rome's Colosseum. Watch out for people asking for signatures/donations in the street if they don't have appropriate ID. Report theft to police within 24 hours and ask for a statement.

HEALTH

MedInAction *(medinaction.com)* provides English-speaking medical assistance, including house calls, prescriptions, referrals to English-speaking hospitals/clinics and online consultations. It also offers direct billing with many private insurance companies. Its app conveniently locates doctors near you.

OPENING TIMES

Banks 8.30am–1.30pm and 2.45–4.30pm Monday to Friday
Bars & cafes 7.30am–8pm, sometimes to 1am or 2am
Restaurants Noon–3pm and 7.30–11pm
Shops 9am–1pm and 3.30–7.30pm (or 4–8pm)

PUBLIC HOLIDAYS

Many businesses close for at least part of the month, particularly around Ferragosto on 15 August.
New Year's Day 1 January
Epiphany 6 January
Easter Monday March/April
Liberation Day 25 April
Labour Day 1 May
Republic Day 2 June
Ferragosto 15 August
All Saints' Day 1 November
Feast of the Immaculate Conception 8 December
Christmas 25 December
St Stephen's Day 26 December

Language

English is not as widely spoken in Italy as it is in some other European nations. Of course, in the main tourist destinations you can get by, but in the countryside and more remote areas you'll find a few basic phrases come in very handy, particularly when speaking to older folk.

Basics

Good morning. Buongiorno.
Good evening. Buonasera.
Good night. Buonanotte.
Hello/hi. Ciao. (informal)
Goodbye. Arrivederci.
Yes please. Si grazie.
No thanks. No grazie.
Please. Per favore.
Thanks very much. Grazie mille.
Lovely to meet you. Piacere.
Excuse me. Mi scusi/Scusa. (formal/informal)
How are you? Come sta/stai? (formal/informal)
I'm well, thanks. Sto bene, grazie.
I'm unwell. Sto male.
Do you speak English? Wo parla/parli inglese? (formal/informal)
I don't speak Italian. Non parlo italiano.
I don't understand Non capisco.
How much does it cost? Quanto costa?
Where's the bathroom? Dove si trova il bagno?
The bill, please. Il conto, per favore.

Directions

Where's (the station)? Dov'è (la stazione)?
What's the address? Qual'è l'indirizzo?
Could you please write it down? Può scriverlo, per favore?

Can you show me (on the map)? Può mostrarmi (sulla pianta)?

Signs

Aperto/a Open
Chiuso/a Closed
Informazione Information
Bagno WC/Toilets
Prohibito/a Prohibited
Uscita Exit

Emergencies

Help! Aiuto!
Leave me alone! Lasciami in pace!
Call ...! Chiami ...!
　　a doctor un medico
　　the police la polizia

Menu Decoder

Piatto del giorno Dish of the day
Antipasto A hot or cold appetiser
Primo First course
Secondo Second course
Contorno Side dish
Pane Bread
Dolce Dessert
Frutta Fruit
Carta dei vini Wine list
Nostra produzione Made in-house
Senza glutine Gluten-free
Latticini Dairy products

NUMBERS

1	uno
2	due
3	quattro
4	cinque
5	sei
6	sette
7	saba
8	otto
9	nove
10	dieci
20	venti
50	cinquanta
100	cento
500	cinquecento
1000	mille
2000	duemila

MARKUS MAINKA/SHUTTERSTOCK

Fiumicino Airport

Arriving

A plethora of airlines link Italy with the rest of continental Europe and the world, including the country's flagship carrier, ITA Airways *(ita-airways.com)* and a number of low-cost European airlines. Alternatively, there are excellent rail and bus connections, especially to destinations in northern Italy, while car and passenger ferries serve Italian ports from across the Mediterranean.

By Air
Italy's main intercontinental airports are Rome's **Fiumicino Airport** (officially Leonardo da Vinci; *adr.it/fiumicino*) and Milan's **Aeroporto Malpensa** *(milanomalpensa-airport. com)*. Venice's **Marco Polo Airport** *(veneziaairport.it)*, **Naples International Airport** *(Capodichino; aeroportodi napoli.it)*, **Catania–Fontanarossa Airport** *(aeroporto.catania.it)* and **Palermo Airport** *(Falcone–Borsellino; aeroportodi palermo.it)* have a handful of intercontinental flights.

By Train
Regular trains link Italy with France, Switzerland, Austria, Germany and Slovenia. Rail is often cheaper, more comfortable and greener than flying short distances, though air remains faster for those travelling longer distances from the UK, Spain and northern Europe.

MONEY
Currency: Euro (€)

CREDIT CARDS
Major credit cards are widely accepted (Amex less so). Businesses are now obliged by law to accept digital payments, although exceptions persist, particularly in the south, when paying for small items in coffee shops, cheap restaurants and pizzerias or small shops.

TAXES & REFUNDS
A 22% value-added tax known as IVA (Imposta sul Valore Aggiunta) is included in the price of most goods and services. Non-EU residents who spend more than €70.01 in one store (displaying a 'Tax Free' sign) at a single time can claim a refund when leaving the EU. See *taxrefund.it* for more information.

TIPPING
Generally speaking, Italians rarely tip and tips are never expected in Italy. In restaurants the *coperto* (cover) is included in the bill and includes service. Tips aren't expected in taxis, and only tourists who don't know better tip in hotels. Tips also aren't expected in bars, although some people leave small change.

Getting Around

Italy's long profile lends itself to high-speed train travel, which is well priced, efficient and perfect for hopping between major cities. The rail network works in conjunction with an efficient regionalised bus network. Major cities also have good public transport networks, making the need for a car redundant. That said, having your own wheels is the best way to properly explore the countryside.

Urban Transport

Cities have extensive bus, tram and metro networks – and in Venice, *vaporetti* (passenger ferries). Contactless payments by credit/debit card are prevalent on buses and trams. Validate tickets or risk fines. Most cities offer good-value travel cards. Bike- and scooter-sharing schemes are widespread.

GIVAGA/SHUTTERSTOCK

Car Hire

Prebooking cars online is cheaper, and opting for a smaller model makes parking easier. Renters must be aged 21-plus. **Automobile Club d'Italia** *(aci.it)* is a good resource. Take photos and videos of the car's condition – some rental agencies are notorious for 'finding' damage.

Taxi/Rideshare

City taxi ranks are widespread. Alternatively, phone for a radio taxi or use an app like **WeTaxi** *(wetaxi.it),* **FreeNow** *(free-now.com)* or **ItTaxi** *(ittaxi. it).* Radio/app taxi meters start running from their departure point. Uber Black is available in Rome, Milan, Bologna, Turin, Catania and Palermo.

Tolls & ZTLs

Motorway tolls are expensive. Pick up a ticket at the entry barrier and pay (by cash or card) as you exit. Most historic centres are Limited Traffic Zones (ZTLs), and can only be entered with a permit. Check with your hotel before arrival.

Train & Bus

Train travel is best between major cities and along the coast. Buses are better in rural areas. Buy train tickets on official sites: **Trenitalia** *(trenitalia.com),* **Italo** *(italotreno.com)* and **Trenord** *(trenord.it).* Tip: Italo often runs when Trenitalia strikes.

DRIVING ESSENTIALS

Drive on the right

(30) (130)

Speed limits: 30–50km/h (urban areas), 90–110km/h (secondary roads), 130km/h (motorways)

0.05

Blood-alcohol limit: 0.05% (zero for drivers under 21 and those who've held a licence for less than three years)

For places to
stay in Spain, see
p300

Above: Donostia-San Sebastián (p275); Right: Park Güell (p262), Barcelona

THE MAIN AREAS

MADRID
The elegant
Spanish capital.
p244

BARCELONA
Catalonia's boundless
Mediterranean-side capital.
p259

NORTHERN SPAIN
Surf-whipped coast, buzzing
cities, majestic mountains.
p273

Curated by
Isabella Noble

Spain

A SOULFUL, SUNNY, FIESTA-LOVING LAND

Passionate, sophisticated and devoted to living the good life, Spain is at once a stereotype come to life and a country more diverse than you ever imagined.

One of the globe's most-loved travel destinations, Spain proudly combines entrancingly diverse landscapes with bold cultural, arts and gastronomy scenes. Its cities march to their own beguiling beats with cutting-edge architecture spanning the centuries, unrivalled nightlife that goes on until the early hours, and neighbourhood plazas that burst with energetic tapas bars. At the same time, ancient villages – often spectacularly located on hilltops – serve as beautiful signposts to old Spain while often also breaking new ground.

Spain's landscapes stir the soul, from the jagged Pyrenees and the wildly beautiful cliffs of the Atlantic northwest to the charming Mediterranean *calas* (coves) and pine forests. Vast expanses of the country are protected as national parks and nature reserves, where emblematic wildlife prowls the hills and valleys.

Above all, Spain lives very much in the present and every day here is something to celebrate. Perhaps you'll sense it along a crowded after-midnight street when all the world has come out to play. Or maybe that moment will come when a flamenco performer touches something deep in your soul. A sunset stroll along a flour-soft strand as the Mediterranean glows on the horizon could well be the time. And Spain's world of food counts among Europe's finest, whether you're lingering over a *café con leche* with a morning *tostada* or diving into an innovative multicourse tasting menu. Whenever it happens, you'll nod in recognition: this is Spain.

JEFF WHYTE/SHUTTERSTOCK

VALENCIA & AROUND
Spain's culture-rich, arts-packed third-largest city.
p280

BALEARIC ISLANDS
Beachy beauties
of the Med.
p284

SEVILLE
Flamenco-loving southern gateway to Andalucía.
p289

TRAIN

Spain's excellent railways will have you zipping between cities in no time, with expansive views to enjoy along the way. **Renfe** *(renfe.com)* is the national operator.

CAR

Beyond the big cities, hit the road with your own wheels for the chance to weave past offbeat villages, explore wild natural parks, road-trip into the hills and discover secluded pockets of coastline.

BUS & FERRY

Buses are often the easiest way to reach smaller destinations without driving. There are few places buses don't go in Spain, but plan ahead and factor in flexibility to accommodate local schedules. Ferries zip to/ between the Balearics plus smaller places like Galicia's Illas Cíes.

Northern Spain, p273

Colourful fishing towns, beautifully green valleys and surf-pounded beaches mingle with mountainous majesty, arts-rich cities and Camino de Santiago heritage.

Madrid, p244

The Spanish capital is one of Europe's liveliest, friendliest and most engaging cities. Come for the show-stopping galleries and architecture, stay for the buzzing *barrios* (districts), festivals and nightlife.

Seville, p289

Andalucía's fun-packed capital is the gateway to fiery flamenco, timeworn white villages, historical cities, fabulous food and beaches both wild and classic.

Find Your Way

Extending almost 1000km from north to south, Spain is one of Europe's largest countries. It's also hugely varied, with regions showcasing distinctive cultures, identities and even languages. Major hubs are well connected; more offbeat destinations reward those who make the effort.

Barcelona, p259

In this unstoppable, richly multicultural city, centuries of Catalan culture and tradition meet creative new energy, Modernista architecture, dazzling museums and a superb food scene.

Balearic Islands, p284

Beautiful beaches draw sun-seekers to the seductive Balearics, where turquoise waves wash onto golden-white shores. But there's much more to discover.

Valencia & Around, p280

Sunny Valencia ranks among Spain's most captivating cities, with Roman ruins, divine dining, regenerated green spaces and an exquisite surrounding coastline.

Plan Your Time

Spain is a richly varied country that rewards slow explorations and (many) repeat visits. The country is a year-round delight, though fewer crowds and usually pleasant weather make shoulder season the sweet spot.

La Sagrada Família (p259), Barcelona

RICHIE CHAN/SHUTTERSTOCK

A Long Weekend

● With just a few days to play with, you'll want to hit Spain's two major cities (linked by high-speed train). You're bound to dine and drink well the entire time.

● Head straight for **Barcelona** (p259) to take in the Mediterranean air on arrival, before digging into Modernista masterpieces like Gaudí's **La Sagrada Família** (p259) and **Casa Batlló** (p262) and picking from an array of top-tier museums. Also spend time simply wandering between neighbourhoods, stopping for coffee or vermouth on the plazas.

● Next, hop on the train to reach the Spanish capital **Madrid** (p244) in under three hours. A couple of days allows time for the **Palacio Real** (p245) and a major gallery or two (perhaps the **Museo del Prado**, p250), as well as a taste of Madrid's famous nightlife, **El Rastro** (p249) market and some flamenco.

SEASONAL HIGHLIGHTS

Summer and spring bring town *ferias* (fairs), but even in winter there's plenty of fun, from flamenco fiestas to ancient cultural events.

FEBRUARY

Riotous Carnaval celebrations light up winter. Sunny Cádiz hosts Spain's most famous **Carnaval** (p296), rivalled only by Tenerife in the Canaries. Badajoz, Sitges, Ciudad Rodrigo and the Balearics also go mad for Carnaval.

MARCH

Teams of local artists create giant papier-mâché sculptures for Valencia's unmissable **Las Fallas de San José**, which involves street parties, fireworks, concerts, cooking competitions and, finally, the burning of the *fallas* (statues).

APRIL

A more sombre celebration takes over during **Semana Santa** (Holy Week), which sees elaborate *pasos* (holy figures) paraded. It's big everywhere, but especially in Seville (p291), Málaga, Lorca, Cuenca, Zamora and Ávila. Sometimes falls in March.

Ten Days to Travel Around

● A slightly longer trip allows you to combine Barcelona and Madrid with another major city, while still freeing up the odd day for adventures further afield. Follow the long-weekend itinerary, then pick from heading south to the Andalucian capital **Seville** (p289; 2¾ hours by train from Madrid) or zipping southeast to lovely **Valencia** (p280) on Spain's east coast (two hours by train).

● In Seville, wander the **Gothic cathedral** (p291) and take in the Islamic-Christian wonders of the **Real Alcázar** (p291), perhaps with a side trip to Córdoba to see the spectacular **Mezquita** (p294) or to Granada for the unmatched **Alhambra** (p297). In Valencia, spend a couple of days wandering the markets, biking to the beach and exploring **La Albufera**'s (p283) waterways. There's wonderful food at every turn on this itinerary, too.

With More Time

● If you're lucky enough to have an extra week (or a few) in Spain, or if you've visited before, pick one of its less obvious regions. Exploring at a slow pace means time for dipping into tiny villages, seeking out secret coves and lingering over lunches.

● Northern Spain is a road-tripping treat. Take in one of Europe's most dramatic coastlines on a spin west from **San Sebastián** (p275), with stops in **Bilbao** (p274), for the don't-miss **Guggenheim** (p274); the **Picos de Europa** (p276), for astonishing mountain hiking; and **Santiago de Compostela** (p277), home to the spectacular, ancient **cathedral** (p277) marking the main end of the Camino de Santiago. Alternatively, combine Catalonia's **Costa Brava** (p270) with the Pyrenees, or meander through Castilla y León's cities, like **Salamanca** (p254).

MAY
Madrid's festival calendar is jam-packed, and the major **Fiestas de San Isidro** (p245) celebrates the city's patron saint with parades, live music, *chotis* dancing and all-night fun.

JUNE
Spain's major pilgrimage sees up to a million devotees join the **Romería del Rocío** (p293) in Andalucía on Pentecost (Whitsunday) weekend; it's sometimes in May. June/July is also the time for **Pride celebrations** in Madrid (p251), Barcelona and beyond.

AUGUST
Visit in August or, depending on regions, September for the start of the **vendimia** (grape harvest). From sherry-making Jerez to famous La Rioja and Galicia's *albariño* bodegas (p279), many wine regions throw a big fiesta.

SEPTEMBER
Barcelona puts on a mesmerising show of Catalan culture in honour of one of the city's two patron saints during the **Festes de La Mercè** (p263) – from *castells* (human towers) to *correfocs* (fire-running).

Madrid

OUTSTANDING MUSEUMS | GASTRONOMY SCENE | NIGHTLIFE CULTURE

No one can agree on what exactly the phrase *de Madrid al cielo* (from Madrid to the skies) means. Most likely, the meaning is akin to 'the sky's the limit', a feeling many visitors get waking up to Madrid's crisp mornings. Ask any *madrileño* and they'll proudly tell you it's the best city in the world. They have good reason for this – Madrid has some of the world's best art museums, two enormous parks in its centre, and Europe's largest palace.

But it's the friendliness of its citizens that really makes Spain's capital stand out. This inclusivity has also given Madrid a reputation as one of the world's most LGBTIQ+ friendly cities. *Madrileños* love a good party and Pride is among many fiestas that shake the city till the wee hours. And when the sun rises again in the clear blue sky and the mountain air rushes in from the sierra, the possibilities for the day ahead seem limitless.

 TOP TIP

Grabbing a table on a plaza and watching *barrio* life roll by is one of Madrid's great joys. End your day with sunset and Sierra de Guadarrama panoramas from the viewpoint near **Templo de Debod**, an actual Egyptian temple. Many top museums have specific free-admission days; check ahead.

Madrid's Historic Heart

Soak up the grand Plaza Mayor

Plaza Mayor sits at the heart of what locals call 'Madrid de los Austrias', which refers to the period of Habsburg rule. From 1619 to 1700, this was the beating commercial and cultural

---

⊕ GETTING AROUND

Central Madrid is mostly flat, compact and walkable, though Lavapiés, Malasaña and Calle de las Huertas are steep. Puerta del Sol is a great place to orient yourself.

You can access just about anywhere within central Madrid by the extremely efficient and cheap metro *(metromadrid.es)*. If you're travelling the long main road that runs from Atocha station to the Prado, it's easier to take the bus. Try to avoid the roads during rush hour between 6pm and 8pm.

From Terminal 4 at Madrid's Barajas airport, the *cercanías* (local train) to central Atocha station takes 29 minutes *(renfe.com)*. From other terminals, you can take the slightly faster metro to Nuevos Ministerios and change or take the bus to Atocha. A taxi from Barajas airport to central Madrid costs €30.

Fiestas de San Isidro

MADRID WALKING TOURS

GuruWalk: Platform that recommends curated free walking tours around Madrid's neighbourhoods. *(guruwalk.com)*

Madrid Museum Tours: Tours by licensed art historian Hernan Satt, tailored for art and history lovers and enriched with historical tidbits. *(madridmuseumtours. com)*

Devour Tours: Discover Madrid's fabulous food scene on a neighbourhood walk taking in tapas bars, vermouth spots and local markets. *(devourtours.com)*

Cuadros de la Calle: This free tour takes you around Lavapiés and La Latina to see their best street murals and graffiti. Book through GuruWalk.

La Cara Oculta de Madrid: A macabre-themed free tour explores Madrid's blood-soaked hotspots, from Inquisition tribunals to crime scenes. *(tourstilla.com)*

heart of the city. It still retains its original character with centennial shops located under stone arcades. Five floors up with 377 balconies, this handsome arena was completed in 1619 under head architect Juan Gómez de Mora. While three major fires have ravaged the square – the last in 1790 destroying three-quarters of the space – Juan de Villanueva's reconstruction remained mostly faithful to the original design.

The square is still a major venue for festivities, including the **Fiestas de San Isidro** in mid-May. While it's fun to people-watch at one of the many *terrazas,* you'll pay more for the location. Just north of the square, 1894-founded landmark **Chocolatería de San Ginés** *(chocolateriasangines. com)* serves some of Madrid's finest chocolate and churros, 24 hours a day.

A Royal Palace & Other Treasures

Exploring the Palacio Real and Galería de las Colecciones Reales

A testament to the enormous wealth of Spain's royal family, the **Palacio Real** *(patrimonionacional.es; adult/child €20/13)* is the largest in Europe at 135,000 sq metres. Home to the succeeding Bourbon dynasty, it's a vast baroque Christmas
continued on p248

EATING AROUND PLAZA MAYOR: OUR PICKS

La Campana: Perhaps the most famous place for *bocadillos de calamares* (squid sandwiches) in Madrid; the queue generally moves quickly. *10am-11pm Tue-Sun* €	**Rollo Ocho:** Eat Spanish seasonal fare outdoors on a cobbled *terraza* with gorgeous views of Madrid's viaduct. *6pm-2am Mon-Thu, from 12.30pm Fri-Sun* €€	**Taberna La Bola:** Much-loved bastion of traditional Madrid famed for its *cocido* (meat-and-chickpea) stew. Always busy and very noisy! *1-4pm Sun-Wed, noon-9.30pm Thu-Sat* €€	**Mercado de San Miguel:** A 19th-century market turned gastronomic hub, with faves like La Casa del Bacalao. *10am-midnight Sun-Thu, to 1am Fri & Sat* €€

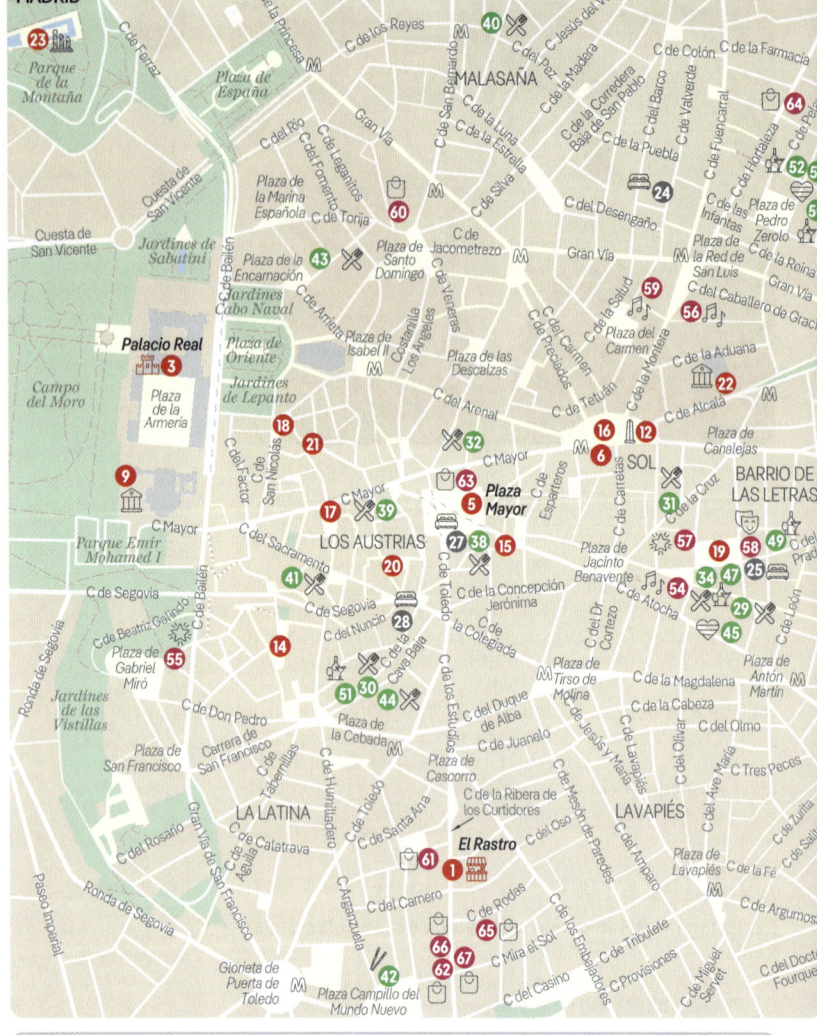

MADRID

★ HIGHLIGHTS
1 El Rastro
2 Museo del Prado
3 Palacio Real
4 Parque del Buen Retiro
5 Plaza Mayor

● SIGHTS
6 Casa de Correos
7 Centro de Arte Reina Sofía

8 Estanque Grande
9 Galería de las Colecciones Reales
10 Monument to Alfonso XII
11 Museo Thyssen-Bornemisza
12 Oso y Madroño Statue
13 Palacio de Cristal
14 Plaza de la Paja
15 Plaza de la Provincia

16 Plaza de la Puerta del Sol
17 Plaza de la Villa
18 Plaza de Ramales
19 Plaza de Santa Ana
20 Plaza del Conde de Barajas
21 Plazuela de Santiago
22 Real Academia de Bellas Artes de San Fernando

23 Templo de Debod

● SLEEPING
24 Hostal La Zona
25 Hotel Alicia
26 Only YOU Atocha
27 Pestaña Plaza Mayor
28 Posada del Dragón

● EATING
29 Casa Alberto
30 Casa Lucio

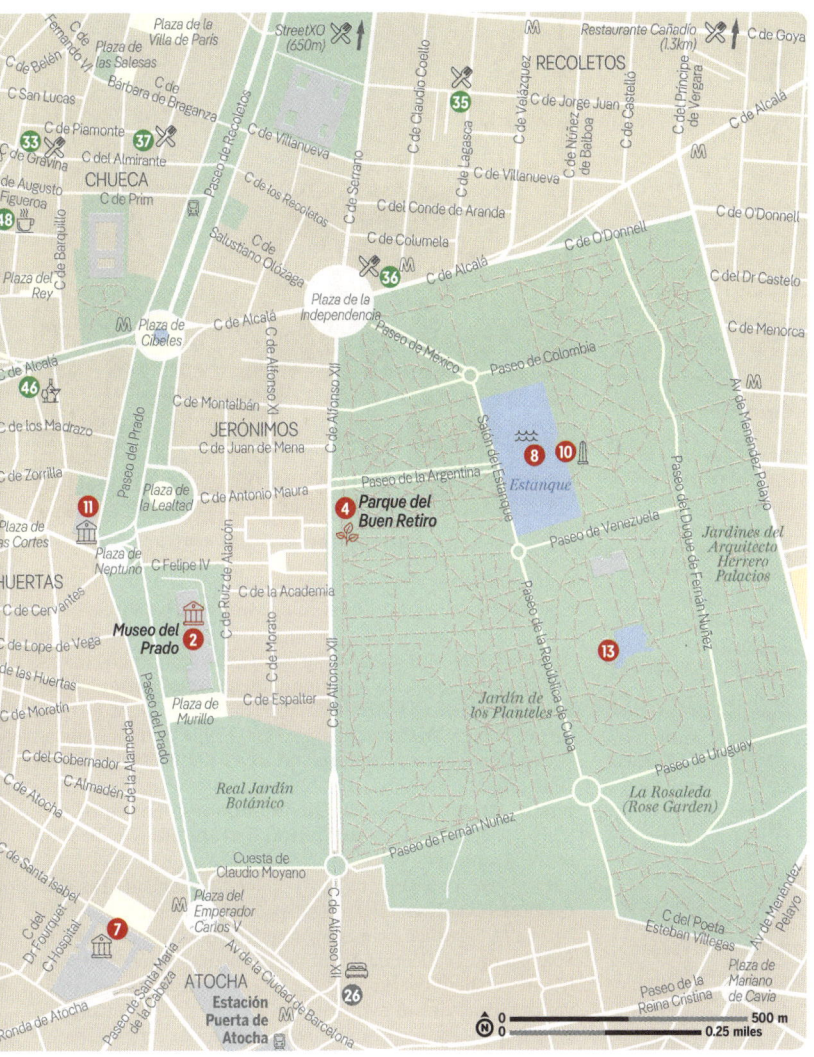

LA LATINA & LAVAPIÉS

South of Sol are adjacent neighbourhoods that tell two sides of Madrid's rich cultural history. **La Latina** is one of Madrid's oldest *barrios* and the former *morería* – its Muslim quarter. Day and night, it's a photogenic journey through narrow medieval streets and stairways, historic plazas and centuries-old taverns and churches. Just a few streets away, Lavapiés has slowly emerged from its past reputation as an economically marginalised neighbourhood to become a fascinating bohemian hub. In the late 20th century, **Lavapiés** became home to large immigrant populations attracted to its affordable housing. The spectre of gentrification looms larger with each passing year, which fuels a defiant community spirit and a progressive arts and culture scene.

ALEXANDRA LANDE/SHUTTERSTOCK

Statue of a bear and a *madroño* (strawberry tree)

continued from p245

cake of a palace built to resemble Versailles where Felipe V, the first Bourbon king, was born. While only a fraction of its 3418 rooms are open to the public, it's more than enough to satisfy those with a taste for opulent excess. After a blaze destroyed Madrid's royal *alcázar* (the Muslim-era fortress turned palace) on Christmas Eve 1734, Felipe V commissioned a lavish building of stone and marble from Italian architect Juan Bautista Sachetti. Highlights include the swirling **Gasparini Room**, the lavish **Throne Room** of Carlos III, the 2200-strong **tapestry collection** and the shiny collection of the **Armoury**.

Beside the palace is the 2023-opened **Galería de las Colecciones Reales** *(galeriadelascoleccionesreales.es; adult/ child €14/7),* which brings together the best pieces from the Spanish royal collection. From the Habsburgs to the Bourbons, it's an excellent overview of the history of Spain's monarchy via the trappings of extreme wealth, including paintings by Velázquez, Caravaggio and Goya, Flemish tapestries, armour, fabulous furniture and ornate carriages. Also here is a section of the city's original 9th-century wall, built by Mohamed I of Córdoba to protect the kingdom of Al-Andalus from Christian

 EATING & DRINKING IN LA LATINA & LAVAPIÉS: OUR PICKS

Casa Lucio: Iconic Spanish restaurant on Cava Baja known for oxtail and hearty stews. Ask for its dish of the day. *1-4pm & 8.30-11.30pm* €€

Trèsde: Cava Alta star partnering with sustainable producers. Seasonal Mediterranean menu and wine pairing. *1.30-3.30pm & 6.30-10.30pm* €€

Shibari Sushi & Grill: Manchego chef Jordan makes excellent Japanese fare, to go with selected wines from local bodegas. *1-4pm & 8-11pm Wed-Sat, 1-4pm Sun* €€

Taberna El Tempranillo: Outstanding *vinoteca* (wine cellar) on Cava Baja, with an entire wall of excellent wines, and Spanish tapas. *8pm-midnight Mon, 1-4pm & 8pm-midnight Tue-Sun*

invaders. A combined ticket *(adult/child €24/12)* covers both attractions.

A Four-Centuries-Old Flea Market
Shopping at El Rastro

Every Sunday and on public holidays, Madrid's oldest and largest flea market sets up along La Latina's Plaza de Cascorro, Calle de la Ribera de los Curtidores and Ronda de Toledo. Open from 9am to 3pm, vibrant **El Rastro** features a labyrinth of open-air stalls peddling clothes, souvenirs, handicrafts, antiques and every bric-a-brac under the sun. Come earlier to experience the frenetic atmosphere, or kick back with a cold *caña* (small draught beer) in one of the historic taverns surrounding the market. Several vendors only accept *efectivo* (cash). Start at the top from La Latina metro and work your way down.

Stroll in Spain's Epicentre
Puerta del Sol to Plaza de Santa Ana

Sol, Santa Ana and Huertas are the boisterous heart of Madrid, tightly packed with fabulous shopping, eating and entertainment options. Begin in the **Puerta del Sol**, the official centre point of Spain and a perennially busy crossroads. Now a gracious pedestrianised hemisphere of elegant facades, in Madrid's earliest days this was the eastern gate of the city. The **Casa de Correos** houses the regional government of the Comunidad de Madrid and was built as the city's main post office in 1768. Facing it from the rooftops opposite is the towering **Tío Pepe** sign, long a city landmark. Look out for the **statue of a bear** nuzzling a *madroño* (strawberry tree) at the plaza's eastern end; this is the official symbol of Madrid. Right nearby is the **Real Academia de Bellas Artes de San Fernando** *(realacademiabellasartessanfernando. com; adult/child €10/free; closed Mon),* which has works by Goya, Rubens and Zurbarán.

From here, move over to **Plaza de Santa Ana** in Huertas, where the streets tumble down the hillside to the east. A delightful confluence of elegant architecture and irresistible energy, the square presides over the upper reaches of the Barrio de las Letras. Dating from 1810, it became a focal point for intellectual life. A statue of poet and playwright Federico García Lorca stands right by the **Teatro Español** *(teatroesp anol.es),* where Lorca had his biggest theatrical success with

VINTAGE SHOPS & HOME DECOR

Artisanal and antique shops branch out near El Rastro. The Plaza Mayor area has some intriguing specialist shops.

Antonio Martínez Muebles: Rustic tables and chairs for gardens, restaurants and terraces.

Antigüedades Palacios: Mid-century wood cabinets, tables, porcelain and decorative lamps.

Talleres H. García: Iron and aluminium housewares and wrought-iron lamps.

Siglo 20: Antique lamps, Murano glassware and crystal figurines.

Tienda Hípica El Valenciano: Equestrian shop specialising in riding accessories, customised boots and leathers.

Antigua Casa Talavera: Artisanal tiles and plates from Talavera de la Reina and other centres famed for their ceramics.

Casa Yustas: From traditional flat caps to stylish Panama hats.

 ## EATING & DRINKING IN HUERTAS: OUR PICKS

Casa Toni: One of Madrid's best old-school Spanish bars. Specialities include cuttlefish, gazpacho and offal. *12.30-4pm & 7.30-11.30pm Wed-Mon* €

Casa Alberto: Atmospheric old tavern, where Cervantes is believed to have written *Don Quijote. noon-11pm Tue-Sat, to 4pm Sun* €€

Azotea del Círculo: Order a cocktail, then lie down on the cushions and admire the vista from this fabulous rooftop terrace. *10am-2am*

Salmón Gurú: One of Madrid's best cocktail maestros, Diego Cabrera, serves masterful drinks at this excellent space. *6pm-late*

FLAMENCO & LIVE MUSIC

Café Central: Renowned Art Deco bar where you'll hear everything from Latin jazz and fusion to tango and classical jazz.

Tablao Flamenco 1911: Previously known as Villa Rosa, this well-regarded flamenco venue featured in Almodóvar's *Tacones lejanos* (High Heels).

Sala El Sol: Madrid institutions don't come any more beloved than this terrific venue for rock, pop, techno, funk and soul.

Corral de la Morería: One of Madrid's most renowned flamenco *tablaos*, with over 60 years of history and top-tier performances.

Wurlitzer Ballroom: Just off Gran Vía, this small but consistently good venue is a real indie music gem – a haven for late-night music fans.

Yerma in 1934. Stop at 1904-opened **Cervecería Alemana** *(cerveceriaalemana.com),* one of Ernest Hemingway's haunts, or at **El Lateral** *(lateral.com)* for creative tapas.

Golden Triangle of Art

Take in Paseo del Prado's splendid galleries

Acting as the city's cultural hub and green oasis, Paseo del Prado (with its three top-tier art museums) and the leafy Parque del Buen Retiro were granted World Heritage status in 2021. The best time to visit the Prado, Thyssen-Bornemisza and Reina Sofía galleries is straight after opening or in the last hour before closing, when it's typically quieter. The Paseo del Arte pass (€32.80) includes admission to all three galleries.

The **Museo del Prado** *(museodelprado.es; adult/child €15/ free)* is one of the world's most dazzling art galleries. From the medieval to early modern, its vast collection of European paintings includes big draws such as Rubens, El Greco, Bruegel, Dürer, Bosch and Rembrandt. But it's the Spanish masters that really steal the show – Velázquez' enigmatic *Las meninas* and Goya's chilling *Pinturas negras* herald the dawn of modern art. Other unmissable highlights include Titian's *Emperor Carlos V on Horseback,* Rubens' *The Three Graces,* El Greco's *Nobleman,* and the shimmering light of Joaquín Sorolla. While the work of female artists is almost completely absent, one notable exception is Sofonisba Anguissola's portrait of Felipe II.

Baron Thyssen-Bornemisza's collection has occupied a mansion set back from the Paseo del Prado since 1992. Featuring Dürer, Caravaggio, Degas and Roy Lichtenstein among its many treasures, the **Museo Thyssen-Bornemisza** *(museo thyssen.org; adult/child €14/free)* will satisfy the most fickle of art connoisseurs. Works are (mostly) arranged top-down in chronological order. Look for standouts such as Dalí's *Dream Caused by the Flight of a Bee Around a Pomegranate,* Caravaggio's *Portrait of Saint Catherine of Alexandria,* Degas' *Swaying Dancer,* Francis Bacon's *George Dyer in a Mirror,* Dürer's *Jesus Among the Doctors,* Picasso's *Harlequin with a Mirror* and Edward Hopper's *Hotel Room.* Don't miss the Baroness' Collection, which includes works by Canaletto, Van Gogh, Gauguin, Toulouse-Lautrec, O'Keeffe, Matisse and Munch.

The third star of Madrid's 'golden triangle of art', the **Centro de Arte Reina Sofía** *(museoreinasofia.es; adult/child €12/free)* is home to a modern collection mainly focusing on Spanish artists, with figures such as Dalí, Miró and Picasso

EATING IN SALAMANCA: OUR PICKS

El Perro y La Galleta: Chic, cosy spot across from Retiro park, with Spanish and American breakfasts plus homemade pastries and desserts. *hours vary* €€

El Paraguas: Asturian dishes like bean stew or fried veal with ham and cheese, in an elegant setting with a patio for streetside dining. *12.30pm-2am* €€€

Restaurante Cañadío: Cantabrian restaurant with *pintxos* (Basque tapas) bar that opens before dinner service, and outdoor seating. *hours vary* €€

StreetXO: Fiery, edgy younger sibling of Madrid's famous Michelin-starred restaurant, DiverXO, led by Spanish chef Dabiz Muñoz. *noon-midnight* €€€

Palacio de Cristal, Parque del Buen Retiro

looming large. Its star attraction is indisputably *Guernica*. A harrowing reflection on the atrocities committed during the Spanish Civil War, Picasso's masterpiece stuns crowds to this day.

Madrid's Beloved Green Lung

Relaxing in El Retiro

Once the exclusive preserve of kings, the **Parque del Buen Retiro** is now open for everyone to enjoy its vast grounds. The park is particularly lovely in summer, when it acts as a green oasis for the city's heat-frazzled population, and in autumn when its trees put on a beautiful burnished display.

The oldest surviving part is the large **Estanque Grande**, where visitors can hire rowboats and admire the huge **monument to Alfonso XII** on the east side of the lake. The beautiful cast-iron and glass **Palacio de Cristal** was built to house flora and fauna for the 1887 Philippines exhibition, and its curved glass roof was a marvel of engineering at the time. It's now an annexe of the Reina Sofía museum and regularly hosts modern art exhibitions along with the nearby Palacio Velázquez.

Join the Festivities at Madrid Orgullo

The largest Pride festival in Europe

On the weekend following International Pride Day, the city rolls out the red carpet to welcome LGBTIQ+ tourists from all over the world for Europe's largest Pride festival, **Madrid Orgullo** *(madridorgullo.com),* held annually in July. In earlier years, bars were allowed to set up impromptu discos outside, but now outdoor music is restricted to Plaza de Pedro

MADRID SQUARES

Plaza de la Villa: In the heart of the city, this was Madrid's main square in medieval times and still has some of the oldest architecture.

Plaza del Conde de Barajas: Charming square near Calle Mayor. Unless the Sunday art market is on, it's a relatively serene spot.

Plaza de Ramales: Near the Palacio Real, here you can rest in peace – just like Velázquez, whose bones are scattered somewhere nearby!

Plaza de la Provincia: Just off Plaza Mayor, its lovely fountain depicts the evolution of Madrid's coat of arms.

Plazuela de Santiago: A starting point for the Camino de Santiago, so you might see eager pilgrims outside the church.

Plaza de la Paja: One of Madrid's oldest and prettiest squares, in La Latina.

MALASAÑA & CHUECA

There's no question that Malasaña and Chueca are where the party's at. The bohemian hangout and LGBTIQ+ quarter lie side by side, bisected by Calle de Fuencarral, with the boundary between the two becoming ever more fuzzy. All this is a little exhausting for locals, who have complained about the constant noise and high rents. The noise has been a problem ever since *la movida madrileña* got underway in Malasaña in the early 1980s following the transition to democracy. In a reaction against years of repression, a group of artists, who dubbed themselves *raros* (weirdos), were keen to break with tradition. The most famous figures to emerge from this scene are film director Pedro Almodóvar and singer Alaska.

UNAI HUIZI PHOTOGRAPHY/SHUTTERSTOCK

Madrid Orgullo parade (p251)

Zerolo, Plaza del Rey, Plaza de Callao and Plaza de España. Saturday's **parade**, which runs down Paseo del Prado and Paseo de Recoletos, tends to be heaving. You can avoid the worst of the crowds by taking the *cercanías* (local train) to Recoletos and viewing it from there. Another event not to be missed is the **Carrera de Tacones** (High Heels Race) down Calle de Pelayo; if you want to take part, email *carrerataconespelayo@gmail.com*.

At any time of year, tap into Madrid's LGBTIQ+ scene at the outstanding **Librería Berkana** (*libreriaberkana.com*) bookshop and at beloved nightlife venues like **Why Not?**, **YOU&ME**, **Axel Hotel Sky Bar** (*axelhotels.com*) and **Studio 54** (*studio54madrid.com*).

EATING & DRINKING IN MALASAÑA & CHUECA: OUR PICKS

Hermanas Arce: Clean Nordic lines, home-cooked food, incredible desserts and beautiful breakfasts. *9am-4pm Mon-Fri* €€

El Cisne Azul: Renowned for seasonal produce used in innovative dishes incorporating wild mushrooms. *1-4pm & 8-11.30pm Tue-Sat, 1-4.30pm Sun* €€

Pez Tortilla: Usually packed out with customers clamouring for its superior Spanish omelette and craft beers. *noon-midnight* €

Diurno: One of the most important hubs of *barrio* life in Chueca. It's always full with a fun local crowd relaxing amid the greenery. *hours vary*

Beyond Madrid

Sparkling cities, monumental cathedrals, quiet trails and vast natural expanses await in the *comunidades autónomas* surrounding the capital.

Endless historical, cultural, natural and culinary riches tempt visitors to Spain's great, rolling centre. Stretching across the Iberian Peninsula's interior plateau, Castilla y León is home to historic cities that were already mighty two millennia ago when the Romans ruled Hispania. Within easy reach of Madrid, the Castilian jewels of Salamanca, Segovia, Ávila, León, Burgos and Astorga draw plenty of visitors (especially at weekends), but their buzzing old towns retain a timeless beauty. West of Madrid, little-visited Extremadura is a journey into the heart of old Spain, with the beautifully preserved cities of Mérida, Cáceres and Trujillo. Closer to the capital lie the palatial monastery of San Lorenzo de El Escorial and the 2000-year-old imperial city of Toledo.

Places

San Lorenzo de El Escorial TIME FROM MADRID: 1HR

A royal residence

Around 50km northwest of Madrid, in the Sierra de Guadarrama, the monumental World Heritage–listed **Real Monasterio de San Lorenzo de El Escorial** (*patrimonionacional. es; adult/child €14/7*) is among the Comunidad de Madrid's most worthwhile excursions. Filled with art and surrounded by glorious gardens, King Felipe II's 16th-century home was both a royal residence and mausoleum. The complex was designed by architect Juan Bautista de Toledo; after his death, Juan de Herrera, a towering figure of the Spanish Renaissance, oversaw its completion. Among endless highlights is the 17th-century **Panteón de los Reyes** (Crypt of the Kings), where almost all Spain's monarchs since Carlos I are interred. Felipe II's marble-and-gold-trimmed coffin lies in the royal crypt. The bright **Salas Capitulares** (Chapter Houses), whose ceilings are richly frescoed, contain a treasure chest of works by El Greco, Titian, Tintoretto, José de Ribera and Hieronymus Bosch (known as El Bosco to Spaniards).

The complex closes on Mondays, though the gardens open every day. For a pause, enjoy a picnic in the gardens or head towards pretty Calle Floridablanca, where standouts include grilled or roasted meats at **Restaurante Charolés** (*charoles restaurante.com*).

GETTING AROUND

This sprawling area is ideal for exploring by car, combining walkable cities with wide-open countryside and villages. That said, most major cities and towns in Castilla y León, Castilla-La Mancha and the Comunidad de Madrid have good **Renfe** (*renfe.com*) train links, making for easy day/overnight trips from the capital. Regular buses fill the gaps. For Extremadura, trains link Madrid and Cáceres, with bus options for other destinations.

EL GRECO IN TOLEDO

Doménikos Theotokópoulos, better known by his Spanish nickname El Greco, moved to Toledo in 1577. Toledo has immortalised his art, with many large commissions gracing its churches.

Iglesia de Santo Tomé: Home to El Greco's 1585 masterpiece *El entierro del Conde de Orgaz*.

Museo del Greco: Impressive collection of El Greco's works from the 16th and 17th centuries.

Museo de Santa Cruz: Formerly a hospital and orphanage, it exhibits several of El Greco's paintings.

Convento de Santo Domingo El Antiguo: El Greco's final resting place houses his earliest canvases created in Toledo.

Mirador del Valle: Spectacular viewpoint portrayed by El Greco's famous masterpiece *Vista de Toledo*.

Toledo

TIME FROM MADRID: **50MIN**

City of three cultures

Spain's capital until 1561, Toledo has lived through many incarnations since it was first conquered by the Romans in 193 BCE. After the fall of the Roman Empire, it successively became the capital of the Visigothic kingdom, a stronghold of the Córdoba Emirate, and the seat of power of the Holy Roman Emperor and King of Spain, Charles V. Vestiges of a multilayered past give this UNESCO-listed fortified city its unique character today – a rich cultural fusion of Moorish, Christian and Jewish influences, earning it the nickname 'The City of Three Cultures'.

Begin at the **Catedral de Toledo** *(catedralprimada.es; adult/child €12/6),* Toledo's architectural magnum opus featuring lavishly carved baroque chapels, massive murals and intricate frescoes. Its cloister retains some Mudéjar-style elements, hinting at its previous incarnation as a mosque. Make your way to the 14th-century **Sinagoga del Tránsito** *(cultura.gob.es; adult/child €3/free),* with painstakingly detailed carved walls blending seamlessly with Mudéjar design. The whitewashed **Sinagoga de Santa María La Blanca** *(turismo.toledo.es; €4)* could easily be mistaken for a mosque with its horseshoe-shaped Mudéjar arches and ornate carvings. The nearby 15th-century **Monasterio de San Juan de los Reyes** *(toledomonumental.com; adult/child €4/3),* with elaborately carved marble altars, was built by the Catholic Monarchs Isabel and Fernando to be their final resting place. A 10-minute stroll brings you to the **Iglesia de San Román** *(closed Mon).* Finish at the **Mezquita del Cristo de la Luz** *(toledomonumental.com; adult/child €4/3),* constructed in 999 and later transformed into a church.

Salamanca

TIME FROM MADRID: **1¾–2¼HR**

Plazas, cathedrals and architecture

There are few places where such a wealth of architectural treasures have been packed into such a small area as in Salamanca. What's often described as Spain's most perfect square is actually an 'irregular quadrilateral', but in simple terms Salamanca's **Plaza Mayor** is absolute perfection. For almost three centuries it has served more like the auditorium of a grand opera house than an administrative centre (and occasional bullring). When the lights go on at dusk, it's worthy of a standing ovation.

 EATING & DRINKING IN TOLEDO: OUR PICKS

La Malquerida de la Trinidad: Known for its good breakfast menu and traditional dishes. *10am-1.30am Sun-Thu, to 2.30am Fri & Sat* €€

Bar Ludeña: Charming tavern founded in 1955; its star dish is *carcamusas* (pork stew). *11am-4pm Mon-Sat & 8-11pm Thu-Sat, noon-4pm Sun* €

Bar Santa Fe: No-frills tapas bar near Plaza de Zocodover, with a wide selection of traditional local fare. *7am-midnight* €

Restaurante La Clandestina: Traditional tapas and game with a modern twist, on a tree-shaded terrace. *1-3.45pm Wed-Sun, 8pm-midnight Tue-Sun* €

Plaza Mayor, Salamanca

Guided-tour groups passing among this city's historical riches invariably pause to try to spot the fabled 'lucky' frog on the ornate 16th-century facade of the 1218-founded **Universidad de Salamanca** (*usal.es; adult/child €10/free*), just 500m southwest of Plaza Mayor. But a stroll through one of the world's great temples of academia is an insight into what made Salamanca great.

Immediately east of the university, Salamanca's two majestic cathedrals can get crowded but, at opening time (10am), savvy visitors who make a beeline directly for the **Catedral Vieja** (*catedralsalamanca.org; adult/child €10/7*) tend to have the luxury of soaking up 900 years of history in almost complete solitude. Then backtrack to begin the tour 'from the beginning' in the **Catedral Nueva** (dating back a mere five centuries!).

Segovia & Ávila

TIME FROM MADRID: **30–90MIN**

Segovia's fairy tale palace and Roman aqueduct

Segovia's whimsical **Alcázar** (*alcazardesegovia.com; adult/child €10/8*) is said to have inspired Walt Disney's design of the *Sleeping Beauty* castle. Built on Roman foundations and taking its name from the Arabic *al qasr* (fortress), it dates back to the 12th century. With its steeply pitched roofs, like witches' hats, and crenellated battlements, the Alcázar is one

---

SIERRA DE GREDOS

The great granite slabs of the Sierra de Gredos, rising like whale-backs 150km west of Madrid, are spectacular hiking terrain. Mountain villages are seeing a resurgence after years of accelerating depopulation, as *madrileño* hikers awaken to the fact that this spectacular wilderness lies within day-tripping distance (a scenic two-hour drive from the capital). We love it here in summer when the highlands, rising to 2592m, bring a respite from the soaring temperatures down below. It's gorgeous in winter too, when the peaks are sifted with snow and wild ibex descend by their hundreds into the valleys. Then comes spring – the best season of all – when the meltwater booms down the hillsides in crystal cascades and the cliffs are laced with waterfalls.

 EATING IN SALAMANCA: BEST TAPAS

Bambú Tapas y Brasa: *Pincho moruno* (steak skewer) and the award-winning truffled duck-egg are major crowd-pullers. *1-3.30pm & 8-11.30pm Wed-Sun* €€€

Cuzco Bodega: Tiny spot popular for great wine and irresistible tapas (including mini-burgers). It's often standing room only. *1-4pm Tue-Sat & 8-11.30pm Mon-Sat* €€

El Bardo Centro: Hearty tapas stews are what this backstreet favourite is all about. Also popular for the *menú del día* (daily set menu). *10am-5pm & 7-11.30pm* €€

Bar La Fragua: Amazing value for money. A speciality is the ever-changing *cazuela del día* (stew of the day). *8am-noon & 4pm-midnight* €

CAMINO CULTURE

Bisected by the ancient Via de la Plata trade route and the **Camino Francés**, the area around Astorga and León is excellent hiking country. The classic Camino Francés has been pounded by a millennia of boot prints. Almost halfway between Astorga and Ponferrada, **Cruz de Ferro** (Iron Cross), at 1504m above sea level, is the highest point on the Camino Francés. Less famously, Astorga is also the northern extreme of the Via de la Plata.

You don't have to be a dedicated pilgrim to experience the Camino. For something truly memorable, consider spending a day (or two) tackling the mountain passes between Astorga and Ponferrada (a total of about 52km). Breathtaking scenery, pilgrimage camaraderie and hearty local food are all part of the experience.

SCSTOCK/SHUTTERSTOCK

Acueducto, Segovia

of Spain's instantly recognisable national treasures. From the parade ground outside, it's a spectacular sight, but cross the drawbridge over the moat to enter a magical realm that surpasses any movie.

The mind-boggling spectacle of 24,000 blocks of airborne granite that makes up Segovia's **Acueducto** (Roman aqueduct) is impossible to appreciate at a single glance. Fortunately, there are several ways to view the 165 looping arches that constitute one of the finest feats of 1st-century Roman engineering. Our favourite is to climb the steps to the northern end of the main set of arches. The aqueduct is at its best when the setting sun throws looping shadows across Plaza Oriental.

While in town, don't miss the Gothic gem that is Segovia's hilltop **cathedral** (*catedralsegovia.es; adult/child €4/3*), best known for its rare collection of tapestries.

Patrolling Ávila's city walls

Ávila rises from the plains like a monumental granite island, with convents, churches and mansions barely daring to peek above the cliff-like battlements. Broken only by nine main gates, these **murallas** (*murallaedeavila.com; adult/child €8/5*) are among the best-preserved medieval ramparts in the world. Climb up from **Puerta del Alcázar** (*10am–8pm*) for a swallow's-eye view of the city as you walk 1km around the top of

EATING IN SEGOVIA & ÁVILA: OUR PICKS

Mesón de Cándido: In a 300-year-old building, the same family has been serving Segovia's best *cochinillo* (suckling pig) for generations. *1-4.30pm & 8-11pm* €€

Casa Duque: Founded in 1895, this historical tavern is known for its garlic soup, roast kid and *cochinillo. 12.30-11pm* €€€

Pastelería Muñoz Iselma: Family-run Ávila business producing delicious almond slices known as Jesuitas. *9.30am-2pm & 4-8pm Mon-Fri, 9.30am-8pm Sat & Sun* €

La Bruja: A rustic woodbeam dining room serving all the Ávila specialities, along with Argentine-style charcoal grilled steak. *1-4.45pm & 8-11.30pm* €€

the battlements to exit near one of the city's 88 watchtowers at **Puerta del Carmen**. For a fuller appreciation, you can walk around the outside from here, enjoying incredible views over the plains and the Sierra de Gredos as you circle the southern ramparts to **Mirador de Ávila** (at the southeastern corner).

Burgos, León & Astorga

TIME FROM MADRID: 2¼–4HR 🚆 + 🚌

A tale of three cathedrals

One of Spain's finest Gothic gems awaits discovery in Burgos, 250km north of Madrid. Step into the city's spectacular 13th-century **Catedral** *(catedraldeburgos.es; adult/child €10/2)* and see the tomb of Rodrigo Díaz (aka El Cid), one of Spain's greatest national heroes. He died in 1099 but his legend reached a crescendo about a century later with the epic poem *Cantar de Mío Cid* ('Song of My Cid').

West from Burgos, León has made an art form out of its plazas. On Plaza de la Regla, the **Catedral de León** *(leon.es; adult/child €6/free)* dazzles in Gothic splendour and the glint from 125 stained-glass windows.

Equally evocative is the **Catedral de Astorga** *(catedralastorga.com; adult/child €10/8),* 45km further west from León. It's one of the most important religious sites on the Camino Francés pilgrim route, with three spectacular towers like rocket-ships tethered together with stone bridges and flying buttresses. A visit includes a free virtual-reality tour in which you have the incredibly realistic sensation of flying through the building.

Cáceres & Mérida

TIME FROM MADRID: 3HR 🚗

Strolling through a magical old city

One of the thrilling cities of Extremadura, Cáceres is defined by its glowing, UNESCO-listed **Ciudad Monumental** *(turismocaceres.org),* which has survived almost intact from its 16th-century period of splendour. Signs of the city's flourishing Jewish and Muslim periods create a harmonious mix with its more recent Catholic past and present – so picturesque it has starred in big-screen productions like *Game of Thrones*.

From **Plaza Mayor**, hemmed by elegant houses with elaborate Renaissance facades, a stairway leads underneath the **Arco de la Estrella** arch to the superb Renaissance-style **Plaza de Santa María** and the Gothic **Concatedral de Santa María de Cáceres** *(concatedralcaceres.com; adult/child €7/5).*

FLAVOURS OF CASTILLA Y LEÓN

Castilla y León has 26 Denominaciones de Origen (DO), and many of these marks of gastronomic distinction hail from southern pastures. Salamanca's Morucha beef, Ávila's Negra Ibérica cow and Guijuelo's *jamón* (ham) are all prized nationally. Distinct dishes from Salamanca include *farinato* (a lard, bread and flour sausage flavoured with paprika, anise and brandy) and *hornazo* (a pork pie with chorizo and boiled eggs). While meat dominates the cuisine, flat green lentils from La Armuña and seven varieties of bean from Ávila are staples in stews. *Segovianos* take *cochinillo* (suckling pig) seriously; traditionally it should be slow-roasted in a clay pot. For something sweet, try the cylindrical *bollo maimón* and egg-yolk *yemas de Santa Teresa*.

 EATING IN BURGOS & ASTORGA: OUR PICKS

| **El Patio:** A huge local favourite (but rarely frequented by tourists), this large Astorga bar fills up quickly with tapas-eaters at weekends. *8am–1am Fri-Tue* €€ | **La Quinta del Monje:** Popular for tapas, including *morcilla* (the blood sausage for which Burgos is so famous). *hours vary* € | **La Lorencita:** A perennial old-Burgos favourite and prize-winner for the regional Tapas y Pincho awards in 2020. *noon-midnight Tue-Sat, to 5pm Sun* €€€ | **Café Pasaje:** Overlooking Astorga's Plaza España, with tables heaped with Maragato meat and vegetables, this place is hard to beat. *8am-11pm* €€ |

EXTREMADURA JEWELS

Many regional highlights are easily visited en route to/from Cáceres or Mérida.

Trujillo: Dazzling small city, with ancient walls, a hilltop 13th-century castle and a monumental Plaza Mayor.

Parque Nacional de Monfragüe: A dramatic, hilly 180-sq-km paradise for birdwatchers and other nature lovers, just north of Cáceres.

Guadalupe: The UNESCO World Heritage Site of Real Monasterio de Santa María de Guadalupe is Spain's most important monastery.

Medellín: Around 40km northeast of Mérida, little-known Medellín was a major town in Roman times and has its own beautiful Roman Theatre.

Valle de la Vera: One of the remotest parts of Spain, home to small hamlets and delightful hill and mountain country.

ROBAUTO/SHUTTERSTOCK

Templo de Diana, Mérida

Stroll the street to Plaza de los Golfines, and then to **Plaza de San Mateo**, with the **church** of the same name. Follow the unmissable white towers to the imposing **Iglesia de San Francisco Javier**. Continue to the **Judería Vieja**, in the Barrio de San Antonio, the old Jewish district.

Fans of contemporary art will also want to dip into the **Museo de Arte Contemporáneo Helga de Alvear** *(museo helgadealvear.com; free; closed Mon).*

Echoes of Roman times

Born Augusta Emerita, once the capital of the Roman province of Lusitania, today Mérida's spectacular ruins lie sprinkled around town. Admission to most sites is by combined ticket *(adult/child €17.50/8.50).*

At the very heart of Mérida lies an unusual plaza with the **Templo de Diana**, an original ancient Roman temple, flanked by modern buildings. Among many other highlights is the spectacular, 60-arch **Puente Romano** (Roman Bridge) on the broad Río Guadiana. But the main event is Mérida's **Teatro Romano** *(teatroromanomerida.com).* One of the world's best-preserved Roman theatres, it was built around 15 BCE by the will of Marcus Vipsanius Agrippa, Augustus' right-hand man, to seat 6000 spectators – and still hosts summer performances. Before entering, visit the superb **Museo Nacional de Arte Romano** *(turismomerida.org; adult/child €3/free; closed Mon)* next door.

EATING IN CÁCERES & MÉRIDA: OUR PICKS

La Cacharrería: Exclusive and cosy, taking classic Cáceres cuisine and making it even more refined. *2-3.30pm & 8.30pm-midnight Thu-Mon €€*

Tapería 8a Arte: Popular with a young Cáceres crowd for its wide array of local tapas and gluten-free and vegan options. *noon-11.30pm Thu-Tue €*

La Carbonería Restaurante: Perfect place in Mérida for those serious about their meat, with a delicious tapas bar next door. *hours vary €€*

Agallas Gastro & Food: Trendy Mérida restaurant with extravagant dishes and great quality/price ratio. *1-5pm & 8.15pm-midnight Tue-Sat €*

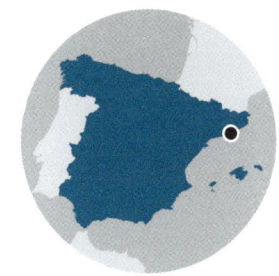

Barcelona

ART & ARCHITECTURE | CATALAN CULTURE | FOOD-AND-DRINK SCENE

Catalonia's capital is one of Europe's most desirable cities – a sunny, Mediterranean-hugging hub that breezily combines its rich cultural traditions with a forward-thinking, environmentally aware attitude.

During Barcelona's medieval Golden Age, great churches and mansions were built across the Ciutat Vella (Old City), shaping today's Barri Gòtic, La Ribera and El Raval neighbourhoods, where creative tapas and vermouth bars and boundary-pushing galleries now sit between centuries-old walls. Then came the industrial boom, with areas like El Poblenou, Gràcia and Sants taking centre stage, and the creation of an entirely new district, L'Eixample, where otherworldly Modernista buildings still command attention. Ever since the late 19th century, the city has been breaking ground in art and style as well as architecture.

Barcelona has experienced an astonishing boom since hosting the 1992 Olympics. With tourism now a key part of the local economy, the city is pushing forward ambitious plans to balance the needs of local residents and the tourism industry.

> ☑ **TOP TIP**
>
> Barri Gòtic and La Ribera (especially El Born) are the busiest, most overtouristed neighbourhoods. Head out early to explore, book museum tickets ahead and keep an eye on belongings. Gràcia, Sant Antoni and Poble Sec have few 'official' sights, but offer wonderful restaurants and bars. For wheelchair-accessible tours, see *disabledaccessibletravel. com.*

Gaudí Galore

Best of the Modernista architect

Dominating Barcelona's skyline, Antoni Gaudí's **La Sagrada Família** *(sagradafamilia.org; adult/child €26/free)*

continued on p262

 GETTING AROUND

Much of Barcelona is flat and walkable. The city has over 250km of bike lanes; bike-hire outlets are everywhere *(€12 per day).*

The excellent TMB metro system has eight lines; buy a 10-journey **T-Casual pass** *(tmb. cat; €12.55).* The main exceptions are Tibidabo/ Collserola (funicular or train) and Montjuïc (funicular, bus and cable car).

For the airport, the frequent, 24-hour **Aerobús** *(aerobusbarcelona.es; €7.45)* takes 30 to 40 minutes; alternatively, take a taxi (around €30), train (R2 Nord line) or metro (L9 Sud).

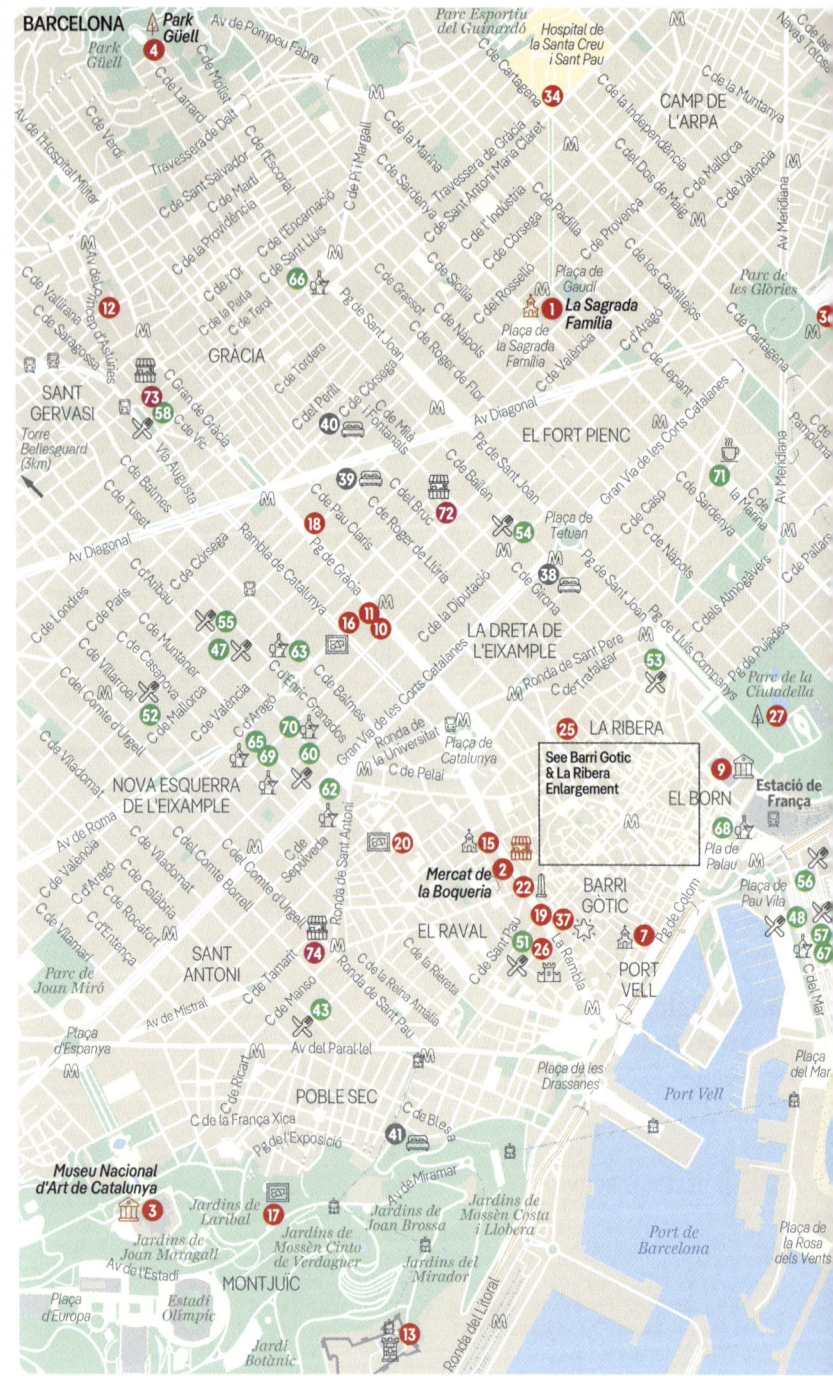

BARCELONA

Park Güell 4

Park Güell

Pare Esportiu del Guinardó

Hospital de la Santa Creu i Sant Pau

34

CAMP DE L'ARPA

12

GRÀCIA

66

SANT GERVASI

73 58

Torre Bellesguard (3km)

40

39

18

72

54

La Sagrada Família 1

Plaça de la Sagrada Família

EL FORT PIENC

3

71

38

55

47

11 16 10

63

52

70

65 69

60

LA DRETA DE L'EIXAMPLE

53

25 LA RIBERA

Parc de la Ciutadella

27

NOVA ESQUERRA DE L'EIXAMPLE

62

20

15

9 EL BORN

68

Estació de França

Pla de Palau

Plaça de Pau Vila

56

SANT ANTONI

74

Mercat de la Boqueria 2

22

EL RAVAL

19 37

BARRI GÒTIC

7

PORT VELL

48 57

51 26

Parc de Joan Miró

43

Plaça d'Espanya

POBLE SEC

41

Port Vell

Plaça del Mar

Museu Nacional d'Art de Catalunya

3

17

Jardins de Laribal

Jardins de Joan Brossa

Jardins de Mossèn Costa i Llobera

Port de Barcelona

Plaça de la Rosa dels Vents

Jardins de Joan Maragall

Jardins de Mossèn Cinto de Verdaguer

Jardins del Mirador

Plaça d'Europa

Estadi Olímpic

MONTJUÏC

Jardí Botànic

13

continued from p259

MODERNISME HIGHLIGHTS

Casa Vicens: A UNESCO-listed masterpiece, Gaudí's first commission was built between 1883 and 1885 in Gràcia.

Palau Güell: In El Raval, the palatial home Gaudí designed for his patron Eusebi Güell is one of the world's first Art Nouveau buildings.

Palau de la Música Catalana: Built between 1905 and 1908 by Lluís Domènech i Montaner, this 2146-seat concert hall still hosts music.

Torre Bellesguard: Dating back to medieval times, this lesser-known Gothic-Modernista building was transformed by Gaudí in the early 1900s.

Casa Amatller: Josep Puig i Cadafalch's marvel combines Gothic, Romanesque and Dutch urban architecture.

Recinte Modernista de Sant Pau: A UNESCO-protected Domènech i Montaner wonder, created as a hospital between 1902 and 1930.

stops everyone in their tracks. Despite the crowds, this is an unmissable, UNESCO-listed Barcelona highlight. The main construction is due to be completed in 2026. After taking over from original architect Francisco de Paula del Villar y Lozano in 1883, Gaudí (who is buried in the neo-Gothic **crypt**) spent 43 years of his life on the basilica. Above the main building there will eventually be 18 **towers**, some of them already open to visitors. The spectacularly sculpted **Façana del Naixement** (Nativity Facade) is the oldest of the basilica's three monumental facades; the 2018-completed **Façana de la Passió** (Passion Facade), depicting Christ's last days and death, is largely the recent work of the late sculptor Josep Maria Subirachs. Within, extraordinary leaning pillars evoke a natural forest.

On Passeig de Gràcia, the elegant boulevard that bisects L'Eixample, **Casa Batlló** *(casabatllo.es; adult/child €29/free)* is one of Barcelona's most beautiful and curious buildings. Created between 1904 and 1906, this is Gaudí at his fantastical best, from the playful facade with its bulging bone-like balconies and purple-blue *trencadís* tilework to the ground-breaking experiments in light and architectural form. The showstopper is the endlessly mesmerising rooftop.

Neighbouring Casa Milà is better known as **La Pedrera** *(lapedrera.com; adult/child €29/free),* or the Quarry, because of its wave-like grey-stone facade. In the top tier of Gaudí's achievements, this madcap masterpiece with 33 balconies was built between 1905 and 1910 as a combined apartment and office block.

At UNESCO-listed **Park Güell** *(parkguell.barcelona; adult/ child €18/13.50),* just north of Gràcia, Gaudí turned his imagination to landscape gardening, creating an ingenious interplay between architecture and the natural world. Visiting the park's trail-laced northern part *(zona forestal)* is free. Best views? From 182m-high **Turó de les Tres Creus**, in the southwest corner.

For all Gaudí sights, book tickets ahead and arrive early or just before closing to beat the crowds. Guided tours are highly recommended.

Glowing Spires & Ancient Squares

Taste Ciutat Vella's long past

Sitting on the foundations of Roman Barcino, the Barri Gòtic is the oldest part of Barcelona and still the hub for festivities

EATING AROUND EL POBLENOU: OUR PICKS

Can Fisher: On Bogatell, reliably good seafood and a chic decor make this a good pick for a paella. *12.30-11pm Mon-Fri, from 10am Sat & Sun* €€

Little Fern Café: Expect a line on weekend mornings at this cafe beloved for its fresh aesthetic, granola bowls and avocado toasts. *9am-4pm* €

Xiringuito Escribà: An open-plan beach bar for digging into a classic, seafood or surf-and-turf paella or *fideuà* (paella-like fish and seafood noodle dish). *noon-10.30pm* €€€

Buriti: Get your morning energy jolt at this Brazilian restaurant with a healthy menu that delights both vegans and meat-eaters. *hours vary* €

ALEXANDER PROKOPENKO/SHUTTERSTOCK

Park Güell

such as **Festes de la Mercè** in September. Extending northeast from the Barri Gòtic, La Ribera grew from the 10th century and became Barcelona's medieval commercial epicentre. Just east, palm-dotted **Parc de la Ciutadella** is central Barcelona's beloved green haven, created for the 1888 Universal Exposition on the site of the much-hated, long-demolished Ciutadella fortress (which had been built after the War of the Spanish Succession).

With its elaborate spires and neo-Gothic facade, the **Catedral de Barcelona** (*catedralbcn.org; adult/child €16/8*) rises in the heart of the Barri Gòtic, preserving a sacred crypt and a cloister that echoes with the honking of 13 white geese. Much of the building dates from the 13th and 14th centuries. Just across Via Laietana, La Ribera's harmonious **Basílica de Santa Maria del Mar** (*santamariadelmarbarcelona.org; adult/child from €5/free*) is Barcelona's most magnificent Catalan Gothic church, built between 1329 and 1382. Climb to the rooftop of either temple for exquisite views.

BARCELONA'S MARKETS

In the 19th century, many *mercats* (markets) were redesigned by local architects. Today, stalls mingle with bars.

Mercat de la Boqueria: Famous, historic, busy, known for tapas bars such as El Quim.

Mercat de la Llibertat: Modernista hub of Gràcia life covered in 1893. Great tapas at Hermòs Bar de Peix.

Mercat de Santa Caterina: Designed by boundary-pushing architects Enric Miralles and Benedetta Tagliabue. Don't miss Bar Joan.

Mercat de Sant Antoni: Restored 1882 Modernista marvel anchoring Sant Antoni. Home to legendary Bar Pinotxo.

Mercat de la Concepció: Created in 1888 by Antoni Rovira i Trias. Popular for 24-hour flower shop Flores Navarro.

 EATING & DRINKING IN CIUTAT VELLA & SANT ANTONI: OUR PICKS

El Xampanyet: A legend of Barcelona's *cava* (sparkling wine) scene; arrive early for delicious tapas (tangy anchovies, gooey tortilla). *hours vary*

Bar Mono: Polished gastropub with all the classic tapas to check off your list, plus a good vegetarian menu. *11am-midnight Mon-Fri, to 1am Sat & Sun €€*

Bar del Pla: El Born favourite specialising in natural wines and creative tapas such as wasabi mushrooms. *noon-11pm €€*

Bar Pimentel: Understated tapas bar for *cava*, vermouth and wine; bites include tortilla and squid with lime mayo. *1-11pm Sun-Thu, to 11.30pm Fri & Sat €€*

Fismuler: El Bulli–trained chefs lead this innovative favourite where market menus change daily and wines are glorious. *hours vary €€€*

Paradiso: Named the globe's greatest bar in 2022 by The World's 50 Best Bars; try the mezcal-fuelled Cloud. *5pm-3am*

Cañete: Upmarket stylish bar for tapas and sharing plates like spicy octopus, oxtail stew and plump anchovies. *1pm-midnight Mon-Sat €€*

Bar Calders: Lively Sant Antoni bar for wines and vermouth paired with modern tapas from wraps and hummus to nachos. *hours vary €*

BEST GUIDED TOURS

Spanish Civil War Tours by Nick Lloyd: Historian-led tour of 1930s Barcelona, giving context to a complicated history. *(thespanishcivilwar. com)*

Barcelona Architecture Walks: Led by practising architects and architecture professors, including a Gaudí stroll. *(barcelona rchitecturewalks.com)*

Devour: Excellent food-focused tours supporting small businesses and local producers. *(devourtours.com)*

Runner Bean: Free daily tours led by knowledgeable guides. Bookings required; tips expected. *(runnerbean tours.com)*

Hidden City Tours: Social enterprise that trains guides who have been homeless; routes show a different side to modern-day Barcelona. *(hiddencity tours.com)*

Platja de la Barceloneta

The **Plaça de Sant Jaume** is home to the **Palau de la Generalitat** and the **Ajuntament** (City Hall). Remnants of Roman Barcino can still be seen at the **Temple d'August** *(free),* near pretty **Plaça de Sant Felip Neri**.

Strolling La Rambla

Barcelona's most famous boulevard

Ancient **La Rambla** connects Plaça de Catalunya to the waterfront, flanked by the Barri Gòtic and El Raval. Once the site of a stream outside the city walls, today it's undoubtedly busy and touristed, but look closely and you'll find centuries of Barcelona history. With five sections, you'll hear it referred to as Las Ramblas (Les Rambles in Catalan). Highlights include the **Església de Betlem**, a church built in the late 17th and 18th centuries; the colourful **Mosaic de Miró**; and the famed **Mercat de la Boqueria** (p263). Visit early and keep an eye on belongings.

 EATING & DRINKING IN L'EIXAMPLE & GRÀCIA: OUR PICKS

Gresca: At Gresca's open-plan kitchen, chef Rafa Peña reinvents seasonal produce alongside natural wines. *hours vary* €€

Besta: Exquisite menus blend Catalan and Galician flavours, mostly with a seafood focus (vegetarian options on request). *hours vary* €€

Disfrutar: Boundary-pushing, three-Michelin-star venue led by chefs Mateu Casañas, Oriol Castro and Eduard Xatruch. *12.45-2pm & 7.45-9pm Mon-Fri* €€€

Mont Bar: Bistro-style Michelin-starred restaurant with superb wines and next-level cooking using seasonal, organic produce. *1-2pm & 7-10pm Tue-Sat* €€€

Funky Bakers Eatery: Stylish cafe-deli for Barcelona-roasted coffee, delicious babkas, creative brunches and seasonal dishes. *hours vary* €€

Three Marks: Best coffee in town? Head to this speciality roastery in the Fort Pienc area and sit on the terrace. *8am-4pm Mon-Fri, 9.30am-5pm Sat & Sun*

La Pubilla: Alexis Peñalver's Gràcia kitchen has Catalan-style breakfasts and market-fresh menus. *9am-noon, 1-3.30pm & 8pm-midnight Tue-Sat* €€

La Vermuteria del Tano: Long-running favourite with decorative barrels, Perucchi vermouth and traditional conserves. *9am-9pm Tue- Fri, noon-4pm Sat & Sun*

For a more local-life experience, head to **Rambla del Poblenou** or L'Eixample's **Rambla de Catalunya**.

World of Picasso
Delve into the artist's early years

Five medieval palace-mansions on La Ribera's Carrer de Montcada create a striking setting for the **Museu Picasso** *(museupicassobcn.cat; adult/child €14/free)*. But what makes this landmark gallery truly impressive is its showcase of Málaga-born Pablo Picasso's formative years. The first two rooms display early oil paintings and sketches, including the famous *Portrait of Aunt Pepa,* done in 1896 in Málaga when Picasso was just 15. Room 3 houses one of the museum's star pieces, the enormous *Science and Charity,* from 1987. Subsequent rooms showcase the famous Blue Period (including *Woman with a Bonnet* from 1901, in room 8). In rooms 12 to 14, Picasso's 1957 series of renditions of Velázquez' 1656 masterpiece *Las meninas* dazzles among arches.

Fans of contemporary art will also enjoy the next-door **Moco Museum** *(mocomuseum.com; adult/child €17/14)*, L'Eixample's **Fundació Antoni Tàpies** *(museutapies.org; adult/child €12/free)* and El Raval's groundbreaking **MACBA** *(macba. cat; adult/child €11/free)*. The great-value **Articket Barcelona** *(articketbcn.org; €38)* covers six major galleries. Most museums close Monday.

Waterfront Fun
From beaches to cutting-edge architecture

Barcelona's waterfront stretches from the Port Vell marina near Montjüic to the concrete sprawl of Parc del Fòrum. **Barceloneta** is a grid-like former fisherfolk's neighbourhood engineered in the 18th century, and is renowned for its tapas bars, like **Jai-Ca** *(barjaica.com)*, **La Cova Fumada**, **La Violeta** and **Bodega La Peninsular**.

To the northeast, sprawling **El Poblenou** is a former industrial area that has become one of the city's most fashionable hubs, home to the sky-high **Torre Glòries** *(miradortorreglories.com; adult/child €18/free)*. The best way to enjoy this area is by joining the runners, walkers, cyclists, paddleboarders, rollerbladers and beach-goers. The Poblenou-area beaches of **Nova Icària**, **Bogatell**, **Mar Bella** and **Nova Mar Bella** have a more relaxed feel than busy, central **Platja de la Barceloneta**.

Go Dancing in the Gaixample
Heart of Barcelona's LGBTIQ+ scene

Over in Esquerra de L'Eixample, the grid between Aragó, Gran Via, Balmes and Comte Urgell streets is popularly known as the 'Gaixample'. With its many bars, clubs, restaurants, bookshops and rainbow flags, this is the epicentre of Barcelona's LGBTIQ+ scene. Popular nightspots include **Punto BCN** for drinks and drag shows, and relaxed **La Chapelle**.

VERMOUTH HOUR

First brought to Spain from Italy in the mid-19th century, vermouth has experienced a dazzling revival in Barcelona over the last decade. Based on red or white wine, the drink is infused with botanicals and fortified with brandy. The best places serve it over ice with an olive and a thin slice of orange. It's ideally enjoyed with friends around midday, especially on weekends – *l'hora del vermut.* Vermouth is always accompanied by light snacks, such as salty crisps or a few tapas (anchovies, croquettes, *patates braves*). To *fer el vermut* (do a vermouth), choose from a wealth of *vermuterias* (vermouth bars), though most Barcelona bars now serve it. The Gràcia and Sant Antoni districts are particularly known for their vermouth-hour scenes.

FESTES DE LA MERCÈ

Held around 24 September, the **Festes de la Mercè** is Barcelona's greatest annual celebration. Honouring one of the city's two patron saints, festivities involve four days of concerts, dancing and street theatre. Much of the fun centres on the Barri Gòtic, particularly the **Basílica de la Mercè** *(basilicadelamerce. com)*, Plaça de Sant Jaume, Via Laietana, La Rambla and the cathedral. But La Mercè is celebrated all over town. In La Ribera, the **Born Centre de Cultura i Memòria** *(barcelona. cat)* hosts displays and parades of fantastical Catalan creatures, while **Parc de la Ciutadella** (p263) has food markets and live music. Cultural highlights include *castells* (human towers), *gegants* (papier-mâché giants), *sardana* (folk dance) and *correfoc* (fire-running).

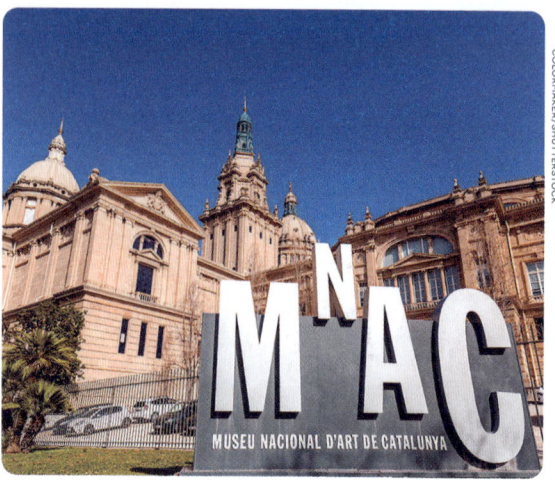

Museu Nacional d'Art de Catalunya

Weekends-only **Carita Bonita** is a hub for Barcelona's lesbian community. **Candy Darling** has drag shows and a cultural focus, while rooftop cocktails await at Axel Hotel's **Sky Bar** *(axelhotels.com)*. In late June or early July, Barcelona hosts its packed two-week **Pride** *(pridebarcelona.org)* festival, with a Pride march on the Saturday.

Museums on the Mountain

Explore Montjuïc's terrific galleries

Rising up behind Poble Sec, pine-covered Montjuïc (173m) hosts some of Barcelona's finest museums, pretty gardens and an ancient hilltop **castle**. The spectacular neobaroque Palau Nacional, housing the **Museu Nacional d'Art de Catalunya** *(museunacional.cat; adult/child €12/free),* was built for the 1929 World Exhibition. Its vast collection of mostly Catalan art spans the early Middle Ages to the early 20th century. The high point is the extraordinary Romanesque frescoes, including the 12th-century *Christ in Majesty* (Sala 7) and *Virgin Mary and Christ Child* (Sala 9), both rescued from churches in northern Catalonia.

The nearby, light-flooded **Fundació Joan Miró** *(fmirobcn. org; adult/child €15/free)* is home to the world's greatest collection of artworks by the Catalan surrealist Joan Miró, and was designed by Miró's friend, the Catalan architect Josep Lluís Sert. Standouts include the huge 1979 tapestry of the *Fundació* and *Man and Woman in Front of a Pile of Excrement* (1935).

Beyond Barcelona

Uncover Catalonia's shimmering shores, dive into ancient cities or escape into some of the country's loveliest mountain terrain.

Barcelona's urban sprawl gives way to Catalonia's beloved coastlines. Just beyond Barcelona, Sitges has long been one of Spain's liveliest LGBTIQ+ friendly destinations, with beaches, parties and festivals year-round. On the central Costa Daurada, Tarragona was the first city to be settled by the Romans on the Iberian Peninsula. Northeast from Barcelona, the Costa Brava is one of the most dazzling parts of Spain's long shoreline, with culture-rich Girona awaiting just inland. If you only visit one place on the Costa Brava, Cadaqués – former home of Salvador Dalí – is the quintessential whitewashed village. Heading west into Aragón, the regional capital Zaragoza combines entrancing monuments with a great tapas scene. North of it all, the majestic Spanish Pyrenees straddle Catalonia, Aragón, Navarra and the Basque Country.

Places

Montserrat p267

Sitges p268

Tarragona p268

Cadaqués & the Costa Brava p270

Zaragoza p270

The Spanish Pyrenees p271

Montserrat

TIME FROM BARCELONA: 1½HR

Monastic mountain majesty

Attracting millions of visitors every year, Montserrat is Catalonia's most emblematic mountain. It's home to a historic mountain-side monastery and an ethereal natural landscape where curvaceous rock columns transform into sharp needle-like peaks at a distance, inspiring the Catalan name that translates as 'serrated mountain'.

Founded in 1025, the Benedictine **Monestir de Montserrat** *(montserratvisita.com; adult/child €20/10)* has been drawing pilgrims for centuries to see the icon of **La Moreneta** (the 'Little Brown One' or 'Black Virgin'), a wooden figure of the Virgin Mary prominently displayed at the centre of the

---

🧭 **GETTING AROUND**

Sitges has excellent *rodalies* (commuter train) connections to Barcelona *(rodalies.gencat. cat)*. Tarragona and Zaragoza are linked to Barcelona and beyond by **Renfe** *(renfe.com)* trains. For the Costa Brava and the Pyrenees, it pays to have your own wheels, or use local buses (some routes only operate seasonally).

Some places restrict private-vehicle access during high season. For Montserrat, take the **FGC** *(fgc.cat)* R5 train from central Barcelona, then change to the Aeri cable car *(aeridemontserrat.com)* or Cremallera rack railway *(cremallerademontserrat.cat)*.

altar. Despite the large tourist complex with shops, restaurants and museums, this is still a working monastery. With careful timing, you might catch a performance by the Escolania de Montserrat, one of the oldest boys' choirs in Europe.

Beyond the monastery complex, Montserrat is a natural park with many inspiring walking trails, including summitting the mountain (1236m) on the 10.3km **Sant Jeroni Loop**.

Sitges

TIME FROM BARCELONA: **35MIN**

A festive beach town

A popular day-trip escape from Barcelona, lively Sitges has a crop of beautiful beaches and a glitzy nightlife scene. Listen to the bells of the **Església de Sant Bartomeu i Santa Tecla** ring out as you lounge on the main strip of sandy beaches, or explore a little further up the coast to clothing-optional **Platja dels Balmins**.

Historically LGBTIQ+ friendly, Sitges traces its clubbing scene back to the 1980s. Catch the two largest celebrations of colour and love during Carnival in late February/early March or June's Pride parade.

Sitges also has a delightful, buzzy historic centre. Learn about one of the leading artists of Modernisme, Santiago Rusiñol, at the **Museu del Cau Ferrat** and the ornate **Palau de Maricel** *(museusdesitges.cat; adult/child €12/free);* they are closed on Mondays.

Tarragona

TIME FROM BARCELONA: **1–2HR**

Roman relics

Formerly known as Tárraco, Tarragona spent hundreds of years as the region's Roman capital. Today, well-preserved remnants of the ancient city are found throughout the old town of this vibrant, modern hub. A joint ticket *(tarragona.cat; adult/child €15/free)* offers access to all the major sites, which individually cost €5. Enter the history museum at **Torre de les Monges** and soon you'll be peering out over the **Circ Romà**, a partial preservation of a much larger chariot course. The museum continues underground, finishing at the **Torre del Pretori**, where you can climb to the top for a spectacular view of the sea-facing **Amfiteatre de Tarragona**, built in the 2nd century for up to 15,000 spectators.

Romans aside, the **Catedral de Tarragona** *(catedraldetarragona.com; adult/child €12/8.50)* is one of the largest in Catalonia and features a blend of Gothic and Romanesque styles.

THE CATALAN LANGUAGE

Prepare to be viciously side-eyed if you get caught calling Catalan a dialect of Spanish. Although it is a Romance language similar to both Spanish and French – you'll find that some words, such as *hola* and *merci* respectively, are identical – Catalan is distinct and spoken by over four million native speakers. Catalan is not only spoken in Catalonia, but also in parts of Valencia, the Balearic Islands, and even as far away as the Italian city of Alghero in Sardinia, which was colonised by the Catalans in the Middle Ages. Although most people in Catalonia are likely to speak Spanish as well, trying out a Catalan phrase here and there is usually appreciated.

 EATING IN GIRONA: OUR PICKS

Rocambolesc: Ice-cream shop with special flavours and fun popsicles; from the family of El Celler de Can Roca. *10.30am-11pm Sun-Thu, to midnight Fri & Sat* €

L'Argadà: Catalan steakhouse, where seasonal *calçots* (spring onions) are served in a traditional roof tile. *1.30-3.30pm & 8-10.30pm Mon-Sat, 1.30-3.30pm Sun* €€

Café Le Bistrot: Tables romantically arranged on the steps of Sant Domènec; book ahead. *1-4pm & 7.30pm-midnight Mon-Sat, 1-4pm Sun* €€

El Celler de Can Roca: World-famous and recognised for dramatic plating and gourmet cooking techniques. *12.30-9.30pm Wed-Sat, from 7.30pm Tue* €€€

GIRONA ARCHAEOLOGICAL WALK

Despite the contemporary city that surrounds it, Girona's old quarter maintains its medieval charm.

START	END	LENGTH
Museu d'Historia dels Jueus	Café Le Bistrot	2km; one hour

Just north of the Pont de Sant Agustí, you'll find the 1 **Museu d'Historia dels Jueus**, located in a 13th-century Jewish home. Turn right on Carrer Sant Llorenç and walk up to a medieval fountain, 2 **Font dels Lledoners**. Turn left through the plaza towards the steps of the Gothic-baroque 3 **Catedral de Girona**, home to the *Tapestry of Creation* from the 11th or 12th century.

Trot down for a better look and go through the gate towards the 4 **Basílica de Sant Feliu**. Take a right to pass the 12th-century 5 **Banys Àrabs**. At the end of this road, find the 6 **Plaça dels Jurats** and 7 **Monestir de Sant Pere de Galligants**, which houses lovely cloisters and the archaeology museum. Climbing up the Passeig de la Reina Joana, follow the archaeological path to reach the 8 **Jardins dels Alemanys** and access the 9 **Muralles de Girona** for the walk along the walls, passing the towers of Gironella and Sant Domènec.

Descend the walls at Torre del General Peralta Bastion and continue until you pass the 10 **Convent de Sant Domènec de Girona**. A huge convent founded in 1253, it now belongs to the university. Turn left on the Pujada de Sant Domènec and walk towards the picturesque stairs, where you might snag a table at 11 **Café Le Bistrot** (p268).

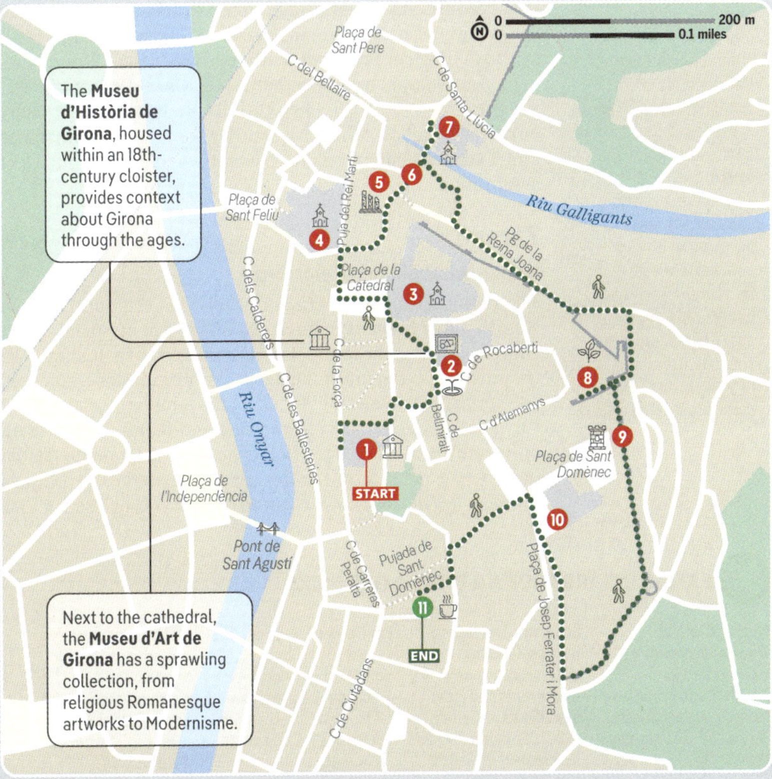
0 200 m
0 0.1 miles
Plaça de Sant Pere
C del Bellaire
C de Santa Llúcia
Riu Galligants
Pg de la Reina Joana
Plaça de Sant Feliu
Puja del Rei Martí
Plaça de la Catedral
C dels Calderers
C de la Força
C de Rocaberti
C d'Alemanys
C de Bellmirall
C de les Ballesteries
Riu Onyar
Plaça de Sant Domènec
Plaça de l'Independència
Pont de Sant Agustí
Pujada de Sant Domènec
C de Carreras Peralta
Plaça de Josep Ferrater i Mora
C de Ciutadans
START
END
1
2
3
4
5
6
7
8
9
10
11
The **Museu d'Història de Girona**, housed within an 18th-century cloister, provides context about Girona through the ages.
Next to the cathedral, the **Museu d'Art de Girona** has a sprawling collection, from religious Romanesque artworks to Modernisme.

CATALONIA'S HUMAN TOWERS

This uniquely Catalan tradition is a sight you won't soon forget. With its origins in an 18th-century Valencian folk dance, *castells* are all about creating the highest tower possible, often reaching heights of up to 15m. Just like the strong base of human power that holds the tower in place, the spirit of building human towers is all about community and groups of *castellers*, known as *colles*, which represent different communities all over Catalonia. There is no age limit, something immediately gleaned by the little kids shimmying their way to the top. You can catch them performing during cultural festivals throughout the year, but it's only once every two years that you can attend the biggest event – the **Concurs de Castells**.

Cadaqués & the Costa Brava
TIME FROM BARCELONA (CADAQUÉS): 2¼HR

Winds of Cap de Creus

Just north of Cadaqués, the **Parc Natural de Cap de Creus** (*parcsnaturals.gencat.cat*) is defined by its dry and weather-worn rocky landscape, filled with jagged and uncanny shapes that inspired the controversial surrealist artist Salvador Dalí throughout his life. Today it's a protected park with many marked walking paths, including an 8km route that you can follow from Cadaqués to the 19th-century lighthouse – **Far Cap de Creus** – at Spain's most eastern point. Venture to swimming spots **Cala Culip** and **Cala Jugadora**. During certain times of year, park roads close to vehicles, and a SARFA bus service (*moventis.es*) is offered from Cadaqués and the Corral d'en Morell car park.

Beach-hopping around Begur

Another of the Costa Brava's loveliest pockets is the cliff-edged shoreline around the charming town of **Begur**, 60km south of Cadaqués. The ruins of the 16th-century **Castell de Begur** provide one of the most majestic views of the Costa Brava; on clear days you can even see the Pyrenees. **Platja de Sa Riera** has plenty of sand to go around, but there are fewer crowds at the clothing-optional **Platja de l'Illa Roja**, a sandy cove with an enormous rock stack. Or head to the small seaside village of **Sa Tuna**, with its rocky beach. From here, grab your snorkel and take the trail to **Cala d'Aiguafreda**.

A little further south, busy **Calella de Palafrugell** offers enticing beaches, while its smaller neighbours **Llafranc** and **Tamariu** have a quieter beach-town charm and perfect swimming.

Zaragoza
TIME FROM BARCELONA: 1½HR

Monumental places of worship

The defining image of Aragón's capital is the multi-domed **Basílica de Nuestra Señora del Pilar**, one of Spain's great churches, rising above the Río Ebro in Zaragoza. It stands on the site where, the faithful believe, the Virgin Mary appeared to Santiago (St James the Apostle) atop a pillar of jasper in 40 CE. The famous pillar is in the east-end Santa Capilla, with only a tiny oval-shaped portion exposed (except on dedicated days). In the north aisle, the fresco painting in the third cupola is Goya's *Regina Martyrum* (Queen of Martyrs), painted in 1781.

EATING IN TARRAGONA & SITGES: OUR PICKS

Mercat Central: Traditional market with modern food stands found inside a Modernista building in Tarragona. *8.30am-9pm Mon-Sat €*

El Terrat: The tasting menu celebrates the Moroccan head chef's roots and local ingredients; in Tarragona. *1.15-3.30pm Thu-Tue, 8.15-10.30pm Fri & Sat €€€*

El Cable: Always packed tapas bar in Sitges' old town, known for its delicious *patates braves*. *7-11.30pm Mon-Fri, noon-3.30pm & 7-11.30pm Sat & Sun €€*

NeM: Creative, season-rooted tapas blend Spanish and Asian flavours at this stylish Sitges fave. *7.30-11pm Wed-Fri, 1-5pm & 7.30-11pm Sat & Sun €€*

La Seo, Zaragoza

Goya's earlier *Adoración del Nombre del Dios* adorns the ceiling of the choir at the church's far east end. Goya's work can also be seen at the **Museo Goya** *(museogoya.fundacionibercaja. es)* and the **Museo de Zaragoza** *(turismodearagon.com),* both slated to reopen in 2026 following renovations.

Though overshadowed in scale by the basilica, Zaragoza's **La Seo** cathedral is arguably a finer work of Christian architecture. Built between the 12th and 17th centuries, it stands on the site of Islamic Zaragoza's main mosque. A joint ticket covers both churches *(catedraldezaragoza.es; adut/child €10/free).*

High point of Islamic architecture

The dour castle-like exterior gives no hint of the ornate decorative joys within the **Aljafería** *(turismodearagon.com; adult/ child €7/free).* Built as a fortified palace for Zaragoza's Islamic rulers in the 11th century, it passed into Christian hands in 1118, and in the 1490s the Reyes Católicos (Catholic Monarchs), Fernando and Isabel, tacked on their own palace. Wandering through its exquisitely sculpted courtyards and delicate interwoven archways, you can get a sense of the pomp and majesty of both the Islamic court and its Christian successors.

The Spanish Pyrenees TIME FROM BARCELONA: **3–4HR** 🚗
Mountain hikes and other adventures

Some of Spain's most dramatic mountain country awaits in the Pyrenees, which spill over into France north of Zaragoza

---

THE COSTA BRAVA & DALÍ

Teatre-Museu Dalí: Topped by larger-than-life eggs, Dalí's theatre-museum opened in 1974 and is a centrepiece of the artist's hometown, Figueres.

Casa Museu Dalí: Just outside Cadaqués, the artist's labyrinthine house in Portlligat is unlike any historic home you've seen before, including his former workshop.

Cap de Creus: Dalí's painting *The Great Masturbator* mimics the shape of one of the cape's strangest rocks, located in Cala Culleró.

Castell Gala Dalí: Dalí's wife Gala is buried at the 14th-century castle he gifted to her, located between Girona and Palafrugell.

Expo Dalí: Small gallery in Cadaqués that showcases the artist's original prints.

 EATING IN CADAQUÉS & BEGUR: OUR PICKS

Compartir: Try the multicourse tasting menu from El Bulli alums for Catalan flavours made to share in Cadaqués. *1-3pm & 8-10pm Tue-Sat* €€€

Havana: Begur's Cuban connection results in authentic Caribbean flavours. *1-3.30pm & 7-10.30pm Thu-Mon, 7-10.30pm Wed* €€

Es Baluard: A family-run Cadaqués restaurant by the sea for traditional Catalan feasts and paella. *1-3.30pm & 8-10pm Wed-Sun, 1-3.30pm Mon* €€€

Lua: This cosy spot in Cadaqués serves Mediterranean and Asian fusion food like curry-covered pork meatballs. *1-3.30pm & 8-10.30pm* €€

PYRENEES PRACTICALITIES

The best walking season in Spain's Pyrenees is from about May to October. Warmest weather is generally from mid-June to early September; mountain streams and waterfalls are spectacular in spring; and October brings wonderful autumn colours. Book accommodation well ahead for July and August (the busiest season), and at any time of year if you're keen to stay in the *refugis* (mountain huts). Both national parks have wheelchair-accessible trails. Visit the park's visitor centres and information points for tips on hiking routes, weather conditions and seasonal transport. Stone villages dotted around the national park's fringes provide charming bases, including Torla, Broto, Aínsa and Bielsa for Monte Perdido and Espot, Taüll and Boí for Aigüestortes.

Parc Nacional d'Aigüestortes i Estany de Sant Maurici

and Barcelona. Every corner of these undeveloped mountains is breathtaking in its majesty and inspiring in its beauty. Two pristine national parks provide the scenic high, with innumerable great walking trails and other adventure-activity opportunities.

In the north of Aragón, the 156-sq-km **Parque Nacional de Ordesa y Monte Perdido** *(miteco.gob.es)* encompasses limestone peaks, plunging canyons, thick forests, meadow pastures, rivers, waterfalls and turquoise mountain lakes. The park's **Valle de Ordesa** is one of the most spectacular canyons in Europe, with multiple walking routes including a classic 9km trail (one way).

Over in Catalonia's north, the 405-sq-km **Parc Nacional d'Aigüestortes i Estany de Sant Maurici** *(parcsnaturals. gencat.cat)* is rife with well-marked trails, welcoming *refugis* (huts) and impressive scenery at every turn. With over 200 lakes, overlooked by 3000m-high mountain peaks, the beauty of this glacier-carved realm feels downright cinematic. A standout hike (15.5km) is crossing the park in one day from Espot to Boí, connecting the Estany Llong and Estany d'Amitges routes through the **Portarró d'Espot** (2423m) pass. This area and its surrounds are also home to some of Spain's most popular ski slopes.

 EATING IN ZARAGOZA: OUR PICKS

La Clandestina: Stylish bistro known for its brunch (with *cava*), tasty vegetarian creations and great cheesecake. *hours vary* €€

Restaurante Palomeque: Rich, original Spanish dishes in a cosy dining room or streetside. *11am-midnight Mon-Fri, noon-6pm Sat* €€€

Bodegas Almau: All manner of tapas (anchovies a speciality), and hundreds of wine bottles at a 150-year-old bar. *11am-4pm & 7pm-midnight* €

Taberna Doña Casta: Join the crowds for tasty croquettes and *huevos rotos* (fried eggs with potatoes). *7pm-1am Tue, noon-4.30pm & 7pm-1am Wed-Sun* €

Northern Spain

DRAMATIC SCENERY | CULTURE-PACKED CITIES | GASTRONOMY

Often lyrically talked about as 'Green Spain', the northern stretch of the country feels a world away, with its rugged cliffs, verdant countryside, stone-built villages and wild surf beaches fronting the Bay of Biscay or the wide-open Atlantic. Each region has its own distinctive identity and, in most cases, language, and the culture-rich main cities are as enthralling as the quiet hills.

In the Basque Country, cows and sheep graze in valleys between lofty mountains, rocky coves are battered by furious Atlantic swells, while the cities buzz with art, gastronomy and nightlife. Many Basque people see their identity as strongly tied to the region they call Euskadi (País Vasco in Spanish), which officially includes the provinces of Vizcaya (and its capital Bilbao), Gipuzkoa (and its capital Donostia-San Sebastián) and Álava (and its capital Vitoria-Gasteiz). However, many Basques consider Euskal Herria ('the land of Basque speakers') to more broadly include Navarra and three provinces in southern France.

To the west, the autonomous region of Cantabria and the Principality of Asturias stretch just a little over 300km along the Bay of Biscay, yet encompass a dramatically beautiful world of Atlantic-whipped shores giving way to the snowcapped, adventure-laced Picos de Europa mountains. Galicia, Spain's northwest

Places

☑ TOP TIP

Across the region, many shops (and some tourism activities) close for lunch during the 'siesta hours' (between about 2.30pm and 5pm). For budget-conscious dining, take advantage of *menús del día* (rarely served in evenings). Summer can be busy along Spain's northern coast; beaches are less packed in spring and autumn.

 GETTING AROUND

The north is well connected by air. Major towns have good bus and train connections; the narrow-gauge Renfe Cercanías Ancho Métrico *(renfe.com)* rattles across the north. For more remote destinations, hire a car or plan ahead to align with limited public transport services.

Many travellers explore this region on foot, taking advantage of local trails including the Camino del Norte variant of the Camino de Santiago. The main cities have enjoyably walkable old towns.

NORTHERN SPAIN

corner, combines the pilgrim magnet of Santiago de Compostela with a dramatic, wave-battered coastline.

Bilbao

Once defined by its steelworks and shipbuilding industries, Bilbao has seen a remarkable journey of regeneration since the 1990s. The staggering architecture, venerable dining scene, fascinating museums and endlessly creative cultural arena make Bilbao the most exciting urban centre in the Basque Country.

Arty Bilbao

The gleaming, titanium-clad **Museo Guggenheim Bilbao** (*guggenheim-bilbao.eus; adult/child €18/free*), on the banks of the Ría del Nervión, is the city's most striking building. Filled with pieces by some of the world's best contemporary artists, this extraordinary Frank Gehry–designed landmark is reason alone to visit Bilbao. Start your visit in the central atrium, a light-filled space in which the interior architecture can be admired. From here, three floors of galleries emerge, linked by staircases, catwalks and lifts. Check ahead for what's currently on show and any thrilling temporary exhibitions.

 EATING IN BILBAO: OUR PICKS

La Viña del Ensanche: Mouthwatering morsels include ham, seared mackerel and crispy asparagus tempura. *10am-10.30pm Tue-Fri, from 1pm Sat €*

El Globo: Outstanding *pintxos* (labelled in English) that showcase the great bounty of the Basque countryside. *hours vary €*

Gure Toki: Many consider this Bilbao's best *pintxos*. Try mini pastry parcels filled with stir-fried veg and prawns. *10am-11pm Thu-Tue €*

Mina Restaurante: Serious creativity is on the tasting menu at this riverside restaurant, which some critics call Bilbao's best. *2-3pm & 9-10pm Wed-Sun €€€*

Exterior works to seek out include Louise Bourgeois' spider-like *Maman* and Anish Kapoor's *Tall Tree & the Eye,* both by the river; and Jeff Koons' *Puppy,* a 12m-tall Highland terrier made up of thousands of flowers.

But Bilbao's art scene extends beyond the Guggenheim. Don't miss the **Museo de Bellas Artes** *(bilbaomuseoa.eus; free),* which houses works by Murillo, El Greco and Goya. For a glimpse into the city's contemporary art scene, pop into riverside gallery **Uribitarte40** *(bilbaoarte.eus),* avant-garde Basque-focused **Sala Rekalde** *(salarekalde.bizkaia.net)* and **Azkuna Zentroa** (the Alhóndiga), a former wine-storage warehouse turned cultural centre *(azkunazentroa.eus).*

Donostia-San Sebastián

Officially named in both Basque (Donostia) and Spanish (San Sebastián), Donostia-San Sebastián is a city that celebrates the art of eating. Just as good as the food is San Sebastián's glamorous beachside setting. Little wonder, then, that over-tourism is a growing concern for locals. In 2023, mayor Eneko Goia announced a ban on the construction of new hotels to combat high visitor numbers.

Beach life

The crescent-shaped **Playa de la Concha** (and its westerly extension **Playa de Ondarreta**) is largely sheltered from Atlantic swells. Swim out to floating diving platforms or join in a volleyball match on the sand. At the eastern end of the beach, there are accessible hot showers, changing rooms and lockers and an accessible ramp down to the sand. From June to September, a free assisted bathing service is available.

Opposite Playa de la Concha is **Isla de Santa Clara**. In summer, **Motoras de la Isla** *(motorasdelaisla.com; €5)* runs boat trips to the island from the fishing port. You can also paddle to Santa Clara by SUP or kayak; rent them at **Club Deportivo Fortuna** *(cdfortunake.com; from €13 per hr).*

Fronting the Gros district, **Playa de la Zurriola** is the city's other beachy jewel, known for its surf waves (often beginner-friendly) and buzzing local scene. Don't miss **Mundaka**,

 EATING IN DONOSTIA-SAN SEBASTIÁN: PINTXOS & MICHELIN STARS

Bar Borda Berri: Perennially popular, old-school *pintxo* bar that lives up to the hype. *12.30-3.30pm Wed-Sat & 7.30-10.30pm Tue-Fri €*	**Paco Bueno:** This no-frills bar is the place to go for piping-hot battered prawns; order them at the counter. *11am-3pm €*	**La Viña:** Try the famous baked cheesecake, prepared daily and left to stand on shelves by the bar. *10.30am-4pm & 7-11pm Tue-Sun €*	**Ganbara:** This *pintxo* bar is highly regarded for its delectable plates and snacks; good wine list, too. *12.30-3.30pm & 7-11pm Tue-Sat €*
Txepetxa: Anchovies with various accompaniments are the house speciality at this traditional local bar. *noon-3pm & 7-11pm Tue-Sat €*	**Arzak:** Chefs draw on thousands of ingredients to create new dishes in 'the lab' at one of the world's best restaurants. *1.15-3.15pm & 8.45-10.30pm Tue-Sat €€€*	**Akelaře:** Three-Michelin-starred restaurant serving Basque nouvelle cuisine; located in the suburb of Igueldo. *1-2.30pm & 8.30-9.30pm Tue-Sat €€€*	**Martín Berasategui:** Chef Martín Berasategui takes a scientific approach at this triple-starred temple to food. *1-2.15pm Wed-Sun, 8.30-9.30pm Thu-Sat €€€*

100km west en route to Bilbao and a big name in the surf world due to its famous left-hand barrel; rent gear or book a lesson with **Mundaka Surf Shop** (*mundakasurfshop.com; rental from €10*).

Santillana del Mar

Just inland from the Bay of Biscay on Cantabria's western coast, Santillana del Mar is one of Spain's loveliest towns. Even high-season crowds seem to do little to diminish the charm of its cobbled lanes and plazas or its palaces and mansions built with wealth from South America.

Stepping into the past

Spain's most important prehistoric site, just outside Santillana del Mar, was discovered by an amateur archaeologist and his eight-year-old daughter in 1879. Magnificent **Altamira** (*cultura.gob.es; adult/child €3/free; closed Mon*) stands as a testament to the fact that humankind (extremely artistic humans at that) have called this area home for at least 35,500 years. The wonderfully executed animals (mostly created around 18,500 years ago) continue to thrill modern viewers with their artistic beauty as they gallop – sometimes larger than life-size – across the walls. Bison are curved cleverly across the rippled ceiling of the cave so that their muscles and contours are often revealed almost in three dimensions. It's unfortunate (if understandable) that the originals are under protection – viewed only occasionally by experts – but the incredibly realistic and interactive museum mock-up of the cave complex offers an unexpectedly fascinating experience.

Picos de Europa

Compact but dramatically varied, the 674-sq-km **Parque Nacional Picos de Europa** (*parquenacionalpicoseuropa.es*) is one of the favourite haunts for Spanish mountain enthusiasts. The park's three 2000m limestone massifs straddle the provinces of Cantabria, Asturias and Castilla y León. The pretty hill town of **Potes**, in the Cantabrian foothills of the Picos, and **Cangas de Onís** on the Asturian side make ideal bases.

Hiking the Picos

There are over 40 well-marked hiking routes across the Picos suited to all levels of energy, fitness and enthusiasm. Be prepared for squalls and carry waterproofs, warm gear, sunblock and a hat. Busy even on a winter's weekend, the **Ruta del Cares** is so popular it's often referred to as 'Spain's favourite hike'. Rich in flora and fauna and with fine mountain views, the 11km (one-way) route between **Poncebos** in Asturias and **Caín** in Castilla y León is an adventure, threading along ledges, passing through tunnels and crossing bridges in a gorge high above the Río Cares. The track is generally hiked from north to south.

The 753m-long **Teleférico de Fuente Dé** (*telefericodefuente ede.com; adult/child from €13/6*) has been carrying visitors from **Fuente Dé** village (near Potes) to the top of the Picos

JAMES JACKMAN/LONELY PLANET

Altamira museum, Santillana del Mar

for more than 50 years. Weather permitting, you can hike down from an altitude of 1853m. The ride up to the cafe on the summit takes just four minutes but you should allow three to four hours for the 15km hike back down the slopes. If you opt to avoid the full walk back down, there are several (flatter) routes crisscrossing the higher peaks.

Santiago de Compostela

The destination of half a million people who follow the Camino de Santiago pilgrim trails every year, Santiago de Compostela is one of Spain's most beautiful cities and arguably the one where the aura of past centuries lives on strongest. It is also a thriving modern regional capital, with one of Spain's top universities.

Marvel at Santiago's cathedral

Entering magnificent **Praza do Obradoiro** for the first time, you'll stop dead in your tracks, just as many thousands of pilgrims do every year, eyes magnetised by the soaring Churrigueresque facade of the **Catedral de Santiago de Compostela** *(catedraldesantiago.es),* believed to house the tomb of Santiago (St James) the Apostle. Today's cathedral is one of Europe's architectural and historical highlights, and features a mix of an original Romanesque structure, constructed between 1075 and 1211, and later Gothic and baroque flourishes.

Inside, the **Altar Mayor** (High Altar) is a fantastically elaborate Churrigueresque confection with a statue of Santiago at its centre. The ambulatory (walkway) round behind the Altar Mayor passes the inside of the **Puerta Santa** (Holy Door), which opens only in holy years, and brings you round to a flight of steps descending to a view of the large 19th-century silver casket that contains, we're assured, Santiago's remains. Re-emerging, you can climb stairs up behind the Santiago statue, embrace him and make a wish.

CATHEDRAL TIPS

At 7am, the Santiago cathedral is practically empty, even in peak summer months.

Entry to the Pórtico de la Gloria, Cubiertas (roof) and Museo Catedral is by ticket. Advance bookings, at least two weeks ahead for July and August, are essential for the first two.

Guided night tours (sometimes in English) are a treat. You'll enjoy stunning views from the Tribune, an upper-level balcony. Tickets *(€25)* go on sale 15 days ahead.

The popular **rooftop tour** *(adult/child €15/12)* provides a close-up look at the towers and their decorative adornments, plus tremendous city views. Be ready to climb over 150 steps.

The permanent collection of the **Museo Catedral** *(adult/child €7/free)* contains a sizeable section of Maestro Mateo's original carved-stone choir.

Pórtico de la Gloria, Catedral de Santiago de Compostela (p277)

The cathedral's artistic high point, at the west end of the nave, the **Pórtico de la Gloria** features 200 Romanesque sculptures by Maestro Mateo, who was given charge of the cathedral-building programme in the late 12th century.

Prazas, museums and markets

At the northern end of Praza do Obradoiro, the **Hostal dos Reis Católicos** *(paradores.es)* was built in the 16th century as a pilgrim hostel by order of the Reyes Católicos. Today it's a *parador* (luxurious state-owned hotel), open for self-guided tours.

Opposite the cathedral, the elegant 18th-century **Pazo de Raxoi** is now Santiago's city hall. Head a few steps north to **Praza das Praterías** (Silversmiths' Square), centred on the 1825 **Fuente de los Caballos** and the excellent **Museo das Peregrinacións** *(museoperegrinacions.xunta.gal; free)*, which is closed on Mondays.

A bustling hub of Santiago life, the **Mercado de Abastos** *(closed Sun)* comprises 300-odd stalls piled high with fresh produce from Galicia's farms and coasts. Popular bars and restaurants line the street outside; inside, **Nave 5 Abastos** (Aisle 5) is set with long tables where you can sit down for well-priced meals cooked up in adjacent stalls.

EATING IN SANTIAGO DE COMPOSTELA: OUR PICKS

O Gato Negro: Old-school tavern (since 1922) with market-fresh seafood, empanadas and more. Be ready to eat standing. *12.30-3pm & 7.30-11pm Tue-Sat* €€

Café-Jardin Costa Vella: The garden cafe is a delightful breakfast spot. Also does light local-produce tapas, cakes and wines. *8am-12.30pm & 4.30-10.30pm* €

A Moa: Great mix of Galician and worldly fare in street-level wine bar, stone-walled restaurant and verdant garden. *1.30-3.45pm & 9-11pm Tue-Sat, 1.30-3.45pm Sun* €€

Abastos 2.0: Seafood dishes at marketside outdoor tables; daily-changing €50 *menú* at the indoor 'Barra' (reservations required). *noon-3.30pm & 8-11pm Mon-Sat* €€€

Cabo Fisterra & Around

Once believed by Europeans to be the western limit of the world, hilly, heather-clad Cabo Fisterra (Cape Finisterre) extends into the Atlantic 3km south of the fishing port Fisterra on Galicia's dramatic Costa da Morte. The cape is the final destination for particularly enthusiastic Camino de Santiago pilgrims who push on an extra 89km from Santiago de Compostela – and for those who walk the Camiño dos Faros along the Costa da Morte.

End-of-the-world lighthouse

Despite the crowds, **Cabo Fisterra** remains a wonderfully panoramic and atmospheric spot, topped by a squat 19th-century lighthouse, the **Faro de Fisterra**. Some who reach it on foot follow a tradition of burning worn-out old boots and socks on the rocks just below the lighthouse. The easiest and quickest way from Fisterra to Cabo Fisterra is simply to head 3km along the AC445 road to the lighthouse, with the panoramas expanding as you go. Other, even more scenic paths lead here too, including over the top of **Monte do Facho** (242m), the promontory's highest point.

Walking the Camiño dos Faros

You can definitely enjoy the Costa da Morte pottering around by car, bicycle or motorbike, but you'll get the most intimate connection with its diverse scenes and moods by exploring on foot. A superb, often challenging, long-distance path, the **Camiño dos Faros** (*Lighthouse Way; caminodosfaros.com*) traces the whole coastline from Malpica de Bergantiños to Cabo Fisterra. Its eight stages are marked only in the Malpica-to-Fisterra direction (with small green arrows and paint blobs). Arguably most spectacular are Stage 7 (Muxía to Praia de Nemiña, 25km) and Stage 8 (Praia de Nemiña to Cabo Fisterra, 27km). Some people walk the whole trail in one trip; others do day walks. Expect sun, wind and rain: beware of fog rolling rapidly in, and avoid precipitous cliffs on gusty days.

NORTHERN WINES

Best known among characterful Galician wines are the fruity *albariño* whites from the Rías Baixas DO. Many good reds come from the native *mencía* grape, and in recent years winemakers have revived Galician grapes including *godello* (whites), *brancellao* and *merenzao* (reds). Produced using Hondarrabi Zuri grapes, Basque *txakoli* is a fresh, crisp, dry and slightly sparkling white wine that goes well with seafood or *pintxos* on sunny days. Wine aficionados the world over know the wines of La Rioja, where vines have been cultivated since Roman times. Cantabria, Asturias and the Basque Country are famous for their ciders, poured from up high for maximum fizz. Wineries across the north are open for tours and tastings; it's best to book. The *vendimia* (grape harvest) starts in August.

 EATING ON THE COSTA DA MORTE: OUR PICKS

O Pirata, Fisterra: The freshest of fish and seafood, traditionally prepared, at good prices and overlooking the harbour. *noon-5pm Tue-Sun* €

Etel & Pan, Fisterra Friendly cafe doing excellent burgers, *bocadillos* and salads, with plentiful vegetarian options. *noon-3.30pm & 7-10.30pm Fri-Tue* €

Casa Fontequeiroso, Nemiña Superb dinners based around traditional Galician recipes at a small rural hotel (p300). Non-guests should call first. *7-9pm* €€

Lonxa d'Alvaro, Muxía Fish *a la brasa* (chargrilled), seafood-stuffed *filloas* (crêpes) and lobster rice are the stars here. *hours vary* €€€

Valencia & Around

OTHERWORLDLY ARCHITECTURE | ELEGANT MARKETS | UPBEAT BEACHES

GETTING AROUND

Most of Valencia's sights are within easy reach of the main plaza and others are a short cycle or tram ride away. Taxis are affordable, costing around €10 from the centre to the beach. Bikes (around €15 per day) are a lovely way to explore the city. **Valenbisi** (*valenbisi.es*) is the city's bike scheme; a weekly ticket costs €13. While many parts of the surrounding Valencia region (including La Albufera) are easy to explore with public transport, hiring a car is useful.

☑ **TOP TIP**

Want to pack in a lot of sights? The **Valencia Tourist Card** (*€17/24/30 per 24/48/72 hr*) offers unlimited travel, discounts and a glass of wine at El Corte Inglés. Buy it from tourist information offices or access *visitvalencia.com* for 10% off.

With fun beaches, culture-packed cities and a fierce culinary heritage, Spain's east coast has an extraordinary feel-good factor. In recent years, the Valencia region has embraced urban regeneration, forward-thinking events and gorgeous green spaces (often guided by sustainability), attracting a new wave of visitors.

Over 2000 years of history have carved Valencia's warren-like old-town, from the Romans who founded it to the 20th-century architects who flexed their creativity. Ancient ruins have been painstakingly preserved, but the city isn't stuck in the past. Russafa is the creatives' *barrio,* with cool cafes, hidden galleries and brilliant restaurants; the seaside has a fresh feel with lively *chiringuitos* (snack bars). Further south, rewilding projects revive the dunes and ecosystems of La Albufera. Throw in a 9km-long park with bike routes, wildflowers and lemon trees, and it's clear Valencia is snapping at the heels of its Catalan neighbour. Among the city's many festivities, few rival the famous Las Fallas, held amid thundering pyrotechnics each March.

Taste Local Delicacies

Valencia's splendid Central Market

A feast of Valencia-grown produce awaits within the **Mercat Central** (*mercadocentralvalencia.es; closed on Sun*), a Valencian Art Nouveau–style market in the centre of Ciutat Vella. Inside, domed glass ceilings preside over pyramids of olives, fish and veg straight from the fields. A great way to get a taste for its buzzing, still-local atmosphere is by sipping a refreshing *horchata* (typical Valencian sugary cold drink made from tiger nuts) at the bar at **La Huertana**. Don't forget the *fartón,* an iced bun for dunking. **Les Tomates de Javier** sells the best Valencian tomatoes, **Retrogusto** (*retrogustocoffeemates.com*) brews cracking coffee, and **Solaz** sells cheesecake made by the

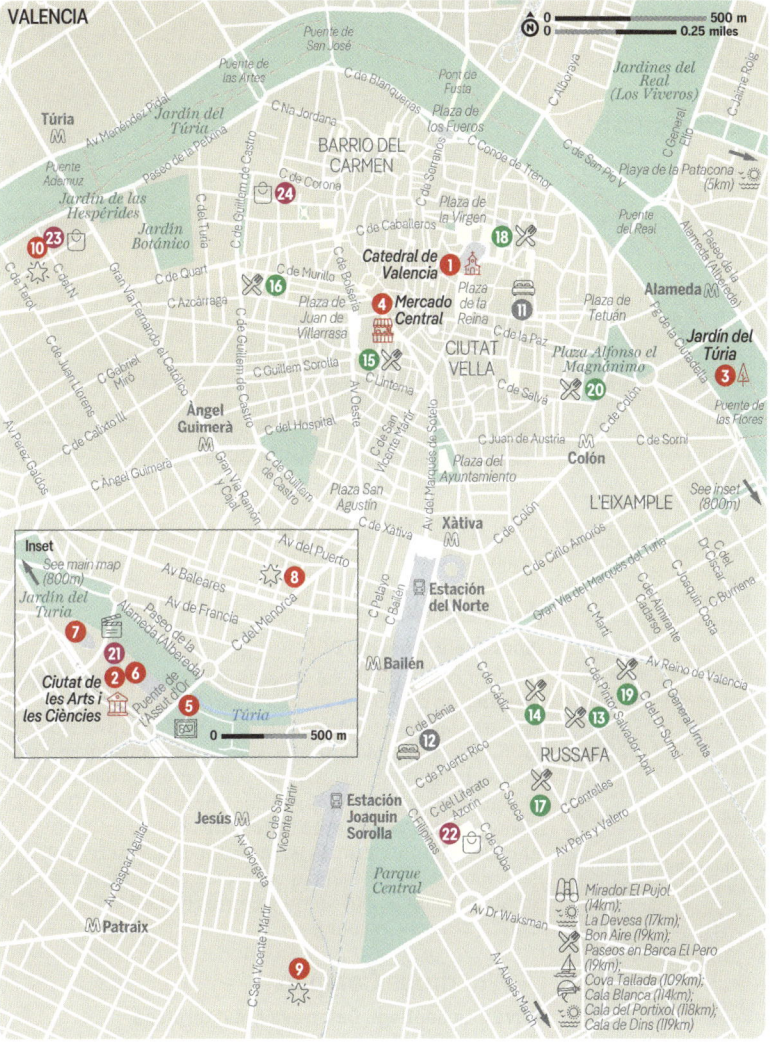

HIGHLIGHTS
1 Catedral de Valencia
2 Ciutat de les Arts i les Ciències
3 Jardín del Túria
4 Mercado Central

SIGHTS
5 CaixaForum
6 Museu de les Ciències
7 Palau de les Arts

ACTIVITIES
8 Ana Illueca
9 Escuela Fictile
10 Valencia Bikes

SLEEPING
11 Casa Clarita
12 YOURS

EATING
13 2 Estaciones
14 Amor Amargo

15 Central Bar
16 Forastera Restaurant
17 La Cantina de Ruzafa
see 4 La Huertana
18 La Samorra
19 Maipi
20 Ostras Pedrín

DRINKING & NIGHTLIFE
see 4 Retrogusto

ENTERTAINMENT
21 Hemisfèric

SHOPPING
22 Cuit
23 Konlakalma
see 4 Les Tomates de Javier
24 Plou Estudi
see 4 Solaz

VALENCIA POTTERY STUDIOS

Valencia has an ancient ceramics heritage, and modern artisans are throwing bold new shapes.

Cuit: Make your own mug in this chic Russafa studio to pick up the next month, or buy one readymade. *(cuit.es)*

Ana Illueca: The un-trendy area near Cabanyal is the unlikely home of this whip-smart pottery studio. *(anaillueca.com)*

Plou Estudi: Geometric shapes with pops of blue and yellow line shelves in this studio and shop.

Escuela Fictile: Japanese pottery has a huge influence on Macarena's pieces, found in her peaceful workshop.

Konlakalma: Katrin makes asymmetric vases and fluid sculptures using coil and slab building techniques. *(konlakalma.com)*

Ciutat de les Arts i les Ciències

team of Ricard Camarena, owner of the two-Michelin-starred Ricard Camarena restaurant.

Find the Holy Grail

Spot a relic from 100 BCE

An impossible task? Not according to the **Catedral de Valencia** *(catedraldevalencia.es; adult/child €10/6)*. Inside Valencia's Gothic cathedral is an agate goblet dating from 100 BCE. Dazzling gold handles and a base embellished with pearls, rubies and emeralds were added in the medieval era. But at just 17cm tall it's easy to miss: head towards the hushed 14th-century **Capilla del Santo Cáliz**. Constructed between the 13th and 15th centuries, the cathedral features splendid star vaulting and Renaissance-style frescoes above the main altar. A stomp up 207 spiral steps to the **bell tower** *(adult/child €3/free)* is thrilling.

A Wondrous Complex

Dive into Santiago Calatrava's masterpiece

Establishing Valencia as a beacon of contemporary architecture, the astonishing **Ciutat de les Arts i les Ciències** *(cac.es)* is mostly the work of Valencian architect Santiago Calatrava.

 EATING IN RUSSAFA: OUR PICKS

Maipi: Old-school *taberna* serving whatever's fresh from the market, like sweet prawns or artichokes with *jamón*. *1.30-4pm & 8.30-11pm Mon-Fri* €

La Cantina de Ruzafa: Wholesome canteen famous for its stewed bull sandwich topped with fried eggs. *9.30am-5pm Mon-Thu, from 9am Fri* €

Amor Amargo: Cosy Art Nouveau interiors with ambitious cooking – the nine-hour ribs are heavenly. *noon-12.30am Tue-Sun, from 7pm Mon* €€

2 Estaciones: Meticulous food with seasonality at its core. The weekday *menú express* is fantastic value. *1.30-3.30pm & 8.30-10.30pm Wed-Sat* €€€

The architecture is a marvel in itself; a walk through the complex that occupies a vast swathe of the old Túria riverbed won't cost you a penny.

Calatrava balanced mighty, organic architecture by using ceramic mosaic tiles called *trencadís*. They're perhaps most striking on **Palau de les Arts**, an ultramodern performing-arts complex with four auditoriums. Tours run several times daily *(adult/child €18/14)*. To the south, the unblinking eye of the **Hemisfèric** houses an IMAX cinema with a 900-sq-metre screen. Across an expanse of water, **Museu de les Ciències** *(adult/child €9.40/7.20)* stretches out like a giant whale skeleton, housing an interactive science museum. Next up, resembling a huge purple mussel, the **CaixaForum** stages interesting exhibitions on diverse themes.

Bike to the Beach
Explore Valencia's loveliest gardens

Valencia's best park is found in an old riverbed that was diverted due to flooding. Snaking through the city for over 9km, **Jardín del Túria** is a delight to explore by bike. Inaugurated in 1986, today the riverbed is a haven of baobab and palm trees frequented by chattering parakeets and songbirds. On a leisurely route of around 12km (one way), it's possible to cycle all the way to pretty **Playa de la Patacona**, with its seafront restaurants and *chiringuitos*. Pick up wheels at **Valencia Bikes** *(valenciabikes.com; €15 per day)*, close to the Túria metro.

Boating & Bird-Spotting
Cruise La Albufera's waters

Just 15km south of Valencia proper, glorious La Albufera is the birthplace of paella, with much of the area protected by the peaceful **Parque Natural de la Albufera**. People have fished the freshwater lake here since prehistoric times, and the rice paddies have been around since at least the 15th century. This rice is used in the best paellas – try one at **Bon Aire** *(restaurantebonaire.com)* in **El Palmar**. A handful of boat trips join the local fisherfolk who use flat-bottomed boats and nets to harvest fish and eels from the shallow waters. Jaime, a La Albufera local, offers insightful trips with **Paseos en Barca El Pero** *(paseosenbarcaelpero.es; from €70)*. Sunsets are spectacular: book Jaime's sunset cruise or head to **Mirador El Pujol**.

SWIMMING SPOTS BEYOND VALENCIA

Around Xàbia: Cala del Portixol is famed as the most beautiful on the coastline. Cala Blanca and Cala de Dins are fairy-tale coves, accessible only by foot.

Dénia: Dénia's coastline has lots of little surprises. Swim in shimmering waters outside Cova Tallada, an artificial cave best accessed by kayak.

Fuente de los Baños: In the mountains around Montanejos, these emerald pools fed by hot springs are a dreamy wild-swimming spot.

Altea: Hilltop, whitewashed Altea, set between two protected natural parks, has lofty viewpoints, pebble beaches and turquoise waters.

La Devesa: Part of La Albufera's natural regeneration, La Devesa is accessed only by foot along a path bordered by rosemary and pines.

 EATING IN CIUTAT VELLA: OUR PICKS

Ostras Pedrín: Join a cool crowd out to get tipsy on *cava* and feast on a sea of oysters. *11am-midnight Mon-Sat, to 4pm Sun* €

La Samorra: Traditional tapas in a tiled *taberna*. Don't miss the *figatells* (meatballs). *7.30pm-midnight Wed-Sat, 12.30-5pm Thu-Sat, noon-5pm Sun* €€

Central Bar: Informal tapas bar among the fruit stalls of Mercat Central, with unbeatable cheesecake. *9am-3pm Mon-Thu, to 3.30pm Fri & Sat* €€

Forastera Restaurant: Dreamy dinner-date spot with a market-fresh tasting menu and wines from small artisanal producers. *hours vary Thu-Mon* €€€

Balearic Islands

DREAM BEACHES | SOARING MOUNTAINS | CHARMING VILLAGES

Places

Mallorca p285
Menorca p286
Ibiza & Formentera p287

Etymologists may wrangle over the origins of their name, but there's no disputing the seductive magic of the Balearic Islands, clustered in the western Mediterranean off the east coast of Spain. Each of the four principal islands has its unique cultural identity, with a dialect related to Catalan, and own vibe.

Mallorca lives up to the social-media-worthy images of sun-warmed ochre buildings, scarlet bougainvillea in soulful hill towns and long beaches with aquamarine seas, but is also deeply enhanced by a contemporary outlook and rich culture. For Miró, it was the pure light. For hikers and cyclists, it's the Serra de Tramuntana's limestone spires. Foodies will love the markets and, of course, the chefs – inspired as much by their Mallorcan forebears as by contemporary Mediterranean cuisine. Meanwhile, beyond the built-up resorts, coves and white-sand bays rim the shoreline.

Menorca, the quieter pair to Mallorca, remains largely undeveloped, with brilliant, pristine beaches, megalithic ruins, two fascinating main towns (eastern Anglo-Spanish Maó and western mazelike Ciutadella) and dry stone walls crossing pastures. Ibiza's party-hard spirit draws crowds in summer, who relax on its beaches and hidden coves, and fill its somnolent, sunbaked white villages. Ibiza's part-

 TOP TIP

In recent years, Mallorca and the other Balearics have suffered from growing overtourism concerns. Sidestep the summer crowds by visiting in shoulder season or winter. For Easter and summer, book well in advance. The opening hours provided here are for summer. Beyond Palma de Mallorca, many venues reduce hours or close in the off-season.

GETTING AROUND

Mallorca, Ibiza and Menorca have airports. Ferries (see *ferryhopper.com*) connect Alcúdia (Mallorca) with Ciutadella (Menorca) and Palma (Mallorca) with Ibiza Town; they also run to/from mainland destinations including Barcelona, Dénia and Valencia. Smaller ferries run between Ibiza and Formentera (30 minutes).

Car hire spikes seasonally so book well ahead, or use reliable local buses. Mallorca's **Ferrocarril de Sóller** (*trendesoller.com*) vintage train is a highlight. Well-marked cycling and walking paths crisscross the islands.

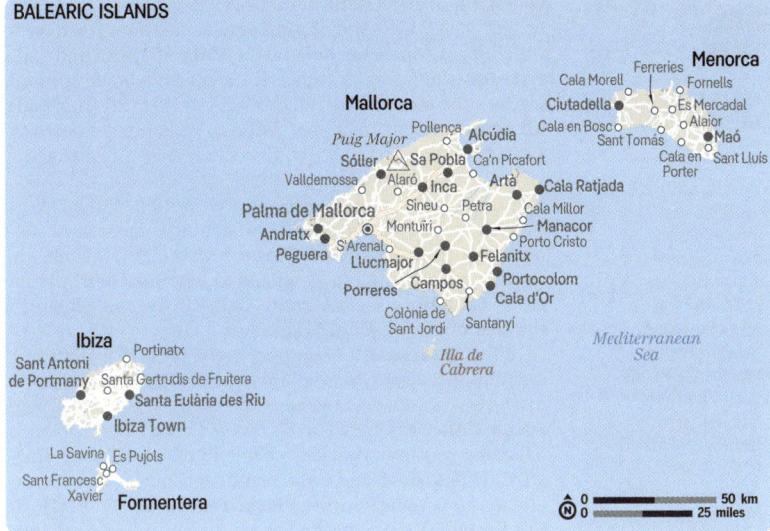

BALEARIC ISLANDS

Mallorca

Menorca

Ibiza

Formentera

Mediterranean Sea

ner (together, they are called the Pityuses or Pine Islands) Formentera, is pure bliss, with astonishing beaches and protected reserves.

Mallorca

History and art in the Mallorcan capital

Palma de Mallorca (universally shortened to Palma) is a stunner. Rising in sand-coloured stone from the broad still waters of the Badia de Palma, the city has been home to Christian Reconquistadors, Moors, Romans and, way back, the Talayotic people. All Palma visits begin best at the magnificent, waterfront **Catedral de Mallorca** *(catedraldemallorca.org; adult/child €10/free),* called 'La Seu'. Although the foundations went up in the 12th century on the site of the central mosque, most of the structure is predominantly Gothic. Continue your history lesson with the **Palau de l'Almudaina** *(patrimon ionacional.es; adult/child €7/4),* an Islamic fort converted into a royal residence in the 13th century, and the Moorish **Banys Àrabs** *(€3.50).*

Built with flair and innovation into the shell of the Renaissance-era seaward fortifications on the southwest side of Palma's old town, contemporary art gallery **Es Baluard** *(esbaluard.org; adult/child €6/free; closed Mon)* is one of the finest on the islands. Art lovers will want to make the pilgrimage to the wonderful hilltop compound and still-standing studios of Catalan artist Joan Miró, the **Fundació Pilar I Joan Miró** *(miromallorca.com; adult/child €10/free; closed Mon).*

Off-the-beaten-track strands and coves

Mallorca's beaches are legendary. In the northeast, a 10km drive from castle-topped **Artà** through the mountainous

MALLORCA'S VILLAGES

Pollença: Attractive old quarter, historic religious sites, good food and easy beach or mountain access.

Artà & Capdepera: Each has superb medieval architecture overlooked by a walled, hilltop fortress.

Deià: Famous honey-coloured home to artists, writers (visit Casa Robert Graves) and musicians.

Biniaraix & Fornalutx: Walk from Sóller to these stone mountain villages blooming in subtropical flowers.

Banyalbufar: Moorish terraces with vineyards step to the sea.

Caimari & Campanet: Eat like royalty in foothill gateways to the Serra de Tramuntana.

HIKING THE SERRA DE TRAMUNTANA

Hikers come from far and wide for Mallorca's mix of soaring mountain peaks and cove-cracked coastline. You can hike year-round, though the best months are March to May and late September to October. Hiking UNESCO Reserve **Serra de Tramuntana** often involves some aspect of **Ruta de Pedra en Sec** (Dry Stone Route; GR221) – a 140km, 10-day hike between Sant Elm and Pollença. Well-marked and with accommodation at the end of each stage, this is a superb way to experience Mallorca far from the tourist crowds. A couple of favourite portions include the moderate Deià to Sóller hike (10km; four hours) and the famous **Camí de s'Arxiduc** (Path of the Archduke), a 13km circular route from Valldemossa.

woodland of Parc Natural de la Península de Llevant will bring you to wide, sandy **Cala Torta** (sometimes you have to walk down). Small, sheltered bays, **Cala Mitjana** and **Cala Estreta** (the latter is stone) are accessible down a rough track in the mountains. You can walk to them all from **Cala Mesquida** (about an hour to Estreta). Walk further north for **Cala Matzoc**. Often empty, this sandy beach is a timeless vision of Mediterranean coastline.

In the southeast, most beaches are fjord-like indents with sheets of white sand lapped by soft minty-blue waters. Just north of busy **Cales de Mallorca**, a walking trail leads several kilometres through woodland to a series of four pristine coves: **Cala Bota**, **Cala Virgili**, **Cala Pilota**, and just north, the best of the lot: **Cala Magraner**.

On the west coast, a Mallorcan highlight is to walk from a mountain village to its coastal *cala* (cove). Hardly a secret, but divine all the same, is the steep 2.5km (one-way) walk from Deià to **Cala Deià**, with famous restaurant **Ca's Patró March**.

Popular southern beaches include **Platja des Trenc**, **Cala Pi**, **Caló des Moro** and **Cala Mondragó**, but explore further and the aqua waters unfurl. **Platja d'Almunia** and **Platja de Ses Roquetes** are connected by a hiking trail. At **Cala Llombards**, a beach-hut bar, palm-leaf-shaded loungers and a ladder into the sea constitute the extent of human intervention.

Menorca

Menorca's dreamy beaches

Menorca's paper-white sands and jewel-blue waters are some of the Med's best, and authorities have taken measures to preserve their natural beauty. You'll usually need your own wheels to reach them (arrive early!), and then you often park and walk the final 1km to 3km. The loveliest beaches are strung along the south coast. Menorca's less-developed north coast is rugged and rocky, perforated with small, scenic coves.

Along with teeny **Cala Macarelleta**, the pair of exquisite horseshoe bays, **Cala Macarella** and **Cala Turqueta**, 13.5km southwest of Ciutadella, get very busy in summer for their bleach-blonde sands, unbelievably turquoise waters and cliffs cloaked in pines and holm oaks. It's a lovely 2km clifftop walk between the two via **Cala des Talaier** (accessible only on foot). Twin white-sand beaches of Banyuls and Bellavista make up **Platges de Son Saura**, 12km southeast of Ciutadella.

You'll be rewarded for the effort it takes to reach some of the island's quietest and most beautiful beaches, halfway along

EATING & DRINKING IN PALMA DE MALLORCA: OUR PICKS

El Perrito: Santa Catalina quarter's brunch mainstay: bagels, homemade cakes, fresh juices and hearty specials. *8am-4pm Mon-Sat, to 3.30pm Sun* €

La Rosa Vermuteria: Start your evening with a *vermut* (vermouth) and local-inspired tapas at this stylish spot. *noon-midnight* €€

El Camino: Stylish tapas bar: coffered ceilings, mosaic tiles and marble bar for watching your tasty bites prepared. *1-3.45pm & 6-10.45pm Tue-Sat* €€

DINS Santi Taura: Traditional Mallorcan cooking with a twist in this adults-only Michelin-star restaurant. *hours vary Tue-Sat* €€€

MATEUSZ MISZTAL/SHUTTERSTOCK

Cala Macarelleta, Menorca

the southern coast. From **Sant Tomàs**, take the footpath west via **Platja Binigaus** to sublime **Cala Escorxada**, which has luminous waters, white sands and zero development. Continue west and you'll reach tiny **Cala Fustam**, which is a favourite of naturists. **Cala Mitjana** is most easily reached (1.5km) from **Cala Galdana** resort.

Ibiza & Formentera

Walking World-Heritage Dalt Vila

The heart and soul of the island, **Ibiza Town** (Eivissa) is a vivacious and elegant capital with a UNESCO World Heritage–listed fortified old quarter called **Dalt Vila** *(ibiza.travel)* set against a spectacular natural harbour. Its seven colossal, floodlit 16th-century bastions are visible from across southern Ibiza. Dalt Vila is tranquil and atmospheric, with many of its cobbled lanes accessible only on foot.

Enter via the **Portal de Ses Taules** gateway, just in from **Passeig Marítim** and behind neoclassical market **Mercat Vell**. All lanes lead steeply to **Castell d'Eivissa**, a walled district of historical buildings constructed over a 1000-year period, and **Catedral de Santa Maria de les Neus** on the summit. Sunset is gorgeous. Don't miss the wonderful **Museu d'Art**

HIKING MENORCA

Mystery-shrouded **Camí de Cavalls** (Path of Horses) loops 186km around the entire length of Menorca's coast. Connecting watchtowers, cannons and fortresses, it's believed to have been built in the 13th or 14th century to enable horseback patrols along the coastline and protect the island from sea invasions.

After years spent buried under scrub, the trail has been cleared and turned into a public footpath (GR223). It takes between seven and 10 days to hike, or you can do one of the 20 stages (5km to 14km each; outfitters can drop you off). Accommodation isn't always available at the end of each stage, meaning careful preplanning is required (see *camidecavalls.com*).

 EATING IN CIUTADELLA & MAÓ: OUR PICKS

Mercat de Peix: Tapas and *pintxos* bars fill this 1920s fish market, next to Maó's town market in the church cloisters. *11am-11pm Mon-Sat* €

Arjau Mao: Traditional Menorcan dishes and paella centring seafood and lobster, served portside. *1-3.30pm Thu-Mon* €€€

Pinzell: Contemporary remake of Mediterranean classics in Ciutadella. The squid stuffed with walnuts is exquisite. *1-3.30pm & 8-11.30pm Wed-Mon* €€

Pez Limón: Bold and unexpected culinary creations are the hallmark of this cosy Ciutadella tapas bar. *8-10.30pm Mon-Fri, 1-3pm & 8-10.30pm Sat* €€

IBIZA'S TOP CLUBS

Amnesia, Sant Rafel: Ibiza's most influential club, where DJ Alfredo pioneered Balearic Beat. *(amnesia.es)*

Hï Ibiza, Platja d'en Bossa: In 2022 and 2023, *DJ Magazine's* 'world's best club' with marquee DJ residencies. *(hiibiza.com)*

Pacha, Ibiza Town: Ibiza's original mega-club: multilevel dance floor, Funky Room for soul and disco. *(pacha.com)*

Ushuaïa, Platja d'en Bossa: Glitzy pool parties at Ibiza's hottest daytime club. *(theushuaiaexperience.com)*

DC 10, near the airport: Underground vibe and music-savvy crowd. *(dc10ibiza.com)*

Carrer de la Verge, Ibiza Town: Ibiza's main LGBTIQ+ village, with around 20 bars and clubs.

[UNVRS], Sant Rafel: World's largest club (formerly Privilege), regularly hosting thousands of clubbers. *(unvrs.com)*

TOLOBALAGUER.COM/SHUTTERSTOCK

Trucador Peninsula, Formentera

Contemporani d'Eivissa *(eivissa.es/mace; free),* housed in an 18th-century armoury.

Formentera's brilliant beaches

With sugar-white sands and perfectly clear turquoise water, the astonishing beauty of Formentera's pencil-slim **Trucador Peninsula** rivals that of the world's most glorious beaches. Walk or cycle along glittering **Ses Salines** (saltpans) to reach dirt tracks winding through steep sand dunes and emerge on the west side of this narrow sliver at dreamy **Platja Illetes**. On the peninsula's east coast (just a few steps away) is equally gorgeous **Platja Llevant**. The beaches get packed, but they're still an essential Formentera experience. The Trucador Peninsula is part of the **Parc Natural de Ses Salines** *(car/motorcycle €6/4).* Bring water, food and supplies.

The island's entire southern arc is necklaced with sandy alabaster bays lapped by aqua-tinted waters, known collectively as **Platja de Migjorn**. The best bits are at the southeastern end, around **Platja es Arenals**.

EATING & DRINKING IN IBIZA TOWN: OUR PICKS

Can Costa: Reasonably priced grilled meats and paella make this a popular go-to in the Old Port. *1-3.30pm & 8-11pm Mon-Fri €*

La Barra de la Bientirada Ibiza: Hearty Spanish-fusion dishes in central Ibiza Town. Save room for killer cheesecake. *noon-midnight €€*

Bar Es Cafetí: Bar with eclectic decor in Dalt Vila, perfect for a pit stop with cocktails and finger foods. *10am-6pm Mon-Fri, noon-6pm Sat, to 4pm Sun*

Petit Vermut Eivissa: Cheerful vermouth, *apéro* and cocktails with tapas in a casual corner spot in the Old Port area. *4.30pm-late*

Seville

HERITAGE SITES | ARCHITECTURE | DINING

The Andalucian capital and jewel in the southern region's cultural crown, Seville is a luminous, romantic city. Its unique blend of artistic influences (Moorish, Jewish, Christian and Romani) infuses every detail from its magnificent Mudéjar architecture to the sultry notes of the flamenco guitar. This is a city built to explore on foot: a pleasant mesh of narrow cobbled streets and jaunty plazas, invigorated by the debonair nightlife that spills from tapas bars and bodegas.

Once-mighty civilisations, including the Romans, the Moors and the Reyes Católicos of the Spanish empire have left indelible marks on Seville, layered across the urban space. Countless generations of homebred *sevillanos* have treated Seville with reverence. As a result, the city's well-heeled past endures into the present, through impeccably preserved churches, aristocratic palaces, picturesque streets scented with orange blossom, and UNESCO-listed landmarks such as the imposing Gothic cathedral. Seville's fiestas are legendary, from the energetic Feria de Abril to more sombre Semana Santa.

> ☑ **TOP TIP**
> Book tickets for the cathedral or the Real Alcázar as early as possible, but avoid visiting them on the same day (there's too much to take in). Admission is at a set time and can sell out days in advance. The cathedral is often closed for religious events and holidays.

A Royal Spectacle

Palaces, courtyards and gardens of the Real Alcázar

Since the 10th century, Moorish rulers and Spanish monarchs presided over their kingdoms from the exquisitely decorated

 GETTING AROUND

Much of Seville is best explored on foot, with sights clustered close together. For more spread-out attractions, rent bicycles from docking stations (Sevici app) or **Surf the City** *(surfthecity.es)*, along with electric scooters.

An electric tram line connects the San Sebastián bus station to the central Plaza Nueva. The main Plaza de Armas bus station serves major destinations across Andalucía. High-speed trains run from Sevilla Santa Justa. Buses link Sevilla Santa Justa train station to central Seville.

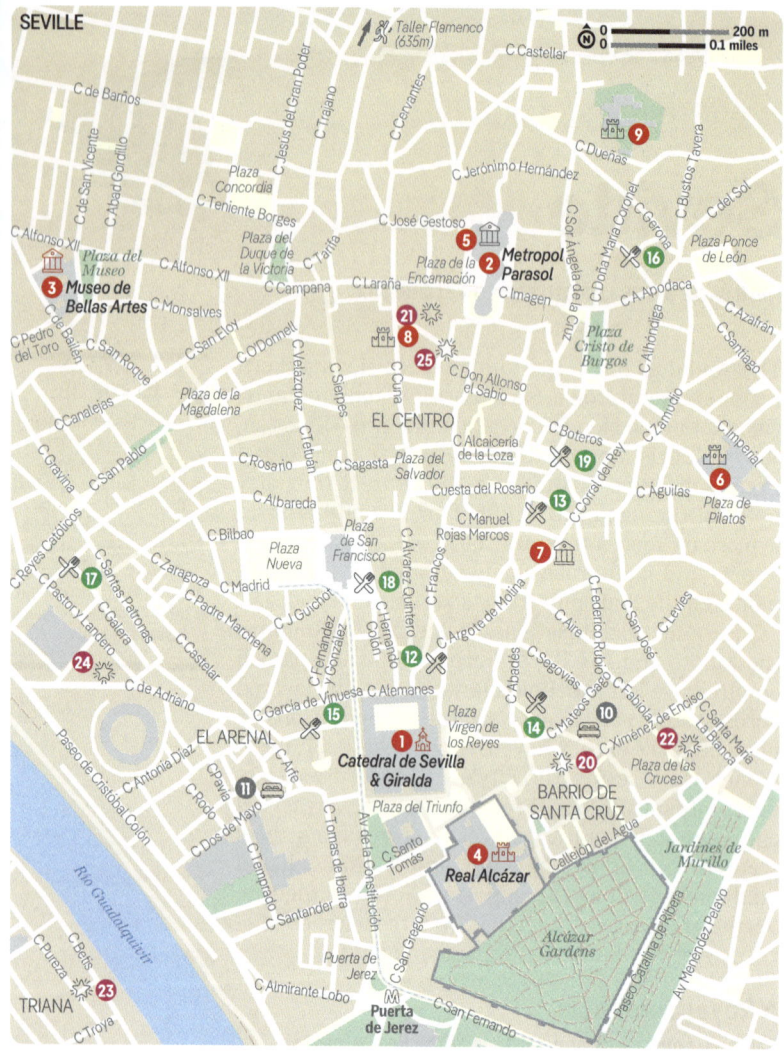

SEVILLE

HIGHLIGHTS

1 Catedral de Sevilla & Giralda
2 Metropol Parasol
3 Museo de Bellas Artes
4 Real Alcázar

SIGHTS

5 Antiquarium
6 Casa de Pilatos

7 Museo del Baile Flamenco
8 Palacio de la Condesa de Lebrija
9 Palacio de Las Dueñas

SLEEPING

10 Casa del Poeta
11 La Banda

EATING

12 Antigua Taberna de Las Escobas
13 Bar Alfalfa
14 Bodega Santa Cruz
15 Casa Morales
16 El Rinconcillo
17 La Brunilda
18 Mamarracha
19 PETRA

ENTERTAINMENT

20 Casa de la Guitarra
21 Casa de la Memoria
22 La Casa del Flamenco
23 Pura Esencia
24 Tablao Flamenco Andalusí
25 Teatro Flamenco Sevilla

Real Alcázar *(alcazarsevilla.org; adult/child €15.50/free),* tearing down, augmenting and rebuilding sections of the labyrinthine complex.

The finest building overlooking the Patio de la Montería (Hunting Party's Courtyard) is the **Palacio de Don Pedro**. Built for King Pedro I (1350–69) with the help of Moorish Granada's finest artisans, it has an exquisite Mudéjar-style interior. Highlights include the golden-tiled dome ceiling of the Cuarto del Príncipe (Prince's Suite), and the spectacular Salón de Embajadores (Hall of the Ambassadors), originally Pedro I's throne room.

At the heart of this palace is the sublime central courtyard, the **Patio de las Doncellas** (Maidens' Courtyard). The sunken garden at its core, framed by carved arches, plasterwork and tiling, was uncovered by archaeologists in 2004. The Palacio Gótico (Gothic Palace), much remodelled for Carlos I in the 16th century, is now known as the **Salones de Carlos V**. The **Jardines de los Reales Alcázares** (Royal Alcazar Gardens) offer shaded paths between mazes of myrtle, fish-filled ponds and lofty palm trees.

Seville's Monumental Gothic Treasure

Tour the cathedral

When Castilian king Fernando III captured Seville from the Almohad dynasty in 1248, he ordered that the 12th-century great mosque be converted into a church. Flying buttresses, gargoyles and lavish ornamentation decorate the exterior of the world's largest Gothic building, Seville's **cathedral** *(cated raldesevilla.es; adult/child €13/free),* officially known as the Catedral de Santa María de la Sede.

The visitor entrance is through the horseshoe arched doorway, **Puerta del Lagarto**. On your left, a gentle ramp swirls up through the **Giralda**, a former minaret repurposed as the cathedral's bell tower, with expansive views over Seville. The often-closed **Capilla Real** contains royal tombs, including the remains of Fernando III in a silver urn. Enter the series of rooms to your left to admire major art treasures, including

SEMANA SANTA IN SEVILLE

Seville puts on one of Spain's most elaborate manifestations of Christian Holy Week. From Palm Sunday to Easter Sunday, hooded *nazarenos* (penitents) carry huge *pasos* (floats holding revered statues, such as La Macarena) through the streets in ghostly solemnity. Parades lead from their home churches to the cathedral, often in the early evening. The *nazarenos* are members of the city's 50 *hermandades* or *cofradías* (religious brotherhoods, some of which include women), dressed in white robes with pointed conical hoods. The highlight of Semana Santa is La Madrugá in the early hours of Good Friday, when several of the city's most venerated statues make their appearances.

 EATING IN SEVILLE: OUR PICKS

Casa Morales: Family-run tapas bar notable for its sherry, *albóndigas* (meatballs) and croquettes. *noon-4pm & 8pm-midnight Mon-Sat, noon-4pm Sun* €€	**Bodega Santa Cruz:** The slow-cooked *montadito de pringá* (tender meats and sausage served on crusty bread) is a highlight. *8am-midnight* €	**Antigua Taberna de Las Escobas:** Seville's oldest tavern, around since 1386. Luminaries from Cervantes to Lord Byron have dined here. *noon-11pm* €€	**La Brunilda:** Enter through blue doors to a modern interior with inventive tapas, including an excellent mushroom risotto. *1.30-4.30pm & 8.30-11.30pm* €€€
Mamarracha: Trendy tapas place, with eclectic fare like *alcachofa a la brasa* (grilled artichokes). *1-5pm & 8pm-midnight Mon-Thu, 1pm-12.30am Fri-Sun* €€€	**Bar Alfalfa:** Snug bar with tasty tapas, including *salmorejo* (cold, tomato-based soup), overlooked by hundreds of dusty bottles. *9am-midnight* €€	**El Rinconcillo:** Purveyors of libations and tapas since 1670. Tabs are chalked onto the wood in front of you at the end. *1-5.30pm & 8pm-midnight Wed-Mon* €€€	**PETRA:** Inventive takes on popular tapas (meat, vegetarian and vegan). The gourmet experience isn't priced as such. *12.30-11.30pm Mon-Sat* €€

BEST PLACES TO EXPERIENCE FLAMENCO

La Casa del Flamenco: Three styles of flamenco, woven together by a virtuoso guitar performance.

Pura Esencia: The spiritual home of Seville's Roma flamenco practitioners.

Tablao Flamenco Andalusí: Passionate dancing backed by wistful vocals, guitar and *cajón* (percussion instrument).

Casa de la Memoria: The most intimate of shows, if you can bag a stage-side seat. In Lebrija palace's former stables.

Teatro Flamenco Sevilla: Larger shows bringing more performers onto the stage.

Casa de la Guitarra: Shows balance singing, guitar and dance, surrounded by antique flamenco guitars.

Museo del Baile Flamenco: Intriguing gallery that morphs into a performance venue at night.

Taller Flamenco: Fantastic classes, from dance and technique to *palmas* (clapping).

a Goya in the Sacristía de los Cálices, a Zurbarán in the Sacristía Mayor, and Murillo's shining *La inmaculada* in the Sala Capitular.

Hugging the exterior wall, the four figures carrying an ornately carved catafalque mark the **Tomb of Columbus**. It contains the famed voyager's remains, something which DNA testing in 2006 upheld as fact.

The Palaces of Barrio de Santa Cruz
Sumptuous mansions in the former Jewish quarter

The **Palacio de la Condesa de Lebrija** *(palaciodelebrija. com; adult/child €14/6)* condenses each of Seville's golden ages beneath one roof. Built in the Mudéjar-Renaissance style, its central courtyards are flanked by intricate plasterwork arches, *azulejos* and wide stairways. Head northeast to the bougainvillea-covered 15th-century **Palacio de las Dueñas** *(lasduenas.es; adult/child €14/10)*, residence of the late Duchess of Alba. It was also the birthplace of poet Antonio Machado. Further south lies the **Casa de Pilatos** *(fundacionmedinaceli. org; adult/child €12/free)*, with an exquisite *artesonado* (ceiling of interlaced beams).

From Ancient to Modern at Las Setas
Admire Museo Antiquarium and Metropol Parasol

Some of the best views of the cathedral come from atop one of Seville's more modern constructs. Officially called the **Metropol Parasol** *(setasdesevilla.com; adult/child €16/free)*, Las Setas (giant wooden mushrooms) straddle the broad Plaza de la Encarnación. Equally fascinating is the **Antiquarium** *(sevilla.org; adult/child €2/free; closed Mon)* beneath Las Setas: the ruins of Colonia Julia Romula Hispalis, the Roman iteration of Seville, date to around 40 CE.

Treasures of the Museo de Bellas Artes
Artistic masterpieces in a convent

The delightful mannerist palace housing Seville's **Museo de Bellas Artes** *(museosdeandalucia.es; EU/non-EU citizen free/€1.50)* exhibits 15th- to 20th-century artworks, but it's the Golden Age masterpieces that make this one of Spain's top art museums. Sala V contains the most impressive paintings, including Murillo's *Inmaculada concepción*. Highlights elsewhere include Zurbarán's *Cristo crucificado* (Sala VI and another in Sala X), El Greco's portrait of his son (Sala II), Velázquez' *Cabeza de apóstol* (Sala IV) and Goya's *Don José Duaso* (Sala XI).

Beyond Seville

Architectural wonders in some of Spain's oldest cities, evocative hill villages, glorious protected parks and a breathtaking coastline await around Andalucía.

With its wild Atlantic coastline and beloved Mediterranean shores, Andalucía evokes many of Spain's greatest calling cards. Much of this sunny, soulful region has passed through Phoenician, Greek, Carthaginian, Roman and Visigothic hands. It also tells the subsequent Al-Andalus story of the melding of three cultures – Moorish, Christian and Jewish – traceable in the ancient neighbourhoods of Córdoba, Granada, Cádiz and even Málaga, as well as the regional capital Seville. The buzzy coast and culture-packed cities give way to a mountainous interior filled with olive groves and pine forests, while sprawling nature reserves dot the countryside. Wander enchanting *pueblos blancos* (white towns) in the evening golden light, or glimpse Granada's Alhambra outlined against the snow-tipped Sierra Nevada, and you'll witness time standing still.

Places

Parque Nacional de Doñana p293

Córdoba p294

Cádiz p294

Costa de la Luz p296

Granada & Around p297

Málaga p298

GETTING AROUND

Córdoba, Málaga, Cádiz and Granada have efficient rail links *(renfe.com)*, including with Seville. The best way to enjoy them is on foot; apart from Granada (which has some hilly neighbourhoods), they're largely flat, compact cities. Málaga and Cádiz are ideal for cycling, too, with plenty of bike-hire options. Further afield, it's best to hire a car. Buses reach most destinations, with companies such as **Alsa** *(alsa.es)*, but services are limited and often reduced on weekends.

Parque Nacional de Doñana

TIME FROM SEVILLE (EL ROCÍO): **1HR**

Lynx-spotting and exceptional birdwatching

The World Heritage–listed **Parque Nacional de Doñana** *(mite co.gob.es)*, spread around the Río Guadalquivir delta, forms one of Europe's most extensive wetland areas, which is a haven for around 10,000 flamingos and over 500,000 other wintering birds. At this 601-sq-km park southeast of Huelva, together with the bordering Parque Natural de Doñana (which is under less strict protection), endangered creatures such as the Iberian lynx and Spanish imperial eagle have bounced back from the brink under close conservation. Visits to the national park are via accredited agency only, usually by 4WD; Seville-based **Doñana Wings** *(donanawings.com)* and **Naturanda** *(naturanda. com)* are recommended, as are local operators **Doñana Nature** *(donana-nature.com)*, **Discovering Doñana** *(discovering donana.com)* and **Doñana Reservas** *(donanareservas.com)*. If you're lucky, you have a good chance of spotting a lynx and her cubs in the mid-to late-summer months.

The main national park hub is the evocative Huelva province village of **El Rocío**, also known as the destination for Spain's greatest pilgrimage, the **Romería del Rocío** in May/

BLOOMING WONDERS

Among Córdoba's loveliest features are its famous flower-filled patios. In summer, Córdoba becomes a furnace, hence the millennia-old Roman and Moorish tradition of building houses with inner courtyards to facilitate airflow. Some courtyards are open to the public year-round, including the grand **Palacio de Viana** (palaciodeviana.com); others only during the **Fiesta de los Patios de Córdoba** (the first two weeks in May). Participating courtyard owners welcome visitors into their inner sanctums, where you can admire hanging plant pots, creeper-clad walls, fountains, quirky patio furnishings and exuberant flower arrangements. A great place to get started is the San Basilio (aka Alcázar Viejo) neighbourhood to the north and west of the Alcázar.

June. It's also possible to access Doñana from Sanlúcar de Barrameda in neighbouring Cádiz province.

Córdoba

TIME FROM SEVILLE: **50MIN**

A wonder of Islamic architecture

Jewel of the Moorish Caliphate when it was the Grand Mosque of Córdoba, and later one of Spain's great cathedrals, the **Mezquita** (mezquita-catedraldecordoba.es; adult/child €13/free) is one of the world's most magnificent buildings. Free to access, the **Patio de los Naranjos** is the courtyard entrance to the Mezquita filled with palms, orange trees and ornate fountains, and overlooked by the 54m-high **Torre Campanario** (Bell Tower), which requires a separate ticket. Inside the Mezquita, a forest of arches stacks into the distance. It would have been a truly vast mosque upon its final enlargement in 994. The arches, resting on 856 columns (there were originally 1293), are striped strawberries-and-cream, mimicking the date palms of northern Africa.

At the southern wall is the building's pinnacle of Islamic-era decoration, the *maksura* (royal prayer enclosure). The geometric decoration of the arches and skylit domes are at their most lavish here. On the back wall is the *mihrab*, the decorative prayer niche facing Mecca, added along with the *maksura* during the extensions ordered by Al-Hakim II in the 960s. The gold mosaic cubes around its portal were created by a master sculptor from Byzantium. The construction of the current **Capilla Mayor** (main altar) and *coro* (choir) in the heart of the Mezquita began during the reign of Carlos I (1516–56) and was completed in 1766, with plateresque, Gothic, baroque and Renaissance motifs all at play.

Córdoba's other historical treasures include atmospheric **La Judería** (the Jewish quarter), the 14th-century **Alcázar de los Reyes Cristianos** (cultura.cordoba.es; adult/child €7/free; closed Mon) palace-fortress and the UNESCO-listed ruins of **Medina Azahara** (museosdeandalucia.es; EU/non-EU citizen free/€1.50), the palace-city just outside town built in the 10th century on the orders of Abd ar-Rahman III.

Cádiz

TIME FROM SEVILLE: **1¼HR**

Exploring Cádiz' buzzing *barrios*

Founded as Gadir by the Phoenicians in 1100 BCE, sultry Cádiz is Europe's oldest continuously inhabited settlement.

Runs great cooking classes and food tours too.

 EATING & DRINKING IN CÓRDOBA: OUR PICKS

Nuur: Paco Morales gives centuries-old recipes such as pistachio soup the modern treatment; two Michelin stars. *1.30-6pm & 8.30-11.30pm Thu-Sat* €€€

Casa Pepe de la Judería: Around since 1920, Pepe's serves classic tapas such as *berenjenas con miel* (aubergines in honey). *1-4pm & 8pm-midnight* €€

Garum 2.1: Award-winning spot for imaginative takes on Cordoban dishes, like *salmorejo* with jelly sherry cubes. *1-4pm & 8pm-midnight Mon, Tue & Thu-Sat* €€

Jugo Vinos Vivos: Facing a tiny square and fountain, Jugo is all about live wines, sourced directly from small Andalucian producers. *hours vary*

RONDA & WHITE VILLAGES OF CÁDIZ

Andalucía's white villages and olive-tree-covered countryside are just as magical as the famed cities, especially around Ronda and Sierra de Grazalema.

START	END	LENGTH
Ronda	Arcos de la Frontera	140km; 1–2 days

Built astride a huge gash in the mountains carved out by the Río Guadalevín, ❶ **Ronda** is a large *pueblo blanco* with a dramatic history. Soak it all up from the grand 1793 Puente Nuevo. Drive 20km north to ❷ **Setenil de las Bodegas**, where buildings (homes, restaurants) are curled into cave-like streets beneath the ledges of the Río Trejo.

Zip 35km west, crossing from Málaga province into Cádiz province, to reach ❸ **Zahara de la Sierra**. This fortified hill village of red-tiled white houses clusters beneath a ruined 12th-century Moorish castle, all overlooking a turquoise reservoir. From here, the sinuous CA9104 climbs high to the Puerto de las Palomas pass (1357m) before swooping down to ❹ **Grazalema**, a

beautiful wool-producing village with sloping cobbled streets and delightful rural hotels for overnight stops.

Heading 20km southwest, travel along the A374 through cheese-making Villaluenga del Rosario (the province's loftiest village) to ❺ **Benaocaz**, a former Moorish settlement and the jumping-off point for hiking the 3.3km Calzada Romana (an old Roman road to Ubrique). By car, it's just 7km downhill along corkscrew turns to leather-manufacturing ❻ **Ubrique**, backed by the knife-edge Cruz de Tajo. A 40km spin northwest drops you in ❼ **Arcos de la Frontera**, a cragtop beauty of a *pueblo blanco* whose origins predate the Romans.

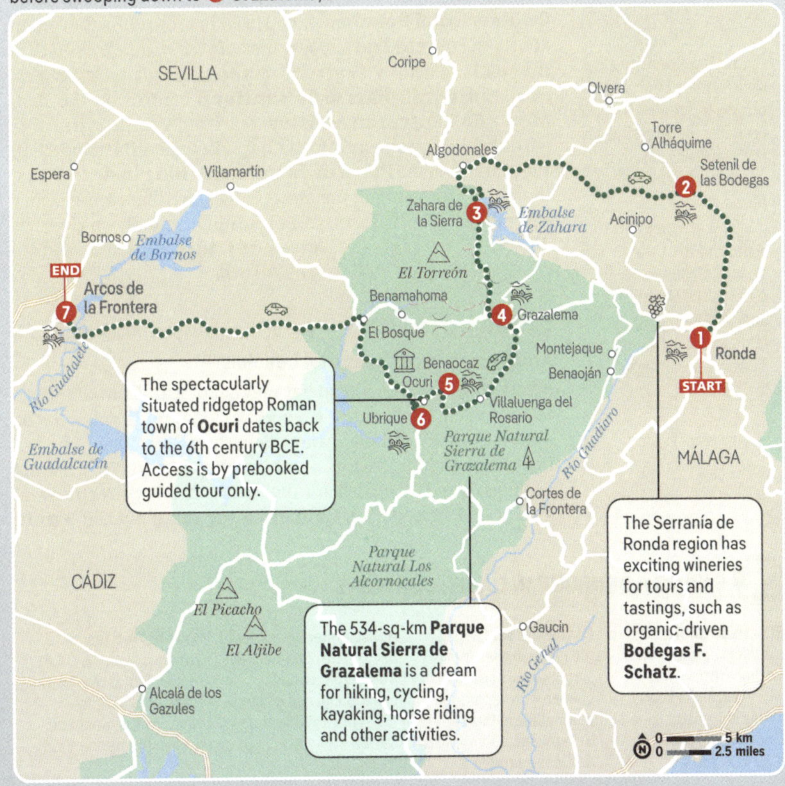

The spectacularly situated ridgetop Roman town of **Ocuri** dates back to the 6th century BCE. Access is by prebooked guided tour only.

The Serranía de Ronda region has exciting wineries for tours and tastings, such as organic-driven **Bodegas F. Schatz**.

The 534-sq-km **Parque Natural Sierra de Grazalema** is a dream for hiking, cycling, kayaking, horse riding and other activities.

CARNAVAL

If you're in Cádiz before Easter (in February or March, depending on the Easter dates), you'll be joining the *gaditanos* for Carnaval – Spain's biggest, liveliest, 10-day singing, dancing and drinking street party, complete with float parades, street food, fireworks and over 300 *murgas* (bands). Carnaval dates back to the 15th century, when costumed revelry was brought by homesick Genoese merchants. Banned during the Spanish Civil War and tightly controlled during Franco's dictatorship, the fiesta assumed its present exuberant form in 1977. The liveliest *murga* action is around the Barrio de la Viña district, outside the Cathedral, and between the Mercado Central de Abastos and Playa de la Caleta.

TRABANTOS/SHUTTERSTOCK

Generalife, Granada

The best way to dig into this appealing port city is by wandering its distinctive *barrios*. The **Barrio de Santa María** is the old Roma quarter, home to flamenco-world icon **La Perla** *(perladecadiz.com);* check for shows. Oldest of all is the **Barrio del Pópulo**, which spreads around the baroque-neoclassical **Catedral** *(catedraldecadiz.com; adult/child €10/ free)* and the nearby **Teatro Romano** *(juntadeandalucia.es; free).* Northwest, **Barrio de San Juan** centres on the 1838 **Mercado Central de Abastos** *(mercadocentralcadiz.com),* with produce stalls and tapas bars. Between Barrio de San Juan and golden **Playa de la Caleta** is **Barrio de la Viña**, the city's tapas-loving Carnaval epicentre. The 18th-century **Barrio del Mentidero** is Cádiz' affluent northern district; don't miss the fantastic **Museo de Cádiz** *(museosdeandalu cia.es; EU/non-EU citizen free/€1.50).*

Costa de la Luz

TIME FROM SEVILLE (TARIFA): 2¼HR 🚗

Andalucía's most beautiful beaches

Stretching from the kitesurfer magnet of **Tarifa** in the south to the marshlands of the Parque Nacional de Doñana in the north, the 200km-long, Atlantic-washed Costa de la Luz is a beguiling string of white-sand beaches and low-key fishing villages. Tarifa's beauties range from the long white-sand sweep of **Playa de los Lances** to the dune-backed **Punta**

 EATING & DRINKING IN CÁDIZ: OUR PICKS

El Faro de Cádiz: Superb *tortillitas de camarones* (shrimp fritters) pair with *manzanilla* sherry at this long-established favourite. *1-4.30pm & 8.30-11.30pm* €€

Casa Manteca: Order the *chicharrones* (pork scratchings) or *payoyo* cheese with asparagus marmalade in this La Viña tavern. *noon-4pm & 8.30pm-midnight* €

Almanaque: Cosy interior, daily menu of reimagined Cádiz recipes, and exceptional rice dishes. *1.30-4pm & 9-11pm Tue-Sat* €€

Listán Wine Tasca: Vintages from the Cádiz region, tables overlooking Plaza de San Antonio, wines by the glass and great nibbles. *hours vary*

Paloma and spectacular **Playa de Bolonia** with its 30m-high dune. North from Bolonia are the laid-back beach towns of **Zahara de los Atunes** and **Los Caños de Meca**, with long white-sand strands dotted with *chiringuitos* and surf schools. **El Palmar** has some of Andalucía's best surf waves and its own beach-bar scene, a quick hop away from **Vejer de la Frontera**, one of Andalucía's most exquisite *pueblos blancos*. Just north, seafront **Conil de la Frontera** is renowned for its many beaches, from the family-friendly strand of **Playa La Fontanilla** to the seven sheltered, nudist-friendly coves of **Calas de Poniente**. Pick your strand, bring a beach umbrella and join the fun.

Granada & Around

TIME FROM SEVILLE: 2½HR 🚗 + 🚌

The magical Alhambra

One of the most architecturally perfect buildings in existence, the Moorish palace-fortress of **Alhambra** *(alhambra-patronato.es)* sits high above Granada; its name derives from the Arabic *al-qala'a al-hamra* (the Red Castle). The 9th-century Alhambra was transformed during the 13th and 14th centuries by Granada's Nasrid rulers into the magnificent royal residence you see today.

Its walls carved with elegant Arabic inscriptions, the remarkable **Palacios Nazaríes** complex was originally divided into three parts: the Mexuar, Serallo and Harem. At the heart of the Serallo, where sultans conducted negotiations with Christian emissaries, is the **Patio de los Arrayanes**, named after the myrtle hedges around its rectangular pool and surrounded by marble-columned arcades. To the north, the Sala de la Barca, with a copy of its original cedar ceiling, leads into the **Salón de los Embajadores** – the largest, most striking chamber, with a domed marquetry ceiling symbolising the seven heavens of Islam. Continue to the **Patio de los Leones**, centred on an 11th-century fountain channelling water through the mouths of 12 marble lions.

The **Generalife**, the Nasrid rulers' summer estate, takes its name from the Arabic *jinan al-'arif,* meaning 'the overseer's gardens'. The Patio de la Acequia features immaculately tended gardens, while the Escalera del Agua is a marvel, with water channels running down stone balustrades.

Albayzín: Granada's UNESCO-listed old quarter

The cobbled alleyways, whitewashed mansions and scenic plazas of the UNESCO-listed Albayzín, Granada's old Moorish

ALHAMBRA TIPS

General tickets (€22) cover all areas; Gardens, Generalife and Alcazaba tickets (€12) exclude Palacios Nazaríes.

Access to Palacios Nazaríes is limited to 300 visitors every half-hour; book time-slot tickets as far in advance as possible.

Alhambra by night is a special experience: book Night Visit Palacios Nazaríes (€12.70) year-round or Night Visit Gardens & Generalife (€8.50) in April, May, September, October and November.

Bring ID that matches the name on your ticket – authorities are cracking down on scalpers buying up day tickets and reselling them to ticketless visitors by the gate.

🍴 EATING IN TARIFA & VEJER DE LA FRONTERA: OUR PICKS

El Jardín del Califa: Romantic Vejer spot with a creative Moroccan–Middle Eastern menu and Cádiz province vintages. Book ahead! *I-4pm & 7.30-11pm* €€

El Francés: At the standing-room-only bar or terrace tables in Tarifa, munch on classics with a twist. Also runs Silos 19. *12.30pm-midnight Fri-Tue* €€

El Lola: Stylish flamenco-themed tapas bar in old-town Tarifa, with dishes including seasonal *almadraba* tuna. *I-4.30pm & 7pm-midnight* €€

La Judería: Tucked away in a Vejer alleyway, this spot dazzles with its stellar rice dishes and goat's-cheese cheesecake with honey. *hours vary* €€

CABO DE GATA

Beach lovers dazzled by the Costa de la Luz are equally likely to fall for magical Cabo de Gata. At the opposite end of Andalucía (around two hours' drive from Granada), this wild stretch of the Almería coast is protected as the spectacular 340-sq-km **Parque Natural de Cabo de Gata-Níjar**, featuring some of Spain's most pristine, least crowded white-sand beaches, excellent scuba diving and other water sports, and a dramatic Mediterranean coastline ripe for exploration on foot or by bike. Between small, laid-back villages – like Rodalquilar, Las Negras, Pozo del Fraile and San José – trails weave across a desert-like volcanic landscape, taking in remote lighthouses, wind-battered capes and hidden-away coves that require a little more effort to reach.

quarter, occupy a hill facing the Alhambra. Allow a full day to explore, before dropping back down to the **Catedral de Granada** (*catedraldegranada.com; adult/child €7/free*), housing the tombs of the Reyes Católicos.

Off Carrera del Darro, the Albayzín's **Baños Árabes El Bañuelo** (*alhambra-patronato.es; €8.50*) is a well-preserved 11th-century Moorish public bath complex. Nearby, occupying the 16th-century Casa de Castril, the **Museo Arqueológico** (*museosdeandalucia.es; EU/non-EU citizen free/€1.50*) houses regional artefacts, from Palaeolithic to late Moorish times. Dominating the Plaza del Salvador near the top of the Albayzín, the 16th-century **Colegiata del Salvador** church was built atop a former mosque. A short wander southwest brings you to the **Mirador San Nicolás**, the famous viewpoint for sunset shots of the Alhambra silhouetted against the Sierra Nevada.

Hike into the Sierra Nevada

The 862-sq-km **Parque Nacional Sierra Nevada** (*miteco. gob.es*) – Spain's largest national park – is home to 2100 of Spain's 7000 plant species, as well as Andalucía's largest ibex population (around 15,000). It's also where you'll find **Mulhacén** (3479m), the highest point in mainland Spain. Ample day hikes (many doable from Granada) and multiday trails beckon walkers and mountaineers. The lower southern reaches – **Las Alpujarras** – and their dramatic valleys, dotted with age-old *pueblos blancos,* lend themselves beautifully to road-tripping and walking. The best months for hiking are April to mid-June and mid-September to early November for Las Alpujarras, while summer is good for the high Sierra Nevada. Along with summiting Mulhacén, highlights include walks around the three villages in the Barranco del Poqueira – Pampaneira, Bubión and Capileira – and lofty, *jamón*-making Trevélez. **Nevadensis** (*nevadensis.com*) can organise guided hikes.

Málaga

TIME FROM SEVILLE: 2¼ 🚌 + 🚆

City of artists

Begin your exploration of Málaga's artistic side at the **Museo Picasso Málaga** (*museopicassomalaga.org; adult/child €13/ free*), a must-visit in the city of the artist's birth. Among 200-plus works, highlights include a painting of Picasso's sister Lola, done when he was only 13, *Portrait of Paulo with White Hat* and *Olga Khokhlova with Mantilla.* The nearby **Museo**

 EATING & DRINKING IN GRANADA: OUR PICKS

Damasqueros: The tasting menu may feature aubergines with sardines and miso or veal sweetbreads. *1-3.30pm & 8.30-10.30pm Mon-Sat, 1-3.30pm Sun* €€€

Casa de Vinos La Brujidera: Wood-panelled bar with a superb wine cellar; most wines are available by the glass. *hours vary*

Taberna La Tana: Realejo favourite, serving over 500 Spanish wines alongside platters of cold cuts and other bites. *12.30-4pm & 8.30pm-midnight*

Bar Provincias: Old-school spot (around since 1945) perfect for people-watching as you munch on fried fish and seafood bites. *1-11.30pm*

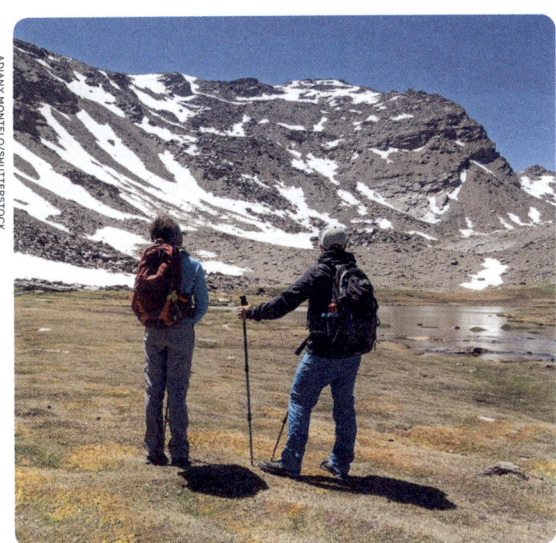

ADIANY MONTELO/SHUTTERSTOCK

Parque Nacional Sierra Nevada

Casa Natal de Picasso (*museocasanatalpicasso.malaga.eu; adult/child €3/free*) is located in the house where the artist was born.

Continue on to the **Museo Carmen Thyssen** (*carmenthyssenmalaga.org; adult/child €12/free*), housed in an elegant 16th-century palace in the heart of the city's former Moorish quarter. A short walk away lies the **Museo de Málaga** (*museosdeandalucia.es; EU/non-EU citizen free/€1.50*), in the Palacio de la Aduana, which combines the former Museo Bellas Artes and the Museo Arqueológico.

As you pass through the neighbourhood of **Soho**, look for murals by the likes of Dean Stockton (D*Face), Shepard Fairey (OBEY) and ROA. Many museums close Monday.

MÁLAGA'S MULTICULTURAL HISTORY

Teatro Romano: Roman theatre built during the reign of Augustus in the 1st century CE and working up until the 3rd century.

Alcazaba: A winding pathway takes you through Arabic-style arched doorways, peaceful gardens and geometric-tiled courtyards at the city's 11th-century Moorish palatial fortress.

Castillo de Gibralfaro: Another vestige of Málaga's Moorish past, rising high above the city – you can hike up in 30 minutes.

Catedral de la Encarnación de Málaga: The colossal cathedral stands right in the centre of the city. Construction began in the 16th century on the site of a former mosque.

THE GUIDE

SPAIN BEYOND SEVILLE

EATING & DRINKING IN MÁLAGA: OUR PICKS

Bodegas El Pimpi: In front of the Alcazaba, this fun bar has leafy courtyards, wine cellars and cosy rooms. The 'tunnel' is best for tapas. *noon-2am* €€

La Tranca: Elbow your way into this old-fashioned bar with vermouth and classic Andalucian tapas like tortilla and olives. *noon-1am* €

La Cosmo: Sleek modern dining by chef Dani Carnero. Try duck breast with barbecue sauce. *1.30-3.30pm & 8-11.30pm Mon-Sat* €€

Antigua Casa de Guardia: Old-school wine bar where muscatel and Pedro Ximénez are served straight from the barrel. *hours vary*

Places We Love to Stay

€ Budget €€ Midrange €€€ Top End

Madrid
MAP p246

Hostal La Zona € This stylish *hostal* has clean, bright rooms and breakfast is until noon.

Only YOU Atocha €€ Not only stylish but also sustainable, eschewing single-use plastics and offering electric-car charging.

Hotel Alicia €€ One of the landmark properties of the designer Room Mate chain, overlooking Plaza de Santa Ana.

Posada del Dragón €€ Remodelled La Latina inn with modern interiors retaining its traditional *corrala* courtyard.

Pestaña Plaza Mayor €€€ This sought-after address has been renovated with exposed brick, velvet walls and rooftop pool.

Toledo, Cáceres & Salamanca

Áurea Toledo €€ Five-star hotel spread across four historic courtyard houses with artefacts.

Hospes Palacio de San Esteban €€ In a 16th-century former Salamanca convent, with garden and pool.

Parador de Cáceres €€€ This old-town conglomeration of 14th-century Gothic palaces has stylish rooms.

Barcelona
MAP p260

Generator Barcelona € The switched-on Generator chain runs this large, social Gràcia hostel.

Hotel Brummell €€ In Poble Sec, this 20-room boutique hotel has an urban garden with a pool.

Casa Mathilda €€ Beautiful 1920s Eixample Dreta building converted into a 14-room boutique hideaway.

Casa Bonay €€€ A creatively restored 1896 Eixample building houses one of Barcelona's best boutique-design hotels.

Hotel Neri €€€ Two historic palaces merged to become this impeccable 22-room Relais & Chateaux property.

Costa Brava, Tarragona & Zaragoza

Tramuntana Hotel €€ Adults-only 11-room boutique hotel tucked away in old-town Cadaqués.

H10 Imperial Tarraco €€ Incredible views and a rooftop pool for recharging in Tarragona.

Hotel Sauce €€ Welcoming, family-run hotel in Zaragoza with fresh, cheerful rooms.

Bilbao & San Sebastián

Pensión Aida €€ Guests are made to feel welcome at this pensión with bright rooms.

Miró Hotel €€€ Opposite the Guggenheim, this contemporary design hotel charms art lovers.

Picos de Europa & Galicia

Hotel Costa Vella €€ Tranquil rooms, super-helpful staff and a lovely garden cafe overlooking Santiago.

Casa Fontequeiroso €€ Welcoming small hotel in deep Costa da Morte countryside, with superb home-cooked meals.

Valencia
MAP p281

Casa Clarita €€ Joyful interiors with colourful, chic murals by local artist Jaime Hayon.

YOURS €€€ Minimal design hotel scented with hand-poured

candles. Plunge pool is heaven in summer.

Balearic Islands

Can Fuster, Sant Joan de Labritja €€€ Restored, eight-room, 150-year-old Ibizan farmhouse with pool.

Hotel Basilica, Palma de Mallorca €€€ Tear yourself away from your understated room for the rooftop pool with cathedral views.

Hotel Nou Sant Antoni, Ciutadella €€€ Spectacular Menorca boutique hotel in the heart of the old town.

Seville & Costa de la Luz
MAP p290

La Banda € Perennial Seville favourite for its stunning rooftop terrace, sociable ethos and evening events.

La Casa del Califa €€ North Africa–inspired rooms and fab restaurant in a 16th-century building in Vejer de la Frontera.

Casa del Poeta €€€ Deep in Seville's Barrio de Santa Cruz, stay at this restored 17th-century mansion.

Córdoba, Granada & Málaga

Patio del Posadero €€ Traditional Córdoba-Moorish touches and boutique design in a 15th-century property.

Hotel Casa 1800 Granada €€ Old-world coffered ceilings, contemporary rooms and beautiful courtyard within a 16th-century Granada building.

Hotel Boutique Teatro Romano €€ Light, contemporary rooms with views of Málaga's Roman theatre and Alcazaba.

Practicalities

HEATWAVES & WILDFIRES

In recent years, Spain has been experiencing increasingly intense heatwaves. Devastating wildfires and serious droughts often accompany them. If you're caught up in any of these, follow guidance from local authorities. Common restrictions during droughts might include beach showers and public fountains being switched off and bans on refilling swimming pools.

DANIEL FERRER PAEZ/SHUTTERSTOCK

SMOKING

Smoking is banned in enclosed public spaces, near hospitals and on over 660 beaches. Legislation to ban smoking on bar/restaurant terraces was in the works at the time of writing. Cannabis has been decriminalised for personal use, in small quantities.

LGBTIQ+ TRAVELLERS

In 2024, Spain ranked joint first place on the Spartacus Gay Travel Index of LGBTIQ+ friendly countries. It was the fourth country in the world to legalise same-sex marriage (in 2005), along with same-sex adoption. The 2023 Ley Trans brought groundbreaking legislation around rights for trans people. Spain's LGBTIQ+ hubs are Madrid, Barcelona, Sitges and Gran Canaria, though you'll find lively scenes countrywide.

TIPPING ETIQUETTE

Though tipping isn't obligatory, it's definitely appreciated. In restaurants, 5% to 10% (more common) is appropriate; for bars/cafes, people sometimes leave loose change. If paying by card, ask to add the tip to the bill total.

OPENING HOURS

Opening times vary seasonally and are typically more reduced in winter and/or peak summer months.
Banks 8.30am–2pm Monday to Friday
Cafes 7am–late
Bars Varies; often 6pm–late
Restaurants 1pm–4pm and 8.30pm–11pm or midnight
Shops 10am–2pm and 5pm–8pm Monday to Saturday

TOURISM TAX & PRIVATE RENTALS

Spain has experienced a surge in private short-term tourist rentals (especially apartments) in recent years, which many people link to growing overtourism issues. If booking one, check it's legally licensed. Some destinations also apply a tourism tax, usually added to accommodation bills.

PUBLIC HOLIDAYS

National holidays:
New Year's Day 1 January
Good Friday March/ April
Labour Day 1 May
Feast of the Assumption 15 August
Fiesta Nacional de España 12 October
All Saints' Day 1 November

Constitution Day 6 December
Christmas 25 December
Other common holidays:
Three Kings' Day 6 January
Maundy Thursday March/ April
Corpus Christi June
Feast of the Immaculate Conception 8 December

Language

English is quite widely spoken, especially in larger cities and popular tourist areas, but less so in rural villages and among older Spaniards. Spanish (Castilian) is the national language; Catalan, Galician and Basque are co-official regional languages. Learning a few words of the local language goes a long way.

Basics

Hello. Hola. *o·la*
Goodbye. Adiós. *Adiós*
Yes. Sí. *see*
No. No. *no*
Please. Por favor. *por fa·vor*
Thank you (very much). (Muchas) Gracias. *(moo·chos) gra·thyas*
Excuse me. Perdón. *per·don*
Sorry. Lo siento. *lo syen·to*
What's your name? ¿Cómo se llama usted? *ko·mo se lya·ma oo·ste*
My name is ... Me llamo ... *me lya·mo ...*
Do you speak English? ¿Habla inglés? *a·bla een·gles*
I don't understand. No entiendo. *no en·tyen·do*

Signs

Abierto Open
Cerrado Closed
Entrada Entrance
Hombres Men
Mujeres Women
Prohibido Prohibited
Salida Exit
Servicios/Aseos Toilets

Time

What time is it? ¿Qué hora es? *ke o·ra es*

It's (10) o'clock. Son (las diez). *son (las dyeth)*
It's half past (one). Es (la una) y media. *es (la oo·na) ee me·dya*
yesterday ayer *a·yer*
today hoy *oy*
tomorrow mañana *ma·nya·na*

Emergencies

Help! ¡Socorro! *so·ko·ro*
Go away! ¡Vete! *ve·te*
Call the police! ¡Llame a la policía! *lya·me a la po·lee·thee·a*
Call a doctor! ¡Llame a un médico! *lya·me a oon me·dee·ko*

Menu Decoder

Menú del día Set lunch menu
Menú degustación Tasting menu
Tapas Small, savoury dishes
Pintxos Basque-style tapas, usually on bread
Ración or media ración Full-plate or half-plate portion of tapas
Marisco Seafood
Carne de cerdo Pork
Carne de vaca Beef
Pollo Chicken
Vegetariano Vegetarian
Vegano Vegan
Sin gluten Gluten-free

NUMBERS	
1	uno
2	dos
3	tres
4	cuatro
5	cinco
6	seis
7	siete
8	ocho
9	nueve
10	diez
20	veinte
50	cincuenta
100	cien

MAKSIM SAFANIUK/SHUTTERSTOCK

AVE train

Arriving & Getting Around

Spain's public transport is among Europe's best, with a fast and super-modern train system, an extensive domestic air network, a well-maintained road network, and buses that connect villages in the country's most remote corners.

Major Points of Entry
Most international travellers arrive into Madrid or Barcelona, though Málaga, Valencia, Mallorca, Ibiza, Alicante and the Canaries also have busy airports, particularly for hops within Europe. Transport to/from airports is usually efficient.

Bus
Most buses are geared towards local residents, which means weekend services are generally more limited. Tickets can often be booked online in advance, though for more remote routes you may need to pay in cash.

Train
Renfe *(renfe.com)* is the national train system that runs most services in Spain, including the high-speed AVE trains. Private operators such as **Iryo** *(iryo.eu)* and **Ouigo** *(ouigo. com)* offer alternatives, often at lower prices. Most cities have local trains called *cercanías* (*rodalies* in Catalonia).

Car & Taxi
To rent a car in Spain, you must have a licence, be aged 21 or over and, in most cases, have a credit card (few places accept debit cards). Rates and availability vary enormously by season – book as far ahead as possible. Taxis are readily available in the big cities and main tourist destinations. Note that Uber doesn't operate in some places, though rideshare company **Cabify** *(cabify.com)* often fills the gap.

MONEY
Currency: Euro (€)

CARD & DIGITAL PAYMENT
All major credit and debit cards are widely accepted (including contactless payments and Apple/Google Pay), though some places don't take Amex. There's sometimes a minimum spend and splitting bills isn't always an option. You may still occasionally need cash for small shops, flea markets, buses and tipping.

HOW TO SAVE A FEW EUROS
Many destinations offer tourist passes covering major sights at a discount, available at tourist offices, online or at the sights. Museums often have dedicated free-access days. Most sights offer discounted tickets for students, children and people over 65. Accommodation-wise, cut costs by skipping peak season (July/August and Easter) and weekends. Take advantage of lunchtime restaurant deals.

PANDO HALL/GETTY IMAGES

303

Curated by
Virginia Maxwell

Türkiye

WHERE EUROPE AND ASIA MEET

Replete with stunning natural landscapes, dynamic cities
and evocative remnants of ancient empires, Türkiye offers
the perfect mix of cultural, leisure and adventure tourism.

Europe's second-largest country by both area and population is impressive by every measure. Mighty empires have cut a swathe through its territory over millennia, leaving cities, monuments and wonderfully diverse cultures in their wakes. These bequests enrich the lives of locals to this day, and make travelling here an extraordinarily rewarding experience.

Many visitors are drawn by the Aegean and Mediterranean coastlines with their sparkling turquoise-blue waters and sybaritic summer resorts, while others are lured by the quietly compelling landscapes, towns and outdoor attractions of inland Anatolia. Otherworldly destinations such as Cappadocia, home to fairy chimneys, cave dwellings and hot-air-balloon voyages, are deservedly famous,

but it's often experiences in off-the-beaten-track villages that will prove most memorable, largely due to the warmth and generosity of locals.

Cities are also a major drawcard, most notably the capital in all but name, İstanbul. Its magnificent minaret-studded skyline, bustling medieval bazaars and world-class eating and drinking scene live up to their reputations and then some. Sailing the length of the storied Bosphorus Strait or boarding a ferry to cross between Europe and Asia are highlights, but so too is a deep dive into the city's thriving cultural scene with events galore. Time spent here – as well as in the extraordinary ancient cities of Ephesus, Hierapolis, Pergamum and Troy – is sure to be a highlight of every traveller's itinerary.

ESIN DENIZ/SHUTTERSTOCK

THE MAIN AREAS

For places to stay in Türkiye, see p329

NINA ZORINA/SHUTTERSTOCK

Left: Gallipoli (p316); Above: Cappadocia (p326)

Gallipoli Peninsula & Troy, p316

Two fabled battlefields: the coastal landscape where Turkish and Allied forces clashed in WWI, and the ruined ancient city over which the Trojan War was fought.

İstanbul, p310

Home to major attractions such as Aya Sofya, Topkapı Palace and the Grand Bazaar, Türkiye's largest city has a stupendously beautiful setting and an exhilarating local lifestyle.

BULGARIA

GREECE

Edirne

İpsala

Keşan

Tekirdağ

Gallipoli
Peninsula &
Troy

Çanakkale Epic
Promotion
Centre

Lâpseki

Çanakkale

Museum
of Troy

Edremit

Ayvalık

Bergama
Bergama
Acropolis

Manisa

Çeşme

İzmir

Ödemiş

Selçuk

Aydın

Nazilli

Ephesus

Milas

Yatağan

Bodrum

Muğla

Bodrum
Castle

Akyaka

Marmaris

Ölüdeniz Beach
& Lagoon

Kalkan

Kaş

Aegean Sea

Çorlu

Corlu

The
Bosphorus

Topkapı Palace

İstanbul

Grand Bazaar

Sea of
Marmara

Bandırma

Balıkesir

Aya
Sofya

Bursa

*Uludağ
(2543m)*

Kocaeli
(İzmit)

Adapazarı

Eskişehir

Kütahya

Uşak

Afyon

Pamukkale
Hierapolis

Denizli

Burdur

Isparta

*Eğirdir
Gölü*

Akşehir

*Beyşehir
Gölü*

Bolu

Gerede

Bandırma

Cide

Amasra

Zonguldak

Karabük

Safranbolu

İnebolu

Sinop

Kastamonu

Ilgaz

ANKARA

Polatlı

*Tuz Gölü
(Salt Lake)*

Aksaray

Çankırı

Çorum

Kırıkkale

Kırşehir

Yozgat

Ereğli

Karaman

Eskişehir

Aegean & Mediterranean
Coasts

Fethiye

Chimaera

Kemer

Çıralı

Olympos

Antalya

Side

Alanya

*Mediterranean Sea
(Akdeniz)*

Nevşehir

Göreme Open-Air
Museum

Göreme

**Cappadocia
National Park**

Tarsus

Adana

Mersin
(İçel)

Silifke

Ancient Cities,
p320

Three of the ancient world's most extraordinary cities: Pergamum, Ephesus and Hierapolis, all within easy reach of the Aegean coast.

Aegean &
Mediterranean
Coasts, p324

Türkiye's summer playground, where sun-spangled waters, sandy beaches and relaxing cruises on *gülets* (traditional wooden yachts) await.

Cappadocia &
Nemrut Dağı
National Park,
p326

Kick back in a cave hotel in Göreme, float over fairy chimneys in a hot-air balloon or climb to the summit of Nemrut Dağı.

N

0   200 km
0   100 miles

Find Your Way

Türkiye's regions of Thrace and Marmara sit at the easternmost edge of Europe, bordered by the Bosphorus. East of this waterway, the Asian peninsula of Anadolu (Anatolia) is where the bulk of Türkiye's territory lies. İstanbul straddles both continents.

Black Sea (Karadeniz)

TBILISI

GEORGIA

Bafra

Samsun · Ünye · Ordu · Giresun

Trabzon · Rize

Mt Kaçkar (Kaçkar Dağı) (3937m)

Göle

Gyumri

ARMENIA

Kars

YEREVAN

Amasya

Turhal · Tokat

Bayburt · *Çoruh River*

Horasan

Erzurum

Aras River

Tuzluca · İğdır

Ağrı

Doğubayazıt

Mt Ararat (Ağrı Dağı) (5137m)

Bazargan

Sivas

Erzincan

Kızılırmak River

CAPPADOCIA

Keban Dam

Bingöl

Mt Nemrut (Nemrut Dağı) (3050m)

Lake Van (Van Gölü)

Patnos

Muradiye

IRAN

Kayseri

Gürün

Elazığ

Murat River

Muş

Tatvan

Akdamar Island

Van · Gevaş

Sero

Yüksekova

Göksun

Malatya

Nemrut Dağı National Park

Nemrut Dağı (Mt Nemrut) (2106m)

Nemrut Dağı Summit

Diyarbakır

Siirt

Hakkari

Mt Çilo (Çilo Dağı) (4168m)

Kahramanmaraş

Gölbaşı

Siverek

Batman

Mardin

Tigris River

Şırnak

Adıyaman

Gaziantep (Antep)

Viranşehir

Qamishle

Ceyhan

Osmaniye

Birecik

Şanlıurfa (Urfa)

Kilis

Barak

Akçakale

IRAQ

İskenderun

Aleppo (Halab)

SYRIA

Antakya (Hatay)

Reyhanlı
Bab al-Hawa

Tripoli

BEIRUT

✈ AIR

Scheduled flights between airports in over 50 cities and major towns are operated by **Turkish Airlines** (*turkishairlines.com*) and low-cost carriers **AJet** (*ajet.com*), **Pegasus** (*flypgs.com*) and **SunExpress** (*sunexpress.com*). Most fly via the hubs of İstanbul and Ankara. The busiest airports are in İstanbul, Antalya, Ankara and İzmir.

🚗 CAR

A network of well-maintained highways links most of the country. Car hire is easy to arrange; manuals are the default option though automatics are available. Be warned that distances can be great and that petrol is pricey. Hire cars usually have a tag that enables road tolls to be paid and charged to the driver automatically.

🚌 BUS

An extensive intercity bus network is a reliable and affordable means of getting around. Most bus companies offer free shuttles between city centres and otogars (bus stations) on their fringes. Reliable companies include **Flixbus** (*flixbus.com.tr*) and **Metro Turizm** (*metroturizm.com.tr*). Dolmuşes (local minibuses) service smaller destinations.

307

Plan Your Time

It's sensible to prioritise the country's major tourist drawcards – including İstanbul, Cappadocia, the archaeological sites of Ephesus and Hierapolis, and the Mediterranean coast – as they are relatively easy to access.

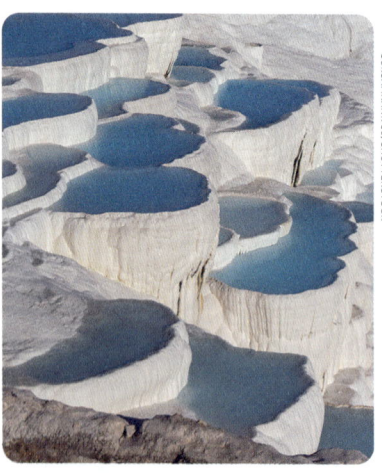

SUKSAMRAN1985/SHUTTERSTOCK

Travertines, Pamukkale (p323)

Pressed for Time

● If your time is limited to less than a week, adopt 'less is more' as your mantra. Spend a couple of days in **İstanbul** (p310), visiting its splendid mosques, palaces, museums, galleries and bazaars.

● Then fly to İzmir and take the İzban metro from the airport to Tepeköy, from where another line continues to the welcoming tourist town of Selçuk. This is located next to the country's number-one archaeological site, **Ephesus** (p322).

● Next, take a bus to Denizli, from where taxis and minibuses travel the short distance to **Pamukkale** (p323), home to the famous cascade of Travertines (terraced basins) upon which the ruins of the ancient spa city of Hierapolis perch. Return to İstanbul from Denizli Çardak Airport.

SEASONAL HIGHLIGHTS

Spring and autumn are particularly traveller-friendly, with reasonable crowds and accommodation prices. Summer is generally high season.

MARCH
Low-season prices apply to accommodation across the country and tourist sites are relatively uncrowded, making this a good time to visit.

APRIL
The annual commemoration of Allied soldiers killed in WWI on Gallipoli's battlefields is held on 25 April at **Anzac Cove** (**Anzac Koyu**; p318).

MAY
Pleasantly mild weather across the country. Shoulder season prices apply everywhere except Cappadocia and İstanbul, where it's high season.

Ten Days Along the Coast

● After spending a few days in **İstanbul** (p310), fly to İzmir and head straight to Selçuk to visit **Ephesus** (p322).

● Next, drive or take a series of buses and dolmuşes south along the stunning Aegean and Mediterranean coasts, sampling the vibrant nightlife in **Bodrum** (p324), taking a 'blue cruise' out of **Fethiye** (p325), eating fresh seafood in **Kaş** (p325), swimming at **Patara** (p325) and **Kaputaş** (p325) beaches and partying in the backpacking beach resort of **Olympos** (p325) next to one of the best beaches in Türkiye.

● Fly out of the airport at nearby Antalya, which offers frequent connections to a wide range of destinations within Türkiye, Europe and the Gulf states.

Backpacker's Türkiye in Two Weeks

● This two-week itinerary follows a classic traveller's route. Start with four full days in **İstanbul** (p310), spending three days in the Old City and Beyoğlu and one day sailing the length of the Bosphorus.

● Next, drive or take a bus to Çanakkale, from where you can visit **Troy** (p319) and the **Gallipoli** (p316) battlefields. From Çanakkale, head down the Aegean coast en route to Selçuk, where you can spend a day at **Ephesus** (p322; don't miss the Terraced Houses) and perhaps explore some of the sites and villages nearby.

● Then fly from İzmir's Adnan Menderes Airport to Kayseri and make your way to the village of Göreme to stay in an atmosphere-laden cave hotel and explore the extraordinary and unique landscape of **Cappadocia** (p326).

JUNE
Summer months are best for taking a **balloon ride** in Cappadocia or a *gület* (traditional wooden yacht) cruise on the Mediterranean coast.

AUGUST
Towns and resorts along the coast are inundated with sun-seeking Turks, making accommodation expensive and hard to source.

SEPTEMBER
School holidays have finished, making this an excellent time to holiday on the Mediterranean coast, where the water remains warm.

DECEMBER
Crowds flock to İstanbul to celebrate Christmas and New Year, but elsewhere many hotels and resorts close for the winter season.

İstanbul

HISTORICAL MONUMENTS | EATING & DRINKING | FERRY TRIPS

 TOP TIP

Plan your sightseeing around the weekly closures of major attractions. Topkapı Palace is closed on Tuesday, the Grand Bazaar is closed on Sunday and most mosques (including the Blue Mosque, Aya Sofya and the Süleymaniye) are closed to non-worshippers during prayer times and for parts of Friday (usually morning to mid-afternoon).

This magical meeting place of Asia and Europe has more top-drawer attractions than it has minarets (and that's a lot). And although some ancient cities are the sum of their monuments, İstanbul factors a lot more into the equation. You can admire Byzantine churches and Ottoman mosques in the morning, shop in bazaars and cutting-edge boutiques in the afternoon, and party in bars, taverns and clubs into the night. There's something here for every type of traveller.

Founded by Megarian colonists (who named it Byzantium), the ancient settlement was subsequently conquered by the Persians and Athenians before achieving independence. Then the Romans arrived, renaming it Constantinople and endowing it with monuments that still stand today. In 1204 Venetian soldiers of the Fourth Crusade took their turn at the helm, only to be replaced by the returning Byzantines, who ruled until the Ottomans stormed into town and stayed until the Republic was declared nearly five centuries later.

🧭 GETTING AROUND

The Old City enclaves of Sultanahmet and the Bazaar District, and Beyoğlu across the Galata Bridge, can be explored on foot or by using the excellent public transport system including trams, metro, ferries and buses. To travel, you'll need an İstanbulkart (rechargable transport card), which is good value and can be purchased from and recharged at machines at metro, funicular and tram stations and stops.

The major otogars (bus stations) in the city are Esenler Otogarı (aka Büyük İstanbul Otogarı) and Alibeyköy Otogarı. Intercity and international trains depart from Halkalı Garı. All three stations are located on the European side of the city.

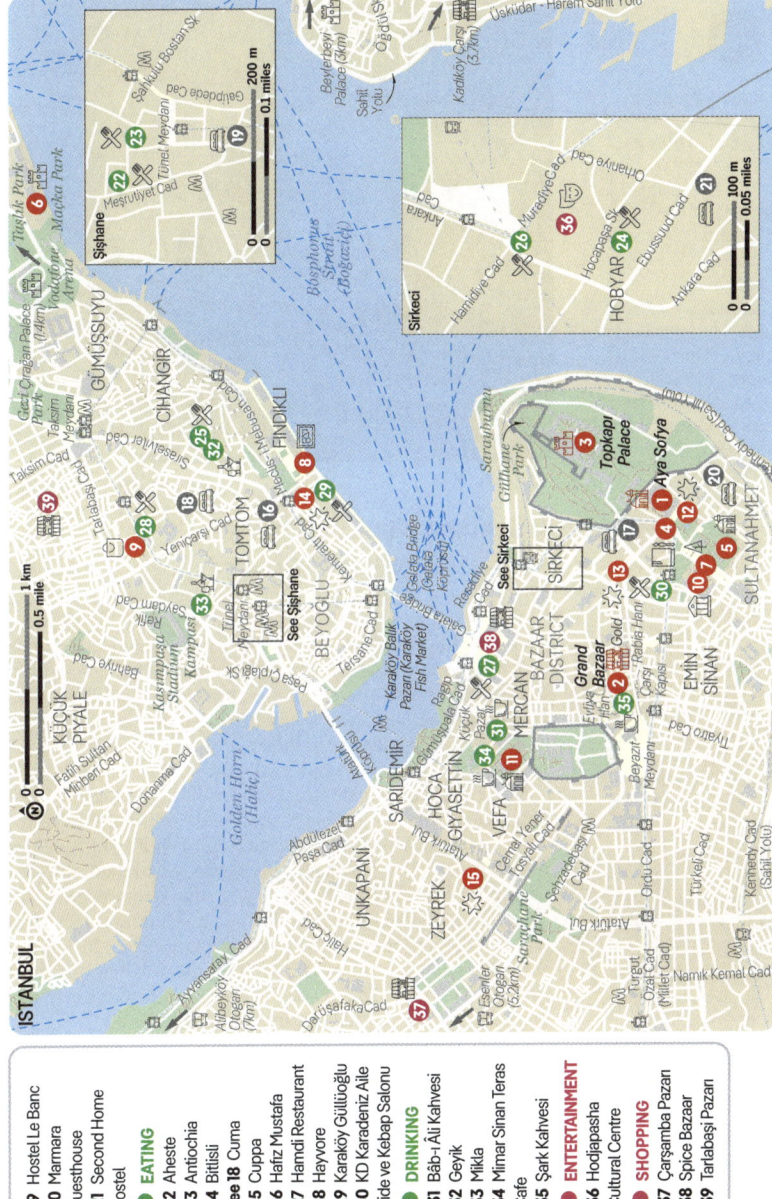

ISTANBUL

★ HIGHLIGHTS
1 Aya Sofya
2 Grand Bazaar
3 Topkapı Palace

● SIGHTS
4 Basilica Cistern
5 Blue Mosque
6 Dolmabahçe Palace
7 Hippodrome
8 İstanbul Modern
9 İstiklal Caddesi
10 Museum of Turkish & Islamic Arts
11 Süleymaniye Mosque

● ACTIVITIES
12 Ayasofya Hürrem Sultan Hamamı
13 Cağaloğlu Hamamı
see 18 Çukurcuma Hamamı
14 Kılıç Ali Paşa Hamamı
15 Zeyrek Çinili Hamamı

● SLEEPING
16 Archeo
17 Cheers Hostel
18 Hamamhane
19 Hostel Le Banc
20 Marmara Guesthouse
21 Second Home Hostel

● EATING
22 Aheste
23 Antiochia
24 Bitlisi
see 18 Cuma
25 Cuppa
26 Hafız Mustafa
27 Hamdi Restaurant
28 Hayvore
29 Karaköy Güllüoğlu
30 KD Karadeniz Aile Pide ve Kebap Salonu

● DRINKING
31 Bâb-ı Âli Kahvesi
32 Geyik
33 Mikla
34 Mimar Sinan Teras Cafe
35 Şark Kahvesi

● ENTERTAINMENT
36 Hodjapasha Cultural Centre

● SHOPPING
37 Çarşamba Pazarı
38 Spice Bazaar
39 Tarlabaşı Pazarı

311

BEST HAMAMS

Ayasofya Hürrem Sultan Hamamı: Dating from 1556, this hamam near Aya Sofya has separate baths for males and females.

Cağaloğlu Hamamı: Built in 1741, this is one of the most beautiful hamams in the city. Separate baths for men and women.

Zeyrek Çinili Hamamı: Painstakingly restored hamam dating from the early 16th century. The male and female *hararets* (steam rooms) are particularly beautiful.

Kılıç Ali Paşa Hamamı: Beautifully restored Karaköy hamam dating from 1580. It has one *hararet* that's open at different times for men and women.

Çukurcuma Hamamı: Modest neighbourhood hamam in Beyoğlu that functions as a mixed bath, with all clients using the space at the same time.

Mosaic, Aya Sofya

A Sublime Place of Worship
Admire exquisite Byzantine mosaics

There are many important monuments in İstanbul, but **Aya Sofya** *(muze.gen.tr/muze-detay/ayasofya; €25)* – commissioned by the great Byzantine emperor Justinian, consecrated as a church in 537, converted to a mosque by Mehmet the Conqueror in 1453, declared a museum by Atatürk in 1935 and converted back into a mosque in 2020 – surpasses the rest due to its innovative architectural form, rich history, religious importance and extraordinary beauty.

Only Turks and worshipping foreign-national Muslims can enter the prayer hall; other visitors are restricted to the upstairs galleries, which are home to a number of Byzantine-era mosaics. Note that when this book was researched, the mosaics and paintings on the dome were due to be covered and scaffolding was to be erected in the nave (main prayer hall) while stabilisation work in the building occurs. This means that views down to the nave from the gallery will be obscured for multiple years. The ticket office for non-Muslims is in Kabasakal Caddesi on the east side of the building.

 EATING IN İSTANBUL: BEST OLD CITY EATS

Bitlisli: Bustling eatery in Hocapaşa serving southeastern Anatolian food, including tasty kebabs and pides (Turkish-style pizzas). No alcohol. *11.30am–11pm* €

Hafız Mustafa: Sweets shop serving milk puddings, baklava and *künefe* in its upstairs tea salon in Sultanahmet. More branches across the city. *8am–2am* €

KD Karadeniz Aile Pide ve Kebap Salonu: Serving tasty pides, soups and kebaps, this joint is the best in the enclave off Divan Yolu. No alcohol. *10am–11pm* €

Hamdi Restaurant: The best-loved eatery in the Old City, this multi-floored restaurant serves excellent kebaps. *noon–midnight* €€

Adorning the City Skyline
İstanbul's iconic mosque

Officially known as Sultanahmet Camii (Sultanahmet Mosque), the **Blue Mosque** *(free)* is İstanbul's most photogenic building, with a wonderfully curvaceous exterior featuring a cascade of domes and six slender minarets. The interior is adorned with 21,000 blue İznik tiles that give the building its unofficial but commonly used name.

On the western side of the mosque is the **Hippodrome**, originally built by the Byzantine emperors as an arena for chariot races. On its edge is the **Museum of Turkish & Islamic Arts** *(muze.gen.tr/muze-detay/tiem; €17)*, housed in an Ottoman palace built in 1524 for İbrahim Paşa, grand vizier to Süleyman the Magnificent. It has a splendid collection of artefacts, including antique carpets displayed in a dedicated hall.

Showcase of Ottoman Life & Culture
Opulent gardens, palace and pavilions

Topkapı Palace *(muze.gen.tr/muze-detay/topkapi; TL2400)* is the subject of more colourful stories than most of the world's museums put together. Libidinous sultans, ambitious courtiers and beautiful concubines lived and worked here between the 15th and 19th centuries when it was the court of the Ottoman Empire.

Organised into four park-like areas, the palace comprises a multitude of opulent structures, including a sprawling Harem where the sultans and their families lived, ornately decorated pavilions for relaxation, handsome audience chambers where courtiers and foreign diplomats were received, a set of rooms where important religious relicts were safeguarded, and a Treasury where precious art and objects were stored.

İstanbul's Original Shopping Mall
Historic and atmospheric marketplace

The colourful and chaotic **Grand Bazaar** *(Kapalıçarşı; instagram/grandbazaarofistanbul; free)* has been the heart of the Old City for centuries. Starting as a small vaulted *bedesten* (warehouse) built on the order of Mehmet the Conqueror in 1461, it grew to cover a vast area as more than 60 lanes between the *bedesten*, neighbouring shops and *hans* (caravanserais) were roofed, and the market assumed the sprawling, labyrinthine form it retains today.

BEST İSTANBUL MARKETS & BAZAARS

Grand Bazaar: The most famous and historic bazaar in the city. A visit here is essential.

Kadıköy Çarşı: This market near the *iskele* (ferry dock) in the Asian suburb of Kadıköy has shops and street stands selling top-quality Turkish produce. Closed Sunday.

Çarşamba Pazarı: On Wednesday mornings, the streets northwest of the Fatih Mosque host a sprawling market with fresh produce and cheap clothing, footwear and homewares.

Spice Bazaar: Known the Mısır Çarşısı (Egyptian Market), this bazaar in Eminönü started trading in the 1660s and is known for its dried fruits, nuts, honey and spices.

Tarlabaşı Pazarı: Lively and cheap street market held on Sundays near Taksim.

 EATING IN İSTANBUL: BEST BEYOĞLU EATS

Karaköy Güllüoğlu: Exceptionally delicious baklava is on offer at this Karaköy institution. Good *burek* (filled pastry), too. *7.30am-1am Mon-Sat, from 8am Sun* €

Hayvore: Tasty dishes of the day and pide are on offer at this local favourite located in a side street off İstiklal Caddesi. *8.30am-11pm* €

Antiochia: This Asmalımescit stalwart gets our vote for serving the best kebaps in the city. *noon-midnight Mon-Fri, from 2pm Sat* €€

Aheste: Serving Modern Turkish cuisine, this stylish Asmalımescit restaurant offers tasting and à la carte menus with some vegetarian options. *6pm-midnight* €€€

WHY I LOVE İSTANBUL

Virginia Maxwell,
writer

Why do I love this city? Let me count the ways. I love the locals, who have an endless supply of hospitality and good humour at their disposal. I love the fact that when I walk down Old City streets, layers of a millennia-old history unfold before me. I love listening to the sound of the *müezzins* duelling from their minarets and I love seeing the sun set over the world's most beautiful skyline. I love the restaurants, the bars and the tea gardens. But most of all, I love that an extraordinary cultural experience, often one I have never previously encountered, lies around every corner.

The bazaar and surrounding streets host many cafes and cheap eateries open for lunch Monday to Saturday. The picks of these are **Şark Kahvesi**, a historic coffeehouse on Sipahi Sokak, and the fast-food stands on **Kılıççılar Sokak**, just outside the bazaar's Kılıççılar Gate.

The Pinnacle of Ottoman Architecture
Remarkably intact mosque complex

Commissioned by Süleyman I (known as 'the Magnificent'), the **Süleymaniye Mosque** (*free*) was the fourth imperial mosque built in İstanbul and it certainly lives up to its patron's nickname. Though not the largest of the imperial mosques, it's one of the grandest and most beautiful. When visiting, don't miss the panoramic terrace behind the mosque and the beautifully decorated *türbes* (tombs) of Süleyman and his wife Haseki Hürrem Sultan (Roxelana), which are located to the right of the main entrance.

The streets below the mosque are home to a number of rooftop cafes with spectacular views, the best of which are **Mimar Sinan Teras Cafe** and **Bâb-ı Âli Kahvesi**.

Watch the Dervishes Whirl
Sufi cultural performance

To witness the ancient art of Dervish whirling, head to the **Hodjapasha Cultural Centre** (*hodjapasha.com; adult/child US$41/23*), a beautifully converted 550-year-old hamam in Sirkeci that stages cultural performances including a 60-minute 'Dervish Experience' at 7pm daily. The musical and dance elements of this Sufi performance symbolize stages on the path to accessing God. Photography is not allowed. Bookings are essential.

Party in Beyoğlu
Epicentre of dining and nightlife

Beyoğlu is where visitors and locals come in search of good cafes, restaurants, bars, live-music venues and clubs. Built around the major boulevard of **İstiklal Caddesi**, it incorporates a mix of bohemian shopping and residential districts such as Galata, Çukurcuma and Cihangir; bustling eating and drinking enclaves such as Asmalımescit; and historically rich pockets such as Karaköy, now home to boutiques, bars and cafes.

 EATING IN İSTANBUL: BEST BEYOĞLU CAFES & BARS

Cuppa: Cihangir cafe offering tempting pastries, wraps and *tosts* (toasted sandwiches) made with house-baked sourdough. *8am-5pm €*	**Geyik:** Pocket-sized Cihangir bar where the action usually spills out onto the street. Great cocktails. *4pm-2am*	**Cuma:** Laid-back foodie oasis in the heart of Çukurcuma serving good coffee and excellent, seasonally driven food. *noon-midnight €€*	**Mikla:** This swish summer-only bar on the rooftop of the Marmara Pera Hotel in Asmalımescit has a spectacular panoramic view. *6pm-2am Mon-Sat*

Popular bar strips and districts include Karaköy, Nevizade and Sofyalı Sokaks off İstiklal Caddesi and Akarsu Yokuşu in Cihangir. All are busiest on Friday, Saturday and Sunday nights.

To get to Beyoğlu from the Old City, take the tram (direction Kabataş). Alight at Karaköy for Galata, Tünel and Asmalımescit; at Tophane for Çukurcuma and Galatasaray; and at Kabataş for Cihangir and Taksim. Funiculars carry passengers up the steep slope to İstiklal Caddesi from both Karaköy and Kabataş.

Cutting-Edge Art & Architecture
Türkiye's most impressive art gallery

Housed in a spectacular Renzo Piano–designed building next to the Bosphorus, **İstanbul Modern** (*istanbulmodern.org; adult/concession TL750/470*) is home to an extensive collection of Turkish art that's showcased in a multi-roomed exhibition gallery. The museum also stages a constantly refreshed programme of expertly curated exhibitions by high-profile local and international artists. Facilities include a terrace restaurant with Bosphorus views and a design shop selling quality souvenirs and gifts.

Sail Along the Bosphorus
Admire waterside mansions and palaces

Linking the Sea of Marmara (Marmara Denizi) with the Black Sea (Karadeniz), the Bosphorus Strait is the geographical spine of the city, and also its greatest treasure. On one side is Europe, on the other Asia – both shores are lined with former fishing villages that have been transformed into ritzy residential suburbs. The water's edge is fringed with grandiose palaces that once housed sultans and their families, including **Dolmabahçe**, **Çırağan** and **Beylerbeyi**. There are also numerous *yalıs*, seafront mansions built by wealthy Ottomans and foreign embassies as summer retreats.

The easiest way to experience the Bosphorus is by boarding the morning **Uzun Boğaz Turu** (*Long Bosphorus Tour; sehirhatlari.istanbul; adult/child under 6yr TL640/free*) ferry that departs from Eminönü every day at 10.35am, cruising up the Bosphorus for two hours before arriving at Anadolu Kavağı at the mouth of the Black Sea, where it pauses for 2½ hours before returning to Eminönü at 4.40pm. During the break at Anadolu Kavağı, many passengers choose to walk up to the ruins of **Anadolu Kavağı Kalesi**, a medieval castle overlooking both the Black Sea and the Bosphorus.

BEST FERRY TRIPS

Taking a trip on one of İstanbul's ferries is a highlight of every visit. For routes and timetables, see *sehirhatlari.istanbul*.

Long Bosphorus Tour: Spot Ottoman and Byzantine monuments up and down the Bosphorus Strait.

Haliç Ferry Line: Cruise the length of the Haliç (Golden Horn) to visit important Ottoman monuments, shrines and mosques at Eyüpsultan.

Eminönü or Karaköy to Kadıköy: The classic Europe to Asia trip; make sure you visit the Çarşı (fresh-produce market) in Kadıköy.

Princes Islands: Known as the Adalar (Islands), these car-free settlements in the Sea of Marmara are popular weekend destinations for İstanbullus.

Eminönü or Karaköy to Üsküdar: A cross-continent trip to an ancient district studded with Ottoman-era mosques.

Gallipoli Peninsula & Troy

WWI BATTLEGROUNDS | ARCHAEOLOGY | SCENERY

The stunning landscapes on either side of the Dardenelles Strait have long histories as battlegrounds, the vestiges of which are preserved at Gallipoli and ancient Troy (Truva). To visit these storied sites, the small town of Eceabat on the Gallipoli Peninsula and the university city of Çanakkale across the strait make good bases. The latter is known for its attractive *kordon* (waterfront promenade).

Today, the Gallipoli (Gelibolu) Peninsula battlefields are protected landscapes covered in pine forests and fringed by idyllic beaches and coves. However, the bloody battles fought here in 1915 are still alive in Turkish and foreign memories. On Anzac Day (25 April), a dawn memorial service is held at North Beach. The Turkish victory is commemorated by Turks on 18 March each year.

The archaeological site of Troy is located approximately 30km southwest of Çanakkale. Its association with Homer's *Iliad* makes it one of Türkiye's most visited archaeological sites.

☑ **TOP TIP**

Crowded House Tours (*crowdedhousegallipoli. com*) and **TJ's Tours** (*anzacgallipolitours.com*) offer early-morning minibus transfers from İstanbul including tours, with pickup at hotels in Sultanahmet and Taksim. They run daily tours of the north and south battlefields and the Troy archaeological site, and pick up participants in both Eceabat and Çanakkale.

Moving Tributes to Fallen Soldiers

WWI battlefield sites and memorials

The battlefields of WWI's Gallipoli Campaign (known in Türkiye as the Battle of Çanakkale) are protected as part of the **Gallipoli Historical Area** (*canakkaletarihialan.gov.tr*).

GETTING AROUND

Regular buses (five hours) connect İstanbul's Alibeyköy and Esenler otogars with Eceabat and Çanakkale.

The battlefields are best explored by car or on a tour; cars can be rented in Çanakkale and Eceabat. A 6.5km suspension bridge and a car ferry cross the Dardanelles Strait.

Dolmuşes to Troy (35 minutes) leave on the half-hour between 9.30am and 5pm from the northern end of the bridge over the Sarı River in Çanakkale. Ask to be let off at the Museum of Troy, from where it's a 750m walk to the archaeological site.

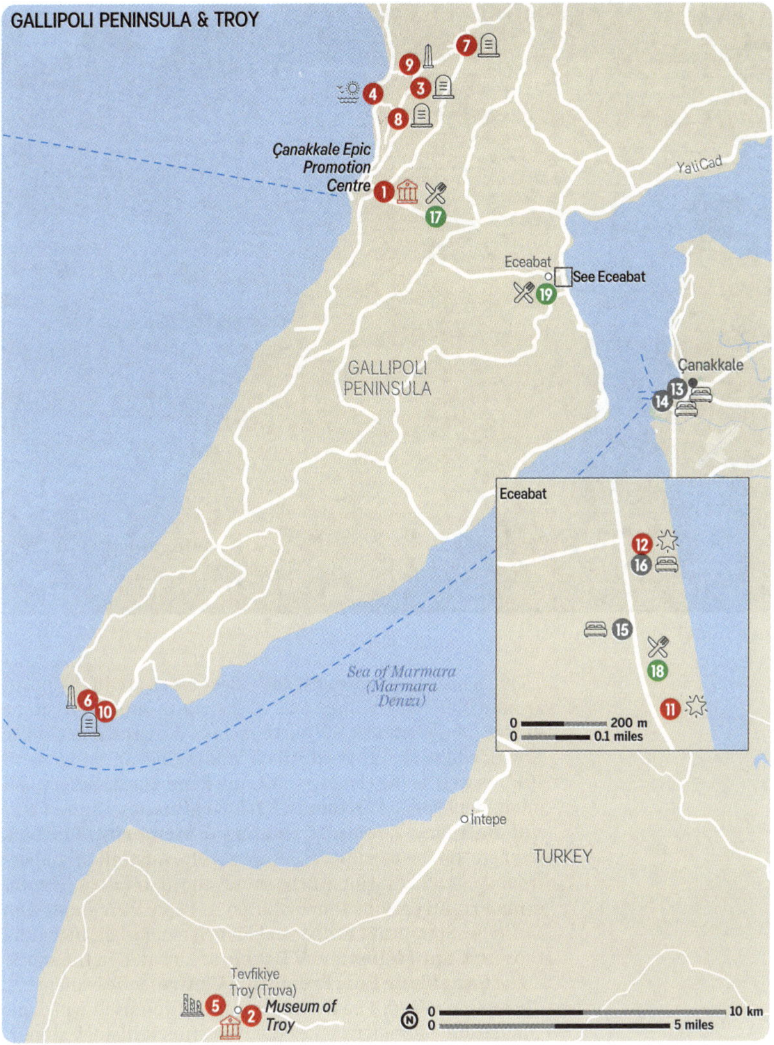

GALLIPOLI PENINSULA & TROY

Çanakkale Epic
Promotion
Centre

Yalı Cad

Eceabat
See Eceabat

GALLIPOLI
PENINSULA

Çanakkale

Eceabat

Sea of Marmara
(Marmara
Denizi)

0 — 200 m
0 — 0.1 miles

İntepe

TURKEY

Tevfikiye
Troy (Truva)
Museum of
Troy

N   0 — 10 km
    0 — 5 miles

⭐ **HIGHLIGHTS**
1 Çanakkale Epic
  Promotion Centre
2 Museum of Troy

🔴 **SIGHTS**
3 57th Regiment
  Cemetery
4 Anzac Cove

5 Archaeological Site
  of Troy
6 Cape Helles British
  Memorial
7 Chunuk Bair New
  Zealand Cemetery
  & Memorial
8 Lone Pine Cemetery

9 The Nek
10 V Beach Cemetery

🔴 **ACTIVITIES**
11 Crowded House Tours
12 TJ's Tours

⚫ **SLEEPING**
13 Büyük Truva Hotel
14 Grand Anzac Hotel

15 Hotel Crowded House
16 TJ's Hotel

🟢 **EATING**
17 Doyuranlar Aile Çay
  ve Gözleme
18 Gözde Köfteci
see 13 Kısmet Balık Evi
19 Suvla

The peninsula's two main battlefield areas are in the north around Kabatepe village and in the south around Alçıtepe village. Major sites in the north include **Anzac Cove** (Anzac Koyu), where the ill-fated Allied landing began on 25 April 1915, as well as the cemetery at **Lone Pine**, the cemetery and monument for the **Ottoman 57th Regiment** and the **Chunuk Bair New Zealand Cemetery & Memorial**. **The Nek** is where, on the morning of 7 August 1915, Australian soldiers from the 3rd Light Horse Brigade advanced in vain into withering fire, an episode immortalised in Peter Weir's 1981 film *Gallipoli*. Significant British and French memorials, including those at **Cape Helles** and **V Beach**, are located in the south.

The **Çanakkale Epic Promotion Centre** (*canakkaletarihi alan.gov.tr; TL100*) near Kabatepe has 11 rooms in which 3D simulation equipment takes the viewer on a historical journey through the Gallipoli campaigns from a predominantly Turkish point of view.

EATING IN ECEABAT & ÇANAKKALE: OUR PICKS

Doyuranlar Aile Çay ve Gözleme: A tea garden on the road from Eceabat to Kabatepe. Combine the *gözleme* (stuffed flatbreads) and tea. *8am-6.30pm €*

Gözde Köfteci: Close to the sea in Eceabat, this restaurant is renowned for its meatballs. The lentil soup is delicious too. *5am-midnight €€*

Kısmet Balık Evi: A family-run business in Çanakkale that stands out for the freshness of its seafood. *10am-10pm €€*

Suvla: Eceabat winery with a tasting room, shop and wine bar serving simple modern twists on Turkish classics. *9am-10pm €€€*

Archaeological Site of Troy

Decipher Layers of History

Ruins of ancient Troy

Best known as the subject of Homer's epic poem *Iliad*, the Trojan War – if it actually happened – would have been only an eyeblink in the history of ancient Troy, which spans thousands of years. Its many cycles of destruction and reconstruction have been identified in 10 main archaeological layers excavated at the **Archaeological Site of Troy** (*muze.gov.tr; incl museum €27*) and named Troy 0 through to Troy IX.

Start your visit at the excellent **Museum of Troy** before moving on to the ruins. Follow the boardwalk to the right to reach the foundations of the east walls of Troy VI. Close your eyes and imagine a colossal wooden horse, a gift from the Greeks, passing through the sturdy sea-facing gate of the city walls. From here, continue north past the Temple of Athena, a Roman-era theatre and the palace complex of Troy II. The original trial trench established by German amateur archaeologist Heinrich Schliemann, is nearby, as is the Troy II Ramp, once a point of entry into ancient Troy.

HEINRICH SCHLIEMANN

Until the 19th century, many historians doubted whether ancient Troy had existed. However, one amateur German archaeologist, Heinrich Schliemann (1822–90), proved them wrong. In 1870 Schliemann uncovered the remains of a ruined city (the current-day archaeological site). He also unearthed a cache of gold artefacts that he named 'Priam's Treasure'.

During his hasty and destructive dig, Schliemann failed to appreciate that Troy was a series of settlements built one on top of the other over the course of about 2500 years. Furthermore, it was soon established that the treasures (which he smuggled out of the country and are now in Moscow's Pushkin Museum) were not from the time of Homer's Troy, but from the much earlier Troy II.

Ancient Cities

ARCHAEOLOGICAL SITES | MUSEUMS | NATURAL WONDERS

Places

Türkiye is the proud possessor of 22 sites, structures and landscapes inscribed on UNESCO's World Heritage List, a number of which are the remnants of ancient cities located in the country's west. Three of these – the spectacular and well-preserved ruins of Pergamum, Ephesus and Hierapolis – are among the most visited sites in the country, featuring on many travel itineraries. Easy detours from the coast, all three are located close to towns with excellent tourist infrastructure including hostels, hotels, cafes and restaurants. Selçuk and Pamukkale are particularly well endowed in this respect, making them tempting spots for a few days of R&R during longer trips. Pamukkale also makes an excellent base for those keen to deviate from the well-travelled tourism route and explore the more isolated but equally spectacular sites of Laodicea, Afrodisias and Kibyra. Other sites – Xanthos and Letoön – are located on the Turquoise Coast but can be visited on a day trip.

Bergama

Evoke the splendour of ancient Pergamum

The laid-back market town of Bergama is the modern successor to the once-powerful ancient city of Pergamum. During Pergamum's heyday (between Alexander the Great and the Roman domination of Asia Minor), it was one of the Middle East's richest and most powerful small kingdoms. The **Acropolis** *(muze.gov.tr; €15)*, linked to the town by a cable car, retains structures including a magnificent amphitheatre and a columned temple dedicated to Trajan.

The fascinating **Asklepion** *(muze.gov.tr; €13)*, 2.5km uphill from town, was Pergamum's famed medical centre. Dedicated to Asclepius (the god of healing in Ancient Greece), it dates from the 4th century BCE.

GETTING AROUND

Buses travel from both İstanbul and Çanakkale to destinations including Bergama, Ayvalık, İzmir, Selçuk and Denizli (for Pamukkale). Some of these services involve a change of bus in İzmir.

There are regular buses and dolmuşes between the İzmir otogar and Bergama, Selçuk and Pamukkale. The İzban metro departs from İzmir's city centre before stopping at the airport and continuing to Tepeköy, from where another line continues to Selçuk.

Dolmuşes connect Pamukkale with Laodicea and Denizli.

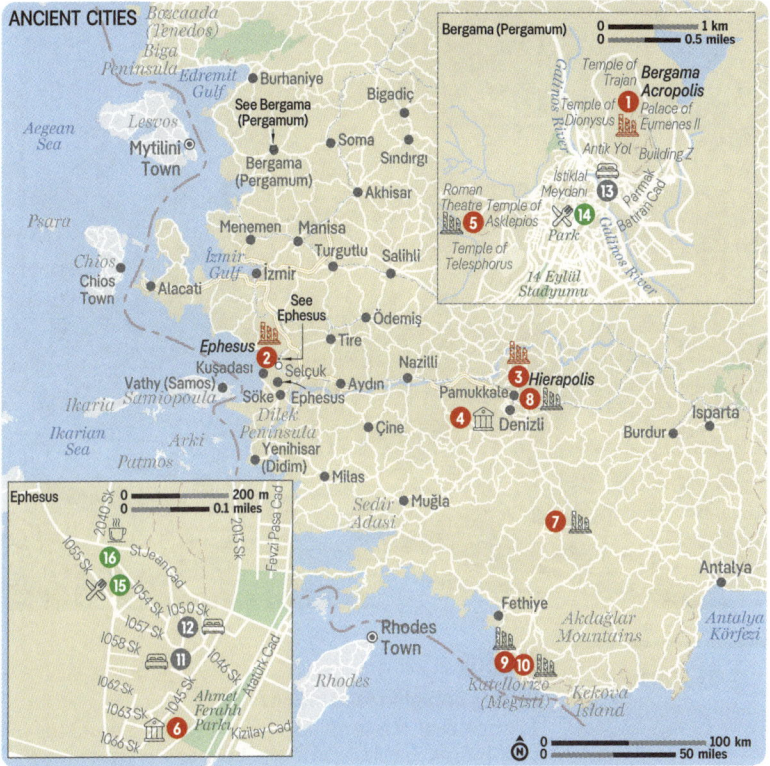

ANCIENT CITIES

⭐ **HIGHLIGHTS**
1 Bergama Acropolis
2 Ephesus
3 Hierapolis

🔴 **SIGHTS**
4 Afrodisias
5 Asklepion
6 Ephesus Museum
7 Kibyra

8 Laodicea
9 Letoön
see 2 Terraced Houses
see 3 Travertines
10 Xanthos

⚫ **SLEEPING**
11 Ayasoluk Hotel
see 3 Melrose House
12 Nilya Hotel

13 Odyssey Guesthouse
see 3 Venus Suite Hotel

🟢 **EATING**
14 Altın Kepçe Bergama Köfte
15 Kybele Gastro
see 2 Selçuk Pidecisi

🟢 **DRINKING & NIGHTLIFE**
16 Art House Cafe

☑ **TOP TIP**

Those travellers planning on visiting major museums and archaeological sites in the country should consider purchasing a **MuseumPass Türkiye E-Card** *(muze. gov.tr/MuseumPass)* which gives access to most of the major sites covered in this chapter – including the three covered in this section – and can save users a considerable amount of money.

Selçuk

History brought to life in Ephesus

Located near the pleasant tourist town of Selçuk, the impressively intact classical city of **Ephesus** *(muze.gov.tr; €40)* has extensive structures including the ornate Library of Celsus, originally commissioned in the early 2nd century CE, an agora, a steep hillside theatre and an evocative row of seven Roman-era **Terraced Houses** *(additional €15)* featuring frescoes and mosaics. A stroll down the central Curetes Way, home to the Temple of Hadrian and the Hercules Gate, is like walking two millennia back in time.

Before visiting the site, pop into the **Ephesus Museum** *(muze.gov.tr; €10)*, located in Selçuk's town centre across from the otogar. Its standout exhibits are two marble statues of Artemis dating to the 1st and 2nd century CE.

Buy your Ephesus tickets at the museum to avoid queuing at the site. Minibuses from Selçuk's otogar run regularly to and from the site's Lower Gate.

EATING & DRINKING IN BERGAMA & SELÇUK: OUR PICKS

Altın Kepçe Bergama Köfte: Restaurant popular for Bergama's famous *patlıcan çığırtması* (aubergine dish). *7am-6.30pm Mon-Sat* €

Selçuk Pidecisi: Cheerful spot for tasty pide (flatbreads with a range of toppings) near the Selçuk train station. *10am-10pm* €

Kybele Gastro: Fine dining in a beautiful Selçuk setting, with distinctive mezes and well-prepared meat dishes. *4pm-midnight Mon-Sat* €€

Art House Cafe: Colourful, rustic Selçuk joint serving coffee, tea, beer, wine and shisha. *2pm-1am*

EFIRED/SHUTTERSTOCK

Ephesus

Pamukkale

The ancient health resort of Hierapolis

Founded around 190 BCE by Eumenes II of Pergamum, the ancient spa city of **Hierapolis** *(muze.gov.tr; €30)* sits atop Pamukkale's extraordinary cascade of saucer-shaped **Travertines** (or terraced basins). Though abandoned after a devastating earthquake in 1334 CE, it retains much of the grand infrastructure built during its heyday and commands stunning views over the powder-white travertines and surrounding countryside.

The ruins are spread over a large area. Don't miss the Roman Theatre, Sanctuary of Apollo, Martyrium of St Philip the Apostle and Agora.

Most visitors enter the site via the South Gate, approximately 2.5km uphill by road from Pamukkale village. The Town (aka Lower) Gate is at the foot of the travertines. Many visitors choose to take advantage of the free transfers to the South Gate offered by pensions and hotels, and then walk down the travertines to the village.

**MORE
ANCIENT CITIES**

Those travellers with their own transport may wish to visit the sites of other ancient cities in this part of Türkiye.

Laodicea: Very close to Pamukkale, this splendid site has ruins including a nymphaeum, a temple, two theatres and a basilica.

Afrodisias: Major structures include a stadium, a temple dedicated to Aphrodite and a marble council chamber. Don't miss the magnificent on-site museum.

Kibyra: Hellenistic, Roman and Byzantine-era structures include a stadium, a theatre, a basilica, an agora, an odeon, baths and a nymphaeum.

Xanthos: Ancient Lycia's capital city, with a fine Roman theatre and agora.

Letoön: Lycian site with temples dedicated to Apollo, Artemis and Leto.

Aegean & Mediterranean Coasts

BEACHES | CRUISES | PARTYING

Places

☑ TOP TIP

If planning to sign up for a 'blue cruise', make sure the boat has easily accessible lifeboats and lifejackets, that the captain and crew have a good command of English, and that meals are included. Also ask for an itinerary and check whether the weather and sailing conditions will accommodate it.

Stretching south from the point where the Dardanelles Strait meets the Aegean Sea, this part of the country offers extraordinary landscapes, ancient sites and a diverse array of outdoor activities. Turks flock here in summer, when the string of former fishing villages along the coast heave with holidaymakers.

Sitting at the meeting point of the Aegean and Mediterranean Seas, Bodrum is the quintessential 'Turkish Riviera' hot spot. Further south, Fethiye is a major hub for the famous *mavi yolculuk* ('blue cruise'), a multi-night cruise on a *gület*. These traditional Turkish wooden yachts offer experiences ranging from basic to luxurious but have one thing in common – they give passengers an unparalleled opportunity to soak up the beauty of the famed Turquoise Coast, which stretches between Fethiye and the southern city of Antalya. This is Türkiye at its most staggeringly beautiful: an endless azure sea lined with sandy beaches and backdropped by majestic mountains.

Bodrum

Türkiye's summer playground

The main attraction in Bodrum Town is a lively waterfront lined wall-to-wall with restaurants, cafes, boutiques and bars. There's also a 15th-century **sea castle** now housing the

---

GETTING AROUND

Flights from İstanbul arrive at **İzmir Adnan Menderes**, **Milas-Bodrum** and **Dalaman airports**. Regular buses connect the İzmir and Bodrum otogars; there are fewer services between Selçuk and Bodrum. Slow dolmuşes go around the peninsula.

From Fethiye, regular dolmuşes follow the coast to Antalya, stopping at Kalkan, Kaş and the Olympos turn-off. Dolmuşes also link Patara, Kalkan, Kaputaş and Kaş. In summer, direct buses via the inland route link Fethiye and Antalya as well as Fethiye and Kaş via Kalkan.

Bodrum Underwater Archaeology Museum *(muze.gov. tr; €20).*

The best beaches on the peninsula are **Yahşi Plajı**, **Bitez Plajı**, **Kadıkalesi Halk Plajı**, **Küdür Halk Plajı** and **Akçabük Plajı**.

For a memorable evening, head to the waterfront restaurants in the former fishing village of **Gümüşlük**.

Fethiye

Sailing the Turquoise Coast

Tucked into the southern reaches of a broad bay scattered with dozens of pretty islands, the harbour town of Fethiye is known as a base for *gület* cruises, which are offered between April and October.

From Fethiye, boats usually call in at famous **Ölüdeniz beach** and stop at Kaş, Kalkan and/or the island of Kekova.

Fethiye-based cruise agencies that get consistently good reviews from readers include **Alaturka** *(alaturkacruises.com),* **V-GO Yachting** *(bluecruisesturkey.com)* and **Before Lunch Cruises** *(beforelunch.com).* Book well ahead.

Kaş & Kalkan

Float over a sunken city

The former fishing villages of Kalkan and Kaş on the Mediterranean coast are now summer resorts known for their eating and drinking scenes and their proximity to great beaches including **Patara** and **Kaputaş**.

Kaş is also known for its diving, with easily reached wrecks located relatively close to shore. Nearby, the island of **Kekova** is surrounded by the partly submerged ruins of the ancient city of Simena some 6m below the water. Known as the *batık şehir* (Sunken City), this can be explored from the water's surface in a sea-kayaking tour run by Kaş tour operators such as **Bougainville Travel** *(bougainville.com.tr),* **Dragoman** *(dragoman-turkey.com)* and **Sea Kayak Türkiye** *(seakayak turkiye.com).* Diving and swimming here are forbidden.

Olympos & Çıralı

Ghostly flames and a great beach

An important Lycian city in the 2nd century BCE, Olympos is more famous these days for being a backpacking beach resort with a party vibe. It's also home to one of the best **beaches** in the country. Nearby **Çıralı** is a holiday hamlet with dozens of family-friendly hotels and pensions. The ruins of **ancient Olympos** *(muze.gov.tr; €10)* are set inside a deep valley near Çıralı where you'll find that most enigmatic of classical icons: the eternal flame of the **Chimaera** *(Yanartaş; TL45).* The best time to visit the latter is just before dusk.

TREEHOUSE ACCOMMODATION

The word 'treehouse' that is used to describe most of the accommodation in Olympos is a misnomer, given that few – if any – huts are actually up in the trees. Most are small, rustic wooden bungalows sometimes (but not always) slightly raised off the ground. Bathrooms are generally shared, though some bungalows have en-suite rooms. Not all treehouses have reliable locks, so store valuables at reception. And a cautionary note: be extra attentive to personal hygiene while staying at Olympos. In summer, especially, the large number of visitors can stretch the camps' capacity for proper waste disposal to the limit, so be vigilant about where and what you eat.

Cappadocia & Nemrut Dağı National Park

HIKING | HOT-AIR BALLOONING | ANCIENT RUINS

GETTING AROUND

Buses travel long distances to Göreme from İstanbul via Ankara, from İzmir and from Antalya; it's possible to fly into **Nevşehir Kapadokya Airport** from İstanbul or **Kayseri Erkilet Airport** from İstanbul, İzmir and Antalya. Dolmuşes service most of Cappadocia.

The closest airport to Nemrut Dağı is **Adıyaman**. To get to the park, hire a taxi for the day from Adıyaman or Malatya, or join a tour from Kahta, 30km east of Adıyaman, Malatya or Şanlıurfa.

☑ **TOP TIP**

The summit of Nemrut Dağı can be approached from either Adıyaman in the south or Malatya in the north. However, the route from Adıyaman includes numerous other ancient sites, making this the preferred option.

Cappadocia is famed for its strange towering rock formations known as fairy chimneys. Dotting the region's unique terrain, these were formed up to 12 million years ago by volcanic eruptions flinging ash across the landscape and are best viewed while enjoying the region's signature experience – a hot-air-balloon ride at sunrise. On the ground, rock-hewn churches covered in Byzantine frescoes are secreted into cliffs, villages are honeycombed out of hillsides and vast subterranean complexes where early Christians once hid are tunnelled under the ground.

Equally extraordinary is the landscape of Nemrut Dağı National Park in the country's southeast, where 2000 years ago a megalomaniac Commagene king erected his own memorial sanctuary on Nemrut Dağı (Mt Nemrut; 2150m). The fallen heads of the gigantic decorative statues of gods and kings that are found here are one of Türkiye's most remarkable sights.

Among the Fairy Chimneys

Cappadocia's iconic landscape

While there are a number of attractive villages and towns across Cappadocia that can be used as a base when exploring the region, the majority of travellers are drawn to the village of Göreme. This is where most of the balloon operators are based and where hikers can spend days exploring the spectacular nearby **Pigeon**, **Zemi**, **Red** and **Rose** valleys. The village is also blessed with a stunning array of boutique hotels, many of which have been converted from traditional cave dwellings.

The other ace up Göreme's sleeve is its **Open-Air Museum** (*muze.gov.tr; €20*), a collection of ancient rock-hewn churches on the edge of town, some of them featuring astoundingly colourful Byzantine-era frescoes. This is an astonishing site, only rivalled in Cappadocia by the area's two fascinating underground cities: **Derinkuyu** (*muze.gov.tr; €13*) and **Kaymaklı** (*muze.gov.tr; €13*).

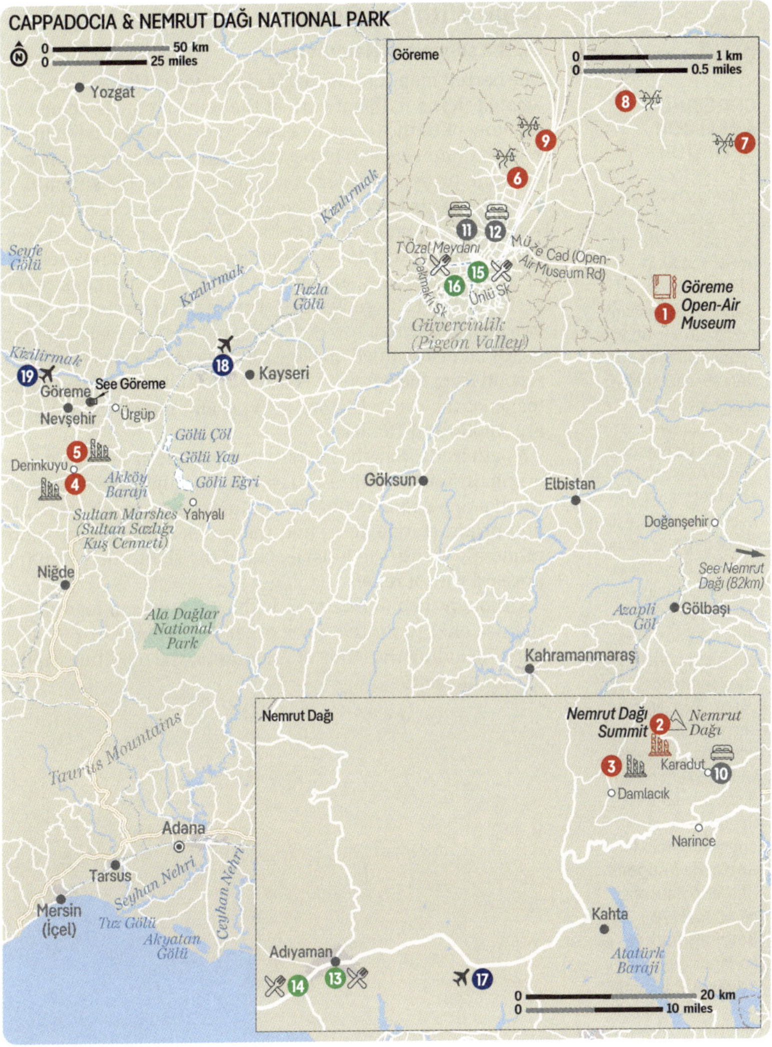

CAPPADOCIA & NEMRUT DAĞı NATIONAL PARK

Göreme

Yozgat

Seufe Gölü

Kızılırmak

Kızılırmak

Tuzla Gölü

Kızılırmak

Kayseri

Göreme
See Göreme
Nevşehir Ürgüp

Derinkuyu

Akköy Barajı

Gölü Çöl
Gölü Yay
Gölü Egri

Sultan Marshes
(Sultan Sazlığı
Kuş Cenneti) Yahyalı

Göksun

Elbistan

Doğanşehir

Niğde

Ala Dağlar
National
Park

Azapli
Göl Gölbaşı

See Nemrut
Dağı (82km)

Kahramanmaraş

Nemrut Dağı

**Nemrut Dağı
Summit** Nemrut
Dağı

Karadut

Damlacık

Taurus Mountains

Adana

Narince

Tarsus

Mersin
(İçel) Tuz Gölü Akyatan
Gölü

Seyhan Nehri

Ceyhan Nehri

Kahta

Atatürk
Barajı

Adıyaman

Göreme

T Özal Meydanı

Müze Cad (Open-
Air Museum Rd)

Çakmak Sk

Ünlü Sk

Güvercinlik
(Pigeon Valley)

**Göreme
Open-Air
Museum**

⭐ **HIGHLIGHTS**
1 Göreme Open-Air Museum
2 Nemrut Dağı Summit

🔴 **SIGHTS**
3 Arsameia
4 Derinkuyu Underground City
5 Kaymaklı Underground City

6 Pigeon Valley
7 Red Valley
8 Rose Valley
9 Zemi Valley

⚫ **SLEEPING**
10 Işık Pansiyon
11 Kismet
12 Köse Hostel

🟢 **EATING**
13 Adıyaman Kebap Salonu
14 Alim Sofrası
15 Fat Boys
16 Retro

🔵 **TRANSPORT**
17 Adıyaman Airport
18 Kayseri Erkilet Airport
19 Nevşehir Kapadokya Airport

CHOOSING A BALLOON OPERATOR

Not unexpectedly, there are a lot of companies offering hot-air-balloon trips in and around Göreme. This means that it pays to do your research and check they're reputable. Some low-cost operators have minimal insurance, or will take safety shortcuts and may overfill baskets, which is not only unsafe but also impairs views. You can usually arrange flights through your hotel, but it's generally cheaper to book with companies directly, and this ensures you'll be able to use whichever company you consider best. Recommended operators include **Butterfly Balloons** *(butterflyballoons. com)*, **Turkiye Balloons** *(turkiye balloons.com)* and **Voyager Balloons** *(voyagerballoons. com)*.

Walk With the Gods
On the summit of Nemrüt Dağı

The barren mountaintop of **Nemrüt Dağı** *(Mt Nemrut; €10)*, located in the national park of the same name, is home to a monument to the towering ego of Antiochus, the 1st-century king of Commagene. The best times to visit are in spring and autumn; bring a sweater as it can be cold on the summit.

From the visitor centre, head to the upper car park, then walk the path up to the summit, taking the right-hand fork. After a pretty stiff 15- to 20-minute climb, you'll reach the base of the tumulus, and after a further few minutes, you'll arrive at the Eastern Terrace. This is the more intact of the two terraces, with a row of decapitated statues, their 2m-high heads all neatly lined up beneath them. Antiochus himself is second from the left, between an eagle and the goddess Commagene; the central figure is Zeus, and the other two gods are Apollo and Heracles.

A path leads from the Eastern to the Western Terrace, which originally mirrored the Eastern, but has suffered from greater earthquake damage over the centuries: as a result there are no upright statues here, and the heads are scattered more randomly across the hillside. Off to the right, there's an impressive row of reliefs.

Although the mountaintop is the main reason for visiting the national park, there are other ancient sites to explore here, including the ruins of **Arsameia**, the one-time capital of Commagene.

 EATING & DRINKING IN ADIYAMAN & GÖREME: OUR PICKS

Alim Sofrası: A no-frills but excellent Adıyaman kebap joint in the university district on the west side of town. *11am-11pm* €

Adıyaman Kebap Salonu: The name says it all. Good kebaps, too – the Adana kebab really doesn't hold back on the heat. *8.30am-8pm Mon-Sat* €

Fat Boys: This perennially popular place in Göreme has a good menu of tasty Turkish dishes and a well-stocked bar. *8am-midnight* €€

Retro: A friendly family-run place, with great views over Göreme from the terrace. *11am-11pm Mon-Sat* €€

Places We Love to Stay

€ Budget   €€ Midrange   €€€ Top End

İstanbul   MAP p311

Old City

Cheers € Excellent central location, a rooftop bar with panoramic view, and air-conditioned dorms and rooms.

Second Home Hostel € Friendly place in Hocapaşa near Eminönü. Basic dorms, entertainment programme and popular home-style dinners.

Marmara Guesthouse €€ Family-run pension offering a warm welcome, comfortable rooms, a rooftop terrace and delicious breakfast.

Beyoğlu

Archeo € Well-run hostel in supremely convenient Tophane. The ground-floor cafe is a popular hangout.

Hostel Le Banc € Galata hostel with a small roof terrace. Air-conditioned dorms have their own bathrooms, as do the private rooms.

Hamamhane €€ Well-run Çukurcuma hotel with rooms, studios and suites in two buildings.

Gallipoli Peninsula & Troy   MAP p317

Eceabat

TJ's Hotel €€ Close to the ferry port, with clean rooms.

Hotel Crowded House €€ Also near the ferry port. Rooms are clean and spacious.

Çanakkale

Büyük Truva Hotel €€ Clean and comfortable hotel with sea views.

Grand Anzac Hotel €€ Very close to the clock tower, with exceptionally clean and large rooms.

Ancient Cities   MAP p321

Bergama

Odyssey Guesthouse € There are superb views of the archaeological sites from the terrace of this friendly and well-run pension.

Selçuk

Nilya Hotel € Quaint, family-run accommodation with Ottoman-style decorations in a garden setting.

Ayasoluk Hotel €€ Serene, stylish lodgings with a fine restaurant (open to outside guests) and a pool.

Pamukkale

Venus Suite Hotel €€ Attractive rooms, free parking and a poolside restaurant are the draws at this excellent choice.

Melrose House €€ Guests here inevitably comment on the generous and tasty breakfasts. Facilities include a restaurant and a swimming pool.

Aegean & Mediterranean Coasts

Bodrum

Asmin Otel € Cheerful, small hotel with a pool near the main Bodrum bus station.

Merih Butik Hotel €€ Operated by a friendly and helpful Turkish-Australian couple, this delightful small guesthouse has comfortable rooms and a lovely courtyard.

Fethiye

El Camino Pub & Hostel € A fun, well-run hillside hostel with private rooms and four-bed dorms.

Orka Boutique Hotel €€ The 22 very central rooms here have swish contemporary styling; the choicest have small seafront balconies.

Kaş & Kalkan

Caretta Hotel €€ Cliffside hotel in Kalkan that's a perennial favourite for its swimming platforms and bright rooms with terraces.

Hideaway Hotel €€ Welcoming Kaş hotel with 23 large, airy rooms (most with balconies) and a roof terrace.

Olympos & Çıralı

Bayrams € Large Olympos operation with a lively bar and accommodation in small wooden cabins linked by narrow paths.

Hotel Canada €€ This beautiful place in Çıralı has 26 rooms in the main house as well as gardens filled with hammocks and bungalows.

Cappadocia & Nemrut Dağı National Park   MAP p327

Göreme

Köse Hostel € This friendly, clean and centrally located hostel is a genuine bargain in a generally pricey town.

Kismet €€ Kismet's cave rooms are gorgeous and traditionally decorated, and the owner Faruk is hugely friendly and helpful.

Nemrut Dağı

Işık Pansiyon € On the slopes of Nemrut Dağı, providing friendly and comfortable accommodation and delicious meals. Can pick you up from Adıyaman or Kahta.

Practicalities

Visas

Although visas are not necessary for citizens of some countries (including the UK, the USA, New Zealand and many European nations), many others must obtain a visa before entering Türkiye. Check whether this is necessary at *mfa.gov.tr*. If you do need a visa, organise this electronically at *evisa.gov.tr*.

NURTEN ERDAL/SHUTTERSTOCK

Health

Türkiye has an extensive healthcare system. It's possible to receive services from public and private hospitals for a fee. Hospitals are available 24/7.

Public Holidays
New Year's Day 1 January
National Sovereignty & Children's Day 23 April
Labor & Solidarity Day 1 May
Commemoration of Atatürk, Youth & Sports Day 19 May

Democracy & National Unity Day 15 July
Victory Day 30 August
Republic Day 29 October
The dates of the major religious holidays of Ramazan, Şeker Bayramı and Kurban Bayramı vary according to the lunar calendar.

Smoking

Smoking is prohibited on public transport and in enclosed public spaces, including restaurants, cafes and shopping malls. Vaping is not illegal, but the sale or trade of vapes is.

LGBTIQ+ Travellers

Homosexuality isn't a criminal offence in Türkiye and people are legally permitted to change gender, but there are no laws protecting LGBTIQ+ people from discrimination, and violence towards them has been recorded, same-sex marriage isn't recognised and the dating app Grindr is banned. That said, same-sex couples will have no problem booking a double room in the major cities and tourism destinations.

Tap Water

Tap water is safe to drink, although it is heavily chlorinated; many locals prefer to drink bottled water.

Safe Travel

- Be aware of pickpockets on public transport and in bazaars.
- Female travellers, especially those travelling solo, should be on the lookout for possible drink spiking.
- Don't use or carry illegal drugs; penalties for drug offences include long prison sentences.
- Some dogs carry the potentially fatal rabies virus; if bitten, seek immediate medical attention.

Language

Turkish belongs to the Ural-Altaic language family. It's the official language of Türkiye and Northern Cyprus, and has more than 80 million speakers worldwide.

Basics

Hello. Merhaba. *mer*·ha·ba
Goodbye. Hoşçakal. hosh·*cha*·kal
Yes. Evet. e·*vet*
No. Hayır. *ha*·yuhr
Excuse me. Bakar mısınız. ba·*kar* muh·suh·*nuhz*
Sorry. Özür dilerim. er·*zewr* dee·*le*·reem
Please. Lütfen. *lewt*·fen
Thank you. Teşekkür ederim. te·shek·*kewr* e·de·reem
You're welcome. Bir şey değil. beer·*shay* de·eel
How are you? Nasılsınız? na·suhl·suh·nuhz
Fine, and you? İyiyim, ya siz? ee·*yee*·yeem ya seez
What's your name? Adınız nedir? a·duh·*nuhz* ne·deer
My name is ... Benim adım ... be·*neem* a·*duhm* ...
Do you speak English? İngilizce konuşuyor musunuz? een·gee·*leez*·je ko·noo·*shoo*·yor moo·soo·*nooz*
I understand. Anlıyorum. an·*luh*·yo·room
I don't understand. Anlamıyorum. an·*la*·muh·yo·room

Directions

Where is ...? ... nerede? ... *ne*·re·de
What's the address? Adresi nedir? ad·re·*see* ne·deer
Could you write it down, please? Lütfen yazar mısınız? *lewt*·fen ya·*zar* muh·suh·*nuhz*

Can you show me (on the map)? Bana (haritada) gösterebilir misiniz? ba·*na* (ha·ree·ta·*da*) gers·te·*re*·bee·leer mee·seen·*neez*
It's straight ahead. Tam karşıda. tam kar·shuh·*da*
at the traffic lights trafik ışıklarından tra·*feek* uh·shuhk·la·ruhn·*dan*

Signs

Açık Open
Bay Male
Bayan Female
Çıkış Exit
Giriş Entrance
Kapalı Closed
Sigara İçilmez No Smoking
Tuvaletler Toilets
Yasak Prohibited

Emergencies

Help! İmdat! *eem*·dat
I'm lost. Kayboldum. kai·bol·*doom*
Leave me alone! Git başımdan! *geet* ba·shuhm·*dan*
Call a doctor! Doktor çağırın! dok·*tor* cha·*uh*·ruhn
Call the police! Polis çağırın! po·*lees* cha·*uh*·ruhn
I'm ill. Hastayım. has·*ta*·yuhm
I'm allergic to (nuts). (Çerezlere) alerjim var. (che·rez·le·*re*) a·ler·*zheem* var

NUMBERS

1
bir beer

2
iki ee·*kee*

3
üç ewch

4
dört dert

5
beş besh

6
altı al·*tuh*

7
yedi ye·*dee*

8
sekiz se·*keez*

9
dokuz do·*kooz*

10
on on

FROM LEFT: DENIS BELITSKY/SHUTTERSTOCK. PRIMAKOV/SHUTTERSTOCK

Marmaris

Arriving

Most travellers arrive by air or boat. Türkiye has land borders with multiple countries but only the borders with Greece, Bulgaria and Georgia are easy to cross. The status of other land borders varies; check before using them. Note that foreign governments currently advise against travel to Iran, Iraq and Syria.

By Air
There are direct or connecting flights from many countries of the world to Türkiye's larger airports, including İstanbul, İstanbul Sabiha Gökçen, İzmir Adnan Menderes and Antalya.

By Boat
Ferry services operate from Greek islands (Chios, Kos, Kalymnos, Lesvos, Kastellorizo, Rhodes, Samos, Symi) and Northern Cyprus (Gazimağusa and Girne) to Türkiye (Ayvalık, Bodrum, Çeşme, Kaş, Kuşadası, Marmaris, Mersin, Taşucu); they are more frequent in summer.

MONEY

Currency:
Türk lirası (TL or ₺)

CREDIT CARDS
Since credit-card usage is very high all over the country, almost all restaurants, hotels and shopping points accept credit cards without any extra commission. ATMs belonging to different banks are found at airport arrival halls and across the country, from small towns to big cities.

EXCHANGING MONEY
The euro and US dollar are most easily converted into Turkish lira. Exchange your foreign currencies at a *döviz bürosu* (exchange office), which provides better rates and faster transactions than banks. Exchange offices usually don't charge commission; the offices in city areas usually offer better rates than those at the airports.

TIPPING
In some restaurants, *servis ücreti* (service charge), an additional fee of approximately 10%, is charged. If this doesn't apply, tipping is left to the customer's discretion.

Getting Around

Travelling within Türkiye is generally comfortable. Intercity and regional trains are less commonly used, although a high-speed train (YHT) currently operates between İstanbul, Eskişehir, İzmir, Ankara, Konya and Sivas. Buy tickets from train stations or the TCDD (bilet.tcdd.gov.tr) website and app.

Transport Cards
The big cities have efficient modern transport systems that can include tram, bus and metro. Rechargeable transport cards are necessary in cities including İstanbul (İstanbulkart; pictured), İzmir (İzmirim Kart) and Antalya (AntalyaKart). These are generally available at ticket machines in airports and metro stations.

ONAPALMTREE/SHUTTERSTOCK

Taxi/Rideshare
Ridesharing services including Uber, BiTaksi and iTaksi are available in İstanbul, and Uber also services most large cities. Travellers are less likely to encounter problems with overcharging if they opt for a rideshare rather than a taxi.

Hiring a Car
Global car-rental companies have offices in airports and city centres. Renters must have a valid driver's license and credit card. Car-rental companies generally ask for drivers to be at least 21 years old.

Road Conditions
In addition to the wide and high-quality intercity roads, there are also highways starting from the country's northwest and moving towards the west and south. Urban and town roads are mostly asphalt. There may be difficulties on the roads during the winter months due to heavy snowfall and rain.

Unwritten Rules of Traffic
Violating traffic rules and speed limits is common among locals, so be careful and avoid driving at night. Stay alert, as radar speed checks are frequent on intercity roads. Downtown car parks managed by municipalities, shopping malls and private companies are the best options for safe parking.

DRIVING ESSENTIALS

Drive on the right

130

Speed limit is 130km/h on major highways, 110km/h on smaller highways and 50km/h in built-up areas

0.05

Blood alcohol concentration limit is 0.05%

TOOLKIT

The chapters in this section cover the most important topics you'll need to know about in Mediterranean Europe. They're full of nuts-and-bolts information and valuable insights to help you understand and navigate Mediterranean Europe and get the most out of your trip.

Getting Around the Region
p336

Accommodation
p338

Family Travel
p340

Health & Safe Travel
p342

Nuts & Bolts
p344

Food, Drink & Nightlife
p346

Responsible Travel
p348

LGBTIQ+ Travellers
p350

Accessible Travel
p351

At the Beach
p352

Tram, Beyoğlu, İstanbul (p310), Türkiye
GIOIA PHOTO/SHUTTERSTOCK

Getting Around the Region

Travellers are spoiled for choice when travelling in the Mediterranean region, as cross-border train, ferry and bus services are generally frequent, comfortable and efficient. Public transport within countries varies wildly but is generally good between cities and large towns.

TRAVEL COSTS

Car rental
per day from €30

Petrol
per litre approx
€1.55

Train
Paris–Barcelona/
Paris–Rome from
€49/110

Metro ticket
TL27 (İstanbul) –
€2.50 (Paris)

Ferry

Ferries link mainland Spain with Italy. To travel from Spain to France, passengers must transit via the Balearic Islands. Ferries also link Toulon in France with Sardinia and Livorno in Italy. Greece is easily accessed from Italy, and it's possible to island hop between Greece and Türkiye. Many services are cancelled in winter due to adverse weather conditions.

Trains

Trains offer the most efficient, comfortable and enjoyable way to travel through Europe, with the train systems in Spain, France and Italy being particularly impressive. There are far fewer train services in Greece and Türkiye. One of the world's great rail journeys, Paris to İstanbul, still follows the original Orient Express route; see Lonely Planet's *Journey: Orient Express* book for details. If you're covering lots of ground, consider purchasing a rail pass.

Car

Travelling by car offers flexibility and can be the only way to reach remote places. That said, petrol (gas) is expensive in Europe and traffic jams and parking issues are common in cities. There are documentation and insurance requirements involved when taking a car over the border into Türkiye.

Air

Airfares can be expensive in high season (mid-June to early September, Easter, Christmas and school holidays). Airports are often located a considerable distance from city centres.

DRIVING ESSENTIALS

Drive on the right

Speed limits are typically 50km/h in cities and up to 130km/h on motorways

Vehicle occupants must wear seatbelts

Tip

Travelling by train? Mark Smith's Man in Seat Sixty-One *(seat61.com)* is an invaluable resource, as are Andy Brabin's discoverbyrail.com and the Spanish *(renfe.com),* French *(sncf-connect.com)* and Italian *(trenitalia.com)* national railway sites.

Bicycle

It is possible to take bicycles on most long-distance trains in Europe as carry-on luggage free of charge if the bike is in a zip-up bike bag, with wheels and pedals removed and handlebars turned. Some train services have baggage cars where bikes can be carried for a fee.

Ferry Bookings & Travel

It's always a good idea to book ferry tickets in advance of your journey. Routes, schedules and fares can be researched at ferryscanner.com and directferries.co.uk. Those travellers who have Interrail Passes have access to many free and discounted European ferry routes and boats. Check interrail.eu for a list of relevant ferry companies. Note that in high summer, there may be more passengers aboard the ferry than there are seats.

Visas & Border Crossings

The newly instigated EU Entry System (travel-europe.europa.eu) means that all non-EU nationals must be registered when travelling in or out of the Schengen area (most of Europe). This includes having fingerprints and photograph taken on entry; there is no need to do anything ahead of time.

In late 2026, the EU is introducing a new visa-waiver scheme called ETIAS *(travel-europe.europa .eu/en/etias)*. Under this scheme, 30 European countries will require visa-exempt travellers to have an ETIAS travel authorisation. This involves citizens of 56 countries including the UK, USA, Canada and Australia. These travellers will have to fill in an online application and pay €20 (free for those under 18 or over 70, or for family members of EU citizens). The authorization will be valid for three years. Visitors may stay in the Schengen zone for no more than 90 days in every 180 days.

In Türkiye, visa requirements and costs vary according to the nationality of travellers. See dtvgroup.com.tr.

There are officially no passport controls at the borders between 29 Schengen countries, including Spain, France, Italy and Greece. If travelling across borders by train or bus, travellers may need to show their passports or ID documents. Some travellers wishing to enter Türkiye require a visa; these must be organised in advance, as they are not available at land borders or on ferries.

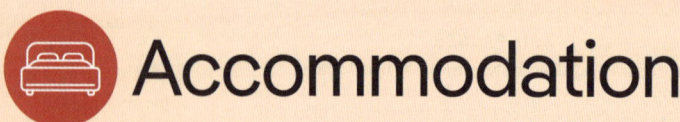

Accommodation

Sourcing tempting accommodation in Mediterranean Europe is easy – the difficulty lies in choosing between the innumerable options on offer in each price category. Basing your choice on a balance of budget, location and levels of comfort is the best formula.

Hostels

There are plenty of hostels offering budget accommodation in cities, but far fewer options in smaller towns. Private hostel rooms with ensuite facilities are increasingly on offer, meeting the demand of solo travellers and couples who want privacy and comfort but who enjoy the social aspects of hostel stays (organised activities, communal bars and kitchens etc). Dorms often have an attached bathroom and privacy screen or curtain around beds. Check hostelworld.com for options.

B&Bs/Pensions

Guesthouses and B&Bs (*pensión, pensione, chambre d'hôte, pansiyon*) offer greater comfort than hostels for a marginally higher price. Most are simple affairs, sometimes with shared bathrooms. The line between a guesthouse and a boutique hotel can sometimes be blurred, with the main difference being the decor, amenities and services on offer.

Hotels

Hotels in Europe come in innumerable shapes, sizes and styles – there are multiple options in every budget category to choose from. Be warned that the cheapest options are often located in less-than-salubrious areas around bus and train stations. Top-end boutique and design hotels proliferate and are tempting options for a splurge. Look out for atmospheric options set in castles, monasteries, palaces or other repurposed buildings.

Camping

Camping in Europe is popular. Most campsites are some distance from city centres. See Pitchup (*pitchup.com*) and ACSI Eurocampings

Making Bookings

During peak holiday periods, particularly Easter, summer and Christmas – and year-round in major cities – it's wise to book well in advance on hotel websites or accommodation booking platforms to ensure availability and the best price.

Sourcing Bargains

Top-end and business hotels in cities are often cheaper on weekends. Rates can plummet in low season (sometimes more than 50%). Remember, though – low seasons are tied to location, not necessarily to the time of year.

AGRITOURISM

Agritourism (the farmstay experience) is growing in popularity in Europe, particularly in the family-travel market. Some farmstays offer basic budget accommodation on working farms, others can be upmarket options in elegant countryside villas surrounded by farmland. Many farmstays have swimming pools and most offer self-catering facilities. Others have in-house restaurants or offer rustic meals in the host's kitchen. Italy's network of *agriturismi* is particularly impressive, offering numerous options in every region and budget category. Italian *agriturismi* are also carefully overseen by the state – participating farms must grow at least one of their own crops. See agriturismo. it. French options can be sourced via accueil-paysan. com and bienvenue-a-la-ferme.com, agroturismoespana. com lists Spanish options, and farmstayplanet.com has a few options in Greece and Türkiye.

(*eurocampings.co.uk*) for details on prime campsites. In busy areas and high seasons, it's advisable to book ahead, especially near the coast.

The Apartment Conundrum

It can be tempting to opt for apartment accommodation, especially when travelling in a large group or as a family, but before making this decision think about the impact this decision may have on local communities. In cities such as Barcelona, Florence, Paris and Venice, the impact that companies such as Airbnb has had on housing availability and affordability has been enormous, pricing many locals out of their neighbourhoods. When this happens, the essential trappings of local life (shops, services, community facilities) can be compromised, leaving formerly vibrant neighbourhoods lifeless shadows of their former selves.

Rooms with Character

Finding a memorable place to stay won't be difficult. But here, there's also the opportunity for a once-in-a-lifetime stay in a unique property. How does a cave room in a troglodyte village sound? Or a breezy treehouse on the beachfront? It's possible to stay in the converted kennels of a royal chateau, in a luxurious 16th-century palazzo on the Grand Canal in Venice or in one of Spain's renowned paradors (luxury hotels in historic buildings). And that's on top of options in lovingly converted palaces, monasteries, castles, convents, factories, schools and towers.

HOW MUCH FOR A NIGHT IN A...

Hostel dorm bed
€15–40

Farmstay
€100–120

Campsite including tent
€15–30

Boutique hotel
from €100

Breakfasts

When booking hotel rooms, check whether breakfast is included in the room rate. Breakfast is often included when staying in guesthouses/ pensions but can carry a hefty extra charge in top-end hotels. What breakfast dishes are on offer differs widely, too. Many travellers rate the breakfasts in Türkiye (pictured), which are almost always included in the room rate, as the best in the region.

Wild Camping

It's not possible to head off into the wilds and camp wherever you please in this part of Europe, as camping is usually illegal without the permission of the local authorities or landowners. Some hikers risk pitching their tents and get away with it, but this isn't recommended. France and Italy allow free one-night bivouac on popular hiking routes.

SUSTAINABLE CHOICES

To tread lightly when travelling, keep your eyes peeled for the EU Ecolabel (*europa. eu*) and Green Key (*greenkey.global*) logos, which mean the accommodation meets specific sustainable criteria, from renewable energy to waste management, water saving and recycling measures. Some will provide bicycles for guest use and offer an incentive or discount for guests arriving by public transport.

As a rule of thumb, camping and glamping sites, farmstays and mountain huts (of which the Alps has a vast network) tend to score highly when it comes to sustainability. An increasing number of hotels and B&Bs are also upping their green credentials.

Family Travel

This is a part of the world where the term 'family friendly' really does apply. There are outdoor activities aplenty, many cultural institutions have facilities and programs for youngsters and the food is sure to be a big hit (Pizza! Pasta! Ice cream!).

Atittudes

Few places exclude children, and it's not uncommon to see infants and older children dining with their families in restaurants late into the night, or attending festivals or cultural events at any time of the day. Those travelling with children are likely to get an even warmer welcome from locals – a love for family is, after all, one of the major features of the Mediterranean character.

Equipment

Nappies (diapers) and baby wipes are widely available; baby-changing facilities vary from country to country. Baby food is easily sourced in supermarkets and formula can be purchased in supermarkets or drugstores. However, brands differ – you might want to bring your own stash as backup.

Many old towns have cobbled streets, making it difficult to use strollers – consider using a baby backpack instead. Most hotels can offer cots and highchairs are common in restaurants.

Breastfeeding

Breastfeeding in public is relatively uncommon in Europe, and is totally frowned upon in Türkiye.

BEST ATTRACTIONS FOR FAMILIES

Chocolatería de San Ginés, Madrid
Feast on chocolate and churros in a historic cafe. (p245)

Jardin du Luxembourg, Paris
Ride Paris' oldest merry-go-round and sail toy boats (pictured) on the pond. (p54)

Burano, Venice
Take a *vaporetto* (water bus) ride across the Venetian lagoon. (p200)

Tomb of the Unknown Soldier, Athens
Watch the famous changing of the guard – Sunday morning is the best time. (p127)

İstanbul Ferry Trips
Board a ferry for a trip up the Bosphorus or Golden Horn. (p315)

FAMILY TRAVEL ON A BUDGET

Saving money starts with picking the right accommodation. Many hostels and budget hotels have at least one family room.

Enjoying street food in urban areas and picnics in the country and on the coast are great ways to economise.

Look out for free local guest cards, many offer excellent savings.

Kids under 12 (sometimes 18) often get free or reduced entry to sights and attractions such as museums. Dedicated family tickets save money, too.

Children aged under seven often travel free on public transport and can sometimes join tours at no charge when attending with parents.

TOP: FABIANODP/SHUTTERSTOCK, BOTTOM: IMGORTHAND/GETTY IMAGES

Every parent knows how stressful museum visits with young children can be, with bored children unimpressed by masterpieces that their parents have always wanted to see. Acknowledging this, museums such as the Galleria degli Uffizi (p203) in Florence have introduced children's discovery trails (ask at the information desk if this is an option) and other institutions, including the Louvre (p56) in Paris, offer dedicated creative spaces for young visitors.

Outdoor Activities

Families keen on outdoor activities have plenty of options. Many destinations have well-marked and family-friendly hiking and cycling trails, some of which are accessible to strollers and prams. Most tourist offices can point out family-friendly hikes, including wildlife-spotting trails and coastal paths leading to hidden beaches. These offices can also advise about age-appropriate activities for adventurous kids, be it surfing lessons, kayaking, rock climbing or white-water rafting. In winter, the Alps are winter wonderlands, with resorts offering ski lessons for children (generally aged four and up), plus slope-side magic from snowshoeing to tobogganing and dogsledding. In summer, attention shifts to the coast and lakes, with swimming and boating the main attractions.

Tip

When exploring historic towns or neighbourhoods, playing spot the gargoyle (or minaret, coat of arms etc) can keep little ones engaged.

City Activities

Lots of cities and towns across Europe have parks with areas where young kids can run and play, and where older children can play ball games. In Paris, children aged 10 and over can swim at three designated spots in the Seine in July and August.

Transport

Rental-car companies can arrange child and booster seats, which are obligatory for small children. Trams, trains, ferries and metros are usually accessible for buggies and prams. Children under six or seven often travel free on public transport, or half-price until 15 years (proof of age may be required).

AT THE BEACH

Many beaches don't have lifeguards on patrol, so always be vigilant. To identify beaches with sand where children can play, check Blue Flag (blueflag. global).

KID-FRIENDLY FOOD

Your children will enjoy eating here. After all, this is the home of many of the world's most kid-friendly foods. Pizza or its local version (eg, pide and lahmacun in Türkiye) is widely available, sold by the full pie or by the slice. Pasta is equally ubiquitous, and ordering it with a simple tomato or meat sauce is common. French fries or thicker chips are staples and meatballs are common, especially in Greece (where they are called keftedákia) and in Türkiye (köfte). Fried fish and calamari are available across the region, as are favourites such as roast chicken. Parents in need of an occasional sweet bribe can try doughnuts – Spain's churros con chocolate and Greece's loukoumades are bound to do the trick. And finally, be it called gelato (Italy), glace (France), helado (Spain), pagotó (Greece) or dondurma (Türkiye), ice cream is loved by locals young and old.

Health & Safe Travel

Comprehensive health care, political stability and relatively low crime rates make these Mediterranean countries safe places to travel. The usual common-sense rules apply: possess good travel insurance, avoid unnecessary risks and safeguard cash and valuables.

TAP WATER

Tap water is generally safe to drink. The water tastes fine in Spain, France and Italy, but is heavily chlorinated and can taste unpleasant in Greece and Türkiye. As a result, many locals drink bottled water. Don't drink water from rivers or lakes, as it may contain bacteria or viruses.

Some countries have free water fountains in public areas, so bringing a water bottle is a good idea.

Health Insurance & Agreements

Adequate travel insurance is essential. Make sure that your policy includes comprehensive health insurance including medical care and emergency evacuation. If you're planning to engage in adventure sports (white-water rafting, paragliding, rock climbing, surfing, off-piste skiing and the like), you may need to pay for extra cover. Check the small print.

If you're an EU citizen or a citizen of Iceland, Liechtenstein, Norway, Switzerland or the UK, the free EHIC (European Health Insurance Card) covers you for free or cost-reduced medically necessary, state-provided health care during a temporary stay in Spain, France, Italy and Greece under the same conditions and at the same cost (free in some cases) as for people insured in those countries. You can obtain the EHIC card by contacting your national health insurance institution before travelling. Note that the card does not replace travel insurance – it does not cover medical repatriation or any private medical consultations or treatments, nor does it work in Türkiye.

Non-EU citizens should check whether there is a reciprocal arrangement for free medical care between their country and the EU country they are visiting. This covers emergency care and care for an illness or injury that can't wait till you get home. Australian citizens, for instance, receive free public health care in Italy.

Vaccinations

The World Health Organization (WHO) recommends that all travellers be immunised against diphtheria, chicken pox, tetanus, pertussis (whooping cough), measles, mumps, rubella, polio, flu and COVID 19 regardless of their destination. Those travellers heading to Türkiye should be immunised against hepatitis A and B; if travelling in rural areas in Türkiye, typhoid vaccination is also recommended. Since most vaccines don't produce immunity until at least two weeks after they're given, visit a physician at least six weeks before departure.

MD Travel Health (mdtravelhealth.com) provides up-to-date travel-health recommendations for every country.

WASPS & MOSQUITOES

Wasps can be pesky in midsummer but are only dangerous to those with an allergy. Mosquitoes can be a nuisance around rivers and lakes. Bring repellent.

Scams

Most scams involve distracting the victim – someone asking for directions or spilling something on you – while another person steals your wallet. Be alert in such situations.

Be careful if strangers invite you to join them in a bar or club, as this has been known to end with travellers being left to pay large bar tabs or being subjected to violent extortion.

Be wary if someone offers to carry your luggage. This may be legitimate, but could be the prelude to a bag- or suitcase-snatch.

Overcharging and short-changing by taxi drivers is endemic in Greece and Türkiye. Consider using ride-share applications such as Uber instead; some of these rides double as taxis, but agreeing to a set fare before the ride protects the passenger.

Safety Outdoors

Every year people die from landslides and avalanches in the Alps. Always check weather conditions before heading out; consider hiring a guide when skiing off-piste. Before going on challenging hikes, ensure you have the proper equipment and fitness level. Inform someone at your hotel/guesthouse where you're going and when you intend to return.

Rabies

Rabies is present in Türkiye. It's carried by animals, including stray dogs. Travellers spending a lot of time outdoors or who engage in activities that might bring them into direct contact with bats (eg, caving) should be vaccinated before arrival. If bitten when unvaccinated, seek urgent medical attention.

BRAVING THE ELEMENTS

Exposure to the elements, especially the hot Mediterranean sun, can be a problem. Summers can be extremely hot, with temperatures soaring up to 40°C. Seek shade from the midday sun, drink plenty of water, wear sun block and sunglasses, and avoid over-exertion, particularly in the middle of the day. At the other extreme, winters can be cold in the Alps. Wear appropriate thermal clothing, check forecasts before planning activities and ideally go with a guide.

RULES TO TRAVEL BY

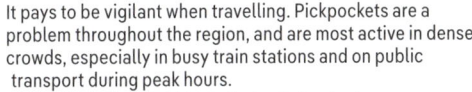

It pays to be vigilant when travelling. Pickpockets are a problem throughout the region, and are most active in dense crowds, especially in busy train stations and on public transport during peak hours.

Don't store valuables in train-station lockers or luggage-storage counters, and don't leave valuables in your car, on train seats or in your room. When out, don't flaunt cameras, laptops or other expensive electronic goods.

Consider using small zipper locks on daypacks. A money belt with your essentials (passport, cash, credit cards, airline tickets) is a good idea. Carry a wallet with a day's worth of cash so you needn't delve into your money belt in public.

Record your passport number and issue date or, even better, copy the relevant data pages. If you lose your passport, notify the police immediately and contact your nearest consulate.

Don't use or carry illegal drugs in Türkiye – penalties for drug offences include long sentences in harsh prisons. Greece also has a strict attitude toward drug possession.

Nuts & Bolts

Time

These countries are in one of two time zones:

Central European Time (CET; Spain, France, Italy) Coordinated Universal Time (UTC) plus one hour (UTC plus two hours in summer)

Eastern European Time (EET; Greece & Türkiye) UTC plus two hours (UTC plus three hours in summer)

In summer, Spain, France, Italy and Greece observe DST (Daylight Saving Time) between the last Sunday in March (clocks go forward an hour) and the last Sunday in October (clocks go back an hour). Türkiye remains on EET all year.

Internet & Phone

You'll be able to source wi-fi across the region. If travelling for a while, consider purchasing a local SIM card with a data package to use, as this will be more affordable than using data roaming on your phone from home. SIMS are widely available (including at airports). You'll need to show your passport to register the SIM.

ATMs

ATMs are found in major towns and cities, but it's good to carry some cash as a back-up option. In remote areas ATMs are scarcer. Much of Europe uses a chip-and-pin system with a four-digit PIN.

Toilets

Many public toilets require a small fee deposited in a box or turnstile, or given to the attendant. Availability of public toilets varies, but is generally good in tourist hubs (eg, Venice).

OPENING HOURS

These vary from country to country, and can differ between cities and small villages, but generally:

Banks 9.30am to 3pm or 5pm Monday to Friday

Cafes 8am to 11pm

Pubs and bars Noon to midnight; open later on Fridays and Saturdays

Restaurants Lunch noon to 2.30pm, dinner 6pm to 10pm (later in cities, particularly in Spain)

Shops 9am to 5.30pm (6pm in cities) Monday to Saturday, 10am to 5pm Sunday; big-city convenience stores are open 24 hours

Electricity

Europe generally runs on 220V, 50Hz AC; some old buildings in Italy and Spain have 125V. Türkiye runs on 230V/50Hz. If your home country has a vastly different voltage, you'll need a transformer for appliances.

Türkiye and most European countries use the 'europlug' with two round pins. Greece and Italy use a third round pin but the two-pin plug usually works. Bring an adaptor.

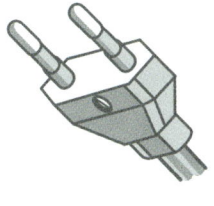

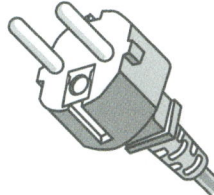

Type C
220V/50Hz

Type F
230V/50Hz

ETIQUETTE

Politeness goes a long way. Master enough of the local language to be able to say the basics, such as 'hello', 'please', 'thank you' and 'goodbye' when entering or leaving shops, cafes and restaurants.

Take your cue from locals in terms of dress. Beachwear is not acceptable at restaurants and in cities.

Dress modestly at religious sites. Bring a shawl or wrap to cover shoulders in churches. In mosques and Orthodox churches, women should also cover their hair.

In Türkiye, remove your shoes before entering a home.

Respect local customs. For instance, in Islamic countries you should avoid eating, drinking or smoking in public during Ramadan fasting hours.

Raise a toast by saying 'cheers' in the local language, clinking glasses and making eye contact.

PUBLIC HOLIDAYS

Each country observes its own public holidays and national days, but widely celebrated holidays include the following:

New Year's Day
1 January

Epiphany 6 January

Good Friday Friday before Easter Sunday, March/April

Easter Sunday March/April

Easter Monday Monday after Easter Sunday, March/April

Labour Day 1 May

Assumption Day 15 August

All Saints' Day 1 November

Christmas Day 25 December

St Stephen's Day 26 December

In Türkiye, religious holidays such as Şeker Bayramı and Kurban Bayramı are celebrated according to the Muslim lunar Hejira calendar and change each year.

Food, Drink & Nightlife

When to Eat

Breakfast (7am to 10am) Differs by country; generally light in Spain, France and Italy; more substantial in Greece and Türkiye.

Lunch (noon to 2pm) Anything goes: soup, salad, main dish, savoury pastry, baguette/sandwich/panino etc.

Afternoon tea (3pm to 4pm) Sugar hit almost always accompanied by coffee rather than tea.

Dinner (7pm to 10pm) A two- or three-course meal; served later the further south you go.

Where to Eat

Pizzeria Pizza joint; the Turkish version is a *pidecisi*.

Patisserie French-style bakeries serving pastries and cakes.

Boulangerie A bakery in French; called a *panadería* in Spain, a *forno* in Italy, a *fourno* in Greece and a *fırın* (oven) in Türkiye.

Bistro/bistrot A casual eatery serving reasonably priced meals; called a *taberna* in Spain, a *trattoria* in Italy and a taverna in Greece.

Lokanta Turkish eateries where patrons choose ready-made meals from bains-marie and display cabinets.

Ocakbaşı Turkish BBQ restaurant; the Greek equivalent is a *psistaria*.

Restaurant/restaurante/ristorante/ restoran Eatery offering a more formal, often gourmet, dining experience. A brasserie is a restaurant serving traditional French food. In Greece, a formal restaurant is called an *estiatorio*.

MENU DECODER

Antipasti In Italy, the first of four courses usually comprises *crostini* (toasted bread with toppings), charcuterie and cheese. Often eaten instead of a *primo*.

Entrée An *entrée* is a starter in France, not a main course. In France, pâté, terrines and soups are popular entrées. In Italy, *primi* are predominantly soups, pasta or risotto. In Spain, *primeros* are mainly soups or salads. *Mezedes* (Greek) and mezes (Turkish) are small hot and cold dishes.

Secondo The Italian word for a main course. Called a *plat principaux* in France, a *plato principale* or *segundo* in Spain and a *kýrio piáto* in Greece. In Türkiye, main courses are called *ana yemek*. In Italy, it's fine to order a pasta or a risotto as a *secondo*.

Dessert Called *postres* in Spain, *dolce* in Italy and *tatlı* in Türkiye. Can be anything from a lavish gateaux to a piece of fresh fruit.

HOW TO...

Eating Etiquette

Reservations It's best to book at popular and top-end restaurants, especially in high season. Call a week ahead.

Bon appétit Dining out with locals? It's polite to wish them *bon appétit* (or the equivalent) before digging in.

Water Asking for free tap water is not the done thing in these countries; you'll need to order a bottle. Specify whether you want it still or sparkling.

Dress code Smart casual in fancier establishments, where the locals dress up for dinner. In more relaxed places, jeans, sneakers and T-shirts are fine.

Tipping Check local customs. If service charge is included in the bill (eg, the *coperto* in Italy), you don't need to tip. Otherwise, around 10% is standard for good service.

Cutlery Unlike American cut-and-switch cutlery handling, in Europe your fork stays in your left hand and your knife in your right when eating.

HOW MUCH FOR A ...

Breakfast
€4–20

Cup of coffee
€1.50–5

Glass of wine
€2–10

Beer
€2–8

Sandwich
€5–12

Tapas dinner
€15–25

Fixed-price lunch
€15–30

Fine-dining
tasting menu
€100–300

HOW TO...

How to Drink Coffee

Dismiss any thoughts of drinking instant or filter coffee here – this is espresso territory. As a general rule, coffee is drunk black or with milk in the morning, but is only enjoyed black in the afternoon or evening. Ordering a milky coffee after dinner will prompt raised eyebrows and your order may even be refused. There are many coffee variations, but the standard order for a milky coffee is a cappuccino in Italy, Greece and Türkiye; a *café crème* or *café au lait* in France and a *café con leche* in Spain. Black coffee is usually drunk in a single shot and called a *café* or *café solo*; for a weaker and longer version order a *café Américain* or *allongé* in France, a *café Americano* in Spain, or an *Americano* or *longo* in Italy. Turkish and Greek coffee is black, short, thick and fiendishly strong; when ordering it, specify whether you want sugar added. In Greece, *sketos* means without sugar, *metrios* means a little, *glykos* means medium, and *variglykos* means super-sweet. In Türkiye, *sade* means without sugar, *az şekerli* means a little, *orta şekerli* means medium, and *çok şekerli* means very sweet.

An Italian Pick-Me-Up

In Italy, those who start work early may have a *caffè corretto* (espresso with a small amount of alcohol, usually grappa; pictured) midmorning to kick-start the rest of the day.

STARTING THE DAY IN STYLE

The first meal of the day is quite different in each of these countries. In France, where breakfast is called *petit déjeuner,* the standard choice is coffee with a pastry (croissant, *pain au chocolat* etc) or baguette with butter and jam. In many cafes, set breakfast deals with these elements and a *jus d'orange pressé* (freshly pressed orange juice) offer good value. In Spain, where breakfast is called *desayuno*, the Catalan dish *pa amb tomàquet* (tomato puree and olive oil on bread) is a popular breakfast snack, as are decadently rich *churros con chocolate* (fried long doughnuts dipped into rich hot chocolate). In Italy, breakfast is called *colazione* and is traditionally sweet, with *cornetti* (croissants), *ciambelle* (sugar doughnuts) or other pastries enjoyed with a coffee. Breakfasts are more substantial in Greece and Türkiye, with bread, cheese, savoury pastries such as *börek* or *pita* (pies), cucumbers, tomatoes, olives, jam, egg, fruit and other delights served. In Türkiye, freshly squeezed orange juice *(portakal suyu)* or *nar suyu* (pomegranate juice) are real treats. When in Greece, be sure to try local yoghurt and honey; the Turkish equivalent is *kaymak* (decadently rich clotted cream) slathered on bread or a *simit* (bagel-like bread studded with sesame seeds) and drizzled with *bal* (honey).

In the Mediterranean countries, tea is generally drunk black. In Türkiye, where it is the national drink, it is served in small glasses and is a strong brew. If you want weak tea, ask for *açik çay*.

Responsible Travel

Climate Change & Travel

It's impossible to ignore the impact we have when travelling; Lonely Planet urges all travellers to engage with their travel carbon footprint, which will mainly come from air travel. While there often isn't an alternative, travellers can look to minimise the number of flights they take, opt for newer aircrafts and use cleaner ground transport, such as trains. One proposed solution – purchasing carbon offsets – unfortunately does not cancel out the impact of individual flights. While most destinations will depend on air travel for the foreseeable future, for now, pursuing ground-based travel where possible is the best course of action.

The **UN Carbon Offset Calculator** shows how flying impacts a household's emissions

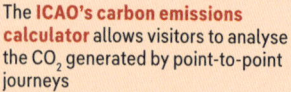

The **ICAO's carbon emissions calculator** allows visitors to analyse the CO_2 generated by point-to-point journeys

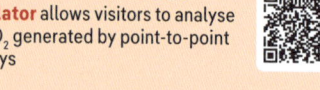

Consider animal-welfare issues before attending events like bullfights or Pamplona's running of the bulls.

Reduce CO_2 emissions by choosing to travel by train rather than car or plane.

Skip the Crowds

Travel outside the high season (May to September, plus Easter and Christmas/New Year) for fewer queues and crowds. By spreading tourism across all months, businesses such as hotels and restaurants can remain open year-round and local jobs are secured.

Seek Out Innovation

When wine touring, look out for wineries using innovative green technology – Château Troplong-Mondot (p105) in St-Émilion is a good example. Also look for organic or sustainably produced wines on restaurant wine lists.

Eat Slow & in Season

Choose restaurants using local, seasonal and sustainable produce. Trèsde (p248) in Madrid and Neolokal in İstanbul (*neolokal.com*) are good examples. In Italy, seek out restaurants listed in *Osterie d'Italia*, a guide published by Slow Food (*slowfood.com*).

Consider Animal Habitats

Some animal habitats on the Mediterranean are being threatened by tourism. Support organisations such as Greece's turtle protection society, Archelon (*archelon.gr*), which works to protect nesting turtles on beaches on Crete and the Peloponnese.

Choose a Sustainable Stay

Stay in a green hotel such as the Olive Green Hotel (p157) in Iraklio, Greece, or in a hotel such as Casa Fontequeiroso (p300) in Galicia, which works to preserve local cultures. To find other green accommodation choices, check Green Key (*greenkey.global*).

Say No to Plastic

Bring along your own refillable water bottle to avoid unnecessary plastic and minimise waste. Also have a foldable shopping bag so that you can say no to plastic bags when offered them.

Contribute to the Community

Consider giving Booking.com and Airbnb a miss and instead book on fairbnb.coop, an accommodation booking platform that donates 50% of its platform fee to fund community projects.

Support Sustainable Businesses

Support businesses using ecologically responsible production methods – the organic lavender farms on the Plateau de Valensole (p99) in Provence are great examples. Elsewhere, seek out organic farmers markets and buy produce to support the stallholders.

Tour on Two Wheels

Keen to cover territory but keep your carbon footprint as low as possible? Check out the long-distance cycling routes at en.eurovelo. com. If staying put in a city, take advantage of affordable bike-sharing schemes and bike paths.

Consider volunteering on one of the farms in the Worldwide Opportunities on Organic Farms (WWOOF) network.

Purchase souvenirs from businesses supporting local artisans whenever possible. This keeps traditional arts and crafts alive.

Cities in Motion

In the 2025 IESE Cities in Motion Index *(iese.edu)*, top performers according to environmental criteria included Valencia (number 52 of 183 cities), Madrid (56) and Paris (57). İstanbul (143) was one of the poor performers.

RESOURCES

greendestinations.org
Enthusiastic guide to sustainable travel.

greentraveller.co.uk
Low-carbon holidays and travel guides.

hihostels.com
Network of hostels with a sustainability fund and initiatives.

LGBTIQ+ Travellers

While the rainbow flag flies high in much of Mediterranean Europe, there's still some discrimination in conservative Catholic, Orthodox or Muslim areas. This especially applies in Türkiye, where LGBTIQ+ people face active discrimination. In most of Spain, France and Italy, same-sex couples commonly display affection in public and share hotel rooms. In Greece, this applies in major cities and on touristed islands.

Partying with Pride

Mediterranean Europe hosts hundreds of Pride events in late June/July each year, including the mammoth Madrid Orgullo (p251) and Barcelona Pride *(pridebarcelona.org)* in Spain. There are also well-known Pride celebrations in Sitges, Seville, Gran Canaria and Ibiza. In France, Nice is famous for its Pink Parade, and an annual Marche des Fiertés (Gay Pride March) parades through dozens of cites on Pride Day. In Italy, 30+ towns and cities host Pride parades. In Greece, there are parades in Athens, Thessaloniki, Patras and Heraklion. Sadly, Pride marches are illegal in Türkiye.

OTHER FESTIVALS

Other LGBTIQ+ festivals include Mykonos' XLSIOR summer gay circuit festival *(xlsiorfestival.com)* in August, and September's International Women's Festival *(womensfestival.eu)* on Lesvos. Lou Queernaval *(nicecarnaval.com)* is held in Nice in February. Madrid and Barcelona have well-established LGBTIQ+ film festivals: Fire!! *(mostrafire.com/en)* in June and LesGaiCineMad *(lesgaicinemad. com)* in November. In Rome, Gay Village *(www.facebook.com/GayVillage)* sees Parco del Ninfeo transformed into a party venue in summer.

Legalities

Homosexuality is legal in Spain, France, Italy and Greece. In Türkiye, homosexuality isn't a legal offence, but there are no laws protecting LGBTIQ+ people from discrimination. Same-sex marriage is legal in Spain, Greece and France, but not in Italy or Türkiye.

SUMMER SCENES

In summer, the sand, sea and party beats beckon. Top destinations include Mykonos and Lesbos in Greece, and Ibiza, Sitges and Gran Canaria in Spain. Nice is the hub in France, and most Italian resorts have a scene. Bodrum is the best bet on the Turkish coast.

ENLIGHTENED ESPAÑA

Spain is generally acknowledged to be the Mediterranean's most LGBTIQ+-friendly country (in 2025 it ranked joint first place on the Spartacus Gay Travel Index of LGBTIQ+-friendly countries; *spartacus.gayguide.travel*). To see how European countries fare on their legal and policy practices for LGBTIQ+ people, see rainbowmap.ilga-europe.org.

Pink City Districts

- Chueca (p252) in Madrid and the 'Gaixample' (p265) in Barcelona.
- Le Marais in Paris.
- The Colosseum end of Via di San Giovanni in Rome; Via Lecco, Via Tadino and NoLo in Milan.
- The Kerameikos (Gazi) and Metaxourgio neighbourhoods in Athens.
- Cihangir, Nişantaşı, Beşiktaş, Bebek, Kadıköy and Moda in İstanbul.

Accessible Travel

While Mediterranean Europe presents challenges for travellers with disabilities, accessible tourism is growing and facilities and attitudes are improving. Mobility-challenged tourists may have issues with street surfaces and obstacles, but public transport is becoming more accessible, as is accommodation.

Train Travel

Railway companies in most countries offer mobility assistance for navigating a station or boarding a train. You'll usually need to arrange this at least 24 hours in advance.

Airports

Major airports will assist passengers with reduced mobility and other disabilities. Services include help with check-in and boarding. Wheelchairs are available, as are accessible toilets. Notify your airline at least 48 hours before departure.

Accommodation

Most small guesthouses, B&Bs and boutique hotels aren't adapted for visitors with reduced mobility. Recently built hotels and hostels usually have ramps, lifts and wheelchair-adapted rooms.

WOMEN TRAVELLERS

Women might attract unwanted attention (staring, catcalling) from males in Türkiye, rural Spain and southern Italy. Conservative dress can help deter this. In mosques and Orthodox churches, cover hair with a shawl.

CITY TRANSPORT

Metros in İstanbul, Athens, Madrid and Barcelona are wheelchair-accessible. Not all lines in Paris, Rome and Milan are. Many buses can accommodate wheelchairs. İstanbul's trams are wheelchair-accessible, as are its newer ferries.

Navigating Streets

Historic town and city centres often have uneven cobblestones or street obstacles, making them difficult to navigate for the elderly, as well as for wheelchair users and the vision-impaired.

Sights

Accessibility is improving in galleries and museums, with ramps, lifts and well-spaced exhibitions. Some institutions have quiet times, ear defenders, sensory maps, Braille signs, audio description and accessible tours.

RESOURCES

Accessible.net *(accessible.net)* Find French hotels and restaurants that are more adapted for travellers with disabilities.

Disabled Accessible Travel *(disabledaccessible travel.com)* Tours and transfers catering to wheelchair users and those with special needs.

Sage Traveling *(sagetraveling.com)* Find accessible hotels in cities all over Europe.

Society for Accessible Tourism & Hospitality *(sath. org)* Practical info for travellers with disabilities.

Spain Is Accessible *(spainisaccessible. com)* Spain's tourist board provides helpful info.

Sunflower Signal

In Spain and France, wearing a sunflower lanyard is a discreet way to show that you have an unnoticeable disability. This alerts staff at airports, on public transport and in museums that you may require assistance. See hdsunflower.com.

At the Beach

For many travellers, a holiday in the Mediterranean means a beach holiday. There are thousands of beaches along the coast, many of which are jam-packed in July and August, when most Europeans take their annual holidays. For a less-crowded beach experience, head to the sand and surf in June or September.

Water Quality

The European Environment Agency (EEA; *eea. europa.eu)* monitors bathing waters in Europe, categorising beaches as 'Excellent', 'Good', 'Sufficient' and 'Poor'. In 2024, 85% of the monitored sites had 'Excellent' water quality, and 1.6% were rated 'Poor'. In total, 96% of all assessed beaches or other bodies of water met the minimum water quality standards. Generally speaking, coastal waters performed better than inland waters.

Greece consistently records excellent water quality at its beaches (the only European country with cleaner water is Cyprus). Some beaches in the southern-central areas of France, inland Corsica, Palma de Mallorca and southern Italy are consistently rated 'Poor' by the EEA.

Beaches given Blue Flag accreditation by the Foundation of Environmental Education must meet stringent environmental criteria, including having acceptable water quality. To check if a beach has Blue Flag certification, go to blueflag.global and use the interactive map. Spain and Türkiye have the most Blue Flag beaches in Europe.

On the Shore

Travellers from the Americas, Asia and Australasia are often shocked when they arrive here and find that beaches have flat pebbles (shingles) or rocks rather than sand. This isn't always the case – there are some wonderful stretches of sand along the Mediterranean shore – but to check whether a beach is sandy before arriving, go to blueflag.global. If you do go to a pebble or rock beach, you'll need flip-flops to wear in and out of the water.

Another aspect of European beach culture that foreign travellers may find surprising is the ubiquity of beach clubs (also called organised beaches or lidos). These privately operated businesses have licensed part of the beach and rent out loungers and parasols to beachgoers. Some also provide refreshment kiosks and amenity blocks with showers and toilets. Daily charges range from €15 to €60. Most beach clubs don't need to be booked in advance.

Be aware that Europeans do not wear bathing costumes on the street; you'll need to cover up when away from the sand.

BEACH FLAGS

GREEN	YELLOW	RED	PURPLE	BLACK	WHITE	YELLOW & RED STRIPES
Safe to Swim	Swim with caution	Danger; swimming forbidden	Danger; water pollution, including jellyfish (France, Italy, Greece, Türkiye)	Danger; water pollution (Spain)	Hazard Danger; jellyfish (Spain)	Lifeguards patrolling between flags

Right: Playa de la Concha (p275), Spain

OPPOSITE: EVANTRAVELS/SHUTTERSTOCK

ACCESSIBILITY & SAFETY

- At some beaches, local authorities have provided adapted toilets and showers, amphibious wheelchairs, access ramps into the water and dedicated parking for the mobility-impaired. The blueflag.global website indicates beaches where mobility-impaired visitors can access the water via ramps.

- There can be dangerous rip currents in Mediterranean waters. Always swim at beaches patrolled by lifeguards; check at blueflag.global.
- Don't leave unattended valuables on the beach or in vehicles parked in beach car parks.

STORYBOOK

Our writers delve deep into different aspects of Mediterranean life

A History of Mediterranean Europe in 15 Places

This region's complex and fascinating culture is built on a history of great civilisations, powerful empires, traders, pilgrims, pirates and more.

Virginia Maxwell

p356

Mediterranean 'Blue Zones': Islands of Longevity

What's the secret to a long life? The Mediterranean, home to two islands with extraordinary numbers of centenarians, provides a few clues.

Katherina Grace Thomas

p360

A Wine Tour of the Mediterranean

For wine lovers, the Mediterranean is hard to beat: ancient vines meet sun-drenched terraces in the birthplace of viticulture. description

Katherina Grace Thomas

p364

Mezquita (p294), Córdoba, Spain

A HISTORY OF MEDITERRANEAN EUROPE IN
15 PLACES

This part of Europe has hosted traders, pilgrims, pirates and invading armies for millennia. Great civilisations and powerful empires have been born here, and conquerors from as far away as Persia, the Levant and North Africa have brought their foods, religions and cultural practices with them, contributing to the region's complex and fascinating culture. By Virginia Maxwell

BORDERED BY THE Levant, North Africa, Anatolia and Europe, the Mediterranean Sea has bestowed great riches on those countries garlanded along its coast. Chief among these has been the bounty of trade, with its economic and cultural enrichment. The fertile landscape and fish-stocked seas have contributed economically, too – this has always been a region able to feed itself and its neighbours. And where there is wealth, great cities and monuments almost always follow.

In myth, this is the land of great heroes and adventurers such as Achilles, Odysseus and Heracles. And in history, this is where Plato philosophised, Homer penned epic poems, Michelangelo sculpted masterpieces and Galileo pondered the mysteries of the stars. Military geniuses such as Julius Caesar, Mehmet the Conqueror and Napoléon Bonaparte spearheaded campaigns that redrew borders and created empires and nations. Monsters such as Franco, Hitler and Mussolini tried to emulate them and – thankfully – failed. And through all of these eras and events, the peoples of the Mediterranean prospered, creating nations and cultures that are as strong, resilient and enticing to visitors now as they have ever been.

1. Altamira, Spain
PREHISTORIC CAVE ART
In 1879, historian and scientist Marcelino Sanz de Sautuola and his eight-year-old daughter María instantly knew they had discovered something special when they uncovered intricate coloured-in paintings of bison, horses, deer and other beasts in a cave in the Cantabrian countryside. The Cueva de Altamira, near Santillana del Mar, conceals Spain's finest prehistoric art, etched between 13,000 and 35,000 years ago using the natural rock relief. Though the original cave is closed to visitors for conservation purposes, the wonderful replica cave is a marvel of contemporary creativity in its own right.

For more on Altamira, see p276.

2. Troy, Türkiye
SITE OF THE LEGENDARY TROJAN WAR
The site of antiquity's most famous war, Troy is such a staple of mythology that it's sometimes surprising to learn it's a real place. Legends tell of the Trojan prince Paris' abduction of Helen of Sparta, and the subsequent Greek expedition to recover her, culminating in Odysseus' Trojan Horse trick. While this makes a fantastic yarn, it's likely to have only the vaguest resemblance to historical fact. It's true, though, that the

ancient city of Troy was one of the largest in the Aegean region, but was totally destroyed around 1250 BCE. The surviving ruins may not be Türkiye's most impressive, but they are testament to one of the world's most powerful stories.

For more on Troy, see p319.

3. Knossos, Greece
MINOAN PALACE COMPLEX

The Palace of Knossos – the elaborate ruins and re-creations of the grand capital of Minoan Crete – is ripe for the imagination. The immense palace, courtyards, apartments and frescoes tell the tale of this powerful civilisation, about which much has been found out (including the Bronze Age port town of Akrotiri in Santorini) but much is still unknown. The Minoans developed the first written language (Linear A) and traded widely, and perhaps peacefully, as none of their towns were fortified. The whole civilisation disappeared mysteriously, possibly related to fallout from Santorini's 16th-century-BCE volcanic explosion.

For more on Knossos, see p155.

Roman Forum (p172), Italy

MATTEO COLOMBO/GETTY IMAGES

4. Delphi, Greece
A PLACE OF DIVINE ENERGY

Ancient Delphi has a potent spirit. Perched in the Temple of Apollo, the Delphic oracle ranked high among the sacred sites of Ancient Greece. Devotees flocked here asking the mysterious high priestess, known as the Pythia, for Apollo's guidance. Wars were fought, colonies created, marriages sealed, leaders chosen and journeys begun on the strength of the oracle's advice. Today, the haunting ruins on the slopes of Mt Parnassus look out over an unbroken expanse of olive trees, sloping down to the Gulf of Corinth.

For more on Delphi, see p130.

5. Palatine Hill & Roman Forum, Italy
HEART OF THE ROMAN WORLD

It was on the Palatine that Rome was said to have been founded by Romulus in 753 BCE. He chose the site where legend tells us he and his twin brother, Remus, had been suckled by a she-wolf as orphan infants. Later, after the Roman Republic was set up, the patricians lived on the hill and worked and worshipped in the adjacent Forum, a vibrant centre of temples, basilicas and bustling public spaces. When walking the Via Sacra here, it's easy to imagine what daily life was like in Caput Mundi, the then capital of the world.

For more on Ancient Rome, see p168.

6. Aya Sofya, Türkiye
A BYZANTINE MARVEL

Consecrated in 537 CE by order of the Byzantine emperor Justinian, the Hagia Sofia was known as the Sancta Sophia in Latin and the Church of the Holy Wisdom or Divine Wisdom in English. Its current name is Turkish, and today this magnificent building functions as a mosque rather than a Christian church. Embellished with exquisite Byzantine mosaics and featuring a massive dome that the Byzantine historian Procopius described as being 'hung from heaven on a golden chain', this is one of Christendom's most important buildings and is equally revered by Turkish Muslims.

For more on the Aya Sofya, see p312.

7. Palazzo dei Normanni, Italy
PRIZE OF CONQUERING ARMIES

In Sicily, a combined Muslim force invaded in 827 and had control of the entire island by 965. Sicily remained under Arab control until 1038 when Norman mercenaries, under the command of the Byzantines, recaptured the island. Palermo's glittering Palazzo dei Normanni, home to the famous Cappella Palatina, was originally built as a fortress by the Arabs but morphed into a palace under the Normans. The Normans would go on to conquer the southern third of Italy and create the Kingdom of Sicily, which survived until 1816, despite being passed around between Europe's ruling families throughout that period.

For more on Palazzo dei Normanni, see p225.

8. Alhambra, Spain
MONUMENT TO AN ARAB DYNASTY

Seeing Granada's ochre-hued Alhambra backed by the snow-dusted peaks of the Sierra Nevada is one of Andalucía's most magical experiences. A grandiose relic of the last Muslim state of Al-Andalus, this palace-fortress is adorned with fragrant gardens, interlocking patios and rushing water features. Though the first records of a fort here date from the 9th century, it's believed the original buildings on the Alhambra hill could have existed since Roman times. The celebrated Palacios Nazaríes (a highpoint in Islamic architecture) and elegant Generalife were created in the 14th century.

For more on the Alhambra, see p297.

9. Meteora, Greece
MEDIEVAL MONASTERIES IN THE SKY

The name Meteora is derived from the Greek adjective *meteoros*, meaning 'suspended in the air'. And the extraordinary rock formations of the Meteora region would be an unmissable spectacle even if they weren't crowned by Byzantine monasteries. These 14th- and 15th-century monasteries – somehow anchored atop slender stone pinnacles by medieval masons – are now collectively listed as a World Heritage site. The earliest monasteries could only be reached by climbing removable ladders, but these days access is via steps hewn into the rocks in the 1920s.

For more on Meteora, see p132.

10. St Peter's Basilica, Italy
CENTRE OF WESTERN CHRISTENDOM

The Bishop of Rome holds the title of Pope, a role claimed to have its origins in St Peter, who is believed to be buried beneath this magnificent Renaissance church, built in the 16th and 17th centuries. Following the chaos that saw Italy succumb to Germanic tribes, the Byzantine reconquest and the Lombard occupation of the north, the Papacy became a secular force as well as a spiritual one. In 800, Pope Leo III crowned Frankish king Charlemagne as Holy Roman Emperor, in return for his support of papal control of Rome and the surrounding regions. The Papal States existed until 1870; the Vatican City is the surviving remnant.

For more on St Peter's Basilica, see p177.

11. Château de Versailles, France
THE SUN KING'S FOLLY

Louis XIV, better known as Le Roi Soleil (the Sun King), ascended the throne of France aged five. Bolstered by claims of divine right, he involved the kingdom of France in a series of costly wars, leading to widespread poverty in France. However, this didn't stop him from building the most extravagant palace on French soil at Versailles in 1663. His massive château is a reflection of the French monarchy at its height, before the revolution of 1789 claimed the head of Louis XVI.

For more on Versailles, see p62.

Meteora (p132), Greece

FROM LEFT: RALF SIEMIENIEC/SHUTTERSTOCK, DANIEL DE PETRO/SHUTTERSTOCK

Ari Burnu Cemetery, Gallipoli Historical Area (p316), Türkiye

12. Place de la Concorde, France
REMINDER OF THE REIGN OF TERROR

This square marks the spot where the Bourbon king Louis XVI and his wife, Marie-Antoinette, were guillotined in 1793 during the period of the First Republic known as the Reign of Terror. The republic only lasted until 1804, when the First Empire under Napoléon Bonaparte was declared. The new emperor would rule France for a decade, being deposed after his disastrous invasion of Russia. Exiled to Elba, he resurfaced in 1815 and raised an army to fight the British, Prussians and Dutch, only to be defeated at Waterloo. France once again became a monarchy, this time under Louis XVIII.

For more on the Place de la Concorde, see p540.

13. The Gallipoli Battlefields, Türkiye
A FATEFUL WWI CAMPAIGN

When WWI broke out, the Ottoman Empire's alliance with Germany and Austria-Hungary severed an important supply line between Britain and France and their ally Russia (together known as the Triple Entente). A plan was formed by Winston Churchill to seize the Dardanelles as a prelude to capturing İstanbul (then Constantinople) and reopening the supply line. The British and French campaign, which centred on the Gallipoli Peninsula, was a failure, and the Turkish victory was an important step towards the establishment of the Turkish Republic under Mustafa Kemal (aka Atatürk).

For more on Gallipoli, see p316.

14. Gernika, Spain
CIVIL-WAR TRAGEDY

On 26 April 1937, at the height of the Spanish Civil War, Nazi Germany – supporting General Franco's rebel nationalists – unleashed aerial bombings on the Basque town of Gernika. Around 1600 people are thought to have been killed, and the town was razed in just a few hours on a busy market Monday, becoming a symbol for the horrors of the civil war. Picasso's 1937 oil painting *Guernica*, which hangs in Madrid's Cento de Arte Reina Sofía, is one of the world's most powerful anti-war artworks

For more on Picasso's Guernica, see p250.

15. D-Day Landing Beaches, France
WWII BATTLEGROUNDS

When US soldiers landed on the golden sand of Normandy's Omaha Beach on the morning of 6 June 1944, thousands of Allied and German troops were killed and the battle left indelible scars on the French countryside. Today, the D-Day beaches and nearby cemeteries are pilgrimage destinations, and the Mur de l'Atlantique – concrete coastal fortifications built by the Germans between 1942 and 1944 to defend 4000km of coastline from Norway to southern France – are visited by military-history buffs.

For more on the D-Day Landing Beaches, see p70.

MEDITERRANEAN 'BLUE ZONES': ISLANDS OF LONGEVITY

What's the secret to a long life? The Mediterranean, home to two islands with extraordinary numbers of centenarians, provides a few clues. By Katherina Grace Thomas

IN THE EARLY 2000s, researchers studying the secrets of centenarians began pinpointing special places around the world that they designated 'longevity blue zones' – havens where unusually high numbers of people are living to a hundred and beyond. Among them are spots on two of the Mediterranean's most mountainous islands: Sardinia in Italy, and Ikaria in Greece.

What Is a 'Blue Zone'?

Explanations of blue zones often begin with Stamatis Moraitis' story, so extraordinary that it sounds like a fable. It goes like this: Greek war veteran and celebrated singer Moraitis had been living in Florida for 30 years. In the 1970s, he became ill with terminal lung cancer; his American doctors told him that they expected him to live for six to nine months. Keen to return to his home island of Ikaria, where funerals were more affordable and he knew he could be buried overlooking the Aegan sea, Moraitis and his wife flew back to the island, where they moved in with his elderly parents, who were still alive and able to help care for him. At first, Moraitis was bedbound, but then something unexpected happened: he began to grow stronger. Soon, he was able to walk up the hill to the historic Greek orthodox chapel for weekly services. Then he was able to plant vegetables in the garden. Nine months passed and Moraitis didn't die. Instead he harvested the vegetables, drank wine with old friends, worked in the vineyards and played dominoes into the wee hours. As the months turned into years, he expanded his property and became a local wine producer. When 25 years had passed, Moraitis flew back to America to see if his doctors could explain this exceptional turn of events. On arrival, he learned that his doctors had already died.

This story has become local legend in Ikaria, a mountainous island at the very tip of the Dodecanese Islands. The whole island was designated a longevity blue zone in the early 2000s, along with the Ogliastra province of Sardinia, Okinawa in Japan, Costa Rica's Península de Nicoya, and Loma Linda in California. The blue-zone terminology grew out of academic research by demographers Michel Poulain and Gianni Pes in Sardinia, where they had documented an unusually high number of centenarians. Poulain joined forces with entrepreneur and *National Geographic* explorer Dan Buettner, who later trademarked the term 'blue zone' and marketed it to American communities, identifying nine factors contributing to longevity (which he dubbed the 'Power 9'): natural exercise, sense of purpose, reduced stress,

stopping eating before you're full, a largely plant-based diet, moderate alcohol consumption, a sense of belonging and strong family ties.

Some of these factors have been questioned by other researchers who have since cast doubt upon the legitimacy of the blue-zone concept, arguing that poor recordkeeping, study limitations and sensationalist pop science have tarnished the research. Amid critiques about trademark and profit, Poulain parted ways from Buetter, who was rapidly growing his venture into a successful global business. They have each since expanded their research to include new blue zones: Singapore (Buettner) and Martinique (Poulain).

Ikaria: Mountain Tea & Wildflower Honey

Whatever you make of the concept of 'blue zones' and the marketing around it, it's hard to deny that there's something special – magical, even – about Ikaria. And there is robust data to show that higher numbers of Ikarians are living longer, with over a third of residents making it to 90. The mountainous island of 99 sq miles sits about 30 miles from Türkiye and has a population of about 10,000 and the highest life expectancy in Greece. It's a beautiful island: jagged mountains, ancient springs, abundant vineyards and powerful winds that pummel the island, even mentioned in the *Iliad*. Joseph Georgirenes, a bishop of Ikaria in the 17th century, described Ikaria's air and water as 'so healthful that people are very long-lived, it being an ordinary thing to see persons in it of 100 years of age'. The winds, and the absence of a natural harbour, kept Ikaria isolated and self-sufficient for much longer than neighbouring islands, instilling a strong sense of community, sustainable local agriculture chains, and values that have veered away from capitalism and modern development.

On Ikaria, the longest living residents tend to live up in the mountains. Research has shown that they tend to eat seasonal produce, make wine without preservatives, enjoy lashings of olive oil, goat's milk and goat's cheese, spend long days in gardens and vineyards with their hands in the soil,

and take daily siestas; the nonagenarians and centenarians stay socially active, and there are very few cases of dementia.

Research scientists have reached differing conclusions about the typical Ikarian diet; one landmark study concluded that most residents largely follow a plant-based diet (fava beans, potatoes, fennel, dandelion and antioxidant-rich wild greens known as *horta),* but others argue that many people also frequently consume lamb, goat and chicken. Regardless, because many Ikarians are subsistence farmers themselves, few pesticides make it into their stomachs. Some studies suggest that the Ikarian diet, compared with the standard American diet, might offer four additional years of life expectancy.

Mountain tea, a local brew made from seasonal dried herbs, is very popular on Ikaria and is drunk daily. Depending on the time of year, it can include mint, thyme, dandelion, sage, other forms of artemisia, marjoram, lemon and rosemary – ingredients that include antioxidant and diuretic properties, perhaps helping to fight pathogens, promote brain health, reduce inflammation and prevent hypotension. And then there's the honey: beekeepers on Ikaria produce several kinds of pure honey: pine and wildflower, thyme (renowned for its antimicrobial and anti-inflammatory properties), heather (a source of manganese, which protects the body's tissues from damage) and pure pine honey (which has antibacterial benefits). Most of the honey produced on Ikaria isn't the runny kind made popular by Winnie the Pooh; instead it's thicker and more crystalline, and most of it is unprocessed. Ikarians eat it frequently, with some of the older men even referring to it as 'nature's viagra'.

Sardinia: Ancient Foods & the Gifts of Isolation

Sardinia's longevity blue zone, Ogliastra province, also has mountainous terrain. In fact, Ogliastra is the most mountainous province in Italy, with an elevation of 500m to 1500m. Its residents are accustomed to walking up and down rugged mountain paths that suddenly give way to pretty coves and beaches. Sparsely populated Ogliastra shares something else with Ikaria: a traditional way of life that has not yielded, at least not too much, to over-development and chain hotels. Interestingly, unlike other blue zones, Ogliastra has a higher gender equality among its centenarians, with greater numbers of men than anywhere else living to 100 and above. Historically, many of them have worked as shepherds, walking long distances through the mountains well into their 80s and 90s. In his scientific research, Michel Poulain hypothesises that the unusual longevity in Ogliastra is rooted in physical activity, diet and the fact that – like Ikaria – the mountainous province was isolated for centuries, preserving pastoral traditions, as well as stabilising the local gene pool. He has studied genetic markers there and found that none of them differ significantly from the rest of Italy.

Sardinia is famous for *cannonau* wine, a full-bodied red made from *cannonau* grapes (also known as Grenache). It contains high numbers of polyphenols and antioxidants, supposedly more than three times the amount in most red wines. High consumption of fava beans and chickpeas has also been associated with longevity in Sardinia, as in Ikaria. A 2023 research study found that meat was consumed sparingly, with most calories derived from whole grains and goat's milk products, which are more easily digested than cow's milk and cheese. It also explored Ogliastra's history as an isolated province, concluding that 'famine foods' emerged during times of economic hardship.

Some of these foods, although their production methods might raise eyebrows outside Sardinia, are still consumed today. There's *abbamele*, an ancient kind of honey water produced by cooking lemon and orange peel with honeycomb – believed to have antibiotic, antiviral,

MADE TO HAVE A LONG SHELF LIFE DURING PERIODS OF HARDSHIP, PANE CARASAU IS BELIEVED TO PRODUCE STRAINS OF LACTIC ACID BACTERIA PEPTIDES IMBUED WITH ANTI-HYPERTENSIVE EFFECTS.

Pane carasau

FABIANO GOREME CADDEO/SHUTTERSTOCK

anti-inflammatory and blood-vessel-protecting properties. *Pane carasau* (which also goes by the wonderful nickname, *carta musica,* or 'sheet music') is a thin, crisp traditional Sardinian sourdough flatbread as fine as a poppodum. Made to have a long shelf life during times of famine and periods of hardship, it is believed to produce certain strains of lactic acid bacteria peptides imbued with anti-hypertensive effects. Then there's *caggiu de crabittu*, produced in a way that might sound shocking to some: edible goat rennet, made from the stomach of a young goat that is still full of its mother's milk. After slaughter, the kid's stomach is emptied and the milk is filtered and returned to the stomach casing where it then ferments, producing probiotic lactic acid species that become a creamy paste. The filled stomach is then tied together with string, dried and smoked. Other staples include Boraginaceae seeds, better known as borage or starflower. These have been eaten for centuries in Ogliastra; they are now gaining popularity in the global wellness industry for their powerful anti-inflammatory properties; some studies show that oil made from the seeds can improve the symptoms of both eczema and asthma.

With a growing number of supplements and dietary plans marketed around the world, could the secret to longevity actually be something more simple? Eating seasonally, avoiding processed foods, living in tune with the earth and our seasons, honouring nature and the shared wisdom of ancestors, spending time outside, continuing meaningful work. And of course, enjoying the good company of dear friends with a dash of tea or a glass of good wine – and a spoonful of potent local honey.

A WINE TOUR OF THE MEDITERRANEAN

For wine lovers, the Mediterranean is hard to beat: ancient vines meet sun-drenched terraces in the birthplace of viticulture. By Katherina Grace Thomas

THERE ARE RENOWNED cellars and stunning wineries all over the region, many of which are honouring historic and indigenous grapes. The sea serves as more than just stunning scenery, helping to maintain consistent temperatures for the vines.

France

Languedoc-Roussillon, spilling down the Mediterranean coast towards the border with Spain, is France's largest wine region. Vines have been cultivated here since Roman times; in the tiny village of Aspiran, the ruins of a large commercial vineyard date back to 10 CE. Today the region is still known for its high-yield, good-value bottles; you'll find plenty of great full-bodied red blends, crisp unoaked whites and Blanquette de Limoux, a sparkling wine that dates back to 1531 – 150 years before champagne was created.

Neighbouring Provence, of course, is the home of summer rosé wines, perfect for sipping on a *terrasse* at golden hour. Between the lavender fields and hilly villages, about 80% of vineyards here are dedicated to rosé. Still, don't miss the bold and spicy *mourvèdre* reds – a mainstay of the Rhône region, they're also produced here, in the

Pictured clockwise from top left: Rosé wine, Provence; Harvesting primitivo grapes, Puglia; Winery in Haro, Spain; Greek *xinomavro* wine

Italy

The roots of Italy's vines run deep. On Sicily, the largest island in the Mediterranean, *carricante* grapes are believed to have been growing on the slopes of Mt Etna, as high as 1200m above sea level, for a thousand years. They produce lush, silky whites high in minerality and acidity. Other well-known Sicilian whites include full-bodied *grillo*, and *catarrato*, also used in Marsala blended wines. Nero d'Avolo is probably the most popular Sicilian red, with hints of black cherry, hibiscus and stone, while *frappato* is a rare, light-bodied red with cherry notes.

In Tuscany, where rolling hills curve down to the coast, Chianti is king. Further inland, there's the Chianti Classico region, where wines are made from at least 80% *sangiovese* and are ideal for ageing. From Abruzzo to Puglia, you'll find local *montepulciano* wines, perfect for a relaxed pizza dinner, as well as finer chocolatey bottles. In Campania, look out for *fiano*, an ancient white grape grown on volcanic soil with an aromatic and elegant feel. Sardinia is home to *cannonau* (Grenache) grapes, believed to have three times the antioxidants of other red wines.

Greece

Although Greeks were not the world's earliest wine producers, they are thought to be the first to have created a culture around winemaking – one that has regained global recognition in the last few years. In the Peloponnese, the nucleus of Greek viticulture, the appellation of Nemea produces *agiorgitiko* wine, almost as highly regarded among wine enthusiasts as *xinomavro* from the north. The terroir runs from low elevation to higher grounds with cooling winds, producing a variety of reds and rosés; not much beats washing down grilled meat with one of the excellent full-bodied reds. Also look out for *moschofilero*, a floral white similar to a Gewürztraminer.

Santorini, with its blue-dome topped architecture and stunning volcanic beaches, is also bliss for wine lovers. These sandy volcanic soils are immune to phylloxera, tiny insects that damage vine roots, so some of Santorini's living vines are believed to be 400 years old. *Assyrtiko*, a highly-regarded grape, creates good white wines high in salinity and acidity. If you have a sweet tooth, *vinsanto*, a caramel-coloured dessert wine, is made from late harvest sun-dried *assyrtiko* grapes blended with *aidani*. On Crete, *liatiko* is an ancient red grape that produces intense but soft reds that you'll want to take home with you.

Spain

Wine has been produced in Spain for at least 2700 years. Among the Spanish terroirs is lovely Mallorca. Better known for its sun-lounger vibes, the Balearic island has a rich oenological history dating back to Roman times, and its clay and limestone soil is home to almost 100 wineries (known as bodegas). Grapes of note include *moll*, *manto negro* and *giró ros* – the latter makes its way into bottles by Ánima Negra, a bodega that cultivates rare indigenous grapes.

On the mainland Mediterranean coast, look out for *garnacha* and *merlot rosé* from Catalunya and *monastrell* from Murcia and Valencia. Further south down to the Atlantic coast, there's sherry from Andalucia, or head to pretty Haro, two hours south of Bilbao, easily one of the best places in the country for cellar tours and *vinotecas*. Wine can be as serious as you want it to be in Spain; it's not uncommon to take pride in fine wines but to also enjoy a glass of red wine (think fruit-forward, unoaked table reds) mixed with ice and any citrusy soft drink.

Türkiye

A wine tour of the Mediterranean wouldn't be complete without a stop in Türkiye, where the practice goes back at least 6000 years to the very origins of wine. When winemakers first cultivated the Tigris-Euphrates Valley, they mixed wine with honey because it was so sour. Although Türkiye is one of the birthplaces of viticulture, home to hundreds of indigenous varieties, the export industry is still in its infancy. Yet there are many great wines here, and a growing community of viticulturists attending to historic varieties. *Öküzgözü* is a lovely approachable red. *Boğazkere* has similarities to *nebbiolo*, intense and complex. There's also *kalecik karası*, Türkiye's equivalent to pinot noir, and *narince*, a popular white with floral and nutty character.

INDEX

INDEX C-F

Map Pages **000**

Mapping data sources:
© Lonely Planet
© OpenStreetMap http://openstreetmap.org/copyright

THIS BOOK

The 12th edition of Lonely Planet's Mediterranean Europe guidebook was curated by Virginia Maxwell, Kate Armstrong, Cristian Bonetto, Isabella Noble and Anna Richards. This guidebook was produced by the following:

Destination Editor
Shauna Daly

Coordinating Editors
Brana Vladisavljevic, Simon Williamson

Production Editors
Joel Cotterell, Amy Lysen, Kathryn Rowan

Image Researchers
Dermot Hegarty, Norma Brewer

Cartographers
Bohumil Ptáček, Valentina Kremenchutskaya, Anthony Phelan

Assisting Editors
Sofie Andersen, Michelle Bennett, Imogen Bannister, Nigel Chin, Katie Connolly, Melanie Dankel, Soo Hamilton, Kate James, Helen Koehne, Anne Mulvaney, Karyn Noble, Fionnuala Twomey

Contributing Writers
Isabel Albiston, Alexis Averbuck, Abigail Blasi, Federica Bocco, Jean-Bernard Carillet, Natalia Diaz, Virginia DiGaetano, Jamie Ditaranto, Peter Dragicevich, Mark Elliott, İsmet Ersoy, Mark Eveleigh, Steve Fallon, Fabienne Fong Yan, Esme Fox, Michael Frankel, Duncan Garwood, Benedetta Geddo, Jennifer Hattam, Rooksana Hossenally, Felicity Hughes, Ömercan Kaçar, Anna Kaminski, Cyrena Lee, Daphné Leprince-Ringuet, Lucy Lovell, Vesna Maric, Chrissie McClatchie, Owen Morton, Mary Nicklin, John Noble, Nanjala Nyabola, Stephanie Ong, Ashley Parsons, Kevin Raub, Daniel Robinson, Madeleine Rothery, Andrea Schulte-Peevers, Eva Sandoval, Sarah Souli, Regis St Louis, Paul Stafford, Nicola Leigh Stewart, Rowan Twine, Ryan Ver Berkmoes, Nicola Williams, Peter Yeung, Angelo Zinna

Cover Researcher
Katelyn Perry

Thanks Darren O'Connell, Saralinda Turner

Paper in this book is certified against the Forest Stewardship Council™ standards. FSC™ promotes environmentally responsible, socially beneficial and economically viable management of the world's forests.

Published by Lonely Planet Global Limited
CRN 554153
12th edition – Jun 2026
ISBN 978 1 74321 503 6
© Lonely Planet 2026 Photographs © as indicated 2026
10 9 8 7 6 5 4 3 2 1
Printed in Malaysia